W9-AXI-284

The Blue Ridge & Smoky Mountains

The Blue Ridge & Smoky Mountains

Jim Hargan

The Countryman Press ✳ Woodstock, Vermont

SECOND EDITION

ISSN 0-88150-666-4
ISBN 1538-8395

Maps by Moore Creative Designs, © The Countryman Press
Text and cover design by Bodenweber Design
Composition by PerfecType, Nashville, TN
Front cover and interior photographs © Jim Hargan

Published by The Countryman Press,
P.O. Box 748, Woodstock, VT 05091

Distributed by W. W. Norton & Company, Inc.
500 Fifth Avenue, New York, NY 10110

Printed in the United States of America

10 9 8 7 6 5 4 3 2 1

EXPLORE WITH US!

Welcome to the second edition of *The Blue Ridge and Smoky Mountains: An Explorer's Guide*, the definitive guide to the tallest mountains in the East. It's the perfect companion for exploring the Great Smoky Mountains National Park, the Blue Ridge Parkway, and all the ridges in between. Here, you'll find thorough coverage for both sides of the Tennessee–North Carolina state line, with detailed listings on the best sight-seeing, outdoor activities, restaurants, shopping, and B&Bs. Like all Explorer's Guides, this book is an old-fashioned, classic traveler's guide, where an experienced and knowledgeable expert helps you find your way around in a new area or explore some fascinating corners of a familiar one.

WHAT'S WHERE

In the beginning of the book you'll find an alphabetical listing of special high-lights and important information that you may want to reference quickly. You'll find advice on everything from Area Codes to Wildlife.

LODGING

We've selected lodging places for inclusion in this book based on their merit alone; we do not charge innkeepers for inclusion. **Prices:** Please don't hold us or the respective innkeepers responsible for the rates listed as of press time in early 2005. Changes are inevitable. At the time of this writing, the state and local room tax ranged from 6 to 11 percent.

RESTAURANTS

In most chapters please note the distinction between Eating Out and Dining Out. By their nature, restaurants included in the Eating Out group are generally inexpensive. A range of prices is included for each entry.

KEY TO SYMBOLS

   Child-friendly. The crayon denotes a family-friendly place or event that welcomes young children. Most B&Bs prohibit children under 12.

   Handicapped access. The wheelchair icon denotes a place with full Americans with Disabilities Act (ADA) standard access, still distressingly rare in these remote areas.

   Rainy day. The umbrella icon points out places where you can entertain yourself but still stay dry in bad weather.

   Pets. The dog's paw icon identifies lodgings that allow pets—still the exception to the rule. Accommodations that accept pets may still charge an extra fee or restrict pets to certain areas, as well as require advance notice.

Author's Choice: Sidebars mark the author's personal favorites in each chapter—a subjective selection, but good guidance when you only have a day or so to spend in an area.

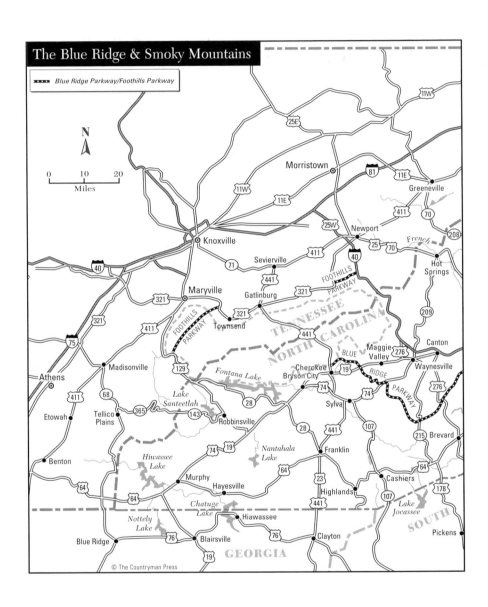

The Blue Ridge & Smoky Mountains

▬▬▬ *Blue Ridge Parkway/Foothills Parkway*

N

0   10   20
Miles

11W

25E

Morristown

81   11E

Greeneville

11W

411   70

11E

25W   Newport

25   70

French

208

Knoxville

Sevierville   411

40

441

Hot
Springs

71

Maryville   Gatlinburg   321

FOOTHILLS
PARKWAY

209

321

321

411

Townsend

TENNESSEE

441

NORTH CAROLINA

Canton

75

129   Fontana Lake

Cherokee

Maggie
Valley   276

Madisonville   Bryson City   19   BLUE

Waynesville

Athens

Lake
Santeetlah   28   74

RIDGE

276

74

68   365   143

Sylva

PARKWAY

Etowah   411   Robbinsville

28   441   107

215   Brevard

Tellico
Plains   Nantahala
Lake   Franklin

74   19

64

64

Benton   Hiwassee
Lake   64   23   Cashiers

Murphy   Highlands   107   178

64   Hayesville   441   Lake
Jocassee   SOUTH

Chatuge
Lake   Pickens

Nottely
Lake   Hiawassee

76   76   Clayton

Blue Ridge   76   Blairsville

19   GEORGIA

© The Countryman Press

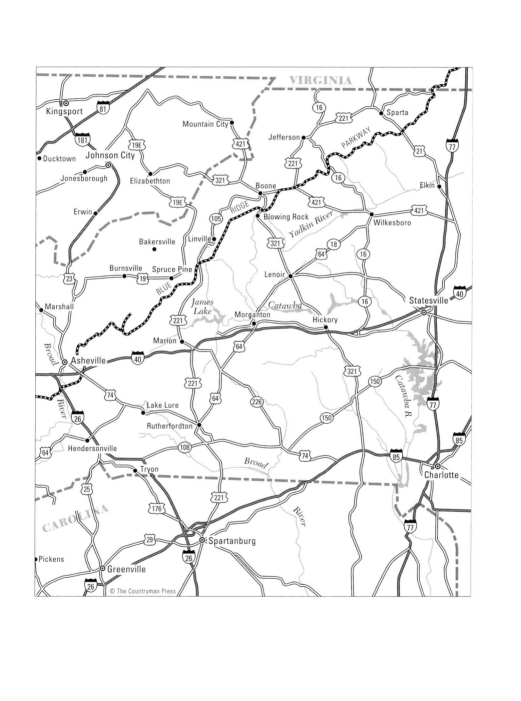

The Blue Ridge & Smoky Mountains Regions

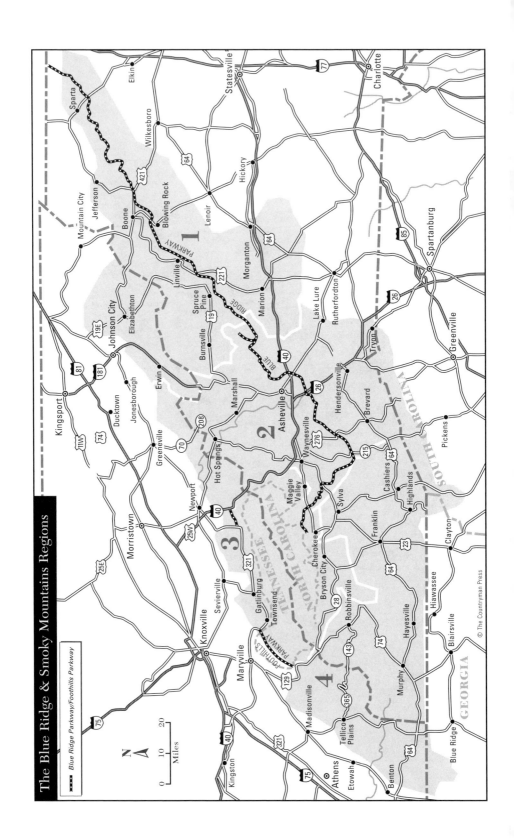

Blue Ridge Parkway/Foothills Parkway

© The Countryman Press

CONTENTS

INTRODUCTION

Some travel experiences are for passive enjoyment, for being gently led from meal to pastime to meal. Not so the Blue Ridge and Smoky Mountains. This area is for involvement—for finding the perfect little inn with broad views from an antiques-furnished room, for discovering the wonderful meal superbly prepared at a little roadhouse, for digging up the odd little corner, the unforgettable museum, the remarkable site. The Blue Ridge and Smoky Mountains are for exploring.

And this is a guide for explorers. It is a guide for finding your way down a winding mountain road to a beautiful river, a quiet log cabin, or a wide view. This guide seeks out the memorable, the unique, and the worthwhile—whether it be a place to visit, a place to shop, a place to eat, or a place to stay. It excludes the ordinary or routine places—after all, there are plenty of those back home. And unlike many guides, it doesn't charge fees or accept advertising. This is a collection of personal recommendations.

This guide centers on two of the most popular national park lands in the nation: the Great Smoky Mountains National Park, and the Blue Ridge Parkway. In doing so it covers the 40 highest peaks of the East, the most biodiverse forests in temperate North America, scores of waterfalls, and hundreds of panoramic views. We go well beyond the boundaries of the national parks, however, to cover all of the surrounding mountains and forests, the small towns and the settled valleys. Here you will find tidy county seats, brick-front downtowns little changed in half a century, artists' colonies hidden away in remote valleys, and well-tended farms and old log cabins that welcome overnight visitors. You'll find the homes of Carl Sandburg and Daniel Boone, the summer estate of an aristocratic South Carolina governor, and the log cabin of a frontiersman North Carolina governor. And you will find lots of outdoor activities as well— whitewater sports, horseback riding, stillwater boating, fishing, rock climbing, snow skiing, and golf.

Specifically, this guide covers the most rugged areas of the South's two great mountain ranges, the Blue Ridge and the Smokies/Unakas. The Blue Ridge, with its long series of gray cliffs facing the distant Atlantic, defines the eastern edge of the region. A set of mile-high ridges defines the western edge, variously named (from south to north) the Unicoi Mountains, the Great Smoky Mountains, the

Bald Mountains, the Unaka Mountains, the Yellow Mountains, and the Stone Mountains. Together, these are commonly called the Unakas (*you-NAY-kuhs*) by geologists, and the Smokies by ordinary folk; this book splits the difference and calls them the Smokies/Unakas.

This guide divides this 10,000-square-mile area (larger than New Jersey) into 20 chapters. Each chapter takes in a coherent area with a good range of sites, activities, and places to stay. The chapters are grouped into four broad areas, each a major region worthy of a long trip. The Great Smoky Mountains National Park gets four chapters to itself, making up one entire part of the book. The Blue Ridge Parkway, over 250 miles long and very skinny, also gets four chapters, spread throughout the first half of the book; these chapters always have "Blue Ridge Parkway" in their titles. The remaining chapters cover the areas between the two great national parks—frequently as rugged, as wildly beautiful, and as entertaining as the parks themselves.

This guide gains strength from being part of an established series known for its high standards—The Countryman Press's Explorer's Guide series. As part of this series, *The Blue Ridge & Smoky Mountains* shares a format polished from long experience and honed to the needs of adventurous travelers. Each chapter covers an area that can be conveniently explored from any of its listed inns. The chapter starts with an overview, then follows with general descriptions of exploring the scenery (*Wandering Around*), the major areas of natural scenic beauty (*Wild Places*), and the major settled places (*Villages*); the titled paragraphs let you go straight to the parts that interest you. After that, the chapter gets down to specifics: sites and attractions worth a visit (*To See*); outdoor activities (*To Do*); the most interesting of the area's best lodging (*Lodging*); places to get good, fresh food prepared from scratch (*Where to Eat*); places with regular evening entertainment

THE BLUE RIDGE PARKWAY IS LINED WITH MILES OF SPLIT-RAIL FENCE.

Jim Hargan

(*Entertainment*); unique shops and worthwhile shopping districts (*Selective Shopping*); and some of the best of the annual festivals (*Special Events*).

Readers experienced with our New England guides will immediately notice that this guide spends a lot more time in the woods, and a lot less time in the towns. Travelers experienced with the American South will see nothing odd in this; in much of the South, the woods are the good part. Yet this guide finds much to recommend in the towns and villages of the Blue Ridge and Smoky Mountains. Most remarkable are the busy, well-tended brick-front downtowns that appear in one country town after another, from Sparta in the far north to Copperhill, 290 miles south. Equally amazing are the artists' colonies spread throughout these hills, from Penland with its 100 or more studios to Tellico Plains with a dozen impressive local crafters. Not surprisingly, good shopping can be found in some unexpected places.

Our author, Jim Hargan, lives deep in the Blue Ridge and Smoky Mountains, near the small town of Mars Hill. A travel photographer and writer with a background in geography, he's been involved with the Smokies since vacationing there as a small boy and attending one of the mountain universities. The Blue Ridge and Smoky Mountains region remains one of his core specialties (Great Britain being the other), and he brings his own local insights to his recommendations.

Appalachians or Alleghenies? Are these really the Appalachian Mountains? Or are they the Alleghenies? Or perhaps the Alleghenies are farther west, and the "Appalachians" include them, along with the Great Valley (Knoxville and Chattanooga), the Smokies/Unakas, and the Blue Ridge. All such usages can be found in contemporary writing. So what's the real name of these mountains?

In 1565 French cartographer Jacques Le Moyne published a map of Florida in which he identified a mountain range, far to Florida's north, which he labeled the "Montes Apalatchi." Evidently the Apalachee Indians of the Florida Panhandle had boasted to Le Moyne that they owned these mountains, an obvious tall tale.

A MOUNTAIN MEADOW.

Jim Hargan

At any rate, both Le Moyne and his Florida informants had been referring to the Georgia Blue Ridge, not the entire mountain chain that stretches from Alabama to Nova Scotia. Five years later, however, Gerard Mercator repeated "Montes Apalatchi" on his landmark map; the term stuck, and the mountains became known as the Appalachians.

If only the story were that simple. The fact was, the name *Appalachian* was a silly one and nobody liked it. By the late 1700s it had died out in favor of the Allegheny Mountains, and the term *Appalachian* disappeared from use. By the late 19th century, only antiquarians knew the meaning of *Appalachian*.

And that is exactly where it came from. In 1861 Swiss geographer Arnold Guyot revived the term and applied it to "the Appalachian Mountain System," which he identified as consisting of the eastern mountains (the Blue Ridge and Smokies/Unakas), the Great Valley of Tennessee (Knoxville and Chattanooga), and a plateau escarpment farther west whose heavily dissected edge has a mountainous look. The mountain people disliked Guyot's new terms (if they ever heard of them), and continued to use *Allegheny* well into the 20th century (one of North Carolina's mountain counties is named Allegheny). But it was no use, as academics of the era had their own ideas. Twentieth-century geographers followed Guyot's lead and ignored common usage, even taking the liberty of moving the term *Allegheny* westward from the Blue Ridge to the plateau escarpment. Sociologists followed, professing to discover a unified social and cultural region in Guyot's "Appalachian Mountain System." They dubbed this purported region "Appalachia," a place they described as characterized by social atavism and extreme poverty—". . . a strange land inhabited by a peculiar people" as one writer put it. No wonder terms remain confusing.

With all this, you will be pleased to learn that both the names *Blue Ridge* and *Smoky Mountains* are authentic early terms, in common usage by the mid–18th century. Cherokee names still abound, and some, such as Nantahala (*nanta-HAY-la*) and Unaka (*you-NAY-ka*) retain their original pronunciation.

About This Book. Unlike many other guidebooks, Explorer's Guides are not collections of paid advertising. No establishment has been charged a fee or allowed to supply copy. Rather, these entries are the personal recommendations of the author, a geographer, travel specialist, and longtime resident of the Smokies and Blue Ridge.

This guide does all it can to include phone numbers, addresses, and prices. You can be safely assured that, by the time you read this book, some of this information is out of date—especially the prices. Use them for comparison, with each other and your budget. Make a little inflation adjustment in your head; these prices were quoted to the author in mid-2004.

Here are a few notes about the organization of this book.

Wandering Around—The one thing you can always rely on in the Blue Ridge and Smoky Mountains is some first-rate sightseeing. This section orients you to an area's scenic qualities while steering you toward the best of the roads and trails.

Wild Places—In the Blue Ridge and Smoky Mountains, settled areas can be widely separated islands in a sea of trees—"plowed spaces" or "paved spaces" in an area where wildlands are the norm. This section describes, in broad terms, the qualities of the giant wild tracts of publicly accessible lands, and follows this with the best of the parks and picnic areas. (New visitors should note that picnicking is an excellent alternative in a land where restaurants are far apart and may not be very good.)

Villages—Of course, the American South doesn't really have villages in the northern sense. More typical is a small county seat with a courthouse and a brick-front downtown, surrounded by many miles of dispersed farms and houses in which settlements are names on the map without specific centers. The mountains are no different. This section describes all places with well-defined centers that a visitor might want to visit or stumble into by accident, plus a few dispersed settlements that feature notable sites mentioned elsewhere in the text. In congested areas, this section gives tips on parking.

To See—Worthwhile destinations are listed here. To get in, a place must be unique and interesting in some mountainy way—the sort of thing you traveled here to see. After all, there are plenty of water slides and miniature golf places back home. Listed places must be reasonably authentic, and not exploitative to either the mountain folk or their own customers. You won't find any salted gem mines or "hillbilly hoedowns" in these pages (but there are several authentic local gem mines and mountain music venues).

To Do—These entries list outdoor activities for those who get antsy with too much relaxing. This book tries to include all outdoor sports that are quiet and noninvasive, as well as some golf courses and ski slopes.

Lodging—This book lists only independent, local establishments with high standards of comfort, cleanliness, and hospitality. Not all worthy establishments can be listed; we've tried to give a good selection of different types of places, emphasizing character and uniqueness. Unless noted, listed lodgings have private baths for all rooms. We make a special effort to find places that are disabled accessible, family friendly, and/or pet friendly, but we are not always able to find such places in each chapter.

Where to Eat—This section emphasizes food made fresh from scratch, using fresh ingredients. It lists places in two categories: casual, inexpensive places in *Eating Out*, and formal, expensive places in *Dining Out*. In *Eating Out* the occasional catered (premade) side is allowed if the price is right and the atmosphere nice; in *Dining Out* catered or precooked food is unforgivable.

Entertainment—The Smokies are not noted for their lively nightclub scene. This section lists places that have authentic mountain music and bluegrass (*mountain music* being the old-time folk music on which bluegrass is based), as well as summer theater, regular classical music schedules, and some miscellaneous neat stuff.

Selective Shopping—As with other entries, this section emphasizes the unique and unusual. Rather than a complete listing, it's typically a few suggestions to help get you started in the right direction. Sometimes it lists individual shops; in other places it gives a general description of a shopping district as an aid in exploration. You'll find a lot of craft galleries listed, as this region is a major center of the Fine Crafts movement.

Special Events—Again, this is not a complete listing, but rather a selection of some of the most worthwhile annual events and festivals.

WHAT'S WHERE IN THE BLUE RIDGE & SMOKY MOUNTAINS

AREA CODES No fewer than six area codes extend into the Blue Ridge and Smoky Mountains from nearby urban areas. In North Carolina most areas are in the **828** code, while the northernmost mountain counties are in **336**. In Tennessee the southern and the northern Smokies/Unakas use **423**, while the central Smokies/Unakas are included with Knoxville's **865**. South Carolina's mountains are in area code **864**, while the northern Georgia mountains are in **706**.

AIRPORTS AND AIRLINES There are six airports with scheduled passenger service in or near this region, five of which have jet service. Most visitors will want to fly into either the **Asheville Regional Airport** or the **Mc-Ghee Tyson Airport** in Knoxville. There are, however, some exceptions: the **Greenville-Spartanburg International Airport** (South Carolina) is the closest to Brevard and Cashiers/Highlands; Tennessee's **Chattanooga Metropolitan Airport** is closer to Copperhill and Murphy; and the **Tri-Cities Airport** (Johnson City, Bristol, and Kingsport, TN) is closest to the northernmost counties. **Hickory Regional Airport** (North Carolina) has regular commuter

flights from the **Charlotte/Douglas International Airport** in Charlotte, NC, and leaves you just underneath the Blue Ridge near Boone and Morganton. Bargain hunters should consider flying into the nearest major hubs (either Charlotte or Atlanta) and driving from there into the mountains (typically 2 to 4 hours). In any case, expect to rent a car; these mountains have virtually no regional or local bus service.

AMTRAK There is no passenger train service to these mountains; not even Chattanooga gets a choo-choo these days. The closest approach is at **Greenville** and **Spartanburg**, SC, about 45 minutes south of Asheville, NC, where the Crescent stops twice a day.

AMUSEMENT PARKS This book does not cover amusement or theme parks, as a modern intrusion from the outside having nothing to do with mountain wilderness or culture. Still, there are several such parks within this region, of varying quality. For those who like such things, look for amusement parks outside the main gates of the Great Smoky Mountains National Park, at Gatlinburg and Pigeon Forge,

TN, and at Cherokee and Maggie Valley, NC—Pigeon Forge's **Dollywood** being the largest and best of this bunch. Aficionados of Wild West attractions will find three to choose from, at Boone, Maggie Valley, and Franklin (all in North Carolina). The Boone Wild West attraction features the **ET & WNC (Tweetsie Railroad)**, a historic steam locomotive that was in local, commercial use through most of the first half of the 20th century (see *Historic Sites* in "The Mountains of Northern Tennessee").

ANTIQUES Antiques lovers used to the rich selections in the Virginia Blue Ridge and the mountains of New England may find this region disappointing. Truth is, most of these valleys were unspeakably poor until the 1950s and '60s, and folk did not buy a lot of fancy furniture. Still, this is a good area to look for old farm implements; animal-drawn plowing did not die out in most of these valleys until the 1960s and '70s.

APPALACHIAN TRAIL Blazed in the 1930s as the world's first long-distance recreational footpath, the Appalachian Trail stretches for well over 2,000 miles along the East's wildest and toughest mountains, from Georgia to Maine. Although officially part of the National Park System (as a National Scenic Trail), the Appalachian Trail is mainly a private volunteer effort, blazed and maintained by 31 hiking clubs that make up the **Appalachian Trail Conference** (304-535-6331; www.atconf.org), 799 Washington St., Harpers Ferry, WV 25425. This book covers 365 miles of the trail, including the ultra-popular stretch through the Great Smoky Mountains National Park. Various chapters include rewarding day hikes along bits of the trail.

APPLES Cherokees introduced apple growing to the Blue Ridge and Smoky Mountains in the early 18th century, having picked it up from the Creeks (who had learned it from Spanish missions in "La Florida"). While English settlers dismissed apple horticulture as impractical in the cold mountain climate, the Cherokees learned to grow trees in special valleys turned warm by persistent air inversions. Nineteenth-century mountain folk took up the Cherokee techniques in a big way, creating the beginnings of a mountain apple industry. Today the **Brevard** area has the largest commercial orchards (see "Chimney Rock & Saluda"), while a fine heritage orchard is open to the public at **Altapass**, along the Blue Ridge Parkway (see"Blowing Rock & Grandfather Mountain"). U-pick-ems are a common site in the Brevard area, and are found in most parts of this region; look to pick apples late August through early October.

Jim Hargan

ARTISTS AND ART GALLERIES In the 1920s and '30s, folk crafts were widely seen as a way of bringing hard cash into remote mountain coves. Folk art schools and guilds founded in that era to support the economic development of poor mountain families survive today as centers of the Fine Crafts movement, dominated by university-educated artists building on mountain traditions. The remaining major schools include the **Penland School of Crafts** in Penland, NC, and the **John C. Campbell Folk School** in Brasstown, NC; the **Southern Highland Crafts Guild** promotes craft artists from its headquarters in Asheville, NC.

BALDS, GRASSY While most of these mountains are covered in dense forest, an occasional grassy meadow will cling to a high ridgeline. Known as grassy balds, these high meadows furnish wide panoramas across swaths of wildflowers, framed in spring by bushes purple with Catawba rhododendrons and orange with flame azaleas. These balds may be as small as a few dozen acres, but may also sweep for miles along a high ridge. Their origin is unclear. Grassy balds were far more common in the 19th century, when 100,000 cattle grazed along the crest of the Great Smoky Mountains every summer. Left ungrazed, these great fields have been returning to forest since the start of the 20th century. The grassy balds may have been created by the Cherokees, burned out to create wildlife habitat for hunting. Or they may have been formed by grazing elk and buffalo in the 16th–18th centuries, then maintained by cattle after the elk and buffalo had been hunted to extinction. The largest surviving grassy balds are in the **Roan Highlands** (see "Spruce Pine & Burnsville").

BALDS, ROCKY Unlike grassy balds, rocky balds are a completely natural phenomenon. Common to the Blue Ridge, a rocky bald consists of a broad expanse of smoothly curving, exposed bedrock, elevated at any possible angle from dead flat to totally vertical. A typical rocky bald will extend 1–5 acres, with the bare rock covered by patches of moss and an occasional dwarf pine. The rock looks like granite, but isn't; it's gneiss (pronounced *nice*), a metamorphosed granite whose peculiar geology causes this unusual formation. Along the Blue Ridge, this ancient gneiss has been compressed under immense pressure for most of the last quarter billion years, only to be raised up and exposed by erosion during the last 50 million years or so. This great relief of pressure has allowed the gneiss to expand like a spring, in the stateliest of slow motion, exfoliating in thinly compressed layers. This exfoliation is just fast enough to slough off soil as fast as it forms, leaving the bedrock smooth and bare. Needless to say, rocky balds furnish some of the most dramatic views anywhere. One of the most impressive sights along the Blue Ridge is an entire dome of rock exposed in this way, such as **Looking Glass Rock**, visible for miles from the Blue Ridge Parkway (see "Waynesville & the Blue Ridge Parkway").

BARBEQUE People who've heard of the wondrous qualities of North Carolina barbeque will be unpleasantly surprised to learn that this rich and varied tradition seldom extends into the mountains. Instead of the piquant, slow-cooked Piedmont barbeque with its vinegar-cayenne baste

Jim Hargan

and a gregarious host who never seems to tire of meeting new people and giving a helping hand to visitors.

By the way, you might want to check the Internet for a B&B web page before calling for a reservation. Nearly all of them have one, and most show photos of the individual rooms.

BERRY PICKING Wild berries are available for the picking throughout the public lands of the Blue Ridge and Smoky Mountains. Old fields and grassy balds offer **wild strawberries** in June, then **blackberries** in mid-August, with **blueberries** in the high grassy balds in late August and early September Wild strawberries, tiny and intensely flavored, hide low among the grasses in old fields. Blackberries grow on thorny canes in old fields that are full of chiggers. Blueberries grow on low, woody bushes on grassy and rocky balds, and like the cool, wet weather above 4,000 feet. There are lots of other edible berries; look for a ranger-led talk in a national park or forest. You can collect up to a gallon of each type of berry per day without a permit in the national park and forest lands—free fun that kids love.

and its coleslaw made fresh with the barbeque sauce, mountain visitors are more likely to find gas-grilled meat smothered with a ketchupy tomato sauce, served with sweet, mayonnaisey coleslaw. Good barbeque, slow-cooked over wood, does exist in the mountains, and we highlight it when we find it.

BED & BREAKFASTS A rare sight 20 years ago, bed & breakfasts are now found in every part of the Blue Ridge and Smoky Mountains except Cherokee. They are generally price-competitive with local motels, and a whole lot nicer. Small and friendly, a B&B is a good way to relax and meet the locals. A typical mountain B&B will have a wide porch with rocking chairs and a view over a garden, a great room with comfortable sofas and chairs grouped around a wood fire, a friendly group of guests who swap experiences over a luxurious breakfast or an evening glass of wine,

BICYCLING The Blue Ridge and Smoky Mountains offer wonderful opportunities for bicyclists. Back roads, increasingly paved, have wonderful scenery and light traffic, with a downside of narrow, shoulderless lanes and the occasional mean farm dog. The premier road biking experience is the **Blue Ridge Parkway**, where the scenery is nonstop and wide shoulders, gentle curves, and frequent pullovers reduce traffic problems. The huge tracts of national forest land found throughout this region offer many miles of trail biking, mainly down old logging roads. Finally, a few places offer dedicated bicycle trails, most notably the Nantahala National Forest's **Tsali Recreation Area**. For those who don't travel with their bicycles, this book lists rentals in most areas.

THE BLUE RIDGE PARKWAY The 469-mile Blue Ridge Parkway stretches from the southern edge of the Shenandoah National Park (in Virginia, near Washington, DC) to the North Carolina gateway of the Great Smoky Mountains National Park. Over 250 miles of the parkway cross this book's region, following the crest of the Blue Ridge from the North Carolina–Virginia state line to Asheville, NC, then climbing a series of remote mile-high peaks over to the Smokies.

Constructed between 1936 and 1989, the parkway was originally intended as a Depression make-work project, with a long-range goal of bringing tourist dollars to the depressed mountain coves of Virginia and North Carolina. By this standard, it's a roaring success; the parkway gets 20 million recreation visitors a year, the largest of any National Park Service property, and comparable to New York City and Disney World.

Built and operated by the National Park Service, the parkway's typical 1,000-foot width has been carefully and unobtrusively landscaped over its entire length for a continuously beautiful drive. The effect is subtle, but remarkable. Grassy verges curve into forests, giving views deep into the trees; split-rail fences line pastures and farmlands; forests drop away suddenly to give wide and dramatic mountain views over low stone walls. Bridges, tunnels, and abutments are clad in hand-laid stonework, done by

artisans brought in from Europe. Commercial intrusion is virtually non-existent, and modern buildings a rare sight. The National Park Service furnishes a small number of concession areas, widely spaced, where food, gasoline, and lodging are available.

BUGS First the good news. The Blue Ridge and Smoky Mountains are largely free of swarming blackflies, midges, and mosquitoes—the kind that form clouds around your face and fill your nose when you try to breathe. What's more, flies and roaches are less of a nuisance here than in warmer parts of the South. This is not to say that these mountains are free of all pests, however. You are likely to get **chiggers**—microscopic larvae buried in your skin—anytime you sit on the ground in even slightly warm weather. **Ticks** are very common, and likely to jump on you anytime you brush against a plant in warm weather. Chigger bites itch like crazy, and can last for weeks if you have an allergic reaction (most people do). Ticks spread diseases, some of them crippling or fatal. Your best defense

Jim Hargan

against both chiggers and ticks is to wear long sleeves and pants, and spray insect repellent around your neck, belt, and cuffs.

BUS SERVICE There is only one scheduled passenger bus route in this region, a **Greyhound** line from Greenville, SC, to Asheville, NC, then northward out of the mountains into Tennessee. Along the way, the bus stops at the mountain towns of Hendersonville and Waynesville, NC.

CAMPING Campgrounds are found in abundance throughout this region. The national parks and forests contain scores of public campgrounds, generally cheap and scenic but without hookups. (The popular campgrounds within the Great Smoky Mountains National Park don't even have showers.) While many of the public campgrounds stay booked up all summer, you can always find a good site in a remote, beautiful little national forest campground down a gravel road somewhere; ask a ranger at the nearest district station (listed in this book under *Guidance*). Private campgrounds are the best bet for RVers who insist on electricity and running water.

Jim Hargan

CANOEING AND KAYAKING This region has abundant whitewater and stillwater, with suitable streams in nearly every chapter. Famous whitewater streams include the **Ocoee**, site of the 1996 Summer Olympics; the **Nantahala**, well known as a training ground for Olympic medalists; and the **Chattooga**, made famous in the novel *Deliverance*. Two other rivers, the **New River** and the **French Broad River**, offer excellent areas for long, scenic canoe trips, perfect for overnight camping. Places to hire canoes and kayaks, join a whitewater rafting party, or have your boat shuttled to a drop-off point are noted throughout this book.

CHEROKEES This entire region was the core home of the Cherokees, centering on the fertile valleys of the Little Tennessee River south of the Great Smoky Mountains. The Cherokees lived in villages ranging from half a dozen to several score houses, made of logs and surrounded by cultivated fields. These were organized along clan lines, similar to the Scottish Highlands but without the constant warfare; the Cherokee villages shared a traditional legal code, enforced through consensus and the leadership of chiefs. Until the wars of the late 18th century, the Cherokees had three major settlement areas: an area of villages in upstate South Carolina, a second area in the deep mountains to the immediate south of the Smokies, and a third area (called the Overhill area) at the foot of the mountains in Tennessee. The more northern mountains, around present-day Burnsville and Boone, were kept as a hunting ground.

In the late 18th century the Cherokees tried to defeat the European invaders in battle, with disastrous consequences. After that, tribal consensus swung toward working within the invaders' legal system. Led by wealthy, Europeanized chiefs, the tribe formed itself into a quasi-autonomous legal entity known as the **Cherokee Nation**, located in northern Georgia, southeastern Tennessee, and the westernmost corner of the North Carolina mountains. In 1838 President Andrew Jackson's administration expelled the Cherokee Nation to Oklahoma, forcing the Cherokees into a deadly winter march known as the Trail of Tears.

About 600 Cherokees remained in the deep coves of the Smokies, and their descendants still live, work, and thrive in these mountains. The **Eastern Band** of the Cherokee Nation, some 10,000 strong, inhabits a sizable reservation, properly called the **Qualla Boundary**, located on the North Carolina side of the Great Smoky Mountains National Park.

CHILDREN, ESPECIALLY FOR I spent many a summer as a child in these mountains, and vividly remember the things I found the most fun: splashing in mountain streams, exploring the forests, picking berries, visiting log cabins, sifting for rubies, and climbing around on rocky crags with dramatic views.

Whitewater rafting hadn't been invented yet, else that would have made the list as well. Rustic cabins were a lot neater than motel rooms, especially on cool, rainy days when we played board games by the wood fire. Home-cooked suppers at our cabins were more fun for us than eating out, and picnics in a national park were more fun than burgers in a tourist town. Museums could be patience

Jim Hargan

testers, but log cabins and pioneer log farms were endlessly fascinating—particularly those with farm animals, or gristmills that worked. We liked to walk down short, easy trails, particularly to cliffs or waterfalls, or just get out of the car and run around. We gained these tastes as small children, and retained them as teenagers; perhaps if we had first seen the mountains at age 14 we would have been too cool for any of this.

This region is jammed with child-appropriate, family-friendly stuff. The text makes a serious effort to mention anything that will challenge a child's patience, endurance, or safety, making it easy to judge what's right for your kids. Please note that most B&Bs do not accept children under 12; the text notes those that do with a crayon icon ✎.

COTTAGE RENTALS Cottage rentals have long been a tradition in these mountains, and have become increasingly popular in recent years. In some places small compounds of log cabins, recently built in traditional styles and luxuriously furnished, have been springing up faster than chain motels. A rental cabin can be a pleasant retreat for a couple, with its ample space, separate living room, and porch; for a family with kids, it can also be a major money saver, allowing breakfasts and dinners at home with picnic lunches on the road.

This book includes a selection of good cabin compounds throughout the region. Many of these cottages can be rented for only a night or two; others require rental periods of up to a week.

COUNTRY STORES As towns thrive and prosper, country stores decline and disappear. However, country stores continue to survive in some of our most remote rural areas, serving the needs of residents who live too far from town. Others, such as the famous **Mast General Store** (see "Boone & Banner Elk") near Boone, NC, have survived and thrived by combining the tourist trade with their local business. This book mentions a number of general stores.

Jim Hargan

DRY COUNTIES These mountain regions are a patchwork of local liquor laws. Both North Carolina and Tennessee allow local options on beer, wine, and liquor sales, and North Carolina still has a socialized liquor control system. Depending on where you are, you may be able to buy wine and beer but not liquor, liquor but not wine or beer, wine or beer in a store but not a restaurant, or in a restaurant but not a store—or all sales may be banned outright. That is, except for golf clubs, tennis clubs, or hotels and restaurants within 3 miles of the Blue Ridge Parkway. This book tries to mention whether wine is available at a fine dining spot, but it's best to check in advance.

EMERGENCIES There is nothing more frightening than having a serious medical emergency and not knowing where the nearest emergency room is. For this reason, each chapter introduction includes the location of the nearest emergency room, as well as the walk-in clinic if one exists.

FALL FOLIAGE The Blue Ridge and Smoky Mountains boast one of America's outstanding autumn color displays—the result of a large variety of species, spread over a large range of elevations and habitats. Look for color to begin in early October and reach its peak in the middle of the month. From then, colors will last until the first strong wind, generally in the third or fourth week of October. Most years color is nearly gone by early November.

FISHING This region is a wonderful place for fly-fishing, and this book tries to include contact information

Jim Hargan

The mountains being what they are, this book frequently recommends touring on gravel-surfaced roads. These are roads that have been improved by pounding in a mixture of gravel and rock dust, the rock dust acting as a sort of temporary cement. Gravel roads form potholes and washboardlike ridges if not graded once or twice a year, a condition most apt to occur on Forest Service roads. The text will highlight known problems. In general, if a road starts looking too rough for you, don't hesitate to turn around and go back.

for guides. You will need a state fishing license everywhere but within the Cherokee Reservation, where you will need a tribal license instead.

HIGHWAYS AND ROADS This region is crossed by **Interstate 40** from east to west, and by **Interstate 26** from north to south; they intersect at Asheville, NC. I-26 now extends north from Asheville to cross into Tennessee, intersecting with I-81 north of Johnson City.

Apart from interstates and US highways, this book follows a welter of road types. State highways are designated, say, NC 80 or TN 70. Although these are supposed to be main through-highways, some are no better than local roads with fancy signs, and three of them in North Carolina are gravel surfaced (NC 281, NC 197, and NC 90). Local roads have names in Tennessee, Georgia, and South Carolina, but four-digit numbers in North Carolina. National Park Service roads always have names. National Forest Service roads have numbers such as FS 712; please note that many Forest Service roads are not passable for passenger autos.

HIGHWAYS AND ROADS IN NORTH CAROLINA Unlike other states, North Carolina has no local roads. All of its rural roads are state roads, from the largest freeway down to the roughest dirt rut. The state's Department of Transportation (known as NCDOT, or NickDot) distinguishes state highways from state roads. **State highways** are considered major thoroughfares, with regular state highway signs and two- or three-digit numbers, such as NC 90 or NC 197. **State roads** have four-digit numbers, typically marked on stop signs with those little home address stick-on numbers. In this book, state roads are denoted as, for example, SSR 1300 or SSR 1407, the

Jim Hargan

SSR standing for "state secondary road." We've tried very hard to get the state road numbers right, because—unlike road names—they are almost always present at intersections. Don't expect locals, however, to direct you to an SSR number; no one in the state pays attention to them.

HIKING Sooner or later, nearly everyone gets out of their car and walks through the woods. The Blue Ridge and Smoky Mountains are laced with footpaths, up creeks and along ridges. There are thousands of miles of walking trails to choose from, with good choices in every chapter of this book. The *Wandering Around* section contains a suggestion or two, very rewarding and not particularly difficult. Other sections will mention still more trails, each with a brief indication of the type of scenery, as well as its difficulty and length.

HORSEBACK RIDING Most parts of this region have at least one horseback riding stable. Some offer trail rides on their own property, while others outfit longer expeditions on national forest lands. Nearly every chapter lists at least one stable under *To Do*. In addition, there are several listed accommodations that offer stabling for people who travel with their horses.

HUNTING The main hunting season runs from **September through January**. Remember that hunting is allowed in all national forest lands, including the 16 wilderness areas; you should always wear hunter orange in these areas during the season. If you wish to avoid hunting areas altogether, stay in the three national parks and 11 state parks (which, fortunately, offer plenty of outdoor opportunity). Hunting is also prohibited on Sunday in North Carolina, making that a good day to enjoy God's creation (but wear hunter orange anyway, just in case).

INFORMATION As much as we like to be encyclopedic in our coverage, we admit that there is nothing like fresh, local information. Each chapter of this book lists the relevant chambers of commerce, along with their toll-free numbers and web page, under *Guidance*. We also describe the local tourist information center, so you can drop by and talk to someone friendly and in the know.

LAKES There are no natural lakes in this region. All the lakes in the Blue Ridge and Smoky Mountains are human-made, mostly for hydropower. Typically the lake drowns a steep-sided mountain valley, twisting upstream for miles through roadless areas into steep-sided woodlands, poking little inlets up side valleys. In many cases the shores are national forest lands, with no restrictions on boatside camping. Other lakes are privately owned, however—and this may include the lake's surface as well as

Jim Hargan

Jim Hargan

by allowing rainwater to run straight down, rather than beading up on the underside of a round log. While barns frequently used round logs, a round log cabin is invariably modern.

This book will sometimes describe a log cabin in terms of its cribs. A **crib** is the rectangle made when the logs are fit together; doors and windows are then cut out of the cribs. The simplest cabins had one crib, covered with a roof. Larger cabins had two cribs, and the cribs could be placed together to form a two-room cabin, separated by a chimney (a rare form in the South), or (most commonly) separated by a roofed central breezeway, or **dogtrot**.

Log cabins were an important part of mountain life—but today all the log cabins you will see will be carefully restored museum pieces, or else abandoned hulks. Not so with log barns; keep an eye peeled for log barns still in use along any back road, and particularly in the areas covered by Part 1.

LOST Even with the best maps, you are likely to get lost once you stray from a main highway. On these twisting roads, even the sharpest explorers will lose their sense of direction. Your best defense is a compass—one of those round ones you stick on your dashboard. Pay attention to it along several twists, and take an average. This will at least tell you if you are going generally toward your destination or away from it. And relax. How bad can it be? Getting lost is an adventure, not a disaster.

MAPS: ROAD MAPS Really good road maps can be a problem in the mountains. Main highways are easy enough to follow, but back roads are a twisty

the surrounding shore. This book will point out interesting opportunities as they arise, as well as give contact information for lake-oriented fishing guides.

LOG CABINS While most of us associate log cabins with the first generations of settlers, log construction continued in these mountains into the early 20th century. This was not a matter of isolation or tradition so much as saving money: Logs were free, while milled studs required scarce dollars. **Mountain Farm Museum** in the Great Smoky Mountains National Park displays a superbly crafted log cabin built by its owner in 1902 (see "Cherokee & the Southeast Quadrant").

In these parts, all vernacular log cabins were built with planked logs— that is, logs that had their vertical sides hewn flat. Planking reduced rot maze, frequently with no regular names. Once you start exploring a back road, your folding highway map won't help you much. The great paper atlases from **DeLorme** (www .delorme.com) show all the back roads as well as the shapes of the mountains, giving extra clues for your party's navigator to analyze. Unfortunately, you'll have to buy four individual state volumes to cover the entire Blue Ridge and Smoky Mountains area; this will give you a bonus (possibly unneeded and unwanted) of incredibly detailed coverage of the entire Mid-South from the Atlantic seaboard to the Mississippi River.

A computer street atlas of the U.S. is much cheaper, if you can get used to using your laptop in a moving car. But whatever map you use, be prepared to get lost every once in a while.

MAPS: USGS TOPOS

Of course, no serious outdoors enthusiast will step away from the parking lot without a U.S. Geological Survey topographic map, showing every detail of mountain slopes at 2.66 inches to the mile. Unfortunately, the USGS hasn't gotten around to updating some of these mountain topos since the Great Depression; the slopes haven't changed much, but don't expect anything else to be very accurate. The good news: The U.S. Forest Service has marked up black-and-white copies of the USGS maps with their own information, giving accurate local road data as well as Forest Service roads, trails, recreation sites, and landownership. To get these first-rate maps, inquire at the local ranger district office, listed under *Guidance*; each office has the maps for their area, and no other.

MOUNTAINTOPS

Nearly all of the Blue Ridge and Smoky Mountains are covered in dense forest. You can walk for miles along a high ridgeline without ever having a view. Of course, the forests are a prime attraction of these mountains, endlessly varied and with more tree species than Europe. However, the occasional overwhelmingly dramatic panorama is certainly welcome, the more so if you don't have to hike all day to find it. The best views are from balds, great sweeps of open grass or rocky ground. Other views are intentionally created and maintained by the National Park Service within the Great Smoky Mountains National Park or along the Blue Ridge Parkway. This book highlights the best of the views, both roadside and from the easier paths.

MUSIC

This guide tries to find and describe worthwhile music venues throughout the region. These range from rural dance halls, to weekend bluegrass jams, to large-scale classical music festivals. Mountain music is featured most often, along with bluegrass—the local favorite, more popular than Nashville-style country. Classical music is found near the universities, along with jazz, and the

Jim Hargan

Jim Hargan

Brevard Music Center hosts a major classical music festival every summer.

MUSIC, MOUNTAIN Mountain music isn't bluegrass, and it definitely isn't country. Mountain music is the music people knew before radios came along, the music they used to play deep in the coves and hollows. Mountain music was already a fast-disappearing anachronism when Mars Hill, NC, native Bascom Lamar Lunsford started his vast collection of mountain folk music, mixing heavily with nationally circulating sheet music and radio broadcasts. Today it represents a carefully preserved folk tradition, still popular and readily available throughout this region. This book cites mountain music venues wherever it can.

PETS Only a few B&Bs will allow pets, and these are highlighted in the text with a dog-paw icon 🐾. You will have better luck with a cottage rental, which fortunately are very common in this area, but verify in advance that your pet will be welcome. Of the places that allow pets, many charge an extra fee or restrict pets to special units. The Great Smoky Mountains National Park prohibits pets on all hiking trails with no exceptions, and requires dogs to be kept on leashes at all times anywhere else.

PUBLIC LANDS: THE NATIONAL PARK SERVICE The National Park Service (www.nps.gov), a bureau of the U.S. Department of the Interior, maintains three properties in this region: the Great Smoky Mountains National Park, the Blue Ridge Parkway, and Carl Sandburg Home National Historic Site. Each has its own management style. **Great Smoky Mountains National Park**— the only designated national park of the three and the most visited national park in America—has always been maintained as a wilderness park with the emphasis on hiking, camping, picnicking, and fishing. The **Blue Ridge Parkway** (the most visited

Jim Hargan

property managed by the NPS) is more purely recreational, with hotels, restaurants, and even gas stations along its length. The **Carl Sandburg Home**, small and little visited, faithfully preserves the great poet's historic antebellum estate the way he knew it—including an active goat farm. All three share one major characteristic with each other and every other NPS property: They are all preserves, each safeguarding a precious resource for the future. All prohibit hunting, gathering plants, rockhounding, and picking wildflowers.

PUBLIC LANDS: THE NATIONAL FOREST SERVICE People frequently confuse the National Forest Service with the National Park Service—yet the two agencies couldn't be more different. While the National Park Service preserves our finest natural and historic lands, the National Forest Service—part of the Department of Agriculture—manages forestlands for sustainable exploitation. The National Forest Service logs many of its tracts, getting much of its operating revenues from timber sales. It allows hunting on virtually all its lands, including congressionally declared wildernesses. The actual uses allowed on any tract of national forest land—logging, recreation, preservation—is set by a plan that is revised every 8 years.

This region has five national forests, any one of which dwarfs the local national parks in size: the **Cherokee** in Tennessee, the **Chattahoochee** in Georgia, the **Sumter** in South Carolina, the **Nantahala** in the southern half of the North Carolina mountains, and the **Pisgah** in the northern half of the North Carolina mountains. Nearly every chapter in this book

includes huge tracts of national forest land, some with many wonderful things to do and see.

PUBLIC LANDS: WILDERNESS Maybe only God can make a tree, but only the U.S. Congress can create a wilderness. Under the Wilderness Act of 1964, Congress sets aside large, contiguous tracts of federal land as perpetual wilderness preserves. Each of the tracts remains under the management of the original agency, but is managed under rules that prohibit all logging, all mechanization, and all roads. There are 16 congressionally declared wildernesses in this book, totaling 185,000 acres (289 square miles), all of which are managed by the National Forest Service and allow hunting. Typically, these are the most rugged, remote, and beautiful areas of the mountains—very special places (see www.wilderness .net).

RAILROADS Blue Ridge railroads are very special for railroading buffs. Rugged topography, thousands of feet of climbing, and an irregular, unpredictable geology posed special challenges to the railroad builders. Some railroads, such as the narrow-gauge **ET & WNC (Tweetsie Railroad)**, mastered the terrain by conforming to it; others, such as the ultra-modern **Clinchfield Railroad Loops**, blasted through in uncompromising straight lines. The big timber companies built elaborate, but very temporary, railroads throughout these mountains, and some of the old grades—including the **Little River Railroad**—survive as modern automobile roads. You can get a good long taste of an old-fashioned mountain railroad on the 53-mile-long **Great Smoky**

Jim Hargan

Mountain Railroad, which runs passenger excursions by day and freight by night.

ROCKHOUNDING Eons ago, columns of molten magma broke into veins throughout the mountain bedrock, crystallizing out quartz, garnets, rubies, sapphires, beryl, and gold along with the granite. None of these valuable minerals has been found in large quantities, although optimists formed small commercial mines in the 19th century. Instead, the mountains have always been mined for the cruder minerals associated with such magmatic intrusion: **Granite**, **feldspar**, **mica**, and **kaolin** are all still mined. In past decades rockhounds have loved the old abandoned feldspar and mica mines for the occasional precious stone or valuable specimen found in the tailings. Few sites today allow such casual and dangerous trespassing; instead entrepreneurs offer sites where tourists can sift for rubies, selling buckets of "pay dirt" salted with cheap foreign stones (which they will cut for you, for a fee). There are a few authentic **ruby** mines, as well as an excellent **placer gold** mine, that offer unsalted dirt from on site, and these are cited in the text.

Old-fashioned rockhounding remains legal on national forest lands, with many restrictions. If this is your interest, inquire at the local ranger district.

SKIING Many people think that the Blue Ridge and Smokies are too far south for skiing. They're right: Snow seldom sticks around more than a week or so at even the highest elevations, and cold rain is a lot more common than fleecy blizzards. Still, a number of ski slopes stay in business using manufactured snow. Mostly the result of a speculative boom in the 1960s, some of these slopes are old and unpleasant, while others keep themselves up. None is particularly fancy. Winter skiing isn't really an environmentally friendly sport, as it carves great scars on hillsides and breaks the winter silence with the sideshow roar of diesel generators and massive snowblowers. For those so inclined, however, this book lists several of the better slopes.

SIX-THOUSAND-FOOT PEAKS Most of the East's mountains stay below 4,000 feet. Of those that rise higher, a handful reach the mile-high mark, and only 41 top 6,000 feet. Of these 6'ers, 40 are within this region, including the 1st–16th tallest peaks. (The 17th tallest peak in the East, Mount Washington, is located in New Hampshire.) Bagging 6'ers is

THE AUTHOR'S FAVORITE TRIP
A Week in the Mountains

This weeklong trip takes you past the author's favorite sites, from south to north. Not surprisingly, it follows the Blue Ridge Parkway for most of the way. This itinerary assumes a weeklong trip bracketed by two weekends; this gives you a travel-there day, 7 days in the mountains, and a travel-back day.

Travel there: Your destination is **Townsend**, TN, for a stay at a modern log cabin. Use I-75, I-81, and/or I-40 to reach the Knoxville, TN, area, where you will pick up I-140 to Maryville, TN. From the end of I-140, take US 129 south 7 miles to US 321, then go left (east) 18 miles to Townsend. Hire a modern log cabin for your arrival night.

Day 1: **Cades Cove** and **Gatlinburg**, TN. Visit Cades Cove early this morning. When you finish, take the **Little River Rd.** to **Sugarlands**. If you have any time left, enjoy Tennessee's permanent unofficial state fair, Gatlinburg. Then return to your cabin. Relax on the porch and enjoy the mountain air. Grab some barbeque, then have a soak in your whirlpool bath or hot tub.

Day 2: **Over the Smokies to Bryson City**, NC. Take US 321 east 23 miles to the Gatlinburg Scenic Bypass, then continue straight ahead 18 miles to Newfound Gap; allow 90 minutes for this 41-mile segment. Explore down the Clingmans Dome Spur Rd. (14 miles round trip), then continue south 17 miles on the Newfound Gap Rd. to US 441 in Cherokee. Follow US 441 south 8 miles to US 23/74; go west 7 miles to the Bryson City exit.

You'll be crossing **Newfound Gap** this morning; be sure not to miss the side trip to **Clingmans Dome**. Early risers will want to enjoy a dawn drive and a high sunrise. Then visit **Mingus Mill** and **Oconaluftee Farmstead** on the North Carolina side. Skip through Cherokee for the time being and head to Bryson City for lunch, followed by a train ride up the **Nantahala Gorge**. Stay at one of the excellent B&B hotels in Bryson City, with an evening stroll downtown and dinner at the Randolph or Frymont.

Day 3: **The Tuckaseegee Valley**. Return to Cherokee, NC, the way you came, or follow US 19 east. The Blue Ridge Parkway starts at the north end of town. For Dillsboro, NC, take US 441 south 14 miles, staying on it as it merges with, then leaves, US 74. The Balsam Mountain Inn is just off the parkway at Balsam Gap, NC, US 23/74, 13 miles east of Dillsboro.

Take time this morning to visit the tribal museums in **Cherokee**, and be sure to include the craft shops. If you need more shopping, head on over to **Dillsboro** for lunch and a stroll. Otherwise, get on the **Blue Ridge Parkway** and get your fill of Smoky Mountain views.

Be sure to take the Heintooga Spur at least as far as **Mile High Overlook**, and don't miss the spur to **Waterrock Knob**. Whether you choose Dillsboro or the parkway, end your day at the **Balsam Mountain Inn**, with a fine dinner and a glass of wine on the porch.

Day 4: **The highest mountains on the Blue Ridge Parkway**. From Balsam Gap (US 23/74), take the parkway in the direction marked northbound (south by your automobile's compass), 33 miles, to the Pisgah Inn.

This is your day for hiking as you follow the Blue Ridge Parkway along mile-high ridgelines with panoramic views. Get the Balsam Mountain Inn to pack you a picnic lunch. Enjoy the sunrise from the Waynesville Overlook, then stretch your legs at **Richland Balsams**. Follow the **Mountains-to-Sea Trail** for wildflower meadows in the South Fork Wilderness, then admire the view from the **Devils Courthouse**. When you reach US 220, visit **The Cradle of Forestry in America** and **Looking Glass Falls**. Then return to the parkway for dinner and head back to your room at the **Pisgah Inn**.

Day 5: **Asheville**, NC. Follow the Blue Ridge Parkway in the direction marked northbound to US 25, 20 miles, then go north 4 miles to the Biltmore Estate; allow an hour for this leg. Downtown Asheville is north of the Biltmore Estate on US 25, 3 miles.

Begin day 5 by enjoying the sunrise from the Pisgah Inn, then follow the parkway into Asheville for an early start in your exploration of the **Biltmore Estate**. Be sure to take one of the special tours, and leave plenty of energy for poking around the gardens. Eat lunch on the estate, and visit the winery on your way out. In the afternoon check into downtown's **Haywood Park Hotel**, then stroll and shop through Asheville's **Battery District**. Be sure to visit the newly renovated **Grove Arcade**, America's first (and most beautiful) mall. Finish with dinner at one of downtown's many wonderful small restaurants—perhaps a pub meal at the **Jack of the Wood**, or fine dining at **The Market Place**.

Day 6: **Up the parkway to Blowing Rock**, NC. From downtown Asheville return to the Blue Ridge Parkway by following US 25 south for 7 miles. Then take the parkway northbound 103 miles to Blowing Rock.

Today it's back to the Blue Ridge Parkway for some wonderful scenery. An early-morning start will reward you with a sunrise from **Craggy Gardens**; on the other hand, you'll miss the shrimp and brown gravy over grits at the **Early Girl Café**, a block's walk from your hotel. Oh well, choices can be difficult. If you are lucky enough to be traveling in late June, schedule some time to enjoy the **rhododendron display** at Craggy. Then go on to the Mount Mitchell Spur, for a spectacular drive and a short, beautiful walk to the **highest point in the East**. Back on the parkway, be sure to stop at **Altapass Orchards** for views and heritage apples. You can get lunch at Little Switzerland, the orchard snack bar, or Linville Falls, depending how late you're running. But leave plenty of time for the stunningly beautiful **Grandfather Mountain**, perhaps the world's premier private theme park devoted exclusively to conservation. Stay at one of Blowing Rock's little bed & breakfast inns; be sure to have dinner at **Crippen's**, topping it off with a cigar and a malt whiskey, if you like, on the porch.

Day 7: **Doughton Park**. Continue northbound on the Blue Ridge Parkway. To reach the Glendale Springs Inn, take NC 16 westbound off the parkway. Doughton Park is 22 miles farther on the parkway.

Early risers will want to enjoy a sunrise stroll this morning around the lake on the parkway's **Moses Cone Estate**, just west of the town of Blowing Rock. After breakfast, spend a relaxing morning strolling and shopping in town, and visiting the Moses Cone mansion. After lunch in Blowing Rock, take a leisurely drive up the parkway. Be sure to see the frescoes at **Glendale Springs**, but leave late afternoon free to wander the wildflower meadows of **Doughton Park**. Enjoy dinner and a relaxing final night at the **Glendale Springs Hotel**.

Travel back: For points north, south, and east, take NC 16 east for 16 miles to a left onto US 421, a superhighway. US 421 reaches I-77 in 25 miles for points north and south; I-40 at Winston-Salem in another 30 miles, for points east. For points west, take NC 16 south 55 miles to I-40 at Hickory.

beginning to catch on as a hobby, akin to bagging Scottish Munros or Coloradan 14'ers, only easier. If you are looking for a reason to choose one mountain walk over another, bagging 6-ers will lead you to a lot of really great places, and the **Tennessee Eastman Hiking and Canoeing Club** will give (well, sell) you a neat patch (www.tehcc.org/Beyond6000 .htm; P.O. Box 511, Kingsport, TN 37662); $5 for a patch, plus a lot of walking. This guide points out the location of all 40 of the 6'ers.

WALKING Frequently the best way to enjoy the mountains is to get out and walk around. Each chapter of this Explorer's Guide offers a few good walks, mainly short and easy, that highlight major features of the locale. This listing is by no means encyclopedic; rather, it's more by the way of a sampler, oriented toward the rushed

Jim Hargan

traveler who doesn't have time to spend on a long, hard hike. There are numerous specialized hiking guides for the enthusiast, starting with *50 Hikes in the Mountains of North Carolina* and *50 Hikes in the Tennessee Mountains*, both from The Countryman Press.

WATERFALLS Erosion—50 million years' worth—has not yet smoothed away all the rock ledges in these mountain valleys.

Waterfalls abound throughout this region, ranging from half a dozen feet high to over 400. Many require difficult hikes down gorges, but some can be reached by an easy path, and a few can be viewed from the roadside. The text highlights dozens of these waterfalls, with something in nearly every chapter.

WEATHER These mountains have long been a summer retreat because of their famously cool weather—but your results may vary.

In general temperatures are cooler farther north, and at higher elevations. Lower elevations are hotter, as are places farther south. The lowest elevations and hottest temperatures are along the base of the Smokies in Tennessee, where 90° weather can linger late into August.

Temperatures are lower on the North Carolina side, with 90° a regular event along the low elevations of the Little Tennessee and Tuckaseegee Rivers, and a rarity on the 4,000-foot crest of the Blue Ridge near Cashiers and Highlands.

Asheville suffers from air inversions, and is quite hot. North of Asheville, temperatures seldom reach 90°, and the mile-high peaks—Roan Mountain, Mount Mitchell, Elk

Jim Hargan

Mountain—are always cool. To sum up: Escape the heat by going uphill and north. Expect hot weather below 2,000 feet.

There *is* life after summer. The hot weather can start in mid-June, but normally waits for the Fourth of July weekend; it can linger into September, but normally departs by late August. Spring and fall are cool, with highs between 40° and 65°, and lows occasionally dipping below freezing.

Consistent freezing weather starts sometime in November, with most days having highs between 25° and 35°. Snow can happen anytime between October and April, with January through March getting the worst of it. January snows are fluffy and clean, while April snows are a soggy mess.

SOME WEB PAGES

These web pages cover most or all of this book's area. Other pages, specific to a limited area, are included in the chapter listings.

Great Smoky Mountains National Park Official Web Site (www.nps.gov/grsm/). This official National Park Service site gives general information on the park, such as travel basics, camping, and facilities. Click on IN DEPTH to go to a much larger NPS site dedicated to the Smokies, with a very wide range of information.

John William Uhler's Great Smoky Mountains National Park (www.great .smoky.mountains.national-park.com). This excellent page contains all the basic information on the park in a well-organized format that loads fast. Uhler runs a large series of similar web pages on other national parks, supported by discreet advertising.

The Blue Ridge Parkway Official Site (www.nps.gov/blri/). As with the Great Smoky Mountains, the official National Park Service site offers basic information on facilities, campgrounds, lodgings, and fees, and an IN DEPTH link to a larger and more elaborately detailed site.

Kathy Bilton's Appalachian Trail Site (www.fred.net/kathy/at.html). Kathy Bilton has run this enthusiast's site since 1994, making it the oldest web site on the subject. It's mainly a links page nowadays, with hundreds of trail-related links in a fast-loading and well-organized format.

www.MtBikeWNC.com (www.mtbikewnc.com), Weaverville, NC. This personal web site—run by Jordan Mitchell, an Asheville-area resident and enthusiastic mountain biker—gives a lot of information about biking the western mountains of North Carolina, including detailed trail descriptions.

WNCTrout.Com (www.wnctrout.com). This thorough-going and well-designed site, run by a Marion, NC, fly-fisherman, covers all of the western North Carolina mountains with information on locations, flies, techniques, regulations, and fishing in the Great Smoky Mountains National Park, as well as links to other sites.

www.SwimmingHoles.Org (www.swimmingholes.org/index.html). Tom Hillegass's wonderfully detailed exploration of the East's best wilderness swimming includes 37 locations within this book's coverage areas. Anyone who wants a cool dip in a mountain stream would do well to consult these web pages.

www.NCRoads.Com (www.ncroads.com/index.html). This hobby page describes most of the state and U.S. highway in North Carolina, in detail, including history and scenery. Huge and easy to navigate, it's a great place to start planning a scenic drive or bicycle ride. And it will answer any question you might possibly have about how those crazy highway numbers got assigned.

Jim Hargan

weekend trip might cover 30 miles of stunning river scenery, quite a contrast to a 6-mile whitewater thrill ride. The New River, the more popular of the two, flows gently through rugged wilderness gorges and narrow pastoral valleys, while the French Broad (upstream from Asheville, NC) meanders through a wide farming valley framed by tall peaks. (Downstream from Asheville, the French Broad is a Class IV whitewater stream.)

WHITEWATER RAFTING This region includes the 1996 Summer Olympics whitewater competition site, as well as the training site of several of our American whitewater medalists. No wonder whitewater rafting is available in nearly every chapter of this book. Rivers range from Class II (a few easy ripples), through Class III and IV (fun, and more fun), to Class V (expect to get very, very wet). Outfitters will put your group into a raft with other customers, put you in the river, and pick you up (typically 6 miles downstream). Some outfitters put a guide in each raft, some in each group of rafts, and some just put you in and let you float—it depends on the difficulty of the river, and how much you pay. With few exceptions this is a family-friendly excursion, although infants and toddlers are not allowed, and the more violent rivers may have higher age restrictions. Most of the outfitters also rent and shuttle kayaks, and offer kayaking lessons.

Two long Class II rivers, the **French Broad** and the **New**, offer miles and miles of easy canoeing. This allows a family group to hire a canoe, paddle gently downstream, and camp for the night along the way. A good

WILDFLOWERS Wildflower season starts late in the mountains, with daffodils finally starting to decorate the drab winter roadsides in mid-April. By mid-May all the trees are in leaf, and the spring wildflowers are under way in earnest. The high grassy balds become colorful by the end of May, with the rhododendrons and azaleas bursting out in mid-June. At that time, natural rhododendron "gardens" in the mile-high grassy balds become dotted with clouds of purple, framing the wonderful views. Color fades slowly into August, then bursts out again in mid-September as the goldenrods and asters make one last fine show under the turning leaves. These

Jim Hargan

will last until late October, before the last of the blooms fade and winter returns.

WILDLIFE Bears, of course. People are sometimes surprised to learn that bears are common enough to be hunted in parts of our national forests (and a bear hunt is a massive enterprise, resembling a military search-and-destroy mission). Bears are common enough that you might walk up onto one by accident in the backcountry; treat it as very, very dangerous, and get away without showing panic or fear. The infamous begging bears of the Great Smoky Mountains National Park are less of a pest now than in the past, but are still to be avoided as dangerous.

Wildlife is common, but timid. The author has seen, on his small rural property, foxes, groundhogs, rabbits, skunks, turkeys, and a bobcat—a pretty typical cross section. Deer are also very common, particularly in the national parks. Rangers offer regular wildlife walks in all the national parks and forests, with schedules available at park offices and web sites.

The Northern Mountains

Jim Hargan

THE NORTHERN MOUNTAINS

At their northern end, the Blue Ridge and the Smokies/Unakas draw together and grow taller, and the high valleys between them become narrow and rugged. The New River drains the northernmost part of this area—a wide, rolling valley that becomes increasingly higher and more rugged toward its south. The first of many mile-high peaks appears at the end of the New River's drainage and the start of the Tennessee River's. From this high watershed all the way south to Georgia, the Tennessee River and its tributaries drain the land west of the Blue Ridge.

Here the Blue Ridge Parkway follows the Blue Ridge on its 469-mile journey from Virginia's Shenandoah National Park to the Great Smoky Mountains National Park in North Carolina. Conceived in the mid-1930s as a work relief project for desperately poor mountain counties, its location along the Blue Ridge was far from assured. Tennessee's aggressive and powerful congressional delegation lobbied hard to place it along the Smokies/Unakas instead, but their heavy-handed power plays alienated the National Park Service, while North Carolina's State Road Department (now NCDOT) officials quietly finessed the federal park bureaucracy. The result: a beautifully landscaped route, with roadworks clad in hand-cut stone, stretching through some of the most remote and stunning scenery in the mountains. Typically miles from any settlement (the exceptions being Blowing Rock and Asheville, NC), the parkway winds slowly through mountain farms and high meadows, across torrential rivers and quiet creeks, through ancient forests and along high cliffs with wide views. Sometimes the parkway hugs the Blue Ridge; in other places it will stray far away.

In this area the parkway follows the actual Blue Ridge very closely. Typical of this old and unusual mountain, the Blue Ridge's eastern slope is a rugged and clifflike wilderness covered in trees and nearly empty of people, while its western slope is a series of grass-covered hills, with more farms than forests. When the parkway follows the eastern side of the Blue Ridge, it slabs across rugged wilderness with wide views, as at Grandfather Mountain. When it follows the western side, it rolls through pastoral countryside with wide meadows, as it does near Linville or Sparta, NC. And when it follows the crest of the Blue Ridge, as it does in Doughton Park, it yields the best of both worlds—rolling ridgeline meadows with wide views over rugged mountains and peaceful little farms.

THE BLUE RIDGE PARKWAY
ENTERS NORTH CAROLINA

The first 75 miles of North Carolina's Blue Ridge Parkway passes through one of the mountains' least visited corners. On the eastern, Atlantic side of the parkway, the land drops straight down to a series of rugged, broken mountains, covered in thick forest and lightly settled. On its western side, the land rolls away in gentle hills covered in farms and pastures, broken only occasionally by an isolated massif large enough to be called a mountain. Despite its pastoral appearance, this western plateau is merely a high, wide bowl, blocked by mountains in all directions, difficult to reach and little visited. In the areas traversed by this section of parkway, only one town has a definite center with a downtown, the handsome county seat of Sparta, NC. The scenery, on and off the parkway, is almost without exception beautiful and little touched by the tourist industry. Nevertheless, there are ample facilities for the most discerning traveler, with a good selection of B&Bs and restaurants.

GUIDANCE **Allegheny County Chamber of Commerce** (800-372-5473 or 336-372-5473; fax 336-372-8251; www.sparta-nc.com/index.html), 58 Main St., P.O. Box 1237, Sparta, NC 28675. This is the only tourist information center that treats the Blue Ridge crest region as its central concern. If you are interested in the Glendale Springs, NC, area of this chapter, contact the Ashe County Chamber of Commerce (see "Boone & Banner Elk").

GETTING THERE *By car*: This area is best approached from **I-77**. Take **NC 89** (Exit 100) if you are trying to reach the north end of the Blue Ridge Parkway or Sparta, NC, from the north. Take **US 21** (Exit 83) to reach Stone Mountain State Park or Sparta from the south.

By air: The **Charlotte/Douglas International Airport** in Charlotte, NC, is probably your best bet. A major regional hub, it's only 100 miles away, straight up I-77. **Piedmont Triad Airport** in Greensboro, NC, also has good service, and is about the same distance away.

MEDICAL EMERGENCIES **Allegheny Memorial Hospital** (336-372-5511; fax

336-372-6032), 233 Doctors St., Sparta, NC. This small regional hospital is located just north of Sparta off NC 18.

Ashe Memorial Hospital (336-246-7101; www.ashememorial.org), 200 Hospital Ave., Jefferson, NC. If you are in the Glendale Springs, NC, area, Ashe is probably closest. A full-service 76-bed hospital with a 24/7 emergency room, it serves the rural northwest corner of the North Carolina mountains.

Watauga Medical Center (800-443-7385 or 828-262-4100; www.wataugamc .org/index.html), 336 Deerfield Rd., Boone, NC. Two miles south of Boone on US 221/321, then a block north on Deerfield Rd. This full-service regional hospital is convenient to the south end of this section of the parkway. It offers a wide range of surgical and medical specialties as well as 24/7 emergency room services at its main building.

✳ Wandering Around

EXPLORING BY CAR **The Blue Ridge Parkway**. From NC 18, 14.8 miles east of Sparta, NC, turn south onto the Blue Ridge Parkway. Follow the parkway southward for 75 miles to the US 321 exit at Blowing Rock, NC.

Along this leg the Blue Ridge is a sharp barrier of hard old rock, a 2,000-foot escarpment facing the Atlantic and gentle hills rolling westward. When the parkway follows the crest, its scenery is wild and its views are long, with deep forests and sharp crags. When the road swerves west, it suddenly enters a land of gentle hills, lush meadows, and rich farms. The first site, only a mile from NC 18, is **Cumberland Knob Recreation Area**, with a good view from its visitors center. For the next 12 miles you will be on the first segment of the Blue Ridge Parkway ever built, in 1934; the last segment, Grandfather Mountain, opened in 1987. On this original stretch, **Fox Hunter's Paradise Overlook** gives wide views, and a lovely path circles a millpond. The parkway regains the crest just in time for a spectacular view over the edge to **Stone Mountain**; use US 21 to visit this remarkable site. **Brinegar Cabin** (MP 238.5) on the left, one of the parkway's most attractive and worthwhile log cabins, marks the beginning of Doughton Park, with its beautiful mountain meadow walks. After Doughton Park there's more farmland, then the **Sheets Cabin** (MP 252.3), a log cabin built in1815 and occupied until 1940. The parkway passes the **Northwest Trading Post**, a local craft shop, then the wonderful views from **Jumpinoff Rocks** and **The Lump**. Beyond The Lump, the parkway swerves behind the crest for wide views westward over the New

THE VIEW TOWARD BLUFF MOUNTAIN FROM THE BASIN COVE OVERLOOK.

Jim Hargan

camping, historic sites, and a network of loop trails exploring the granite dome area—including waterfall paths and views both of and from Stone Mountain. The Blue Ridge slopes towering above the granite dome to its north have only one public footpath, a rugged, rocky path to backpacking camps; the rest of the backcountry remains little-visited wilderness. Free.

STONE MOUNTAIN AS VIEWED FROM THE WEST.

Jim Hargan

PICNIC AREAS 🐾 **Picnicking on the Blue Ridge Parkway**. Picnickers will find a number of good sites along this 75-mile stretch of the parkway. From north to south, these include **Cumberland Knob Recreation Area**, MP 217.5; **Little Glade Mill Pond**, MP 230.1, with five tables and a short path by a pond; **Doughton Park**, MP 241.1; and **Cascades Area**, MP 271.9. See *To See* for more on all these sites.

✳ To See

BLUE RIDGE PARKWAY The 1,000-acre **Cumberland Knob Recreation Area** was the first segment of the Blue Ridge Parkway opened to the public, being the site of the dedication ceremony in 1935. It's a forested knob located a mile south of the Virginia border, adjacent to the parkway's NC 18 exit. It has a visitors center with exhibits, and a very nice picnic area. You'll also find two pleasant trails, a 1-mile stroll to the top of Cumberland Knob (only 2,840 feet, but the highest point in the area), and a more strenuous 2-mile loop down to **Gully Creek**—the latter an 800-foot return climb, offering mountain views, deep forests, attractive small waterfalls, and a log barn.

Doughton Park. Originally named Bluff Mountain, this 6,000-acre Blue Ridge Parkway tract includes 6 miles of the Blue Ridge crest and the watershed beneath it. Typical of all the Blue Ridge, the Atlantic side is a rugged, broken drop of 2,000 feet, while the western side is little more than rolling hills. The crest is especially notable for its large meadows and heaths, and its rocky outcrops with wide views. Paths link the meadows and the outcrops, forming multiple loops that plummet into the stream basin beneath and climb back out again. At the center is a classic parkway recreation area—picnic area, camping area, gas station, store, two coffee shops, and a motel-style lodge.

At the north end is the **Brinegar Cabin** (MP 238.5), built in 1885 and one of the loveliest log cabins in the region; it's the site of weaving demonstrations during summer. In 2 miles the parkway enters meadows, with a parking area and path on the left (MP 240.6). You'll reach the main area of meadows, heaths, rocky outcrops, and grand views in another half mile; take the road to the lodge on the left. The stunning **Fodderstack Trail**, with its panoramic view centering

THE VIEW WEST ALONG THE BLUE RIDGE FROM THE LUMP.   Jim Hargan

on a log cabin far below, starts at the lodge. The meadows follow the ridgeline from the lodge south toward the picnic area, extending for nearly a mile along the crest of the Blue Ridge. Along this stretch, the parkway descends the gentle western side of the mountain, staying discreetly out of the wild and windy views. The meadows end at a cliff, with the parkway dropping below it to a narrow spine passing more overlooks with impressive views back toward the mountain.

Jumpinoff Rocks and **The Lump**. The Jumpinoff Rocks are a set of outcrops that form a rocky bald on the crest of the Blue Ridge, with wide views over the valley far below. The level half-mile walk leads through galax and wildflowers; you'll find it at the Jumpinoff Rocks Overlook (MP 260.3), just north of the parkway's NC 16 exit. Four miles farther south, The Lump (MP 264.4) is a knobby peninsula that projects 1,000 feet out from the crest of the Blue Ridge. Covered in meadows and surrounded by 2,000-foot drops, The Lump affords views both wide and spectacular. It's a short walk up a small hill from the overlook parking lot; in summer there's a good chance you'll see people flying powered model airplanes from it.

E. B. Jeffress Park. The 500-acre E. B. Jeffress Park, actually part of the Blue Ridge Parkway, is named for the 1935 North Carolina Department of Roads chief who championed the parkway and insisted that it be a free road instead of a tollway. Located along the parkway just north of its intersection with US 421, it preserves a 2.3-mile stretch of the Blue Ridge crest with its typically steep plummet on the Atlantic side and gentle swale toward the back. A late-19th-century log cabin and a rough log structure used as a church and revival site sit in a flower-studded meadow by the roadside (park at the Thomkins Knob Overlook and follow the path). Half a mile north, the **Cascade Picnic Area** has well-kept tables with excellent views over the edge of the Blue Ridge toward the Piedmont. The park's most popular site, however, is the 1-mile loop path that leads from the picnic area through junglelike old-growth forests and heavy rhododendrons to **Cascade Falls**, a lacy waterfall over a 50-foot gray outcrop.

✏ **Stone Mountain: Hutchinson Homestead** and **Garden Creek Church** (336-957-8185). Located within Stone Mountain State Park, these two historic sites present a picture of late-19th-century community life in the Blue Ridge area. Hutchinson Homestead is a mid-19th-century farm in scenic meadows underneath the cliffs of Stone Mountain. Preserved for decades as a park maintenance area, it was restored in 1998 to its original form as a pioneer farmstead. It has a log cabin, barn, corncrib, meat house, and blacksmith shop, all furnished in period. Stunning views over the meadows to the massive monadnock, Stone Mountain, add to its charm. A mile down the park road, the 1897 Garden Creek Baptist Church gives a rare opportunity to visit an authentic 19th-century country church. Nearly unchanged in over a century, the small crackerbox building is of unpainted clapboards, and has a lovely display of daylilies in early summer. It's still used for Sunday services in warm weather.

The Edwards-Franklin House (336-789-7034), 4132 Haystack Rd., Mount Airy, NC. Open the second weekend each month, Apr.–Sep. Built in 1799, this handsome white wood farmhouse with a full porch and shake roof has its original decorative painting on the doors, mantels, and wainscoting. Owned by the Surry County Historical Society, it's 12 miles off the parkway's NC 18 exit at the edge of the Blue Ridge Mountains, in the back road community of Blevins Store, NC. Its location way down a back road gives you a chance to see the Blue Ridge backcountry and the scenic **Fisher River Valley**; go 0.65 mile east on NC 18; then right 5.2 miles on NC 89; then right 5.2 miles on Hidden Valley Rd. (SSR 1338) following the Fisher River; then left onto Haystack Rd. (SSR 1331).

Whippoorwill Academy and Village (Tom Dooley Museum) (336-973-3237; www.wilkesnc.org/history/whippoorwill.htm), 11929 Hwy. 268 W., Ferguson, NC. Located at the edge of the twisted Blue Ridge Mountains, it's 12 miles from the parkway's US 421 exit as the crow flies, and 32 miles as the crow drives a car down good-quality highways. Take US 421 about 20 miles to the Piedmont town of Wilksboro, then go west on NC 281 another 12 miles or so. Open Sat.–Sun. 3–5 PM; closed Jan.–Mar. This open-air museum, a collection of late-19th-century buildings with fascinating exhibits, marks the hometown of "Tom Dooley"—Tom Dula, the subject of the mountain folk song made popular by the Kingston Trio. Tom, a Civil War veteran and lady's man, was unfortunate enough to have planned to elope with Laura Foster the night she was stabbed through the heart. Even a defense by North Carolina's popular Civil War governor Zeb Vance (see "Asheville & the Blue Ridge Parkway") didn't save the poor boy from the hangman's noose. The old one-room schoolhouse of unpainted clapboard (called the Whippoorwill Academy for its remoteness), authentically furnished downstairs, has a museum to local-boy-made-bad Dula in its loft. Also on site is a general store with period products and locally canned goods, a replica of an 18th-century smokehouse with local art exhibits, a forge and weaving shed, a chapel, and an authentic reconstruction of the home of another famous local boy—Daniel Boone, who lived here with his wife in the 1760s. Free (donations appreciated).

Fort Defiance (828-758-1671; fax 828-759-1792), 1792 Fort Defiance Dr. (on Hwy. 268), Lenoir, NC. Apr.–Oct., Thu.–Sat. 10–5, Sun. 1–5; Nov.–Mar., weekends only. Not a fort at all, but the 18th-century home of Revolutionary War hero

General William Lenoir, this simple, handsome colonial homestead is located on NC 268, the scenic state highway that runs along the foot of the Blue Ridge between US 321 and US 421. Twice a month, costumed docents give tours of this authentically furnished house, including 250 items of General Lenoir's. The site is beautiful and the drive well worthwhile for scenic interest; time it right and you can combine it with a visit to Tom Dooley's hometown (above), just 9 miles east on NC 268. Admission charged.

CULTURAL SITES **The Parish of the Holy Communion (The Churches of the Frescoes)** (336-982-3076; fax 336-982-9870), 120 Glendale School Rd., Glendale Springs, NC. These two rural parish churches close to the parkway's NC 16 exit at Glendale Springs are noted for their exquisite frescoes in the classic Italian Renaissance manner. Constructed between 1901 and 1905, both still serve Episcopalian congregations in Ashe County. Artist Ben Long created the frescoes between 1971 and 1980, choosing themes that mirrored the annual cycle of Episcopalian liturgy. The larger of the two churches, **St. Mary's Church** in West Jefferson, NC, has three large frescoes, each depicting a stage in the life of Christ: *Mary Great with Child*, *John the Baptist*, and *The Mystery of Faith*. The tiny **Holy Trinity Church** in Glendale Springs is decorated with one giant fresco behind the altar, a moving and original interpretation of the *Last Supper*. These remarkable works of art have become an attraction—or perhaps a pilgrimage site—of great popularity, receiving 60,000 visitors a year. Free.

FRESCOES OF THE LAST SUPPER ARE ON VIEW AT HOLY TRINITY EPISCOPAL CHURCH IN GLENDALE SPRINGS.

Jim Hargan

GARDENS AND PARKS ✿ **Rendezvous Mountain Educational State Forest** (336-667-5072), 1956 Rendezvous Mountain Rd., Purlear, NC. Mar.–Nov., Tue.–Sun; closed Dec.–Feb. This 3,000-acre mountaintop forest sits in the Blue Ridge Mountains, 12 miles east of the parkway's NC 16 exit. The "educational" part is a 150-acre open-air museum, developed and run by the North Carolina Forest Service (a state agency that promotes sylviculture and good forestry practices). Oriented toward children and families, the museum's four loop paths lead through exhibits on forest ecology and logging practices. Loops include "talking trees" who explain who they are and how they fit in the forest, a fire tower and CCC cabin with fine views, and a logging demonstration with an operating sawmill. Much of the museum area is located on the summit of Rendezvous Mountain, with excellent views from the picnic area. The remainder of the tract preserves a beautiful old-growth oak–hickory forest, with 20 miles of hiking, horseback riding, and mountain biking trails. Free.

❋ To Do

BICYCLING **Buffalo Bob's Mountain Store** (336-372-2433; fax 336-372-7820), MP 232, Blue Ridge Parkway, Sparta, NC. May–Oct.; call for operating hours. This gift shop rents bicycles.

GOLF **Old Beau Golf Club** (336-363-3333), Hwy. 21, Roaring Gap, NC. Open all year. Located in Roaring Gap, a short distance off the parkway on US 21, this 18-hole resort course is remarkably scenic, with wide mountain views. $47 weekdays, $62 weekends. After 2 PM $35.

STABLES **Mountain View Riding Stables** (866-686-8724 or 866-686-8724; www.mtnviewstables.com/info.htm), 6345 Elk Creek–Darby Rd., Darby, NC. Open daily, all year. Reservations required. Located in the remote tangle of mountains beneath the Blue Ridge, this stable offers trail rides graded by the rider's ability, from easy, scenic meadow ridges to strenuous mountain climbs. It's in a very rural and mountainous area about 15 miles south of the Blue Ridge Parkway's US 421 exit. $45 for 2 hours, $65 for 3 hours, $90 for 4 hours, and $130 for 6 hours. Novice meadow trail rate: $30 for 1 hour.

❋ Lodging

COUNTRY INN

Glendale Springs Inn (800-287-1206 or 336-982-2103; fax 336-982-4036; www.glendalespringsinn.com), 7414 NC 16, Glendale Springs, NC 28629. This historic 1892 country inn sits a quarter mile off the Blue Ridge Parkway. It's a large, gabled Victorian structure with a wide front porch, furnished throughout in a turn-of-the-20th-century style. Downstairs is a full-service gourmet restaurant (see *Dining Out*) and one guest room; upstairs are four more guest rooms and private common areas for the lodge guests. Next door, a recently built guest lodge looks like a country cottage, with its own full porch; it has four more rooms, furnished in a country style. Some rooms have whirlpool tub and fireplace. $95–135.

BED & BREAKFAST INNS **Burgiss Farm Bed and Breakfast** (800-233-1505; www.breakfastinn.com), 102 Thistle Meadow, Laurel Springs, NC 28644. This 1899 farmhouse sits on 200 acres in Laurel Springs, 3 miles off the Blue Ridge Parkway's NC 18 exit. Handsome and well kept, it's surrounded by lawns and framed by wood fences and green hills. The 1,200 square feet of living space is available to only one party at a time, and includes two bedrooms and an ample common area in an informal country decor. Amenities include a large stone fireplace, hot tub, bumper pool, and satellite TV. Guests have their choice of seven different hearty, full breakfasts. The Burgiss Farm also includes the Burgiss Barn Mountain Music Jamboree (see *Entertainment*), a unique and lively Saturday-night mountain music venue with homestyle barbeque. They've recently started their own winery on the premises, and their wines are now available for purchase. $90 per room for the first night; $80 for each additional night.

Doughton-Hall Bed and Breakfast (336-359-2341; www.doughtonhall .com), 12668 NC 18 S., Laurel Springs, NC 28644. Located less than 2 miles from the parkway's NC 18 exit, Doughton-Hall B&B occupies the 1898 National Register–listed home of Robert L. Doughton, the powerful congressman who helped write the Social Security Act and who brought the Blue Ridge Parkway to North Carolina. Tucked into a quiet rural location and surrounded by lawns, this red-trimmed Queen Anne house has wide wraparound porches. A stocked trout stream crosses the property, and guests are welcome to try their luck. Its common areas and four guest rooms are furnished with antiques, and the guest rooms each have whirlpool tub. Guests are greeted with wine and hors d'oeuvres when they arrive and given a full breakfast at the time they choose. $90 per night.

Mountain Hearth Lodge (336-372-8743; www.mountainhearthlodge .com), 110 Mountain Hearth Dr., Sparta, NC 28675 (MP 231.5). Open all year. Call for seasonal rate info. This modern log lodge sits by the Blue Ridge Parkway near its exit onto US 21. Made of local hemlock logs with hardwood floors, the lodge has a common living room and restaurant-style dining room. Its seven rooms consist of three normal-sized guest rooms, a suite, and three log cabins (no kitchens). All seven rooms are en

suite and furnished in antiques; the suite and the cabins have fireplace and whirlpool tub, and each cabin has a porch. A full breakfast is included. Rooms $80–120; cabins $120–140.

CABIN RENTALS ✿ **Fall Creek Cabins** (336-877-3131; www.fall-creek -cabins.com), P.O. Box 190, Fleetwood, NC 28626. Seven cedar log cabins sit on 54 acres deep in the Blue Ridge Mountains, not 5 miles from the parkway's intersection with US 421. These modern two-story cabins, all individually decorated, have full porch and wood floors, as well as fireplace and hot tub; some have mountain views, while others look out on forests or streams. $175–200 per night. Weekly rates also available.

Adele's Cabins at Turkey Hill (828-263-8633; www.turkeyhillcabins.com), 1991 Ben Miller Rd., Deep Gap, NC 28618. These three modern log cabins sit near the top of the Blue Ridge, 2 miles from the parkway's exit onto US 421. All are carefully decorated, with full front porch, hardwood floors, and fireplace, with views of the wooded property or over the mountains toward the parkway. $140–160 per night. Weekly rates also available.

❋ Where to Eat

EATING OUT **The Pines Restaurant** (336-372-4148), 501 S. Main St., Sparta, NC. Mon.–Thu. 7 AM–8:30 PM, Fri. and Sat. 7 AM–9 PM, Sun. 7 AM–8 PM. This southern-style eatery on the south edge of Sparta, 7 miles off the parkway on US 21, offers fresh country cooking and hand-chopped barbeque.

DINING OUT **Glendale Springs Inn and Restaurant** (800-287-1206 or

336-982-2103; www.glendalesprings inn.com), 7414 NC 16, Glendale Springs, NC. Lunch and dinner. Closed Wed. This historic 1892 inn, a quarter mile off the Blue Ridge Parkway, offers casual fine dining for lunch and dinner. Guests are seated in three dining rooms, furnished in a turn-of-the-20th-century style, including one overlooking the garden used to grow the fresh herbs for the kitchen; on a pleasant summer's day, tables are available on the wide porch as well. The menu emphasizes a wide choice of fresh seafood, as well as chicken, pork, and beef, typically prepared with an appropriate sauce or married with complementary tastes. The dessert menu is wide ranging, with all desserts made fresh by the restaurant's pastry chef. An extensive wine list is available, with most bottles less than $25. Entrées, served with soup or salad, $11–12.

✳ Entertainment

Laurel Springs

♪ ♪ **Burgiss Barn Mountain Music Jamboree** (800-233-1505; www.break fastinn.com/barn.htm), 102 Thistle Meadow, Laurel Springs, NC. Sat. 7–11 PM. This large, plain modern barn hosts a dinner and a bluegrass and mountain music dance every Sat. night. Bands from all over the mountains furnish the music, and the food is cooked fresh in a large pit barbeque. It's located just off the Blue Ridge Parkway, 3 miles north on NC 18 to NC 113. The 200-acre Burgess Farm B&B is next door. $5 adults, children under 12 free. Barbeque dinner $5–7 extra.

✳ Selective Shopping

This deeply rural section of the Blue Ridge defines the periphery of this region's market areas. Its residents are used to driving some distance for even basic goods, while tourists tend to pass through on the parkway without straying from it. First-rate shopping is available in abundance at Blowing Rock, NC, at the southern end of this section.

Northwest Trading Post (336-982-2543), Glendale Springs, NC. Apr.–Oct. This gift shop, looking like an old country store, fronts the Blue Ridge Parkway at MP 259. Run by the Northwest Development Association as a nonprofit to promote local mountain crafts, it features lots of handmade art and craft items, as well as baked goods, from the northwestern counties of North Carolina's Blue Ridge.

✳ Special Events

SUMMER **Allegheny Quilter's Show and Blue Ridge Mountain Craft Fair** (336-363-2312), US 21 north of Sparta. Third weekend in June, 10–5. This Fri. and Sat. event combines a craft show and a quilters' meet with live bluegrass and mountain music, at the county fairgrounds in Sparta. Free.

Sparta Lions Club Game Show (843-332-0020 or 336-961-2449), Sparta, NC. First week in July. A horse show held in the county fairgrounds in Sparta, with barrel racing and pole bending. $5.

Allegheny Fiddler's Convention (www.ls.net/~fiddler/), 334 Reynolds Rd., Sparta, NC. Third weekend in July. Old-time mountain and bluegrass bands come from all over to compete for cash prizes at the county fairgrounds at Sparta. There's also a dance competition. Fri. night $6, Sat. $7, both days $10.

AUTUMN Mountain Heritage Festival (800-372-5473). This annual street fair in downtown Sparta features live bluegrass and mountain music, craft demonstrations, 100 or more art and craft booths, and food vendors. Contact the Allegheny County Chamber of Commerce at the number shown for annual dates and times.

Sonker Festival at the Edwards-Franklin House (800-948-0949 or 336-786-6116; www.carolinamusic ways.org/events/surry/events_Sonker_ fest.html), 4132 Haystack Rd., Mount Airy, NC. First Sat. in Oct., 1–5 PM. A *sonker* is a deep-dish fruit pie. This festival celebrates the sonker with old-time mountain music (and lots of home-cooked sonkers) at Surry County's 18th-century Edwards-Franklin House, at the foot of the Blue Ridge. Free.

THE BLUE RIDGE PARKWAY:
BLOWING ROCK & GRANDFATHER
MOUNTAIN

This 50-mile stretch of the crest of the Blue Ridge has been attracting summer visitors since the late 19th century. First the resort village of Blowing Rock, NC, emerged on the Blue Ridge crest just south of Boone, NC; then, 12 miles down the crest, a mountain family settled the summer cottage village of Linville, NC, and surrounded it with thousands of acres of wilderness preserve. Many of the hardscrabble ridgetop farms were absorbed into large estates surrounding summer homes—later to become parts of the Blue Ridge Parkway, further preserving the crest scenery. Another 12 miles down, the spectacular Linville Falls attracted more summer cottages; and 12 miles below that, Little Switzerland, NC, became a magnet for early-20th-century automobile tourists.

This section of the Blue Ridge Parkway is varied and exciting, with rugged, wild scenery alternating rapidly with more settled and pastoral views. Off the parkway, Blowing Rock remains the main focus of interest. Still a popular resort appealing to the wealthy, it features a good selection of gourmet restaurants, luxurious small B&Bs, and fascinating shopping.

GUIDANCE Blowing Rock Chamber of Commerce (800-295-7851 or 828-295-7851; fax 828-295-3198; www.blowingrock.com), P.O. Box 406, Blowing Rock, NC 28605. This chamber runs a visitors center half a block from downtown, in an old house.

GETTING THERE *By car*: The Blowing Rock, NC, area is best approached via **US 321**, a reasonably good highway that extends south from I-81 and north from I-40 and Charlotte, NC.

By air: You have a choice of three airports, two regional and one international. **Hickory Regional Airport** (828-323-7408) is only 35 miles away from Boone, NC, and gets several commuter hops a day from Charlotte, NC, via US Airways Express. Car rentals are inside the terminal. **Charlotte/Douglas International Airport** is another 40 miles farther, and is usually much cheaper. Don't neglect

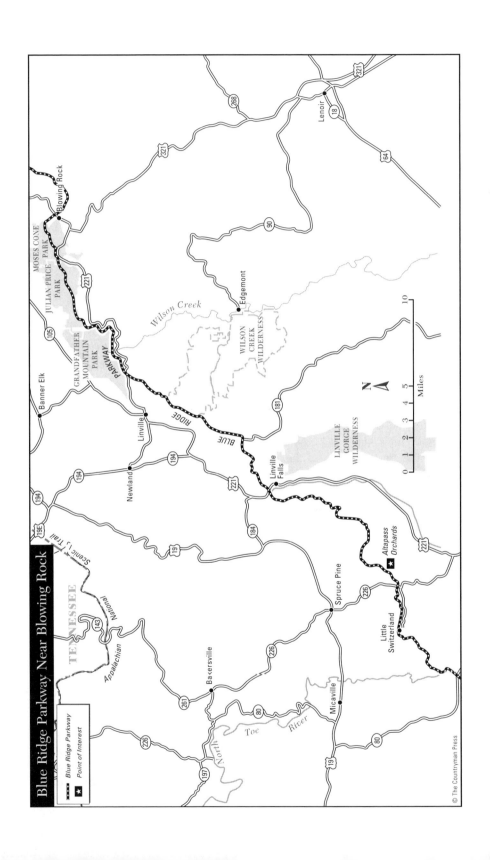

Blue Ridge Parkway Near Blowing Rock

- ●●●●● Blue Ridge Parkway
- ★ Point of Interest

© The Countryman Press

to check out the **Tri-Cities Airport** (423-325-6000), 2525 Hwy. 75, Blountville, TN; much bigger than Hickory, it may offer cheaper fares than Charlotte.

By bus or rail: There is no scheduled bus or rail service in this area.

MEDICAL EMERGENCIES **Watauga Medical Center** (800-443-7385 or 828-262-4100; www.wataugamc.org/index.html), 336 Deerfield Rd., Boone, NC. Two miles south of Boone on US 221/321, then a block north on Deerfield Rd. This full-service regional hospital is convenient to Blowing Rock, NC, and the northern half of this section of parkway. It offers a wide range of surgical and medical specialties as well as 24/7 emergency room services at its main building.

Spruce Pine Hospital (828-765-4201), 125 Hospital Dr., Spruce Pine, NC. Located near the south end of this section of the parkway, this small regional hospital furnishes 24/7 emergency room service. You'll find it off US 19E on the south edge of Spruce Pine.

❋ Wandering Around

EXPLORING BY CAR **The Blue Ridge Parkway**. *Leg 1*: Enter the Blue Ridge Parkway at US 321 in Blowing Rock, NC, and go south 20 miles to NC 181. *Leg 2*: Continue south 32 miles to NC 18. Burnsville, NC, is 20 miles north via US 19E.

The parkway immediately enters the civilized meadows of **Moses Cone Park**, with its 1890s neoclassical mansion (now a craft center) and miles of carriage trails. From there the parkway passes into **Julian Price Park**, with its lovely lake views, then enters more rugged scenery as it approaches **Grandfather Mountain**, the tallest peak on the Blue Ridge at 5,960 feet. The parkway slabs the high eastern slopes of Grandfather, a wild and impressive drive of wide views and great crags, with viaducts over the most rugged cliffs and a downhill view over the **Wilson Creek National Wild and Scenic River**. Beyond, US 221 leads right to the entrance of **Grandfather Mountain Park**; at this intersection, **Beacon Heights Overlook** gives one of the best views of Grandfather Mountain, plus a little side trail leading half a mile to another viewpoint. In 3 more miles the Flat Rock parking lot on the right marks a short, worthwhile walk to **Flat Rock Overlook**, a gardenlike rocky bald.

Past NC 181, the scenery becomes more pastoral, passing meadows and farms with pleasant views over split-rail fences. A spur road to the left leads to the giant **Linville Falls waterfall** at the mouth of the Linville Gorge Wilderness. Beyond the falls the scenery becomes rugged again. Look for impressive gorge views over the Catawba River to your left, climaxing with the dizzying view from **Chestoa Overlook** in 3 miles, and a 270° panorama from **Bear Den**

LOOKING FROM FLAT ROCK OVERLOOK TOWARD GRANDFATHER MOUNTAIN.

Jim Hargan

Overlook 2 miles later. After Bear Den, look for your first of many views over the 2-mile-long **Altapass Orchards**, a stunningly beautiful heritage orchard with hayrides, a café and gift shop, and free live music on summer weekends. The historic **Clinchfield Railroad Loops** are visible below, as is the gravel roadbed of the 1913 predecessor to the parkway, the Crest of the Blue Ridge Highway. At the NC 226 intersection, the **Museum of North Carolina Minerals** and services at Spruce Pine, NC, are to the right. From there the parkway parallels the settlement of Little Switzerland, NC, then enters another wild and rugged area with fine views in all directions. The parkway passes **Crabtree Falls Recreation Area**, then reaches **Black Mountain Overlook** for its best view of Mount Mitchell, the tallest peak in the East. NC 80, the end of this section, is 2 miles away. The easiest way to get back to Blowing Rock is to return the way you came.

EXPLORING ON FOOT Daniel Boone Scout Trail (800-468-7325 or 828-733-4337; fax 828-733-2608; www.grandfather.com/hiking/east-side.htm#boone), 2050 Blowing Rock Hwy., Linville, NC. Daily 8 AM–closing. This National Recreation Trail runs from the peak of Grandfather Mountain through the Grandfather Park backcountry to the Blue Ridge Parkway. It's owned and maintained by the private **Grandfather Mountain Park**; admission fees pay for its upkeep and patrol, and hikers are required to pay the fee. Hikers who start on the parkway and walk uphill can get permits in Blowing Rock at half price at High Mountain Expeditions (see *Rafting and Kayaking*)—but face an uphill climb on the **Boone Trail** of 2,000 feet in 2.6 miles. Many hikers find that it's worth it; the trail features high meadows and cliffs with stunning views, through scenery so rugged that the trail uses cables and ladders to cross it. Uphill hikers can get a good taste of the Grandfather backcountry by taking the **Nuwati Trail** instead, a short distance before the Boone Trail. Nuwati climbs gently and evenly for 1.2 miles to **Storyteller's Rock** for first-rate views over this virgin backcountry. On the return hike, **Cragway Trail** branches off right to climb 500 feet in a mile to reach the Boone Trail, passing through crags and boulder fields with wide views.

The Tanawha Trail. The Lin Cove Viaduct engineers built this 12-mile hiking trail as part of the viaduct project in 1987, and to the same high standards. Staying on the National Park Service's Blue Ridge Parkway properties throughout, this moderately easy path wanders through every type of Blue Ridge scenery from rough crags to soft meadows. It starts at the **Linn Cove Viaduct** Visitors Center, then passes under the viaduct, giving a close view of the bridge and the ecology it protects. It ascends a boulder wall using stone steps, then passes by a small waterfall on a flagstoned path—the headwaters of **Wilson Creek National Wild and Scenic River**. It climbs up to **Rough Ridge** and crosses its rare and fragile mountain heather ecology on a 200-foot boardwalk, with continuous panoramic views off the Blue Ridge, over the viaduct and the Wilson Creek watershed, and into the Piedmont. Beyond, the path goes through New England–style forests and Blue Ridge–style rhododendron tunnels as it approaches **Price Park**, then passes through a long series of old meadows, fields, and apple orchards before ending at the **Boone Fork Overlook** (MP 297.1). This makes a fine 1-day hike if you can arrange to be picked up.

Blowing Rock, NC, sits in a shallow bowl just behind the crest of the Blue Ridge, a short distance off the parkway. It's been around since the 1890s, a resort town from the first, and many of the buildings are very historic. The model for novelist Jan Karon's Mitford, Blowing Rock's old village center remains attractive and busy, with a four-block downtown and a city park at its center. It has always been a gathering place for the wealthy, so that both quality and prices tend to be high. Parking can be difficult, even in the off-season, and you may find yourself forced into a hilly two- or three-block walk to reach the downtown shops.

Linville, NC, was founded as a resort town in the 1890s, about the same time as Blowing Rock; it was the Linville resort that constructed US 221 between the two, the earliest automobile road in the mountains. Linville was conceived as a summer village around the **Eseeola Lodge**, and a collection of early summer homes still exist at the far end of the lodge. In those days the resort company controlled the entire valley surrounding Linville, including Grandfather Mountain, and managed it as a wilderness park of great beauty. Today that resort company survives as **Grandfather Mountain Park**, still a privately owned wilderness park, while Linville has declined into a sleepy little village with little beyond the typical roadside services.

Linville Falls, NC. Twelve miles south of Linville on US 221, and just off the Blue Ridge Parkway, Linville Falls is the third in this series of 19th-century Blue Ridge resorts, and the least successful survivor in the series. Formed on the Crest of the Blue Ridge Highway, it was expected to be a major tourist stop as visitors took time to view the **Linville Falls waterfall**. Today it is little more than a name on a crossroads, with a couple of restaurants and handful of motels; a group of stone buildings and a wide scattering of 19th-century summer houses attest to its historic origins. Linville Falls is the most convenient village for both the Linville Falls waterfall and the **Linville Gorge Wilderness** (see "The Catawba River Valley"), justly popular for its wild, craggy beauty.

Little Switzerland, NC. The western end of the abandoned Crest of the Blue Ridge Highway continued as a toll road to nowhere as late as the mid-1920s. Passing above the cliffs of the Blue Ridge, this early automobile road gave flat-landers easy access to cool summer air and wide views. It still does, and the settlement of Little Switzerland has formed from the people attracted to this high perch. Unlike the other villages in this chapter, Little Switzerland is a linear settlement of a type familiar in the automobile era, stretched along NC 226A (as this section of the Crest of the Blue Ridge Highway is now designated) mainly as a series of motels and restaurants. The town center consists of four or five interesting shops gathered around the post office.

❋ Wild Places

THE GREAT FORESTS 🐾 **Grandfather Mountain Park—the backcountry** (800-468-7325 or 828-733-4337). The privately owned Grandfather Mountain Park supports over 4,000 acres of primitive backcountry as an environmental preserve, centered on the 5,900-foot central ridge of Grandfather Mountain.

This unique area has been managed as a preserve since it became part of the Eseeola Lodge property in 1892, and is still owned by the heirs of the founding family. Today the preserve is run in partnership with The Nature Conservancy and the United Nations—it's the world's only privately owned International Biosphere Reserve.

Viewed from any direction, Grandfather Mountain's most distinctive characteristic is the line of rugged cliffs and bare rock along its main crest and extending down its side ridges. Up close, these become the center of a fantasy landscape of broken rock and sheer drops, with nonstop views that change constantly. These outcrops and boulder fields nurture 16 distinct habitats, creating one of North America's most biologically diverse environments. The preserve shelters 42 rare and endangered species, with 11 listed as globally imperiled—including the beautiful wildflowers Heller's blazing star, Gray's lily, and pink-shelled azalea.

The Grandfather backcountry is open to hikers and campers only. The park maintains a 13-mile system of trails, some in territory so rugged that cables and ladders have been permanently installed. Because this is an admission-supported park, you have to pay to hike in it. You can buy a less expensive hiking permit at several local stores (including High Mountain Expeditions—see *Rafting and Kayaking*—and the Banner Elk Eckerd) that let you hike the trails from the valley up. There are two routes for this, both of them spectacular and strenuous. The **Daniel Boone Scout Trail**, the east-side route starting on the Blue Ridge Parkway, is shorter, less difficult, and more popular. The **west-side route**, starting on NC 105, is a mile longer and 400 feet taller; it passes the view of an old man's profile that gave Grandfather Mountain its name. If you pay the full admission, you get to start at the **Mile High Swinging Bridge** and take 1,000 feet off your climb; from there, the ladder and cable ascent of the 5,940-foot peak is only a mile away and 600 feet uphill.

Wilson Creek National Wild and Scenic River drains the southeast slope of Grandfather Mountain, dropping 4,000 feet in a 23-mile run through the **Pisgah National Forest** to its end at the **Johns River**, the upper edge of the Piedmont. It drains a rugged and little-visited watershed, remarkable for its waterfalls, cliffs, and gorges. From the Piedmont, NC 90 winds slowly northward to the heart of this region to end at its center, in the rural community of Edgemont. From it, good gravel roads and rough national forest tracks twist uphill in various directions; Blowing Rock, Linville, and Linville Falls, NC, are all possible destinations.

Wilson Creek has two halves. The upward half, from Grandfather Mountain to Edgemont, is remote and rugged, with much of the western watershed protected in the **Wilson Creek Wilderness Study Area**. The lower half, starting at the **Mortimer Recreation Area**, is a deep gorge famous for its Class II–V whitewater. Pleasantly enough, a good road (SSR 1328) runs along the bottom of the gorge, making it easy to park, sunbathe on a rock, and watch the more vigorous among us kayak through the rapids.

Many of the best sightseeing opportunities are in the 21-square-mile Wilderness Study Area. Containing much of the western half of Wilson Creek's watershed, it's a tangled series of rugged ridges and V-shaped valleys. It has over 30 miles of Forest Service–maintained trails (including 10 miles of the **Mountains-to-Sea Trail**), leading to six waterfalls and three clifftop views. FS 464, a good gravel road, follows a ridgeline uphill through the center of the study area, starting at NC 90 in Edgemont and ending 11.4 miles later, where NC 181 intersects with the Blue Ridge Parkway. It's a lovely forest drive with good views and access to a number of good trails, including **Darkside Cliffs Trail** (#272), a nearly level mile round trip to a cliff view of Grandfather Mountain and the Wilson Creek basin.

RECREATION AREAS **Bass Lake**. This lovely little lake, in Cone Park adjacent to the village of Blowing Rock, NC, is ringed by carriage paths that are wide, flat, and immaculately kept. Popular with joggers, it's a wonderful place to stroll and unwind for those staying in town. It has its own parking lot, half a mile west of downtown Blowing Rock on US 221. There's a first-rate picnic area just across US 221 from it, run by the North Carolina Department of Motor Vehicles.

PICNIC AREAS The village of **Blowing Rock**, NC, offers two convenient and attractive picnic areas. The **town park** at the center of downtown is convenient for shoppers, and gives nice views of Main St. **Broyhill Park** has large and lovely gardens as well as a challenging waterfall hike; you'll find the tables at its north end, two blocks west of downtown off US 221, on the left.

The Blue Ridge Parkway. On this section, picnic areas are located at **Price Park**, **Linville Falls**, and **Crabtree Falls Recreation Area**, all three of which are large and well kept.

Mortimer Recreation Area (Wilson Creek Area). This pretty Pisgah National Forest recreation site is in the Wilson Creek area, on NC 90 at the rural settlement of Edgemont. It has a nice riverside picnic area as well as tent camping. It's at the site of a large CCC camp and marks the head of the scenic **Wilson Creek Gorge**. Two other national forest recreation sites in this remote area also offer picnicking: **Mulberry** and **Boone's Fork** are both off NC 90 east of Edgemont, along SSR 1368.

✳ To See

ALONG THE BLUE RIDGE PARKWAY 🐾 **Moses Cone Park**. In the 1890s Greensboro, NC, denim manufacturer Moses Cone and his wife, Bertha, started to accumulate a large estate along the crest of the Blue Ridge above the new resort village of Blowing Rock. The pair built a summer home for themselves second only to Biltmore in resplendence, with Grecian columns framing a view that not even the Vanderbilts could command. The Cones converted the tired old farmlands they had purchased into wildflower meadows and laced these meadows with miles of carriage paths. Without any close heirs, they decided to will their estate to their favorite charity, a Greensboro hospital, under the condition that it remain intact, a recreation ground for the American people. In 1949 hospital managers did the best thing they could to fulfill the Cones' wishes: They donated the property to the National Park Service to become part of the Blue Ridge Parkway—the present Moses Cone Park.

THE MANOR HOUSE AT MOSES CONE PARK.

Jim Hargan

This is not a wild place. It is a cultured place, a cultivated place, a place where a human-made landscape of great beauty and richness spreads over thousands of acres. At its base, the lovely **Bass Lake** sits on the edge of Blowing Rock, ringed by carefully planned carriage paths. From it, meadowlands stretch uphill, broken and framed by forests and rhododendrons, woven by carriage paths, to reach the beautiful mansion, simple and elegant, now a craft center run by the **Southern Highlands Craft Guild**. Crossing the parkway behind the manor, the meadows continue uphill as the carriage path forks to two high peak views—a 3-mile switchback to **Flat Top**, and a 5-mile spiral to **Rich Mountain**.

The manor and its craft center get much of the visitor attention—deservedly so, with its shop of fine crafts from throughout the Appalachians, its summer craft demonstrations, and its wide views from a porch well outfitted with rockers. The carriage paths, however, are the real marvel of the park. Evenly and gently sloped, they wander through the carefully planned landscape in a series of amazing turns and twists, switchbacks, loops, and spirals. They allow a modern walker to meander up the face of the Blue Ridge while hardly breaking a sweat. The paths are also open to horses, which can be hired in Blowing Rock (see *Stables*).

Julian Price Park. Part of the Blue Ridge Parkway, 6.5-square-mile Julian Price Park fills the gap between Moses Cone Park and the privately owned Grandfather Mountain Park. It does this in the most literal sense, filling in the mountainous spaces between these two better-known areas; and it does it in a more metaphoric sense as well, being less tame and civilized than Cone Park, yet not so wild as the windswept cliffs of Grandfather Mountain. It is more of a typical Blue Ridge landscape, with fields left from grazing and woods left from logging, crossed by trails that are rough and rolling. The middle of the park is taken up by a rolling plateau surrounded by slightly taller peaks, containing a pleasant lake, a large picnic area framed by split-rail fences, and a campground. The parkway runs close by the edge of the lake and over its stone dam—a popular and scenic stop. From the picnic area a path runs 2.5 miles (round trip) along Boones Fork to a pretty 25-foot waterfall, from there connecting to a number of rougher backcountry trails.

& **Linn Cove Viaduct**. One of the most remarkable and important bridges of its era, the Linn Cove Viaduct came about from an environmental dispute between the National Park Service and a local man. In the late 1960s the NPS tried to replace its 1930s-era right-of-way (never used) with a much higher route, slashing across the virgin preserve of Grandfather Mountain in giant cuts and fills. The local man—Hugh Morton, owner of Grandfather Mountain—was determined to protect his mountain. Although the NPS believed it had the right to simply condemn Morton's land, they quickly found out that this power did not extend to relocating the right-of-way; yet they refused to budge from their concept of a high-mountain slash. Finally the governor of North Carolina forced a compromise, a middle route that avoided environmental problems by bridging them. The longest of these bridges is the Linn Cove Viaduct.

The viaduct took a radical new approach to protecting the environment. It's set on towering pillars, installed without a construction road, each one disturbing only a tiny 50-foot circle of land. Every roadway section was precast in concrete and lifted into position; when one section was attached to a pillar, the work crews would move onto it to move the next section into position, cantilevering out from the pillars. The roadway sections curve slightly to conform to the environmental needs of the land below. The resulting bridge is very beautiful, a soft line curving gently against the wild mountain.

As you approach from Blowing Rock, NC, you will see the viaduct as you get beyond the **Rough Ridge Overlook** (MP 303); then, a mile later, you'll be on it with no opportunity to stop and admire it. To get a good look, stop at the **Yonalossee Overlook** (MP 303.5), where a roadside path leads to its beginning, and the view you see in postcards. Once you've crossed it, you will reach the **Linn Cove Viaduct Visitors Center** on the left on the opposite side, with an information desk and exhibits. A disabled-accessible trail leads a short distance to an overlook.

Flat Rock Overlook. You have to work for this view, but it's worth it. A half-mile circular walk takes you to a large rocky bald with the beauty of a Japanese garden, its dwarfed pines and azaleas (May–June blooms) framing 270° panoramic views that include Grandfather Mountain.

Linville Falls Recreation Area. The Blue Ridge Parkway has a large recreation area along the Linville River, centering on the tall plunge of Linville Falls. As the parkway approaches the river, it enters lovely meadows with split-rail fences. A spur road to the left leads 1.5 miles to the waterfall; just beyond, a side road leads right to the riverside picnic area, where you can get a good view of the parkway crossing the Linville River high above on a stone-clad arched bridge. The picnic area is nice, and the Linville River Bridge is impressive, but the waterfall is the real attraction.

THE LINN COVE VIADUCT AS VIEWED FROM YONALOSSEE OVERLOOK.

Jim Hargan

The trails to Linville Falls start at a small visitors center at the end of the spur. The falls occur as the Linville River reaches the upper edge of Linville Gorge (see "The Catawba River Valley") and plunges straight down into it. The trails spread out in fingers from the visitors center to various viewpoints, starting as paths along both banks of the river. The left-bank paths lead first to a ledge and pool at the top of the waterfall, with a view out over the gorge and a

✒ **Grandfather Mountain Park** (800-468-7325 or 828-733-2013; fax 828-733-2608; www.grandfather.com), Linville, NC. Daily. Summer 8–7, winter 8–5. Owned by noted conservationist Hugh Morton and his family, Grandfather Mountain Park describes itself as "a scenic travel attraction"—a theme park where the theme is nature, the environment, and incredible natural beauty. There's a spectacular drive up, a nature center, a first-rate habitat zoo, and a mile-high suspension bridge. Four thousand acres of the park is a permanently protected wilderness preserve recognized by the United Nations as an International Biosphere Reserve (the only such privately owned tract in the world).

The attraction area starts at the park entrance on US 221 (1 mile west of the Blue Ridge Parkway and 2 miles east of Linville), and centers on a 2.2-mile road that climbs 1,000 feet up the mountain in eight tight switchbacks. This section of the Blue Ridge crest has spectacular, sheer cliffs facing west, getting larger as the mountain gets higher. The road gains views of these cliffs on its westward curves (including a clifftop **picnic area**), while eastward curves wander through lovely forests broken by large rock formations. The road's last half mile swags steeply up the mountain with wide views over high meadows.

Halfway up is the outstanding **habitat zoo**, open to visitors at no extra charge. Grandfather's large animal enclosures feature native mountain critters in their actual habitats, with the human visitors separated by moats or elevated walks. Animals include black bears, bear cubs, deer, panthers, and river otters (with an underwater viewing area), as well as golden eagles and bald eagles. The adjacent **nature center** presents the history of Grandfather Mountain (both natural and human) in a museum designed by the Smithsonian's former chief of natural history exhibits. It includes a section on Daniel Boone, a display of North Carolina minerals and gems, and an operating real-time weather station. Works of art, rather than dead things, illustrate the flora and fauna of Grandfather: Paul Marchand's artificial wildflowers, songbird woodcarvings by Bill Chrisman, Hugh Morton's photographs of endangered species. There's also a **restaurant**.

The road ends at almost exactly 1 mile in elevation, in an area of great open views, meadows, spruce–fir forests, cliffs, and strange rock formations. In the middle of it all is the **Mile High Swinging Bridge**, almost 100 yards long, crossing a rocky chasm 80 feet deep. An easy 2.5-mile walk goes through the chasm under the bridge, then through boreal forests and across rocky outcrops to a viewpoint overlooking the Blue Ridge Parkway. Adults $12, children $6. Hiking permit half price.

lovely little cascade upstream. Then the path continues to a view toward the falls from the gorge rim and two views over the gorge. The right-bank paths lead to a rimtop view toward the waterfall, then a drop to the bottom of the gorge for a view from beneath. The shortest walk is a mile round trip, while visiting all six overlooks will require about 5 miles of walking.

✔ ⛑ **Museum of North Carolina Minerals** (828-765-2761), 79 Parkway Rd. (MP 331), Spruce Pine, NC. Located near the parkway's exit onto NC 226 at Little Switzerland, NC (MP 331). Daily May–Oct. This small museum, built of local stone in the shape of a cottage, marks the center of North Carolina's mountain mining industry. It was erected in 1953 as a joint project between the parkway and the state; National Park Service experts designed the exhibits with

THE UPPER FALLS SEEN FROM THE CHIMNEY VIEW OVERLOOK.

Jim Hargan

extensive input from local gem collectors and mining industry officials. Displays included careful descriptions of the mountain mining industry, the minerals they extracted, and the rare and fascinating gemstones that resulted as a by-product. The most interesting displays are those of the local gem collectors, a fascinating exhibit of rare stones and strange crystals.

By the time you visit the museum, this may be changed, updated to reflect the passage of half a century of time. Then again, it may not. At this writing the 1953 exhibits are all still there, an immaculately kept window into the mid–20th century. Free.

Crabtree Falls Recreation Area, MP 340, contains a picnic area, a snack bar and store, a gas pump, and a campground. Its main feature of interest is a 2.5-mile loop trail to Upper Crabtree Falls, a very beautiful cascade popular with photographers and valued by waterfall aficionados. The return requires a 500-foot climb.

HISTORIC SITES **The Clinchfield Railroad Loops**. The Clinchfield Railroad, built in the first decade of the 20th century, climbs the Blue Ridge in an amazing series of loops and tunnels just beneath the Orchards at Altapass. The Clinchfield's plan was to link the Atlantic South with the Midwest by attacking the Appalachian barrier head-on, using all the techniques of modern engineering. Building north from Marion, NC, they pushed their road straight up the sheer face of the Blue Ridge; in the 6 linear miles between the bottom and the crest, they built 23 miles of road with five hairpin curves and 17 tunnels. Although

⚓ **The Orchards at Altapass** (888-765-9531; fax 888-766-9455; www.altapass orchard.com), Little Switzerland, NC. At the turn of the 20th century, the Clinchfield Railroad built an amazing grade up the face of the Blue Ridge, with 17 tunnels in 23 miles of hairpin loops. Above the last loop, the railroad planted an apple orchard that followed the crest of the Blue Ridge for 2 miles. Then, in the 1930s, the Blue Ridge Parkway passed through the middle of the orchard—2 miles of sweeping views over large apple trees heavy with fruit, one of the great sights of the parkway.

Sixty years later the orchard had suffered from years of neglect, the trees ignored and allowed to grow wild. In 1994 Kit Carson Trubey bought the orchard to restore and preserve it, under the management of her brother and sister-in-law Bill and Judy Carson. Their plan: Restore the orchard and welcome in the public.

Today it's a wonderful place. The heritage apple trees, nearly a century old, are again healthy and beautiful, framing unimaginable views with bright red fruit in huge clusters. **Hayride tours** wind through the orchard, with orchard storytellers telling the lively history of this important pass. In-season, warm weekend afternoons ring to the sounds of local country musicians in **free concerts** by the apple packing house. Behind the packing house is a **monarch butterfly garden** (the staff hand-raise monarchs in a special area of the packing house), an **herb garden**, and a **spring wetland**. The packing house holds a remarkable **gift shop**, with apple products made in the orchard, local honeys and preserves, craft art from local crafters (four of whom have been declared North Carolina Living Treasures), and neat stuff from all over. It also has a small **café** if you are feeling peckish. Free admission and weekend music; hayrides $3.

THE ORCHARDS AT ALTAPASS WITH LINVILLE MOUNTAIN IN THE DISTANCE.   Jim Hargan

enormously expensive, this superbly engineered road gave the Clinchfield a
short, direct route between two major markets, while their competitors mean-
dered around the mountains. The road, now part of the CSX System, remains a
heavily used freight line. The Blue Ridge Parkway parallels it closely for 4 miles,
from MP 327 to MP 331; look for it from the **North Cove Valley Overlook**
(MP 327.4), **Altapass Orchards Overlook** (MP 328.4), and **Table Rock Overlook** (MP 329.8).

The Crest of the Blue Ridge Highway. In 1910 North Carolina state geologist
Dr. Joseph Hyde Pratt came up with a wonderful idea—a scenic road following
the crest of the Blue Ridge, specifically designed to attract wealthy adventurers
driving their newfangled automobiles. This was at a time when farmers struggled
down muddy ruts to get their crops to railheads, and through-highways were a
starry-eyed dream. Spend state money on a tourist road? The toll road would pay
for itself, however, and would bring in out-of-state money to some of the state's
poorest areas. The state approved Pratt's plan, dubbed it the Crest of the Blue
Ridge Highway, and built a chunk of it before World War I ended construction.

In a very real sense the modern Blue Ridge Parkway is the realization of Dr.
Pratt's vision. A section of the original Crest of the Blue Ridge Highway survives,
paralleling the parkway from Altapass to Little Switzerland, NC. To follow it, exit
the parkway at McKinney Gap (MP 327.7), go under the parkway, and turn right
onto SR 1567 to Altapass Orchards. This gravel section must look very much like
it did in 1913, passing through the heart of the orchards, then continuing (across
the parkway) through farmlands. At its end, turn left onto NC 226 to return to
the parkway; or continue under the parkway and take a right onto NC 226A
through Little Switzerland, another section of the Crest Highway, still charging
tolls in the mid-1920s.

GARDENS AND PARKS Broyhill Park and **Annie Cannon Gardens**. This
large and attractive town park in central Blowing Rock, NC, has informal gardens and a gazebo around a lovely lake. Below the dam lies Annie Cannon Gardens, a native flower garden. Downstream from Cannon Gardens, a hiking path
leads steeply downhill to two large
and beautiful waterfalls, a worthwhile
if strenuous hike (3 miles round trip,
800-foot climb). A park that any town
would be proud of, it's located one
block west of downtown.

The Blowing Rock (828-295-7111;
fax 828-295-4007), Blowing Rock, NC.
Mar.–Dec. daily, Jan.–Feb. weekends.
This privately owned attraction features a 1-acre garden and short trails
around the rock formation that gave
the village of Blowing Rock its name.
The views are excellent. A large gift
shop is on the premises. $5 adults.

ALTAPASS ORCHARDS AS SEEN FROM THE
NORTH COVE VALLEY OVERLOOK.
Jim Hargan

OTHER ✍ **Linville Caverns** (800-419-0540 or 828-756-4171; www.linvillecaverns .com), Marion, NC. Mar.–Nov., daily 9–5; Dec.–Feb., weekends. Located south of Linville Falls on US 221, this show cave features elaborate dripstone formations along nearly level paths. It's lighted in the most natural way possible, to better show off the subtle colors and shapes of the strange rock formations. The endangered eastern pipistrelle bats, harmless and tiny, are found in this cave. The attractive park-style reception building, made of stone and gray wood, has a nice gift shop. $5 adults, $3 children, $4 seniors.

✳ To Do

GOLF Golfers may think it odd that no courses are listed for the Blowing Rock, NC, or Grandfather Mountain area—considering that several are clearly visible from the main road. In fact there are six golf courses, all of them either largely or completely closed to casual visitors. The two listed courses are some distance south of the ritzily exclusive Blowing Rock area.

Blue Ridge Country Club (800-845-8430 or 828-756-4013; www.blueridgecc .com), Linville Falls, NC. Located near Linville Falls, on US 221. All year. This 18-hole course, built in 1995, features wide mountain views and a mountain river in play on eight of the holes. $25–45.

Mount Mitchell Golf Club (828-675-5454; fax 828-675-0458; www.mount mitchellgolfresort.com), 11484 NC 80 S., Burnsville, NC. Just off the NC 80 exit from the Blue Ridge Parkway. Open Apr.–Nov. This 18-hole golf course sits at the foot of Mount Mitchell with wide views toward the East's highest peak. $40–80.

RAFTING AND KAYAKING **High Mountain Expeditions** (800-262-9036 or 828-295-4200; fax 828-295-4437; www.highmountainexpeditions.com), Main St., across from The Speckled Trout, Blowing Rock, NC. Various hours; check the web site or call. They furnish rafting trips—calm, family-oriented floats on the Watauga River, or wild, whitewater trips on the Nolichucky. They also offer a whole lot of other stuff: caving tours, hiking tours, mountain bike tours, mountain bike rentals, flatwater (mountain lake) kayaking tours, and—note this, hikers—shuttle services. Rafting $49–67, caving $45, hiking tours $35–75, mountain bike tours $35–75, mountain bike rentals $19 per hour, $29 for 8 hours. Ask about children's rates.

ROCK CLIMBING **High South Mountain Guides** (828-963-7579), Linville, NC. This guide service centers in the Linville Gorge area, and will provide equipment. An instructional session takes students to Table Rock.

STABLES **Blowing Rock Stables** (828-295-7847). Located on the western edge of the village of Blowing Rock off US 221, this stable offers trail rides through the stunning Moses Cone Park section of the Blue Ridge Parkway.

✳ Lodging

RESORTS **Westglow Spa** (800-562-0807 or 828-295-4463; www.westglow.com), 2845 US 221 S., Blowing Rock, NC 28605. Located 3 miles west of Blowing Rock, Westglow is a European-style spa in a beautifully restored 1916 mansion surrounded by 20 landscaped acres. The National Register classical-style house, with Greek columns framing the front porch, was the summer home of American impressionist artist Elliott Daingerfield, who named it Westglow. Seven suites are furnished in antiques; more modest cottages near the mansion have lower prices. The three meals a day are healthy, balanced—and gourmet, enough so that the restaurant, **Elliot's Place**, is open to the public for dinner as a fine-dining experience. Spa services, included in the tariff, are both wide ranging and less structured than many American-style spas; a new **Life Enhancement Center** contains an indoor pool, weight and exercise equipment, whirlpools, saunas, a hair and nail salon, an aerobics studio, a café, and nearby tennis court. Prices include three meals and all fully staffed spa facilities. Unlike other prices quoted in this book, these include taxes and gratuities. Mansion $816–906 per night for two adults in one room. Cottages and lodge $712–790 per night for two adults in one room. Significant discounts for stays longer than 1 night.

✍ **Clear Creek Guest Ranch** (800-651-4510 or 828-675-4510; www.clearcreekranch.com/main), 100 Clear Creek Rd., Burnsville, NC 28714. This beautiful classic dude ranch sits in the shadows of Mount Mitchell, the tallest peak in the East, on a back road at the far southern end of this section of the parkway. The property has meadows, streams, mountains, and wide, wide views. It also has horses. The tariff includes a full slate of trail rides and ranch activities. Accommodations are in log-sided cabins with full front porches, new and immaculately kept, with one to three bedrooms. Rates include hearty ranch meals, served three times a day, family style in the central lodge, or on the trail, or at an outdoor barbeque (including a weekly steak barbeque). The ranch has wide decks spreading downhill from the lodge to surround a pool, as well as a stocked pond. This family-friendly resort offers a full program for children ages five and up. $370 per night for two adults in one room.

✍ **Eseeola Lodge** (800-742-6717 or 828-733-4311; fax 828-733-3227; www.eseeola.com), 175 Linville Ave., Linville, NC 28646. Open May–Oct. In existence since 1892, the Eseeola remains a summer playground for the wealthy in the village of Linville. It's surrounded by historic homes, the summer homes of its early-20th-century patrons, whose heirs still own it. The present lodge, dating to 1926 and on the National Register, has 24 elegant rooms with all amenities. All rooms have a private porch, and many have a separate living room. The rates include breakfast and dinner (coat and tie required) at the lodge's gourmet restaurant; menus change daily, and always include a choice from seven entrées. Guests have access to tennis courts, exercise rooms, and a fishing lake (all at a separate charge), and there's a day camp for children. Guests also have access to the 18-hole private golf course ($80 per round), little changed since Donald Ross designed it in 1924. Rooms $300–335, suites $400–450, including two meals a day.

Blowing Rock, NC 28605

Crippen's Country Inn (877-295-3487 or 828-295-3487; fax 828-295-0388; www.crippens.com), 239 Sunset Dr. Located in a restored turn-of-the-20th-century home, Crippen's offers a European-style experience in the center of Blowing Rock. Located between downtown and US 321 on quiet Sunset Drive, it's a large bungalow-style structure with a full front porch, green clapboarding and shingle gables, and a lovely little garden in the postage-stamp area between the porch and the stone wall bordering the sidewalk. Inside, two front parlors are comfortably furnished with sofas, fireplaces, art on the wall, and coffee table books. The right-hand parlor opens up into a comfortable and intimate bar with a good selection of cognacs and single malts, part of the superb restaurant that comes alive in the evening (see *Dining Out*).

Upstairs are the rooms, each carefully and comfortably furnished, with modern and antique furniture and quilts on the beds; regular rooms are normal sized, while deluxe rooms are large enough to include roomy sitting areas with sofas. The continental breakfast, served in the restaurant, consists of baked goodies made on the premises. Regular rooms $99–119, large rooms $129–149, private cottage $159–179.

Gideon Ridge Inn (828-295-3644; www.ridge-inn.com), 202 Gideon Ridge Rd. Located just south of Blowing Rock off US 321, near the entrance to the Blowing Rock attraction, Gideon Ridge Inn straddles the Blue Ridge with sweeping views off the edge of the world. This low stone building sits among 5 acres of native gardens, accessible from wide stone terraces. While the terraces, with their views framed by gardens, serve as the focal point for the common areas, there is also a large library with a stone fireplace and a breakfast room with original art. Rooms are comfortably furnished with country-style antiques and reproductions; the least expensive are modest upstairs rooms with wide views from dormer windows, but most rooms are larger, with a choice of amenities such as terrace doors, whirlpool bath, and fireplace. Rates include a full breakfast and afternoon tea. $125–285.

The Inn at Ragged Gardens (828-295-9703; www.ragged-gardens.com), 203 Sunset Dr. This elegant B&B, a short stroll from downtown Blowing Rock, is surrounded by gardens and walled off from the world. It's a large, square manor, clad in shingles, with an oversized porte-cochère topped by a balcony/deck. The large common rooms are elegantly furnished with Edwardian antiques—a spirit carried into the 12 individually decorated rooms, each with a turn-of-the-20th-century theme. Rooms range in size from normal to large; each has a fireplace, goose down comforter, bathrobes, and seasonal fresh flowers, and the majority have private balcony, whirlpool bath, and sitting area. Breakfast includes homemade granola and bread, plus a choice of two hot entrées. There's also an evening wine serving with hors d'oeuvres, and two stocked butler's pantries for guests who need munchies. $170–310.

Springhaven Inn (828-295-6967), P.O. Box 2726. Located at the south edge of downtown Blowing Rock on Main St., this little B&B occupies a stagecoach inn built in the earliest

THE GARDENS AT THE INN AT RAGGED GARDENS.

Jim Hargan

days of the village; Martha Mitchell was one of its guests. It's a handsome shingle-sided two-story structure with wide porches overlooking Main St., on a lot surrounded by giant pines. Decorated throughout with antiques, the five rooms all have private bath. Breakfast, typically fruit, muffins or breads, and a breakfast casserole, is included. $69–99.

Maple Lodge Bed and Breakfast
(828-295-3331; www.maplelodge.net), 152 Sunset Dr. This 11-room early-20th-century inn is located just behind downtown Blowing Rock. Separated from the street by a white picket fence and surrounded by wildflower gardens, it's a simple and attractive two-story colonial structure furnished with antiques, including a library with fireplace, and two parlors. The rooms are also furnished with antiques and Oriental rugs; some are quite large, with sitting area, while others are cozier. Full breakfast, included in the price, is served in the dining room overlooking the wildflower garden. $90–180, depending on size and season; weekday discounts.

&. **Stone Pillar Bed and Breakfast**
(800-962-9955 or 828-295-4141; www.stonepillarbb.com), 144 Pine St. Located just off downtown Blowing Rock, this 1920s-era home is furnished with antiques, including its six guest rooms. Although the cheapest room is very small, other rooms are comfortable and beautifully decorated. The price includes a full breakfast. May–Oct., $65–110; Nov.–Apr., $60–95.

Rocksberry Bed and Breakfast
(828-295-3311; www.rocksberry.com), P.O. Box 1417. This seven-room B&B occupies a large old mountain farmhouse, white clapboard with a two-story porch, down a back lane close to Blowing Rock. It's on its own private road, surrounded by 3 acres of tree-shaded landscaping and gardens, including fruit trees and berry patches. It's furnished throughout with antiques, including the seven guest rooms. A full breakfast is included. $120–130.

Little Switzerland, NC 28749
The Alpine Inn (828-765-5380),
P.O. Box 477, Hwy. 226A. Located
just off the Blue Ridge Parkway, the
modest Alpine Inn was built in 1929
and once furnished lodgings to the
Blue Ridge Parkway workers. Today it
is a homey, well-kept, low-cost B&B
with 14 rooms, nearly all with breathtaking panoramic views from their
balconies. $50.

CABIN RENTALS ♪ **Bear Den
Creekside Cabins** (828-765-2888;
fax 828-765-2864; www.bear-den
.com), Rt. 3, Box 284, Spruce Pine,
NC 28777. Open all year. Located on
a remote stretch of the Blue Ridge
Parkway between Linville Falls and
Little Switzerland, this set of modern
pine log cabins with oak floors is part
of a 400-acre camping resort with a
lake, a sand beach, canoes, and lots of
on-site walking paths. The comfortable and fully furnished cabins—each
with full kitchen, fireplace, whirlpool
bath, and front porch—are isolated
from the camping area, along a creek.
There are also some "campin' cabins,"
described by the owners as "tents
with a tin roof." $110–200 per night,
2-night minimum; price depends on
size and season.

✳ **Where to Eat**

EATING OUT **Storie Street Grille**
(828-295-7075). This downtown
Blowing Rock, NC, storefront restaurant prides itself on its fresh food
prepared from scratch. Soups, sandwiches, and special entrées are prepared to order with imagination and
flair—definitely a good Main Street
choice.

**The Original Emporium Restau-
rant** (828-295-7661). If you're looking

for a beer, a burger, and a view, this
popular restaurant south of Blowing
Rock, NC, on US 321 is definitely
your spot. The menu may be fairly
standard, but the burgers, salads, and
sandwiches are fresh and good. And
the view . . . well, it's the kind you
came here for, with a large deck hanging over the edge of the Blue Ridge
just a wee bit, giving an unobstructed
180° panorama down into the Catawba Valley.

The Gamekeepers Restaurant
(828-963-7400; www.gamekeeper
-nc.com), 3005 Shull's Mill Rd.,
Boone, NC. Located in a remote
mountainous area north of Blowing
Rock, across from the Yonahlossee
Resort, the Gamekeeper occupies a
large wooded site, well up from its
country road. Its menu puts a modern
twist on mountain favorites, featuring
game, fish, vegetarian entrées, and
fresh seasonal vegetables cooked on a
wood-fired grill. The winding drive
out is very beautiful, passing through
and then along the boundaries of
Moses Cone Park; from Blowing
Rock, just follow the signs to the Yonalossee Resort.

**Famous Louise's Rockhouse
Restaurant** (828-765-2702), US 221
and NC 183, Linville Falls, NC. This
landmark stone building by the Blue
Ridge Parkway once furnished a
hearty good time to the parkway's
WPA construction crews—an en-
deavor helped by its position straddling three county lines, discouraging
unwanted snooping by county sher-
iffs. Now it's a popular southern-style
restaurant serving good home-style
food three meals a day.

**Chalet Restaurant at Switzerland
Inn** (800-654-4026 or 828-765-2153;
www.switzerlandinn.com), Little

Switzerland, NC. Open for lunch and dinner. Just off the Blue Ridge Parkway at MP 334, this restaurant is part of the Switzerland Inn. Nicely decorated, it's mainly noted for its panoramic views off the Blue Ridge, which at this point is directly underfoot. The straightforward menu has a lot of old favorites and some pleasant surprises as well—local trout smoked on the premises, a knockwurst and bratwurst plate on fresh sauerkraut, a bowtie pasta dish with andouille sausage, chicken, and shrimp in a tomato Creole sauce. They have a Friday prime rib and seafood buffet for the all-you-can-eat crowd, and a Saturday outdoor barbeque during summer (weather permitting). Weddings a specialty.

DINING OUT **Crippen's Country Inn and Restaurant** (877-295-2487 or 828-295-3487; fax 828-295-0388; www.crippens.com), 239 Sunset Dr., Blowing Rock, NC. Located on Sunset Dr., a side street running between downtown Blowing Rock and US 321. Dinner only. July–Oct., daily; June, Tue.–Sun.; Nov.–May, Thu.–Sun. Owner Jimmy Crippen and chef James Welch have created one of the finest and most exciting restaurants in the mountains, in this beautifully restored boardinghouse. Occupying much of the first floor of this fine European-style inn, the restaurant features an elegant yet casual atmosphere perfect for Blowing Rock. A wide front porch welcomes diners, as does a comfortable small bar facing a comfortable parlor sitting area. Past the bar, the roomy dining area has old-fashioned full-length windows and wood floors, simple wood furniture, and fine art on the walls. Each evening's menu is unique, selected from Chef Welch's large repertoire of adventurous, boldly flavored creations. Appetizers range from inexpensive grilled duck quesadillas (with charcoaled onions, chilies, and Jack cheese, served with roasted corn and tomato salsas and lime chili sour cream) to the pricey Coca-Cola-marinated grilled kangaroo (with black-eyed peas and red bliss mash). Entrées center on beef and seafood (with chicken, duck, pork, and lamb also appearing on the menu) married with fruits, vegetables, nuts, cheeses, and sauces; there is also a pasta dish, typically less expensive. Selections may include a grilled pork tenderloin marinated with rosemary and garlic, served with a rosemary Zinfandel sauce, a mash of goat cheese and chives, and baby vegetables; or a grilled beef tenderloin, crusted with espresso and infused with bittersweet chocolate, served with an Irish cream sauce, French beans, and walnut goat cheese au gratin potatoes. Desserts are decadent, rich combinations of caramel and chocolate and cream and pecans—only part of a dessert menu that also lists ice creams and sorbets made on the premises, fine brandies, single-malt scotches, ports and dessert wines, and fine cigars (smoking on the porch only). The menu is à la carte. Soups and salads $5–8, appetizers $7–14, entrées $16–26.

✳ Entertainment

The Blowing Rock Stage Company (828-295-9627; fax 828-295-9104; www.blowingrockstage.com), Blowing Rock, NC. This nonprofit professional theater company performs four plays (two of them musicals) each summer season.

Geneva Hall (828-668-7223). The Little Switzerland, NC, town hall hosts weekly clogging all summer long, just across from the Switzerland Inn.

✳ Selective Shopping

Blowing Rock, NC

Blowing Rock's elegant little downtown stretches along four blocks of US Business 321, opposite the town park. It's built up from numerous small buildings—old brick fronts, houses, renovated gas stations, even a vacant lot or two—now given over to catering to the needs of the village's well-heeled visitors. Galleries, gift shops, antiques shops, and restaurants dominate the street.

☂ **Main Street Gallery/Expressions Craft Guild** (828-295-7839). Located in downtown Blowing Rock in an old stone building across from the post office, this fine craft cooperative features a wide selection of local artists' pottery, jewelry, glass, wood, fiber, and photography. It's owned and managed by its members, and a member should be on the floor to talk with you when you drop in.

Man in the Moon (828-295-9229; fax 828-295-3699), 1087 Main St. This downtown Blowing Rock shop is a rarity—a gift shop where husbands want to stay longer than their wives. No sports memorabilia or NASCAR souvenirs here, just a wide range of doodads and whatchamacallits tailored

ARTISTS' POTTERY AT THE EXPRESSIONS GALLERY.

Jim Hargan

to men's tastes. Be sure to come in to enjoy the large kinetic sculptures with marbles dropping down copper rails; the cheery little noises they make are part of the fun. Now, if they would just add a selection of power tools . . .

☂ **Sunset Tees and Hattery** (828-295-9326), 1117 Main St. Another masculine favorite in downtown Blow-ing Rock, Sunset Tees features a huge selection of first-rate men's hats in a large room in the back. There are plenty of cowboy hats and baseball caps—but also derbies, bowlers, top hats, berets, jazzy hats, Sunday-go-to-meeting hats, leather hats, cloth hats, straw hats, and lots of felt hats. A fun shop.

Lenoir, NC

Bolick Family Pottery (828-295-3862), 4884 Bolick Rd. You'll find this studio 3 miles south of Blowing Rock on US 321, then left on Blackberry Rd. (SSR 1500) for half a mile. Mon.–Sat. 8–5, Sun.1–5. Fifth-generation potter Lula Owens Bolick and her husband, Glenn, moved from Seagrove, NC, to this spot down a back road in 1973. They specialize in traditional shapes—mugs, bowls, pitchers, candleholders, tea sets—in colors of gray, oatmeal, and cobalt blue.

Linville, NC

One World Bookstore and Soup Bar (828-733-8897). Wed.–Sat. 11–4. This unique shop down a residential street combines a bookshop specializing in regional, Native American, cooking, health, children's, and metaphysical titles with a soup bar offering fresh, homemade soup, baked goods, and fresh coffee. It also has local art, pottery, antiques, and gifts.

Little Switzerland, NC

Trillium Gallery (828-765-0024), Blue Ridge Parkway MP 334. May–Oct. daily, call for hours; changeable for summer. Located in the set of shops associated with the Switzerland Inn, the Trillium Gallery represents a dozen or more local fine crafters, including some associated with the Penland School. You'll find original works of art in pottery, basketry, glass, and jewelry. The Trillium sits in an interesting collection of shops, including a craft shop and a gem shop.

Grassy Mountain Bookshop (828-765-9070). May–Oct., daily 10–5. This bookshop at the center of Little Switzerland (on NC 226A) specializes in used, rare, and out-of-print books.

✳ Special Events

SPRING **Blowing Rock Art in the Park**. One Saturday a month, May–Oct. This juried art show features 100 contributors over its 6-month run in downtown Blowing Rock's beautiful park.

SUMMER **Singing on the Mountain** (800-468-7325 or 828-733-2013). Fourth Sunday in June. Held annually since 1924, this all-day gospel sing and church bazaar at the foot of Grandfather Mountain features a dozen gospel groups. Free.

Grandfather Mountain Highland Games and Gathering of the Clans (828-733-1333; fax 828-733-0092; www.gmhg.org), Linville, NC. Second weekend in July. For nearly half a century the Grandfather Mountain Highland Games have been held on MacRae Meadows at Grandfather Mountain Park. A highly popular 5-day fete with attendance in the tens of thousands, events include classic Scottish athletics, bagpipe demonstrations and competitions, Highland dancing, a 5-mile footrace and a marathon up Grandfather Mountain, ceilidhs (Celtic jam sessions), Scottish harp, Scottish fiddling, Gaelic song, and sheep herding demonstrations. There are a large number of vendors and clan tents. The event is sponsored by the nonprofit Grandfather Mountain Highland Games, Inc., which uses proceeds to run the games and a scholarship fund. Every day requires a separate ticket, as do many special events; tickets typically range $10–20 apiece, and eventwide passes are not available.

Blowing Rock Charity Horse Show (828-295-9861; www.blowing rockhorseshow.com), Blowing Rock, NC. Late July–mid-Aug. An annual event since 1923, this horse show consists of two AA-rated Hunter/Jumper shows (5 days each) and one A-rated

4-day Saddlebred Show. Although the emphasis is on fun, the first Hunter/Jumper show is a World Champion Hunter Rider event, and the Saddlebred show is part of the American Saddlebred Grand National Series. Charities supported include the local volunteer fire department and rescue squad, Moses Cone trail maintenance, and a riding program for the disabled.

Grandfather Mountain Amateur and Professional Camera Clinic (800-468-7325 or 828-733-2013). Third weekend in Aug. For over half a century Grandfather Mountain Park has hosted this annual photojournalism convention, open to all serious photographers. Free. (Participants must register for free admission to park.)

WINTER ❧ **Blowing Rock Winterfest** (888-465-0366 or 828-295-9168; www.blowingrockwinterfest.com). Mid-Jan. For a 3-day weekend during the coldest part of the year, the village of Blowing Rock, NC, celebrates the fun part of winter, with hayrides and hot chocolate, bonfires, a parade, dogsledding, ice sculpting, street musicians, dances, live jazz, live theater, a chili cookoff—and (hopefully) lots of snow.

BEHIND THE BLUE RIDGE:
BOONE & BANNER ELK

On the back of the Blue Ridge, westward from Blowing Rock, NC, the Watauga and New Rivers drain a wide, perched bowl of a valley. Each river runs in a separate direction—the New River northward toward the Ohio River, the Watauga River westward toward the Tennessee. Nevertheless, their headwaters come within a few hundred yards of each other in a wide, level gap at the center of this region. This location, long a wilderness crossroads, now holds the college town of Boone, NC.

North Carolinian Daniel Boone explored this high, mountainous bowl in the years before the Revolution. He wasn't the first European to do so; he was just the most important. His pa, Squire Boone, had created a prosperous farmstead at the foot of the Blue Ridge, and young Daniel spent his youth poking up every little game trail he could find within a 2-week walking distance. Daniel established reasonably good trails up the Blue Ridge into the Watauga lands, and helped European settlers find their way into these Cherokee hunting grounds (in violation of English laws). The settlers negotiated a private peace with the Cherokee chiefs (money played a large part in the transaction) and settled down the Watauga into Tennessee. Boone went on to blaze more trails, moving into western Virginia and the empty Kentucky hunting lands.

Today the town of Boone sits at the center of this rugged valley, a small town with a busy brick-front downtown and a largish state university, Appalachian State. Nearby, the settlement of Valle Crucis (pronounced *valley crew-sis*), NC, preserves a lively and beautiful historic landscape that mixes farmhouses from Boone's era with general stores dating to the 1930s. Still farther back, a couple of those 5,000-foot peaks harbor ski slopes—about as snowy and nicely kept as you will find in the warm latitudes of the American South. To the north of Boone stretches beautiful rural countryside, little visited by tourists, dominated by the ancient New River and the little county seat of Jefferson, NC.

GUIDANCE **Boone Convention and Visitor's Bureau** (800-852-9506 or 828-264-2225; fax 828-264-6644; www.boonechamber.com), 208 Howard St., Boone, NC 28607. Located on a back street in downtown Boone, this friendly information desk will help you with the town of Boone and its surrounding area.

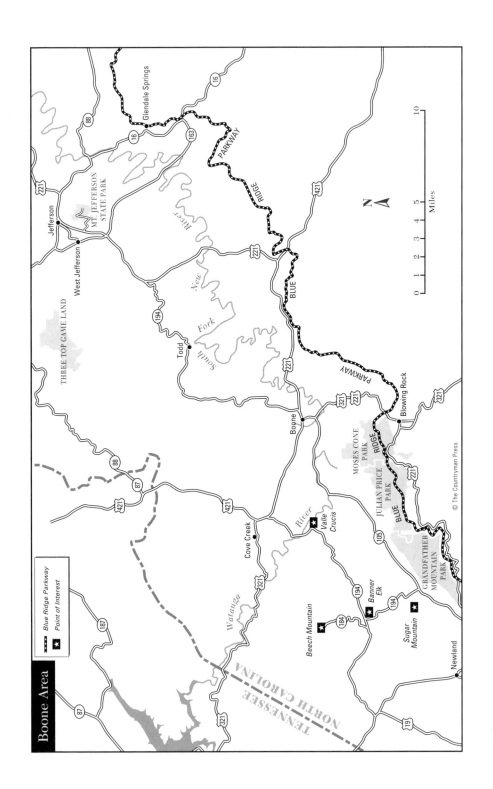

Boone Area

Blue Ridge Parkway
Point of Interest

Glendale Springs

16

88

163

PARKWAY

221

Jefferson

MT. JEFFERSON
STATE PARK

BLUE

RIDGE

New

West Jefferson

421

THREE TOP GAME LAND

194

River

221

Todd

South

Fork

221

BLUE

Boone

PARKWAY

88

Blowing Rock

87

221
221

MOSES CONE
PARK

221

421

RIDGE

421

JULIAN PRICE
PARK

221

River

Valle
Crucis

BLUE

Cove Creek

105

421

GRANDFATHER
MOUNTAIN
PARK

© The Countryman Press

221

Beech Mountain

184

Watauga

194

Banner
Elk

187

Sugar
Mountain

Newland

321

87

321

19

N

TENNESSEE
NORTH CAROLINA

0   1   2   3   4   5   10

Miles

Beech Mountain Chamber of Commerce (800-468-5506 or 828-387-9383; fax 828-387-3572; www.beechmtn.com), 403A Beech Mountain Parkway, Beech Mountain, NC 28604. Mon.–Fri. 9–4. This small-town chamber welcomes visitors from an office within city hall. You'll find it at the top of the mountain on the left on NC 184.

Avery/Banner Elk Chamber of Commerce (800-972-2183 or 828-898-5605; fax 828-898-8287; www.banner-elk.com), P.O. Box 335, Banner Elk, NC 28604. Covering all of Avery County (the rural areas west of Valle Crucis), this visitors center is hidden away in the shopping center at the corner of NC 105 and NC 184.

Ashe County Chamber of Commerce and Visitors Center (336-246-9550; www.ashechamber.com), 6 N. Jefferson Ave., West Jefferson, NC 28694. Located off the main highway in West Jefferson's redbrick downtown, this visitors center offers help and advice for the Jefferson area.

GETTING THERE *By car*: The main highways into this region are **US 321** and **US 421**, which converge at Boone, NC. Within the region, **NC 105** (a surprisingly unattractive roadway) is the easiest way to drive south from Boone to Banner Elk, NC, while **US 221** is the easiest route north from Boone to Jefferson, NC.

By air: You have a choice of three airports, two regional and one international. **Hickory Regional Airport** (828-323-7408) is only 35 miles away from Boone, NC, and gets several commuter hops a day from Charlotte, NC, via US Airways Express. Car rentals are inside the terminal. The **Charlotte/Douglas International Airport** is another 40 miles farther, and is usually much cheaper. Don't neglect to check out the **Tri-Cities Airport** (423-325-6000), 2525 Hwy. 75, Blountville, TN; much bigger than Hickory, it may offer cheaper fares than Charlotte.

By bus or train: There is no scheduled bus or train service in this region.

MEDICAL EMERGENCIES **Watauga Medical Center** (800-443-7385 or 828-262-4100; www.wataugamc.org), 336 Deerfield Rd., Boone, NC. Two miles south of Boone on US 221/321, then a block north on Deerfield Rd. This full-service regional hospital, with a wide range of surgical and medical specialties, offers 24/7 emergency room services at its main building.

Ashe Memorial Hospital (336-246-7101; www.ashememorial.org), 200 Hospital Ave., Jefferson, NC. This full-service 76-bed hospital with a 24/7 emergency room serves the rural northwest corner of the North Carolina mountains from its campus at the center of Jefferson.

✳ Wandering Around

EXPLORING BY CAR **NC 194**. *Leg 1*: Starting at Jefferson, NC, take US Business 221 through West Jefferson, NC, to US 221; turn right onto NC 194; then follow 194 to Boone, NC. *Leg 2*: Continue on NC 194, coterminous with US 421 through Boone; continue on NC 194 when it turns left off US 321/421; continue to Banner Elk, NC. *Leg 3*: Turn right off NC 194 onto NC 184, climbing to Beech Mountain, NC.

NC 194 passes through the center of this region for 48 miles, from Jefferson to Boone, then on to Valle Crucis and Banner Elk. It's a very slow and twisty road, but exceptionally pretty, with pastoral vistas over streamside meadows framed by low mountains and dotted with old barns and farmhouses. Start at the northern end of this region, at **Jefferson**, lightly built with scattered businesses and homes, dominated by its great domed redbrick courthouse. In 2 miles US Business 221 reaches **West Jefferson**, a busy little former rail depot, with a three-block redbrick downtown that is coming back to life. As the road narrows and enters the mountains, it climbs a little valley then switchbacks down to the National Register village of **Todd**, NC, a tiny collection of historic buildings off the road on the left. On a side lane through Todd, the **South Fork of the New River** makes one of its characteristic 180° curves, doubling back on itself around steep mountain slopes. Eleven miles later NC 194 twists out of the mountains to reach US 221/421 at Boone.

NC 194 follows US 421 through **Boone**, a busy college town, passing right up the middle of its crowded downtown and out the other side. Five miles beyond Boone, NC 194 turns off the main highway to the left and once more becomes a mountain road, curving down to the wide meadows of the Watauga River at **Valle Crucis**, NC, passing the **Mast General Store**. The pastoral beauty and historic structures continue for 7 miles past the Mast Store, as the road twists sharply around meadows and up mountain slopes to **Banner Elk**.

On the far side of Banner Elk, this route climbs NC 184 to Beech Mountain, using five switchbacks in 3 miles to rise 1,400 feet above the valley. The road tops out at 5,000 feet above sea level, at the center of the highest village in the East; to the right, Blackberry Ridge Rd. leads a short distance to superior views. The main road continues through the village to switchback down the back of the mountain, with more good views. You'll find **Ski Beech** down this way, where a summer ride up a ski lift leads to a mile-high panorama.

EXPLORING ON FOOT **Mount Jefferson Summit**. This mile-long walk along the summit of 4,600-foot Mount Jefferson climbs 350 feet in elevation on its way to two spectacular viewpoints. It starts at the picnic area on the top of the mountain in **Mount Jefferson State Natural Area**, a mile outside Jefferson, NC. The trail proceeds along an old roadbed at the far end of the picnic area, climbing uphill at a fairly steep 15 percent—mercifully, for only 1,000 feet or so—to a viewpoint at the highest point of Mount Jefferson. The trail continues along a high rocky ridge, forested with some very tough old hardwoods, for another half mile to **Luther Rock**, a rocky outcrop and cliff with very wide views over Jefferson and northward over the New River Valley. A loop returns through rhododendron tunnels.

☙ **Lee and Vivian Reynolds Greenway Trail (The Boone Greenway)**. This 2.2-mile (one way) urban greenway follows the headwaters of the New River just east of Boone, NC. An attractive and well-kept riverside walk, the paved and gravel trails cross the river three times on handsome pedestrian bridges to find wildflower fields, river glades, and vistas. Popular with locals and college students, it has plenty of benches for enjoying the view. The upstream end is the easier to find; take US 321 south 2 miles from downtown Boone to a left turn onto Deerfield Rd., then four blocks to a left onto State Farm Rd., then one block to the start of the greenway.

✳ Villages

Boone, NC. This college town and county seat sits in a high valley straddling the headwaters of the Watauga and New Rivers. Not that many years ago it was a sleepy mountain town, but the explosive growth of **Appalachian State University** has left Boone bursting at the seams with 13,400 residents, its overflow sprawling down US 321 toward Blowing Rock and NC 105 toward Banner Elk. This is a lot of people for a mountain town that can only be reached down two-lane highways, and traffic can be bad. On the bright side, it has a neat downtown shopping district and plenty of interesting shops and restaurants. The compact campus of 13,000-student Appalachian State sits only three blocks from downtown, paralleling it along a stream and up the opposite mountain slope. The university-sponsored **Summer Festival** brings a wide variety of performing artists and lecturers into Boone each July.

Valle Crucis, NC. This rural settlement is nearly unique in the Appalachians—a popular tourist destination that remains unspoiled by success. Pronounced *Valley Crew-sis*, it's a dispersed rural settlement along the Watauga River, its center 9 miles west of Boone, NC, on back roads. It has become popular for its lush pastoral scenery, historic buildings, unique small shops and B&B inns, and general store and post office, the famous **Mast General Store**. It has a prosperous look more common to New England than Appalachia, but there's nothing fake about it; this area's been settled since the late 1700s, and surviving buildings date to that earliest period. To find it from Boone, take NC 105 west for 4.75 miles to Broadstone Rd. (SSR 1112), just over the Watauga River, and turn right. Valle Crucis stretches along Broadstone Rd. 2.8 miles to NC 194 and the Mast General Store, generally taken as the center of the village.

Banner Elk, NC. For many years a quiet little village centered on a small liberal arts college, today Banner Elk is main street for the **Sugar Mountain** and **Beech Mountain** ski slopes. Banner Elk's original village center sits at the intersection of NC 194 and NC 184, by tiny **Lees-McRae College**, and this remains the best place to look for shops, cafés, or quaint old B&Bs. It's also the location of **Mill Pond**, a very scenic picnic spot run by the college and open to the public. Modern-day Banner Elk scatters south from its old center along NC 184 for 2.6 miles to the entrance to Sugar Mountain, then beyond another 1.5 miles to the urban sprawl along NC 105.

Beech Mountain, NC. In all likelihood the highest town in the East, Beech Mountain's town hall sits just barely above 5,000 feet in elevation—and a third of a mile higher into the sky than nearby Boone, NC. This ski village is reached by taking NC 184 north from Banner Elk, NC, straight up five switchbacks and 1,500 feet. The village sits on a high, flat shelf about 200 feet shy of the summit, a small scattering of modest shops and motels surrounded by condos and second homes. The ski slope starts some distance downhill (toward the back of the mountain) and rises directly behind the town hall, making it easy to watch the skiers from the little town square. In fact, the town government provides a children's sledding slope behind the town hall, complete with artificial snow. The temperature difference is very noticeable, with Beech Mountain being long-sleeved cool and breezy in the warmest of summer weather. Beech Mountain is an isolated mile-high peak surrounded by much lower terrain, so good views are a given from just about anywhere near the village center.

Jefferson and **West Jefferson**, NC. Twenty-five miles north of Boone, NC, and far off the beaten tourist paths, these little-developed redbrick sister towns retain their old mountain look and feel. They complement each other: Jefferson, with 1,400 residents, has the government functions and the historic domed courthouse, while West Jefferson, with 1,000 citizens, has the downtown main street (called Jefferson Street). Once a railroad depot, West Jefferson's old-fashioned redbrick downtown is surprisingly interesting, with a scattering of galleries representing local artists. **Mount Jefferson** looms above both towns, a state park with magnificent views from four overlooks.

✳ Wild Places

THE GREAT FORESTS Wild places abound along the Blue Ridge, a scant half a dozen miles to the south of Boone, NC, including some of the most remarkable in the Southern Appalachians—the privately owned scenic park of Grandfather Mountain, the Blue Ridge Parkway with its stunning views, and the deep woods and waterfalls of the Pisgah National Forest. These are described in the chapter devoted to the Blue Ridge Parkway as it runs through this area: "Blowing Rock & Grandfather Mountain."

Once you've backed away from the Blue Ridge, large public wild places become scarce. Much of the Watauga and New River Valleys has been heavily settled and farmed since the time of Daniel Boone in the late 18th century; the lovely pastoral landscapes are dotted with historic old buildings, but wilderness has long since given way to woodlots. To the south of this area, the high, wild peaks of Sugar and Beech Mountains have been converted to ski-oriented tourist attractions and thickly built up, their former wilderness dissected by closely spaced roads and small building lots.

THE ASHE COUNTY COURTHOUSE IN JEFFERSON.

Jim Hargan

To the north of Boone, tall mountains retain their wild character. Forests tend to be old and lovely, with rich and diverse ecosystems; the scenery is dotted with beautiful waterfalls, odd little perched valleys, and impressive cliffs. Unfortunately for travelers, virtually all of these wild places are privately owned and closed to the public. Only one large tract welcomes the public to explore at their leisure— Three Top Mountain Game Lands, near Todd. A second tract, The

Nature Conservancy's Bluff Mountain Preserve, is open only to guided walks (which, fortunately, occur all summer long).

Three Top Mountain Game Lands (919-733-7291). Take NC 194 north of Boone, NC, to Todd, NC, then head north on Three Top Rd. for 8.7 miles. The public access parking lot is on the right, just before a bridge over Three Top Creek. This 2,300-acre tract (about 3.6 square miles) between Todd and Jefferson preserves the impressive 4,800-foot craggy peak known as Three Tops and its surrounding slopes. The tract's public hiking trails lead through rich forests to wildflower meadows, crags, and views. The Nature Conservancy started assembling this impressive tract in 1989 from a mosaic of donations, cooperative local owners, and a couple of busted subdivisions; expect some of the lower walking to be on old subdivision tracks. It's currently owned by the North Carolina Wildlife Resources Commission, whose main mission is maintaining public land for hunting and fishing.

Bluff Mountain Preserve (The Nature Conservancy) (919-403-8558; fax 919-403-0379; http://nature.org/wherewework/northamerica/states/northcarolina/preserves/art5590.html), 1 University Place, 4705 University Dr., Suite 290, Durham, NC 27707. This 2,000-acre privately owned preserve, located in the same mountain range as the Three Top Mountain Game Lands, protects an unusual flat-bottomed valley perched just below the 4,800-foot peak of Bluff Mountain. The site offers wonderful views from rocky outcrops, and a variety of beautiful and unusual ecosystems—a mature hemlock forest, a dwarf oak forest, rocky bald plant communities, and a rare example of the Southern Appalachian fen, protected in the high valley. Owned and managed by The Nature Conservancy, Bluff Mountain is not open for casual visits from the public. Both the Conservancy and the Ashe County Chamber of Commerce, however, host regular guided walks.

THE GREAT RIVERS The South Fork of the New River. The most remarkable thing about the South Fork of the New River is the way it meanders, acting as if it is lazily wandering through a level plain before finally reaching an ocean. This is not the case. The New River rises more than 3,100 feet above sea level, just behind the Blue Ridge, and follows the Blue Ridge for nearly 90 miles. Of course, those are meandering river miles; the actual linear distance covered is 29.43 miles. Those distance-tripling meanders reduce the slope of the river to the point that canoes commonly replace kayaks; much of the river is flatwater, and most of its rapids are a mild Class I. Despite their flatland shapes and slopes, these meanders have managed to cut straight down into the hard rock of the Blue Ridge, leaving the river surrounded by clifflike slopes. Occasionally the river will make a sharp 180° curve, cutting a gorge that doubles back on itself. The easy paddling couples with the prime mountain scenery to offer 90 miles of day explorations and overnight adventures.

This stretch of river has long enjoyed the reputation as the second oldest river in the world, and the oldest in North America—claims repeated by President Clinton when, from its banks near Jefferson, NC, in 1998, he declared it a National Heritage River. Some have objected to this, claiming that there is no agreed-upon

NC & BANNER ELK

measure of a river's age—and even if there was, it has never been used in a world survey. Well, picky, picky, picky. Those 90 miles of meanders formed when the New River flowed through a flat plain. The meanders cut into the rock as the mountains rose underneath them—in this case the Blue Ridge Mountains, 220 million years old. You do the math.

RECREATION AREAS **Mount Jefferson State Natural Area** (336-246-9653; fax 336-246-3386; http://ils.unc.edu/parkproject/visit/moje/home.html), Jefferson, NC. This isolated mountain rises just south of Jefferson, its peak 1,400 feet above the wide valleys that surround it. A paved lane climbs the west slope of Mount Jefferson in seven switchbacks, with two overlooks giving broad views over West Jefferson and Bluff Mountain. At the top you'll find a tree-shaded picnic area, a nature trail, and walking paths along the narrow half-mile-long summit to two more overlooks.

PICNIC AREAS **Mill Pond Picnic Area.** This lovely little picnic area sits at the center of Banner Elk, NC. It's a landmark along NC 184, with a barn-red cottage sitting under great trees by the reflecting surface of the small lake. Its scattered lakeside tables are a great place to picnic, or just sit and relax.

Howard Knob Park. This 6-acre county park sits high above Boone, NC. Its main feature is a large outcrop and cliff with stunning views over Boone and Valle Crucis, NC. It can be difficult to find, but is worth the effort. From downtown Boone, head uphill on Waters St. (away from the university) to its end, then continue steeply uphill on Junaluska Rd.; when it tops out, go right to Howard Knob Park.

✳ To See

HISTORIC SITES **Todd National Historic District**. Located halfway between Boone and Jefferson on NC 194, Todd, NC, is a former depot town on a long-defunct mountain railroad that followed the New River to Jefferson and over the mountains to Virginia. A bit of a ghost town, Todd today is a collection of late-19th- and early-20th-century vernacular buildings that somehow manage to preserve the look and feel of an old rural railroad siding village. While most of the buildings are private, the general store is still going strong, and the depot houses a local craft gallery and New River outfitter. The New River comes right up to the town's lower edge and makes one of its unique hairpin turns around a cliff—an interesting site. It was at this point that the railroad started following the New River, and its old grade is now a narrow country lane with sweeping river views; you can rent bicycles at the depot for a lovely riverside jaunt.

✐ **Hickory Ridge Homestead** (828-264-2120), 591 Horn In The West Dr., Boone, NC. Located by the Horn In The West amphitheater (see *Cultural Sites*) and the Daniel Boone Gardens; go east of downtown on US 421 and turn right (south) onto Horn In The West Dr. Summer, Tue.–Sun. 1–8:30; spring and fall, Sat. 9–4, Sun. 1–4. Closed in winter. This living history museum in Boone re-creates a late-18th-century pioneer farmstead. Owned by the Southern Appalachian Historical Association, it preserves two historic log cabins and several

✐ ☂ **Mast General Store** (828-963-6511; www.mastgeneralstore.com), NC 194, Valle Crucis, NC. Mon.–Sat. 7–6, Sun. 1–5. You may have seen various Mast General Stores selling outdoor and gift items in downtown Boone, Hendersonville, Asheville, and Waynesville, NC. Make no mistake: The 19th-century frame store at the center of Valle Crucis is the real Mast General Store and always has been—the primary general store for the community of Valle Crucis since 1882 (when it replaced a smaller structure across the street). This National Register structure is really a collection of white clapboard buildings sort of stuck together, with doorways passing through common walls on the inside. The outside has a false front, plate-glass windows, a wood boardwalk, and a hand-crank gas pump that no longer works. Inside, it combines the items needed by the Valle Crucis community—groceries, mail, fishing licenses, burning permits, and a checkers set by a potbellied stove—with local canned jellies and honeys, barrels of marbles, bulk candy, local arts, outdoor products, and all sorts of other stuff. The Mast family owned it until 1973 and is still involved in its management. Its current owners, John and Faye Cooper, have taken the Mast's longtime formula of "Everything from Cradles to Caskets" and used it to create a general store marketing powerhouse with branches in five mountain towns. Still, they've kept the original Mast General Store true to its heritage, one of the few general stores to make it successfully into the 21st century.

THE MAST STORE IS LISTED ON THE NATIONAL REGISTER OF HISTORIC PLACES.

Jim Hargan

outbuildings on an attractive wooded slope near the center of town. The build-ings are beautifully and authentically furnished, and have period vegetable and herb gardens. Guides in period clothing explain the pioneer way of life, demon-strate crafts, and perform authentic music. Visitors are invited to participate in activities such as carding and spinning wool, weaving on a loom nearly two cen-turies old, candle making, or cooking over an open hearth. Summer visitors should look into an evening visit followed by a performance of Horn In The West—for the same cost as a ticket to Horn In The West alone. $2 per person.

CULTURAL SITES **Appalachian State University** (828-262-2000; www.appstate .edu), Boone, NC 28608. The parklike main campus of Appalachian State stretches the length of central Boone, along a stream two blocks downhill from downtown. Compact and modern, the 50 or more university buildings squeeze onto a 75-acre site, landscaped with a plentiful number of hardwood trees and rhododendrons. The attractive campus is studded with sculptures and contains several galleries of student and faculty art. On-campus accommodations are available at the tree-shaded, hilltop **Broyhill Inn**, with a first-rate restaurant (see *Lodging*). A member of the University of North Carolina, ASU has nearly 13,000 students and 175 degree programs.

& ⊤ **The Appalachian Cultural Museum** (828-262-3117; www.museum .appstate.edu), University Hall, Appalachian State University, Boone, NC. Lo cated off US 321 south of Boone; take US 321 south from downtown, turning left onto University Hall Rd. Tue.–Sat.10–5, Sun. 1–5; closed Mon. Sponsored by Appalachian State University, this museum has exhibits on every aspect of Appalachian history and culture: Blue Ridge geology, Native American settle-ment and culture, early settlers, Daniel Boone, Daniel Boone's mythologizer James Daugherty, the Civil War, African Americans in Appalachia, moonshine (including an authentic 100-year-old still), mountain crafts and music, story-telling, a reconstructed general store from 1911, NASCAR racing, the local ski industry, and modern logging and tourism (including an exhibit on the Land of Oz, a failed theme park on Beech Mountain). Of particular note is a gallery of self-portraits of local people, ranging from professional artists to ordinary folk. $4 adults, free Tue.

Horn in the West (888-825-6747 or 828-262-2120; fax 828-262-0105; www .boonenc.org/saha/hitw/index.htm), 591 Horn in the West Dr. (off US 321), Boone, NC. Evening performances June 22–Aug. 11, Tue.–Sun. For over half a century the Southern Appalachian Historical Association has presented Kermit Hunter's large-scale outdoor musical drama of the early settlement of the Wa-tauga Valley, centering on Daniel Boone and the American Revolution. Held 6 evenings a week through summer, the performance is preceded by an evening tour of the historically authentic reconstructed pioneer farmstead, Hickory Ridge Homestead (see *Historic Sites*)—actually an extension of the perform-ance, with period-costumed guides demonstrating the pioneer way of life. $12 adults, $6 children under 13, includes entrance to Hickory Ridge Homestead.

⊤ **The Jones House Community and Cultural Center** (828-262-4576), 604 W. King St., Boone, NC. Wed.–Sat. noon–5. This 1908 local doctor's home sits incongruously in the center of Boone's brick-storefront downtown, a genteel white clapboard mansion with a wide porch overlooking its high lawn toward busy King St. Today this National Register structure is owned by the Town of Boone and run by the Watauga County Arts Council. While much of the large house is given over to community center uses, several rooms serve as a gallery for local artists, while others are furnished in period. It's definitely worthwhile to take a time out from King Street shopping and pop up for a visit. Free.

⇑ **The Turchin Center for the Visual Arts** (828-262-3017; fax 828-262-2848), Boone, NC. Affiliated with Appalachian State University, this arts center occupies the 100-year-old octagonal brick Methodist church that has long been a prominent downtown landmark. Meant as a center for campus–community interaction, it has a main gallery and six smaller galleries, plus two terraces for displaying sculpture, a lecture hall, and a wing for classrooms and studios.

GARDENS AND PARKS Daniel Boone Gardens (828-264-6390), downtown Boone, NC. May–Oct., 9–6; 9–8 PM on days with Horn in the West performances. Closed Nov.–Apr. Owned and run by the nonprofit Garden Club of North Carolina on land contributed by Horn in the West (Southern Appalahian Historical Association), the Daniel Boone Gardens presents native Appalachian plants in a free-flowing, informal landscape. Opened in 1966, the gardens have had nearly four decades of growth and improvement, offering season-long displays of every native flower imaginable. The gardens now include a bog garden, a fern garden, a sunken rock garden with a tiny pond, a mountain spring, a reflecting pool, and a meditation garden. The large wrought-iron entrance gate with the initials DB was handmade by artist and Daniel Boone descendant Daniel Boone VI. $4.

✳ To Do

BICYCLING Magic Cycles (828-265-2211; www.magiccycles.com/main.html), 208 Faculty St., #1, Boone, NC. This full-service bicycle shop, located south of downtown Boone on Faculty St. just off US 321, offers both mountain bike rentals and guided bicycle trips. The Boone area offers a wide variety of bicycle paths and trails, and this is a good place to find out about them all. Rentals: $15 for 4 hours, $25 for 8 hours, $30 for 24 hours, $60 for 3 days. Guided trips cost $50 per person, with a minimum of two people.

Beech Mountain Biking Trails (828-387-2795), 325 Beech Mountain Parkway, Beech Mountain, NC. The Beech Mountain Biking Club maintains over 30 miles of mountain biking trails on the high slopes of Beech Mountain—many (or most) on a busted subdivision abandoned since the 1970s. These trails offer a wide range of technical challenges and mountain scenery. The Beech Mountain Chamber (see *Guidance*) offers a good brochure with very clear and detailed maps.

FISHING Whitetop Laurel Fly Shop (366-246-3475), 210 S. Jefferson Ave., West Jefferson, NC. This full-service fly-fishing shop at the center of West Jefferson offers guided trips throughout the New River region.

GOLF **Village of Sugar Mountain Golf Course** (828-898-6464), Sugar Mountain Dr., Banner Elk, NC. Open Apr.–Oct. This 18-hole course, designed in 1974 by Duane Francis and Arnold Palmer, sits just beneath the ski slope at Sugar Mountain. $22.

Willow Creek Public Golf Course (828-963-6865; www.willowvalley-resort .com), Bairds Creek Rd., NC 105, Boone, NC. Open May–Oct. Part of a resort development, this nine-hole course west of Boone off NC 105 features country scenery and well-kept fairways. $14.

Boone Golf Club (828-264-8760), 433 Fairway Dr., Boone, NC. Open Apr.– Oct. This 18-hole course, situated just south of Boone on US 321, was designed in 1959 by Ellis Maples. $43 weekdays, $48 weekends.

Hawksnest Golf Resort (828-963-6565), 2058 Skyland Dr., Seven Devils, NC. Open Apr.–Oct. A 4,200-foot-high, 18-hole course boasting stunning scenery and lots of dramatic elevation change. $35 weekdays, $39 weekends.

Jefferson Landing on the New River (336-982-7767), Hwy. 16/88, Jefferson, NC. Open mid-Mar.–mid-Nov. This 18-hole course, built in 1991 on the site of a former dairy farm, offers wide views toward Mount Jefferson, as well as water hazards on 15 holes. $42 weekdays, $62 weekends.

Mountain Aire (336-877-4716; www.mountainaire.com), 1104 Golf Course Rd., West Jefferson, NC. Open mid-Mar.–mid-Dec. This 18-hole course, built in 1950 in the remote mountains near Jefferson, offers first-rate scenery. $32 weekdays, $39 weekends.

ROCK CLIMBING **Footsloggers** (828-262-5111; www.footsloggers.com), 139 S. Depot St., Boone, NC. Tower open spring–fall, noon–5. This downtown Boone outdoors store, in addition to offering a full line of climbing gear and encyclopedic knowledge of local routes, has a 35-foot climbing tower and an enclosed bouldering cave. Tower: $9 plus rentals.

Rock climbing guides. Several of the rafting outfitters also offer guide and/or instruction services for rock climbers. Be sure to check the listings.

SKIING ✺ **Ski Beech** (800-438-2093 or 828-387-2011; www.skibeech.com), 1007 Beech Mountain Parkway, Beech Mountain, NC. 8:30 AM–10 PM. Located downhill behind the village center, Ski Beech stars a group of two-story 1960s Alpine vernacular buildings grouped around an outdoor skating rink, with a snack bar and a number of shops. The main lodge is up a set of outdoor wooden stairs—a rambling, 1960s-style three-story structure with broad and impressive views from many decks and windows. The whole complex is clean and well kept, full of adults and families with children; happy kids cover the bunny slope, giggling and screeching. Its run is 3,600 feet with a drop of 750 feet from a summit of 5,505 feet to a base of 4,700 feet, the highest ski elevations in the Smoky Mountains region (and probably in the East). Day lift tickets $28–45 adults, $21–32 children and seniors.

✺ **Sugar Mountain** (800-784-2768 or 828-898-4521; www.skisugar.com), Banner Elk, NC. The Sugar Mountain ski lodge is easily accessible from NC 184 in Banner Elk, not that far a distance uphill or off the main road. It's a three-story wood building with gray pressboard paneling in an early-1970s style, perhaps a bit down at the heels but very clean. It's busy with adults and families, but handles crowds well. It has the longest run and the farthest drop in the area—1.5 miles and 1,200 feet, from a summit at 5,300 feet to a base at 4,100 feet.

STABLES **Banner Elk Stables** (828-898-5424) offers trail riding along the slopes of Beech Mountain from their stables at the end of Shomaker Rd. in Banner Elk, NC. $15 per hour.

Smith Quarter Horse Farm (828-898-4932). A mile outside Banner Elk, NC, off NC 194, Smith Quarter Horse Farm offers trail rides on the slopes of Beech Mountain.

WHITEWATER SPORTS The Watauga River and the New River—both rising from the town of Boone, NC—offer radically different whitewater opportunities. The **South Fork of the New River** meanders through a cliff-sided gorge, but with so many twists that its 30 miles of travel is lengthened to 90 miles of riverbed of an exceedingly gentle gradient and with hardly any rapids. Indeed, it almost qualifies as stillwater, and most people prefer to travel along it in canoes. It is so stunningly beautiful that it's been declared both a National Wild and Scenic River and a National Heritage River, and at 90 miles it allows some great overnight canoe trips. The **Watauga River** offers shorter and more action-packed runs, with some Class II–III rapids to get your adrenaline running.

✺ **Appalachian Adventures** (336-877-8800; www.appalachianadventures.com), Todd, NC. Located in the 1888 train depot at the historic center of Todd, midway between Boone and Jefferson on NC 194, Appalachian Adventures furnishes tubing, kayaking, and canoeing on the South Fork of the New River, as well as bicycling on the scenic lanes in the area.

✺ **Appalachian Challenge** (888-844-7238 or 828-898-6484; www.appalachian challenge.com), Banner Elk, NC. This guide service offers whitewater rafting on the mild and beautiful Watauga River, and special trips on the technically challenging Wilson Creek. They also offer guide services for rock climbing and cave exploring (the latter in Virginia and Tennessee caves). Watauga River rafting $39 adults, $29 children.

Edge of the World (800-789-3343 or 828-898-9550; www.edgeoworld.com rafting.htm), Banner Elk, NC. Guided raft floats on Class II–III rapids on the Watauga River; the 4-hour trip includes a fried chicken lunch made fresh that morning. They also offer regular daylong rock climbing and rappelling instructional trips. Watauga River rafting $52 adults, $42 children, including lunch. Rock climbing $75 adults.

✺ **Wahoo's Adventures** (800-444-7238 or 828-262-5774; www.wahoos adventures.com), Boone, NC. Wahoo's offers a wide range of rafting experiences throughout the Smokies, with branches in Gatlinburg and Ducktown as well as their GHQ in Boone. In the Boone area, they offer gentle family trips on the New and Watauga Rivers, and fierce rapid-runners on Wilson Creek, Russell Creek, and the Watauga River Gorge.

✐ **Zaloos Canoes** (800-535-4027 or 336-246-3066), 3874 NC 16 S., Jefferson, NC. Located on the South Fork of the New River, at the corner of NC 16 and NC 88 (5 miles east of Jefferson), Zaloos offers tubing and canoe trips (including camping trips) along the New River.

✴ Lodging

HOTELS The Broyhill Inn and Conference Center (800-951-8048 or 828-262-2204; fax 828-262-2946; www.broyhillinn.com), 775 Boden-heimer Dr., Boone, NC 28607. Open all year. The Broyhill is a full-service 83-room inn and conference center on the attractive campus of Appalachian State University. This modern building of rock-clad concrete, with a pitched roof mirroring the surrounding peaks, sits on a parklike hilltop landscaped to appear like a mountaintop meadow. Its charming dining room (see *Dining Out*), with a large wood-burning fireplace, has sweeping mountain views over a small sculpture garden. Common areas, including the spacious lobby, are roomy and comfortable, with plush chairs and sofas, decorated with local art. A recent renovation has turned the formerly Spartan rooms into the comfortable quarters you'd expect from a high-end business hotel. While standard rooms remain smallish, they are furnished with new, elegant furniture, including a king or two double beds, desk, two phones, a computer dataport, and a recliner chair facing the TV. The tariff does not include meals, but this can be changed by adding a set surcharge of $40–50. Winter and spring $90–95 for standard rooms, $130–175 for suites. Summer and fall $135 for standard rooms, $165–220 for suites.

The Mast Farm Inn (888-963-5857 or 828-963-5857; fax 828-963-6404; www.mastfarminn.com), P.O. Box 704, Valle Crucis, NC 28691. This popular and respected small country inn at the heart of Valle Crucis has so many historic buildings that it's listed on the National Register as a Historic District. The 1880s farmhouse holds nine comfortable rooms furnished in country antiques. Adjacent historic log cabins and farm outbuildings, original to the site and as old as 1812, have roomy cottage accommodations furnished with mountain country antiques; one- and two-bedroom floor plans have separate living rooms and wet bars, but no kitchens. The grounds are beautifully landscaped, and the farmhouse's wide wraparound porch is a perfect place to sit and rock. Their restaurant is noted for its organic gourmet regional cuisine. Rooms $125–195, cottages $195–380.

✐ **Archers Mountain Inn** (888-827-6155 or 828-898-9004; www.archersinn.com/index2.htm), 2489 Beech Mountain Parkway, Banner Elk, NC 28604. Halfway up Beech Mountain, this

ENJOYING A CUP OF COFFEE ON THE PORCH OF THE MAST FARM INN.
Jim Hargan

group of 1970s-vintage lodge buildings offers a wide variety of room types (and prices). All rooms are individually decorated with antiques and reproductions, typically in a country or farmhouse style, and all have fireplace and either a deck or a porch. Features available in some rooms include separate sitting area, kitchen, structural cedar beams, whirlpool bath, feather bed, and private mountain-view porch. A full breakfast is included. The lodge's restaurant, the Jackalope View (see *Dining Out*), is first-rate, and has a weekend jazz bar. $70–195.

BED & BREAKFAST INNS Lovill House Inn (800-849-9466 or 828-264-4204; www.lovillhouseinn.com), 404 Old Bristol Rd., Boone, NC 28607. All year. This AAA four-diamond-rated inn retains the look and feel of the mountain countryside while sitting on the edge of downtown Boone. Its 11 acres of property has a perennial flower garden, barn, stream, and waterfall, with woodland views on all sides. The 1875 Victorian farmhouse with wraparound porches and rockers, built by one of Boone's most prominent citizens, has hardwood pine and maple floors, and wormy chestnut moldings and doors. Public areas are elegant and roomy, with lovely period antiques. The six en suite rooms are large, with fireplaces (half wood, half gas) and elegant antiques and reproductions. An outbuilding, once a feed store on the 19th-century farm, has been renovated as a self-catering cottage, carrying the same theme of 19th-century country elegance. A full gourmet breakfast is served in the sunny dining room, and a social hour—by the fire in bad weather, on the porch in good—greets guests in the evening. $125–185.

Window Views B&B (800-963-4484 or 828-963-8081; www.windowviews .com), 204 Stoneleigh Lane, Boone, NC 28607. This two-room private home B&B perches on a high mountainside with stunning panoramas from the decks and full-length windows of the 1992 house. A large common room lets out onto a deck with an unobstructed 180° panorama over Valle Crucis and the valley of the Watauga River. The bright, cozy rooms, decorated with modern furniture and antiques, have similarly wide views through glass French doors that lead to decks. Afternoon cookies are served on the deck, and a full breakfast in the morning. $75–100, including full breakfast.

The Baird House (800-297-1342 or 828-297-4055; www.bairdhouse.com), 1451 Watauga River Rd., Valle Crucis, NC 28679. All year. This 1790 farmhouse sits above the Watauga River in the lovely rural mountain community of Valle Crucis. Its 16 acres includes 500 feet of Watauga River frontage— here a clear, rocky stream alive with fish. Uphill, a barn with a red tile silo sits near a 130-year-old apple tree, loaded with heritage Yellow Transparent apples in early fall. On the hilltop sits the old Baird family cemetery, whose earliest stones mark the graves of the couple who first settled this farm in 1780 and built the large and beautiful house a decade (and five children) later. The house they built— The Baird House—survives in a remarkably pristine condition, a very early example of planked lumber construction (as opposed to log cabins). While the stunning two-story-high porch with its round columns is a bit of dressing up by an early-20th-century judge, the old house's two original cribs and center dogtrot-style hall survive intact—as do the original 18th-century planking on the walls of one of the elegantly furnished common rooms. The guest rooms, ranging in size from normal to large, are elegantly furnished with antiques and reproductions typical of prosperous 19th-century farms. Two rooms are in the main house, while three more rooms (one a kitchenette) occupy a renovated 20th-century outbuilding. $95–145 per night, including a full country breakfast.

Alta Vista (828-963-5247; www .altavistagallery.com), 2839 Broadstone Rd., Valle Crucis, NC 28691. Located upstairs from the Gallery Alta Vista, this comfy B&B has large rooms with country antique furniture, beadboard walls and ceilings—and lots of original art on the walls. In fact, having a fine gallery on site is part of the charm of this 1923 brick bungalow in the center of the settlement. Another part of the charm— the large front porch overlooking the Watauga River and the old general store now occupied by the Mast General Store Annex. An upstairs common sitting room serves as the venue for the full hot breakfast, as well as a great place to sit and read. $100-150, varies by date.

♿ **Azalea Inn** (828-898-8195; www .azalea-inn.com), P.O. Box 1151, Banner Elk, NC 28604. All year. This large 1937 bungalow, rated three diamonds by AAA, sits at the very center of the village of Banner Elk, by a stone WPA school built the same year and still in use. The roomy and cheerful house, furnished with country antiques and quilts, has wormy chestnut trim in the front parlor, while three other common rooms offer

sunny places to relax. Within the main house are two downstairs rooms, plus one upstairs room with a strange and wonderful attic tunnel sitting area. An addition has more rooms, including one with a whirlpool bath and a full-sized private porch. A detached cottage, over a garage, offers a very high level of self-catering. $99 per night and up.

✿ **Banner Elk Inn Bed and Breakfast** (828-898-6223; www.banner elkinn.com), 407 Main St. E. (NC 194W), Banner Elk, NC 28604. All year. Built in 1912 as a country church, this large wood house was moved to Banner Elk from a site farther up the mountain to take advantage of the new automobile road— now the Old Toll Road east of town. Beautifully restored, this pink house with green shutters recalls the elegant, comfortable living of a country lawyer or doctor. A breakfast area is flooded with light from large windows; plush chairs face a fire; stained beadboard covers the walls and ceilings. Two standard rooms are ample sized, while a two-bedroom room suite (never offered as separate rooms) offers comfortable quarters for families or couples traveling together. A honeymoon suite, taking up most of the low-ceilinged attic, offers special privacy (and a whirlpool bath) for those willing to take on the extra-steep and narrow steps. Pets must be arranged in advance. Rooms $95–145, two-bedroom suite $140–180.

The River Farm Inn (336-877-1728; www.riverfarminn.com), 179 River Run Bridge Rd., Box 2, Fleetwood, NC 28626. This renovated 19th-century dairy barn sits on a beautifully landscaped property on the South Fork of the New River, off a lovely country lane in the community of Fleetwood, 17 miles northeast of Boone. The beautifully renovated barn holds two large suites, each elegantly decorated with antiques, and each with a full kitchen. A nearby building holds a third suite, while a modern log cabin is also available. A continental breakfast is included. Suites $175–195, cabin $250.

Buffalo Tavern Bed and Breakfast (877-615-9678 or 336-877-2873; fax 336-877-2874; www.buffalotavern .com), 958 West Buffalo Rd., West Jefferson, NC 28694. Built in the 1870s, this large wooden house in the rural Bluff Mountain area (6 miles west of Jefferson) was a popular 19th-century coaching inn and Prohibition-era tavern. Today it's an elegant three- room B&B surrounded by azaleas, its first- and second-story porches shaded by large old trees. It's decorated in the country Victorian style, and all rooms have down comforters and log fireplaces. A gourmet breakfast is served by candlelight in the dining room. $115–135.

French Knob Inn (336-246-5177; fax 336-246-5087; www.frenchknob inn.com), 133 Ferguson Rd., West Jefferson, NC 28694. This three-room B&B sits in a scenic location amid the low mountains of the New River Valley, 5 miles south of Jefferson on NC 163. A modern farm-style home with dormers, its rooms and common areas are elegantly decorated with Victorian antiques and reproductions. Two of the three rooms are large, with whirlpool tubs. A full breakfast is included. $95–150.

CABIN RENTALS **The Cottages at Glowing Hearth** (828-963-8800), 171 Glowing Hearth Lane, Vilas, NC

28692. All year. Bill and Pam Moffit host five luxurious cottages on 40 acres of mountaintop land. At 3,700 feet above sea level, these mountain-top meadows offer sweeping views north over the scenic coves of Valle Crucis—then cross the ridgeline for more sweeping views south toward Foscoe. Each cabin has a 30-foot covered porch facing the Valle Crucis view, and a picnic area on the ridgeline facing the Foscoe view. The cabins are powder-blue modern structures, reminiscent of farmhouses with picket rails, but with an 18-foot peaked ceiling faced with broad windows over the view. White pine tongue-and-groove paneling covers the ceiling, with 1,500 feet of floor space beneath. The main living area stretches from the huge window to the stone wood-burning fireplace, with plush sofas and chairs. The fully equipped kitchen has a cooking island covered in hand-painted western tiles. The master bedroom, decorated in soft floral prints, centers on a four-poster king bed, with a 100-gallon whirlpool bath in the master bath. This remote Baird Creek site, up winding paved roads, is an easy, scenic 10-minute drive from Valle Crucis to the west and Boone to the east; ask for directions. From $200 per night.

✳ Where to Eat

EATING OUT **Red Onion Café** (828-264-5470), 227 Hardin St., Boone, NC. Weekdays 11–9, weekends 11–10. This casual downtown restaurant reuses a 1960s-era barbeque as an upmarket sandwich-and-pasta café. Well decorated and well kept, quiet and comfortable, the Red Onion is a good break from the ordinary. A tuna salad features grilled and marinated yellowfin tuna on mixed greens with hearts of palms, mushrooms, olives, scallions, and tomatoes; the less extraordinary mayonnaisey tuna salad is available, too. The menu offers a variety of such adventurous fare balanced by familiar favorites within a core of salads, soups, sandwiches, and pasta dishes. Personal-sized pizzas on whole wheat crusts come with a variety of toppings, from traditional and pesto to southwestern and Creole. Desserts are made on the premises. Sandwiches and salads $6.95–7.95; pastas, 10-inch pizzas, and specialties $9.95–15.95.

Our Daily Bread (828-264-0173), 627 West King St., Boone, NC. Mon.–Fri. 8–6, Sat. 9–5; closed Sun. When Sam and Jennifer Parker bought this small downtown storefront café in the center of Boone, they knew what they wanted—fresh produce from local farms, lots of choice, and great food prepared from scratch. Their menu centers on breakfasts, soups, salads, and sandwiches, with everything done up right. Not just a cup of homemade soup—three different homemade soups and two chilies, and cream soup made with whipping cream a house specialty. Not just half a dozen sandwiches—25 different sandwiches, including 12 vegetarian choices, hot dogs, a generous build-your-own, and grilled cheese made with local farm cheese (and under $3). Their carefully decorated interior is bright and welcoming, with plenty of blond hardwood. Prices are low—all part of the small-town main-street atmosphere. "That's why we like it here," says Jennifer. "King Street is like Mayberry; you can't walk two blocks to the bank without seeing someone you know."

Breakfast $1.45–3.95, lunch $2.25–5.50.

✿ **Dan'l Boone Inn** (828-264-8657; www.danlbooneinn.com), 130 Hardin St., Boone, NC. June–Oct., weekdays 11:30 AM–9 PM, weekends 8 AM–9 PM. Nov.–May, weekdays 5–8 PM, weekends 8 AM–8 PM. A popular family eatery since 1959, the Dan'l Boone Inn occupies a large former boardinghouse at the south edge of downtown Boone. Inside, it's plain and straightforward, with several large rooms paneled in tongue-and-groove pine, floors covered with linoleum. Although seating is at individual tables, all food is brought out in bowls family style. Fried chicken, corn, whipped potatoes (with lumps), green beans (soft, with fatback, southern style), country-fried steak and gravy, coleslaw, a superb country ham on biscuit (the only thing *not* all-you-can-eat), plain biscuits (wonderful!), jelly, baked apples, gravy—all brought out in large bowls, until the oversized tables are filled with food. Beverage, soup or salad, and dessert are also included. You take what you want, and if the bowl goes empty they bring you some more. Dinner $12 adults, $0–6 children under 12, depending on age. Breakfast $8 adults, $0–5 children under 12.

The Corner Palate (828-898-8668). Located at the corner of NC 184 and NC 194 (between Sugar Mountain and Beech Mountain). Lunch and dinner; may keep shortened hours in winter. A casual atmosphere and an intelligent, imaginative menu. Like an English pub, it allows you to pick your atmosphere; it combines a lively "village local" in back with a quiet and atmospheric dining room in front. In both areas you'll be treated with the same gourmet approach to all meals, combining fresh local ingredients and a creative interpretation to popular American dishes. Like a good English local, the Corner Palate has quite a list of specials that change daily, with different specials for lunch and dinner. Lunch $5–10, dinner $8–20.

DINING OUT **The Broyhill Inn** (800-951-6048 or 828-262-2204; fax 828-262-2946; www.broyhillinn.com), 775 Bodenheimer Dr., Boone, NC. Open all year. The recently renovated Broyhill Inn, on a hilltop inside Appalachian State University, now sports an elegant dining area off the main lobby. Quiet and pleasant, with simple, attractive decor, it's anchored by a giant hearth with a wood fire at one end and a glass wall at the other, with a view over the inn's sculpture garden and parklike grounds to Howard Knob and the mountains beyond. Breakfasts can be either a buffet or à la carte, while lunches center on an ample buffet, and a Sunday brunch buffet includes an omelet chef. Dinners are the main event, however—elegant entrées served with live piano and a crackling wood fire. Appetizers might include a wild mushroom ragout in puff pastry or sautéed Maryland-style crabcakes. Entrées, served with potato, mixed green salad or freshly made soup, and vegetables, include farm-raised quail stuffed with wild rice; grilled rainbow trout with baby shrimp, leeks, and amaretto butter; and braised veal shank with a white wine tomato demiglaze. If you aren't feeling quite that fancy, simpler (and cheaper) fare includes a half-pound burger, and a black pepper fettuccine. Dinner $10–22; lunch and breakfast also available.

The Jackalope View (888-827-6155 or 828-898-9004; www.archersinn .com/jackalopes/), 2489 Beech Mountain Parkway, Beech Mountain, NC. The first thing you notice at the Jackalope View is—the view. Located halfway up Beech Mountain on NC 184, this casual fine-dining restaurant at Archer's Mountain Inn has glass walls and a deck hanging over a 180° open south-facing panorama toward Sugar Mountain and the Blue Ridge. Everything about the Jackalope, however, impresses. Three wine cellars offer 300 different wines (with a large selection under $25 a bottle), and 28 wines by the glass. The menu presents exotic and original preparations of beef, trout, fresh seafood, and game. A chili is made with venison and black beans, with their own tortilla chips on the side; a risotto includes lump crab, shiitake mushroom, and asparagus. A mountain trout may be crusted with walnuts and almonds, and drizzled with citrus butter; a veal chop may be grilled, stuffed with prosciutto ham and Gorgonzola cheese, and served with a Marsala mushroom sauce. Upstairs is a large and comfortable bar, with even more great views, a wide selection of microbrews, and live jazz on weekends.

✳ Selective Shopping

Boone, NC
Stretching for four long blocks along US 321/421, downtown Boone marks the former location of Daniel Boone's Wilderness Trail. Today it's a classic turn-of-the-20th-century brick-front downtown, lively and active with interesting shops. The main street is a simple two-laner with parallel parking, named King St.; behind it on the

downhill side is alleylike Howard St., where most of the off-street parking is to be found; Appalachian State University starts on the next block down. With a 13,000-student university two blocks downhill, parking is very bad and regulations are aggressively enforced. There's a trick to it, however: Stop by the Chamber of Commerce on the western end of Howard St. and get a permit that lets you park to shop downtown.

Farmers Hardware (828-264-8801), 661 West King St. This is one of those places you brag about finding. After all, at least one hardware shop graces virtually every small-town center in these mountains, and you don't expect the next one to be special. For Farmers Hardware, part of Boone since 1924, expect it; it's special. And not just for its classic main-street storefront, with well-worn hardwood floors, old wood cabinetry, and wide stairs descending downward in the middle of the store. Inside, and to the left, a "housewares department" occupies the former home of the Watauga County Bank, with the sort of kitchenware you normally find only in specialty catalogs, a range of Disney and Coke licensed collectibles, and a section of wild birdhouses and feeders. Inside the old safe (with inspection stickers from 1924 to 1953) are fine decorative items. Then down the stairs, behind the paints section (this is a working hardware store), is another strange and funky selection of pottery and garden decorations.

Row by Row Bookshop (828-265-2154), 641 W. King St. This modest used-book shop, the last in a series of small alternative shops occupying the same downtown Boone storefront, deserves a visit from any book lover.

Its books are well kept and well organized, with a wide range of unusual topics—from a wall full of obscure history titles to a good selection of hardbound mysteries and science fiction. It's a good place to look for firsts, or just for a nice reading copy of that long-out-of-print title.

The Watauga County Farmer's Market. Sat. morning, May–Oct. Held at the Horn In The West for more than 25 years, the farmer's market features fresh, locally grown produce and local crafts. Go there for organically grown produce, fresh herbs, fruits, flowers, honey, eggs, preserves, fresh-baked goods, bedding plants, and farm crafts. You can talk with the actual growers, buy some baked goodies, and have a picnic at the adjacent Horn In The West picnic area.

Valle Crucis, NC

Gallery Alta Vista (828-963-5247; www.altavistagallery.com), 2839 Broadstone Rd. This lovely gallery occupies the parlors and dining room of a large 1923 farmhouse. It features a large selection of realistic and impressionistic watercolors and oils, mainly by local and regional artists, but also by artists from around the nation and the world. It's a good place to browse for fine art original paintings of mountain scenics—the technical quality and originality are consistently high.

West Jefferson, NC

De Pree Studio and Gallery (877-639-5808 or 336-246-7399; www .depreestudio.com), 109 N. Jefferson Ave. Weekdays 9–5, Sat. 9–4. This large and beautiful gallery occupies a 1930s brick storefront at the center of the small rural town of West Jefferson. Its roomy display areas highlight the paintings of co-owner Lenore De Pree, brilliantly colored scenes of Blue Ridge life and landscapes, stylistically influenced by medieval Persian art. The gallery also features large and small wood sculptures by local artist Tom Sternal, and handwoven Persian rugs.

Ashe County Cheese Company (336-246-2501), 106 E. Main St. The mountain region's only cheese manufacturer has been in business in West Jefferson since 1930. They offer factory tours, fresh cheese for sale, and a gift shop.

✳ Special Events

SUMMER **Lees-McRae Summer Theater** (828-898-8721; www.lmc .edu/jspeer/summer.html), Lees-McRae College, Banner Elk, NC. June–Aug. Lees-McRae College, a small liberal arts college, sponsors this summer theater festival. They typically perform three musicals, each for a 5-day run toward the end of a month. $18 adults, $10 children.

An Appalachian Summer Festival (800-841-2787 or 828-262-4046). July. Affiliated with Appalachian State University at Boone, NC, the Appalachian Summer Festival fills the July calendar with music, dance, and the visual arts. Music is the main focus, with classical symphonic performances, pop orchestras, jazz, and mountain music, with a mix of regional and national performers. Modern dance and serious theater stud the program, along with lecture series, workshops, and visual arts displays. The festival ends with an outdoor fireworks concert featuring a major headliner.

Doc Watson Music Fest. Third Sat. in July, proclaimed "Doc Watson Day" by the North Carolina legislature.

This annual celebration of Doc Watson is held on the lawn of the old Cove Creek High School, not too far from Doc Watson's home, as a fundraiser to establish the Doc and Marie Watson Museum inside the old school. The 2-day event features music by Doc Watson and his friends—about 20 bluegrass and mountain bands in all. Craft vendors are present (with the emphasis on music), and food is available.

Firefly Festival. First Sat. in Aug. Held at the Hickory Ridge Homestead, Boone's annual Firefly Festival includes storytellers, musicians, mountain crafters, and folk artists, with guides dressed as 18th-century pioneers to help things along. It's an afternoon event, sandwiched between the morning farmer's market and the evening performance of Horn In The West, both on this site, as a fundraiser for this outdoor museum of 18th-century life.

Barbershop Bonanza. Mid-Aug. This annual Boone, NC, event features a day of barbershop quartet competitions, followed by an evening performance by the winners.

AUTUMN **Cove Creek Farm Heritage Days**. Historic Cove Creek High School, Sugar Grove, NC. Mid-Sep. weekend. This annual event celebrates the rich agricultural heritage of the coves and mountains northwest of Boone, known locally as Cove Creek Community. Sponsored by Cove Creek Preservation and Development, a nonprofit organized by residents in 1996 to save the old stone high school, this fund-raiser on the high school lawn is patterned after the local agricultural fairs of 100 years ago. It has mountain music and clogging (under a tent with plenty of seating), all sorts of farm exhibits, farm craft demonstrations, old-time games and activities, a petting zoo, local crafts, and canning judging. The day after the fair, local farms open their doors to strangers for afternoon farm tours; participants get a map and plan their own route, dropping by the farms that interest them.

Old Boone Streetfest (828-262-4532). Last weekend in Sep. This street fair celebrates downtown Boone, NC. It features free concerts on the Jones House lawn and near the Turchin Center, and craft vendors and food on downtown's back street, Howard St.

Banner Elk Woolly Worm Festival. Third weekend in Oct. Held in Banner Elk, NC, for the last quarter century, this celebration of the furry caterpillar draws more than 15,000 people every year. Although there are

vendors and food, interest centers on the worm races—50 heats of the worms racing up strings, bringing cash prizes to their owners. When a champion is finally declared, the festival's official forecaster uses its stripes to predict the coming winter weather. It's a fund-raiser for local schools, held on the elementary school grounds at the center of the village.

WINTER Cut and Choose Christmas Tree Celebration (828-264-3061). Mid-Nov.–mid-Dec. Each Christmas season, 16 or so Watauga County Christmas tree growers organize an old-fashioned family Christmas-tree-cutting celebration, holding a special welcome for families coming from the warm flatlands to choose a tree and maybe see some pre-Christmas snow. A brochure describes each farm in detail, telling how to get to it and how you will be welcomed.

BEHIND THE BLUE RIDGE: SPRUCE PINE & BURNSVILLE

The Toe and the Cane Rivers drain some of the East's tallest mountains. The Black Mountains, with 10 peaks above 6,000 feet, sit on the south edge of the Toe–Cane drainage.

The Highlands of Roan, with three peaks above 6,000 feet, loom over the north edge of the drainage, with miles of mountaintop meadows and hundreds of acres of natural rhododendron gardens. Between these two great ranges is a broken land of 4,000-foot peaks and 2,000-foot valleys, an area little visited by tourists. On the west, the Cane River and its tributaries drain rich, narrow valleys with bottomland farms beneath tall peaks; here the lovely little county seat of Burnsville gathers around an old town square still dominated by its 172-year-old inn. Farther east, the South Toe River drains northward off the forested slopes of Mount Mitchell, the tallest peak in the East, and enters a difficult and broken country linked to the notorious lives of Frankie and Charlie Silver. Still farther east, the North Toe River drains a rough and forested land, dominated by feldspar, rock, and gravel mining, centering on the terraced town of Spruce Pine. Here the famous Clinchfield Railroad cuts through the mountains by following the North Toe River as it merges with the South Toe and Cane to become the roaring Nolichucky River, powerful enough to carve a deep gorge through the mountains and out into the plains of Tennessee.

GUIDANCE **Yancey County Chamber of Commerce** (800-948-1632 or 828-682-7413; fax 828-682-6599; www.yanceychamber.com), 106 W. Main St., Burnsville, NC 28714. The Yancey Chamber of Commerce runs an attractive visitors center in a restored early gas station on the western edge of downtown Burnsville.

Mitchell County Chamber of Commerce (800-227-3912 or 828-765-9483; fax 828-765-0202; www.mitchell-county.com/north-carolina), 79 Parkway Rd., Spruce Pine, NC 28777. The Mitchell County Chamber of Commerce, covering the Spruce Pine and Bakersville areas, maintains an information desk for visitors just off the Blue Ridge Parkway in the Museum of North Carolina Minerals (see "Blowing Rock & Grandfather Mountain").

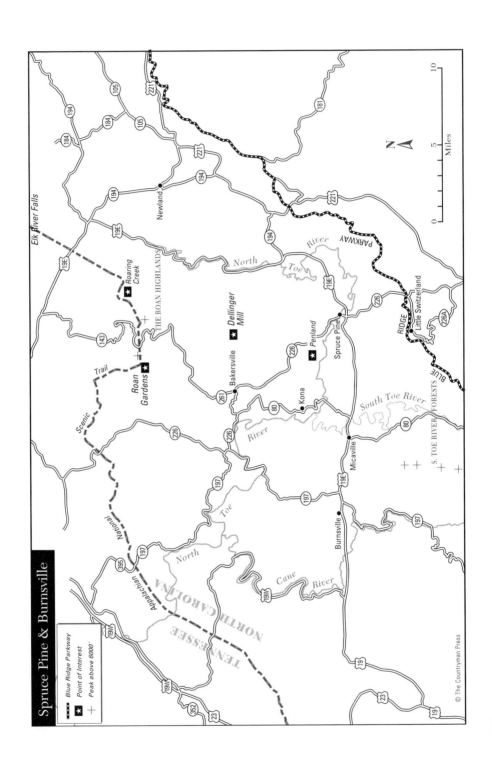

Spruce Pine & Burnsville

Legend:
- ▓▓▓ Blue Ridge Parkway
- ★ Point of Interest
- + Peak above 6000'

Elk River Falls

Roaring Creek ★

THE ROAN HIGHLANDS

Roan Gardens ★

Scenic Trail

Appalachian

National

Newland

North River Toe

Dellinger Mill ★

Bakersville

Penland ★

Spruce Pine

Kona

Micaville

Burnsville

South Toe River

S. TOE RIVER FORESTS

BLUE RIDGE PARKWAY

Little Switzerland

TENNESSEE
NORTH CAROLINA

Cane River

North Toe River

N

0   5   10
Miles

© The Countryman Press

Toecane Ranger District, Pisgah National Forest (828-682-6146), P.O. Box 128, Burnsville, NC 28714. This small ranger station, the administrative headquarters for the Pisgah National Forest in the Toe and Cane River Valleys, maintains an information desk and welcomes travelers with questions. You'll find it in Burnsville, on the US 19E Bypass.

GETTING THERE *By car*: The Toe and Cane River Valleys are linked by **US 19**, marked as US 19E over much of this segment. It runs from Mars Hill, NC, north of Asheville, through Burnsville, Micaville, and Spruce Pine, NC, then into Tennessee near Elizabethton.

By air: **Asheville Regional Airport** (828-684-2226; fax 828-684-3404), 708 Airport Rd., Fletcher, NC. Located 15 miles south of downtown Asheville off I-26, Exit 9 (NC 280). This lovely little airport is virtually unchanged since the 1950s—a low, rambling, white concrete structure with orange stripes, its boarding gates rambling outward from a central lobby. Despite its old-fashioned appearance, it has daily service from Atlanta, Cincinnati, Pittsburgh, Raleigh, and Charlotte, with 20 to 25 flights daily. Several car rental agencies are located within or near the airport.

Tri-Cities Airport (423-325-6000; fax 423-325-6060; www.triflight.com), 2525 Hwy. 75, Blountville, TN 37617. The Tri-Cities are Johnson City, Kingsport, and Bristol. Tri-Cities Airport is located in Tennessee's Great Valley in the middle of the triangle formed by the three cities, off I-81's Exit 63. Tri-Cities has four commuter airlines furnishing nonstops to six different hubs, so it's not uncommon to find good and/or cheap connections to it.

By bus or train: The Clinchfield Railroad eliminated passenger service on what had been one of the most scenic rides in the East over half a century ago. Bus service is long gone as well. You will need a private car to see this region.

MEDICAL EMERGENCIES **Spruce Pine Hospital** (828-765-4201), 125 Hospital Dr., Spruce Pine, NC. This small regional hospital furnishes the only 24/7 emergency room service in the region. You'll find it off US 19E on the south edge of Spruce Pine.

✳ Wandering Around

EXPLORING BY CAR **NC 80**. *Leg 1:* From the NC 80 exit from the Blue Ridge Parkway, take NC 80 north 28.3 miles to its end at Loafers Glory, NC. Sections are very twisty and narrow. *Leg 2:* Turn right onto NC 226; go 2.6 miles east to Bakersville, NC, then turn left onto NC 261; go 12.8 miles to the top of Roan Mountain at Carvers Gap, at the Tennessee state line. Easy. The total drive is 43.6 miles.

THE CLINCHFIELD RAILROAD RUNS THROUGH NOLICHUCKY GORGE.

Jim Hargan

LOOKING TOWARD THE BLACK
MOUNTAINS PAST A ROW OF
RURAL MAILBOXES.

Jim Hargan

From the parkway, NC 80 quickly drops into the lovely South Toe River Valley, with fine views over the river to **Mount Mitchell**, the highest peak in the East (see Mount Mitchell State Park in "Asheville & the Blue Ridge Parkway"). From here the highway descends through the scattered rural community of **Celo**, NC, noted for its fine craft community, reaching the old railroad siding town of **Micaville**, NC, in 14 miles. After that, NC 80 becomes a narrow country lane of astonishing twistiness, coiling past cemeteries and churches, through forests, and into fields with wide mountainy views. A new bridge crosses high above the **South Toe River**, with views of the historic **Clinchfield Railroad** running through its gorge. Just beyond, country lanes lead 5 miles to the famous **Penland School of Crafts**. (Side trip: Go right on Snow Hill Rd., SSR 1170, for 2.4 miles to a right on Conley Ridge Rd., SSR 1164; the campus is 2 miles farther.) Then NC 80 reaches the attractive village of **Kona**, NC, with excellent views, a neat artist's gallery, and a **museum to Frankie and Charlie Silver** in an old church.

Seven twisty, view-studded miles later, NC 80 ends at the settlement of **Loafers Glory**, named for the gang of old-timers who once gathered in front of its (now defunct) general store. The charming, down-at-the-heels county seat of **Bakersville**, is just beyond; **Dellinger Mill**, a 1901 overshot waterwheel still in operation, is 4 miles west. North of Bakersville, the route sweeps through lovely rural valleys, then climbs up to the mile-high **Carvers Gap** deep in the **Roan Highlands**. At the top, wide mountaintop meadows sweep uphill to the right, with incredible panoramic views. To the left, a paved side road leads to **Roan Mountain Gardens**, a 600-acre natural rhododendron garden with wide views from two 6,000-foot peaks. Crossing into Tennessee, the highway becomes TN 143, a ledge carved into the clifflike side of **Roan Mountain**, descending steeply with incredible views.

NC 197. Pick up NC 197 north of Asheville, NC, at Barnardsville, NC, and follow it 52 miles to its end at Indian Grave Gap, at the Tennessee state line. Very twisty, and part gravel.

Like nearby NC 80, NC 197 is remarkably primitive for a road marked as a major highway. In fact, a section of it is gravel—one of the few dirt-surfaced state highways left anywhere in the South. It gives the drive a certain charm. From **Barnardsville** the highway is straight and easy at first, but quickly becomes a switchbacked gravel track as it climbs 2,000 feet up to **Cane River Gap**, then descends more switchbacks with views toward the **Black Mountains**. NC 197 finally regains its paved surface and crosses the **Cane River** (already quite large), then hugs the river for 11 miles, with many lovely views. The road enters the outskirts of **Burnsville**, NC (whose town square is worth visiting), then passes a small textile mill (they make sailcloth) as it climbs **Green Mountain**, giving good views both north and south.

Past Burnsville, the highway continues through attractive rural countryside for half a dozen miles, then reaches the wide and beautiful **Toe River**; at this point NC 197 turns right to follow the Toe upstream for 4 miles, with unobstructed views over the river. After crossing the river, it reaches the community of **Red Hill**, NC (whose general store makes good sandwiches), then turns back on itself to twist and turn 6 miles in the opposite direction, through some very remote, rugged, and beautiful farmland. It finally regains the **Toe River** at **Relief**, NC, a point 5 miles downstream from its first Toe intersection, after 10 miles of driving. NC 197 follows the Toe for another mile or so downstream, then turns sharply right to once again twist into the mountains. Actually, it's cutting across a large horseshoe bend in the river, and will regain it (now merged with the Cane and dubbed the **Nolichucky**) at **Poplar**, NC, where the Forest Service maintains a kayak launch site at the start of the Nolichucky Gorge. From Poplar, the highway swerves and switchbacks uphill to cross the **Unaka Mountains** into Tennessee, at 3,370-foot **Indian Grave Gap**. **Erwin**, TN, is 7 miles ahead on TN 395.

EXPLORING ON FOOT **The Roan Highlands on the Appalachian Trail**. Starting at **Carvers Gap** on NC 216, this walk goes eastward through the wide meadows of the Roan Highlands to the northernmost 6,000-foot summit in the South, **Grassy Ridge Bald**. This undulating trail is a 5-mile round trip, with 1,000 feet of climbing (a third of it on the way back). Park in the Forest Service picnic area on the left side of the road, and take the Appalachian Trail (AT) across the road, through a split-rail fence, and into the mountaintop meadows. Both the views and the wind will increase steadily as you climb 300 feet up **Round Bald**, reaching the first of several 360° views from its summit in just under half a mile.

The trail continues down to a small gap, then uphill to **Jane Bald** (1.1 miles), staying in grassy meadows with wildflowers and wide views the entire way. After a shallow gap, the trail starts on a long climb (600 feet in three-quarters of a mile) up Grassy Ridge Bald; when the AT slabs off the ridge crest to the left, continue on the side trail along the ridge. After passing through thick rhododendrons, the trail tops out on the 6,200-foot summit, with a full-circle view from the top of the world. Return the way you came.

The Overmountain Victory Trail. In the colonial era, a footpath known as Brights Trace crossed the Roan Highlands through its center at Yellow Gap, following flood-prone Roaring Creek on the eastern side. In September 1780 the frontier militia crossed the mountains on Brights Trace and united with Piedmont militias in an attack on British forces at Kings Mountain, SC—one of the most important American victories in the Revolution. The surviving segment of Brights Trace in the Roan Highlands is commemorated as the Overmountain Victory National Historic Trail.

LOOKING TOWARD MOUNT MITCHELL FROM THE SUMMIT OF ROAN MOUNTAIN.

THE ROAN HIGHLANDS

The 15,000 protected acres of the Highlands of Roan contain the largest con-centration of grassy mountaintop balds in the East, 600 acres of natural rhodo-dendron gardens, large tracts of Canadian-style spruce–fir forests, and more rare species than the Great Smoky Mountains National Park. John Fraser dis-covered the Catawba rhododendron here in 1787, and great early scientists such as Asa Gray and Elisha Mitchell studied its unique environments. Gray called it "without doubt the most beautiful mountain east of the Rockies, while Mitchell wrote, "It is the most beautiful of all the high mountains."

The Roan Highlands consist of a single wall of remote, high mountains along the NC–TN state line, stretching from **Hughes Gap** (SSR 1330, Buladean Rd.) eastward to the deep gap that carries US 19E. Most of it is within the Pisgah National Forest, with significant tracts protected by the Southern

The trail begins at the end of Roaring Creek Rd. (SSR 1132), a left turn off US 19E, 14 miles eastward from Spruce Pine; there's an OVERMOUNTAIN VICTORY plaque at the proper intersection. The trailhead is at the end of the road in 4.6 miles, the last part of which is a steep gravel road. A turnaround area here offers wide views over the head of Roaring Creek Valley. Now part of the Pisgah National Forest, this area was a private farm until the mid-1990s. It's still cov-ered in meadows, with an apple orchard just below and a bright red barn sur-rounded by wide fields on the mountaintop opposite. The formal trail follows the

Appalachians Highlands Conservancy, The Nature Conservancy, and the State of Tennessee. Made up of hard old rocks more characteristic of the Blue Ridge than the Smokies, the crest of the Roan Highlands stays above 4,000 feet for nearly its entire length, with 5 miles of it more than a mile high. Its three peaks that top 6,000 feet are the last in the Appalachian Mountains until Mount Washington in New Hampshire, 800 miles to the north.

Despite heavy exploitation between 1890 and 1940, the Roan Highlands look much the same today as they did 170 years ago. In 1836 Mitchell wrote, "The top of the Roan may be described as a vast meadow without a tree to obstruct this prospect, where a person may gallop his horse for a mile or two with Carolina at his feet on one side and Tennessee on the other, and a green ocean of mountains rising in tremendous billows immediately around him." Gray rocky crags stick out of the knee-high grasses; wildflowers form carpets whipped by winds that average 25 mph. Most astonishing are the panoramas, frequently extending in a complete circle around the viewer, continuing unbroken for mile after mile. Even the bureaucracy of the U.S. Department of Agriculture is impressed, writing in a 1974 planning document, "There is no other area that offers such extensive panoramic views of the high country of the Southern Appalachians. Unique is not, in this sense, misleading."

The Roan Highlands are bordered by two roads (Buladean Rd. on the west and US 19E on the east), and crossed by one other—NC 216/TN 143, making the climb at mile-high **Carvers Gap**. Carvers Gap is the Roan's main access point for recreationalists, with a side road leading west to **Roan Gardens** and the **Appalachian Trail** leading east through miles of open meadows. The crest of the Roan is followed closely by the Appalachian Trail for its entire length, a very difficult through-walk that traverses 2,000-foot climbs up over steep and rocky paths. Side trails tend to be even worse, and the rugged slopes are seldom visited. One notable exception to this is the head of **Roaring Creek Valley**, extremely scenic and easily reached, the location of a colonial-era trace that the Overmountain militia followed on their secret march to attack the British at Kings Mountain.

gated Forest Service road gently uphill through forests. A much more interesting alternative is to take the informal trail downhill into the fields, then follow it up through wildflower meadows and apple orchards to the barn. Now an Appalachian Trail (AT) shelter, the barn gives a panoramic view over Roaring Creek Valley and toward the Blue Ridge beyond. To continue, take the blue-blazed trail east, recovering the Overmountain Trail in couple hundred yards. The path continues uphill through open woods to **Yellow Mountain Gap** on the crest of the Roan. Here you will intersect with the AT, in the broad ridgetop meadows so characteristic of the Roan Highlands. Head east along the AT, going steeply uphill through wide open meadows, to reach the peak of **Little Hump Mountain**, with panoramas in all directions. Return the way you came. If you go all the way to Little Hump Mountain's main summit, you will walk 5 miles round trip with a 1,200-foot climb.

✳ Villages

Burnsville, NC. This beautiful little village centers on its classic town square, a large, well-kept strolling space with lawns, trees, and flowers surrounding its statue of an early-19th-century sea captain (Otway Burns, the town's namesake). Grouped around the square are the county courthouse, city hall, public library, and the town's 172-year-old coaching inn, the **Nu Wray Inn**. There are also several nice restaurants, gift shops, and craft galleries. Parking is free, with overflow parking two blocks west of the square.

Micaville, NC. This tiny town sits along the South Toe River bypassed by US 19E, halfway between Burnsville and Spruce Pine. It was for many years an important siding on the Yancey Railroad, a spur from the Clinchfield, and it is from those early years that much of Micaville's small center dates. During the 1970s the Yancey Railroad was abandoned so quickly that the tracks were left behind with a pony engine still sitting on them (and there to this day). The old **Micaville General Store**, attractively restored, is now a combination real estate office and craft cooperative, while the **Micaville Grille** across the street is popular with locals.

Spruce Pine, NC. This railroad town along the North Toe River has long been supported by mineral mining, particularly feldspar. The mining continues today, with a large strip mine scarring the mountainside immediately above downtown, and another strip mine greeting tourists who approach the town from the west on US 19E. Modern Spruce Pine, still dominated by mining, is struggling to create an interesting and vibrant downtown—with some success. Downtown Spruce Pine consists of two long blocks paralleling the riverside depot (still active with freight trains), with a lower level facing the depot and an upper level one story above that. There are a number of interesting shops on both levels, and plenty of free parking by the depot.

Bakersville, NC. The seat of Mitchell County, Bakersville is a tiny town with a scant one-block downtown next to its old courthouse. Located on NC 216, 10 miles north of its much larger sibling Spruce Pine, Bakersville is best known for the large number of fine-craft artists who live in the surrounding valleys.

✳ Wild Places

THE GREAT FORESTS **South Toe River forests**. South of Burnsville and Micaville, NC, looms the tallest summit in the East, **Mount Mitchell**, one of the ten 6,000-foot peaks in the **Black Mountains**. The eastern base of the Blacks, rising out of the South Toe River, is almost entirely owned by the Pisgah National Forest. The Blacks typically rise 3,000 feet above the Toe River in a linear distance of 3 miles, creating an unbroken barrier 7 miles long. This great steep slope is banded with forests, each band appropriate for the climate induced by its elevation and topography—the bands occasionally broken by great rockslides at the steepest slopes. While much of the area was logged, the very steepness spared large tracts along these slopes, and some trails climb through old-growth forests. Five paths make the 3,000-foot climb up the face of the Blacks, all of them scenic, and all of them difficult all-day slogs. The whole wall of the Blacks can be admired from the South Toe River at **Carolina Hemlocks Recreation Area**, a great swimming hole.

The Nolichucky Gorge. At the end of their long run, the Toe and the Cane Rivers merge to become the Nolichucky River, large enough to carve a gorge straight through the high Unaka Mountains. The Pisgah National Forest owns nearly all of the land on both sides of the gorge, as well as the gorge itself. No roads or paths penetrate the bottom of the gorge—just the **Clinchfield Railroad** hugging tight to the riverbank, still under very heavy use as a through goods line (and ludicrously dangerous for walking). A small village, known as **Lost Cove**, thrived for many years at the bottom of the gorge with no automobile access of any sort—until the railroad ceased passenger service, and its inhabitants had to walk in and out. The upper edge of the gorge can be reached on foot for stunning clifftop views, though not without difficulty; the easiest route is a Forest Service logging road that runs west from NC 197 at the state line (see NC 197 under *Exploring by Car*), dropping 1,000 feet in 6 miles.

Yet more remarkable views can be found from the easily accessible top of **Flattop Mountain**, a large Pisgah National Forest tract on the west side of the gorge. Here a good gravel road leads to an old farm site near the top of the mountain. The shortest of climbs uphill leads to broad meadows (maintained by the Forest Service for wildlife), stretching for a mile along the rolling top of this tablelike mountain. Explore around—it will take a while to find all the vistas from all the fields. Views include panoramas west over the Nolichucky Gorge to the Highlands of Roan, then east toward the Bald Mountains. The marked footpath leads downhill to the remains of Lost Cove village—a very difficult walk by all reputes. The access road to Flattop Mountain, Howell Branch Rd. (SSR 1415),

THE END OF A GRAVEL ROAD ON THE NOLICHUCKY RIVER.

Jim Hargan

starts 5.3 miles along US 19W on the North Carolina side of the state line; when you pass through a gate after 1.2 miles, you'll be on the gravel FS 278 for 3 more miles to its end at a closed gate. This is the old farmstead; the path is uphill to your right.

RECREATION AREAS Carolina Hemlocks Recreation Area. Apr.–Nov. This picnic and camping area on NC 80 is maintained by the Pisgah National Forest adjacent to its large South Toe River holdings. Its main attraction is a long and lovely stretch of the South Toe River, with wonderful views toward Mount Mitchell (the tallest peak in the East), and several good swimming holes. There's also a riverside path and a nature trail. $3 per car.

Elk River Falls Recreation Area. Open all year. Located off US 19E near the Tennessee border, this lovely little recreation area offers several picnic tables, a long stretch of the Elk River with grassy banks for fishing—and a large waterfall, where this wide and powerful river pours over a 50-foot rock ledge. A short path clambers down to the base of the falls, and a long rocky spur leads out to a fine view. Free.

PICNIC AREAS Ray-Cort Recreation Park, Burnsville, NC. This county park centers on a handsome small mountain stream flowing gently through a tree-shaded draw, with picnic tables scattered along its length. It has a fine large playground, as well as volleyball and basketball courts. Picnic tables are under the trees surrounded by closely cropped grass, or under shelters (including one made of stone and logs, with a shake roof). To find it, take the side street north from the town square about five blocks.

Riverside Park, Spruce Pine, NC. Located across the North Toe River from downtown Spruce Pine, and linked to it by a 410-foot footbridge, Riverside Park offers a shelter and a row of shaded picnic shelters, as well as a paved walking/jogging loop that runs by the river.

✳ To See

HISTORIC SITES Kona, NC (Frankie and Charlie Silver) (www.frankiesilver.com). Kona resident Frankie Silver (Mrs. Francis Stewart Silver) may not have been the first woman hanged in North Carolina, but she was certainly the most notorious. Three days before Christmas 1832, in her Kona log cabin and with her infant daughter looking on, the petite 18-year-old chopped her husband, Charlie, into pieces and burned him in the fireplace. The mountain folk song "Ballad of Frankie Silver" (not to be confused with the Delta blues song "Frankie and Johnny") attributed the murder to jealousy—but the real motive was Charlie's brutal abuse of his wife. Best-selling author Sharyn McCrumb, whose grandparents lived nearby, has written a fine (and very insightful) novel on the subject, *The Ballad of Frankie Silver*.

Modern-day Kona is a lovely little mountain settlement straddling scenic NC 80, 6 miles north of US 19E. Kona occupies a set of meadowy hilltops that drop from the old Baptist church, past the new Baptist church, then straight down to the gorge of the Toe River and the Clinchfield Railroad below. The old Baptist

Jim Hargan

MUSEUM DIRECTOR JIM PRIES-
MEYER IN HISTORIC GARB AT
THE MCELROY HOUSE.

church sits by NC 80 surrounded by the **Silver Cemetery**. The Silver family gives pride of place to their common ancestor, Revolutionary War veteran George Silver, who was rewarded the surrounding square mile of land for his service in the Patriot army. Most tourists, however, are interested in his grandson Charlie's graves—three of them, as they kept finding bits of Charlie hidden in the snow. (After Frankie was hung, she was buried behind a tavern near Morganton, now on private land.) The Silver Cemetery is extremely well kept, with banks covered in wildflowers and broad views westward from its grassy top. The old wooden church serves as a museum for the Silver clan, with many interesting exhibits on the notorious murder. The original Silver homestead, built by George in 1806, still stands in the village, on private lands. South of the cemetery is the colorful **Mountain Hill Country Gallery**, the working studio of painters Pat and Dan Dowd.

By the way, that infant daughter survived, was raised by Frankie's mother, and prospered as much as anyone could in the mountains after the Civil War; she has left more than 100 known descendants.

The McElroy House (828-682-3671), Burnsville, NC. Located two blocks off Burnsville's town square above the Yancey County visitors center, this large 1840s-era farmhouse is home to the **Rush Wray Museum of Yancey County History**. It's now a simple and attractive home, but in the antebellum era it was the fanciest mansion in this poor, remote corner of the world. During the Civil War it served as the headquarters for the Home Guard, the state forces charged with securing the (largely Unionist) mountain coves and hollows for the Confederacy. Today its kitchen and living area have been restored to exhibit early mountain farm life, while other exhibits are being prepared on Cane River archaeological sites, the Civil War in the Toe and Cane Valleys, and the history and people of the McElroy House. Traditional food and craft demonstrations are offered through summer and fall; call for details.

Dellinger Mill (828-688-1009), Bakersville, NC. Four miles east of Bakersville on Cane Creek Rd. (SSR 1211). June–Sep., every third Sat. 10–5; Oct.–Nov., Mon.–Sat. This operating overshot water mill has been grinding corn for the Bakersville area since 1867. Still owned by its original family, the current National Register structure was built of chestnut in 1901, when the original mill was washed out in a flood. All but the flume and milldam are original to the 1901 structure, including the giant metal overshot wheel and the huge granite millstones. This is a working mill, producing stone-ground corn throughout the corn harvest season.

CULTURAL SITES **Penland School of Crafts** (828-765-2359; fax 828-765-7389; www.penland.org), 816 Penland School Rd., Penland, NC. Gallery and visitors center, Tue.–Sat. 10–noon and 1–5 PM, Sun. noon–5; closed Mon. Campus tours Tue. and Thu. by appointment. One of the most distinguished craft schools in America, Penland was founded as a weavers' cooperative in 1923, by local schoolteacher Lucy Morgan. Miss Morgan brought in instructors to improve the weavers' skills—and was surprised by the outpouring of interest in professional-level craft instruction. In 1929 she formally opened the Penland School to offer regular schedules of instruction. Over the years nine other craft areas have been added: books and paper, clay, drawing, glass, iron, metals, photography, print-making, and wood.

Then as now, Penland is a serious school for craft professionals and dedicated amateurs. Completely residential, its classes, studios, and student buildings wander over a pastoral 400-acre campus 5 miles northwest of Spruce Pine, NC. Straddling both sides of a twisting country lane, the campus has an informal, slightly shabby look, with buildings of every conceivable 20th-century style. Intense summer programs are 1–2 weeks in length, while autumn and spring see 8-week in-depth sessions in selected subjects. An old school houses the gallery and visitors center, with excellent rotating displays of affiliated artists.

GARDENS AND PARKS ❀ ♿ **Roan Mountain Gardens**. Closed in winter. Six hundred acres of natural rhododendron gardens cover two 6,000-foot peaks deep within the Pisgah National Forest. Just off NC 216 on the state line (see *Exploring by Car*), Roan Mountain Gardens offers a mile of high ridgetop meadows and rhododendron balds, with stunning views. Managed as a park by the Forest Service (which levies an admissions charge), this site has three major activity areas. First after the entrance station is a ridgetop parking lot with picnic tables; a trail leads right over meadows to the site of a long-gone 1880s hotel, and left uphill to more meadow views. It is here that the **Appalachian Trail** climbs up to its last two southern peaks above 6,000 feet— **Roan High Knob** (6,285 feet, 18th highest in the East), a short hill walk to the east, and **Grassy Ridge Bald** (6,180 feet, 27th highest), a handful of miles farther on. Half a mile up the road, a small information booth, toilets, and picnic area on the left mark

GLASS AND CERAMICS AT THE PENLAND GALLERY, PENLAND SCHOOL OF CRAFTS.
Jim Hargan

the center of the gardens. Here a disabled-accessible trail loops a third of a mile through spectacular rhododendrons (blooming mid- to late June), with a platform giving wide views across the Toe River Valley to the Black Mountains. Continuing to the end of the road and the park's third and final picnic area, an easy walking path leads 1.2 miles round trip to **Roan High Bluff**, at 6,367 feet the 12th highest summit in the East. Here a platform overlook built over rocky crags gives a clifftop view over the broken mountains of the Toe Valley. $3 per car.

✳ To Do

FISHING **Main Street Outpost** (828-682-1206; fax 828-682-9813), 392 West Main St., Burnsville, NC. Located just off the town square in downtown Burnsville, this attractive outdoors shop offers fly-fishing guide service as well as guided hiking trips and shuttle service.

GOLF **Grassy Creek Golf and Country Club** (828-765-7436), 101 Golf Course Rd., Spruce Pine, NC. Apr.–Oct. This 18-hole course, built in 1957 by Ross Taylor, sits a mile south of Spruce Pine on NC 226, near the Blue Ridge Parkway. You'll find it a hilly course with good views of the surrounding mountains. $34–39.

Mountain Glen Golf Course (828-733-5804), NC 194, Newland, NC. This well-kept 18-hole course, located a few miles north of Newland, offers surprisingly level fairways and water hazards on 16 of its holes. $45.

THE OUTDOOR LIFE **Toe River Lodge** (828-682-9335), Rt. 1, Green Mountain, NC. This 117-acre outfitter caters to those who long for a true outdoor experience. Located on the banks of the Toe River near NC 197, in the remote mountains north of Burnsville, the lodge offers single-day and overnight clinics and guide services in kayaking, fly-fishing, and upland bird hunting. Accommodation is in canvas tents set on wood platforms near a mountain stream, with a pavilion nearby where meals are served. Guests can mix and match the lodge's specialties, with fly-fishing float trips or kayaking instruction on the Class III–IV waters of the Nolichucky Gorge (only 4 miles away). Kayak instruction costs vary. Fishing $175–250 for 1 day, $550 for 2 days with accommodation. Upland bird hunting $200–300.

STABLES **Springmaid Mountain** (828-765-2353), 2171 Henredon Rd., Spruce Pine, NC. These stables offer 1- and 1½-hour trail rides on their own 400-acre property, south of Spruce Pine near Altapass. $12–17.

✳ Lodging

COUNTRY INNS AND HOTELS **The Nu Wray Inn** (800-368-9729 or 828-682-2329; www.nuwrayinn.com), Town Square, P.O. Box 156, Burnsville, NC 28714. Open all year. No one knows exactly how old Burnsville's Nu Wray Inn may be. It appeared in the history books in 1833, when its first innkeeper sold it to Milton Penland. Then, 35 years later, Penland sold it to Garrett Ray, who changed its name to the Ray Hotel.

When Garrett's children inherited it in 1912, they refurbished it and renamed it the Nu Wray Inn. And so it remains today: one of the oldest and most gracious historic hotels in the Smokies.

The Nu Wray Inn occupies a fine old three-story white frame structure, its full-height brick-columned entry porch facing the town square. Behind the inn is a large, well-maintained garden. Inside, its 32 en suite rooms are comfortably furnished with country antiques, with a large guest lounge on each floor. Guests are welcomed with an authentic English tea in the afternoon, and greet the new day with a choice of English, southern, or continental breakfasts. $70–95.

Pinebridge Inn (800-365-5059 or 828-765-5543; www.pinebridge inn.com), 207 Pinebridge Ave., Spruce Pine, NC 28777. This AAA three-diamond-rated hotel occupies a two-story brick high school in a quiet residential neighborhood at the cen-

ter of town. Beautifully landscaped and kept, the 44-room hotel is linked with Spruce Pine's terraced downtown by a lighted 400-foot footbridge across the North Toe River. The hotel's two buildings, separated by a courtyard, are lovely 1920s-vintage school district Gothic, and the rooms retain their high ceilings and large windows. Next door, the former school's former gymnasium, a plain modern structure, houses a recreation center under separate management. Wooded riverside parks, also adjacent to the end, offer walking and jogging paths. The nicely decorated rooms range from normal sized to large, and two housekeeping units are available as well. Room rates include a continental breakfast. Rooms $59–70, suites $84, housekeeping units, $139.

BED & BREAKFAST INNS **The Terrell House** (828-682-4505; www .terrellhousebandb.com), 109 Robertson St., Burnsville, NC 28714. Built in the early 1900s as a dormitory for a

THE NU WRAY INN ON THE TOWN SQUARE IN BURNSVILLE.

Jim Hargan

private girls' school, this large old Colonial-style home sits on a quiet residential street. Reminiscent of an old plantation house, it's clad in white clapboard and surrounded by well-kept gardens; white columns hold a two-story roof over its front porch. Common areas include a back garden with a gazebo, a cozy parlor with late-Victorian antiques and facing sofas, and a formal dining room where a full breakfast is served on fine china. The six guest rooms are all normal to cozy in size, and are furnished individually in country-style antiques and repro-ductions. $75–85.

🖉 **The Celo Inn** (828-675-5132), 1 Seven Mile Ridge Rd., Burnsville, NC 28714. This five-room B&B occu-pies a long two-story log frame build-ing, sitting by the South Toe River, in a grove of old trees. Located in the remote Celo community, about 8 miles south of Burnsville on NC 80 and not far from the Blue Ridge Park-way, the inn is well known and well respected in the small, but national-caliber, artists' community that spreads itself through Celo. The inn, a co-sponsor of the Burnsville Metric, is particularly welcoming to bicyclers. $30–75.

🖉 **Estes Mountain Retreat** (828-682-7264), 822 Winterberry Rd., Burnsville, NC 28714. A modern log cabin off a quiet back road in the high mountains west of Burnsville. This planked white cedar structure sits on 4 acres at 3,800 feet—high enough for good views off its wide front porch, and high enough to be notice-ably cooler than Asheville. Both of its two en suite rooms are roomy and comfortable, with simple country fur-nishings and handmade quilts on the bed. The tariff includes a full break-fast and a homemade dessert in the evening. $59–72.

🖉 **Richmond Inn Bed and Break-fast** (877-765-6993 or 828-765-6993; fax 828-766-7224; www.richmond-inn .com), 51 Pine Ave., Spruce Pine, NC 28777. Rated three diamonds by AAA, this eight-room B&B sits on a residential back lane, three blocks uphill from downtown Spruce Pine. It's a large, white clapboard Dutch Colonial house from the mid–20th century, sitting on a high stone terrace with dormers, bay windows, and a wide porch looking out over Spruce Pine to the mountains beyond. Guests share a comfortable parlor, furnished with antiques in a restrained country style. Rooms range from comfortable sized to large, and are individually decorated with antiques. The full breakfast is served in a formal dining room overlooking the garden.

CABIN RENTALS **Laurel Oaks Farm** (800-528-7356 or 828-688-2652; www.laurel-oaks.com), 7334 NC 80, Bakersville, NC 28705. These two cabins sit on a sheep farm in the wooded hills south of Bakersville, on scenic NC 80. One modern and one an old-style log cabin, both of these comfortable, fully equipped cabins have views from their porches. The farm has two trout ponds, on-property walking paths, and a border on the Toe River, as well as a sheep herd and a llama. $85–130 per night.

✳ **Where to Eat**

EATING OUT **The Garden Deli** (828-682-3946; www.garden-deli .com), 107 Town Square, Burnsville, NC. Mon.–Sat. 11–2. A Burnsville lunchtime fixture since 1987, the Gar-den Deli features patio seating shaded by willows and wisterias, overlooking the lovely town square. Indoor seating for this year-round café is in a wood-paneled room with bay windows and a large fireplace. The menu consists of soups, salads, and sandwiches, with a selection of fresh-made sides and desserts. Many of the sandwiches are New York deli style, with good-quality meat that's sliced thin and piled high. The menu also has specialty items, such as pork barbeque pit-smoked on the premises. $3–5.

Afternoon Delight (828-765-7164), 14701 NC 226 S., Spruce Pine, NC. Mon. and Wed.–Sat. 7 AM–9 PM, Sun. 9–3. Despite its name, this is an all-day, full-menu restaurant with a tilt toward southern-style food. Neat and attractive, this new building is located along NC 226 a few miles south of Spruce Pine, between the Blue Ridge Parkway and the Wal-Mart. Menu service or full buffet breakfast, all very reasonably priced, while the lunch menu features sandwiches and salads. Dinners also offer a full range of sandwiches, along with such entrées as slow-cooked roast beef, grilled pork chops, country-fried steak, and (of course) fried chicken. Breakfast $2–4, lunch $3–5, dinner salads and sandwiches $6–7, full dinners $9–13.

✳ Entertainment

Parkway Playhouse (828-682-4285), 202 Green Mountain Dr., Burnsville, NC. Plays start at 8 PM most summer weekends. Reservations are required; call on weekday afternoons. Founded in 1947 as a summer outlet for Greensboro university students, the Parkway Playhouse is the state's oldest continuously operating theater. Now a semiprofessional company, it features a combination of old Broad-

way standards, children's plays, and Appalachian-themed plays from its giant barnlike theater down a (well-signposted) back street in Burnsville.

Young's Mountain Music (828-765-4365), US 19E, Micaville, NC, halfway between Burnsville and Spruce Pine on the Yancey–Mitchell County line. Sat. from 7 PM. A revered mountain tradition, Young's is noted as a venue for authentic, old-time (pre-bluegrass) Appalachian music from serious local musicians. The large, nondescript building features live mountain music and dancing (clogging, two-step line, and square) every Saturday night, with nonalcoholic beverages, a snack bar, and homemade desserts. $2 donation.

✳ Selective Shopping

Burnsville, NC
Silent Poetry (866-442-9336 or 828-682-7998; www.silentpoetry.com), 120 W. Main St. Located just off Burnsville's town square in a plain old brick (white) commercial building, this well-known and respected craft gallery assembles the work of a number of local fine art and craft artists—potters, glass artists, jewelry, visual artists, and garden art. In addition, they maintain a gallery of fine antiques.

The Country Peddler (828-682-7810), 3 Town Square. This small shop on Burnsville's town square sells custom-made quilts, as well as quilting supplies and patterns—a good source for those who want a real Appalachian quilt instead of something from an Asian sweatshop.

Micaville, NC
Toe River Crafts (828-675-4555), NC 80 S. Fri.–Sat. 10–5, Sun. noon–5. Limited off-season hours.

This modest old board-and-batten building, 7 miles south of Micaville on NC 80, is home to a cooperative of local artisans who specialize in a variety of contemporary crafts. Staffed by cooperative members, this gallery features pottery, woodworking, textiles, fibers, glass, paper, metals, toys, photography, prints, watercolors, and needlework.

Spruce Pine, NC

Twisted Laurel Gallery (828-765-1562), 221 Locust St. Apr.–Dec., Tue.–Sat. 10–5; Jan.–Mar., Fri. and Sat. 10–5. Established in 1989 by third-generation clock maker Luther Stroup, this downtown gallery, just across from the railroad depot, features the work of over 130 craft artists, all from the Spruce Pine and Penland area. Beautifully displayed in a large, airy storefront, the art covers just about every medium and style imaginable, with a particularly rich selection of glass art.

Blue Moon Book Store (828-766-5000), 271 Oak Ave. Mon.–Sat. 10–6. Located on the upper level of Spruce Pine's terraced downtown, this large storefront bookstore offers a wide selection of regional titles and children's books, used books, art (particularly notecards) by local crafters, and a good café. Blue Moon sponsors a program of music, storytelling, and readings in the store all year long.

Bakersville, NC

Potters of the Roan (www.potters oftheroan.homestead.com). This cooperative unites 11 potters—all with ties to the Penland School— with studios scattered throughout the mountain valleys surrounding Bakersville. All members open their studios (many of them in extraordi-

narily scenic locations) to the public. For a brochure giving contact information, a map and directions, and pictures of the work of all 11 potters, e-mail the cooperative at: info@ pottersoftheroan.com, or ask the Mitchell County Chamber of Commerce (see *Guidance*).

✳ Special Events

SPRING Spring Studio Tour. First weekend in May. Sponsored by the local nonprofit Toe River Arts Council, this annual event opens more than 50 artists' studios and galleries to the public, spread throughout the Burnsville and Spruce Pine, NC, areas.

Spring Arts Festival. Last Sat. in May. This annual arts festival, held in front of the Yancey County Courthouse in Burnsville, NC, combines local artists, live art demonstrations, and food sponsored by local nonprofits.

Avery Heritage Fest. First Sat. in June. Held in the beautiful town square of Newland, NC, in front of the old Avery County Courthouse, this festival emphasizes genealogy and mountain history, with local history writers, genealogy tents, Civil and Revolutionary War reenactors, and an authentic 19th-century circuit-riding preacher. The local church serves up a barbeque lunch.

SUMMER ⚓ Burnsville, NC, Fourth of July Celebration. This lively town square celebration includes an all-day band competition, craft booths, local nonprofits selling homemade items and food, fire trucks, a wagon train, and special activities for children.

Spruce Pine, NC, Independence Day Celebration. This downtown street celebration includes square dancing, food, and fireworks. It's preceded by a 3-day townwide sidewalk sale.

Rhododendron Festival (www .bakersville.com/rhod.html). Last weekend in July. For more than half a century the little mountain town of Bakersville, NC, has celebrated the magnificent rhododendron display with a large street fair, including street dancing, a car show, a beauty pageant, and a number of bicycling events.

🐾 ✂ ♿ **Mount Mitchell Crafts Fair**, Mount Burnsville, NC. First weekend in Aug. This town square craft fair, founded in 1956, features over 200 local and regional craft artists chosen by the Crafts Fair Selection Committee for quality, originality, and variety. You'll find ongoing bandstand entertainment that emphasizes moun-

tain music and dance, as well as a number of food vendors. Free.

AUTUMN Overmountain Victory Trail March. Mid- to late Sep. Every year the Overmountain Victory Trail Association commemorates America's amazing Revolutionary War victory at Kings Mountain, SC, by reenacting the frontier militia's cross-mountain march. The festivities start with a mid-Sep. reenactors' camp at the Museum of North Carolina Minerals, in which both the British and Patriot sides plot strategies, drill, and practice shooting their black powder muskets. Then a week later (roughly around the anniversary of the events on Sep. 25), the frontier militia marches across the mountains to dinner and encampment at Spruce Pine, NC, followed by a march at the Orchards at Altapass.

THE MOUNTAINS OF
NORTHERN TENNESSEE

M ountains guide the TN–NC state line along a series of 5,000- and 6,000-foot peaks, with a 4,000-foot drop down to the valleys of East Tennessee. It's an impressive sight, but it doesn't end there. Yet more mountains rise to 3,000 and 4,000 feet—some a rough jumble, others running straight as a stick for many miles. The four wild places give a good sampling: Big Laurel Branch Wilderness for a linear mountain with craggy views, Pond Mountain Wilderness for a rough jumble of wildlands, Unaka Mountain Wilderness for a 5,000-foot state-line ridge, and the famous Highlands of Roan for 6,000-foot peaks, rhododendron gardens, and crestline grassy balds.

This is also a land of deep history. Settled in the 18th century, Elizabethton, TN, has a 1770s "mansion" with its original interior, a reconstructed fort, a 134-foot 19th-century covered bridge, and a historic district of antebellum and Victorian houses. Nearby Erwin, TN, has strong links to one the Appalachian's great railroads, the Clinchfield, still one of the East's great freight lines. Just outside town, the Nolichucky River Gorge is increasingly prized for its challenging whitewater and stunning scenery.

GUIDANCE **Elizabethton–Carter County Chamber of Commerce** (888-547-3852 or 423-547-3850; fax 423-547-3854; www.tourelizabethton.com), 500 E. Bypass, P.O. Box 190, Elizabethton, TN 37644. The chamber maintains a welcome center (including picnic facilities) on the eastern edge of Elizabethton, on US19E/321.

Unicoi County Chamber of Commerce (423-743-3000; fax 423-743-0942; www.unicoicounty.org), 100 S. Main Ave., Erwin, TN 37650. The Unicoi County Chamber maintains a visitors center and information desk in one of downtown Erwin's restored historic buildings.

Watauga Ranger District, Cherokee National Forest (423-735-1500), P.O. Box 400 (TN 173, north of town center), Unicoi, TN 37692. Mon.–Fri. 8–4:30. This large modern office, just east of US 23 (future I-26) off Exit 23, has a friendly information desk and bookshop, with full information on the forests in this chapter.

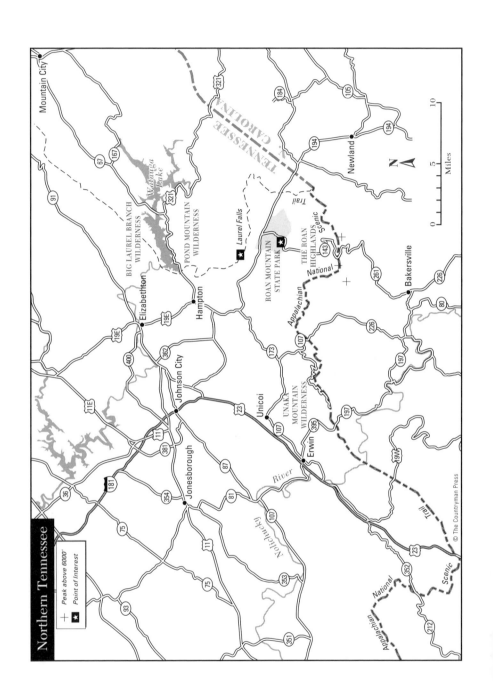

Northern Tennessee

- Peak above 6000'
- ★ Point of Interest

Mountain City

67
167
91

Watauga Lake

321

BIG LAUREL BRANCH WILDERNESS

POND MOUNTAIN WILDERNESS

Elizabethton

Hampton

Laurel Falls ★

★ ROAN MOUNTAIN STATE PARK

THE ROAN HIGHLANDS

Appalachian National Scenic Trail

143

261

Bakersville

80

226

226

197

107

173

19E
400
362
Johnson City

111E

111
381

Jonesborough

87

354

81

181

36

75

111

75

93

351

Unicoi

23

UNAKA MOUNTAIN WILDERNESS

107

Erwin

395

River

Nolichucky

107

333

19W

23

352

212

Appalachian National Scenic Trail

321
184
105

194

194

Newland

N

0   5   10
Miles

TENNESSEE
NORTH CAROLINA

© The Countryman Press

GETTING THERE *By car*: **I-181/US 23** provides freeway access to Erwin, TN, and the western parts of this area. **US 19E** and **US 321**, mostly four lane, link Elizabethton, Roan Mountain, and Lake Watauga, TN, to the rest of the world.

By air: **Tri-Cities Airport** (423-325-6000; fax 423-325-6060; www.triflight .com), 2525 Hwy. 75, Blountville, TN 37617. The Tri-Cities are Johnson City, Kingsport, and Bristol. Tri-Cities Airport is located in Tennessee's Great Valley in the middle of the triangle formed by the three cities, off I-81's Exit 63. Tri-Cities has four commuter airlines furnishing nonstops to six different hubs, so it's not uncommon to find good and/or cheap connections to it.

By bus or train: **Greyhound Bus** service runs to Johnson City, TN, immediately outside this area. There are no passenger trains in East Tennessee. (Not even Chattanooga!)

MEDICAL EMERGENCIES **Sycamore Shoals Hospital** (423-542-1300; www .msha.com/facilities/ssh.htm), 1501 W. Elk Ave., Elizabethton, TN. This 121-bed hospital offers full emergency service from the west end of town on US 321.

Unicoi County Memorial Hospital (423-743-3141; fax 423-743-1244; www .unicoicounty.org), Greenway Circle, Erwin, TN. Erwin's 48-bed hospital is located in town, 1 mile south of downtown via TN 81 (former US 23) and two blocks to the left. It has full emergency services.

✳ Wandering Around

EXPLORING BY CAR **The Unaka Mountains** loom 3,000 feet above Erwin, Tennessee. This drive circles the Unakas, explores the historic railroad town of Erwin and its surrounding valleys, then climbs up to the very top of the mountain for some wonderful views from the Appalachian Trail (AT).

Start on I-26 at the state line, a place known as **Sams Gap**. The AT crosses here, and a short walk up to the west leads to some nice views from an old cemetery. From here you can see the interstate slabbing down a side ridge, blowing through everything in its path; to its left, the old U.S. highway drops straight down into the valley, steeply and with many curves. Take the interstate down toward Erwin for many fine, wide views. The official overlook is definitely worth a stop, with a short ridgeline path to a variety of views up to the Unakas and down into the settled valleys.

When you reach the bottom, take the first **Erwin** exit and follow TN 81 (the former US 23) through this well-kept railroad town; as you pass along its classic small-town Main Street, the railroad yards are a block to your left. Continue out of town on TN 107 (still the old main highway), quickly passing through suburbs to regain mountain valley scenery. The county's worthwhile **Heritage Museum** is 3 miles from Erwin at the old Federal Fish Hatchery, with exhibits on the Clinchfield, local history, and a log one-room schoolhouse. The small town of **Unicoi**, TN, is 5 miles from Erwin, off TN 107 to the left, with an antiques shop and a couple of restaurants.

Continue on TN 107 through lovely mountain valleys. When you begin to climb out of the valley (12 miles from Erwin), look for a gravel road on your right, possibly marked with a brown recreation sign. This is the **Unaka Mountain Scenic Rd.**—supposedly a scenic tourist route, but in reality a rough gravel road, very badly maintained by the U.S. Forest Service. At this writing (mid-2004) it is nearly impassable for anything but high-clearance vehicles such as SUVs, and is unsafe for any vehicle in bad weather. If you have the right sort of vehicle, it's worth the bother. After the first switchback, look for a parking area on the right, for a short trail to the 100-foot-tall **Red Fork Falls**, noted for its sunset rainbows. From there the road runs through dense valley forests, then climbs to a ridgeline in two hairpin switchbacks. Two more hairpin switchbacks ladder you up to **Stamping Ground**, a high rocky heath bald with unusual gardenlike vegetation and breathtaking views over the Unaka Mountain Wilderness. This is the high point, staying just shy of 5,000 feet for the next mile, with Canadian-style spruce–fir forests crowning Unaka Mountain on your left. Then you drop down Unaka Mountain in two more hairpin switchbacks to the meadowed **Beauty Spot Gap**, with nice views into North Carolina and easy access to the AT. In another mile a spur road to the left follows a split-rail fence to aptly named **Beauty Spot**, for easy walks through a huge grassy bald with stunning views in all directions.

From here the "Unaka Scenic Highway" becomes overly steep and very badly potholed (as well as passing no more points of interest), and you may want to turn back; four-wheel-drive vehicles can continue to come out on TN 395, a short distance south of Erwin.

EXPLORING ON FOOT **Laurel Falls on the Appalachian Trail**. The trailhead parking is 3 miles up paved Dennis Cove Rd. (FS 50), which intersects US 321 five miles south of Elizabethton, TN, in the small town of Hampton, TN, marked by a brown recreation sign. This short section of the Appalachian Trail (AT) follows an old logging railroad grade along the rim of the Laurel Fork Gorge,

LOOKING SOUTH FROM THE UNAKA MOUNTAINS TOWARD THE BLACK MOUNTAINS OF NORTH CAROLINA.

Jim Hargan

to end at the lovely Laurel Falls. It is 2.5 miles long with no meaningful elevation change until the steep and difficult plunge down to the foot of the falls; the walk out on the railroad bed is worthwhile in itself. Take the AT to the left (north), along a level railroad grade. The trail quickly reaches Laurel Fork, an impressively large and violent stream noted for its trout fishing. At this point the trail enters the **Pond Mountain Wilderness** and stays there for the rest of the walk. After three-quarters of a mile the trail enters a cut, then drops steeply down into a gorge as the old railroad grade ends at a long-vanished trestle. The trail crosses the stream at an impressive footbridge on two rock piers, leading to a ledge in a sheer quartzite cliff; then it rises again to the rail-road grade in a flight of 60 stone steps. From this point on the gorge drops away from the level trail very quickly, showing large white quartzite cliffs through the trees. At 1.25 miles the AT plunges steeply off the railroad grade and down into the gorge, reaching Laurel Falls after 265 very difficult stone steps. Alas, there are no views of the falls from the top of this drop, and those determined to see the falls have quite a climb in front of them. Most will find it worth the work. Laurel Fork stair-steps down a 30-foot thickness of plunging quartzite, forming a waterfall about as wide as it is high and framed by gray-white cliffs. Return the way you came.

Historic Elizabethton Walking Tour (888-547-3852 or 423-547-3850). Eliza-bethton's chamber of commerce (888-547-3852) has established one of the nicest and best-marked historic town walks of the mountains. The short path, starting at the downtown city hall, wanders past 30 historic buildings and sites along this small town's three-block downtown and along the elegant Doe River. Highlights include elegant southern mansions, lovely riverside parks, an authen-tic covered bridge, and a red 1921 fire engine (not to mention the tallest fir tree in Tennessee, in front of one of those mansions). The excellent brochure is avail-able from the chamber, just east of town on US 19E/321.

✳ Villages

Erwin, TN. Located at the foot of the Unaka Mountains not far from the TN–NC line, Erwin is, and always has been, an industrial town. It is in no way polluted, defaced, or ugly; but neither does it make much of an attempt to put on a pretty face for visitors. Purposely founded as Unicoi County's seat in 1879, Erwin became a small city when, in 1908, the **Clinchfield Railroad** chose it as its major repair yard (a big deal in the days of temperamental steam engines), and later its corporate headquarters. The Clinchfield's bold attempt to slice straight through the heart of the Appalachians was a financial success, and Erwin thrived along with its railroad. During this period, Southern Potteries operated a successful hand-painted china factory in Erwin, turning out the **Blue Ridge China** now prized by collectors. The pottery closed in 1957, however—a victim of postwar foreign competition—and the Clinchfield offices closed in 1983 when CSX bought it out. Not that Erwin suffered much from these closures; it had already acquired a new major industry—uranium processing (mainly for naval ships). CSX still maintains a yard in town, servicing the very busy line that the Clinchfield built. Erwin has an attractive, old-fashioned downtown, with several shops that are worth a visit. You will find Erwin just off the US 23 freeway (which will be redesignated I-26 at some time in the future).

✳ Wild Places

THE GREAT FORESTS **Big Laurel Branch Wilderness** is located 6 miles east of Elizabethton, TN, via Siam Rd.; follow the signs for Watauga Dam. Cliffs rise straight up out of still lake water; a stream plummets over the edge and falls 50 feet straight down. Such is the dramatic edge of the Big Laurel Branch

ELIZABETHTON, TENNESSEE

Viewed from the main highway, Elizabethton appears to be a modest factory town, a bit on the skids. Early-20th-century rayon factories line US 321, shielding drivers from any accidental views of the Watauga River paralleling the highway. The highway continues to bypass the center of town through modest industrial suburbs until it leaves it altogether. Elizabethton holds a secret, however: Turn off the highway, wander into its center, and a charming historic village opens up—a brick-front downtown with a riverfront park, a beautiful white clapboard covered bridge reflected in a weir, a line of Victorian and antebellum homes, and a large Veterans Monument in a circle by the old brick courthouse. Elizabethton's center looks as if it would be more at home in New England than in the rural South.

Located at the confluence of the **Watauga** and **Doe Rivers**, Elizabethton was one of the earliest transmountain settlement south of Virginia. These settlers were well west of any law or government, in Cherokee lands where settlement was prohibited by British law, so they formed the Watauga Association to establish and enforce laws, and lease land from the Cherokees. The association held its first court under a sycamore tree near the current downtown, a site marked by a section of the original tree (which died in 1987). Guarded by the British army at nearby Fort Watauga and with good fords over two difficult rivers, Elizabethton became an important frontier settlement. The **old fort**, at Sycamore Shoals on the western edge of town, has been reconstructed and now houses a fine local museum.

Elizabethton remained small throughout most of the 19th century, acquiring several antebellum mansions that still stand today, as well as a fine **covered bridge** that still crosses the Doe River in a single 134-foot span. The town quickly became a lumbering and factory center, however, when the railroad arrived in the late 1880s. The first railroad was the famous **Tweetsie**, a narrow-gauge line that crossed the mountains from Boone, NC. The two large rayon factories furnished prosperity during the 1920s, and still dominate the town east of the reconstructed fort.

Wilderness, taking up the southernmost 10 square miles of heavily wooded **Iron Mountain** (with an additional 8 square miles of the mountain classed as a "roadless area"). Iron Mountain climbs 1,400 feet above the waters of **Lakes Watauga** and **Wilbur**, then extends northeast, straight and true, with a narrow crest that never swerves. Big Laurel Branch itself is a bowl-shaped drainage cut into the southern edge of the mountain, trailless and inaccessible to all but the most experienced cross-country hikers. The **Appalachian Trail** follows Iron Mountain through the wilderness, however, furnishing good access and a first-rate day hike. You can pick up the trail at **Watauga Dam** and follow it uphill along the crest for 4.5 miles to a trail shelter, a fairly steady climb of 1,200 feet. The trail passes through a varied and interesting dry hardwood forest, broken by large outcrops and cliffs with dramatic views down to the lake below. The trail shelter, located at the edge of the wilderness area, has a particularly wide and impressive clifftop view.

Pond Mountain Wilderness is 6 miles south of Elizabethton, TN, via US 321, on the south side of the highway. Pond Mountain is not a linear mountain like that of the Big Laurel Branch Wilderness; instead, it's a wild jumble of peaks and valleys, ridges that run every which way, valleys perched on high crests, outcrops projecting from deep forests, and gorges cut straight through ridges. From the valley below it doesn't look taller than linear Iron Mountain—but it is, a 2,200-foot climb from nearby **Watauga Lake** to its vaguely crescent-shaped crest. The U.S. Congress has protected nearly 11 square miles of this difficult area as the Pond Mountain Wilderness.

Of the many interesting features of the wilderness, the strangest may be the deep gorge carved through its western edge by Laurel Creek—a gorge that includes a couple of deep horseshoe curves at the center of the crestline. The **Laurel Creek Gorge** features an impressive waterfall, sheer cliffs, and some strange rock formations, as well as a historic old railroad bed. The **Appalachian Trail** follows that old railbed for a fine hike, then curves around to the top of Pond Mountain for some wide views.

Highlands of Roan. This large area of high, rugged wilderness straddles the TN–NC state line 25 miles south of Elizabethton, TN, via US 19E and TN 143. With three peaks above 6,000 feet and 6 miles of mile-high crest, the Highlands of Roan make up one of the great sights of the Southern Appalachians. Nearly 10 miles of the Roan Mountain crest is covered with wide grassy balds and rhododendron heaths; one heath forms a 600-acre natural garden that turns brilliant pink every June. With 23 square miles of protected land, there's plenty to see.

On the Tennessee side, **Hampton Creek Cove State Scenic Area** includes an operating mountain farm that merges with the forests above, its access track leading still higher to the grassy balds along its crest. Nearby, Tennessee's **Roan Mountain State Park** protects 2,000 acres along the lower slopes, including a reconstructed 19th-century homestead, the **Dave Miller Farmstead**.

From the state park, TN 143 climbs a dramatic mile-high gap to enter North Carolina, an impressive scenic drive. From the gap, the **Appalachian Trail** heads east through wide-open meadows, on one of the most breathtaking walks in the East. A paved road leads west from the same gap along the crest to a 600-acre rhododendron garden with wide views in North Carolina's **Pisgah National Forest** (see "Spruce Pine & Burnsville").

A long drive around on the North Carolina side leads to the head of Roaring Creek Valley, with stunning views over an apple orchard and a red barn, as well as a walk along the Revolutionary War–era **Overmountain Victory Trail**.

Unaka Mountain Wilderness. The 5,160-foot peak of Unaka Mountain looms above Erwin, TN, its summit clothed in black-green firs and spruces. The

Unaka Mountain Scenic Rd. follows its crest, linking a series of heaths and grassy balds with wide views, paralleled by the **Appalachian Trail** on its uphill side. Downhill from this stretches the Unaka Mountain Wilderness, known for its rugged terrain, steep cliffs, dramatic waterfalls, and wide views from heath balds. It's a surprisingly popular place for hikers, with its beauty outweighing its remoteness and difficulty. One popular trail starts at the wilderness's low point, the **Rock Creek Recreation Area**, and climbs 1,000 feet in a 5-mile round trip to **Rock Creek Falls**, a beautiful cliff cascade. Another trail from the same recreation area climbs the exposed backbone of **Rattlesnake Ridge** to reach the scenic drive after a 2,500-foot climb and a lot of spectacular views (6 miles round trip).

RECREATION AREAS **Roan Mountain State Park** (800-250-8620 or 423-772-0190; www.state.tn.us/environment/parks/RoanMtn/), 1015 TN 143, Roan Mountain, TN. Wed.–Sun. 8–4:30; closed Mon. and Tue. Located 21 miles south of Elizabethton, TN, via US 19E and TN 143, this state park preserves 3 square miles of the middle slopes of the Roan Highlands. It has an attractive visitors center graced by an old-fashioned overshot wheel, a number of hiking trails, and several good picnic areas. Considered a "resort park," it also has a set of 30 cabins as well as tennis courts and a swimming pool. Roan Mountain is particularly noted for its wide-ranging program of activities, including workshops in traditional mountain crafts, a spring Naturalists Rally, and a fall Rhododendron Festival. The state park is 10 miles from the crest of Roan Mountain and its famous gardens, via TN 143—one of the most spectacular 10 miles in the mountains.

Wilbur Lake and Watauga Dam Recreation Areas. Three miles east of Elizabethton, TN, via Siam Rd.; follow the signs for Watauga Dam. The Tennessee Valley Authority (TVA) maintains a large and attractive recreation area stretching from Wilbur Dam, along the 3-mile length of Wilbur Lake, then over a gap to a hill above Watauga Lake. It starts with views of Wilbur Dam, a 1912 concrete structure 77 feet high, with a canoe launch at its foot. From there the road closely follows the banks of narrow Wilbur Lake, with several picnic areas, boat launches, and places to park and fish. The scenery here is particularly attractive, with cliffs rising out of the opposite shore of the lake, and the impressive, 50-foot **Laurel Branch Waterfall** opposite one of the picnic areas. At a fork in this road, the right-hand road continues along Wilbur Lake for more picnicking and fishing, while the left-hand road climbs to Iron Mountain Gap. Here the **Appalachian Trail** crosses the park road; to the right it goes 1 mile

WILD GERANIUM IN BLOOM.

Jim Hargan

to cross the top of Watauga Dam, while to the left it enters Big Laurel Branch Wilderness. Beyond the gap, the park road drops to the Watauga Lake at a large and well-kept TVA picnic area, with wide views from a glassed overlook, and a short trail to a view over the 330-foot earthen Watauga Dam.

PICNIC AREAS **Rock Creek Recreation Area**. This attractive picnic and camping area, heavily shaded, sits at the lowermost edge of the **Unaka Mountain Wilderness** and serves as one of the area's trailheads.

Shook Branch Recreation Area. This Cherokee National Forest picnic area marks the place where the **Appalachian Trail** crosses US 321, 8 miles southeast of Elizabethton, TN. It's located on **Lake Watauga** with pleasant lake views, as well as access to the **Pond Mountain Wilderness**. As you follow US 321 eastward along the lakeshore, you will find two more lakeside picnic areas in the next 3 miles, plus a boat ramp and a campground.

✳ To See

BIG DAMMED LAKES **Lake Watauga**. This Tennessee Valley Authority (TVA) lake 6 miles west of Elizabethton, TN, covers just 10 squares miles, but has 100 miles of shoreline—half of it owned by the Cherokee National Forest. With miles of fiddley little indents and coves and lots of forested shoreline, it's a fun lake to explore. It has numerous recreation sites for picnicking, boat launching, and camping, the three largest being along US 321, 21 miles east of Elizabethton. The TVA built the Watauga Dam in 1948 for flood control and hydropower. This earthen dam stands 100 yards high and 1,000 feet wide at the top; you can visit the dam by hiking out the **Appalachian Trail** from Iron Mountain Gap, or view it from above at **Overlook Picnic Area**. On the road to the dam, **Lake Wilbur Picnic Area** gives views of Little Laurel Branch throwing itself out of an adjacent wilderness area and over a 50-foot cliff into the lake below.

HISTORIC SITES **Doe River Covered Bridge**. In continuous use since its construction in 1882, this 134-foot wood truss bridge spans the Doe River a block south of downtown Elizabethton, TN. Clad in white clapboard, the bridge looks absurdly elongated and flimsy—but it survived intact the fierce, deadly floods of 1901 and 1998, when more modern structures were swept away. The secret of its success: its massive trusses, made up of coupled 8x8 oak beams that tower 10 feet over the deck. The trusses suspend the deck across the entire width of the river, far above the highest floodwaters. The white clapboard cover exists for one reason only—to protect the wood truss from rot. Without the cover, the beams' slanted joints would pick up rain and snow, rotting away at the points where the strain is greatest. Because of its wood cover, this bridge remains strong enough to carry automobiles after 120 years and two major floods.

The bridge is flanked by lovely riverside parks on both banks, and framed on its downstream side by a weir that fed a 19th-century millrace. On the Elizabethton side of the river, rows of beautifully kept Victorian houses stretch along the water, facing across the road to the riverside park. A block north is Elizabethton's reviving brick-front downtown, with several antiques shops. A walk through the park along the river is a delight, with views that are simply beautiful, particularly in fall when brilliant colors frame the bridge.

Sycamore Shoals State Historic Site (423-543-5808; fax 423-543-0078), 1651 W. Elk Ave., Elizabethton, TN. Park open 8–dusk; visitors center open Mon.– Sat. 8–4:30, Sun. 1–4:30. On the western outskirts of Elizabethton (a mile west of downtown on US 321), Sycamore Shoals was the center of the colonial trans-mountain settlement of Watauga. The British built **Fort Watauga** here in the early 1770s to control a frontier that was supposedly closed to white settlement; white settlement had already begun, however, and the settlers relied on the fort for safety. Sycamore Shoals became of the most important frontier sites of the Revolutionary period. It was here that the private Transylvania Corporation, made up of North Carolina land speculators, bought Kentucky and West Tennessee from a group of Cherokee chiefs; years later, it was here that settlers sheltered from Cherokee attacks during the Revolution; and it was here that the Overmountain Boys mustered for their successful march to Kings Mountain, SC, to defeat a loyalist army poised to harry the mountain settlements.

Today Sycamore Shoals is a small, well-kept state park centered on a reconstruction of Fort Watauga and a small museum with a number of rotating local displays. In mid-July an outdoor drama featuring local amateur actors tells the story of the Watauga settlement. Sycamore Shoals offers a full calendar of activities, including some very imaginative ones (Flint Knapping Day comes to mind; see *Entertainment*). The park is beautiful and well kept, on a rolling, tree-shaded site by the Watauga River. It has good day-use facilities, including a picnic area and a riverside jogging path. Free.

Carter Mansion (423-543-6140), 1651 W. Elk St., Elizabethton, TN. Located at the end of Broad St. (US 321); go straight through the traffic light at US 19E and continue for one block. (The contact information is for Sycamore Shoals, which administers the site.) Tours daily May–Aug. The oldest frame house in Tennessee, the Carter Mansion was built by John Carter, a leader of the Watauga Association, in 1780. Astonishingly, over 90 percent of the interior of this modest frontier "mansion" dates from the original 1780 construction. This includes the hand-carved paneling, the crown molding, and the chair rails—and it definitely includes the two landscape paintings over the fireplaces, executed directly on the wall paneling. It also includes the plumbing; there isn't any, and never has been! Last occupied in 1966, the house was acquired by the State of Tennessee in 1973 along with 4.6 acres of land, and restored it to its original appearance in 1978. Free.

Dave Miller Farmstead. Adjacent to Roan Mountain State Park, on TN 143, 3 miles south of the village of Roan Mountain, TN. Memorial Day–Labor Day, Wed.–Sun. 9–5. This lovely early-20th-century farmstead, immaculate white with stylish little gable dormers over its front porch, is the successor to two pioneer log cabins, the homes of the Millers since 1870. The first cabin was on land leased from Roan Mountain's land baron, Gen. John Wilder; the Millers bought their farm from the general in 1904, and built the second cabin. The present house succeeded it, the home of later generations of Millers. Now it's an open-air museum, demonstrating a turn-of-the-20th-century mountain farmstead. Try to stop by on a summer Sat. between noon and 2 PM, when artists and musicians are present. Free.

The ET & WNC (Tweetsie Railroad) (423-928-8936), Elizabethton, TN. Although the initials stood for "East Tennessee and Western North Carolina," to mountain folk they stood for "eat 'taters and wear no clothes." It was also known as the "Tweetsie" for the peculiar sound made by the whistle of its main steam engine. One of the legendary lines of the Southern Appalachians, the Tweetsie was a narrow-gauge railroad originally built to haul iron ore from a mine north of Spruce Pine, NC, to Johnson City, TN; eventually it was extended as far as Boone, NC. A friendly, local line that wandered slowly through the mountains, it linked communities in a way that the more serious-minded Clinchfield did not. The Tweetsie's crew (the same men for many years) would take orders from locals along the line and deliver the goods to their door. The Tweetsie survived surprisingly late into the 20th century, losing its line to Boone, NC, in a 1944 flood and closing its last section in 1950. Still, in a sense it survives to this day— as the roadbeds of US 19E, NC 194, and NC 105, all major highways.

With most of its bed superseded by highways, little remains to be seen—with one spectacular exception: the **Doe River Gorge**. To visit this exception, call the Doe River Christian Camp and Conference Center to get permission to park your car on their land and walk through their property (and to get directions to the trailhead, near the village of Roan Mountain, TN). Oh, and don't forget your flashlight—the railbed trail immediately dives into a long tunnel (the first of three) to enter the rugged gorge. From there it traverses 2.4 miles of stunning cliff-sided gorge scenery, with spectacular views and lots of railroad artifacts along the way. Turn around when you reach a rickety trestle; no wood structure can be trusted after half a century's abandonment in the heavy damp of the Southern Appalachians.

A final note: Some readers will associate *Tweetsie Railroad* with a Blowing Rock, NC, tourist attraction, a cowboy theme park that features the actual, original steam locomotive from the Tweetsie. The attraction has beautifully restored the old engine and keeps it in top shape—and it still makes that strange "tweetsie" sound. If you care to visit it, it will carry you in a fine circle to an Olde West town.

CULTURAL SITES **Heritage Museum** (423-743-9449; www.unicoi.tn.us/heritage .html). Located in the 1903 Superintendent's Residence of the U.S. Fish Hatchery, off US 23's Exit 19 between Erwin and Unicoi, TN. May–Oct., Tue.–Sun. 1–5. Nine of its 10 rooms are open to the public. Railroad buffs will head immediately to the Railroad Room on the second floor, with exhibits on the old **Clinchfield Railroad**. The Clinchfield was (and remains) one of the greatest lines in the East, running straight through the Appalachians like a hot wire through butter; formerly an independent company headquartered in Erwin, it's now a heavily used main line for the CSX. In the next room is a reconstruction of Erwin's Main St., from about the period when the fish hatchery (and the Clinchfield) were built. Other rooms display home-canned and -preserved food; another type of preserve—artifacts of nature, including a stuffed bear (killed by

accident); period furniture; local arts and crafts; turn-of-the-20th-century costumes; and just a lot of neat stuff. Individual rooms are sponsored by local civic
organizations. A one-room log schoolhouse sits outside (moved in from Greasy
Cove), and a nature trail is on the property. Free.

GARDENS AND PARKS **Hampton Creek Cove State Natural Area** (423-323-
4993), 804 Rock City Rd., Kingsport, TN. Unique among the State of Tennessee's 60 natural areas, Hampton Creek Cove contains a working farm, still
run by the family that has farmed this land for the last century. A state-owned
part of the 15,000-acre **Highlands of Roan**, Hampton Creek demonstrates
mountain farming practices that conserve natural ecosystems and improve bio-
diversity. A track runs uphill through the farmlands and into the woods above,
eventually reaching the famous ridgetop meadows of the Roan at the **Overmountain Victory Trail**. You will find the natural area at the end of Hampton
Creek Rd., which starts at the village of Roan Mountain, TN.

✸ To Do

GOLF **Elizabethton Municipal Golf Course** (423-542-8051), Golf Club Rd.,
Elizabethton, TN. This fairly hilly 18-hole par-72 course overlooks the Watauga
River on the west side of Elizabethton, off US 321. $15–23.

Buffalo Valley Golf Course (423-743-5021), 90 Country Club Dr., Unicoi, TN.
Eight miles north of Erwin, this 18-hole public course sits on the level floor of
the oddly riverless valley that stretches north from Erwin to Johnson City. It's an
attractive rural location, convenient to the US 23 freeway that's destined to
become I-26 someday. $17–19.

STILLWATER BOATING **Watauga Kayaking** (423-542-6777; www.trouttown.com/
watkay/wkhome.htm), 1409 Broad St., Elizabethton, TN. Watauga Kayaking
offers calm-water lake and river tours on area waters, including Lake Watauga,
for a peaceful enjoyment of nature. They also rent kayaks for calm-water use.

WHITEWATER ADVENTURES There are good choices for whitewater excursions
in this area. The **Nolichucky River** enters TN by passing through a deep
wilderness gorge, a wild 12-mile stretch of Class III–IV rapids. Downstream
from Erwin, TN, the Nolichucky continues through beautiful mountain scenery
at a much more leisurely pace, suitable for families with small children. Finally,
the **Watauga River** near Elizabethton, TN, has an attractive 9-mile stretch of
water with Class I–III rapids.

Cherokee Adventures, Inc. (800-445-7238 or 423-743-7733; www.cherokee
adventures.com), 2000 Jonesborough Rd., Erwin, TN. This outfitter specializes
in fully guided trips on the Nolichucky River—wild rides on the Nolichucky
Gorge, or gentle, scenic floats farther downstream. Most floats include lunch.
With 50 riverside acres, they have packages that combine primitive camping or
simple cabin accommodations with meals and float trips. They also offer mountain bike tours and a roping school. Half day $16–36, whole day $31–63.

B-Cliff Whitewater Rafting (800-592-2262 or 423-542-2262), 390 Wilbur Dam Rd., Elizabethton, TN. Memorial Day–Labor Day, B-Cliff offers whitewater rafting and kayaking on the Watauga River 5 miles east of Elizabethton. $30.

Nantahala Outdoor Center at Erwin, TN (800-232-7238 or 828-488-2175; fax 828-488-0301), 4 Jones Branch Rd., Erwin, TN. This major regional company, headquartered in Bryson City, NC, maintains an outpost at the head of the Nolichucky Gorge 4 miles south of Erwin—a base for trips through the gorge.

USA Raft (800-872-7238 or 828-488-2175), 2 Jones Branch Rd., Erwin, TN. This West Virginia whitewater rafting chain operates an outpost at the mouth of the Nolichucky Gorge, 4 miles south of Erwin.

✳ Lodging

BED & BREAKFAST INNS 🐾 **Iron Mountain Inn** (888-781-2399 or 423-768-2446; fax 423-768-2451; www.bbonline.com/tn/ironmtn/), 138 Moreland Dr., P.O. Box 30, Butler, TN 37640. Open all year. This modern log structure, purpose-built as an inn by its current proprietor, sits on 140 acres in the Iron Mountains, 12 miles south of Mountain City, TN. It has a porch and a deck with views, a great room with a fireplace, and a library. Its four rooms, individually decorated and themed, have handmade quilts and whirlpool bath; two rooms have steam shower, and three have private balcony. Guests are treated to afternoon refreshments as well as a three-course breakfast, and the cookie jar is always full. Dinner and picnic lunches are available with 24-hour notice (fee). Pets and small children require prior arrangement. $125–250 per room, per night. Rates are lower on weekdays and off-season, higher on weekends, on holidays, and in Oct. AAA discounts.

Doe River Inn (423-543-1444; www.doeriverinn.com), 217 Academy St., Elizabethton, TN 37643. This 1894 Victorian house faces the Doe River in Elizabethton's historic district, within site of the covered bridge. Built on the site of the original ford over the Doe River, it was once known as the Crossover. Today's inn has two rooms, each elegantly furnished with antiques and its own bath. Common rooms, also furnished in high-Victorian style, include a living room, a sunroom, and a formal dining room where the full breakfast is served.

General Wilder's Bed and Breakfast (423-772-3102; www.generalwilder.com), 200 Main St., Roan Mountain, TN 37687. Built in 1880, this National Register Victorian country house in the village of Roan Mountain was probably the most elegant structure in the rural Doe River area. Its original owner, Civil War general John Thomas Wilder, built it as he formed plans to exploit his 7,000-acre property on the crest of the Roan Highlands—the core of today's national forest holdings. It's a simple two-story white frame house with a hip-roofed front porch and simple gingerbread details, located at the center of this mountain gorge village, several blocks removed from US 19E. Inside, four rooms with private bath are elegantly furnished with Victorian antiques to a level of comfort General Wilder would appreciate. $79–99, including breakfast.

☙ ✍ **Mountain Harbour B&B** (866-772-9494 or 423-772-9494; fax 423-772-9451; www.mountainharbour.net), 9151 US 19E, Roan Mountain, TN 37687. This four-room B&B inn is in a farmhouse-style home with stained clapboarding, dormers, and a wraparound porch. The four rooms, ranging in size from cozy to large, are individually furnished in a country antique style, with the largest room having a whirlpool tub and a fireplace. Two rooms are en suite, while two others share a bath. $70–120.

CABIN RENTALS ☙ ✍ ♿ **Roan Mountain State Park Cabins** (800-250-8620 or 423-772-0190), 1015 TN 143, Roan Mountain, TN 37687. Open all year. This 2,000-acre state park has 30 rustic cabins available by the day. Each is a modern-built structure in a classic park style with full front porch, living room, full kitchen, and two bedrooms. They are attractively set in a wooded glade, with a stream nearby and a large, well-kept lawn area. Ten cabins are available with phone. Only one cabin is approved for pets. $65–95 per night.

☙ ✍ **Mountain Lake Wilderness Resort** (800-381-6751 or 423-768-3030; www.mountaincityonline.com/mountainlake/), 166 Wilderness Trail, P.O. Box 300, Butler, TN 37640. These modern log cabins are on the site of Wilderness Ranch, an outdoor family resort with horseback rides, hayrides, exotic animals, covered wagon rides, and a wagon train ride. Each cabin has a full front porch, living room with fireplace, full kitchen, and two bedrooms, with a picnic area outside. Pets require prior approval and an extra $10 per night fee. $85 per night; discounts for longer stays.

Cherokee Forest Mountain Cabins (423-768-4484; www.cabin4me.com/index.html), 1423 TN 167, Butler, TN 37640. Open all year. These two modern log cabins are located at the far northern end of Watauga Lake. Both have wide views from their front porches, with wood-finished interiors furnished in a simple, elegant country style. Living areas have cathedral ceilings and fireplaces, and kitchens are full sized. $130–170 per night; discounts for longer stays.

Bee Cliff Cabins (423-542-6033; www.beecliffcabins.com), 106 Bee Cliff Lane, Elizabethton, TN 37643. These three cabins are located on a rural stretch of the Watauga River, 5 miles east of Elizabethton. It's a bit like an old-time fish camp; modest log-sided cabins group tightly around a central drive, sharing a common dock on the river. Inside, they are simply and comfortably furnished, wood walled, with full kitchens. $75 per night; discounts for longer stays.

✳ **Where to Eat**

EATING OUT **Ridgewood Barbeque** (423-538-7543), 900 Elizabethton Hwy., Bluff City, TN. Lunch and dinner Tue.–Sun.; closed Mon. The Proffit family of Bluff City founded this popular pit barbeque in 1948, and still own it today. They run a friendly, family-oriented place, sitting underneath the last of the mountain ridges on the old US 19E (now called Elizabethton Hwy.) 7 miles north of Elizabethton. They barbeque pork and beef in the two original pits, using their own sauce recipe and slicing it to order. The sides are made fresh as well.

The Coffee Company (800-358-3709; www.experiencingcoffee.com) 444 East Elk St., Elizabethton, TN.

Breakfast and lunch. This coffee shop in downtown Elizabethton serves breakfast and lunch along with a full line of coffees roasted on the premises. Breakfasts are limited to muffins and other goodies baked fresh each morning. Lunches are more elaborate, with homemade soups, sandwiches, desserts, and a daily special.

✳ Entertainment

Elizabethton, TN

Special Events at Sycamore Shoals (423-543-5808). This fascinating historic site runs a full slate of events, with something happening every month. Its reconstructed fort hosts several reenactments, including the famous **Overmountain March** each Sep. 23. There is a **Native American Festival** in June, a **fine art show** in July, a **Celtic Festival** in Sep., and a **quilt show** in Oct.

The Wataugans Outdoor Drama (423-543-5808). Tennessee's official outdoor drama and the oldest outdoor drama in the state, *The Wataugans* tells the story of the 18th-century Watauga Settlements that brought Europeans into the lands now known as Tennessee. It's held in July at Sycamore Shoals. $5 adults, $3 children.

The Elizabethton Twins (423-547-6440), 208 N. Holly Lane. Elizabethton is one of only two cities in this guide to have its own minor-league team (Asheville, NC, is the other). A farm team of the Minnesota Twins since 1937, the Elizabethton Twins are part of the rookie-level Appalachian League, one of America's last remaining old-time small-town leagues.

✳ Selective Shopping

Duck Crossing Antique Mall (423-542-3055), 515 East Elk Ave., Elizabethton, TN. Mon.–Sat. 10–5. Various dealers of antiques and gift items inhabit this three-story downtown building.

Farmhouse Gallery and Garden (800-952-6043 or 423-743-8799; www.farmhousegallery.net/navigation.htm), 21 Covered Bridge Lane, Unicoi, TN. Located north of Unicoi on Erwin Hwy., the Farmhouse Gallery features the wildlife art of Johnny Lynch. The gallery is located in a restored log cabin, surrounded by 3 acres of perennial and water gardens, and set in a 75-acre preserve. The complex includes an events venue for weddings, meetings, and such.

The Hanging Elephant (423-743-9661), 219 S. Main St., Erwin, TN. This downtown shop offers antiques and collectibles, including Blue Ridge Pottery—hand-painted china made in an Erwin factory from the 1920s through the 1950s.

✳ Special Events

Also see Special Events at Sycamore Shoals under *Entertainment*.

SPRING **Peters Hollow Egg Fight** (423-547-3852). Easter. This annual event, held at Sycamore Shoals, started in 1823 when an Easter egg hunt got out of hand. Or maybe it was a competition to see whose hen laid the strongest egg; traditions vary. Some people like to watch, while others join in.

Fiddlers and Fiddleheads Festival (423-743-8799). Late Apr., 10 AM– 9 PM. This annual event at Johnny Lynch's Farmhouse Gallery and

Gardens features music, a vintage car show, antiques sales, flower sales, storytelling, and food. Free.

Roan Mountain (State Park) Spring Naturalists Rally (423-772-0190). First weekend in May. Roan Mountain State Park sponsors a weekend of nighttime nature lectures and daytime naturalist-led hikes through the early-spring wildflowers.

Unicoi Strawberry Festival. Second weekend in May. This street fair in the small town of Unicoi, TN (5 miles north of Erwin, TN) celebrates the strawberry with live entertainment, a Sun. gospel sing, craft and fair booths, a citywide yard sale, and strawberries.

SUMMER Covered Bridge Celebration. Early June. Elizabethton, TN, celebrates its beautiful old covered bridge with a 4-day annual festival.

Annual Rhododendron Festival at Roan Mountain State Park (423-772-0190). Last weekend in June.

This annual festival at Roan Mountain State Park celebrates the peak of the rhododendron display, particularly spectacular in nearby Roan Mountain Gardens (part of the Pisgah National Forest across the line in NC). This 2-day event includes old-time mountain music, clogging, crafts, and food. There's another Rhododendron Festival held at about the same time on the other side of the mountain, at Bakersville, NC (see "Spruce Pine & Burnsville"). A true festival enthusiast will want to take in both.

AUTUMN Unicoi County Apple Festival. First weekend in Oct. This 2-day street fair takes over downtown Erwin, TN, with 300 craft and food exhibits, live music, and (of course) plenty of apples.

BENEATH THE BLUE RIDGE: THE CATAWBA RIVER VALLEY

T he mountains begin, and the Piedmont ends, in the valley of the Catawba River. One of the great rivers of the South, the Catawba rises from the upper slopes of the Blue Ridge 15 miles east of Asheville, NC, near the town of Black Mountain, NC. It then drops steeply to Old Fort, NC, and flows eastward into a wide, rolling valley, past the redbrick centers of Marion and Morganton, NC, then out into the Piedmont. The cliffs of the Blue Ridge loom 6 or 8 miles north of the valley bottom; the rugged peaks and clefts of the South Mountains lie the same distance south.

The Catawba Valley has always been the main approach to the Smokies from the thickly settled areas of North Carolina. First wagons, then trains, went up it to reach the rich mountain forests; today a flood of automobiles and trucks follow I-40 in their path. Before the Civil War, some of those wagons carried the North Carolina Supreme Court to Morganton every summer, escaping the downstate heat; the Supreme Court's graceful little courthouse still sits in the middle of Morganton's old-fashioned downtown. After the war, furniture manufacturers built factories along the rail yards beneath the cliffs of the Blue Ridge, the perfect distance between mountain hardwoods and downstate markets. More than 100 years later, furniture manufacturing still leads a laundry list of clean mill industries that continue to dominate the Catawba Valley economy. Today you will find an axis of urban and industrial development stretching lengthwise along the I-40 corridor; leave the interstate corridor to the north or south, however, and modern development drops away as you climb out of the valley floor and into the mountains.

GUIDANCE **Burke County Travel and Tourism Commission** (888-462-2921 or 828-433-6793; fax 828-433-6715; www.hci.net/~bcttc/), 102 E. Union St., Morganton, NC 28655. Mon.–Fri. 10–4, Sat. 10–1. Headquartered in Morganton's fine Old Courthouse, this small agency is delighted to help walk-in visitors with their visits to the eastern half of the Catawba Valley.

McDowell County Tourism Development Authority (888-233-6111 or 828-652-1103; fax 828-652-3862; www.mcdowellnc.org/tda.htm), P.O. Box 1028,

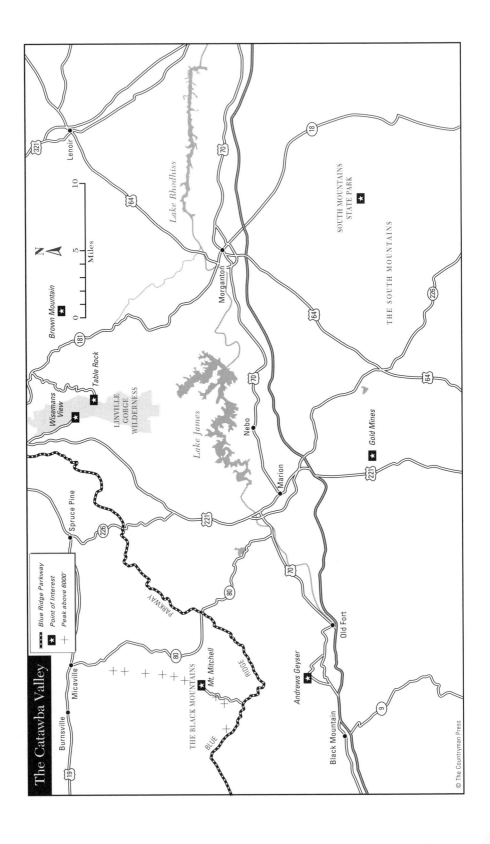

The Catawba Valley

Blue Ridge Parkway
★ Point of Interest
+ Peak above 6000'

N

0 5 10
Miles

© The Countryman Press

Burnsville
Micaville
Spruce Pine
THE BLACK MOUNTAINS
★ Mt. Mitchell
BLUE
RIDGE
PARKWAY
Andrews Geyser ★
Black Mountain
Old Fort
Marion
Nebo
Lake James
Gold Mines ★
THE SOUTH MOUNTAINS
SOUTH MOUNTAINS
STATE PARK ★
Morganton
Lenoir
Lake Rhodhiss
Wisemans View ★
Table Rock ★
LINVILLE GORGE WILDERNESS
Brown Mountain ★

321
19
80
9
70
221
64
70
221
64
64
226
18
226
181
64
321
70
80

EXPLORING BY CAR: THE RIM OF LINVILLE GORGE

Leg 1: From Linville Falls, NC, on US 221, go east on NC 183 for 0.8 mile; then right on the Kistler Memorial Hwy. (SSR 1239) to Wiseman's View, 4 miles. Return to NC 183. *Leg 2:* Continue right on NC 183, 4 miles; then right on NC 181, 3 miles; then right at Table Rock Rd. (SSR 1265), 6.3 miles; then right 1.4 miles to Table Rock Picnic Area. Return to NC 181. *Leg 3:* Right on NC 181, 23 miles to Morganton, NC.

This drive explores both rims of rugged Linville Gorge, the first eastern forest to be declared a wilderness area. It starts at the rural community of **Linville Falls**, noted for its handsome stone buildings constructed by the stonemasons for the Blue Ridge Parkway, and for its simple, turn-of-the-20th-century farm-style houses built as summer homes by an early generation of tourists. Outside the village, this route follows the gravel, poorly maintained **Kistler Memorial Highway** along the western edge of the Linville Gorge Wilderness. This verbosely named back road follows the ridgeline that defines the edge of the wilderness, running through a dry oak forest for the most part. The first path on the left (parking) leads to **Linville Falls** (see "Blowing Rock & Grandfather Mountain"), and all the later paths on the left descend steeply to the gorge bottom. Stop at **Wiseman's View**, on the left, and take the short, easy path to impressive clifftop views over the gorge. Beyond Wiseman's View the Kistler Highway may be impassable to passenger autos; return the way you came.

The route continues through rural countryside to the unremarkable mountaintop settlement of Jonas Ridge, NC, where a brown recreation sign points down the road to **Table Rock Picnic Area**. This good-quality Forest Service gravel road slowly winds its way through a large, handsome hardwood forest. The final mile climbs up seven switchbacks to reach the other side of the Linville Gorge, almost opposite Wiseman's View, at the lovely, tree-shaded picnic area. Here footpaths stretch north and south along the gorge rim to spectacular clifftop views and strange geological formations at **Table Rock** and the **Chimneys**. Return the way you came.

The final leg follows NC 181 downhill to Morganton. In 2 miles the trailhead for **Upper Creek Falls** is on the left, with **Bark House Picnic Area** just beyond. For the next 5 miles the highway follows the top of **Ripshin Ridge**, with excellent views back toward Table Rock and the Chimneys—here more impressive than ever. At the bottom of the mountain, commercial nurseries keep large fields of blooming trees, an amazing sight in spring. NC 181 leads to the center of **Morganton**, with its early-19th-century courthouse once used by the North Carolina Supreme Court for its summer sessions.

Marion, NC 28752. The McDowell County Tourism Development occupies a large, modern hilltop visitors center by a minor exit off US 221 as it bypasses Marion on its west. Covering the western half of the Catawba Valley, it offers friendly help and advice, a small but interesting display of local art and minerals, and a sweeping view north toward the Blue Ridge.

Old Fort Chamber of Commerce (828-668-7223), P.O. Box 1447, Old Fort, NC 28762. Tue.–Sat. 10–4. The town of Old Fort's local chamber offers visitors help and guidance from the railroad depot at the west end of town. It also includes a small railroad museum.

✔ **Pisgah National Forest, Grandfather Ranger District** (828-652-2144), 109 E. Lawing Dr., Nebo, NC 28761. Normal business hours. The Pisgah National Forest includes an arc of large mountainous tracts along the slopes and side ridges of the Blue Ridge, all along the northern edge of the Catawba Valley. The ranger station for these lands is a large building by Exit 90 off I-40, at Nebo. It contains a staffed visitors center with a full range of maps and pamphlets, as well as a small bookstore and exhibits on forestry.

GETTING THERE *By car*: **Interstate 40** runs up the center of the Catawba Valley for its entire length. With rugged mountains lining the valley's north and south edges, I-40 is the easiest approach no matter what direction you are coming from.

By bus: **Greyhound Bus Lines** (800-229-9424; www.greyhound.com) schedules daily service through the Catawba Valley, with stops in both Marion and Morganton, NC. Both of these towns have taxi services and car rentals; check with their visitors centers for details.

By air: **Hickory Regional Airport** (828-323-7408; www.ci.hickory.nc.us/airport/), 25 miles east of Morganton, NC, at the small Piedmont city of Hickory, NC, has five scheduled commuter flights a day from Charlotte, NC, via US Airways Express (fewer on weekends), with car rentals inside the terminal. The **Charlotte/Douglas International Airport** (704-359-4027; www.flycdia.com) is 75 miles from Morganton via four-lane highway.

MEDICAL EMERGENCIES **Grace Hospital** (828-438-2000), 2201 S. Sterling St., Morganton, NC. This major regional hospital, serving the eastern half of the Catawba Valley, is located by I-40, at the NC 18 exit.

The McDowell Hospital (828-659-5000), 100 Rankin Dr., Marion, NC. This fair-sized local hospital with 24/7 emergency room service sits by I-40 at Exit 81 (Sugar Hill Rd.), 3 miles south of Marion, convenient to the western half of the Catawba Valley.

✳ Wandering Around

EXPLORING BY CAR OR BICYCLE ✔ **The Swannanoa Grade**. *Note*: You can rent bicycles in Black Mountain, NC (see "Asheville & the Blue Ridge Parkway").

Leg 1: From Old Fort, NC, take US 70 west 0.25 mile to Old US 70 (SSR 1400); then right 2.5 miles to Mill Creek Rd. (SSR 1407); then right 5.25 miles to Old

US 70 (SSR 1400). Automobiles continue straight to Ridgecrest and I-40. *Leg 2 (bicycles only)*: Turn left as you regain Old US 70, at the white gate. Follow the concrete road, former US 70, now abandoned, downhill for 3.4 miles.

Built in the 1870s with convict labor, the steep railroad known as the Swannanoa Grade takes 10 miles to cover a distance that a crow could fly in just over 4. In doing so it climbs 1,000 feet in elevation, loops back on itself five times, and goes through seven tunnels with a total underground distance of three-quarters of a mile. More to the point, most of these engineering wonders (and the rugged scenery that brought them into existence) can be easily viewed by automobile-bound visitors—just as well, as there's been no passenger service on this line for half a century.

Start at downtown **Old Fort**, where two small museums give historic perspective—on pioneer life at the **Mountain Gateway Museum**, and on 19th-century railroading at the **Old Fort Railroad Museum**. After that, follow the signs westward to Andrews Geyser. You'll be on the former main highway as far as the classic CCC-built **Old Fort Picnic Area**, then up the pastoral Mill Creek valley as far as **Andrews Geyser**. The railroad built the "geyser" (a 30-foot fountain) to impress passengers disembarking at a resort hotel; passengers and hotel are long gone, but the geyser remains, kept in operation by dedicated local residents. It's placed in the center of three pigtail loops, and railroad enthusiasts will enjoy tracing the railroad on its mountain slope gyrations. From Andrews Geyser the road climbs the Blue Ridge as a good gravel lane through **Pisgah National Forest** lands. Attractive hardwood forests surround the road all the way up, except for a small orchard (privately owned) at the luxurious **Inn at Mill Creek**; the small pond behind the inn is the source of Andrews Geyser.

A bit farther you suddenly regain the old paved main highway, open to the right but gated to the left. The gated leftward road is **Old US 70**; a half-mile walk down its old concrete surface will lead to a series of four railroad tunnels, as well as a good view. From here, automobiles should complete the drive by following the old concrete road right to **Black Mountain** and I-40. Bicyclists, however, can follow the abandoned highway downhill for wonderful views and a close look at those railroad tunnels. The old highway circles back to the Old Fort Picnic Area.

EXPLORING ON FOOT **Waterfalls and views in the South Mountains**. The South Mountains offer a wide variety of first-rate walks and hikes; these two, each steep but short, lead to an 80-foot waterfall and a wide panorama. Both are reached from the **Jacobs Creek Picnic Area** within the **South Mountains State Park**, and are well signposted.

Start by following the signs to the **High Shoals Falls Trail**, a well-built waterfall walk that will take you on a 2-mile round trip with many, many steps. Go straight to the falls by taking the left fork of this loop trail—the one marked WARNING: STEEP AND RUGGED PATH. The path follows the violent little High Shoals Creek for a short distance, then turns suddenly and crosses an astonishing field of truck-sized boulders on a long, stepped boardwalk. Here the stream breaks up around the boulders, forming many small waterfalls. From this point up it's all steps, flight after flight, until you reach a large viewing platform at the base of 80-foot High Shoals Falls—where the powerful stream plunges straight down over a vertical gray cliff to a large, deep pool. The steps continue upward, hugging the cliffs near the falls, to reach the top, with a narrow view over the falls into the gorge. The loop trail continues on through second-growth forest; it's more fun to return the way you came, appreciating the fine cliff scenery from a leisurely descent.

If you still have the energy, take **Chestnut Knob Overlook Trail** on the way back for great views across a deep gorge to High Shoals Falls and beyond; you'll pass the trailhead on your return to the picnic area. This trail ascends the dry hemlock and pine forests of the steep south-facing slopes, climbing 1,000 feet in 2 miles to reach the wide clifftop views at Chestnut Knob. You'll reach the first view after a mile of uphill trudging—a fine view over the deep gorge of Jacobs Creek with High Shoals Falls clearly visible on the opposite side. From here the trail continues to ascend gently to the cliffs of Chestnut Knob. Here, more than anywhere else in North Carolina, you can see the end of the mountains, the sudden plunge to the Piedmont, and the endless plains of the Deep South. Return the way you came.

Table Rock walks on the Linville Gorge rim. Table Rock Picnic Area gives access to one of the most interesting and spectacular day hikes in the area, following the rocky, cliff-lined rim of the Linville Gorge. To the north, **Table Rock Trail** climbs steeply (500 feet in half a mile) up to the cliff-lined, flat-topped Table Rock, a remarkable mesalike formation protruding 600 feet above the trees of the surrounding ridge. The clifftops give a sweeping view over the entire gorge and the Blue Ridge beyond, as well as out over the Catawba Valley to the south.

The **Chimneys Trail** heads south along the rim to the rocky hoodoos known as the Chimneys. Much easier and only slightly longer (100 feet up in two-thirds of a mile), the path starts as a gentle ridgetop climb to an exposed rocky cliff with wide views, including one back toward Table Rock. From there the trail descends gently to a gap as the ridge becomes increasingly knifelike. More rocky cliffs give views over the gorge, with tall rock spires eroded along its top edge. The trail continues along the knife ridge to the top of the Chimney, a phallic spire towering above the rest. Return the way you came.

WISEMAN'S VIEW, LOOKING SOUTH DOWN LINVILLE GORGE.

Jim Hargan

✳ Villages

Morganton, NC. Founded in the late 1700s as the pioneer settlement of Morganborough, Morganton gained its prosperity as a furniture mill town in the 19th century. The mountain hardwood forests furnished the raw material, and the railroad shipped out the final product. This is still the arrangement—Morganton and its suburbs retains the corporate headquarters of major furniture manufacturers Henredon and Drexel Heritage. (Alas, neither has a public showroom.) Late-19th-century Morganton also gained major medical centers, and for similar reasons—good rail access, and proximity to the healthful air of the mountains. Today the late-19th-century campuses of the Broughton Hospital (a state psychiatric hospital) and the North Carolina School for the Deaf make up a large National Register Historic District, occupying the same hill on the south end of town. It's a gentle place of stately old buildings, wooded glades, and wide mountain views over grassy meadows.

Settled since the middle of the 18th century, Morganton has several worthwhile historic sites. The main attraction, however, is its downtown—a classic small-town main street, anchored by a lovely Courthouse Square, dominated by the square **Old Burke County Courthouse**. A good-quality shopping district, full of active, interesting stores and cafés, runs along the north side of the Courthouse Square, while two complexes of historic buildings are being renovated into more shops nearby. Parking is plentiful and free, with lots of street parking as well as large municipal lots behind the storefronts.

Marion, NC. This thriving county seat sits on an important railroad junction, where two major freight lines fight their separate ways up the face of the Blue Ridge. It centers on a four-block-long downtown of two-story brick storefronts from the late 19th century, and a golden brick 1920s courthouse faced with 12-foot windows. Downtown shops still center mainly on the old small-town standbys, well kept but lacking restoration. The little downtown has character, however, and improves a bit every year as projects such as the **Shamrock Inn** and **Eagle Hotel** restore the buildings one by one, filling them with interesting and worthwhile things.

Old Fort, NC. Nestled at the base of the Blue Ridge, Old Fort has been a working railroad town since the 1870s. Its large siding, where steam engines used to get a second "pusher" engine to help them up the mountain, has long attracted mills, and modern Old Fort has half a dozen or so clean factories. For a visitor, Old Fort is worthwhile for its two museums (one to pioneer life, another to the railroad) and its attractive little downtown. Downtown Old Fort sports a single block of 19th-century brick storefronts, a bright yellow depot containing the railroad museum, a tiny park with a gazebo, and a 25-foot-tall granite arrowhead set on a 15-foot stone plinth, erected in the 1920s as a memorial to frontier peace.

✳ Wild Places

THE GREAT FORESTS ♿ **Linville Gorge Wilderness**. One of the earliest wilderness areas created by Congress, this 11,000-acre tract preserves a deep, 13-mile-long gorge cut into the face of the Blue Ridge. The gorge starts with the massive 100-foot plunge of the Linville River over **Linville Falls**, then quickly drops away in near-vertical slopes to a river bottom that's a third of a mile below the gorge edge. The fierce river and steep slopes have prevented logging, leaving

☘ ✑ ⚲ **South Mountains State Park** (828-433-4772; fax 828-433-4778; www
.ils.unc.edu/parkproject/visit/somo/home.html), 3001 South Mountains State
Park Ave., Connelly Springs, NC. Located 20 miles south of I-40, Exit 104 (Enola
Rd.): Take Enola Rd. south for 9 miles to its end at Old NC 18, then go right 5
miles; large brown state park signs will guide you in for the remaining 6 miles.
Daylight, all year.

The 16,000-plus-acre South Mountains State Park occupies the rugged central heart of the South Mountains, an outlier of the Blue Ridge. With about 1,000
feet of valley-to-peak relief, the South Mountains are smaller than much of the
Blue Ridge—but they more than make up for it with rugged scenery. Streams
twist and dash through deep gorges; the sharp points of gray cliffs emerge from
deep forests; truck-sized boulders litter the bottoms of steep gulches; great
waterfalls plunge over cliff edges. The mixed forests are dominated by the hemlock, a conifer with pinelike bark and firlike needles that grows rapidly to great
sizes. On exposed cliffs, pines and hemlocks twist into bonsai shapes.

Heavily logged in the 20th century, South Mountains State Park is laced by
a network of slide roads (used to skid timber downhill), jeep trails, and even
automobile roads—nearly all now closed to vehicles. The best of these are
marked as bicycle and/or horse trails, while other paths are strictly for foot

A WATERFALL ON JACOBS FORK ALONG THE HIGH
SHOALS FALLS TRAIL.

travel. The rugged topography makes nearly all paths
difficult, but the short local
relief limits the pain. The
two most popular paths—
High Shoals Falls Trail and
**Chestnut Knob Overlook
Trail**—give breathtaking
(figuratively and literally)
climbs to a high cliff view
and an 80-foot waterfall.
Many other worthwhile
paths exist, some requiring
backpacking. The park
has an information desk
(which may close when
the rangers are busy elsewhere), two picnic areas,
and an equestrian camping
area. Free.

Jim Hargan

the gorge in pristine shape—a rich, riverside old-growth forest. Access to the gorge bottom is by footpaths that go straight down the gorge sides, making for an extremely difficult return. Even the riverside trail can be difficult, finding its way along the rough, rocky gorge bottom. Nevertheless, the gorge bottom is reasonably popular with day hikers, backpackers, and anglers. Fortunately for the less athletic, the gorge rims are easier to reach, and the finest viewpoint, **Wiseman's View**, is disabled accessible.

RECREATION AREAS 🐾 ✿ ♿ **The Catawba River Greenway in Morganton** (828-437-8863; fax 828-437-5264; www.ci.morganton.nc.us/html/greenway_in_ morganton.html), City Hall, 201 W. Meeting St., Morganton, NC. This City of Morganton park stretches along the south bank of the Catawba River for a mile, starting at Judges Barbeque. It's an easy, paved walk with plenty of views over the wide Catawba as it enters the Piedmont. The upstream terminus at Judges has ample parking and picnicking facilities, as well as a canoe launch and fishing docks.

PICNIC AREAS **Table Rock Picnic Area**. This small primitive picnic area sits in a handsome hardwood forest on the rim of the Linville Gorge Wilderness, between the rock pinnacles of Table Rock and the Chimneys. The drive into the picnic area is worthwhile in itself, and short hiking trails lead to stunning views.

Bark House Picnic Area. This small, attractive picnic area sits in a shady hardwood glade atop a small knob, an easy 6 miles south of the Blue Ridge Parkway on NC 181 in the Linville, NC, area. It's a lovely little place, with a low fee (free) that reflects its single pit toilet and water from a hand pump. Nearby, two short but steep hiking trails lead down into the gorgelike Upper Creek Valley to reach the large and beautiful **Upper Creek Falls**.

✿ ♿ **South Mountains picnic areas**. South Mountains State Park has two fine streamside picnic areas. **Jacobs Fork Picnic Area** sits beside the main parking lot, its dozen tables spread widely underneath tall hemlocks and rhododendrons. The first-rate **Hemlocks Nature Trail**, disabled accessible, starts in the picnic area and follows the banks of Jacobs Creek for about a third of a mile. Just beyond the end of the nature trail is the primitive **Shimmy Creek Picnic Area**, with no automobile access, toilets, or water.

Old Fort Picnic Area. This lovely national forest picnic area, on the back road to Andrews Geyser, offers streamside picnicking in an old CCC-style site. Tables sit under tall old trees, spaced well apart, with small stone walls and steps forming scenic accents. The entrance road furnishes

TABLE ROCK MOUNTAIN, SEEN FROM THE CLIFFS LINING THE CHIMNEYS TRAIL.
Jim Hargan

a wonderful view up Mill Creek Valley, past a quiet farming community, to the forested wall of the Blue Ridge.

✳ To See

BIG DAMMED LAKES ✐ **Lake James** (828-652-5047), Nebo, NC. Giant electric utility Duke Power created this huge reservoir at the foot of the Blue Ridge between Marion and Morganton, NC, by damming two separate watersheds—the Catawba River and the Linville River—and linking them with a canal. They actually needed three dams to do this, with the third preventing the combined impoundments from slipping into a side stream. Like all such lakes, Lake James provides lots of room for motorboat-based sports, and lots of public and private boat launches. One of these is at **Lake James State Park**, along with a number of short walking trails, a sandy beach, and a very good picnic area.

Sitting at the foot of the Blue Ridge, Lake James gives exceptional mountain views—particularly toward the cliff-lined mouth of the **Linville Gorge Wilderness**. The easternmost dam, known as **Bridgewater Dam**, gives the best shore views; from the top of this tall earthen dam, traversed by a paved state road, you can see the sweep of the Blue Ridge curving in front of you, from the Linville Gorge cliffs on your right to the mile-high peaks of the Black Mountains on your left. This is a first-rate sunset spot, especially when the air is still and the water glassy. To reach this spot, take NC 126 west out of Morganton for 9 miles, then head left at a fork onto N. Powerhouse Rd.; Bridgewater Dam is 3 miles farther on.

HISTORIC SITES ✐ ⊤ **The Old Burke County Courthouse** (828-437-4104), Morganton, NC. Year-round, Tue.–Fri. 10–4. The tiny old Burke County Courthouse sits at the center of downtown Morganton, on its nicely kept square, with its Civil War statue out front. It's a square structure whose outside stairs lead to grandly columned second-story porches, topped by an elaborate Victorian cupola. It's much older than its Victorian trim, however: It was built in 1837 as a simple, elegant Federal-style structure, and served as the summer seat of the North Carolina Supreme Court until the Civil War. Inside, the Historic Burke Foundation maintains a small historic museum with exhibits that change annually; the second floor

THE OLD BURKE COUNTY COURTHOUSE IS NOW A MUSEUM.

Jim Hargan

is taken up by a single 150-seat auditorium, where you can view a good slide presentation on Burke County history. Also in the building are the offices of the Historic Burke Foundation and the Travel and Tourism Commission, either of which will welcome your visit and your questions. Free.

⊤ **Quaker Meadows Plantation (The McDowell House)** (828-437-4104; fax 828-433-6715), 119 St. Mary's Church Rd., Morganton, NC. Take NC 181 for 4 miles northwest from Morganton's town center to the end of the four-lane, then turn right onto St. Mary's Church Rd. Apr.–Nov., Sun. 2–5; other times by appointment. The 1812 McDowell House sits on the 6 remaining acres of the vast Quaker Meadows Plantation. In colonial times the McDowells were leaders of the western settlers, and their plantation hosted the gathering of the Overmountain Men as they marched to meet the British forces at Kings Mountain. The restored McDowell House reveals the post-Revolutionary success of this early family. In this high-ceilinged two-story structure made of on-site red brick, the two front doors show a Pennsylvania Dutch influence (even though the McDowells were Scots-Irish). Despite encroaching urbanization, the house remains beautifully situated amid rolling lawns. The Historic Burke Foundation has carefully restored it to its 1812 appearance and rebuilt the detached kitchen, and is locating authentic period furnishings; an 1852 corncrib sits behind the house, awaiting its time. $3 adults, $1 students.

Morganton's National Historic Districts. Morganton has nine National Historic Districts listed on the National Register of Historic Places. This adds up to a lot of old buildings. However, it means more than this: A historic district preserves the look and feel of the past, and is an experience in itself. The **Historic Burke Foundation** (828-437-4104) has an excellent color brochure listing all nine districts and giving details of the major buildings in each one. It's a good way to get a deep insight into the way an American small town used to be.

✒ **Andrews Geyser**. Take US 70 west from Old Fort and follow the signs, first onto Old US 70, then up Mill Creek Rd. Built as part of the Swannanoa Grade railroad in the 1870s, Andrews Geyser shoots 30 feet up in the air continuously (that is, as long as it's turned on). The geyser, named for a railroad pioneer, sits in a small park surrounded by railroad; it's in the crook of a hairpin turn that the railroad makes as it climbs the face of the Blue Ridge. In the early days the geyser served as a scenic focal point for railroad passengers entering (or leaving) this spectacular mountain climb, an impressive sight as their train circled it. Today it's a historic artifact from a bygone era, kept in loving repair by locals such as innkeeper Jim Carillon of the **Inn on Mill Creek**; the lovely little lake that feeds the geyser is on the inn's property, and Jim is the one who turns the valve on and off daily. The geyser, shooting straight up in the middle of a pentagonal reflecting pond, is surrounded by shaded picnic tables. If you are lucky, a train will pass while you visit it, looping around you with half its cars coming toward you and the other half going away.

⊤ **Carson House** (828-724-4948), Pleasant Gardens, Old Fort, NC. On US 70 west of Marion, near the intersection with NC 80. May–Oct., Tue.–Sat. 10–5, Sun. 2–5; closed Mon. Nov.–Apr., open by appointment. Revolutionary War soldier and prominent North Carolina politician Col. John Carson built this large family home at the center of his plantation in 1790, an elaborate two-story farmhouse built of 12-inch walnut logs. Fifty years later his son modernized this sophisticated log home by covering it in clapboard and adding the wide first- and second-story porches with their Greek Revival trim. McDowell County was organized in the Carson House; it served as the new county's first courthouse; and the Carsons donated the site of the permanent county seat, Marion, 3 miles to the east (but still on the family plantation). Today the Carson House is an independent not-for-profit museum displaying pioneer objects and furnishings. $3 adults, $2 children.

↑ **The Albertus Ledbetter House** (877-738-9798 or 828-738-9798; fax 828-738-0485; www.springhousefarm.com), Chimney Rock, NC. Each Sat. at 2 PM, innkeepers Arthur and Zee Campbell of the Cottages at Spring House Farm open their private home, the 1836 Albertus Ledbetter House, to the public. It's definitely worth the 15-mile trip south from Marion, NC, to the remote, pastoral Hickorynut Mountains.

Jonathan Ledbetter built his original log cabin in 1826, then (10 years later) used post-and-beam construction to expand it into a two-story farmhouse. That expanded farmhouse, very little altered, is what you see today. Ledbetter, a prosperous farmer and local postmaster, built his house grandly with Greek Revival detailing, but still managed to follow Southern Appalachian traditions. Two rectangular, two-story "cribs"—each an independent structure with its own stairway—were separated by an open dogtrot, a wide hall open on both ends. Stone fireplaces were set in the gabled sides, while a wide porch ran along the long front of the house. A kitchen wing extended to the rear. Alterations in the 1940s enclosed the dogtrot to form more interior space and modernized the kitchen; otherwise the house is unaltered. Amazingly, this includes the original 1836 paint on the planked walls and dogtrot stairs. These elaborate paintings and stencilings combine with a hand-carved vine motif—a rare survival, signed and dated by artist Charles Dunkin. It also includes gunports in the attic gables, possibly used during the anarchy that gripped the Appalachian countryside during the Civil War. These features are set off by the Campbells' 36 locally made quilts, ranging from 50 to 120 years of age—discovered when they salvaged a nearby farmhouse, derelict and junk filled, for its historic timbers. $5 per person.

CULTURAL SITES Senator Sam J. Ervin, Jr. Library (828-438-6000; fax 828-438-6015; www.wp.cc.nc.us), 1001 Burkemont Ave., Western Piedmont Community College, Morganton, NC. Follow the signs from Exit 103 on I-40; once on campus, you'll find the library on the second floor of the Phifer Learning Resource Center. Parking is ample; no permit is needed. Mon.–Fri. 8–5. Those of us old enough to remember Watergate will no doubt recall the late Sen. Sam Ervin, chairman of the Nixon impeachment hearings, for his fairness, shrewdness, sharp intelligence, deep knowledge of the Constitution—and frequent protestations that he was "a simple country lawyer." Senator Sam was a Morganton man born and bred, and Western Piedmont Community College has commemorated its local-boy-made-good in a most appropriate way: by preserving his large personal library. The college has gone well beyond saving the senator's personal papers and 7,500 books. It has faithfully re-created his large, wood-paneled library, every piece of furniture the way the senator left it, every book it its original place on the shelf. Located in its own room within the college's library, the Ervin Library offers a window into a great mind. Free.

Apart from the Ervin Library, **Western Piedmont Community College** is itself worth a visit for its wide views and handsome campus. Crowning a hillock on the southwestern edge of town, its modern buildings form a tight group surrounded by wide meadows. To the north and east are views toward the 19th-century his-

THE OLD FORT RAILROAD DEPOT.

Jim Hargan

toric districts of Broughton Hospital and the North Carolina School for the Deaf, each facing the college with its own farmland and crowning its own hill with cupola-topped buildings. On the horizons are the silhouettes of the Blue Ridge and the South Mountains.

⊤ **Jailhouse Gallery (Burke Arts Council)** (828-433-7282), 115 Meeting St., Morganton, NC. Mon.–Fri. 10–4. No Old Courthouse Square would be complete without an Old Jail. Morganton's 1950s-era Andy-of-Mayberry-style sheriff's office and jail now houses an art museum dedicated to local and regional artists. Expect more than the traditional displays of small-town art students; home as it is to the national headquarters of major furniture manufacturers, Morganton is a serious venue where artists can get their work seen and appreciated by art-buying professionals. The thorough-going displays, professionally presented, wander through two good-sized galleries, while a third room houses a small gift shop. Displays change every 2 months, so it's always worthwhile to stop in for another look.

✒ ⊤ **The Mountain Gateway Museum** (828-668-9259). Located at the center of Old Fort, NC, this small state museum features exhibits on pioneer life and folk culture in a 1936 WPA building made of native stone. Permanent exhibits include mountain folk arts, a log cabin reconstructed from a pioneer church, and a reconstructed still; temporary exhibits, on a variety of topics, change every couple of months. Next door are two beautiful old log cabins, authentically furnished with period antiques.

✒ ⊤ **The Old Fort Railroad Museum**. The canary-yellow depot of Old Fort, NC, sits at the center of its single block downtown, the site of the town's 25-foot-tall granite arrowhead, a monument to frontier peace. Today the depot houses a small but charming railroad museum, with rooms furnished as a late-19th-century depot and exhibits on the dramatic Swannanoa Grade, 10 miles of railroad that loop up the face of the Blue Ridge just outside town.

MYSTERIOUS PHENOMENA The Brown Mountain Lights. Since 1900 (and perhaps earlier, according to local tales), mysterious lights have danced and flickered over the 2,725-foot peak of Brown Mountain, a side ridge off the Blue Ridge 13 miles north of Morganton, NC. Attempts to explain them have all failed, including train lights (they appear when trains don't run), auto headlights (no autos), and swamp gas (no swamps). Most of the remaining explanations involve ghosts in some way. So find a good viewpoint and a clear night, bring to mind your favorite campfire tale, and wait for the lights to come out. With luck, you can view the Brown Mountain Lights from **Wiseman's View** on the rim of Linville Gorge, and from overlooks along NC 181.

✳ To Do

BICYCLING Table Rock Bikes (800-358-2453 or 828-437-7959; fax 828-437-9184), 133 W. Union St., Morganton, NC. Mon.–Fri. 10–5:30. This downtown Morganton bike shop offers trail bike rentals, and has loads of information and help on local trails.

GOLD MINING ✍ **Thermal City Gold Mine** (828-286-3016; www.huntforgold .com), 5240 US 221 N., Union Mills, NC. Daylight hours, all year. The South Mountains, and the hills to their east, formed the site of America's first gold rush, when a 12-year-old boy picked up a 12-pound (yup, that's pounds, not ounces) gold nugget from a Piedmont creek. Within the South Mountains, gold was quickly found along the Second Broad River, 13 miles south of modern-day Marion (and 9 miles south of I-40) just off US 276. One of the first gold mines, the 1830 Thermal City Mine, is still in operation, under the ownership of the same family since 1890. Owner Lloyd Nanney offers recreational gold miners 30 acres of placer deposits along half a mile of the Second Broad River. (In a placer mine, gold dust and nuggets are washed from streamside sediments, not dug out of hard rock.) Panning is done with unsalted on-site deposits in an attractive riverside setting, for an authentic experience. Lloyd has an on-site snack bar and café, and sells a full line of gold mining equipment from a small store in the center of the mine. Serious gold bugs go for the three common digs held each year, where participants pay a $100 fee for 2 days of all-out collective prospecting, everyone splitting the take.

GOLF Silver Creek Plantation Golf Club (828-584-6911; www.silvercreek plantation.com), 4241 Plantation Dr., Morganton, NC. Open all year. This 18-hole, Tom Jackson–designed semiprivate course wanders along hilltops west of Morganton, with sweeping views toward the South Mountains and the Blue Ridge. Fairway Oaks Bed and Breakfast is located on this beautiful course, overlooking the 5th green (see *Lodging*). $19–31.

Pine Mountain Golf Course (828-433-4950), US 18, Connelley Springs, NC. This 18-hole Paul Mallard–designed course rests high in the South Mountains, adjacent to South Mountains State Park. Originally created as part of South Mountains Resort, this golf course with its wide and lovely views continues to thrive even as the resort business is being reorganized (and largely phased out).

Old Fort Golf Course (828-668-4256), Rt. 2, Old Fort, NC. Take Exit 73 (Old Fort) off I-40, then follow the signs south for 3 miles. This semiprivate nine-hole par-36 course, built in 1962, sits south of Old Fort in the rolling hills of the Catawba River Valley, with views toward the Hickorynut Mountains to the south. $12–16.

Marion Lake Golf Club (828-652-6232), US 126, Nebo, NC. This par-70 course, first opened in 1933, wanders along hilltops on the south side of Lake James, with stunning views over the water toward the cliffs of the Blue Ridge. $12 weekdays, $20 weekends.

✳ Lodging

BED & BREAKFAST INNS **Fairway Oaks Bed and Breakfast** (877-584-7611 or 828-584-7677; fax 828-584-8878; www.fairwayoaksbandb.com), 4640 Plantation Dr., Morganton, NC 28655. It only looks like a traditional southern farmhouse, with its wide wood porches and tall windows! Fairway Oaks was built as a four-room B&B inn in 1997. Set inside the gated golf community of Silver Creek Plantation 10 miles west of Morganton, this course-side inn has sweeping views over the links toward the majestic South Mountains. The guest lounge is warm and inviting, with hardwood accents, plush new furniture, and a gas log fireplace. Upstairs, each of the four sizable guest rooms is furnished around its own theme with antiques and reproductions, and has its own phone, dataport, and desk. Guests receive a discount on the semiprivate Silver Creek Plantation Golf Club. $65 per night, including full hot breakfast.

🐾 ♪ **College Street Inn** (828-430-8911), 2041/2 S. College St., Morganton, NC 28655. Located near downtown Morganton in the prestigious West Union Historic District, the four-room College Street Inn occupies a simple, well-kept cottage behind innkeepers Bill and Karen Pizzorni's bungalow. While the exterior may be simple, the inside is nothing less than a road warrior's Valhalla. Handsomely furnished with blond hardwood accents, the rooms are large, comfortable, and business-ready, with desks, phones, and dataports. The smallest room matches that of a good hotel; the largest room has a king bed, a full-sized executive desk, and a separate sitting area with two sofas and full-sized windows. Guests with business meetings can use the cottage's conference room, with its own private entrance, fax, computer, and large-screen TV/video player. Guests receive a hot breakfast in the large and comfortable common room, or can make up their own meals in the fully furnished guests' kitchen. The inn welcomes pleasure travelers as well as business travelers, and is a good choice for touring Morganton's handsome downtown and nine historic districts. $59–69, including breakfast.

The Inn at Old Fort (828-668-9384), 106 West Main St., Old Fort, NC 28762. This large 1880 farmhouse sits on a hill in the center of Old Fort, separated from the historic old depot by its own wide gardens. Simple by Victorian standards, the mountain home has a wide front porch with views over Old Fort, and high peaked gables front and side. Innkeepers Chuck and Debbie Aldridge have surrounded it with gardens—a five-tiered front garden, an English garden around a back deck, a cottage garden, vegetable garden, herb garden . . . Inside, the Aldridges have decorated the three rooms and a suite with Victorian antiques and themed bric-a-brac; hardwood floors (uneven from age) and 19th-century beadboard ceilings add character, as do odd angles from the many gables. Some rooms have shared baths. $50–70, including homemade continental breakfast.

The Shamrock Inn (828-652-5773; fax 828-659-8976), 28 Henderson St., Marion, NC 28752. Open all year. This downtown Marion B&B occupies a simple redbrick boardinghouse from the turn of the 20th century, a few steps down a side street. Outside it appears modest enough, its wide porch overlooking a well-kept front garden. Inside, it is elegantly furnished with antiques and art, with hardwood floors and trim, and hand stenciling rather than wallpaper decorating the walls. A ground-floor suite and four upstairs rooms are all individually themed and furnished with antiques. Gourmet breakfasts are served with crystal and silver. $85–150 a night, including full breakfast.

The Inn on Mill Creek (877-735-2964 or 828-668-1115; fax 828-668-8506; www.inn-on-mill-creek.com), P.O. Box 185, Ridgecrest, NC 28770. Leave I-40 at Ridgecrest (Exit 66) and follow the BED AND BREAKFAST signs east for 3 miles. Open all year. Innkeepers Jim and Aline Carillon have created this peaceful, beautiful haven deep within the Pisgah National Forest, the only home on a country lane that winds up the Blue Ridge through 9 miles of forestland. Beside the inn, a 1916 dam forms a small lake stocked with rainbow and brown trout; its outfall, through a pipe regulated by innkeeper Jim, feeds Andrews Geyser. Uphill, carefully trimmed fruit trees march in neat rows; Aline delights in making gourmet breakfasts from the fresh fruit. Old tracks radiate through the miles of public forest that cover the Blue Ridge slope in all directions—carefully mapped by Jim and perfect for exploring on foot or mountain bike. Jim will even arrange for rental mountain bikes to be delivered to your doorstep. Amazingly, despite all this remoteness, the historic little shopping village of Black Mountain is an easy 10-minute drive.

The home itself, a large modernist structure from the early 1980s, fits the site beautifully, its brown wood sides and high windows blending in with the surrounding forests. Common spaces are large yet comfortable, with the homey touch of two woodstoves and a library balcony. The four en suite rooms are exquisitely furnished with reproduction antiques in a country style; three of the rooms have four-poster beds. The smallest room, Orchard View, is larger than most hotel rooms (with 350 square feet), and the largest room, Lake View, is simply huge at 650 square feet, with broad windows overlooking the lake, a private screened balcony, and a bath with two showers and a Jacuzzi tub. Only slightly smaller is the Terrace Room, with a private terrace, fireplace, and private four-person hot tub. $90–160, including breakfast.

CABIN RENTALS ♪ **Robardajen Woods Bed and Breakfast** (828-584-3191), 5640 Robardajen Woods, Nebo, NC 28761. A 5-minute drive from I-40, halfway between Morganton and Marion, NC. Owner Bill Reep moves historic log cabins onto his large forested property near Lake James, rebuilds them, and renovates them to a high degree of comfort. The result is sort of a log cabin B&B; you stay in a historic pioneer log cabin, with a porch overlooking deep woods, then join the Reeps and the other guests for a fine country breakfast. Or make breakfast in your own cabin—they all have full, well-equipped kitchens. One cabin is a roomy two stories with a wood-burning fireplace and a wide front porch. Another, moved from a nearby mountain, has a billiard table and a library, as well as a porch overlooking the pool. In addition, the Reeps occasionally take guests into their personal home—a 1790 two-story log farmhouse from South Carolina with a stunning interior that meanders through five different levels. All cabins are furnished in country antiques, and have access to a swimming pool and an exercise room.

The Cottages at Spring House Farm (877-738-9798 or 828-738-9798; fax 828-738-0485; www.spring housefarm.com), P.O. Box 130, Chimney Rock, NC 28720. The cottages are located off Sugar Hill Rd. (SSR 1001), 12 miles south of exit 81 off I-40; ask for directions. Open all year. These four luxury log cabins share a wooded 92-acre farm in the Hickory-nut Mountains (part of the South Mountains), 15 miles south of Marion, NC. The 1836 Albertus Ledbetter House, a National Register property, is on the farm, the home of owners Arthur and Zee Campbell. All cabins are privately situated deep in the woods. All have private porch or deck, full-sized outdoor hot tub, and a wood-burning stone stove or fireplace. One boasts a view over a trout pond; another, a tree growing through its deck; a third, a bedroom that opens onto a large, airy porch. The Craftsman-style furniture is handmade locally from lumber salvaged from the Ledbetter House restoration; the massive king-sized beds are particularly impressive. Kitchens are fully furnished and stocked with milk, sausage, Zee's fresh-made bread, real butter, local jams, and brown eggs from a neighbor's farm. $200–265 per night; kitchens are fully provisioned for breakfast.

✳ Where to Eat

EATING OUT ❧ **Yiannis Restaurant** (828-430-8700), 112 West Union, Morganton, NC. Lunch and dinner daily. Greece-native Yianni brings a high degree of sophistication to this casual downtown storefront café. Behind the narrow storefront is a bright, sparkling space with hand-painted murals on white walls, hardwood floors and tables, and an original high ceiling. Behind this roomy main area is an old-fashioned counter, and behind that a flight of steps leads up to a glass-brick bar framed by great floor-to-ceiling windows; then up to a third level of seating, this quieter and more formal than the ground floor. The menu is large and eclectic, with traditional Greek recipes mixing with southern and American favorites, with still other items Yianni picked up from his stints in New York and Maryland (including fresh crabcakes). All dishes, from the simplest American fare to the subtlest European entrées, are made to order from fresh ingredients, and the flavors are delicate and wonderfully blended. Not surprisingly, this bright and airy restaurant has gained a broad audience in this sophisticated little mill town, with its appealing mix of simplicity and sophistication, quality and price. Most sandwiches are under $5; most dinners are under $10. Full bar.

✐ **Judges Barbeque** (828-433-5798), Greenlee Ford Rd., Morganton, NC. Year-round, daily 11–9. This large new restaurant sits on a remote, shaded spot on the south bank of the Catawba River, at the end of Greenlee Ford Rd., hard by the upstream terminus of the Catawba River Greenway. Inside it's an open, wood-paneled layout with hardwood tables and an exposed ceiling; its floor-to-ceiling windows give wide views over the Catawba River, as does its multilevel deck. It features a varied menu and imaginative daily specials, but here's all you really need to know: The barbeque is great. It's fresh made, slow-cooked, mild, smoky, tender, and moist, with just the right amount of crust—chopped pork, beef brisket, chicken, or ribs. They serve sauce on the side, not on the meat, and they make it themselves—a wonderfully spiced hot sauce and a sweeter mild sauce. The homemade sides include a wonderful cayenne-hot coleslaw made not with mayonnaise, but with the vinegar sauce they use to baste the meat (a North Carolina tradition, worthy of imitation elsewhere). The onion rings are also worthy of note—made fresh daily, thick cut, and sweet. If you order a sandwich they'll use a sourdough bun "made special for us by a lady in town," as a waitress put it. "She makes the pound cake, too. You should try it." Good advice. Sandwiches $4.75–5.95, barbeque dinners

$7.25–9.95, other dinners $8.95–13.95. Wine and beer.

✐ **D&B Café** (828-668-7786), 396 S. Railroad St., Old Fort, NC. Tue.–Fri. 9–4, Sat. 9–3; closed Sun. and Mon. Mom (Dee Russell) makes your food from scratch, and her daughter Brandy serves it up with a friendly smile in this delightful storefront café in Old Fort's tiny downtown. It's bright and cheerfully decorated; a table of today's newspapers and shelves of books and magazines invite you to linger. The menu lists all the old favorites of a traditional small-town café, to which Dee adds some more adventuresome specials—like a pork tenderloin, grilled and served over noodles with a bell pepper sauce. Dee makes a wide variety of desserts, all of them wonderful. Be sure to get a few fresh cookies to take with you. Breakfast $0.75–2.25, lunch $1.95–4.25.

The Crooked Door, Marion, NC. Wed.–Sat. 8 AM–10 PM. This attractive second-story coffee shop sits behind the arched windows of Marion's beautiful old Eagle Hotel, an 1895 three-story brick building on the north end of downtown. It features Italian and American coffees and homemade pastries, along with lots of old Victorian wood trim, a sofa'd sitting area by a fire, and good views over downtown.

Carolina Chocolatiers (828-652-4496), 8 N. Main St., Marion, NC. This sandwich- and dessert-oriented restaurant in downtown Marion occupies a restored corner of an old downtown building, with wide windows, handsome interior arches, and a tin ceiling painted shocking pink. They have a large range of deli-style sandwiches and grill items, and they make their own desserts. They also make fancy gift chocolates, a real temptation as you leave.

DINING OUT

King Street Café (828-437-4477), 207 S. King St., Morganton, NC. Wed.–Sat. 5–9. This elegant little café wanders through the ground floor of a small Victorian house in the South King Street Historic District, adjacent to downtown Morganton. Cozy and comfortable, it's a friendly place of quiet, happy conversation. The menu is varied and original. "We've been developing it one item at a time," states owner Margaret Plaomaki, "to make sure we get it right." Indeed, you don't expect a $15 liver entrée in most mill towns—but the King Street Café has two, one sautéed with apples and red onions, served with demiglaze, the other sautéed with mushrooms and onions in a brown sauce. Cornish game hen is served with dates, oranges, cinnamon, nutmeg, and garlic; quail is roasted with chanterelle mushrooms in a lingonberry sauce; chicken is married with shrimp, red bell peppers, and pineapple. Seafood has a special place in Malaysian chef Peter Chang's repertoire: trout, crab, salmon, shrimp, lobster, and sole blend with a variety of sauces, domestic and exotic. True native southerners, however, need have no fear of being overwhelmed by the unfamiliar—pork and steak entrées receive simple, classic treatment. The King Street Café has an intelligent selection of simple and sophisticated wines, $16–42 a bottle. Entrées typically $15–25.

✵ Entertainment

↑ **City of Morganton Municipal Auditorium (CoMMA)** (800-939-7469 or 828-433-7469; www.ci .morganton.nc.us), 410 S. College St., Morganton, NC. This handsome auditorium, larger and nicer than you might expect for a small town, sits on a hill above downtown, surrounded by the well-kept Victorian mansions of the South King Street Historic District. Their summertime Back Porch series features outdoor evening concerts with a picnic dinner. To find it, follow the signs for CoMMA. Back Porch events are $7.50. Other events vary, typically $10–45.

↑ **Old Fort Mountain Music**. Every Fri., from 7 PM until late at night. Old Fort Mountain Music shares space with Old Fort EMS in an old brick building at the center of town. On the one hand, it doesn't provide any on-site parking, as the EMS vehicles can't be blocked. (There's plenty of free parking within half a block, though.) On the other hand, the wide, empty EMS driveways provide a place for the musicians to tune up, practice, and talk. Inside, a long, narrow hall with folding chairs forms the venue for this free weekly mountain concert and jam session. Bands range from first-rate to enthusiastic, playing a variety of mountain music, bluegrass, and country—but the emphasis is on mountain music. Free.

✳ Selective Shopping

Morganton, NC

Downtown Morganton's Old Courthouse Square, well kept and handsomely landscaped in a traditional style, sits at the center of a four-block downtown of turn-of-the-20th-century two-story storefronts. It preserves the charm of a small-town center, its old buildings immaculately kept and filled with clothing stores, restaurants, and boutiques. Shopping is concentrated along Union St. (US Business 70) on the north side of the square. Traditional old storefronts stretch westward from the square; to the east sits the newly restored Morganton Trading Company, offering more specialty shops in a restored 19th-century mill complex that includes the city hall.

↑ **Studio XI** (828-433-0056; www .westerncarolinacenter.org/studioxi), 117 W. Union St. This unique art gallery serves as an outlet and studio for a group of artistically gifted individuals who are challenged by developmental disabilities. Walk into this gallery in the center of downtown, and you will be greeted by sophisticated art in the primitive style, with bold colors and designs and a strong point of view, by artists who exhibit nationally and internationally. Studio XI makes a fine anchor for Morganton's lively little downtown, occupying a Union Street storefront, near the Courthouse Square, surrounded by a variety of restaurants and shops.

Apple Hill Orchard and Cider Mill (828-437-1224), Appletree Lane. Take the Enola Rd. exit (Exit 104) from I-40 south for 4 miles, turning right onto Pleasant Hill Rd. at the large brick church. Business hours, Aug.–Christmas. This working apple orchard, located on the lower slopes of the South Mountains south of Morganton, has been producing apples since the 1930s. During the harvest season they open their orchard to the public and sell a variety of fresh-made apple products—including cider pressed on site. While the well-kept buildings are modern, the site and the orchard are very scenic.

South Mountain Crafts Village (828-433-2836; www.westerncarolina center.org/south_mountain_crafts.html)

409 Enola Rd. Take the Enola Rd. exit (Exit 104) off I-40, then go south a quarter mile. Mon.–Fri. 9–4. This unique craft shop features handmade crafts and furniture produced by the residents of Western Carolina Center, a large regional facility for the developmentally disabled. Founded in 1980, the Crafts Village occupies seven of a mile-long line of small, square wooden houses that face Enola Rd., built half a century ago as employee housing for the center. The Crafts Village exists to give training and work opportunities, and the skilled and original products found in its shop testify to its success. In it you'll find wooden craft items, pottery, weaving, candles, soaps, potpourri, quilts, early American pine furniture, and fine finished oak tables and chairs—all handmade on the premises. In-season, you may find fruits, vegetables, and flowers grown in the village's gardens and greenhouses—although the center's kitchens get first crack at the edibles.

Marion, NC
Marion's downtown spreads along four blocks, centered on a 1903 bank with a fake dome and a wonderful 1922 golden brick courthouse with 12-foot art deco windows. Downtown is busy and improving steadily, but is still recovering its shopping and architecture. Shops tend to be functional rather than funky, and all too many historic storefronts remain barnacled by "modernizing" facades from the 1950s and 1960s.

Old Fort, NC
Old Fort may well have the nicest one-block downtown in the mountains. A single row of one- and two-story turn-of-the-20th-century stores lines a block of US 70, anchored by

the old railroad depot and the giant arrowhead statue at its west end. Half of one side is taken up by a nice little park with a gazebo, while half of the other is occupied by Old Fort EMS and Mountain Music (mixed together in the same old brick building). There is just enough room remaining for three nice, largish shops of antiques, collectibles, memorabilia, and stuff, as well as D&B's Café. It's definitely worth poking around, particularly because it's next door to the Old Fort Railroad Museum and only two blocks from the Mountain Gateway Museum.

✳ Special Events

SPRING **Assault on Mount Mitchell**. Second weekend in May. Sponsored by Freewheelers of Spartanburg, a South Carolina bicycle club, this bicycle race goes from Spartanburg, SC, to the top of Mount Mitchell, NC. The 1,000 or so racers cover 100 miles of road and bicycle 11,000 feet uphill; the final stretch, from Marion to Mount Mitchell, climbs 6,700 feet in 27 miles.

SUMMER **Freedom Celebration and Rodeo**. Fourth of July weekend in Old Fort, NC. Old Fort Ruritans sponsor an old-fashioned cowboy rodeo as the main event in the town's celebration; there's also a parade and fireworks.

Historic Morganton Festival. Weekend after Labor Day. This large street fair in downtown Morganton, NC, features art and craft booths, food vendors, and live music.

AUTUMN **Mountain Glory Festival**. Second Sat. in Oct. This two-block-long street fair in downtown Marion, NC, features 100 booths with crafters, artists, and food vendors, plus live entertainment in front of the County Courthouse. It's held in association with a monthlong **Quilter's Show**.

WINTER **Appalachian Potters Market**, Marion, NC. First Sat. in Dec. Held annually at McDowell High School, this major regional market, open to the general public, is a serious meet between regional potters and their buyers. It draws 60 to 80 potters each year.

Asheville's Mountains 2

Jim Hargan

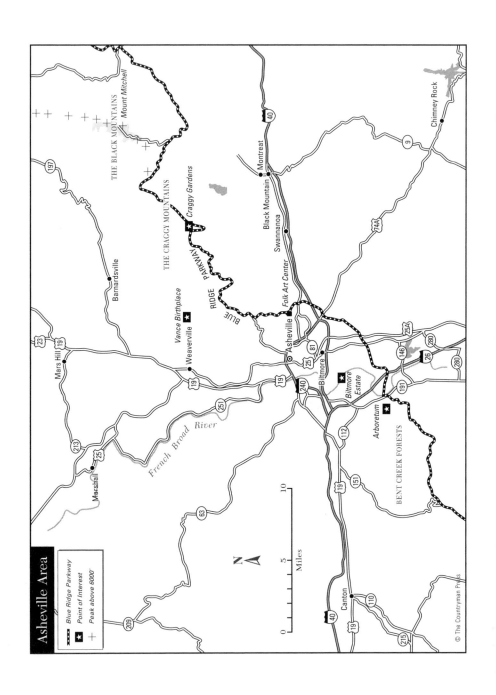

Asheville Area

Blue Ridge Parkway
Point of Interest
Peak above 6000'

Mars Hill
Marshall
Weaverville
Vance Birthplace
Barnardsville

THE BLACK MOUNTAINS
Mount Mitchell

THE CRAGGY MOUNTAINS
Craggy Gardens

BLUE RIDGE PARKWAY

Asheville
Folk Art Center
Biltmore
Biltmore Estate
Arboretum
BENT CREEK FORESTS

French Broad River

Swannanoa
Black Mountain
Montreat

Chimney Rock

Canton

N

Miles
0   5   10

© The Countryman Press

ASHEVILLE'S MOUNTAINS

The highest mountains in the East mark the point where the Blue Ridge enters the Asheville, NC, region. Here the Black Mountains extend a solid wall of 6,000-foot peaks northward, including Mount Mitchell, the highest mountain in the eastern United States. The Craggy Mountains, famous for their natural rhododendron gardens, merge with the Blacks just north of Asheville. The Blue Ridge Parkway hugs these high ridgelines, furnishing easy access to spectacular tracts of Pisgah National Forest land.

Despite this rugged beginning, one of the largest and gentlest valleys in the Smoky/Blue Ridge region forms behind the Blue Ridge—the valley of the French Broad River. A major tributary of the Tennessee, the French Broad River (like the geologically similar New River farther north) is one of the most ancient in North America, and perhaps the world. It twists sluggishly through a wide area, cutting through hard Blue Ridge rock like so much butter. It forms a natural path for transmountain roads and railroads, and the convergence of these roads forms the mountains' only city, Asheville.

The mountain's first stagecoach road, known as the Buncombe Turnpike, was constructed in the 1820s from Charleston, SC, to Asheville and down the French Broad into Tennessee. For decades it made much of its money from drovers, men who would drive hundreds of cattle, pigs, and even turkeys from mountain farms to markets in South Carolina. It quickly generated an unexpected industry, however: tourism. Rich South Carolina plantation owners would take their coaches up the turnpike to large summer estates in the cool mountains. The greatest of such early resort settlements was at Flat Rock, well established by the 1840s, but other great summer estates of the wealthy stretched along the Blue Ridge as far as Cashiers.

Asheville is surprisingly sophisticated for its size (fewer than 69,000 residents in 2000), with a large downtown that's both lively and historically fascinating. While its early tourism industry helped, much of its big-city air comes from its richest homeboy, George Vanderbilt, whose 1890 Biltmore Estate is now the region's premier tourist attraction outside the Great Smoky Mountains National Park. In the decades before World War I, society families flocked to Asheville to be near Vanderbilt, and society architects followed. A century later, Asheville remains a striking early-20th-century city, resplendent in Craftsman and art deco architecture.

AN APPLE ORCHARD IN SPRING BLOOM.

Jim Hargan

The Blue Ridge swings due south from Asheville, once again reverting to type with a rugged, steep eastern face and a gentle, hilly western face. In this area the gentle, western slopes are heavily planted in apple orchards, the subject of apple festivals, roadside stands, and u-pick-ems. The east face is particularly rugged, a gapless cliff that runs due south to South Carolina, then turns westward in a line so dramatic it's known as the Blue Wall.

Meanwhile, the mountains to the west of Asheville and the French Broad Valley rise in a confusing mass of mile-high peaks, carrying names like the Bald Mountains, the Newfound Mountains, the Pisgah Mountains, and the Great Balsam Mountains. The Blue Ridge Parkway leaves the actual Blue Ridge to climb into these high peaks, reaching a mile in elevation in the Pisgahs, then climbing above 6,000 feet in the rugged wilderness of the Great Balsam Mountains. From there, the Smokies are only a short distance away.

ASHEVILLE & THE BLUE RIDGE PARKWAY

A sheville sits behind the Blue Ridge in a huge bowl of a valley. The railroads converged here in the 19th century, followed by the interstates in the 20th. It's the major trade center for the entire mountain region.

You will find it surprisingly sophisticated, especially for a city of 68,000. It has a wonderfully retro downtown, a 60-block area with exuberant little buildings from the 1890s to the 1930s. During the day, shoppers fill a dozen or more shopping blocks lined with small, independent stores; at night, streets bustle as people explore the restaurant and music scene. Some of this sophistication is the natural result of being the only city for miles around. Much of it, however, springs from the influence of George Vanderbilt, who made Asheville his home in 1889 and constructed the spectacular Biltmore Estate, reputedly the largest private home in America.

Northeast of Asheville, the Great Craggy Mountains and the Black Mountains come together to form the highest mountain complex in the eastern United States. This amazing knot of mountains includes Mount Mitchell, at 6,684 feet the highest peak in the East. It also has the 2nd highest peak in the East (Mount Craig), as well as the 5th, 7th, 8th, 13th, 14th, 15th . . . well, honestly, it's hard to come up with an accurate count when 13 miles of near-continuous ridgeline tops 6,000 feet. Easily reached from the Blue Ridge Parkway, this high ridge provides stunning panoramas, deep forests, rough crags, and fields of wildflowers. The section of the Craggy–Black complex known as Craggy Gardens provides a large natural rhododendron garden with wide views; blooms peak in mid-June, with some color lingering into mid-July.

GUIDANCE Asheville Convention and Visitor's Bureau (800-257-1300 or 828-258-6101; fax 828-254-6054; www.ashevillechamber.org), P.O. Box 1010, Asheville, NC 28802. This chamber covers Asheville and the surrounding area. It runs a visitors center in downtown Asheville, just off I-240's Montford Avenue exit.

Asheville Bed and Breakfast Association (ABBA) (877-262-6867; www .ashevillebba.com). This association is made up of 16 small B&B inns, all of

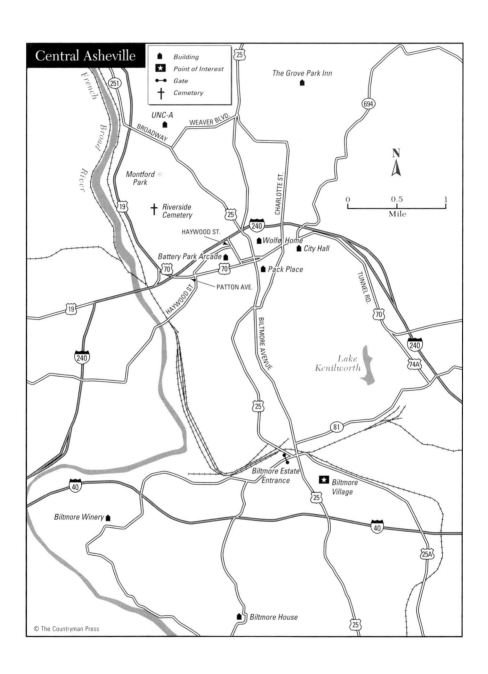

Central Asheville

Building
Point of Interest
Gate
Cemetery

25
The Grove Park Inn
694

251
UNC-A
WEAVER BLVD.
BROADWAY
CHARLOTTE ST.

N

0   0.5   1
Mile

Montford
Park

Riverside
Cemetery
25
240
Wolfe Home
City Hall
19
HAYWOOD ST.
Battery Park Arcade
70
70
Pack Place
TUNNEL RD.
70

HAYWOOD ST.
PATTON AVE.
19
240
74A

BILTMORE AVENUE
Lake
Kenilworth

240
25

81

40
Biltmore Estate
Entrance
Biltmore
Village
25
Biltmore Winery
40
25A

© The Countryman Press
Biltmore House
25

French Broad River

them in private homes located in quiet neighborhoods in and around Asheville. You can use either their web site or the toll-free number to find and reserve the room that's right for you.

Black Mountain/Swannanoa Chamber of Commerce (800-669-2301; www
.blackmountain.org), 201 E. State St., Black Mountain, NC 28711. This chamber runs a visitors center out of a small storefront in the town of Black Mountain, a short distance east of downtown on US 70. It covers the four towns on the uphill side of the Blue Ridge's Swannanoa Gap—Black Mountain, Swannanoa, Ridgecrest, and Montreat, NC.

Pisgah National Forest (828-257-4202; www.cs.unca.edu/nfsnc/), P.O. Box 2750, 160A Zillicoa St., Asheville, NC 28802. The headquarters for all the national forests in North Carolina is located in Asheville, off the US 19/23 freeway (future I-26); take the NC 251 exit and follow the signs. They maintain an information desk and bookstore, and—like all national forest stations—are more than happy to help you. Hikers take note: This office sells USGS topographic maps overprinted with current trail data.

GETTING THERE *By car*: Asheville is located at the intersection of **I-26** and **I-40**. Downtown Asheville is several miles north of I-40 via a spur, **I-240**. I-40 is one of America's major east–west interstates; the recently extended I-26 now runs northward from South Carolina, through Asheville, to end at I-81 in Tennessee.

By air: **Asheville Regional Airport** (828-684-2226; fax 828-684-3404), 708 Airport Rd., Fletcher, NC. Asheville's small regional airport is located 15 miles south of downtown off I-26, Exit 9 (NC 280).This lovely little airport is virtually unchanged since the 1950s—a low, rambling, white concrete structure with orange stripes, its boarding gates rambling outward from a central lobby. Despite its old-fashioned appearance, it has daily service from Atlanta, Cincinnati, Pittsburgh, Raleigh, and Charlotte, with 20 to 25 flights daily. Several car rental agencies are located within or near the airport.

By bus: **Greyhound Bus Lines** (828-253-8451; www.greyhound.com), 2 Tunnel Rd., Asheville, NC. Asheville is served by Greyhound, with several arrivals each day. The terminal is located a mile east of downtown on US 70.

MEDICAL EMERGENCIES **Mission St. Josephs Hospital** (828-213-1111; www.msj.org), 509 Biltmore Ave., Asheville, NC. This major hospital complex has a huge campus south of downtown Asheville, straddling Biltmore Ave. Its Class II trauma center (the only one in western North Carolina) is a left turn as you go south on Biltmore, into the St. Joseph's Hospital area of the campus. You might want to call for directions.

✳ Wandering Around

EXPLORING BY CAR **The Blue Ridge Parkway**. *Leg 1:* Start at NC 80. Follow the Blue Ridge Parkway 37.8 miles to US 70. *Leg 2:* From US 70 outside Asheville, NC, follow the Blue Ridge Parkway 11 miles to NC 191. *Leg 3:* From NC 191, take the Blue Ridge Parkway 11.7 miles to NC 151.

The first leg follows the **Blue Ridge crest**, climbing uphill through increasingly rugged country. The road breaks out of the forest on both sides for frequent views; **Mount Mitchell**, the highest point in the East, can be clearly seen on the right, distinguishable by its tower. In 9.25 miles the parkway leaves the Blue Ridge forever; at **Pinnacle Bald** the Blue Ridge heads south into South Carolina and Georgia, and the parkway climbs northward into the Black Mountains. In 10.2 miles from NC 80, the Mount Mitchell Spur Rd. heads 4.5 miles right to wonderful views from the highest point anywhere east of the Rockies. The parkway continues through high spruce–fir forests and frequent views to **Craggy Gardens**, covered in purple rhododendron blossoms in June. From here the parkway descends from its mile-high perch, passing the **Folk Arts Center** right before the end of Leg 1.

The second leg bypasses Asheville on a series of low mountains (or high hills), a forested section with few views. You'll pass the **Blue Ridge Parkway Headquarters Building**, opened in 2001, in 1.5 miles, with an exit onto US 74A, I-40, and I-240 just beyond. In 4 more miles (after the US 23 exit) the parkway passes through the Biltmore Estate, but with no special views until it reaches the French Broad River and NC 191 in another 4.5 miles. The entrance to the **North Carolina Arboretum** is on this exit ramp.

From here, the third leg climbs steadily away from Asheville and into the wilderness. The views start immediately, over the gorge of the French Broad River; look carefully for the **Biltmore House**. In 6.5 miles, gravel Bent Creek Rd. gives access to **Lake Powhatan Recreation Area**. A series of tunnels brings you above 4,000 feet as you approach the NC 151 exit. Ahead are the **Pisgah Mountains** and the **Great Balsam Mountains**, the grand finale of the parkway. NC 151 provides a beautiful drive back to Asheville.

EXPLORING ON FOOT **Downtown Asheville Urban Trail** (828-259-5855; fax 828-259-5832; www.ci.asheville.nc.us/Asheville/parksrec/urban.htm), Asheville, NC. This 1.6-mile loop is not your ordinary downtown historic walk. A City of Asheville public art project, the Urban Trail marks each of its 30 interpretive stations with a unique work of art. Some are solemn historic statuary with explanatory plaques, such as the monument to Elizabeth Blackwell, MD, the Ashevillian who became the first American woman to get a medical degree. The most notable pieces, however, are whimsical tributes to Asheville's past. A little girl drinks from a fountain in City Hall Plaza; author Thomas Wolfe's size 13 shoes

WOOD FENCING ALONG THE BLUE RIDGE PARKWAY.

Jim Hargan

sit outside his mother's boarding-house; a giant flat iron, accurately reproducing one used in downtown's Asheville Laundry, stands in front of the Flat Iron Building. You might sit down on a bench to rest a spell, only to find yourself beside a bronze fiddle, a bag of apples, or a little boy; or facing dancers swirling to mountain music. Historic buildings, never completed due to timidity, rise in the glorious form imagined by their architects.

✳ Villages

Asheville, NC. Until 1889 Asheville was just another mountain town, a bit larger and more prosperous than most. By then, several rail lines had converged upon Asheville, guaranteeing its future success (at least in comparison to its neighbors). Convenient rail connections gave Asheville more than its share of the emerging mountain tourism market; from this, Asheville gained a couple of truly spectacular hotels (now, alas, gone), which in their turn attracted a more highfalutin clientele. One of these society high rollers was George Vanderbilt, grandson of the railroad magnate, who visited an Asheville hotel in 1888. A year later he returned, buying up over 100,000 acres and creating a grand baronial estate for himself.

CITY HALL PLAZA IN ASHEVILLE.   Jim Hargan

What followed Vanderbilt and his Biltmore Estate wasn't just more tourism—it was a cultural upheaval. Vanderbilt caused part of this directly and intentionally. Unhappy with the way American loggers destroyed their forests, Vanderbilt brought Gifford Pinchot (a German-trained forester, born in America) to his estate to develop European-style forestry and teach forest conservation to the locals. He founded a model village, Biltmore Village, to provide humane and comfortable housing and stores for his workers. He started craft schools and built a cultural center for his African American workers. All these efforts may have fallen short of turning a raw southern town into a sophisticated and diverse European settlement, but they certainly had their effect. Vanderbilt's indirect impact was even more important. He brought America's greatest society architect, Richard Morris Hunt, to Asheville, along with America's greatest landscape planner, Frederick Law Olmsted. Hunt, in turn, hired the immensely talented Douglas D. Ellington as his chief assistant. Hunt, Ellington, and Olmsted all received local commissions, many from socialites attracted to Asheville by the presence of the Vanderbilts. Asheville was raw no more.

In the 1920s Asheville's blossoming attracted investors—including land speculators looking for the next Florida. After 1925, land prices soared and building boomed, and the 1926 collapse of the Florida Land Boom only seemed to bring more land speculators to Asheville. Author Thomas Wolfe publicly ridiculed the speculators—and privately advised his mother (who ran an Asheville boarding-house) to buy more land on credit. Asheville's bubble burst in November 1930, leaving a 60-block downtown so vastly overbuilt that its gorgeous Land Boom architecture remained largely unviolated 70 years later. Careful land-use planning, instituted in the 1990s, has kept it that way, allowing the beautiful old buildings to slowly fill with wonderful small shops.

Black Mountain, NC. The village of Black Mountain sits in a high-mountain valley 15 miles east of Asheville, just off I-40. Located just below Swannanoa Gap on the Blue Ridge, it has historically been a major entry point to the western mountains—first by wagon road, then by the Swannanoa Grade railroad. Today you will find it a handsome small town. Its lively downtown fills two blocks with old brick-front stores, now filled with antiques shops, gift shops, and restaurants, anchored by its historic train depot, now an important regional craft gallery.

Weaverville, NC. Located on the north edge of Asheville's urban area, Weaverville has managed to retain its small-town look and feel. Its one-block-long downtown lines the former US 19 with nice old brick-front stores; its handsome residential districts, with houses dating to the 1840s, host several nice B&B inns that offer a small-town ambience within an easy drive of downtown Asheville.

Barnardsville, NC. This remote village (pronounced *BAR-nurds-vill*), sits along NC 197 well north of Asheville, under the shadow of the Craggy Mountains. It has a recognizable center, but is mainly noted as a gateway to the Pisgah National Forest's extensive and spectacular holdings in the Craggies. You will find the turnoff to Barnardsville well signposted on the US 19/23 freeway 14 miles north of Asheville, then 6 miles east on NC 197. To reach the Pisgah Forest lands, take Dillingham Rd. (SSR 2173) south from the village center—an attractive drive with some lovely surprises.

✳ Wild Places

THE GREAT FORESTS **Mount Mitchell and the Black Mountains**. Quite simply, this is the highest mountain range in the East. In the mid–19th century New Englanders were astonished to learn that Mount Mitchell, the tallest of the Blacks at 6,682 feet, was taller than New Hampshire's impressive Mount Washington (6,288 feet). By the end of that century, people knew that eight Black Mountain peaks topped Mount Washington, and the entire ridgeline stayed above 6,000 feet almost continuously for 13 miles.

The Black Mountains and the Craggy Mountains run together at **Balsam Gap**—a beautiful 22.7-mile drive north of Asheville's US 70 on the Blue Ridge Parkway. The parkway parallels the **Black Mountain crest** for the next 4.6 miles to the Mount Mitchell Spur Rd., NC 128, on the left. This spur road then parallels the crest for 4.8 miles, finally reaching 6,500 feet at a parking lot a quarter mile below Mount Mitchell. A short, easy path leads a quarter mile to the peak, with spectacular views. A hiking trail, made difficult by craggy, boulder-strewn terrain, continues along the crest of the Blacks to its end.

The Craggy Mountains. Rising from the northeast edge of Asheville, NC, the aptly named Great Craggy Mountains quickly reach above a mile in elevation, with the tallest peak topping 6,000 feet. The highest peaks are characterized by sharp crags and thick heath balds—a beautiful but impenetrable combination of rhododendron, mountain laurel, azalea, and blueberry. The most beautiful peak is **Craggy Gardens**, where the thick heath is broken by wide areas of grassy meadows and wildflowers, for wide views framed by deep purple rhododendrons. The Blue Ridge Parkway traverses the high gaps of the Craggies, passing above a mile in elevation in 17 miles from Asheville's US 70—on a hot summer day, an easy and most pleasant drive. It gives easy access to the **Mountains-to-Sea Trail**, running along ridgetops previously too thickly grown with heath to be accessible, now giving wide views from rock ledges. The western slopes of the Craggies are mainly owned by the Pisgah National Forest and have a large number of fascinating hiking trails as well as several gravel forest roads well worth exploring with a high-clearance vehicle; access is mainly from Barnardsville, NC. The east slope, wild and stunningly beautiful, is the Asheville watershed and closed to the public.

The Bent Creek Forests (828-667-5261; fax 828-667-9097; www.srs.fs.fed.us/bentcreek/index.html), 1577 Brevard Rd., Asheville, NC. This tract of the Pisgah National Forest, on the southwest edge of Asheville, centers on the watershed of Bent Creek, a 6,000-acre bowl surrounded by 3,500-foot ridgelines. George Vanderbilt consolidated this tract in 1909 from 70-odd small farms and homes, because it linked his estate with his huge Pisgah Forest holdings, and because it was in the middle of the view from his terrace. Seven years later, his widow sold it to the Forest Service for $5 an acre. Since 1925, the bulk of this land, including

THE ROADSIDE VIEW TOWARD MOUNT MITCHELL FROM LICKLOG RIDGE OVERLOOK (MP 349).

Jim Hargan

all of the Bent Creek watershed, has been managed as the **Bent Creek Experimental Forest**. At first the forest was dedicated to experiments in regrowing healthy hardwood forests on devastated lands, but since World War II the experiments have concentrated on managing mountain hardwood forests for their logging resources. For the last 75 years, most of these experiments have included systematically altering small forest areas and measuring the difference, creating a patchwork of forest scenery. Two large tracts have been carved out of the experimental forest for recreational users: the **North Carolina State Arboretum** and the **Lake Powhatan Recreation Area**. A network of trails wanders through all parts of the forest, most of them open to mountain bikes and horses as well as walkers. Ready accessibility and relatively easy gradients make this a popular area. Free.

RECREATION AREAS **Lake Powhatan Recreation Area**. This Pisgah National Forest recreation area sits just outside Asheville, NC, off NC 191, in the Bent Creek Experimental Forest. It has a large lake with a swimming beach, picnicking, and camping. A large network of hiking trails, very popular with Ashevillians, spreads throughout the surrounding hills, and an easy gravel road leads uphill to the Blue Ridge Parkway.

PICNIC AREAS **Lake Tomahawk Park**, Black Mountain, NC. This town park, located in a Black Mountain neighborhood, centers on a lovely little lake surrounded by a walking path. As well as picnicking, you will find tennis, golf, a swimming pool, and croquet. Lake Tomahawk is the venue for Black Mountain's "Park Rhythms" summer music series.

Montford City Park. This attractive city park has a gardenlike appearance—well kept, deeply shaded, and climbing a steep hill in stone terraces. A full-service recreational park, it's located on Montford Avenue about a mile north of downtown Asheville, NC.

✳ To See

ALONG THE BLUE RIDGE PARKWAY **Mount Mitchell State Park** (828-675-4611; www.ils.unc.edu/parkproject/momi.html), Burnsville, NC. Summer 8 AM–9 PM. Closes earlier at other times of the year. This 1,700-acre state park centers on the highest peak in the East—6,684-foot Mount Mitchell, more than 1.25 miles above sea level. The park stretches along the high ridgeline of the **Black Mountains**, with three other 6,000-foot peaks in its 2.5-mile length. The remainder of the Blacks are largely owned by the Pisgah National Forest, with a large chunk of the western slopes in private hands. A spur road runs from the Blue Ridge Parkway to the park, a 2.5-mile drive through Pisgah Forest lands, just below the crest of the Black Mountain (and beneath two more 6,000-foot peaks). At the park entrance the road passes above 6,000 feet with wide meadow views, and stays above 6,000 feet to its end on Mount Mitchell. The road continues to climb along the Black Mountain crest, through subarctic spruce–fir forests, reaching 6,200 feet at the **Mount Mitchell State Park Restaurant** in 1.25 miles (see *Eating Out*). Beyond, the road slabs up Mount Mitchell to gain the ridge again at 6,400 feet, with some good road-side views. From there it passes 250 feet beneath the peak of Mount Mitchell to end on the ridgeline a bit downhill from the summit. Here you will find plenty of parking, a first-rate picnic area, a snack bar, and a small visitors center. Expect it to be cold and blowy, even in summer. The wide, easy path to the summit passes through forests and wildflower meadows to reach the peak in a quarter mile, after climbing 125 feet. A contemporary-style concrete tower allows you to climb above the trees for a 360° view, with the entire eastern United States beneath your feet.

Jim Hargan

LATE-SPRING RHODODENDRONS IN THE CRAGGIES.

Mount Mitchell is the high point of the dramatic and rugged Black Mountain, 15 miles of high crest named for the dark spruce–fir forest that covers its highest slopes. Eighty percent of the Black Mountain crest exceeds 6,000 feet in elevation, with 10 peaks officially listed as 6'ers. Six of these string out northward from Mount Mitchell, along the rough and difficult ridgeline trail that starts at the picnic area. The first is **Mount Craig**, at 6,647 feet the second highest peak in the East and a popular day hike. Beyond is **Balsam Cone** (ranked 5th at 6,611 feet), near the northern edge of the park; then, in the Pisgah National Forest, are **Potato Hill** (6,475 feet, 8th), **Winter Star Mountain** (6,212 feet, 24th), **Gibbs Mountain** (6,224 feet, 21st), and **Celo Knob** (6,327 feet, 14th). The difficult hike out to Celo Knob, passing over extremely rough ground, is usually done as an overnighter. At the other end, **Mount Hallback** (6,329 feet, 15th) rises above the entrance gate, with an easy trail from the ranger station. Just outside the park gate, in the Pisgah National Forest, is **Mount Gibbes** (6,571 feet, 7th), the official summit in a collection of three peaks. The final Black Mountain 6'er, **Blackstock Knob** (6,359 feet, 13th), is 2 miles west of Mount Gibbes, near the Blue Ridge Parkway. Free.

Craggy Gardens (www.nps.gov/blri/craggy.htm). This recreation area on the Blue Ridge Parkway takes in the three highest peaks of the Craggy Mountains: **Craggy Dome** (6,080 feet, ranked 30th in the East), **Craggy Pinnacle**, and **Craggy Gardens**. Views are great—but there is more here than views from high mountains. Each June, the Craggies have one of the finest rhododendron displays in the mountains.

Driving up the parkway from Asheville, NC, you enter the Craggies at **Potato Field Gap**, MP 368, with views left over the Town of Woodfin's watershed. In half a mile, a paved spur road leads left 1.25 miles to **Craggy Gardens Picnic Area**, a lovely tree-shaded meadow. This is the lower end of the **Craggy Gardens Trail**, climbing 400 feet in half a mile to Craggy Gardens, a stunning natural rhododendron garden. Craggy Gardens mixes clumps of June-flowering heath shrubs with expanses of grassy meadows. The grassy meadows give wide views over lush displays of perennial flowers, framed in June and July by the wild displays from the heath clumps—huge mounds of purple Catawba rhododendrons, mixed with rosebay rhododendrons, flame azaleas, blueberries, and mountain laurels.

Back at the parkway, the road curves wide past Craggy Gardens, out of its view on a breathtaking ledge. In 3 miles the road reaches **Pinnacle Gap**, with wide views in both directions. Here a tiny visitors center has several exhibits about the Craggy Mountains and a gift shop. Here, too, is the uphill end of the Craggy Gardens Trail. From here Catawba rhododendrons line the parkway and frame changing views over the Asheville watershed. The **Craggy Pinnacle Overlook** is half a mile from the visitors center, with wide views that improve dramatically as you walk up the easy path to the rhododendron-covered summit.

 ♢ ☙ **The Folk Art Center and Allenstand Craft Shop** (828-298-7928; fax 828-298-7962; www.southernhighlandguild.org/folkart.html), MP 382, Blue Ridge Parkway, Asheville, NC. Daily 9–6 (Jan.–Mar., 9–5). Founded in 1930 to help poor mountain folk refine their craft skills and find markets for their crafts, the **Southern Highland Craft Guild (SHCG)** has evolved into an juried membership organization of craft artists from a large area centered on the Southern Appalachian Mountains. In the 1970s the National Park Service collaborated with the SHCG to provide a facility to interpret Southern Appalachian mountain culture on the Blue Ridge Parkway. To achieve this, the NPS built the present Folk Art Center, a large building on the Blue Ridge Parkway just north of US 70, and turned it over the SHCG. The Craft Guild has utilized this building by moving their Allenstand Craft Shop into it from downtown Asheville, and by installing a medium-sized gallery in an upstairs mezzanine. Although the gallery features items from the guild's collection of 3,500 mountain craft pieces, for the most part it displays contemporary art by its current members, with university-trained fine artists far outnumbering native mountain folk crafters. Free.

♞ ∙ ♢ **The North Carolina State Arboretum** (828-665-2492; fax 828-665-2371; www.ncarboretum.org), 100 Frederick Law Olmsted Way, Asheville, NC. Gardens open daily 8 AM–9 PM; buildings may keep shorter hours. Founded in 1992, this 426-acre arboretum has elaborate formal and informal gardens, greenhouses, educational programs, and miles of walking paths. As an arboretum (and part of the University of North Carolina), it is dedicated to conserving native plant resources and educating the public.

TULIPS BLOOM OUTSIDE THE VISITORS EDUCATION CENTER AT THE NORTH CAROLINA STATE ARBORETUM.

Jim Hargan

Beyond that, it's darned pretty, even though (at 15 years old) few of the gardens
are mature, and some haven't been built yet. The entrance drive, off the Blue
Ridge Parkway at the NC 191 exit, is spectacular—beautifully landscaped in an
unobtrusive style that blends in with the native habitats, including a viaduct over
a delicate stream environment. The handsome main building, of stone and gray
wood, combines contemporary architecture with such homey touches as a large
porch with rocking chairs; beyond its information desk, this main building mainly
contains classrooms and offices. Outside stretches a series of contemporary formal gardens, designed by the original architect and rather severe and intellectual. More successful is the informal garden beneath the porch and stretching
down the mountainside. Known as "Plants of Promise" (or POP), it contains a
riot of native garden plants, both showy and practical, in a setting designed by
the arboretum staff and maintained with home garden equipment and methods.
Behind the main building are the greenhouses, now the source of nearly all the
seasonal and potted plants in the arboretum, and an active participant in the
campaign to conserve rare and endangered native species. Paths stretch downhill
through forests to reach Bent Creek, where an old road has been converted to a
walking and biking path. Along the creek are more gardens, both existing and
planned. The most interesting for a May visit is the **National Azalea Repository**, containing all but two of the native American azalea species. Free.

THE BILTMORE ESTATE The Biltmore Estate (800-543-2961 or 828-255-3400;
fax 828-255-1139; www.biltmore.com), 1 N. Pack Square, Asheville, NC. Located on US 25, a quarter mile north of I 40, Exit 50; administrative offices are
in downtown Asheville. Open daily, Jan.–Mar. 9–5, Apr.–Dec. 8:30–5. Locations
within the estate may have different hours. In 1889, 28-year-old George Vanderbilt decided to become a medieval nobleman. The grandson of railroad tycoon
Cornelius Vanderbilt, George was a sensitive and intellectual young man who
left the coarse work of running the family enterprises to his older brothers. Like
many of the Victorian aristocracy, he looked back on medieval Europe as a
happy, stable society where the laboring classes found satisfaction through fine
craftsmanship while the nobility watched over all with fatherly concern. Vanderbilt wanted to create such a society with himself as the nobleman, and chose
Asheville as the site.

George Vanderbilt had discovered Asheville on his many travels. He loved the
mild climate and the scenic beauty, and appreciated the advantages of forming a
great estate from cheap Appalachian land. And Vanderbilt had a very large estate
in mind. Before he was done he had purchased 125,000 acres—nearly 200
square miles stretching from the southern edge of Asheville to the Pisgah Mountains on the far horizon. He then assembled a remarkable team of experts to
convert this tired-out land into a noble demesne: leading architect Richard Morris Hunt to design the house; Frederick Law Olmsted, the designer of Central
Park and the U.S. Capitol grounds, to design the gardens and develop a management plan; and America's first forester, Gifford Pinchot, to restore and manage
100,000 acres of logged-out forest (see The Cradle of Forestry in "Hendersonville & Brevard"). He had Hunt build the largest house in America, a 250-room

French château, and emparked this house with several hundred acres of Olmsted's gardens. Beyond the gardens he laid out 1,000 acres of farmland and dairy to establish the self-sufficiency of a great medieval estate. He built a medieval village at the estate gates, today's **Biltmore Village**, to provide his workers with housing and shops.

After George Vanderbilt's death in 1914, his wife continued to live on the estate and manage its farms and forests, becoming the first woman president of North Carolina's agricultural society. Being more of a practical manager than a medieval baroness, she sold 87,000 acres of forest to the U.S. Department of Agriculture (run by her husband's old employee Gifford Pinchot), to form the nucleus of the **Pisgah National Forest**. She sold off Biltmore Village and other holdings as well, shrinking the estate to a mere 11,000 acres. When she remarried and moved north, her daughter and son-in-law, Cornelia and John Cecil, continued to live in Biltmore, opening it to the public in 1930.

The Vanderbilt heirs ceased living at Biltmore in 1958, but have continued to run it as a self-sufficient estate; it is now owned by John and Cornelia's son and grandson, who run it as a profit-making, taxpaying enterprise. Currently possessing 8,000 acres, the estate continues its extensive farming and forestry operations as well as a distinguished winery and vineyard. But the core of the estate remains the house and gardens, carefully preserved and restored to reflect the way it looked to George and Edith Vanderbilt, an Appalachian lord and lady at the height of the Gilded Age.

One-day admission to the grounds, house, and winery costs $29.95 for adults, $22.50 for ages 10–15; children nine and younger are free with a paying adult. A second consecutive day is $7. An annual pass costs less than 2 nonconsecutive days.

&. **The Biltmore House**, Asheville, NC. Daily 9–5:30. Famed architect Richard Morris Hunt personally supervised the construction of this 250-room French château from 1889 to 1895, and helped its owner, George Vanderbilt, pick out the furniture in a series of European buying sprees. Today, still fully furnished as in Vanderbilt's day and immaculately preserved by his heirs, the Biltmore House is completely overwhelming.

The front entrance is a delightful surprise—a bright, open place, where white marble floors surround a glass-roofed atrium, opening into arches that lead into great spaces. This is the **Winter Garden**, with its great palms overhanging rattan and bamboo garden furniture. To one side of the entrance is the grandest room in the house, the baronial **Banquet Hall**—a huge space with a barrel-vaulted wooden ceiling 70 feet high, five gigantic 16th-century Flemish tapestries, and a leaf table that expands to hold 64 guests. Opposite the hall, the **Library** has balconied two-story-tall walls, completely covered with 10,000 books—less than half of Vanderbilt's personal collection.

Walk onto any one of a series of terraces that line the rear of the house, and one of the grandest views in the region opens up. Meadows and glades drop away from the steep stone sides of the terraces to the farmland lining the French Broad River far below. Then, after miles of steeply rolling forestlands, the grand clifflike sides of the Pisgah Range form a tall, unbroken wall along the horizon. Vanderbilt owned this view; every bit of land in this panorama was his.

Upstairs, on the second and third floor, are the family's private quarters and a very large number of guest rooms. Vanderbilt disliked formal entertainment but enjoyed having house guests, informal house parties of the sort popular in the great houses of Europe. There were so many guests, and so many guest rooms, that Vanderbilt had the halls color-coded so that guests would know where they were. Downstairs, the basement housed servants' quarters, kitchen and laundry facilities, and indoor recreation rooms including a swimming pool, bowling alley, and gymnasium.

In all, the self-guided house tour leads through 23 rooms upstairs and 11 rooms downstairs, and has disabled access. Two other tours, each requiring an additional payment and at least six flights of steps, take visitors through closed portions of the house, from the fourth-floor servants' quarters to the Victorian boilers and electric panels in the sub-basement, and up onto the roof for sweeping views. Cost of the tour is included in the estate ticket; Behind the Scenes and Roof tours are extra.

Biltmore Gardens, Asheville, NC. Daily 9 AM–dusk. Designed by Frederick Law Olmsted after he had already completed New York's Central Park, the Biltmore Gardens flow downhill from the house, covering several hundred acres. Formal gardens, patterned after Italian Renaissance styles, frame the house and offer striking views both of the house and the mountains beyond. Then, downhill from the house's Italianate gardens, an informal **Ramble** allows visitors to explore an intimate mountain draw covered with flowering shrubs. Beneath the Ramble is a large, formal **Walled Garden**, patterned after the gardens found in English country houses, and ending in a large and impressive series of glasshouses called the **Conservatory**, with displays of delicate tropical vegetation. Beneath the Walled Garden stretch a series of intriguing informal gardens spread about the mountain slopes and reached down a long series of paths. Most notable here is the stunning **Azalea Garden**, with an extensive collection of local and exotic azaleas, and the beautiful **Bass Pond and Waterfall**, restored to its original appearance.

The exit road takes visitors through parts of the garden, including the Walled Garden, the Conservatory (with a parking lot), and the Bass Pond. The estate's brochure, included with the admission ticket, has an excellent and detailed map of the garden's many twisting paths. Garden visits are included in the admission ticket.

The Biltmore Winery, Asheville, NC. Jan.–Mar., Mon.–Sat. 11–6, Sun. noon–6; Apr.–Dec., Mon.–Sat. 11–7, Sun. noon–7. Biltmore opened its ambitious winery in 1985, in a dairy barn designed by Hunt and built as part of the original estate construction. The short winery tour includes a 7-minute video and a self-guided walk through the wine-making areas and the basement. The tour ends with a delightful private tasting in the old calf barn, where you can interact with wine-serving bartenders at U-shaped bars. The wines include one of Biltmore's top-end estate-grown wines, plus several white and red blends of North

Carolina and California grapes. Those interested in tasting more of Biltmore's estate wines and champagnes can pay $5 for an additional tasting; otherwise winery visits are included in the admissions ticket.

Biltmore Shops and Restaurants, Asheville, NC. Quite a variety of shops and eateries are found within the estate and available only to ticket holders. The largest concentration of these is by the house, in the old stables. Here are shops that specialize in Victorian-style gifts, Biltmore wines, Christmas items, old-fashioned toys, old-fashioned candies, and books related to local sites, Victorian arts and crafts, and the Vanderbilts. Food service includes the **Stable Café** (11–5), an ice cream parlor, and a bakery. In the winery is another gift shop with Biltmore wines and other food and gift items, as well as **The Bistro** (11–9), serving lunch and dinner. Finally, a garden shop located at the Conservatory offers plants from the Biltmore nurseries and a variety of garden items. The **Deerpark Restaurant**, also on the estate, is open to the public for buffet lunches.

The estate's eateries are not cheap. Visitors who wish to spend less on lunch can find a large variety of good local cafés in Biltmore Village immediately outside the main gate. Your ticket allows you to leave the estate and reenter on the same day.

PACK PLACE ✦ ♿ ⬆ **Pack Place** (828-257-4500; http://main.nc.us/packplace/), 2 S. Pack Square, Asheville, NC. Tue.–Sat. 10–5, Sun. (June–Oct. only) 1–5. Closed Mon. Located on downtown Asheville's Pack Square, this arts and sciences center's small entrance is deceiving. Behind the entrance, a large complex of museums, public spaces, and the **Diana Wortham Theatre** stretches back through several buildings, including the marble-clad 1920s neoclassical **Public Library Building**.

PACK PLACE IN DOWNTOWN ASHEVILLE.
Jim Hargan

The not-for-profit Pack Place Foundation runs the multilevel public area at the center of the complex, including the fascinating free exhibition on the history of the square. Off the public area are three indepen-dent museums—the art museum, the gem and mineral museum, and the hands-on health museum—and the Diana Wortham Theatre. Behind this main structure in its own historic building is the YMI Cultural Center, a major part of Asheville's African American community. Pack Place will sell you combined tickets at various complex prices (every tenant sets its own price rules), or you can buy tickets at each venue separately. Combined tickets are cheaper. $14 combined adult ticket.

♿ ⬆ **The Asheville Art Museum** (828-253-3227; fax 828-257-4503; www.ashevilleart.org/index.htm), Pack

Place. Founded in 1948 by a group of Asheville-area artists, the Asheville Art Museum has a permanent collection of over 1,500 pieces of 20th-century art. Part of the Pack Place Center, it occupies much of the old Italian Renaissance public library adjacent to Pack Square. Wandering through three stories of display space, the museum will have two or three exhibitions going at any one time, making the overall experience quite diverse. As you might expect, the permanent exhibitions emphasize western North Carolina, with one gallery displaying art inspired by the Blue Ridge Mountains from the 19th century to the present, and another displaying pieces by the contemporary craft masters of the western mountains. The displays are by no means limited to area artists, however, and pieces by nationally known figures are splashed throughout the museum. $6 adults, $5 children and seniors. Additional fees may apply for selected exhibitions.

✒ ♿ ⬆ **Colburn Gem and Mineral Museum** (828-254-7162), Pack Place. Founded in 1960, this first-rate mineral museum combines an extensive collection of North Carolina gems and minerals with educational and interpretive exhibits aimed at families with children. Exhibits include locally mined precious stones, mountain building, and mountain minerals. Summer field trips lead to some of the most fascinating and little-known corners of the Asheville area. $4 adults, $3 students.

✒ ♿ ⬆ **The Health Adventure** (828-254-6373), Pack Place. Founded in 1968, the Health Adventure is a hands-on health and science museum. Originally a museum for schoolchildren, they have been expanding their exhibits to appeal to adults and older children, and to include biology and physics as well as health. $4 adults, $3 students.

✒ ♿ ⬆ **The YMI Cultural Center** (828-252-4614), Pack Place. George Vanderbilt constructed this National Register Tudor-style brick building as a cultural center for his African American workmen. Originally known as the Young Men's Institute, it continues to this day as the YMI Cultural Center. Exhibitions on African American arts and history, particularly in the Asheville area, are always featured, as are plays, storytelling, and hands-on craft classes. Considered part of Pack Place, its building is across the street to the south. $4 adults, $3 students.

HISTORIC SITES ♿ **Vance Birthplace State Historic Site** (828-645-6706; www.ah.dcr.state.nc.us/sections/hs/vance/vance.htm), 911 Reems Creek Rd., Weaverville, NC. Mon.–Fri. 9–5; closed Sat. and Sun. This log farmstead east of Weaverville accurately reconstructs the early-19th-century birthplace of Zebulon B. Vance, one of North Carolina's most beloved politicians. In the mid–19th century, Vance led the movement to democratize North Carolina's patrician planter-controlled government; during the Civil War, Governor Vance (an anti-Confederate and anti-secessionist, but not a Unionist) protected North Carolina from lawlessness, preserved civil liberties, and sheltered his state from the Confederate government's worst excesses. This state historic site memorializes his life, and presents an accurate picture of the frontier mountain life that shaped his boyhood.

The farmstead is a well-crafted two-story log home, set on a grassy hill, shaded by large old trees, and surrounded by mountains. It has been carefully furnished to reflect the frontier period of Vance's boyhood. A vegetable garden separates the farmhouse from several log outbuildings—a weaving house with period loom, toolhouse, smokehouse, corncrib, springhouse, and slaves' house. Beautiful views stretch from the split-rail "worm" fence, past the log buildings, and to the mountains beyond.

Throughout the season, this is a venue for various programs interpreting early life on the mountain frontier. There's a visitors center with a small museum on Vance's life. Only the visitors center, restrooms, and picnic area are fully disabled accessible. Free.

⭱ **Smith-McDowell House Museum** (828-253-9231; www.wnchistory.org/smithmcdowellhouse/), 283 Victoria Rd., Asheville, NC. May–Dec., Tue.–Sat. 10–4, Sun. 1–4. One of the oldest brick houses in the area, this 1840 home sits on a hilltop south of downtown Asheville, on what is now the campus of Asheville-Buncombe Technical Community College. The postfrontier farmhouse of a prominent family, this handsome, symmetrical structure sports first- and second-story full front porches, and double fireplaces on each gable end. Now a historical museum, different rooms are furnished for different periods of the house's 19th-century heyday. The kitchen shows the earliest period, the 1840s; a bedroom reflects more prosperous antebellum tastes; the parlor and dining room show the style of the succeeding generation. The garden behind the house preserves a design of Frederick Law Olmsted, executed during his days at the nearby Biltmore Estate. $4.50.

THE KITCHEN OF A LOG FARMHOUSE IS ON VIEW AT THE VANCE STATE HISTORIC SITE.
Jim Hargan

Thomas Wolfe Memorial State Historic Site (828-253-8304; fax 828-252-8171; www.wolfememorial.com), 52 N. Market St., Asheville, NC. Apr.–Oct., Mon.–Sat. 9–5, Sun. 1–5; Nov.– Mar., Tue.–Sat. 10–4, Sun 1–4. Author Thomas Wolfe, acclaimed for his auto-biographical novels during the 1930s, spent his childhood in his mother's boardinghouse, My Old Kentucky Home, on the eastern edge of the Lexington Hill section of downtown Asheville. That boardinghouse, and the town of Asheville, became the thinly veiled subject of his most famous novel, *Look Homeward Angel: A Story of the Buried Life*, published in 1929 to high acclaim (and great embarrassment among Asheville's worthies). Today the boardinghouse and a modern visitors center make up the Thomas Wolfe Memorial. For many years the boardinghouse has fronted a pedestrianized street opposite a downtown hotel tower, furnished as it was when Wolfe lived there in the 1910s and housing a considerable collection of Wolfe memorabilia and arti-facts. An arsonist brought this to a halt in 1998, causing massive destruction to the house and collection. Fortunately, most of the collection has been salvaged, and the house has been restored and reopened. The visitors center houses a display of Wolfe artifacts and an audiovisual show on his life and works. Free.

The Grove Arcade (828-252-7799; fax 828-255-7953; www.grovearcade.com), 29½ Page Ave., Asheville, NC. This astonishing 1920s downtown mall, for many decades used as a federal office building, has now been reopened as a shopping center—for the first time in 60 years. It's an elaborately decorated five-story structure, covering two entire city blocks in downtown Asheville's Battery Hill shopping district. Outer walls are covered with terra-cotta tiles and limestone; stone-carved lions and gryphons guard the entrance. Built by the developer of the Grove Park Inn in 1929, it functioned successfully as an "indoor market" throughout the Depression, only to be taken over by the federal government in 1942 as part of the war effort. In 1995 the City of Asheville bought it and restored it to its former glory; it has about 70 stores, many specializing in unique local products.

CULTURAL SITES **Grovewood Galleries** (828-253-7651; fax 828-254-2489; www.grovewood.com), 111 Grovewood Rd., Asheville, NC. Go to the Grove Park Inn, enter its parking lot, and follow the signs. Mon.–Sat. 10–6, Sun. 1–5. This collection of two museums, a gallery, and a lovely little café occupies a group of historic buildings in their own little garden by the Grove Park Inn. The complex was erected by the Vanderbilts in 1901 as a training school for traditional mountain weavers and woodworkers. After George Vanderbilt's death, his widow sold the school to the adjacent inn, which added three English-cottage-style buildings to the complex in 1917. From then until the 1980s, the small complex produced fine homespun cloth for the craft market. Independent of the Grove Park Inn since 1942, Grovewood became a crafters' center again in the 1990s. Its large fine-craft gallery represents regional craft artists in a wide variety of media, including a large furniture gallery. It rotates solo exhibits every two months or so, and has actively supported artists' groups in areas such as wood-working and jewelry. Adjacent are two museums, one dedicated to the Vander-bilts' school and the homespun industry of the early 20th century, and the other with a collection of 30 antique cars. All these buildings front on a lovely tree-shaded garden, with sculptures scattered about and a wide view over the Grove Park Inn and its golf course toward downtown Asheville.

Montreat (800-572-2257 or 828-669-2911; fax 828-669-2779; www.montreat .org), Montreat, NC. Of the 20 or so religious retreats and conference centers in this area, Montreat is one of the two most worthwhile for a casual visit, as well as friendly toward a casual visitor (the other being Lake Junaluska). Founded in 1897 and now run by the Presbyterian Church USA, Montreat is really a town in itself, combining its major retreat center with a liberal arts college and a collec-tion of summer homes, all grouped around a lovely recreation center on Lake Susan. Located at the end of NC 9, 2 miles north of Black Mountain, Montreat features a major concentration of early-20th-century resort architecture, from its impressive front gate (now permanently open) to the large and beautiful Assembly Inn, built of local stone. Historic stone and wood buildings face Lake Susan on one side; a gardenlike park lines the other. Uphill, winding gravel roads lead past early-20th-century cottages to reach various hiking trails. The best-known and most popular trail follows the old Mount Mitchell Rd., abandoned in 1940 in favor of the Blue Ridge Parkway.

GARDENS AND PARKS **The Botanical Gardens at Asheville** (828-252-5190), 151 W. T. Weaver Blvd., Asheville, NC. This 10-acre garden in central Asheville is dedicated to preserving and exhibiting the native plants of the western North Carolina mountains in their natural surroundings. Designed in 1960 by Doan Ogden, the gardens follow a narrow draw formed by Reed Creek. Four bridges cross the creek, each with its own view. Special environments include a Sunshine Garden, a Woods Garden, a Rock Garden, a Heath and Azalea Garden, and a Garden for the Blind, emphasizing textures and smells. Also on the property are a historic log cabin and earthworks from a Civil War skirmish. This volunteer-run garden sponsors regular walks and talks, as well as plant sales. Free.

Asheville City Hall Plaza. This urban park covers four blocks of downtown Asheville, between Pack Square and the seats of local government—the

A FOOTBRIDGE IS SURROUNDED BY SPRING BLOOM AT THE BOTANICAL GARDENS AT ASHEVILLE.
Jim Hargan

Asheville City Hall and the Buncombe County Courthouse. It's a lovely place to stop and rest, with ample tree-shaded benches and well-kept flower beds. Its courthouse is an attractive 1927 neoclassical "skyscraper" of 17 stories, with an elaborately decorated interior. The real star of the square, however, is the Asheville City Hall, a 1927 nine-story art deco masterpiece in rich gold brick, white limestone, and rose terra-cotta trim. Its octagonal stepped roof is topped by a tall torch-shaped carillon belfry, all covered in pink terra-cotta tile with green accents. Its architect, Ashevillian Douglas D. Ellington, designed several other stunners within an easy walking distance—the adjacent **Fire Department**, the octagonal **First Baptist Church** two blocks north, and the **S&W Cafeteria Building** two blocks south.

Riverside Cemetery (828-258-8480; www.ci.asheville.nc.us/parks/riverside.asp), 53 Birch St., Asheville, NC. Mon.–Fri. 8–4:30. This 87-acre historic cemetery, owned by the City of Asheville and operated by Parks and Recreation, features parklike grounds with winding hillside paths, large shade trees, many dogwoods and azaleas—and over 9,000 unusual headstones, monuments, and mausoleums. In use since the Civil War, it holds the graves of such notable Ashevillians as O. Henry, Thomas Wolfe, and Governor Zeb Vance. It's a popular place to stroll on a warm spring day. Free.

✍ ♿ **Western North Carolina Nature Center** (828-298-5600; fax 828-298-2644; www.wildwnc.org), 75 Gashes Creek Rd., Asheville, NC. Open 10–5. Run by Buncombe County Parks and Recreation, this large and sophisticated nature study museum concentrates on the animals and plants of the western North Carolina mountains, occupying 42 acres on the east side of Asheville, off NC 81. Much of the museum is taken up with live animal and plant displays that put their subjects in their environmental context. Habitat displays include predators (red wolves, black wolves, cougars, and bobcats), river otters, turkeys, deer, and bears. A **Nocturnal Hall** displays animals found only at night—bats, owls, rabbits, flying squirrels. The **Educational Farm** has farm animals (including a petting area) and exhibits. The **Main Hall** has 75 live animal exhibits and encourages touching (except for the poisonous snakes and spiders). There are also raccoons, foxes, turtles, hawks, and eagles, as well as a log cabin, herb garden, and nature trail. Their excellent web page has a huge compendium of nature information, a calendar of local nature-oriented events, and a whole lot of links. $5 adults, $3 youths.

✳ To Do

BALLOONING **Mount Pisgah Hot Air Balloons** (828-667-9943; www.go mountains.net/balloons.html), 1410 Pisgah Hwy. (NC 151), Asheville, NC. A hot-air balloon dealer and FAA-certified repair shop with more than 20 years of experience, Mount Pisgah Balloons offers 1-hour flights in one of the most beautiful corners of the Asheville area. Hominy Valley, southwest of town, offers unspoiled pastoral beauty framed by 5,000-foot peaks, including Mount Pisgah. Reservations are necessary. $130 per person.

BICYCLING **Epic Cycles** (828-669-5969; www.epic-cycles.com), 108 Black Mountain Ave., Black Mountain, NC. This full-service bike shop rents bikes and offers detailed information on area trails.

Bio-Wheels (828-232-0300; www.biowheels.com), 76 Biltmore Ave., Asheville, NC. This large bicycle shop on the south edge of downtown Asheville (on US 25) offers rentals and tours, with your choice of off-road mountain biking, road touring, or leisure biking.

Liberty Bicycles (800-962-4537 or 828-684-1085; www.libertybikes.com), 1987 Hendersonville Rd., Asheville, NC. This full-service bike shop on US 25 south of Asheville, popular with the area's serious bicyclists, rents mountain bikes.

FISHING **Lake Julian County Park** (www.buncombecounty.org/governing/depts/parksalive/facilities/parks/Lake Julian.htm). On Asheville's south side, off I-26, Exit 6, then east half a mile on NC 146. This county park centers on a large cooling pond used for a major regional power plant, "Lake Julian," covering some 300 acres. Wilderness it's not, but the fishing is excellent, with an abundance of bass, catfish, brim, crappie, and talapia. Johnboat rentals are available. Fishing permits $3 per day, johnboat rentals $15 per day.

Hunter Banks Co. (800-227-6732 or 828-252-3005; www.hunterbanks.com), 29 Montford Ave., Asheville, NC. This large fly shop, occupying a fine old brick store in Asheville's historic Montford section (just north of downtown, off I-240's Montford St. exit), offers guide services to local trout streams. Their web page is worth a peek for its detailed stream reports and fly recommendations. Half day $150, full day $250, including lunch.

GOLF **Grove Park Inn Resort** (828-252-2711), 290 Macon Ave., Asheville, NC. This scenic course sits in a historic neighborhood a short distance north of downtown Asheville, overlooked by the mammoth stone-built Grove Park Hotel and Beaucatcher Mountain. Built in 1899, it was substantially redesigned by Donald Ross in 1923; a major renovation was completed in 2001. $80.

Great Smokies Holiday Inn Sun Spree Resort (828-253-5874; www.sunspree .com), 1 Holiday Inn Dr., Asheville, NC. In the center of Asheville, it's right off I-240. This 18-hole 1976 course sits on a hilltop overlooking the French Broad River and downtown Asheville. $30.

Buncombe County Golf Course (828-298-1867; www.buncombecounty.org/ governing/depts/parksalive/facilities/bcGolf.htm), 226 Fairway Dr., Asheville, NC. Designed in 1927 by Donald Ross, this 18-hole, par-72 course is located on the east side of Asheville, just off US 70. The front nine parallel the Swannanoa River, while the back nine climb a fairly substantial hill with narrow, short fairways. Built as part of a 1920s subdivision, it's now surrounded by a pleasant urban neighborhood and run by the Buncombe County Department of Recreation as a fully public course. $20.

Reems Creek Golf Course (828-645-4393; www.reemscreekgolf.com), 36 Pink Fox Cove Rd., Weaverville, NC. A 1984 course designed by English firm

Hawtree and Son and set among the Blue Ridge Mountains east of Weaverville. Rated four stars by *Golf Digest*, its scenery is particularly beautiful. $42–49.

Black Mountain Municipal Golf Course (828-669-2710). This 1929 18-hole public course has hilly terrain, water on most holes, and spectacular mountain scenery. While most greens are short, number 17 is 747 yards, par 6. $20.

ROCK CLIMBING **ClimbMax** (828-252-9996; www.climbmaxnc.com), 43 Wall St., Asheville, NC. Located in the Wall Street shopping district, this complete climbing shop has equipment and a large indoor climbing wall in addition to guide services for day trips and overnighters.

Mountain Adventure Guides, Inc. (828-255-7577; www.mtnadventureguides .com), Asheville, NC. This adventure guiding service offers all levels of equipment-assisted rock climbing, with beginner instructions for children as young as eight. They also offer guided day hiking and backpacking.

Black Dome Mountain Sports (828-251-2001; www.blackdome.com), 140 Tunnel Rd. (US 70), Asheville, NC. This large outdoors supplier offers guide services for rock climbing, fly-fishing, and backpacking. Their store is located in its own building just east of downtown Asheville, and is worth a visit.

STABLES **Biltmore Estate Equestrian Center** (828-277-4485), 1 Biltmore Estate Dr., Asheville, NC. The Biltmore Estate's stables offer riding on the 100 miles of estate trails that George Vanderbilt constructed in the 1890s.

Berry Patch Stables (828-645-7271), 300 Bairds Cove Rd., Asheville, NC. Located just north of Asheville off Old US 19, this stable offers trail rides, camps, lessons, and pony rides.

WHITEWATER ADVENTURE The French Broad River, running for many miles straight through the middle of the Asheville area, furnishes a wide range of recreational opportunities, from dramatic Class III–IV rapids near Hot Springs to leisurely canoeing through the heart of the Biltmore Estate. The Buncombe County Recreation Department maintains a number of canoe and kayak launch sites along the river. In addition to these outfitters, check out the listings for the French Broad River in the Hot Springs chapter ("Asheville's Rugged Hinter-lands").

Southern Waterways (800-849-1970 or 828-232-1970; www.paddlewithus .com), 521 Amboy Rd., Asheville, NC. Gentle, self-guided trips on the French Broad River as it cuts through the Biltmore Estate—several miles of private wilderness, little changed since Frederick Law Olmsted designed its landscape in the 1880s. You have your choice of raft, canoe, or kayak, or they will shuttle your private boat for a modest fee. A guided sunset paddle goes down the same stretch in the twilight hours. Partial day $24–48.

Nantahala Outdoor Center in Asheville (888-622-1662 or 828-232-0110), 52 Westgate Parkway, Asheville, NC. This large Bryson City outfitter maintains a base and outdoor shop in Asheville, at the Westgate Shopping Plaza off I-240 just across the river from downtown.

✳ Lodging

Blue Ridge Mountain Host of North Carolina (800-807-3391; www.carolinamountains.org), P.O. Box 1806, Asheville, NC 28802. This organization of independent hotels and B&Bs covers the area around Asheville and Boone.

COUNTRY INNS AND HOTELS ✐ ⅙
The Richmond Hill Inn (888-742-4550 or 828-252-7313; fax 828-252-8726; www.richmondhillinn.com), 87 Richmond Hill Dr., Asheville, NC 28806. Feb.–Dec. This AAA four-diamond inn, centering on an 1890s mansion built by a congressman, occupies 46 private acres on a hilltop just outside downtown Asheville. The Richmond Hill is well known for its gracious hospitality, fine dining, and luxurious comfort; the 2001 Zagat Survey has listed it as one of the top 15 small resorts and inns in America. Its most remarkable feature, however, is its 6-acre Victorian garden, designed and maintained by the inn's

full-time horticulturalist, Hunter Stubbs, and his staff. (Check their web site for Hunter's gardening newsletter.) The inn's 36 rooms are divided among the old mansion at the top of the hill, the new Garden Pavilion at the base of the hill, and a row of tiny cottages around the regulation croquet court. Rooms range in size from normal to large, and all are tastefully decorated with antiques and reproductions; some have fireplace, whirlpool bath, refrigerator, separate sitting area, private rocking porch, and/or garden balcony. The room rate includes a full breakfast in the garden, and afternoon tea. Rooms $155–395, suites $240–450, including breakfast.

✐ ⅙ **The Haywood Park Hotel** (800-228-2522 or 828-252-2522; fax 828-253-0481; www.haywoodpark .com/default.htm), 1 Battery Park Ave., Asheville, NC 28801. This small luxury hotel sits at the center of downtown Asheville's Battery Hill shopping district in a renovated historic four-story brick building. The

THE RICHMOND HILL INN.

Jim Hargan

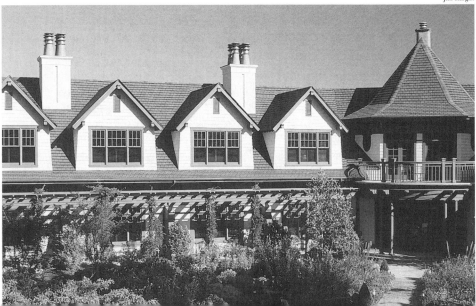

lobby centers on a four-story glass-roofed atrium whose contemporary lines contrast nicely with the historic brick exterior; inside the atrium are exotic shops and restaurants. The hotel has room service, an exercise room, a sauna, and covered valet parking. The 33 rooms are stylishly and elegantly decorated with custom-designed contemporary furniture, and all rooms have sitting area, wet bar, and Spanish marble bath with garden tub (with whirlpool bath in some rooms). Business travelers will appreciate the three room phones and the writing desk with a computer/fax port. A continental breakfast is delivered to each room, included in the room rate. Child care facilities are available. $140–325.

☙ ♿ **The Grove Park Inn Resort and Spa** (800-438-5800 or 828-252-2711; fax 828-253-7053; www.grove parkinn.com), 290 Macon Ave., Asheville, NC 28804. Open all year. This impressive stone inn sits on a hillside above Asheville, just north of downtown. Built in 1913, it was a focal point for Asheville's early development; now it's at the center of an upscale historic neighborhood. The large old inn is built of huge granite stones, some as large as 10,000 pounds, and topped with a bright red roof—a grand sight viewed across its 1899 golf course (redesigned by Donald Ross in 1923). The huge stones form the lobby wall, with a huge fireplace at one end. This old inn is flanked by two modern wings, built in the 1980s; together, they offer 510 rooms. These rooms are all furnished in Arts and Crafts–style furniture—reproductions in the new wings, the hotel's custom-built original furniture in the old inn. Some of the original

rooms are small (labeled "value rooms" in the resort's literature), while others range from normal sized to large suites. Resort activities include the 18-hole golf course with its wide mountain views, three indoor and three outdoor tennis courts, a sports complex with exercise equipment, aerobics classes, racquetball, a swimming pool, and a 40,000-square-foot spa. The hotel also has seven restaurants, cafés, and bars, as well as a number of shops (including a golf pro shop and a tennis pro shop). This child-friendly inn offers fully supervised children's programs (ages 3–12) in a summer camp format for half days, full days, and (some) evenings. Child-averse adults can stay in the child-free Club Floor, which has oversized rooms, its own private lounge, free evening cocktails, and free continental breakfast. Apart from the Club Floor, breakfast is not included in the tariff. Value rooms $135–195, standard rooms $150–299, oversized rooms and suites $235–635.

Inn on Biltmore Estate (800-624-1575; www.biltmore.com/inn/index .html), 1 N. Pack Square (administrative offices), Asheville, NC 28801. This 213-room hotel stands six stories tall on a hillock within the Biltmore Estate, about 2 miles from the house and garden. A monolithic modern structure built in 2001, it has been given exterior decorative flourishes reminiscent of the Biltmore House's French château architecture. The same sort of decorated modern architecture carries on in the interior, where distinctly contemporary lines and room designs serve as backdrops for English and French country house furniture. Apart from the beautiful reproduction furniture, guest rooms are fairly standard and none too large; you will find yourself having to pay extra for a balcony, a whirlpool bath, or a little extra space. Carrying a four-diamond rating from AAA, the Inn on Biltmore has all the attentions and luxuries you expect from a top-flight hotel. Please note: The room rate does *not* include a ticket to the Biltmore House and Gardens, even though the hotel is on the estate grounds. Apr.–Dec., rooms $199–359, suites $595–2,000. Jan.–Mar. rooms $139–269, suites $450–1,400.

BED & BREAKFAST INNS

In Asheville, NC
The Albemarle Inn ((800) 621-7435; (828) 255-0027; fax (828) 236-3397; www.albemarleinn.com), 86 Edgemont Rd., Asheville, NC 28801. Occupying a large Greek Revival mansion in Asheville's elegant Grove Park district, the Albemarle Inn is spacious, elegant, and quiet. Greek columns support its great front porch nearly two stories high, an elegant place to sit and enjoy the westward view; inside, a grand oak staircase winds up past a semicircular sitting area before reaching the second story. A guest lounge has wood paneling, comfortable Victorian furniture, and a gas log fire in the old fireplace. Here guests are served wine and cheese in the early evening; the attached sunroom, roomy and bright, is the site for breakfast. The 11 guest rooms range from spacious to huge, with high ceilings, period furnishings, queen and king beds, and claw-footed baths. Breakfasts are luxurious, ample servings of stunning gourmet treats. These include French toast made of large slices of homemade bread, sandwiching a ricotta-and-cream filling

and topped with a homemade orange sauce.

Abingdon Green Bed and Breakfast Inn (800-251-2454 or 828-251-2454; fax 828-251-2872; www.abbingtongreen.com), 46 and 48 Cumberland Circle, Asheville, NC 28801. This 1908 Colonial Revival mansion, listed on the National Register, sits on a large tree-shaded lot in Asheville's Montford Historic District, not far from downtown. Carefully tended English gardens surround the house and fill the back of the property. Inside, antique furnishings grace the common rooms. The eight guest rooms (including three suites in the separate Carriage House) are theme furnished with antiques, and range in size from cozy to large. Full breakfasts are served in the elegant dining room. Rooms $125–185, suites $225–265.

Chestnut Street Inn (800-894-2955 or 828-285-0705; fax 828-285-3170; www.chestnutstreetinn.com/index.html), 176 E. Chestnut St., Asheville, NC 28801. This large brick Victorian home is located three blocks north of downtown Asheville, in the Chestnut Hill National Historic District. Its wide porch looks out on a large lot landscaped as an English garden. Common areas have their original heavy woodworking and period antiques, and each of the six rooms is theme decorated in Victorian antiques. The tariff includes a full breakfast and afternoon tea. $165–235.

WhiteGate Inn and Cottage (800-485-3045 or 828-253-2553; fax 828-281-1883; www.whitegate.net), 173 E. Chestnut St., Asheville, NC 28801. Located in Asheville's Chestnut Hill National Historic District, just three blocks north of downtown, the hilltop WhiteGate is surrounded by gardens, with the tops of downtown Asheville's tallest buildings visible over the white picket fence. This 1889 shingle-style house, painted brick red, is elegant in-side and out. Gravel paths loop through its English-style gardens, with a 1,200-square-foot greenhouse and conservatory holding a special orchid garden. Inside, the common rooms are wood paneled and decorated with Edwardian antiques. The four rooms in the main house are large, each theme decorated with period antiques; two have separate sitting rooms. A small garden cottage, original to the house, makes up the fifth room in the inn. A full breakfast is included. The WhiteGate Inn is rated three diamonds by AAA. $155–200.

The Wright Inn and Carriage House (800-552-5724 or 828-251-0789; fax 828-251-0929; www.wright inn.com), 235 Pearson Dr., Asheville, NC 28801. Located in Asheville's Montford National Historic District just north of downtown, the National Register–listed Wright Inn occupies one of the largest and most elaborate Queen Anne mansions in the North Carolina mountains. The thickly gin-gerbreaded veranda curves around the front in a witch's-hat turret; on the side, elaborate steps lead down the rock wall foundation to the Victorian garden. The period is carefully maintained inside, with polished hardwood trim setting off the antique and heirloom furniture. The seven rooms and three suites are all elegantly decorated in period, and range in size from cozy bedrooms to multi-room apartments. A full breakfast is included, along with afternoon tea and cookies in the gazebo. The

Wright Inn is rated three diamonds by AAA. $125–235; ask about the five-room suite.

✒ **The Colby House** (800-982-2118 or 828-253-5644; fax 828-259-9479; www.colbyhouse.com), 230 Pearson Dr., Asheville, NC 28801. This four-room inn occupies a 1924 Colonial-style house in Asheville's gentrifying Montford National Historic District, convenient to downtown. An extra-wide side porch is floored with red tile and framed by classical columns; its rockers give views over the private back garden. Common areas, furnished with a combination of Edwardian and 1920s-era furniture, include a parlor, a library, a formal dining room, and a butler's pantry where cookies, coffee, and soft drinks are always available. Rooms, ranging from cozy to large, are decorated with elegant Colonial themes. A full breakfast is served in the dining room, and wine and hors d'oeuvres are served in the evening. A detached garage has been converted to a two-room cottage with a whirlpool tub, where children are welcome; only children over 12 are allowed in the main inn. Rooms $130–150, cottage $235.

1900 Inn on Montford (800-254-9569 or 828-254-9569; fax 828-254-9518; www.innonmontford.com), 296 Montford Ave., Asheville, NC 28801. Tree lovers take note: The 1900 Inn on Montford has the North Carolina State Record Norway Maple in its front yard. Business travelers take note: This century-old historic house a couple of blocks north of downtown Asheville has high-speed Internet ports in every room. This fine old Victorian house in Asheville's Montford National Historic District is painted brick red, has flanking front gables, and features a huge wraparound porch overlooking its English garden landscaping. Common areas as well as the five rooms are elegantly furnished in a turn-of-the-20th-century style, allowing you to plug in your laptop with some homey comfort. A full breakfast is included. Rooms $165–225, suite $295.

North Lodge Bed and Breakfast (800-282-3602 or 828-252-6433; fax 828-252-3034; www.northlodge.com), 84 Oakland Rd., Asheville, NC 28801. This 1904 house sits on a large lot in Asheville's hospital and medical district. It was built in the fashionable cottage style, influenced by the Arts and Crafts movement, with stone walls on the first floor and cedar shakes covering the second floor. Beautifully restored, the house is isolated from the neighborhood by its landscaped lot and long drive. Inside, it's beautifully decorated in a mixture of antiques and contemporary that goes well with its early-20th-century design features. Five en suite guest rooms are theme furnished in the same manner, and range in size from cozy to large. A sixth en suite bedroom has a single twin bed and a reduced price. A full breakfast is included in the tariff. Located halfway between downtown Asheville and the Biltmore Estate, this B&B inn is only a few blocks from both of Asheville's major hospitals. Rooms $105–145, single room $70.

Cedar Crest, a Victorian Inn (800-252-0310 or 828-252-1389). This 1890s Victorian mansion graces its upscale Asheville neighborhood with a full panoply of gables, gingerbread, turrets, balconies, and verandas. The influence of the nearby Biltmore Estate is clearly visible in the elaborate woodwork in the common areas

and on the grand staircase. Gardens surround the property, making for a pleasant view from the rocking chairs on the porch. The nine guest rooms in this huge house are all individually decorated in period antiques. Full breakfasts are served in the formal dining room or on the veranda, and fresh cookies and lemonade are served each afternoon. Rooms $140–190, suite and cottage $205–240.

&. **The Blake House** (888-353-5227 or 828-681-5227; www.blakehouse .com), 150 Royal Pines Dr., Asheville, NC 28704. Built as a summer home in 1847, the Blake House sits in what is now a quiet southern suburb of Asheville, convenient to the airport. Built entirely of granite, it sports 22-inch-thick granite walls and 14-foot-high ornamental plaster ceilings, as well as a wide front porch with rocking chairs. Common rooms are beautifully decorated and quite roomy. The spacious five rooms are individually and elegantly decorated with antiques. A full breakfast is served in the dining room. Rooms $155–185, suite $225.

Engadine Inn (Owls Nest Inn at Engadine) (800-665-8868 or 828-665-8325; fax 828-667-2539; www.engadine inn.com), 2630 Smokey Park Hwy., Chandler, NC 28715. Half a mile from Exit 37 off I-40. This elaborately Victorian 1885 farmhouse sits on the western edge of the Asheville area on 12 acres of meadowed land with beautiful views. Even for a Victorian house the porches are a wonder, wrapping around both floors with a corner turret and plenty of gingerbread and fine wood trim. The five guest rooms, decorated with Victorian antiques, range in size from roomy to large. $120–195, including full breakfast.

In Weaverville

Dry Ridge Inn (800-839-3899 or 828-658-3899; fax 828-658-9533; www.dryridgeinn.com), 26 Brown St., Weaverville, NC 28787. This 1849 farmhouse, rebuilt into a stylish Victorian mansion in 1888, sits in a quiet residential neighborhood blocks from Weaverville's quaint little downtown. Surrounded by a white picket fence, the house's wide front porch looks out on well-kept gardens, with a water garden in the rear. The eight rooms are individually decorated in country-themed antiques, and range in size from cozy to large. Full breakfast is included, served in the brightly lighted breakfast room or on the brick patio by the water garden. $95–155.

The Inn on Main Street (877-873-6074 or 828-645-4935; www.innonmain.com), 88 S. Main St., Weaverville, NC 28787. Built by a local doctor in 1900, this country house in Weaverville, two blocks south of downtown, represented high living in a small town. Today this late-Victorian house, with its two-story projecting bay windows and wide porches, continues to give high comfort in a small town. This seven-room B&B is furnished throughout with antiques. Rooms tend to be normal to large in size, each theme furnished in antiques and reproductions that feel comfortable in a turn-of-the-20th-century home. A full breakfast is included. $95–145.

✳ Where to Eat

EATING OUT Asheville Pizza and Brewing Company (828-254-1281), 675 Merrimon Ave., Asheville, NC. Lunch and dinner. Located in an old neighborhood theater on busy Merrimon Avenue north of downtown, the Asheville Pizza and Brewing Company offers some of the best pizza in town, their own outstanding microbrewed beer, and second-run movies on a full-sized screen. Pizzas are fresh made to order, as are a good selection of hamburgers, veggie burgers, sandwiches, and other bar food—but the really outstanding menu item is their Shiva IPA, an unusually mild and rich version of this heavily hopped English-style brew. You can enjoy your food in the lobby, set up as a regular restaurant and bar with funky movie memorabilia, or in the theater, where movie house rocking chairs face onto bench tables, and beat-up old sofas fill the empty area in front of the screen. There's a slight charge for recent movies, but various other features (including daytime children's movies and late-night *South Park*) are free. $8–14; the movie is $2 extra.

✍ **The Laughing Seed Café** (828-252-3445; www.laughingseed.com), 40 Wall St., Asheville, NC. Mon., Wed., Thu. 11:30 AM–9 PM; Fri., Sat. 11:30 AM–10 PM; Sun. 10 AM–9 PM; closed Tue. Any vegetable lover will enjoy this downtown Asheville vegetarian café for its wide choice of fresh, exotic produce, and its imaginative preparation that fuses a variety of ethnic themes and ideas. It occupies its own little building on Wall Street, reminiscent of a 1940s snack bar; inside, it's bright and sparkling, with a big mural and lots of blond wood. The menu is huge, with plenty of cheese dishes; vegan (no dairy or egg) choices are clearly labeled. All food is prepared from scratch with fresh ingredients (including the bread), and they strive to find local organic suppliers for their huge selection of exotic produce. They offer a superb choice in organic wines, and their own brand of home-brewed beer, the England-inspired Green Man (brewed downstairs). Lunch $5–9, dinner $7–14.

Trevi (828-281-1400; fax 828-281-2818; www.trevirestaurant.com), 2 Hendersonville Rd., Asheville, NC. Lunch weekdays 11:30–2:30, dinner daily 5–9 (until 10 Fri. and Sat.). This Biltmore Village restaurant features Italian cooking from the Apulia region—light sauces, fresh produce, lots of seafood, flavorful cheeses, and intense fresh herb flavors. Even with its serious approach to regional Italian food, the Trevi offers a variety of simple foods at modest prices. The lunch menu includes sandwiches and salads, market-fresh fish, calzones, and a large number of pasta dishes, with few prices straying outside the range of a good deli. Sandwiches disappear from the dinner menu, replaced by a greater choice of entrées. The large and varied wine list is dominated by Italian wines, with nearly every bottle less than $25. Inside the restaurant, the superb little specialty grocer

BaBa Riche offers an amazing array of Italian and international specialty items. Lunch $5–8, dinner $8–15.

Jack of the Wood (828-252-5445; www.jackofthewood.com), 95 Patton Ave., Asheville, NC. Daily 4 PM–2 AM. Free parking adjacent after 6 PM. Unlike many "Irish pubs," this downtown Asheville brew pub has a distinctly Celtic slant. Located in a storefront on Patton Avenue, Jack of the Wood makes its own beer and its own food fresh daily. Simple bar meals of sandwiches, stew, curry, fish cakes, or chili complement the British-style ales brewed in the basement. An interesting and original line-up of bands entertain on Friday and Saturday nights, while jam sessions are a regular feature on Sunday (Celtic, 5 PM), Wednesday (mountain music, 9:30 PM), and Thursday (bluegrass, 9:30 PM). $6–9.

♂ **The Early Girl Eatery** (828-259-9292), 8 Wall St., Asheville, NC. Breakfast weekdays 7:30–11:30, lunch weekdays 11:45–3, dinner Thu.–Sat. 5:30–10, brunch weekends 9–3. This small storefront in the Battery Hill shopping district specializes in original food with a southern twang, made fresh from locally grown ingredients. The café is bright and airy, with windows overlooking a downtown park two floors below; service is fast and attentive. Breakfasts have traditional egg and pancake dishes, complemented with less typical courses such as shrimp in brown gravy over grits. Lunches have fresh soups and sandwiches, plus a large blackboard of specials like shrimp and andouille sausage in a rich brown sauce full of fresh spring onions, served over stone-ground yellow grits. Dinners feature duck, chicken, salmon, and pork in a variety of blackboard specials. There are always vegetarian and vegan choices, and the extensive vegetable list will show you just what the mountain farms are harvesting right now. Beer and wine are available, with a good choice of microbrews and quality wines by the glass. Breakfast $2–7, lunch $3–7, dinner entrées $11–15.

Mount Mitchell State Park Restaurant (828-675-9545; fax 828-682-6510), NC 128 (Mount Mitchell Spur Rd.), Burnsville, NC. In Mount Mitchell State Park; access from the Blue Ridge Parkway (MP 355), Mount Mitchell Spur Rd. May–Oct. daily. Opens at 10 AM. Closes: May, 7 PM;

June–Aug., 8 PM; Sep., 7 PM; Oct., 6 PM. Closed Nov.–Apr. This pleasant lodge-style restaurant sits on the crest of the Black Mountains inside Mount Mitchell State Park, with stunning vistas from its large windows. Inside, it's all native stone and polished wood, kept immaculately clean. The restaurant is uncrowded, and table service is friendly and helpful. The food is best described as Southern Roadhouse, but better than usual. You choose a main dish, then sides from a list—two sides with a dinner, one with a sandwich. This lets you pick fried okra with your hamburger, a surprisingly good combination. Desserts are particularly worthwhile. Prices are higher than most roadhouses, but more than justified by the food's quality and the wonderful views. This is a worthy stop for anyone doing the parkway. Soup $4; salads, burgers, sandwiches $6.50–8.50; dinners $7–15; desserts $2–4. Children's menu.

DINING OUT Gabrielle's (888-742-4550 or 828-252-7313; fax 828-252-8726; www.richmondhillinn.com), 87 Richmond Hill Dr., Asheville, NC. Open 6–10 PM; closed Tue. A coat for gentlemen is suggested. Reservations are required. The elegant paneled dining room of a 19th-century congressman serves as the venue for this classic continental restaurant, one of the few in North Carolina to receive the AAA's four-diamond award. Part of the Richmond Hill Inn, the restaurant occupies part of a hilltop 1890s mansion, whose wide front porch overlooks 6 acres of Victorian gardens. Inside are cherry-paneled walls, crystal chandeliers, and live piano music; double-clothed tables are set with fine china and crystal. The single set price brings six courses: an amusé, a choice of four appetizers, a salad, a seasonal sorbet as a refresher, a choice of four entrées, and a choice of three desserts. From the "Classic Menu," you might choose to follow the amusé with a wild mushroom ravioli served with Parmesan cream and squash confetti; then a simple salad of Bibb lettuce with Roquefort cheese, pecans, and sherry vinaigrette; then follow the sorbet refresher with seared red snapper with lobster risotto, carrot and salsify ragoût, and Parmesan tuile; finishing with warm melting chocolate cake with vanilla bean ice cream and coffee swirl. The more expensive "Grande Menu" features dishes made with caviar, truffles, foie gras, and quail eggs. The final step to this grand meal is a cup of freshly brewed coffee or tea, enjoyed from a rocking chair on the porch. $58–85 for a six-course dinner.

The Market Place Restaurant and Wine Bar (828-252-4162; www.marketplace-restaurant.com), 20 Wall St., Asheville, NC. Dinner Mon.–Sat. One of the attractive storefronts on Wall Street in downtown Asheville, The Market Place offers a fusion of continental and global cuisine with fresh mountain ingredients. Outside, wrought-iron gates welcome Wall St. strollers into a courtyard and dining patio; inside, diners are greeted by cool, contemporary lines in tall spaces, with elegant, muted colors. The dinner menu changes daily, depending on the fresh, seasonal fruits, vegetables, and seafood available. It may feature meats from local farms, perhaps smoked with apple wood, or berries from the Biltmore Estate. The wine list includes hundreds of different bottles, with many rare vintages priced over $100 and a limited choice of wines under $30. Appetizers $7–10, entrées $13–26, desserts $4–7.

✴ Entertainment

Asheville, NC

The Asheville Symphony Orchestra (888-860-7378 or 828-254-7046; fax 828-254-1761; www.asheville symphony.org). Since 1960, the Asheville Symphony Orchestra has been bringing professional symphony to the mountains. Seasons typically include six masterworks concerts, two pops concerts, and a fully staged opera in conjunction with the Asheville Lyric Opera Company. $14–38.

Asheville Community Theatre (ACT) (828-254-1320; www.ashe villetheatre.org), 35 E. Walnut St. Asheville's amateur theater maintains an ambitious program of eight or more sophisticated plays from their permanent downtown theater near the Thomas Wolfe Memorial. $15.

The Diana Wortham Theatre (828-257-4530; www.dwtheatre.com), 2 S. Pack Square. This 500-seat theater, part of the Pack Place complex, hosts around 150 performances a year of every conceivable type.

Shindig on the Green (828-259-6107), July–Aug., Sat. 7–10 PM. Asheville sponsors this weekly outdoor musical get-together on the large green in front of the downtown city hall, featuring old-time mountain music, bluegrass, and dancing. Free.

The Asheville Tourists (828-258-0428; fax 828-258-0320), McCormick Field, 30 Buchanan Place. Asheville's minor-league baseball team has its headquarters in an handsome new redbrick stadium, McCormick Field, just south of downtown off US 25. Founded in 1909 as the Asheville Red Birds, the team's been known as the Tourists since 1915 and has been playing at the current site since 1924. Members of the A-rated South Atlantic League, the Tourists have been affiliated with the Colorado Rockies since 1994.

Black Mountain, NC

Park Rhythms (828-669-2052), July–Aug., Thu. 7 PM. These free concerts at Black Mountain's Lake Tomahawk Park feature a variety of bluegrass and alternative music. Free.

Swannanoa Chamber Music Festival (828-771-3050; www.warren-wilson.edu/~chamber/), June and July. This annual series consists of five weekly concerts, each one performed first at Warren Wilson College (between Asheville and Black Mountain), then repeated at Waynesville and Hendersonville, NC. $15.

✴ Selective Shopping

DOWNTOWN ASHEVILLE, NC

Asheville's 1920s-era downtown spreads over a 60-block area, just south of I-240 at US 25 (Exit 5A). Frozen in time by the Great Depression, it somehow survived the late 20th century with most of its charm intact. Nearly all of the large downtown area is dominated by two- and three-story buildings dating to the early 20th century. "Newer" buildings show art deco's industry-inspired design features, while many of the older structures sport the elaborate fillips of the 19th-century Art Nouveau movement. Indeed, you will find only four modernist block buildings in the entire district, and few buildings higher than 10 stories. Without glass towers to sterilize the streets below, Asheville retains a downtown district of charm and grace. Shoppers stroll past buildings crusted with fancy brickwork, colored tile, stone trim, and sculptures small and large. Sidewalks are filled with people, and storefronts filled with shops.

Asheville's downtown is large enough to split into four districts, each with its own distinct personality. To the west, **Battery Hill** has the largest concentrations of vintage-1920s architecture and small boutiques. **Pack Square** marks the busy heart of downtown, its banking and office district, and its arts district. To the north of Pack Square, **Lexington Hill** houses businesses and people pursuing alternate or New Age lifestyles. And to the east, the **Thomas Wolfe Plaza** area (heavily urban-renewed in the 1960s) holds the institutions of urban life—the city hall, the courthouse, the glass-tower hotel, the YMCA, and lots of parking lots.

Below are descriptions of the main shopping streets of the three shopping districts. Some of the shops are mentioned by name; others are left for you to discover. When visiting downtown Asheville, be sure to park in one of the city-owned garages: 50¢ an hour, with the first hour free.

The Pack Square Downtown Shopping District

Tiny Pack Square sits at Asheville's center, a classic urban square with benches, trees, sculptures, and storefronts—four-story brick buildings from the late 19th century. On its north side, two of Asheville's modernist glass towers choke off interest; paradoxically, the squat anonymous one on the right now houses the corporate offices of the Biltmore Estate,

having been designed by I. M. Pei for a chemical company in 1979. On its south side, the city's Pack Place museum and theater complex sits beside the marble-clad **Asheville Public Library**. Restaurants, including the **Café on the Square**, crowd around its edge.

Asheville's **arts district** extends south of the square along Biltmore Ave. (US 25). Its centerpiece is the large commercial gallery, **Blue Spiral I**, representing major regional artists in a 14,000-square-foot display area that wanders through a three-story brick building. Next door, the **Fine Arts Theatre** plays a full schedule of independent films. Storefronts up and down the street house smaller galleries; but not all is art. A **Mast General Store** (see "Boone & Banner Elk") inhabits a 1940s-era department store building; next door, an architectural salvage firm fills a building with a range of antique items rescued from old buildings being demolished. **Barley's Taproom**, a popular regional franchise, is a good place for a pizza and a microbrew (including Asheville's own Highland Gaelic Ale, brewed in the basement). The district ends at the **French Broad Food Co-op**, with a large line of natural and organic products, and the **Asheville Wine Market**, a large wine shop with a full selection of beers and cheeses as well.

Lexington Park Downtown Shopping District

At one time Lexington Park would have been known as the Bohemian Quarter, or perhaps the hippie district. In the New Millennium it's the place where the New Age hangs out its shingle. The smallest of the districts, it includes Broadway (US 25)

BATTERY HILL DOWNTOWN SHOPPING DISTRICT

The Battery Hill shopping district wanders through back streets lined with fine old 1920s-era buildings in the western part of downtown Asheville. Start your shopping trip at the little triangular-shaped park on Patton Avenue at Haywood Street. Although most of the action is to your north and west, you definitely want to start by going a block east on Patton to the **Kress Emporium**, where the individual booths of handcrafters fill the delicious old Kress Department Store building. Back at the park, **Ten Thousand Villages** carries gifts and art objects from Third World countries.

Go north, then left onto Battery Park. There's an amazing number of good, upscalish restaurants within a block of this corner: **Uptown Café**, **23 Page and The New French Bar**, the **Early Girl Eatery**, the **Laughing Seed Café**, **The Market Place**. In the lobby of the Haywood Park Hotel is **Himalayas Import**, with gift items from Tibet and Nepal. Straight ahead is the amazing **Grove Arcade**, a quarter-million-square-foot 1920s-era mall encrusted with elaborate statuary; it is fully restored and filled with small, independent merchants. When you finish with the arcade, go down the alley-width Wall Street, pedestrianized and lined with shops. **Natural Selections**, a nature store, has regional art, books, telescopes, and optics—everything that has to do with appreciating nature. Rock-climbing store **ClimbMax** has gear and an indoor climbing center. At the end of Wall Street, the monolithic glass walled Federal Building houses the **World Data Center for Meteorology**, our nation's major repository for global warming data.

Return along Battery Park, then go left up Haywood Street. There are several interesting shops and restaurants here. Be sure not to miss **Malaprop's Bookstore**, winner of the *Publishers Weekly* Bookseller of the Year 2000 Award, with a wide selection of hard-to-find titles. At the end of the long block, the **Asheville Public Library** is a friendly refuge, and library patrons who park in the garage behind it can get their parking receipts validated. Beside that is the **Asheville Civic Center and Thomas Wolfe Auditorium**, a popular venue for all sorts of stuff, from symphony orchestra concerts to minor-league ice hockey.

north of the plain modernist glass towers that flank Pack Square, and Lexington Avenue, one block to the west. This is the least boutiquey of the three districts, and the most likely spot to find stores that decorate with spray paint. It's also the best place to find that odd-little-something that would never appear inside a mall shop. The best shopping is on Lexington Avenue. A row of shops (**Native Expressions**, **Cosmic Vision**, and **The Natural Home**) feature gifts, clothing, jewelry, and home accessories from Third

World countries. Beyond that, **Max and Rosie's** offers hearty vegetarian meals in a pleasant, deli atmosphere. **TS Morrison and Company**, a downtown department store in continuous operation since 1891, now specializes in a broad selection of nostalgia items. An equally venerable institution, **The Downtown Bookstore**, anchors the upper end of Lexington with a huge set of magazine racks.

BILTMORE VILLAGE In the 1890s George Vanderbilt constructed Biltmore Village (www.biltmorevillage .com) outside the gates of his Biltmore Estate as the home for his hundreds of workers. Frederick Law Olmsted planned the village, and Richard Morris Hunt designed its buildings, giving it a unique appearance that survives to this day. Though the estate was sold off after Vanderbilt's death in 1914, Hunt's handsome buildings and Olmsted's landscaping remain—now holding an upscale shopping district.

To understand the village, picture the idyllic rural world that Vanderbilt tried to create. Vanderbilt placed his village across from the main gate of his estate, separated from it by an old narrow coach road and an expanse of green lawn. On one side of the village he placed an elegant little train station to serve the needs of the estate. In the ensuing decades, a large industrial rail yard grew up beside the little depot. The narrow coach road became US 25 and slowly expanded to hold 10 lanes of traffic. The grassy lawn, sold off and divided into pieces, came to hold a motel, three gas stations, and two fast-food franchises. Fortunately, the noise and ugliness stop as if cut off by a curtain as soon as you enter the tiny back streets of the village. The center of the village remains pretty much as Vanderbilt left it.

The large selection of independently owned shops includes half a dozen antiques stores, several galleries, five clothiers, and a dozen or so gift shops. If you get a might peckish, there are nine small independent restaurants inside the village. The village features free street parking, usually (but not always) with enough spaces to handle all the shoppers.

New Morning Gallery (828-274-2831), 7 Boston Way, Asheville, NC. New Morning Gallery looks like a tiny storefront sitting half a block from the center of Biltmore Village. Looks can deceive; the gallery stretches back deep into the building, then climbs up the stairs to sprawl through nearly a block of elegant second-floor space. New Morning specializes in "functional art," handcrafted stuff you can use (if only as a paperweight). It features artists from all over America, but with a special emphasis on regional artists. The New Morning Gallery sponsors the annual Village Arts and Crafts Festival. An affiliated gallery in the village, **Bellagio**, offers hand-crafted clothing and accessories.

BLACK MOUNTAIN, NC **The Old Depot Gallery and Museum** (www.olddepot.org). Black Mountain's old-fashioned passenger depot anchors the southern end of this small-town downtown. Painted bright yellow, it sits hard against Sutton Avenue with a row of old brick storefronts across the street. The Old Depot Association, which took it over and renovated it in 1976, runs a good-sized craft gallery there, dedicated to high-quality handcrafts in traditional mountain styles. The works of over 75 local and regional mountain craft artists can be seen at any one time, and artists frequently volunteer to run the gallery. Behind the gallery, a restored caboose houses a local history museum.

✳ Special Events

SPRING Spring Herb Festival (828-689-5974), WNC Farmer's Market, NC 109 at I-26. Early May. This annual gathering brings together all of the region's many herb farmers, selling seedlings and meeting new customers. Free.

✐ **Lake Eden Arts Festival** (828-686-8742; www.theleaf.com), 377 Lake Eden Rd., Black Mountain, NC. Last weekend in May; repeated in mid-Oct. This twice-annual festival is an eclectic mix of New Age and traditional mountain elements, heavy on music and crafts, families, and good times. Limited to 5,000 attendees at any one time, it's held at Camp Rockmont, a large and beautiful facility in the mountains west of the town of Black Mountain. People tent-camp by the lakes, go swimming and kayaking. The 3-day schedule mixes traditional and New Age arts with music, dancing, concerts, handcrafting, healing arts, special children's programs, and workshops. For a full weekend pass, adults pay $80 in advance, $90 at the gate; youths pay $65 in advance, $75 at the gate.

Black Mountain Arts and Crafts Show (828-669-0433; www.olddepot.org/craftshow/). First weekend in June. This juried sidewalk art show, limited to the best 70 exhibitors, occupies downtown Black Mountain's Sutton Avenue by its historic old depot. On Saturday night, "A Taste

of Black Mountain" offers a sampling of foods from a dozen or more Black Mountain restaurants for one ticket price. The art show is free; Taste of Black Mountain $15–18.

Asheville Gem and Mineral Show (828-254-7162). Mid-June. This weekend show at Pack Place's Colbern Gem and Mineral Museum has booths displaying crystals, gemstones, meteorites, and handcrafted jewelry, from collectors and rock shops all over the East. Free.

SUMMER Fourth of July Celebrations. Asheville, NC, has a large downtown party with live entertainment, food, children's activities, and evening fireworks. Montreat, NC, has

THE HISTORIC DOWNTOWN DISTRICT OF BLACK MOUNTAIN.

Jim Hargan

a street parade. Black Mountain, NC, has its celebration at Lake Tomahawk. **Belle Chere** (828-259-5800; www .belechere.com). Last weekend in July. This annual street festival boasts of being the largest free outdoor festival in the South. Taking over most of downtown Asheville for 3 days, Belle Chere is best known for its multiple, ongoing music venues (featuring bluegrass, jazz, rock, pop, and whatever), its street food, its copious beer sales, and its hundreds of art and craft vendors. Free.

Village Art and Craft Fair. First weekend in Aug. This large fine-craft and art show, held on the shaded grounds of the Cathedral of All Souls in Biltmore Village, attracts 140 or more artists from all over America. Held annually since 1972, its posters are notable for their original art featuring cats. It's sponsored by the New Morning Gallery.

The Mountain Dance and Folk Festival (828-257-4530). First weekend in Aug. Founded by Bascom Lamar Lunsford in 1927, this annual festival is dedicated to mountain folk music and dancing. Held in the Diana Wortham Theatre in Pack Place.

Mount Mitchell State Park Heritage Day, Burnsville, NC. Last Sat. in Aug. Traditional mountain music and dancing on the highest peak in the East, along with a variety of traditional foods and crafts, a raptor demonstration, an annual tree-planting event, hikes, and workshops.

Sourwood Festival at Black Mountain (www.blackmountain.org/festivals .php). Last weekend in Aug. This annual street fair, held in downtown Black Mountain, NC, features craft and art exhibits and food vendors. Free.

AUTUMN ♪ **Fall Pioneer Days at Vance Birthplace State Historic Site** (828-645-6706; www.ah.dcr.state .nc.us/sections/hs/vance/vance.htm), 911 Reems Creek Rd., Weaverville, NC. Third weekend in Sep. This annual event has craft and pioneer skill demonstrations, along with a frontier militia encampment, at a fully preserved early-19th-century log farmstead. Free.

Fall! By the Tracks. (www.olddepot .org/fallindex.html) Second Sat. in Oct. Black Mountain, NC's local art and history association, the Old Depot Association, sponsors this annual fall fest, featuring crafter demonstrations, making your own mountain toys, cakewalks, local honey, mountain barbeque, and made-while-you-watch apple cider.

Craft Fair of the Southern Highlands (828-298-7928). Mid-Oct. Founded in 1930 to promote crafters of the southern mountains, the nonprofit Southern Appalachian Craft Guild has been holding these craft fairs since 1948. Held in downtown Asheville, NC's Civic Center, it has a large juried show of member artists, craft demonstrations, and live music. There's a show in mid-July as well. $5.

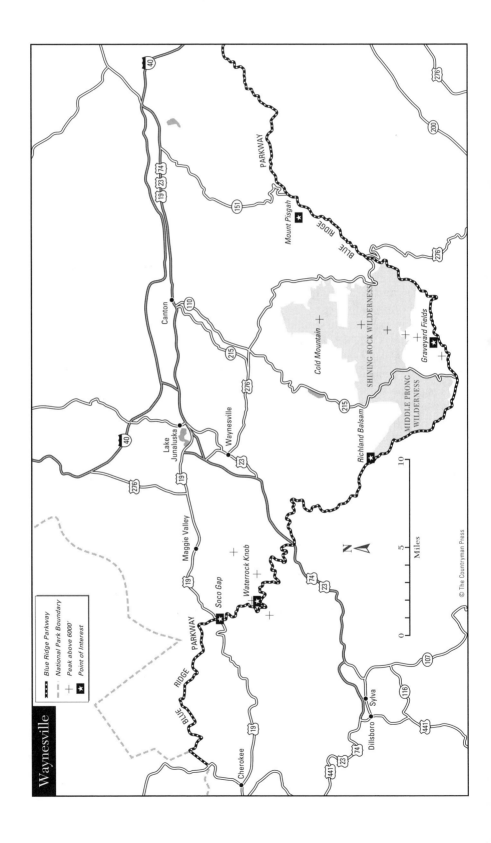

Waynesville

WAYNESVILLE & THE BLUE RIDGE PARKWAY

The penultimate section of the Blue Ridge Parkway forms a high half circle that arcs around Waynesville for nearly 50 miles. It's the parkway's highest section, passing close to 12 peaks above 6,000 feet while peaking out at 6,158 feet (1.16 miles above sea level). Indeed, 19 miles of this drive are a mile or more above sea level, and virtually all of it is above 4,000 feet. As the parkway gets higher, its views get better—broad, panoramic vistas that cover ridge upon ridge, not only from the overlooks, but also from long roadside stretches as the roadway becomes a ledge perched high in the sky. This is the most remote section of the Blue Ridge Parkway, almost continuously bordered by giant tracts of national forest lands, including two large wilderness areas; little wonder that only three roads intersect it between its start and end points.

At the foot of these mountains, Waynesville, NC, is a classic redbrick small town with a bustling three-block Main Street filled with interesting stores; its historic neighborhoods have an astonishing selection of high-quality B&B inns. Nearby is the lovely little Methodist retreat village of Lake Junaluska, NC, with its historic center and landscaped lakeside walks.

GUIDANCE **Haywood County Tourism Development Authority** (800-334-9036 or 828-452-0152; fax 828-452-0153; www.smokeymountains.net), 1233 N. Main St., Suite 1-40, Waynesville, NC 28786. This quasi-governmental agency uses the room tax to promote tourism. They are the people to call to get a packet of brochures and information.

Haywood County Chamber of Commerce (877-456-3073 or 828-456-3021; fax 828-456-7265; www.haywood-nc.com), 73 Walnut St., P.O. Drawer 600, Waynesville, NC 28786. This private not-for-profit promotes business members. It maintains a visitors center in a restored bungalow, on US 276 just north of downtown Waynesville.

Canton Papertown (Canton Chamber of Commerce) (828-648-7925; fax 828-648-6145; www.cantonpapertown.com), 36 Park St., Canton, NC 28716. The Canton Chamber of Commerce shares the town's former public library with the Canton Historic Museum, a Colonial-style brick building on the eastern edge of downtown.

GETTING THERE *By car*: I-40 runs westward from Asheville into this area, then turns northward; at this point, the freeway-quality US 23/74 continues west, past Waynesville to Sylva. The Blue Ridge Parkway follows the southern edge of this area, starting at Asheville and intersecting with US 23/74 at Balsam Gap, west of Waynesville.

By air: **Asheville Regional Airport** (828-684-2226) is just to the east of this region.

MEDICAL EMERGENCIES **Haywood Regional Medical Facility** (828-456-7311), 90 Hospital Dr., Clyde, NC. This major regional hospital has a walk-in clinic on its campus, as well as a full-service emergency room. It's 5 miles east of downtown Waynesville via US 23; take the NC 209 exit, then parallel the freeway to Jones Cove Rd.

✳ Wandering Around

EXPLORING BY CAR **The Blue Ridge Parkway**. *Leg 1*: From the parkway's intersection with NC 151, go right 17 miles to the intersection with NC 215. *Leg 2*: From NC 215, continue along the parkway for 32 miles to US 19.

This starting point, already 2,200 feet above Asheville, NC, is on the crest of the Pisgah Ridge—a crest you'll be following for the next 17 miles. Your first landmark will be the short dead-end **Mount Pisgah Spur Rd.**, on the left. Go down it a few hundred yards for a good view southward over the forests of the Mills River, then continue to the end if you want to pick up the popular (but steep and rocky) 2.5-mile round-trip hike to the 5,720-foot cone of **Mount Pisgah**, where an observation deck offers 360° views only partially spoiled by a TV tower. Back at the parkway, the **Mount Pisgah Picnic Area** is a short distance away, with the **Mount Pisgah Inn** (a good place to grab a meal) a bit farther on. From here the views open up to the south over the rhododendron-covered cove known as **The Pink Beds**, with the enormous rock dome of **Looking Glass Rock** behind it; US 276 furnishes an excellent side trip to **The Cradle of Forestry in America**. Now the parkway climbs to 5,000 feet through increasingly rugged and dramatic scenery, to **Graveyard Fields**, a meadow-covered cove perched high among mile-high peaks. In another mile

LICKSTONE RIDGE FROM MP 439 ON THE BLUE RIDGE PARKWAY.
Jim Hargan

Black Balsam Spur Rd. leads left to the trailhead for the **Shining Rock Wilderness** and access to six peaks topping 6,000 feet. Back at the parkway, look for the great stone outcrop known as the **Devils Courthouse**, and don't miss the short, easy path to its top, with panoramic views.

The second leg follows the crest of the **Great Balsam Mountains**, with seven more 6'ers along its 32 miles of ridgetop wilderness. Built in the 1960s, this modern highway slashes through the wilderness landscape in huge cuts, with long sweeping views from its wide, clear shoulders. The views start suddenly as the parkway turns upward along the clifflike flanks of 6,110-foot **Mount Hardy**, with continuous and wide panoramas southward. More views open up as the parkway sweeps toward 6,000 feet in elevation, with exceptional panoramas near **Caney Fork Overlook** and at **Cowee Mountain Overlook**. After that, the parkway reaches its highest elevation as it crests out at 6,190 feet at the **Richland Balsams Overlook**. From there it follows the mile-high meadows of **The Long Swag** before it starts its long drop to Balsam Gap. On this downward leg the parkway gives impressive views of itself as approaches the long, curving **Pinnacle Ridge Tunnel**; beyond, look for sunrise views at **Waynesville Overlook**.

The parkway dips into **Balsam Gap**, where it intersects with the four-lane US 23/74 and the first services since Mount Pisgah (go right 1 mile). After Balsam Gap the parkway climbs steadily for the next 8 miles, as good views open up. The parkway crests out as it crosses the massive side ridge known as **Plott Balsams**, at 5,710 feet. Here a spur road leads to the impressive **Waterrock Knob Overlook**, with a new visitors center, water, toilets, and picnic tables. To the left, a side trail follows a high, narrow ridgeline to form the **Plott Balsams Walk**, with excellent views back toward Balsam Gap. As the parkway descends from Waterrock Knob, it passes a series of good views west over the Cherokee lands before dropping into the forests of **Soco Gap**.

EXPLORING ON FOOT **A walk around Lake Junaluska**. You'll find Lake Junaluska just off US 19, 4 miles north of Waynesville, NC; turn right onto Lakeshore Drive and proceed to the large public lot by the administration center.

After you've explored the high, windy ridges and mountaintop meadows in the rugged wilderness surrounding

THE PUBLIC PARK ON THE SHORES OF LAKE JUNALUSKA IS A PLEASANT PLACE TO CATCH COOL LAKE BREEZES.

Jim Hargan

TRAILS OF THE GREAT BALSAM MOUNTAINS

Even compared with other parts of the Blue Ridge and Smoky Mountains, this area offers an exceptional variety of walking paths in a small area. Each of these walks gives a comparatively easy taste of a particular type of scenery found here: mountaintop meadows, backcountry waterfalls, wide views, craggy outcrops, and spruce–fir "balsam" forests.

Graveyard Fields and Black Balsam Knob. This high perched valley sits nearly a mile above sea level, flanked by seven 6,000-foot peaks, just off the Blue Ridge Parkway 3 miles east of NC 215. Once covered by huge old-growth forests—*graveyard* refers to the gravelike mounds left by fallen giant trees as they return to the soil—it was devastated by clear-cut fires in the early 20th century and remains meadow covered to this day. A lovely system of hiking trails, most starting at the Graveyard Fields Overlook on the Blue Ridge Parkway, loops around the wildflower-carpeted meadows, along the clear mountain river that cuts through its center, down to the roaring waterfall that marks its foot, and up to the tall, graceful waterfall that sits at its head.

Above the fields, the 6,214-foot **Black Balsam Knob** (23rd highest peak in the East) and the adjacent 6,040-foot **Tennant Mountain** (34th highest) can be easily reached via the **Black Balsam Trail**, starting on the Black Balsam Spur Rd. off the parkway just west of the fields. This 1.75-mile round trip (with 1,200 feet of total climbing) follows the high ridgeline through mountaintop meadows and past large rock outcrops, with nearly continuous views over waving wildflowers. Turn around when you reach the deep gap with the old abandoned road—or continue forward into the stunning high ridge meadows of the **Shining Rock Wilderness** with three more 6,000-foot peaks.

A Walk in the Middle Prong Wilderness. The **Mountains-to-Sea Trail** makes for an easy 3.5-mile round trip to the lush, spreading meadows on the 5,800-foot-tall crest of this otherwise remote wilderness area. Park your car on the Blue Ridge Parkway as it traverses the Great Balsam Mountains, at **Rough Butt Bald Overlook** (MP 425.3) about 2 miles from Beech Gap (NC 215). A path directly opposite the overlook links you to the Mountains-to-Sea Trail with its white circular blazes. Follow the blazes to your right. The trail quickly

the Blue Ridge Parkway, you may find yourself ready for a level walk, on a paved path, through landscaped parklands along a lakeshore. If so, you're in luck. The historic Lake Junaluska retreat, run by the United Methodist Church, maintains a 3-mile parkland walk along their centerpiece lake, open to public use. Admire the stunning mountain view from the parking lot, and the handsome buildings at the center of this retreat; then follow the paved path left. You will quickly reach the monumental cross that serves as the centerpiece for the retreat, on a hill passes into the **Middle Prong Wilderness** and follows an old logging tramway, level, wide, and easy. This balsam forest, like other high-altitude forests on Balsam Mountain, had survived heavy logging and acidic paper mill emissions throughout most of the 20th century, only to fall to a natural enemy—the fir-killing woolly aphid, accidentally introduced to North America around 1900. At 1.2 miles the Mountains-to-Sea blazes turn uphill to the right, climbing half a mile to the crest of **Fork Ridge**, remarkable for its mountaintop meadows. Formed by logging fires in the early 20th century and still occupying most of the Fork Mountain crest, the grassy meadows extend along the top of this high ridge for 2.3 miles, with a maze of paths leading through wildflowers and berries. Views are frequent and stunning, with the best views from rocky outcrops on the east side, looking over the gorge of the West Fork Pigeon River toward the sweeping meadows of the Shining Rock Wilderness.

Richland Balsams Nature Trail. This 1.2-mile nature trail climbs 350 feet to the 6,410-foot peak of **Richland Balsams** (10th highest in the East), the highest point on the lands of the Blue Ridge Parkway. Once a forest walk where giant firs and spruces shaded an open floor of needles and moss, it now crosses an ecosystem undergoing rapid and radical transition. Around 1980 a parasitic insect known as the woolly adelgid or aphid (an exotic introduced into Canada around 1900) reached the Balsam Mountains in its slow southward migration through the Appalachians. Within a few years all the fir trees (more than half the forest) had died, leaving the remaining spruces exposed to harsh weather and high wind, and the forest floor exposed to a whole host of sun-loving competitors. The trail now travels through wildflower meadows, thick patches of blackberry briars, stands of mountain ash (rowan) saplings, occasional groves of old spruces, and thick masses of fir seedlings and saplings competing with each other as well as the aphids. Once viewless because of the dense forest, the path now offers several vistas over newly formed meadows and briar patches; one such view lets you look down on the sign claiming to mark the highest point on the parkway. A guide to this nature loop, available at its beginning, gives full information on the forest succession going on around you.

above you. Then, at a quarter mile, walk across the handsome old dam that impounds the lake. For the next mile the level, paved path goes through landscaped parklands along the lakeshore, with stunning views west toward the 6,000-foot peaks of the Plott Balsams. Then the path crosses the lake on a long footbridge and reenters the main retreat area, passing historic and modern buildings still used as a center for refreshing the spirit. When you regain your car, you'll have walked 2.25 miles.

✳ Villages

Waynesville, NC. In the early days of the Republic, Waynesville sat at the border of the Cherokee Nation, literally the end of the road for European settlers. As the Cherokees were pushed back into Tennessee, and then evacuated to Oklahoma, Waynesville gained in importance as the gateway to the tangled valleys of the Blue Ridge and Smoky Mountains. Today it remains the main gateway and the largest of the traditional mountain towns. At first glance it's more sprawling and industrial than the other Smoky and Blue Ridge Mountain towns; however, attractive and genteel neighborhoods, rich in historic architecture, sit only a scant half a block off the main drag. These historic neighborhoods have become a prime destination for knowledgeable visitors, as a dozen or more bed & breakfast inns have moved in. Waynesville has a charming downtown, three blocks of historic redbrick structures with a good choice of interesting shops. Downtown parking is free, but limited; there is plenty of parking on the back blocks, however. Every July this wonderful town center becomes the main venue for **Folkmoot**, a large-scale gathering of 10 or more national dance troupes with performances throughout the Smoky Mountains region.

The town of Lake Junaluska, NC. This small lakeside town 4 miles north of Waynesville, NC, off US 19 is dominated by its large and historic retreat, headquarters for the United Methodist Church in the Southeast. The 180-acre lake was created in the 1920s as part of a retreat for missionaries; now open to the public, the retreat remains the main focus of the village. The Methodist Church headquarters and retreat sits on the north side of the lake, an impressive grouping of buildings, both historic and modern, dominated by the 1922 **Lambuth Inn** with its giant memorial cross. The south side, a quiet residential area, is lined by landscaped parklands with a 2-mile paved path—a wonderful lakeview walk.

WAYNESVILLE IS SURROUNDED BY THE FORESTED SLOPES OF THE PISGAH RANGE.

Jim Hargan

Canton, NC. Founded as the home of Champion Paper in 1906, Canton remains dominated by its giant mill, still one of the largest in America. Champion located here because the high-altitude boreal forest furnished large numbers of spruce trees, valued for producing a high-quality pulp. Parts of these Champion forests have since become the Shining Rock Wilderness, the Middle Prong Wilderness, and the Smokemont area of the Great Smoky Mountains National Park—all with large areas significantly altered to this day by huge clear-cut fires. Champion Paper finally left this

LOOKING FROM MP 430 INTO THE MIDDLE PRONG WILDERNESS.

Jim Hargan

area in the late 1990s, selling its plant to its employees and divesting itself of its last forestlands in 2001. Still a working mill town, Canton has few tourist facilities, but its small museum is worth a visit.

✳ Wild Places

THE GREAT FORESTS **The Shining Rock Wilderness**. The 18,400 acres of the Shining Rock Wilderness center on the high **Shining Rock Ledge**, a north-trending side ridge of the **Pisgah Range** with three 6,000-foot peaks (and four more in the protected recreation lands on its immediate south). Champion Paper purchased all of these lands in 1906, building the huge paper mill at Canton, NC, to exploit the spruces found in these high-altitude forests. This was not a success, and Champion turned to the Smokies for spruce pulp, selling Shining Rock to a succession of lumber companies. The loggers used tramways and locomotives to clear-cut the area; in 1926 sparks from a locomotive touched off a 25,000-acre wildfire that denuded Shining Rock's mile-high crest, creating the broad grassy meadows that remain the wilderness's most distinctive feature. Logging ceased after the fire, and the tract passed into the hands of the Pisgah National Forest in 1935. Congress created the Shining Rock Wilderness in 1964.

Shining Rock's summit meadows are rich in wildflowers and punctuated by unusual rock outcrops—including the large **Shining Rock** itself, a great mass of quartz that shines in the sun. The meadows extend southward all the way to the crest of the Pisgah Range and the Blue Ridge Parkway, and northward to **Cold Mountain** (6,030 feet, the 40th highest in the East), the same mountain used as the title for the best-selling novel. Because this 12-mile ledge is both stunningly beautiful and easily reached from the Blue Ridge Parkway, it tends to be popular. A good trail follows the crest from Black Balsam Knob all the way to Cold Mountain; it's easy going in its early sections but gets gradually more difficult as it proceeds, with the final ascent of Cold Mountain being notoriously difficult. A number of side trails, very rough and difficult, lead down the ridge to the forested valleys in the wilderness's lower slopes.

The Middle Prong Wilderness (828-877-3265), Pisgah Forest, NC. Created by Congress in 1984, the 7,900-acre Middle Prong Wilderness occupies some of the highest, roughest, and most difficult land in the eastern wilderness system—the southern terminus of the **Great Balsam Mountains**. Within this wilderness the mountains rise from 3,200 to 6,400 feet—over 3,000 feet of local relief—in only 2 linear miles. The **Middle Prong** runs through the center of this wilderness, a mountain river in a deep, gashlike valley; **Fork Mountain** rises from it to the east, wholly within the wilderness, while the Great Balsam Mountains (with the Blue Ridge Parkway on the crest) rings the wilderness to the south and west.

Like the neighboring Shining Rock Wilderness, the Middle Prong was clear-cut in the 1920s, then devastated by fire. The forests have rested since then, becoming very mature and attractive. Upper slopes are covered by balsam forests, while lower slopes are covered in maturing mixed hardwoods. The high crest of **Fork Ridge**, contained within the wilderness, is covered by a series of grassy wild-flower meadows stretching for 2 miles along its ridgeline, affording spectacular views; at the south end of Fork Mountain stands 6,010-foot **Mount Hardy**, the 30th tallest mountain in the East. The **Mountains-to-Sea Trail** gives safe and easy access to these mountaintop meadows; otherwise, the Middle Prong Wilderness trail system, although extensive, consists mainly of unblazed, unmaintained logging tramways, making for difficult and dangerous hiking.

PICNIC AREAS **Mount Pisgah Picnic Area**. This large picnic area on the Blue Ridge Parkway is part of the Mount Pisgah area, the last full-service recreation area on the parkway. It sits in a ridgeline forest just shy of 5,000 feet high—very breezy and cool on a hot summer day.

✸ To See

THE BLUE RIDGE PARKWAY **Caney Fork** and **Cowee Mountain Overlooks** (MP 428 and 431). Although Caney Fork Overlook itself is mildly disappointing, the mile-long stretch of parkway on either side gives dramatic roadside views (with easy verge parking) down a 3,000-foot drop into a mountain valley, and beyond to the Tuckaseegee River, the Cowee Mountains, and the Nantahala Mountains. Sunset lovers will appreciate the way the sun dips down into the lowest part of the deep valley, dropping below the horizon to throw orange sidelights on the tall ridges to its right and left, then falls behind layered mountains that recede endlessly into the background. Two miles later, Cowee Mountain Overlook gives a 270° view from a promontory, nearly 6,000 feet in elevation, that thrusts westward from the parkway over the deep valleys of the Balsams. A quarter mile north, the **Haywood-Jackson Overlook** supplies the missing 90° view, eastward over the deep gorge of the West Fork to the mountaintop meadows of the Middle Prong and Shining Rock Wilderness; fans of the best-selling novel *Cold Mountain* should look for this 6,030-foot peak in the far background.

Balsam Gap. The parkway crosses this deep gap at right angles as it follows the crest of the Balsams, making long ascents on both sides. Balsam Gap was (and is) the gateway to the western mountains of North Carolina, the only good eastern approach to the deep valleys of the Tuckaseegee, the Nantahala, and the Little

Tennessee Rivers. Nowadays it's traversed by a railroad and a four-lane highway, US 23/74. The historic community of **Balsam**, NC, occupies the western side of the gap, where the Balsam Mountain Inn, an old railroad hotel, still thrives. The closest facilities, however, are on the eastern side of the gap, where a wayside park furnishes picnic tables, toilets, and phones, with gas stations only a little farther on.

Waterrock Knob. In its climb northward out of Balsam Gap, the parkway passes a number of good overlooks with views west and south. You might want to save your film for the top, though; as the parkway finally reaches the crest, it sends a third-of-a-mile spur to a series of three overlooks with stunning 270° views. These overlooks (with views west, south, and north over the Balsams) occupy the high, grassy crest of a great wall-like side ridge known as **Plott Balsams**, for the local frontiersman who bred the Plott bearhound for hunting these slopes. The collection of overlooks makes up a small recreation area, with a modest visitors center, water, toilets, several tables, many wildflowers, and large grassy verges perfect for picnic blankets or tossing a Frisbee. Beyond the overlooks a wide, heavily used trail climbs very steeply to the peak of Waterrock Knob, for some good views.

MUSEUMS **The Museum of North Carolina Handicrafts** (828-452-1551), 49 Shelton St., Waynesville, NC. Tue.–Fri. 10–4. Located on the south edge of Waynesville on US 276, the 1875 Shelton House is home to this extensive display of both home crafts and fine art crafts from the Smokies, other parts of North Carolina, and the Navajo Nation. This beautifully restored mountain farmhouse, surrounded by meadows, has two-story verandas along its front and walnut trim throughout its interior. Inside are traditional 19th-century farm furnishings and a wide array of mountain crafts—pottery, baskets, quilts, toys, and dulcimers. It has a large collection of Seagrove pottery, and items from fine-craft artists throughout the state. A gift shop offers handmade craft items for sale. $5.

Canton Historic Museum (828-646-3412), Park St., Canton, NC. Mon.–Fri. 10–noon and 1–4, Sun. 2–4. This small local museum occupies the former public library in downtown Canton, next to the city hall. It has some items from the pioneer era, but most of its exhibits are about its controversial paper mill, often cited as the largest in the South, in operation next door since 1906. Free.

✳ To Do

FISHING **Lowe Fly Shop and Outfitter** (828-452-0039; fax 828-452-2860; www.loweflyshop.com), 977 N. Main St., Waynesville, NC. Roger Lowe acts as a fly-fishing guide from his fishing shop in downtown Wayneville. A specialist in hand-tying flies, he offers encyclopedic information on fly patterns useful in the Smokies. Half day $150 for the first person, $50 per additional person; full day $200 for the first person, $75 per additional person, including lunch.

GEM MINING **Old Pressley Sapphire Mine** (828-648-6320), 240 Pressley Mine Rd., Canton, NC. Take Exit 33 off I-40, then go north 1 mile on Newfound Rd.; from there, follow the signs for another 1.5 miles down back roads. Daily 9–6.

This remote mine has produced record-setting sapphires in years past. It remains one of the few recreational gem mines in these mountains to be located at an authentic mine, using unsalted ore from on site (which you can dig yourself).

GOLF Waynesville Country Club Inn (800-627-6250 or 828-452-4617; fax 828-456-3555; www.wccinn.com), Waynesville, NC. Located on the edge of Waynesville, a mile west of downtown on US Business 23. This golf resort built its first nine-hole course on a dairy farm in 1926; the barn served as the clubhouse. It now has three 9-hole courses, which are played in three 18-hole combinations; views from the links extend to the surrounding mountains. The large resort has buildings from nearly every decade from the 1930s to the 1990s. $28.

Iron Tree Golf Course (828-627-1933), Iron Tree Dr. (NC 209), Waynesville, NC. Located 5 miles north of Waynesville off NC 209 (Exit 24 off I-40). Daily 7–7. This 1991 course recently expanded to 18 holes. The course is hilly, with excellent mountain scenery. $22.

Lake Junaluska Golf Course (828-456-5777), 19 Golf Course Rd., Waynesville, NC. This 18 hole public course, built in 1919, is located 2 miles north of Waynesville on US 19, on the south edge of the Methodist retreat community. $12.

Springdale Resort and Country Club (800-553-3027 or 828-235-8451; fax 828-648-5502; www.springdalegolf.com), 200 Golfwatch Rd., Canton, NC. Opens at 7 AM, all year. Despite its Canton mailing address, this golf resort is deep in the Pisgah Mountains, in a scenic valley 11 miles south of Waynesville, NC, on US 276. The 18-hole, par-72 course offers stunning scenery, with views toward Cold Mountain and the Shining Rock Ledge; play is accentuated by hilly terrain and mountain streams. $45.

✳ Lodging

COUNTRY HOTEL The Old Stone Inn (800-432-8499 or 828-456-3333; www.oldstoneinn.com), 109 Dolan Rd., Waynesville, NC 28786. Apr.–Dec. This Mobil three-star lodge sits off a quiet back street in one of Waynesville's residential neighborhoods, three-quarters mile north of downtown. In operation since 1946, this rustic lodge has 23 rooms and a well-respected gourmet restaurant in its seven buildings scattered over 6 acres. The Main Lodge, with stone walls and tuliptree logs, houses the restaurant, wine bar, and two rooms; its long front porch overlooks the well-kept garden. Seventeen other rooms and four cottages (no kitchens) are found elsewhere on the property. Rooms, frequently small, are deco-rated in a simple, rustic manner, with wood paneling common. Breakfast, included in the tariff and available only to guests, starts with coffee, muffin, and newspaper left outside the room, and continues with a full, gourmet buffet in the lodge (table service on weekends). $89–154 per night, including breakfast.

RESORTS ✐ ♿ The Pisgah Inn (828-235-8228; fax 828-648-9719; www.pisgahinn.com), P.O. Drawer 749, Waynesville, NC 28786. Apr.–Oct. This modern motel-style inn fronts on the Blue Ridge Parkway in the

4,900-foot-high Mount Pisgah area—a national park concessionaire, and a good one. Two long, low buildings face over a sharp drop, giving dramatic views from every room. Standard rooms are normal hotel size, with two double beds and a private balcony with rocking chairs overlooking that fabulous view. The deluxe rooms have the same great views from the balcony but are more spacious, more recently renovated, and have larger windows for an unobstructed inside view. The one suite is a two-roomer with wood-burning fireplace. The attached restaurant (see *Eating Out*) is consistently good, specializing in fresh, simply prepared mountain dishes. This is the Blue Ridge Parkway's final inn, at the start of the stunning, rugged Pisgah/Balsams section—very cool, windy, remote, and quiet. Standard rooms $75, deluxe rooms $87, suites $125.

✧ ♿ **The Lambuth Inn at the Lake Junaluska Assembly** (800-222-4930; fax 828-452-2225; www.lakejunaluska .com), P.O. Box 67, Lake Junaluska, NC 28745. Open all year. This Methodist retreat complex, owned and operated by the Southeastern Conference of the United Methodist Church (whose headquarters are on the premises), is open to individual vacationers and families, whether or not they wish to participate in any of the religious programs. The retreat includes modern motels, apartments, and private cottage rentals—but its most striking property is the 1922 Lambuth Inn, with 130 en suite hotel rooms. This large hilltop hotel dominates the Lake Junaluska skyline with its bright yellow walls, white trim, and neo-Federalist classical styling. Needless to say, views from the Lambuth

are first-rate. The Lambuth has standard hotel rooms for one to four people, plus an on-site restaurant. The tariff includes free access to all the recreation facilities at the retreat, including golf and tennis. Alcohol is prohibited on all retreat properties. The Junaluska Assembly likes to quote prices per person double occupancy including meals; as usual, this entry converts it to two people double occupancy without meals, at the time of writing. In-season $72, off-season $58. To include all meals, add $20 per day per person.

BED & BREAKFAST INNS ✧ **Windsong, A Mountain Inn** (828-627-6111; fax 828-627-8080; www.wind songbb.com), 459 Rockcliffe Lane, Clyde, NC 28721. This handsome modern log lodge sports wide views from its high-mountain meadows, grazed by sheep and llamas. The front of the inn faces uphill toward the small, Oriental-style garden, heated swimming pool, and tennis courts. Inside the inn, timber framing and planked log walls give a rustic counterpoint to an exotic decor that combines western furniture with folk items from around the world, while high picture windows open up the inn to the grand view outside. Four of the five rooms share that view with private decks or patios, while the fifth has a private entrance onto the inn's flower and herb garden. All the rooms have fireplace, large whirlpool tub (with wineglasses and opener on the side), and VCR. Children are welcome in the adjacent **Pond Lodge**, another modern log structure, each of whose two suites has two bedrooms and a full kitchen, along with a wonderful view from a private deck. Main Inn guests have a full gourmet breakfast, delicious and strikingly original; Pond Lodge guests have a continental breakfast delivered to their suite. Llama trek lunches and dinners (extra charge) are a special treat available to guests only—a woodland trek with Russ's sweet and gentle llamas to a special picnic platform over a mountain stream, with a dinner of grilled salmon. Main Inn $120–145 low season, $125–155 high season. Pond Lodge suites $160–170 low season, $170–180 high season. $10 weekday discount.

The Yellow House (800-563-1236 or 828-452-0991; fax 828-452-1140; www.theyellowhouse.com), 89 Oakview Dr., Plott Creek Rd., Waynesville, NC 28786. Open all year. This outstanding luxury B&B occupies a century-old house on a pond, surrounded by beautiful gardens, in the pastoral Plott Creek Valley 3 miles from downtown Waynesville. Built by the prominent Lykes family of Tampa in the late 19th century, the Yellow House is a simple, elegant late-Victorian structure with wraparound porches and a second-story balcony. Common rooms are rich in polished hardwood and Victorian antiques; guests enjoy a wine-and-cheese reception in the afternoon, and a refrigerator full of beverages in the kitchen. The full gourmet breakfast is served on china and crystal in the elegant dining room. All of the six large guest rooms are individually theme decorated by owner Susan Smith, each reminiscent of a favorite place. Two are largish rooms with bay windows, themed after American places. Two others are each two-room suites including a full sitting area with fireplace, wet bar, and luxurious bath. The remaining two rooms are extra-

sized suites with private entrance and views over the lily pond. The cottage, Joy's Place, offers a French country kitchen, two bedrooms and baths, two fireplaces, and views over the pond from every room. Rooms $135–145, suite $175–250, cottage with kitchen $235. Discounts for midweek and off-season.

Andon House Bed and Breakfast (800-293-6190 or 828-452-3089; www.andonhouse.com), 92 Daisey Ave., Waynesville, NC 28786. This large 1902 Victorian-style farmhouse sits in a quiet residential neighborhood three blocks uphill from downtown Waynesville. It features wide porches, tall ceilings, high windows, and lots of wood trim and Victorian furniture in the ample common rooms downstairs. The four rooms range from cozy to large; all are individually decorated and sound-insulated, and two have private sundecks. The full breakfast, served in the dining room, runs to four courses. Low season $85–115, high season $95–125.

⚘ Prospect Hill Bed and Breakfast (800-219-6147 or 828-456-5980; www.mountaininns.com), 274 S. Main St., Waynesville, NC 28786. Built in 1902, this large late-Victorian farmhouse sits on its own hill surrounded by 1.3 acres of lawns and trees, on US Business 23 just south of downtown Waynesville. A large, wide wraparound porch gives fine views over downtown Waynesville, and the first-floor common rooms are decorated with period antiques. The five guest rooms, all upstairs, are individually furnished with antiques and reproductions; all are spacious, and the three more expensive rooms have sitting areas with Victorian sofas.

Morning coffee is brought to your room, and a full breakfast served on china and crystal in the formal dining room or on the porch. While small children are not taken in the main house, they are welcome in the two cottage apartments on the property, both in the heavily modernized carriage house; these full-sized studio apartments have fireplace, kitchen, and great views from picture windows. $95–135 for B&B in the main house; cottage apartments (no breakfast) $170 for 2 nights, $450 per week.

Haywood House Bed and Breakfast (828-456-9831; fax 828-456-4400), 675 S. Haywood St., Waynesville, NC 28786. This large historic house on a busy side street of Wayneville's lovely little downtown was once the home of the local historian; now it houses a bed & breakfast inn. The five cozy rooms are elaborately decorated in high-Victorian style, including antiques; two share a bath. A full home-cooked breakfast is served in the dining room. $75–95 per night, including breakfast.

♿ **Herrin House** (800-284-1932 or 828-452-7837; www.herrenhouse.com), 94 East St., Waynesville, NC 28786. Originally built as a boarding-house in 1897, the completely renovated Herrin House sits a short block off the center of downtown Waynesville, on a quiet residential side street. Its large wraparound porch looks out over a garden, with a roomy gazebo. Decor, both in the ample common areas and in the six guest rooms, is elegantly Victorian, with antiques and reproductions. Rooms are individually decorated, some elaborately and others with a simpler, outdoors theme; one special room is octagonal, with an original 48-light

window. Afternoon tea consists of homemade goodies, and a full breakfast is served in the dining room. $95–140.

Ten Oaks Bed and Breakfast (800-563-2925 or 828-452-9433; www.tenoaksbedandbreakfast.com), 224 Love Lane, Waynesville, NC 28786. This large hilltop Victorian house, built for the mayor of Waynesville in 1898 and listed on the National Register of Historic Places, sits in a quiet residential neighborhood, with views over Waynesville and toward the Pisgah Mountains beyond. Common areas, with elegant Victorian decor, face a large wraparound porch and a gazebo garden. The five large rooms all have sitting area and individual Victorian decor, and two are two-room suites. Rooms $95–110, suites $130–145, including breakfast.

October Hill (800-628-4455 or 828-452-7967; www.octoberhillbedandbreakfast.com), 421 Grimball Dr., Waynesville, NC 28786. This elegant 1920s mansion sits on a hill, surrounded by shaded lawns, 1 mile south of downtown Waynesville just off US Business 23. Its four literary-themed rooms, ranging in size from normal to large, are furnished in high fashion from the 1920s, as are the comfortable common rooms. A full breakfast is served in the dining room, and afternoon refreshments are available in the Grand Room. $95–135.

♨ **The Grange Bed and Breakfast** (828-452-0339; fax 828-452-6999; www.thegrangebb.com), 355 Grassmere Lane, Waynesville, NC 28786. This modern, purpose-built inn sits on its own 60 acres in Oxear Cove, 5 miles from downtown Wayneville. The lands include an English tea garden, meadows, forests, mountain streams, and even a duck pond, all accessible to guests by a network of old farm roads. Wide covered porches offer spectacular views over Waynesville and the Pisgah Ridge, especially good at sunrise in fall, when fog fills the valleys below. Each of the four rooms has its own balcony with a wide mountain view. A full breakfast is included. $100–115; discounts during the off-season.

CABIN RENTALS Rivermont Cabins (828-648-3066; www.rivermont.com), 311 Rivermont Dr., Canton, NC 28716. This 70-acre wooded property has half a mile of frontage on the West Fork Pigeon River in the Sunburst area, 9 miles south of Waynesville. The nine cabins are all individual structures with their own histories, ranging from modest cabins to full-sized houses, and from contemporary log structures to the local 1855 schoolhouse. $415–985 per week; daily rentals only during the off-season.

✳ Where to Eat

EATING OUT Lomo Bakery and Café (828-452-1515; fax 828-452-1746), 44 Church St., Waynesville, NC. Lunch Mon.–Sat. This lunch spot produces fresh breads and pastries, and a fine array of first-rate sandwiches. Its big brother, the nearby Lomo Grille (see *Dining Out*), opens for lunch as well to give customers better seating for the popular sandwiches and pastries, plus burgers and other hot items.

♿ **The Pisgah Inn** (828-235-8228; fax 828-648-9719; www.pisgahinn .com), P.O. Drawer 749, Waynesville, NC 28786. Open Apr.–Oct. 7:30–10:30 (breakfast), 11:30–4 (lunch), 5–9 (dinner). This national park concessionaire sits by the side of the Blue Ridge Parkway, high and remote on the flanks of Mount Pisgah. The casual, simply furnished restaurant has dramatic views from huge windows that cover its entire southern side, flanked by large timber beams. The menu emphasizes fresh ingredients and mountain recipes, although plenty of old favorites are available, too. Full breakfasts can be ordered with fresh mountain trout, and local hickory-smoked trout can be ordered from the appetizer menu. Burgers and sandwiches can be ordered for lunch or dinner, but a more formal dinner is also available, with specials that are prepared from scratch and change daily. Wine and beer are available. Breakfast $4.75–9.95 (pastries $1–2), lunch $4.95–6.95, dinner $4.95–11.50.

Maggie's Galley (828-456-8945), 49 Howell Mill Rd., Wayneville, NC. Lunch and dinner, Tue.–Sun. Despite its name, Maggie's Galley is not located in Maggie Valley; this seafood restaurant occupies a log building just off US 276 a mile north of downtown Waynesville. Built in 1975 from logs salvaged from historic log cabins, this cozy and comfortable eatery features casual dining from a menu heavy with seafood favorites. Don't expect any masterful gourmet specialties here— just good food, prepared in the traditional way.

DINING OUT The Old Stone Inn (800-432-8499 or 828-456-3333; www.oldstoneinn.com), 109 Dolan Rd., Waynesville, NC. Apr.–Dec. 6–8 PM, by reservation only. Part of a rustic lodge, this Golden Fork–winning restaurant sits in a quiet residential neighborhood three-quarters of a mile north of downtown Waynesville. Owner Cindy Zinser serves as the chef, designing a short but selective menu that imaginatively exploits seasonally fresh ingredients. The wine list is excellent, and the **Wine Bar** offers wine by the glass with hors d'oeuvres from 5 PM. The stone-and-log lodge, with a large porch overlooking 6 landscaped acres, has a rustic look and feel. Entrées $15–21.

The Sourwood Grille (800-553-3027 or 828-235-8451; fax 828-648-5502; www.springdalegolf.com), 200 Golfwatch Rd., Canton, NC. Lunch and dinner, Apr.–Nov. Located on the grounds of the Springdale Country Club 11 miles south of Waynesville on US 276, this scenic and popular spot offers fine dining for lunch and dinner. Lunch menus include a range of interesting and unusual hot and cold sandwiches, burgers, fish cakes, salads, and pasta dishes, none of it particularly expensive. Dinners are fancier, with fresh and highly original fare, ranging from a spinach, leek, and goat cheese phyllo pie with charred pepper and tomato coulis, to grilled spice lamb chops with roasted sweet potato and mint cumin yogurt sauce. Lunch $6–8, dinner $13–19.

Lomo Grille (828-452-5222; www.lomogrill.com), 44 Church St., Waynesville, NC. Dinner Thu.–Sat. as well as Mon. This Golden Fork winner in downtown Waynesville specializes in Italian-Argentinian cuisine—the heritage of owner Ricardo Fernandez. Its special feature is its wood-fired oven, imported from Italy. The menu includes imported Argentine beef, as well as lamb, salmon, trout, and pasta. Chef Ricardo is fanatic about using only fresh ingredients, to the point of growing many of his own vegetables and herbs. The restaurant has an extensive international wine list (not surprising, since Ricardo is a retired wine merchant), as well as a wine bar where many of the offerings can be sampled by the glass.

✹ Entertainment
Haywood Arts Repertory Theatre (HART) (828-456-6322), 114 Church St., Waynesville, NC. This local theater group performs seven shows each summer season (including two musicals) in their purpose-built 250-seat theater behind the Museum of North Carolina Handicrafts. $12–15.

Pickin' in the Park (828-646-3411). Every Fri. at 7 PM, May–Aug., the City of Canton, NC, presents local bluegrass, mountain, and country groups, free of charge, by the Pigeon River at the Canton Recreation Park. Bring your own lawn chair. Free.

Mountain Street Dances (828-456-3517). Every other Sat., July–Aug., 6:30–9 PM. Clogging and square dancing to live bluegrass music on the front lawn of the county courthouse, in downtown Waynesville, NC. Free.

✹ Selective Shopping
Waynesville, NC
Downtown Waynesville has one of the more interesting and varied shopping districts in the Smokies. A classic small-town district, it stretches three blocks along the former main highway, from the county courthouse to the city hall. Its 86 retailers and restaurants are dominated by small craft galleries and boutiques, along with antiques stores, kitchen supplies, books, cafés, wine sellers . . . almost anything except the franchised or the dull.

Sloan's Book Shop, 263 N. Haywood St. This bright, pleasant bookstore one block off Main St. goes well beyond the usual stock of best sellers to carry a wonderful selection of local-interest titles. Smoky Mountain history, ecology, folklore, fiction—it's all here.

Craft galleries and studios in downtown Waynesville. Twelve craft galleries and studios group together in the three blocks of downtown Wayneville—a bonanza for the fine-craft shopper. On the edge of downtown (Haywood and Depot), sculptor Grace Cathey exhibits her nature-inspired art in a working gas station (Walker Service Station), with a sculpture garden in back. Then, in a two-block stretch of Main Street (US 276), look for galleries displaying local professional artists' clay sculpture, stoneware, jewelry, textiles, photographs, woodcarving, watercolors, pencil sketches, and numbered prints. Four of these shops incorporate the working studios of their artist-owners. **Twig and Leaves** (98 Main St.) features nature-inspired art, and includes the studio of potter Kaaren Stoner. **Burr Gallery** (136 Main St.) features the studio and work (sculpture and stoneware) of clay artists Dane and MaryEtta Burr. **Hardwood Gallery** (102 Main St.) features craft items and sculptures carved from local woods on the spot. And **Cross-Currents** (84 Main St.) features textiles and rugs, some handwoven on the giant loom upstairs.

✳ Special Events

SPRING The Garden Party (828-642-7925). Second Sat. in May. This Canton, NC, street fair celebrates the coming of spring with plant sales,

craft displays, live music, and a Mad Hatter contest.

SUMMER Art in the Mountains (828-456-3517), 19 South Main St., Waynesville, NC. Third Sat. in June. Downtown Waynesville artists open up their galleries and studios for this annual open house and walking tour.

Fourth of July celebrations. Waynesville, NC, celebrates Independence Day with a downtown street fair, with sidewalk sales, entertainment, and refreshments (11 AM–3 PM). Nearby Lake Junaluska has an 11 AM parade, followed by live mountain music, clogging, and craft displays until 3 PM. Waynesville's fortnightly evening of **Mountain Street Dancing** starts the following Saturday.

⬆ **Blue Ridge Reunion Arts and Crafts Show**, Balsam Gap. July–Oct. The wide halls of the historic Balsam Mountain Inn host this annual juried art show of Jackson and Haywood County artists and crafters.

Folkmoot USA (877-365-5872 or 828-452-2997; fax 828-452-5762; www.folkmoot.com), 112 Virginia Ave., Waynesville, NC. Last 2 weeks in July. This major folk dance event

PARTICIPANTS IN TRADITIONAL COSTUME AT WAYNESVILLE'S FOLKMOOT.

Jim Hargan

brings 10 to 12 national dance troupes to the Smoky Mountains region, with Waynesville at the center of the action. As many as 350 dancers and musicians perform folk music and dance in native costume at venues scattered throughout the mountains. The festivities start with a daylong street fair in downtown Waynesville, with dancers and musicians giving impromptu performances and mixing with visitors and locals. After that, the festival concentrates on indoor performances, with admission charges partially defraying costs.

The Canton Labor Day Celebration (828-648-7925). Canton, NC, with its giant paper mill, makes quite a celebration out of Labor Day. Starting the Thursday before, 5 days of music and special events at Canton Recreation Park climax with a parade down Main Street on Labor Day.

AUTUMN **The Haywood County Fair** (828-456-3575). Last week in Sep. at the Haywood County Fairgrounds in Waynesville, NC, this classic fair has carnival rides, live entertainment, food, livestock shows, home extension exhibits, and agriculture competitions.

Church Street Arts & Crafts Show. Second Sun. in Oct. This Waynesville, NC, street fair features regional crafters along with mountain music and dance, entertainment, and food.

WINTER **Christmas Celebrations**. Waynesville, NC, has its **Christmas Parade** the last week in Nov.; Canton, NC, follows with its **Festival of Lights Night Parade** a week later. The celebration continues throughout December with home tours, lighting displays, and a "drive through Nativity" organized by Canton churches.

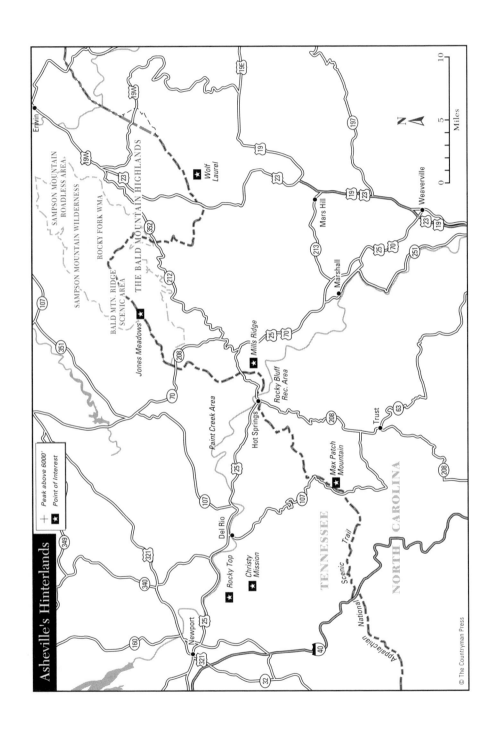

Asheville's Hinterlands

+ Peak above 6000'
★ Point of Interest

SAMPSON MOUNTAIN
ROADLESS AREA

SAMPSON MOUNTAIN WILDERNESS

ROCKY FORK WMA

THE BALD MOUNTAIN HIGHLANDS

BALD MTN. RIDGE
SCENIC AREA

★ Jones Meadows

★ Wolf Laurel

Erwin

Mars Hill

Marshall

Weaverville

★ Mills Ridge

Paint Creek Area

Rocky Bluff
Rec. Area

Hot Springs

Trust

★ Max Patch
Mountain

Del Rio

★ Rocky Top

★ Christy
Mission

TENNESSEE

NORTH CAROLINA

Appalachian   National   Scenic   Trail

Newport

N

Miles

0   5   10

© The Countryman Press

ASHEVILLE'S RUGGED HINTERLANDS

Northof Asheville, NC, the mountains extend in a grand tumble for mile after mile. This is an area of tangled ridgelines where craggy tops can suddenly change to wide, broad meadows, a place where streams drop over waterfalls into sharp-sided valleys. It's also a region of broad rivers that flow through deep gorges to empty into broad, rich valleys, where isolation keeps towns tiny and unspoiled. Opportunities for outdoor enjoyment are remarkable and widespread: the French Broad River, a first-rate kayaking and rafting river with spectacular gorge scenery; the Bald Mountains, straddling the state line with 50,000 rugged acres open to the public; Max Patch, one of the most beautiful sunset peaks anywhere. Most tourism focuses on the tiny, remote town of Hot Springs, NC, where there is a good choice of quality B&Bs and restaurants. High-quality travel services can also be found in Marshall, NC, Mars Hill, NC, and Del Rio, TN—but for the most part this area has more outdoor opportunities than innkeepers and restaurateurs.

GUIDANCE **Madison County Tourism Development Authority** (877-262-3476 or 828-680-9031; fax 828-689-2217), P.O. Box 1527, Mars Hill, NC 28754. This agency maintains a visitors center in a restored farmhouse near the center of Mars Hill.

Pisgah National Forest, Appalachian/French Broad Ranger District (828-622-3202), P.O. Box 128, Hot Springs, NC 28743. The French Broad Ranger District is responsible for all of the Pisgah National Forest lands in this region. It maintains an information desk at its office on US 25 in Hot Springs.

GETTING THERE *By auto*: This area is bisected by **US 25/70**, a two-lane US highway running between Newport, TN and Asheville, NC; all four of the region's villages are on this highway. Tennessee's Bald Mountains, in the northeast quadrant of this area, are best reached from Greeneville, TN, via TN 107 or TN 351.

By air: The closest facility to most of this area is the **Asheville Regional Airport** (828-684-2226; fax 828-684-3404), 708 Airport Rd., Fletcher, NC. Located

15 miles south of downtown Asheville off I-26, Exit 9 (NC 280). This lovely little airport is virtually unchanged since the 1950s—a low, rambling, white concrete structure with orange stripes, its boarding gates rambling outward from a central lobby. Despite its old-fashioned appearance, it has daily service from Atlanta, Cincinnati, Pittsburgh, Raleigh, and Charlotte, with 20 to 25 flights daily. Several car rental agencies are located within or near the airport.

For those who are mainly interested in Tennesse's Bald Mountains, the closest facility is the **Tri-Cities Airport** (423-325-6000; fax 423-325-6060; www.triflight .com), 2525 Hwy. 75, Blountville, TN 37617. The Tri-Cities are Johnson City, Kingsport, and Bristol. Tri-Cities Airport is located in Tennessee's Great Valley in the middle of the triangle formed by the three cities, off I-81's Exit 63. Tri-Cities has four commuter airlines furnishing nonstops to six different hubs, so it's not uncommon to find good and/or cheap connections to it.

By bus or train: This region has no scheduled passenger service by either train or bus.

MEDICAL EMERGENCIES

Hot Springs Health Program

The Hot Springs Health Program (www.hotspringshealth-nc.org) is not a hospital, and does not maintain an emergency room. Rather, it is a rural primary care program with four clinics (listed below)—the only primary care program in the area. It was founded in 1971 by two nurse-practitioners who were distressed by Hot Springs's inability to obtain any sort of medical care from a doctor. The rural clinic they founded—a model of its sort—now employs eleven doctors, a doctor of osteopathy, and a dental surgeon, along with 130 other employees. For routine medical problems in this area, these are good people to contact. Please note that the Mars Hill clinic is open every day.

Mars Hill Medical Center (828-689-3507), 119 Mountain View Rd., Mars Hill, NC. Mon.–Sat. 9 AM–9 PM, Sun 1–9.

Marshall-Walnut Medical Center (828-649-3500), 8625 US 25/70, Marshall, NC. Mon.–Fri. 9–5, Sat. 9–5.

Hot Springs Medical and Dental Center (828-622-3245), 66 NW US 25/70, Hot Springs, NC. Mon.–Fri. 9–5, Sat. 8–noon.

Laurel Medical Center (828-656-2611), 80 Guntertown Rd., Laurel, NC. Mon.–Fri. 9–5.

Nearby Hospitals

Mission St. Josephs Hospital (828-231-1111), 509 Biltmore Ave., Asheville, NC. With western North Carolina's only Level II trauma facility, this huge hospital is located just south of downtown Asheville. This is the closest hospital for Mars Hill and Marshall; for Hot Springs, it's a toss-up between Asheville and the much smaller hospital in Newport, TN (below).

Baptist Hospital of Cocke County (865-625-2200), 435 2nd St., Newport, TN. Located near the center of Newport, this 74-bed hospital has the closest emergency room to the Del Rio area.

Takoma Adventist Hospital (423-639-3151), 401 Takoma Ave., Greeneville, TN. This full-service local hospital within Greeneville is just west of the town center off US 321. It's the closest hospital to Tennessee's Bald Mountains.

✳ Wandering Around

EXPLORING BY CAR **A Hot Springs drive**. *Leg 1*: From Hot Springs, NC, follow US 25 north 13 miles to Del Rio, TN; then right on TN 107 for 13 miles to the state line; then continue straight ahead 3.3 miles on gravel Max Patch Rd. (SSR 1182) to Max Patch Parking Area. *Leg 2*: Continue on Max Patch Rd. 4.5 miles to Meadow Fork Rd. (SSR 1175); then left 3.6 miles to Caldwell Corner Rd. (SSR 1165); then right 2 miles to NC 209; then left 11.6 miles to Hot Springs.

This chapter's featured scenic drive links Hot Springs with Max Patch, visiting the western part of the district on the way there and back. Its first leg starts along the recently rebuilt US 25, switchbacking out of Hot Springs past a monument, then leaving town to make broad sweeps high above the **French Broad River**. As the river drops into a gorge far away on the right, the highway sweeps upward and away from it toward the Tennessee border, marked by a classic state-line bar (once a common sight when much of the rural South was dry). From there the highway curves back to the French Broad River, crossing it on a long, old bridge with good views. The highway now follows the river closely, with broad views over it toward the fields and mountains beyond, reaching **Del Rio** in 4.5 miles. Despite its tiny size and obscurity, Del Rio featured prominently in two pop-culture icons from the late 1960s—Catherine Marshall's best-selling religious novel *Christy* and the ribald bluegrass standard "Rocky Top." From there, the route runs through beautiful, hilly farming valleys, then climbs very steeply uphill to the crest of the **Bald Mountains**. Finally the road crosses the crest of the Bald Mountains into North Carolina, and immediately turns into the gravel Max Patch Rd. (SSR 1182). Max Patch itself, with its wide wildflower meadows and stunning 360° views over the Smokies and the Balds, is just beyond.

Past Max Patch, Max Patch Road becomes a beautiful ridgetop drive that alternates between deep forests and wide views over mountaintop pastureland. From there, your route turns east off the mountaintop, dropping through lovely valleys and over a side ridge to reach NC 209. Here a right turn will take you 2 miles to the tiny village of **Trust**, NC, with a beautiful roadside chapel and, farther down NC 63, a European-style garden. The route goes left instead, however, heading back toward Hot

THIS VIEW OVER THE FRENCH BROAD RIVER AND THE BALD MOUNTAINS FROM A ROADSIDE OVERLOOK ON OLD US 70 IS MAINTAINED BY A LOCAL RESIDENT.

Jim Hargan

Springs. On this stretch NC 209 passes through well-tended farm valleys with some fine old buildings, then curves steeply uphill to run along the top of the dramatic **Spring Creek Gorge**. There are three good views over the gorge, plus more views from the paths in **Rocky Bluffs Recreation Area**. From there, Hot Springs is only 3 miles away, for a total loop of 50 miles.

EXPLORING ON FOOT **Sampson Mountain Wilderness walks** are known for their waterfalls, their handsome forests, their good views—and their steep uphill pulls from the ends of valley roads. The trails that lead into the wilderness from **Horse Creek Picnic Area** possess all these virtues. The easier of the two follows **Squibb Creek** uphill, climbing 600 feet in 2.2 miles, through beautiful cove forests to a small but particularly lovely waterfall. The second path, a mountain climbing loop, leaves Squibb Creek after a third of a mile, marked as **Turkeypen Creek Trail**. This path climbs a steady 18 percent gradient through rich and varied forests, following a small, steep creek to finally gain a ridgeline. Then there's more steep climbing up along the ridge, whose xeric forests give way to large rock outcrops with spectacular views over the **Sampson Wilderness**. The trail reaches a ridgetop intersection at 2.5 miles, having gained 1,600 feet in that short distance. Turn right for a ridgeline walk back down to Squibb Creek.

✳ Villages

Mars Hill, NC. Mars Hill is a handsome hilltop college town, with a one-block downtown adjacent to the tree-shaded, redbrick campus of **Mars Hill College**. Both the college and the village are compact, more like a New England college town than a southern one, and people tend to get around on foot—along the downtown sidewalk with its old redbrick storefronts, through the campus on tree-shaded walks, and into the neighborhoods with their historic old houses. Mars Hill is located a mile off the main freeway, US 23 (the future I-26), on NC 209. Its single traffic light marks the center of town, with the campus straight ahead, the visitors center to the left, and downtown to the right.

Marshall, NC. Madison County's seat sits deep in a gorge, stretching for six blocks along the French Broad River. The river here is broad enough to have an island that holds the local elementary school—a popular venue for festivals. A major railroad line stretches along the river's east bank; then the town's center stretches along the railroad; then the town's residential area terraces up the side of the gorge behind downtown. The handsome old courthouse sits in the middle of downtown, its dome set against the green forests of the gorge wall behind it. A long time ago, the main road from Asheville passed through the center of town, but Marshall was bypassed in the 1950s, then the bypass was bypassed in the 1960s. Now the bypassed bypass's bypass has been bypassed by the new I-26. Nowadays Marshall is a real quiet place. You will find Marshall just off US 25, north of Asheville.

Hot Springs, NC. Hot Spring's old downtown tries to stretch itself to three blocks. On those blocks you'll find a little bit of everything—restaurants, a neat hardware store, a 1950s-style motel, a Forest Service ranger station, some houses, and several shops. This central business district, however, gets an unusual boost

Max Patch walks. A 4,630-foot peak marking the western end of the Bald Mountains, the Pisgah National Forest's Max Patch offers easy and dramatic walking across miles of mountaintop meadows. This walk starts at the trailhead parking lot (see *Exploring by Car*). Go uphill through meadows, climbing 200 feet in a scant half a mile, gaining increasingly spectacular views on the way up. You'll probably pass hay bales; the Forest Service keeps these old cattle pastures from returning to scrubby forests by regular mowing and burning. At the top you will find a surveyor's monument marking the summit, and posts with white blazes marking the route of the **Appalachian Trail (AT)** through the grasses and flowers. Here the view is a complete circle of endlessly receding mountains. The mountains on the west are the Great Smokies; the ridges passing on to the northeast are the Bald Mountains. The **Max Patch summit** is a wonderful place for a sunset, and it's not uncommon to see people all over the ridge, picnicking and camping in an impromptu sunset party.

To extend the walk, follow the AT downhill to the left, dropping 400 feet. As the trail reaches a lower set of meadows it briefly merges with an old farm track running along the ridge. Follow this track along the ridge for another mile of stunning meadow views. When you reach the end, don't try to explore downhill; instead, return by following the farm track all the way back to Max Patch Rd. When you reach the road, your car is parked 1,000 feet to the right.

THE APPALACHIAN TRAIL PASSES OVER THE SUMMIT OF MAX PATCH. Jim Hargan

from its sidewalk; this particular stretch of concrete is known to the world as the **Appalachian Trail**. The famous Georgia-to-Maine path descends into town from the mountains on the west, follows the sidewalk through town and across the French Broad River, then dives into the woods again. You'll see hikers with backpacks walking the sidewalk, sitting and resting on a bench, or inside one of the stores with their gear stored neatly in a corner.

The other notable thing about Hot Springs is its remoteness. It's 30 minutes to the nearest town in either direction, down a twisting, two-lane highway (US 25). After a 1998 ice storm it took 10 days to restore power to parts of the area. Hot Springs tends to attract people who like it quiet and isolated, making for a tightly knit community of mountain people, free spirits, and folk dedicated to some serious relaxing. Most services are available at Hot Springs. US 25 runs through town from Asheville to Newport, TN, and NC 209 forks away at the center of town to wander southward toward Waynesville, NC.

Del Rio, TN. Del Rio is old depot town in the Bald Mountains of Tennessee. Sitting by a siding near the banks of the French Broad River, it consists of a straggle of old buildings along TN 107 just off US 25. While Del Rio itself offers little reason to slow down (aside from an occasional dog sleeping on the road), the surrounding mountains are remarkably scenic. Del Rio was the model for "El Plano" in Catherine Marshall's 1968 novel *Christy*, and the actual mission portrayed in that novel makes for an interesting visit.

✳ Wild Places

THE BALD MOUNTAIN HIGHLANDS For the most part, the steep-sided Bald Mountains are known for two things: dividing North Carolina from Tennessee, and carrying 20 miles of the **Appalachian Trail**. Less well known are its nearly 50,000 contiguous acres of recreational wildlands—about 75 square miles. To the hikers, fishers, hunters, and campers who use this area, it's one giant tract of remote mountain land, a land filled with craggy ridgelines, mountaintop meadows, hidden coves, waterfalls, and a single, continuous hardwood forest that has not been disturbed for more than 60 years. To the powers that be, however, it's five separate tracts: one (Shelton Laurel Backcountry Area) owned by the Pisgah National Forest in North Carolina, three (Sampson Mountain Wilderness Area, Sampson Mountain Roadless Area, and Bald Mountain Ridge Scenic Area) owned by the Cherokee National Forest in Tennessee, and one (Rocky Fork/Cherokee WMA) leased by the State of Tennessee from a lumber company.

APPALACHIAN TRAIL THRU-HIKERS REST OUTSIDE THE BRIDGE STREET LAUNDRY IN HOT SPRINGS.

Jim Hargan

BRIDGE ST. LAUNDRY

Shelton Laurel Backcountry Area. This remote tract of North Carolina's Pisgah National Forest was the site of one of the most notorious of the Civil War's atrocities: the Shelton Laurel Massacre, where Confederate regulars, acting under orders, murdered 13 local Unionist farmers and hid the bodies in a mass grave. The victims were traditionalist mountain folk who believed that God had established the Union and that the flatlander Confederates were rebels against God's will (see Primitive Baptist Church under Cades Cove Historic Sites in "The Northwest Quadrant"). In turn, the most radical Confederates considered these Unionist mountain folk to be traitors who deserved to be killed. These killings occurred throughout the mountains, but were usually done by marauding gangs of irregulars. The Shelton Laurel Massacre was exceptional for its brutality —13 males killed, some of them children—and for being an official act of the Confederate army.

Today Shelton Laurel is a backcountry forest, managed by the Pisgah National Forest for rugged outdoor recreation. Here, mixed-hardwood forests cover the steep southern slopes of the Bald Mountains, crossed by hiking trails that not uncommonly climb 2,000 feet or more. Two popular (and very difficult) loops climb from **Big Creek** to the **Appalachian Trail**, with stunning views back over the Laurel; to find the trailhead, take NC 212 to Big Creek Rd. (SSR 1312, opposite Carmen Church), then north to the trailhead. A second trailhead (NC 212, then north on Hickey Fork Rd., SSR 1310) leads to an easy forest walk up and old road to remote, meadow-covered **Whiteoak Flats**, where a half-mile-long trail goes right to a waterfall.

The Sampson Mountain Wilderness Area and **Roadless Area**. Part of Tennessee's Cherokee National Forest, these two areas protect nearly 15,000 acres of the north slope of the Balds, near Erwin, TN. They cover an area of quickly maturing second-growth forest, last logged in the 1920s. These two areas are noted for their waterfalls, as well as their attractive forests and good views. They are also noted for trails with long, steep uphill pulls, starting at the ends of the valley roads and going straight up the steep flanks of the Balds. The most popular trailhead, at **Horse Creek Picnic Area**, gives a good sampling of all these qualities.

Bald Mountain Ridge Scenic Area. West of the Sampson Mountain Wilderness, the Tennessee Bald Mountains are protected for recreationists as the Bald Mountain Ridge Scenic Area. Unlike a wilderness area, this scenic area allows a broad range of recreation (while prohibiting logging). ORVs are allowed on some trails, and three remote sites can be reached by passenger cars. One, **Forge Creek Campground** (a side road from Horse Creek Picnic Area), is a seasonal campground and trailhead for the notably beautiful **Jennings Creek Trail**. The second, **Round Knob Picnic Area**, features a hair-raising mountain drive to a lovely little CCC picnic spot. The third leads to the remarkable **Jones Meadows**, high on the crest of the Balds.

The Rocky Fork Unit of the Cherokee Wildlife Management Area. This 10,000-acre tract of private land has been leased by the State of Tennessee as a hunting area for the last 60 years. At this writing, the state still leases it, and it remains open to hikers when hunting isn't going on. It's an important tract, separating the Sampson Mountain Wilderness from the Appalachian Trail and abutting the Shelton Laurel Backcountry. It shares the virtues of these publicly owned tracts—spectacular views, waterfalls, rugged and rocky scenery, and deep gorges. Trails are not developed, but hunters' trails exist, and access tracks lead deep into its center. Approach it from the US 23 freeway (future I-26) south of Erwin, TN, by taking TN 352 for 4.4 miles to a right on Rocky Fork Rd., then another 0.9 mile to the trailhead.

THE FORESTS OF HOT SPRINGS, NC **The Paint Rock area**. Just east of Hot Springs a large tract of national forest land extends upward from the French Broad River, with high peaks, wildflower meadows, impressive waterfalls, and a long section of the **Appalachian Trail (AT)**. Historically, its most famous landmark has been Paint Rock, a tall red cliff that loomed above the Buncombe Turnpike, an 1820s road that opened up the mountains. Now the cliff looms above gravel Paint Rock Road, on the east bank of the French Broad River— once well known for its waterfalls and picnic areas, but recently destroyed by flooding.

Over the river from Hot Springs and south of US 25, the AT climbs the bluffs above the French Broad River for wide, clifftop views. From there it wanders into a series of meadows on the rolling 2,500-foot top of **Mill Ridge**. Passenger cars can make it to the near edge of the Mill Ridge meadows by taking US 25 about 4 miles west of town, to make a left onto a side road and cross over the highway on a viaduct; from there it's only a mile up a gravel Forest Service road. There's a loop bicycle path and lots of good exploring. Nearby (at the intersection of US 25 and NC 208), another hiking/biking path leads gently downhill to the French Broad River at the remote, abandoned siding town of **Runion**, NC. The trail follows an old lumber railroad grade along the remarkably beautiful Laurel Creek, gently falling ever deeper into the gorge.

Max Patch. Known as the "Jewel of the Appalachians," remote 4,600-foot Max Patch is crowned with wide wildflower meadows. The best-known and best-loved part of a large tract of Pisgah and Cherokee National Forest lands, Max Patch is an easy introduction to this little-visited corner of the country, with a trailhead on Max Patch Road. scarcely half a mile and 200 feet from the summit. Grasslands cover its wide, rolling summit, and grasslands continue to flow down to the ridgelines 400 feet below. A 360° panorama surrounds a summit nearly always buffeted by high winds; the Great Smoky Mountains National Park is clearly visible to the west. Westward from Max Patch, the **Harmon's Den Area** of the Pisgah National Forest is crossed with hiking and horse trails. To the north, the Cherokee National Forest conceals the lost mountain community of **Wasp**, TN, its ruins hidden deep in the forest that has taken over its high, perched cove. Farther east, the AT pokes its way through a number of interesting little corners before making its final drop into Hot Springs. A private outfitter lets you llama trek this mountain in scenic luxury, with all-day and overnight excursion that feature gourmet meals (see "Gatlinburg & the Northeast Quadrant").

RECREATION AREAS Jones Meadows on the Bald Mountains. Wide grassy meadows top the crest of the Balds at Jones Meadows, a remarkable site within the Bald Mountain Ridge Scenic Area of the Cherokee National Forest. The 8-mile gravel approach road, Bald Mountain Rd. (CR 58), can be charitably described as thrilling, with rough bumps up 4 miles of hairpin switchbacks. Nevertheless, it's worth the thrill, as wide wildflower meadows spread along the 4,500-foot crest. An attempted vacation subdivision went bankrupt here in 1989, to be snapped up by the Forest Service at auction; you'll see abandoned and decaying vacation cottages in the woods on all sides. The **Appalachian Trail** enters the meadows on your right, crosses them, and exits on your left. Park and follow it left (east). You'll quickly come to a side trail that leads 15 yards right to **Whiterock Cliffs**, with wide views south over North Carolina's Shelton Laurel Backcountry. Continue on for another short trail left to the **Blackstack Cliffs**, with panoramic views north over the face of the Balds to Tennessee's Great Valley. There are no formal facilities up here, but plenty of places to spread a picnic blanket.

Rocky Bluffs Recreation Area. NC 209 twists and turns its way south of Hot Springs to hack its way along the cliffs of the **Spring Creek Gorge**, with a couple of impressive views along the way. Three miles south of town along this scenic stretch of highway, the Rocky Bluffs Recreation Area furnishes picnicking and camping on the edge of the gorge. A short loop trail goes to a viewpoint before descending into the gorge, while a longer loop trail explores the steep slopes above the road.

PICNIC AREAS Horse Creek Recreation Area. The Cherokee National Forest's Horse Creek Recreation Area centers on a deep, clear pool in a mountain creek, a popular swimming hole. The picnic area is up the road a short distance, with several tables under tall old trees. A popular Sampson Mountain Wilderness trailhead is here, with some fine walking. To reach it, take TN 107 to Horse Creek Rd., CR 94, and follow the Forest Service signs.

Round Knob Picnic Area. Find the intersection of TN 350 and TN 351 (it will be southeast of Greeneville, TN, on your map). From there, go toward the mountains (southeast) on Jones Bridge Rd.; stay on it 1.25 miles as it curves left and becomes McCoy Rd. In another mile, go right on Greystone Rd., and stay on it 2.5 miles to a right on Round Knob Rd. This tiny CCC-era picnic area snuggles deep under tall trees, halfway up Bald Mountain's steep slopes. While this heavily forested site has no views, it is so high and steep that it gives the impression of an eyrie. It has a shelter built of great logs, and a hand pump,

A SPRINGTIME APPLE ORCHARD OUTSIDE MARS HILL.

Jim Hargan

A MOUNTAIN VIEW FROM HIGH PASTURES.

along with a few tables. The 4.5-mile drive up the mountain is on **Round Knob Rd.** (FS 88), a one-lane gravel road, very steep and narrow, with some stunning views off the side.

Morlay Branch Picnic Area. This Pisgah National Forest area has a number of tree-shaded tables beside the French Broad River, on Paint Rock Rd.

✳ To See

HISTORIC SITES **The "Christy" Mission** (423-487-2648), 1425 Chapel Hollow Rd., Del Rio, TN. To find the mission at Chapel Hollow ("Cutter Gap" in the novel), take TN 107 south from Del Rio for 1 mile, then go right on Old 15th for 4.4 miles to Chapel Hollow Rd. Novelist Catherine Marshall based her best seller *Christy*, about a young teacher in a remote Appalachian mission, on her mother's life and work in a cove above Del Rio ("El Plano"). That original Presbyterian mission site, and all that remains of its buildings, are signposted, interpreted, and preserved by local resident Larry Myers—whom fans of the novel—and fans of the 1996 CBS TV series based on the novel—will be delighted to learn is the grandson of "Fairlight Spencer" (Flora Corn). Such remote missions, bringing education, medicine, and religion to the inaccessible coves, were an important feature of the turn-of-the-20th-century mountains. Times have changed, and formerly well-known missions have been lost; the Salvation Army's Max Patch Mission has long disappeared into the Pisgah National Forest, and the Methodist Church's Pittman Center Mission is now a country club and golf resort. The "Christy" mission is now the best place to get a feel for those difficult times.

A final note for fans of the TV series: The location shots were done at Townsend, TN, 60 miles west of Chapel Hollow. The actual Chapel Hollow sites lack the breathtaking mountain backdrops of the Townsend TV sets. If you want to see the Townsend location sites, ask for directions at the visitors center.

Rocky Top, TN. Felice and Boudleaux Bryant wrote the racy bluegrass standard "Rocky Top" at about the same time Catherine Marshall was writing *Christy*. You might not recognize these two pop icons of the 1960s as being about the same place, but they are. Rocky Top is a 2,400-foot peak separating Chapel Hollow (Christy's "Cutter Gap") from the town of Newport, TN. The real-life Christy, Leonora Whitaker, ran her small mountain school and mission immediately below Rocky Top, on its eastern slope, presumably not far from where the song's good old boys were making moonshine and whooping it up with the girls. Of course, this proximity is complete coincidence; the Bryants picked "Rocky Top" merely because it sounded good in the song, and had no knowledge of the actual locale. Catherine Marshall's version is the one based in fact—not the Bryants'.

CULTURAL SITES Country Workshops (828-656-2280; www.countryworkshops .org), 990 Black Pine Ridge Rd., Marshall, NC. This craft school for serious hand-tooled woodworking occupies a remote farmstead high in the Shelton Laurels area. Founded by Drew Langner in 1978, it offers 2- to 6-day residency seminars and workshops that cover a wide variety of woodworking with hand tools; while most courses deal with furniture making, others deal with folk vernacular styles, woodcarving, green woodworking, making hand tools on a forge, and making a timber frame building. Students stay in a dorm on the property and eat hearty homemade meals together. Anyone serious about woodworking will want to visit the school's store, with a thorough line of high-end woodworking equipment and books. The school welcomes visitors, who should call ahead for directions (and to ensure that someone is there). $300–$850, including dormitory-style accommodations and all meals, for 2- to 6-day courses.

Trust Chapel. On NC 63 just south of its intersection with NC 209 in the community of Trust, NC. Open during daylight hours. Beverly Barutio built this 12x14-foot log chapel, dedicated to St. Jude, in 1990 in thanks for the curing of her cancer. It's a beautiful structure, built of logs and outfitted with a variety of handcrafted art objects. To be in it is to be moved.

&. **Mars Hill College** (800-543-1514). The town of Mars Hill, NC, remains firmly centered on its 150-year-old Baptist liberal arts school, Mars Hill College, a four-year college with 1,100 students. Founded in 1856, it was one of a number of church-run boarding high schools, called "academies," in these mountains; such academies were the only real way that a mountain child could obtain any education beyond the local one-room schoolhouse. Mars Hill College entered its modern phase in 1896, when it began the long journey to becoming a fully accredited four-year college (in 1962). The modern campus evolved over the 20th century. It's dominated by handsome redbrick buildings from every period of the 20th century, from elegant and beautiful late-Victorian structures to recent modernist structures, looking slightly racy on this rural Baptist campus. The grounds are shaded and parklike, beautifully landscaped with native vegetation.

Rural Life Museum (828-689-1424). Mars Hill College's History Department maintains the on-campus Rural Life Museum, dedicated to the history and culture of the Southern Appalachian Mountains. It includes a fascinating section on the hand-hooked rug industry, a Depression-era, $3-million-a-year cottage industry in the Mars Hill area.

Weizenblatt Gallery (828-689-1396). Part of the Art Department at Mars Hill College, the on-campus Weizenblatt Gallery features the works of students, faculty, and regional artists, and has regular exhibits highlighting the works of southern artists. Free.

✳ To Do

FISHING Metcalf Creek Outfitters (828-689-5503), 1911 Metcalf Creek Loop Rd., Mars Hill, NC. Gerald Scott guides fly-fishing trips on the streams throughout this area, including equipment and hand-tied flies.

HORSEBACK RIDING AND LLAMA TREKKING On a horseback ride, the horse carries you around. On the whole, llamas are too small to carry people. On a llama trek, llamas will carry all your food, water, and equipment, while you walk. In this area the picnic lunch is the main point of most llama treks, and the main reason you pay to take those llamas along. Another reason is that llamas are very cute, with an appealing, if unsettling, habit of coming up silently behind you to nuzzle your ear from above.

English Mountain Llama Trekking (828-622-9686; www.hikinginthesmokies .com), 767 Little Creek Rd., Hot Springs, NC. Owner Lucy Lowe leads llama treks in the Pisgah National Forest. Day treks include lunch; overnight treks include all gear and meals. Call or e-mail for rates, which vary.

Little Creek Outfitters (828-622-7606; www.littlecreekoutfitters.com), 767 Little Creek Rd., Hot Springs, NC. Daily during summer. This stable in the rural countryside west of Hot Springs offers half- and full-day trail rides inside the Pisgah National Forest and the Great Smoky Mountains National Park, including trail rides over nearby Max Patch. They also offer trail riding/fly-fishing combinations. Half day $30–40, full day $80–90.

Sandy Bottom Trail Rides (800-959-3513 or 828-649-9745; www.sandybottom trailrides.com), 155 Caney Fork Rd., Marshall, NC. Apr.–Oct. This stable offers half- and full-day trail rides, as well as overnighters, from their location in a beautiful rural valley west of Marshall.

Flintlock Inn and Stables (423-257-2489). This Tennessee stable, off TN 107 east of Greeneville, offers half-day and whole-day trail rides in the rolling hills near the Nolichucky River, and in the forests of the nearby Sampson Mountain area of the Cherokee National Forest. They also have a B&B on their property, in a 200-year-old log cabin.

WindDancers Llama Treks (828-627-6986; fax 828-627-0754; www.wind dancersnc.com), 1966 Martins Creek Rd., Clyde, NC. These half-day llama treks on a beautiful 270-acre private ranch include spectacular views and a gourmet meal. They also offer overnight treks with four meals, coupled with a stay in their lovely B&B. $40, including meal. Overnight: $150 per adult, plus the cost of 1 night in their B&B, including four meals.

East Fork Llamas (828-689-5925), East Fork Rd., Marshall, NC. Gourmet food is part of this llama trek on 60 private acres in the Walnut Mountains between Marshall and Mars Hill, NC. They also offer llama training and breeding, and adventure-based counseling. Half day $50.

Roads End Llama Treks (828-680-9429; www.ashevillellamatreks.com). This outfit offers half-day llama treks with and without picnic lunch, in the mountains between Marshall and Mars Hill, NC. Half day $25; $31 with picnic.

SKIING **Wolf Laurel** (800-817-4111 or 828-689-4111; www.skiwolflaurel.com), Rt. 3, Mars Hill, NC. This ski slope is located on the leeward side of snow-magnet Bald Mountain, just below its crest. Maximum vertical drop is 700 feet from a high elevation of 4,650 feet, with 14 runs and four chairlifts. All runs have artificial snow and night lights. Day lift tickets $24–34.

WHITEWATER ADVENTURES Upstream from Hot Springs, the French Broad River dives into a steep and rugged gorge, surrounded on both sides by large tracts of national forest land. A number of whitewater sports outfitters offer trips on this section, operating from a string of stations along US 25 between Marshall and Hot Springs.

Huck Finn River Adventures (877-520-4658; www.huckfinnrafting.com). Head-quartered in Hot Springs, NC, this outfitter leads whitewater rafting trips on the remote French Broad River upstream from Hot Springs, and float trips on the calm waters downstream from Hot Springs. Special trips include an evening float trip with a sunset steak dinner, and an overnight river camping trip with a steak dinner and pancake breakfast. Half day $25–35, full day $35–50, overnight $125.

WHITEWATER OUTFITTERS LINE THE BANKS OF THE FRENCH BROAD RIVER.

Jim Hargan

French Broad Rafting Company (800-570-7238 or 828-649-3574; www.frenchbroadrafting.com), 7525 Unit 2, US 2570, Marshall, NC. Lo-cated north of Marshall off US 25 near the French Broad River, this outfitter offers both whitewater and calm-water trips on different sections of the French Broad. Prices vary.

Nantahala Outdoor Center (800-232-7238). This large outfitter, head-quartered in Bryson City, NC, has an outpost north of Marshall, NC, on US 25 for whitewater trips on the French Broad River. $33–56.

USA Raft (800-872-7238). This large rafting chain headquartered in Rowlesburg, WV, maintains an outpost north of Marshall, NC, on US 25, for excursions on the French Broad River. $31–38.

✳ Lodging

RESORTS 🐾 ♦ **Gannon's French Broad Outpost Ranch** (800-995-7678 or 423-487-3147; www.frenchbroadriver.com), 461 Old River Rd., Del Rio, TN 37727. Open all year. This dude ranch sits on the French Broad River near Del Rio, extending from the riverside meadows to the ridges above. A classic dude ranch, one price covers accommodation, all meals, and all activities. The ranch has a central lodge and related facilities built to look like an Old West town, which they dub "Rough Cut." Along with the four-room lodge, it contains the dining room, a dance hall, and a saloon. Accommodations consist of four good-sized lodge rooms, four ridgetop cabins, and four tiny log "pioneer cabins" rather like old-fashioned tourist camp units. While all activities are optional, they include 5 days of horseback trail riding, three rafting trips (including one with some Class IV rapids), a 1-mile cattle drive ("it may not be a long drive, but it's the only one east of the Mississippi"), a fishing trip with a chuck wagon lunch, and a guided Appalachian Trail hike on Max Patch. There's also nightly entertainment, which may include live bluegrass, square dancing, campfires, naturalist talks, and wagon rides. Children of all ages are welcome, and there are special activities just for kids under 12. $250–400 per day for two adults; weekly packages at reduced rates; discounts for children; includes all meals and all activities.

BED & BREAKFAST INNS **WindDancers Lodging and Llama Treks** (828-627-6986; fax 828-627-0754; www.winddancersnc.com), 1966 Martins Creek Rd., Clyde, NC 28721. Three modern log lodges group around the high meadows of a llama ranch, with wide views over the remote and little-visited Newfound Mountains, east of the Great Smokies. Each lodge has four large rooms grouped around a central common area, with decor tending toward the western or exotic. All rooms are decorated with art items and artifacts from around the world, with lounge areas, fireplaces, decks with mountain views, and two-person tubs. Two lodges have in-room mini kitchens, in which a continental breakfast is left daily; the third has a pool table and video room, with full breakfast served in the common area. WindDancers is a working llama ranch, offering 1- to 3-day treks with these gentle animals on their 270 acres and in the surrounding Pisgah National Forest. $130–165.

The Magnolia Mountain Inn (828-622-3543; www.mountainmagnoliainn.com), P.O. Box 6, Hot Springs, NC 28743. This elaborate 130-year-old Victorian house in Hot Springs, NC, has been beautifully restored to a five-room B&B. It was built in 1868 by the only member of the SC legislature to vote against secession at the outbreak of the Civil War, and it is no coincidence that it's located in the remote heart of the most Unionist corner of the South. The 3 acres of gardens are beautifully landscaped in flower gardens and shaded lawns, with a 100-year-old boxwood maze, vegetable and herb gardens (used in the food prepared for guests), and rhododendrons, all framed by spectacular mountain views. The house is Victorian at its best, its elaborate exterior trim and porches in authentic multicolored paints; inside, common areas are furnished with period antiques. The five rooms range from cozy to large, each with its own personality, defined by the spaces of the house and the beautiful antiques within. Several of the rooms have a private balcony. There's also a 20th-century Garden Cottage, overlooking the vegetable gardens, with a beautifully decorated open plan very suitable for retreats or family gatherings. A full breakfast is included in the price (except for the Garden Cottage). Dinner is available to guests and nonguests on Friday and Saturday for an extra charge. Rooms $120–175, cottage $250.

The Bridge Street Inn (828-622-0002; fax 828-622-7282; www.bridge streetcafe.com), P.O. Box 502, Hot Springs, NC 28743. Apr.–Oct. The second story of the Bridge Street Café's old general store home has been converted to a four-room bed & breakfast. Rooms are bright and high ceilinged, furnished in turn-of-the-20th-century antiques, with two shared baths. Guests are treated to a continental breakfast at the café downstairs—noted for its fresh-made breads and pastries. Early sleepers should note that the restaurant has live entertainment on Sat. $50–70.

✒ **Duckett House Inn and Farm** (828-622-7621; www.duckethouse-inn.com), 433 Lance Ave., Hot Springs, NC 28743. Open all year. This 1900 Victorian-style house sits by

NC 209 half a mile outside Hot Springs. It's the sort of fancy farmhouse that a wealthy man might have built, with a nicely trimmed wraparound front porch, a full second story, and a fancy third story with a projecting gable and lots of dormers. Today it is beautifully kept, with an eye-catching red tin roof. Inside, six tastefully decorated rooms are furnished with period antiques; all share baths. Breakfasts feature homemade breads and free-range eggs. In addition, there is a two-bedroom cottage on the property. Children of all ages are welcome in the cottage, while the main house is restricted to children over 12. Rooms $85–95, cottage $125.

🐾 ✒ **Marshall House Bed and Breakfast Inn** (828-649-9205; fax 828-649-2784; www.marshallhouse .org), 100 Hill St., Marshall, NC 28753. Located in the center of the quaint and quiet town of Marshall, the Marshall House rises in stone terraces above the handsome old county courthouse. Designed by the same architect who built Biltmore Village, this 1903 National Register mansion is covered with pebbledash, with a 50-foot-long veranda rising from a tall stone wall and turreted on one end. The views from the veranda extend over the courthouse and town below, framed by the French Broad River and the mountains behind. Inside, the home is decorated with period antiques; one interesting feature is the original painting by Liberace of the innkeeper as a young girl. One of the eight rooms has a queen bed, the remainder having twins or doubles; some of the rooms share baths. A full breakfast is included, and pets, children, and smokers are welcome. $40–85.

Flintlock Inn (423-257-2489; fax 423-257-5547), 790 G'Fellers Rd., Chuckey, TN 37641. Located on a stable offering trail rides, the Flintlock has three antiques-furnished rooms in a 200-year-old log cabin, along with a three-bedroom rental cabin on the Nolichucky River. They also offer stables for people traveling with their horses. It's located in the broad, rolling plains of Tennessee underneath Sampson Mountain, near TN 107.

CABIN RENTALS ✍ **Mountain Valley View Cabins** (888-808-8812; fax 828-622-9587; www.ncmountainview.com), 225 Mountain Valley Dr., Hot Springs, NC 28743. Open all year. Two log-clad traditional cabins sit on a grassy and shaded ridgetop 9 miles south of Hot Springs off NC 209. These bright, one-bedroom cabins are nicely decorated in a country style, and have picnic area with barbeque pit, full front porch with rocking chairs, living room with woodstove (plus gas heat), and full kitchen, along with such amenities as phone, washer-dryer, and satellite TV with HBO. $110 per night.

ALONG A COUNTRY LANE IN THE NEWFOUND MOUNTAINS.

Jim Hargan

✳ Where to Eat

DINING OUT **The Bridge Street Café** (828-622-0002; fax 828-622-7282; www.bridgestreetcafe.com), Hot Springs, NC. Apr.–Oct., Thu.–Sun. from 5:30 PM, plus Sun. brunch. Located in a restored general store fronting on the Appalachian Trail in the center of Hot Springs, the Bridge Street Café offers casual fine dining with a Mediterranean flair. The inside dining area is decorated with original art, and complemented by an outside terrace overlooking a small mountain creek—a venue for live music on summer Saturdays. Its menu is noted for its fresh, organically grown produce, breads, and desserts made from scratch, and an Italian-style brick oven. Pizzas are made from fresh dough and wood baked; pastas and entrées feature an imaginative range of fresh, seasonal vegetables and seafood along with free-range chicken. A Shrimp Trieste sautées large shrimp with fennel, sun-dried tomatoes, mushrooms, and capers in a garlic-citrus sauce; a Pizza Gorgonzola combines Gorgonzola cheese with shiitake mushrooms, caramelized onions, and rosemary. The wine list is extensive, with many offerings by the glass, and microbrews are also available. Appetizers and soups $5–7, pastas $9–14, pizzas $10–19, specialties $15–19.

✳ Entertainment

Southern Appalachian Repertory Theater (SART) (828-689-1384; fax 828-689-1272; www.sartheatre.com), Mars Hill, NC. Located in the 175-seat Owen Theater on the campus of Mars Hill College, SART is a non-profit professional theater company whose performance schedule of plays and musicals always includes original plays from Appalachian authors. $18–21.

The Bridge Street Café (828-622-0002), Hot Springs, NC. Apr.–Oct., Sat. from 8:15 PM. The excellent Bridge Street Café in the center of Hot Springs offers live entertainment on its creek-side terrace every Saturday night in-season. It tends toward alternative music, with folk and blues well represented in the schedule.

✎ **Hillbilly's Music Barn** (423-487-5541), Del Rio, TN. Sat. 6–11 PM. Located deep in the mountains behind Del Rio, Hillbilly's Music Barn offers weekly live bluegrass music in the heart of bluegrass country—below the peak of Rocky Top, TN. It has a large dance floor, with country dancing a major part of the event. Family-oriented, there's plenty of munchies and soft drinks, but no alcohol permitted. To find it, take TN 107 5.4 miles south from Del Rio, to make a right on Blue Mill Rd., and follow the signs. Free.

✳ Selective Shopping

The Gallery Main Street (828-689-5520), Mars Hill, NC. Located in Mars Hill's tiny brick-front downtown, adjacent to Mars Hill College, this gallery features fine arts and crafts from local and regional artists. You'll find an interesting selection of painting, sculpture, pottery, jewelry, fiber art, and photographs.

The Yellow Teapot (828-622-9727) Hot Springs, NC. This downtown Hot Springs shop specializes in fine teas, tea accessories, and Appalachian folk art and crafts.

✳ Special Events

SUMMER Fourth of July celebrations. All three Madison County, NC, towns—Mars Hill, Marshall, and Hot Springs—have special Independence Day celebrations that climax with fireworks. Mars Hill and Hot Springs have live music and food (Mars Hill has a fish fry), with special attractions for the kids. Marshall's Volunteer Fire Department sponsors a rodeo on the island in the French Broad River opposite the courthouse.

AUTUMN Madison County Heritage Festival (828-689-9351). First Sat. in Oct. This Mars Hill street festival, just outside the 150-year-old Baptist college, celebrates its mountain heritage and traditions with booths and craft demonstrations from a variety of local mountain people. You'll find rug hooking, spinning, weaving, musical instrument making, mountain music, clog dancing, shape-note singing, quilts, and traditional foods. Admission is free. The evening Bascom Lamar Lunsford Festival honors this famous collector of Appalachian ballads (and Mars Hill native) with a program of mountain music and dancing at Mars Hill College; admission is charged.

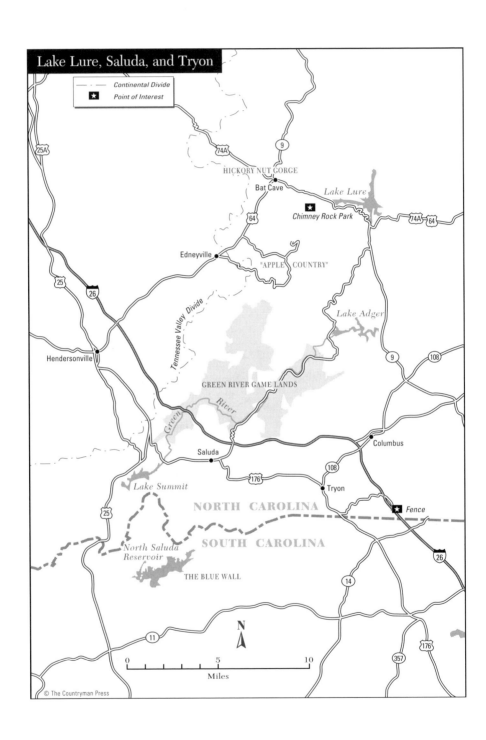

Lake Lure, Saluda, and Tryon

- - - Continental Divide
★ Point of Interest

25A

74A

9

HICKORY NUT GORGE

Bat Cave

Lake Lure

64

★
Chimney Rock Park

74A 64

Edneyville

"APPLE COUNTRY"

25

26

Tennessee Valley Divide

Lake Adger

Hendersonville

9

108

GREEN RIVER GAME LANDS

Green River

Columbus

Saluda

108

176

Lake Summit

Tryon

25

★ Fence

NORTH CAROLINA

SOUTH CAROLINA

26

North Saluda
Reservoir

14

THE BLUE WALL

N

11

357

176

0   5   10

Miles

© The Countryman Press

THE BLUE RIDGE: CHIMNEY ROCK & SALUDA

E ast of Asheville, the Blue Ridge (the mountain, not the parkway) extends due south in a straight line, reaching South Carolina after 50 miles of rugged valleys and gray cliffs. It is quite a barrier, and towns have formed where gorges have broken through it. On its north end, the Hickory Nut Gorge carried a 19th-century coach road up the Blue Ridge, now US 64/74A; along this old road sit the village of Lake Lure, NC, and the settlements of Chimney Rock and Bat Cave, NC. On the south end of the Blue Ridge, the Pacolet River Gorge allowed the railroad to break through, bringing the handsome little depot towns of Tryon and Saluda, NC.

Between these two settled areas stretches 40 miles of empty, rugged mountains. The southern half of this remote stretch is forest-covered wilderness, broken by the deep wilderness gorge of the Green River; much of this wildland is open to the public as part of the 18,000-acre Green River Game Lands, owned by the State of North Carolina. North of these wildlands stretches Apple Country, rolling orchard lands with wonderful views from a confusing network of back roads.

GUIDANCE **Hickory Nut Gorge Chamber of Commerce** (828-625-2725; www.thehickorynutgorge.com), P.O. Box 32, Chimney Rock, NC 28720. This association of merchants from Lake Lure, Chimney Rock, Bat Cave, and Gerton, NC, runs a visitors center and information desk on US 64/74A, at the center of Lake Lure on the west end of the lake.

Polk County Travel and Tourism (800-440-7848; www.nc-mountains.org), 317 N. Trade St., Tryon, NC 28782. This agency, covering the Saluda, Tryon, and Columbus, NC, area, has a visitors center and information desk at the Tryon City Hall, on US 176 at the north end of downtown Tryon.

Rutherford County Tourism Development Authority (800-849-5998 or 828-245-1492; fax 828-247-0499; www.rutherfordtourism.com), 1990 US 221 S., Forest City, NC 28043. This agency provides tourist information for Lake Lure and Hickory Nut Gorge, NC, as well as for parts of Rutherford County east of the mountains. It's located in Forest City, a Piedmont town some distance from Lake Lure.

GETTING THERE *By car*: **I-26** runs north–south up the middle of the region. The interstate-quality **US 74** freeway links this region to Charlotte, NC, and points east, meeting I-26 outside Tryon, NC. Everything else is a back road— including the U.S. primary highways (US 176 from South Carolina to Tryon and Saluda, NC; US 64 from Hendersonville to Lake Lure, NC; and US 74A from Asheville to Lake Lure, NC).

By air: **Greenville-Spartanburg Airport** (GVL) is probably your best bet for an air connection, located only a short distance south of this region. Asheville is also very convenient, but frequently costs more.

MEDICAL EMERGENCIES **Mission St. Josephs Hospital** (828-231-1111), 509 Biltmore Ave., Asheville, NC. Just north of this region in the center of Asheville via I-26 or US 74A. This huge regional hospital offers 24/7 emergency room service as well as western North Carolina's only Level II trauma facility.

Margaret R. Pardee Memorial Hospital (828-696-1000), 715 Fleming St., Hendersonville, NC. Located in downtown Hendersonville, this hospital is convenient to most parts of this region, via US 176 from Saluda, NC; I-26 from Tryon or Columbus, NC; or US 64 from Lake Lure, NC.

Pardee Urgent Care at Four Seasons (828-697-3232; www.pardee-med .org/urgentcr.htm), 205 Thompson St., Hendersonville, NC. Mon.–Sat. 9–9, Sun. noon–6. This walk-in clinic, run by the area's regional hospital, is located near the I-26 intersection with US 64, just off US 64 (behind the Taco Bell), toward Hendersonville.

✳ Wandering Around

EXPLORING BY CAR **The Blue Ridge without the parkway.** *Leg 1*: From Asheville, NC, follow US 74A to Lake Lure, NC. *Leg 2*: East of town center, turn right onto NC 9 for 1.25 miles; then right on Owl Hollow Rd. (SSR 1164) for 1.25 miles; then ahead on Silver Camp Rd. for 6 miles; then right on Green River Cove Rd. (SSR 1151) for 10 miles to I-26. *Leg 3*: Continue straight 1.25 miles to Saluda, NC; then left on US 176 for 8 miles to Tryon, NC; continue on US 176 for 1.4 miles to Ridge Rd. on the state line; then left 0.6 mile to Hunt Country Rd. (SSR 1501); then right 3.4 miles to Foothills Equestrian Nature Center (FENCE).

This 46-mile drive follows the Blue Ridge after the Blue Ridge Parkway has deserted it, using U.S. highways and gravel back roads to stay as close to it as possible. You'll be surprised how different the Blue Ridge looks away from the care of the National Park Service. The first leg follows the **Rocky Broad River** along the base of the **Hickory Nut Gorge**. As you pass the village of **Bat Cave**, NC, you'll get good views of the rough little Rocky Broad; look to your right for views of the 400-foot **Hickory Nut Falls**. Gift shops and motels increasingly block the views as you approach the 1920 stone gates of **Chimney Rock Park** and the western edge of **Lake Lure** a mile later. US 74A follows the lakeshore through the 1927 town center, with views backward over the lake to the cliffs of the Blue Ridge, now behind you.

As you enter the second leg you will be on the western edge of the Piedmont, with the Blue Ridge sometimes visible as a faraway wall that rises out of rolling meadows. This route curves through some lovely farmland then quickly passes **Lake Adger**, a largish 1920s hydro lake. A mile later the route turns to reenter the mountains, following the **Green River** upstream in a deep gorge, surrounded by the **Green River Game Lands** with a few scatterings of vacation cottages. At the end of the gorge, the road climbs steeply up the face of the Blue Ridge, with 17 switchbacks in less than 2 miles—a shocking stretch of road. By rights you should have a grand view from the top of this, but you won't. You will, however, get a chance to stop for a homemade ice cream at a good craft shop—and well earned, too.

The third leg continues on to lovely little **Saluda**, a major craft center despite its tiny size. From there the route once more drops down the Blue Ridge, following US 176 into the **Pacolet River Gorge**. After the Green River this is an easy, pleasant drive; nevertheless, the railroad that wanders in and out of view on the right is the steepest grade in the East. Look for a waterfall in a rocky gorge on your left, after which the road opens up, with broad views over the gorge, right. **Tryon** sits at the bottom of the gorge; this route continues straight through downtown, past Morris the giant toy horse and the old depot. This route continues into "hunt country," using back roads to drive past horse farms and the trails used in the hunt. The drive ends at the unique **Foothills Equestrian Nature Center**, with its combination of nature exploration and horse competitions.

Apple Country. Along the Blue Ridge crest south of Hickory Nut Gorge, a maze of small, deep-sided valleys forms a protected environment perfect for apples, and has been covered with orchards since the late 19th century. The orchards bloom in late April and come into full fruit from mid-August to mid-October. During the harvest, the growers put up stands along US 64 to allow passersby to buy bushels of fresh-picked mountain Rome apples. Behind the main highway, country lanes reach deep into the orchards and along the ridges for some beautiful scenery and stunning views.

Here's a back road orchards tour, a loop just 15 miles long but with lots of scenery (and plenty of places to get lost). To start, take US 64 south from Bat Cave, NC, for 3.5 miles to a left on Hog Rock Rd. (SSR 1703), passing the actual **Hog Rock** on your right at 1.25 miles. From there, go left onto Bald Rock Rd. (SSR 1710), entering a valley bowl with scattered orchards. Passing through a mile of orchards, this road becomes Sugarloaf Mountain Rd. (SSR 1602), reaching a three-way fork in another mile. You'll take the left fork to its end, then backtrack and take the right fork. The left fork, still Sugarloaf Mountain Rd., looks like a gravel farm lane as it climbs through orchards; then it suddenly crosses a ridge and slabs out onto the steep eastern face of the Blue Ridge, with a near-vertical 3,000-foot plummet on the right. The road tops out at meadowed summit of **Sugarloaf Mountain (NC)**, with four or five houses and wide views.

Backtracking to the triple fork, take Spicer Cove Rd. (SSR 1708) south through orchards and along ridges with frequent views, to a right onto Sumners Rd. (SSR 1713) after 2.25 miles. Sumners Rd. twists through two rural valleys with many orchards, then reaches an intersection with yet another section of Sugarloaf

Mountain Rd. (SSR 1602). Turn left. As this road crosses another orchard-clad valley, it will also cross the **Eastern Continental Divide** twice, briefly entering, then leaving, the Mississippi Valley. In 2.5 miles you will regain US 64 at the apple packing town of **Edneyville**, NC, less than 3 miles from where you started. If you are completely turn around at this point, Bat Cave is to your right, and Hendersonville, NC, is to your left.

EXPLORING ON FOOT **Walking the Green River Gorge** (828-692-0385). Fifteen miles of hiking trails loop along the clifftops over the Green River Gorge, climb down to the river's edge, and reach into the 6-foot-wide chasm known as **the Narrows**. Three paths start from **Big Hungry Rd.**, a country lane running from US 64 east of Hendersonville to a dead end in the game lands. The three Big Hungry trails run through rolling terrain covered in rich old forests, typically reaching the cliff edge in 2 miles for some spectacular views over the gorge. Other paths run parallel to the cliffs, linking the main paths into loops, while two more paths make their way down the gorge side to the river's edge. The final trail, reached from the road that follows the gorge bottom, hugs the river's edge for 3.5 miles to reach the Narrows.

All of these remarkable paths, constructed by a local group known as ECO (which publishes an excellent brochure on them), explore but 1,500 acres the huge Green Mountain Game Lands—only about 10 percent of the total public lands. Perhaps we'll be seeing more of this beautiful tract in years to come. To find the Big Hungry trailheads, leave I-26 at Exit 22, Upward Rd., and go east 1.5 miles to a right turn onto Big Hungry Rd. (SSR 1802). The three trailheads are on the right, the first one at 4.25 miles. The riverside trail starts at the new bridge on Green River Cove Rd., 1.25 miles downstream from the Fishtop Access Area.

✳ Villages

☂ **Saluda**, NC. Saluda's short downtown lines one side of US 176 with turn-of-the-20th-century brick buildings, facing the railroad that monopolizes the opposite side of the street. The buildings are immaculately kept and filled with fascinating places to poke into: an old-style country store with a soda fountain; a wood-floored hardware shop; the **Heartwood Contemporary Crafts Gallery**, a fine-craft gallery featuring the works of the nationally known artists who live nearby; the forge of a blacksmith who incorporates his wife's hand-painted tiles in his creations; **The Purple Onion Café and Coffee House**, an elegant little storefront café with live music. The railroad itself is well known as the steepest grade now existing in the East, the notorious Saluda Grade, and Saluda is the siding created to furnish the special services needed for such a steep grade. Across from the railroad, little **McCreery Park** climbs up the hillside with views of downtown, good picnicking, and lots of happy children.

☂ **Tryon**, NC. Located at the base of the Blue Ridge, Tryon has been a summer retreat for South Carolina aristocracy since the turn of the 20th century. The rolling hills that extend from the end of the mountains had immediate appeal to the horse-and-hounds set, and Tryon has long been a center for hunt-oriented equestrian activities. Its short, railroad-facing downtown has art galleries and restaurants, watched over by Morris, a giant toy horse and the town's mascot since 1928. Across the tracks, the old depot holds the **Tryon Depot and Polk County Historical Museum**, an excellent history museum and the hunt club; just uphill is the **Tryon Fine Arts Center**, whose galleries and gardens cover half a block.

Columbus, NC. Located at the foot of White Oak Mountain, Columbus is an attractive, old-fashioned county seat. It has a sleepy, Piedmont flavor, very much an old-fashioned flatland southern town—even though the mountains are in sight from its streets. It centers on its handsome old courthouse, sitting on a square with a Confederate soldier statue, and surrounded by a downtown that's only a scattering of old brick buildings. Tourist services are limited; tourists are the job of Tryon, 8 miles to the west.

THOMPSON'S GROCERY IN DOWNTOWN SALUDA.

Jim Hargan

✳ Wild Places

THE GREAT FORESTS Hickory Nut Gorge. It's best to say it right up front: Hickory Nut Gorge doesn't look the slightest bit like a wild place when you drive through it on US 64/74A. This winding two-lane road that runs down the gorge's bottom has become lined—very close to continuously—by an assortment of businesses clamoring for tourists' attention. What many tourists never realize is that all this development is just one building lot thick. The rest of Hickory Nut Gorge is plain beautiful.

Hickory Nut Gorge is an 8-mile slash through the heart of the Blue Ridge, a U-shaped valley 1.25 miles wide and 1,900 feet deep. Much of the gorge's upper slope is near vertical, and its lowermost 2 miles are framed by sheer gray cliffs. Its stream, the **Rocky Broad River**, is even stranger. Above its short and narrow gorge, the Rocky Broad fans out in a series of parallel and perpendicular tributaries that collect a tremendous volume of water from all over Buncombe and Henderson Counties. You can see the result clearly in the gorge—rocks the size of pickup trucks litter the streambed all the way down. As violent as this river looks on a hot summer's day, it seems unbelievable that it could roll these rocks down from Asheville. Believe it; the Rocky Broad is noted for its devastating floods. It's quite an experience to camp by the Rocky Broad, watch your kids splash around in the water, and listen to an old-timer talk about the flood of 1998.

The Hickory Nut Gorge is privately held in its entirety. The largest tract open to the public is the spectacular **Chimney Rock Park**, a 1,000-acre attraction and nature preserve that has stunning clifftop views, amazing geological formations (including the Chimney Rock, a huge freestanding spire reachable via a long bridge over a chasm), and a 400-foot waterfall. Other areas can be reached by the guests of private resorts. **The Chalet Club** gives its guests access to miles of trails on the north rim opposite the Chimney Rock, while the **Hickory Nut Gap Inn**'s guests can explore the mountains along the upper parts of the gorge. The Nature Conservancy owns a 93-acre preserve that contains a stretch of undisturbed north-facing cliff and the **Bat Cave**, believed to be the largest granite fissure cave in America; this preserve is open only to Nature Conservancy field trips.

Green River Game Lands (919-733-7291). Like the Rocky Broad 13 miles to its north, the Green River drains a wide area above the Blue Ridge, then uses its heavy water flow to cut a long, deep gorge through the hard center of the mountain. The gorge of the Green River remains in a nearly wild state, however, with more than 18,000 acres protected by the State of North Carolina as the Green River Game Lands. Like other Blue Ridge gorges, the Green River Gorge is U shaped with sheer gray cliffs common along its upper slope, its lower slopes clad in botanically rich mature cove hardwoods. The gorge starts a short distance north of Tryon at the **Summit Lake Dam**, is crossed by US 176 on an impressive old bridge, then digs deeply into the mountain wilderness. The Green River becomes increasingly wild, with Class III–IV rapids, as it reaches its deepest and most rugged point—**the Narrows**, where the river rushes between cliffs barely 6 feet apart. After the Narrows, the gorge widens out to form a flat valley floor beneath tall cliffs, the river becoming wider and much less wild. This section, called **Green River Cove**, is traversed by a back road and contains scattered houses between blocks of state game lands. The gorge ends suddenly as the Green River drains into the Piedmont and enters **Lake Adger**.

Kayakers enjoy both the rowdy upper section of the Green River Gorge and

THE SUMMIT OF CHIMNEY ROCK, WITH LAKE LURE IN THE DISTANCE.

Jim Hargan

its somewhat less technical lower section, and the NC Wildlife Resources Commission maintains a launching point just downstream from the Narrows, as well as a nice riverside picnic area. Five miles of hiking paths allow easy exploration of the deepest and most rugged section of the gorge, including the Narrows and the cliffs to its north.

South Carolina's Blue Wall, an impressive mountain escarpment (see "Hendersonville & Brevard") extends into this area as the Saluda Mountains. Lower and less rugged than the mountains near Brevard, they are nevertheless beautiful and full of variety. Most of this section of the Blue Wall is taken up by the City of Greenville's watershed and closed to the public, and much of the remainder is in private hands. A hiking trail known as the **Blue Wall Passage** traverses Nature Conservancy lands and is worth the walk, passing ponds and climbing through old-growth forests to reach stunning mountain views. To reach it, take US 176 south of Tryon to a right at the Lake Lanier entrance just before the state line; follow W. Lakeshore Rd. around the lake for 2 miles to a right on Dug Hill Rd.; follow Dug Hill Rd. to the entrance of the Nature Conservancy's Blue Wall Preserve.

RECREATION AREAS ❦ ✎ ♿ **Foothills Equestrian Nature Center** (828-859-9021; www.fence.org), 3381 Hunting Country Rd., Tryon, NC. This beautiful and unusual center (known as FENCE) sits in the foothills of the Blue Ridge near Tryon. It combines an educational nature center with a large, national-quality horse show and steeplechase venue. Best known as the host of Tryon's famous equestrian events, it also has 320 acres of picnic areas, walking paths, forests, and wildflower meadows. Its rolling foothills location provides an astonishing variety of environments for its 5 miles of paths—hardwood forests, pine forests, hilltops, open meadows (with lovely views), marshlands, and ponds. A historic building at the center, shaped like a stable, holds the offices and a shop; next door, an herb garden surrounds a log cabin. One of the trails is disabled accessible.

On the other side of I-26 sits the equestrian center, with an 8-furlong track and stalls for 200 horses. Some sort of equestrian event is scheduled for almost every weekend, and is worth looking into. Free.

PICNIC AREAS McCreery Park, Saluda, NC. This small park at the center of Saluda climbs a hill opposite downtown, with good views from the picnic tables toward the Main St. shops. It's a popular playground for local kids.

Fishtop Access Area, Green River Cove. Part of the Green River Game Lands, Fishtop Access Area offers

A LOG CABIN AT THE FOOTHILLS EQUESTRIAN NATURE CENTER.

Jim Hargan

LOOKING FROM THE TRAIL DOWN TOWARD CHIMNEY ROCK VILLAGE IN HICKORY NUT
GORGE.

🐾 ✎ ♿ **Chimney Rock Park** (800-277-9611 or 828-625-9611; www.chimney
rockpark.com), US 64/74A, Chimney Rock, NC. Daily. Ticket plaza opens 8:30
AM; closes 5:30 PM May–Oct., 4:30 PM Nov.–Apr. Owned by the same family
since 1902 (and open as a tourist attraction since 1885), Chimney Rock is a
very old, very traditional, and very beautiful scenic attraction off US 74A in
Hickory Nut Gorge. The park centers on a series of stunning cliffs along the

limited riverside picnicking at the deepest and most rugged part of the Green
River Gorge, the mouth of the Narrows.

✳ To See

BIG DAMMED LAKES Lake Lure. The village of Lake Lure, NC, includes the
large hydropower lake of that name and all the land surrounding it. The Morse
family, owners (then and now) of **Chimney Rock Park**, built the lake and
founded the town in 1926. They wanted to expand Chimney Rock's appeal by
adding a scenic lake, recreational opportunities, and upscale vacation development; it was the Morses who created the vintage 1928 town center and the 1926
Donald Ross golf course. The Depression intervened, however, and Lake Lure
was sold off in bankruptcy. That's too bad; the Morses have shown themselves to

south edge of the gorge, where unusual geological formations frame over-whelming panoramas over Lake Lure, Hickory Nut Gorge, and the Blue Ridge. Entering the park in the middle of **Chimney Rock Village**, you'll travel a mile through park lands before reaching the 1920 stone-built ticket booth. Two more miles brings you to the base of the cliffs, with views up to the **Chimney Rock**—a 300-foot rock tower with a flat top, crowned by a giant American flag. From here you walk through a 200-foot tunnel and zoom up a 250-foot elevator to a cliff ledge large enough to hold a gift shop and snack bar. Outside are wide views from large rock-floored balconies placed in the ledge—views over to the Chimney Rock, now only a little way up, along the cliffs, and over Lake Lure. This is the end of the disabled-accessible area. Now a cliffside path and steps climb up to a bridge across the chasm that separates the Chimney Rock from the cliff face; the wide top of the Chimney furnishes more views. From there the trail continues, climbing the cliffs in stairs, looking down on the Chimney Rock, getting even better views from the clifftop, cutting through the cliff face on a narrow ledge, and viewing the unique cliffside forest, stunted into bonsai shapes by harsh winds. The climax of the cliff walk: a huge, violent **waterfall** that plunges straight down for 400 feet without so much as a bounce off a ledge until it crashes to the bottom. (This is the same waterfall featured in the 1992 movie *The Last of the Mohicans*.) A separate (much easier) path leads to the bottom of the falls, with astonishing views upward. The pre-elevator steps to the Chimney, built in 1920, are still there, and are a fun trip down. If you bring your dog, you are required to use the steps instead of the elevator.

Below the cliffs, an area called **the Meadows** provides a large picnic area and a museum that explains the natural history of the cliffs above. Be sure not to miss it on the way out. $11 adults, $5 children 4–12.

be masters of tasteful and environmentally friendly development at Chimney Rock Park.

Lake Lure remains an attractive little resort settlement, despite its haphazard development. The towering cliffs of the Blue Ridge form a crescent around the lake's western end, and Hickory Nut Gorge cuts deeply into this gray-green escarpment. This great wilderness escarpment frames a lakeshore largely encrusted by vacation homes of all types and sizes, extending two to five lots uphill on twisting gravel roads. Access to the town is by US 64/74A, a narrow prewar relic that hugs the lake's southern coastline; travel services stretch out along this highway, but become thicker toward the village center at the lake's western end. The main highway continues westward up the base of Hickory Nut Gorge, past the road-hugging tourist settlements of Chimney Rock and Bat Cave, NC.

HISTORIC SITES ↑ **Tryon Depot and Polk County Historical Museum** (828-859-2287), 22 Depot St., Tryon, NC. Tue. and Thu. 10–noon. Sitting across the tracks from downtown, Tryon's classic turn-of-the-20th-century depot serves as home for a wonderful local historical museum. Exhibits include a reconstructed press for the *Tryon Daily Bulletin*; a section on William Gillette, the famous actor (and Tryon resident) who created Sherlock Holmes for the stage; a local moonshine still, complete and accurate; the depot stationmaster's room, furnished accurately; and a "madstone," a folk remedy for curing rabies. This delightful miscellany is pulled together into a picture of life underneath the Blue Ridge 100 years ago—definitely worth seeing. Also in the depot are the offices of the Tryon Riding and Hunt Club, sponsors of several important horse events including the Blockhouse Steeplechase.

CULTURAL SITES ↑ **The Upstairs Gallery** (828-859-2828; www.upstairsgallery .org), 49 S. Trade St., Tryon, NC. Tue.–Sat. 11–5. This well-respected contemporary art gallery displays the works of professional regional artists and fine crafters from their digs in downtown Tryon.

A not-for-profit art organization, the Upstairs Gallery is in the process of renovating a new three-story home in an old downtown building. The Upstairs Gallery is the venue for the monthly Pickin' Parlor.

SHUNKAWAKEN FALLS ON WHITE OAK MOUNTAIN.

Jim Hargan

↑ **Tryon Fine Arts Center (TFAC)** (828-859-8322; fax 828-859-0271; www.tryontfac.org), 34 Melrose Ave., Tryon, NC. Founded in the mid-1960s, TFAC is an umbrella organization made up of nine local arts groups, including the **Little Theatre**. TFAC occupies a half-block campus a block away from downtown across the tracks, with several public gardens and art galleries. On site is **Tryon Crafts**, a craft school and one of the founding members. Also on site is the gallery for the **Tryon Painters and Sculptors**, a co-op made up of local professional artists.

GARDENS AND PARKS **Pearson's Falls**. Mar.–Oct., Tue.–Sun. 10–6; Nov.–Feb., Wed.–Sun. 10–5. Since 1931 the Tryon Garden Club has preserved this extraordinarily beautiful and botanically rich gorge, located off

US 176 (on Pearsons Falls Rd., SSR 1102) between Tryon and Saluda, NC. From a small picnic area, a quarter-mile trail climbs gently up a limestone ravine, alive with every sort of wildflower and fern imaginable, to the lovely 20-foot Pearson's Falls. $2 per adult.

White Oak Mountain. Long a popular beauty spot outside Columbus, NC, this tall outlier of the Blue Ridge is being loved to death, its summit taken over by condominiums and vacation houses. To find it, take Houston Rd. (SSR 1137) north from Columbus for 1.1 miles, to a left on White Oak Mountain Rd. (SSR 1136)—and a 1,500-foot climb to the summit. As you reach the top of the mountain, the road will cross the beautiful and tall **Shunkawaken Falls**. Then, as you top out on the summit, what's left of a mountaintop meadow sits in front of a condo development, with some truly remarkable views south over the Piedmont.

✷ To Do

GOLF **Lake Lure Municipal Golf Course** (828-625-4472), US 64/74A, Lake Lure, NC. This nine-hole course, designed by Donald Ross in 1929, follows rolling terrain between Lake Lure and US 74A. $11–14.

Colony Lake Lure Golf Resort (828-625-2626), 201 Blvd. of the Mountains, Lake Lure, NC. This golf resort is located north of Lake Lure at the development complex known as Fairfield Mountains. It has two 18-hole courses with notable views of the rock cliffs of the Blue Ridge. $43–46.

Orchard Trace Golf Club (828-685-1006), 942 Sugarloaf Rd., Hendersonville, NC. This 18-hole 1993 course is located in Apple Country, just north of Hendersonville and a mile or so off US 64. It features large greens and sloping terrain. $10.

Pine Links Golf Club (828-693-0907), S. Orchard Rd., Flat Rock, NC. A nine-hole Apple Country course, designed in 1997 by Sidney Blythe, that features short greens and a number of water hazards. $12.

Red Fox Country Club (828-894-8251), 2 Club Rd., Tryon, NC. This 18-hole course, designed by Ellis Maples in 1966, sits in the Piedmont underneath Tryon, with views toward the Blue Ridge some distance away. Described as "scenic and serene," it has a number of streams and a 30-acre lake in play. $30–35.

HORSEBACK RIDING **Cedar Creek Riding Stables** (877-625-6773 or 828-625-2811; www.cedarcreekstables.com), 542 Cedar Creek Rd., Lake Lure, NC. Daily 8–5. Located deep in the mountains north of Lake Lure, Cedar Creek offers scenic 1- and 2-hour trail rides on their own 360-acre ranch. Two-night pack trips in the Pisgah National Forest include all equipment and meals. $25–45 for half-day rides; 2-night pack trips run $400 per person.

STILLWATER SPORTS **Lake Lure Marina** (877-386-4255 or 828-625-1373; fax 828-625-2036; www.lakelure.com), Lake Lure, NC. This marina on Lake Lure rents a variety of human- and machine-powered boats, including canoes and kayaks. Half day $40–50, whole day $65–75.

✳ Lodging

COUNTRY INNS AND HOTELS The Orchard Inn (800-581-3800 or 828-749-5471; fax 828-749-9805; www .orchardinn.com), US 176, P.O. Box 128, Saluda, NC 28773. Sitting on its own little mountaintop at the end of a winding private drive, surrounded by 12 acres of gardens and woods, this 1910 National Register country hotel offers mountain views from its wide, wraparound veranda. Located near Saluda, the Orchard Inn has nine rooms furnished with antiques, along with four small kitchen-free cottages— each with fireplace, whirlpool bath, and private deck—scattered about on the property. Well known for its fine dining (see *Dining Out*), the Orchard serves a wonderful full breakfast, included in the tariff. Second-floor rooms $119–139, first-floor room with sitting area $169–189, cottages $169–245. Includes breakfast.

The Pine Crest Inn (800-633-3001 or 828-859-9135; fax 828-859-9135; www.pinecrestinn.com), 85 Pine Crest Lane, Tryon, NC 28782. This National Register 1917 hotel sits on 3 hilltop acres above downtown Tryon. Built as a meeting place for Tryon's horses-and-hounds set, today it's run as an elegant English-style country inn with a full gourmet restaurant (see *Dining Out*) and an AAA four-diamond rating. The main lodge holds 4 of the 35 rooms as well as the restaurant. Long and deep, its side-on front entrance looks a bit like a farmhouse, but its long side is set upon a stone terrace and covered with a veranda overlooking gardens. Within the lodge, a parlor area is furnished with English-country-house-style furniture, centered on a large stone fireplace, while a library is similarly

furnished and stocked floor to ceiling with books. Most of the rooms are in cottages (no kitchens)—five multi-room and five individual. The cottages range widely in style, from historic log cabins to contemporary, with most in a 1930s style. The rooms range in size from comfortable to very large, and continue the decorating theme of an English country house; many have separate seating area, fireplace, and whirlpool bath. The full breakfast, included in the tariff, is in the restaurant and from the same gourmet menu offered to the public. Rooms $95–190, private cottages $170–370.

🐾 ♪ **The Melrose Inn** (828-859-7014; www.tryon-melrose-inn.com), 55 Melrose Ave., Tryon, NC 28782. This 1889 hotel sits on a hill above downtown Tryon, in a quiet residential neighborhood. It has wide verandas with mountain views as well as a full-service restaurant that serves lunch and dinner. Its guest rooms are individually decorated with antiques and reproductions in a late-Victorian theme. Special guest rooms are dedicated to families traveling with children or pets. $75–115 includes a full breakfast.

The Mimosa Inn (877-646-6724 or 828-859-7688; www.carolina-foothills .com), Mimosa Inn Dr., Tryon, NC 28782. This 1903 mansion, built in the style of an antebellum classical plantation, sits on the north end of Tryon, in 4 acres of landscaped grounds. An impressive sight when viewed from busy NC 108, it is dominated by its 50-foot-tall veranda framed by classical columns—a popular site for breakfast on pleasant summer mornings. Extensive common rooms are furnished in elegant turn-of-the-20th-century antiques. The 10 upstairs guest rooms are also antiques furnished and individually themed. A guest house with kitchen and private entrance is also available on the property. A full breakfast is included in the room rate. $95 and up.

RESORTS ✪ The Chalet Club (800-336-3309; fax 828-625-9373; www.chaletclub.com), P.O. Box 100, Lake Lure, NC 28746. Open all year. The Washburn family has run this intimate resort above Lake Lure on the rim of Hickory Nut Gorge since they founded it in 1934. Even though it's classed as a private club, they welcome all visitors with no restrictions; the modest annual fee is used to maintain the surrounding wildlands. With five guest rooms and six cottages, it is nevertheless a traditional full-service resort, including all meals and all activities in the price; guests can also get a "bed & breakfast" limited to breakfast and only a few of the activities. The main lodge, built in 1927 as the family vacation retreat, is in a chalet style with plenty of period charm and panoramic views. It contains the five comfortable guest rooms and the large common areas with a stone fireplace, comfortable furniture, an ample library, and lots of games. The cottages were all built as private houses, and range from a quaint 1927 log caretaker's cabin to a comfortable 1962 home. Meals are prepared from fresh ingredients, with breakfasts served from a menu and a simple lunch served buffet style or taken as a picnic. Dinners are more formal, with gentlemen expected to wear a coat. Outdoor activities for which there is no extra charge include two tennis courts, a platform tennis court, 7 miles of hiking and biking trails, basketball,

shuffleboard, and horseshoe courts, two swimming pools, lake swimming, waterskiing, canoeing, kayaking, electric boating (for lake fishing), and powerboating. Discounts or special packages are available for golf, horseback riding, rock climbing, and several nearby attractions. Rooms $156–262 per couple, cottages $166–314 per couple. Add $30 per couple membership fee, good for one year. Discounts for children. Includes all meals and activities. "B&B rates" include breakfast and the use of all facilities: $40 less per couple.

Hickory Nut Gap Inn (828-625-9108; www.hickorynutgapinn.com), P.O. Box 246, Bat Cave, NC 28710. This mountaintop lodge with six guest rooms is notable for its remarkable building and guest facilities. It sits above Hickory Nut Gorge near Bat Cave, at the end of a mile-long private drive, with wide views from its 40 acres and extensive recreation on the site and in its elaborate game room. The founder of the Trailways Bus line built the lodge in the 1940s out of wood and stone taken from his surrounding 5,000-acre estate. With a modest exterior, the lodge is sited to gain a stunning view over the cliffs of Hickory Nut Gorge. Its interior is completely paneled with fine hardwoods—including floors and ceilings. The huge living room has a cathedral ceiling and large stone fireplace, and remains furnished in the style of a 1940s vacation lodge; memorabilia includes a platinum record left behind by previous owner Lynyrd Skynyrd, who used it as a retreat and rehearsal studio in the 1970s. The game room downstairs, paneled in gleaming hardwoods, has a full-sized bowling alley as well as pool and ping-pong tables.

All six guest rooms are fully paneled as well, and furnished in simple comfortable period furniture reminiscent of the 1940s. The tariff includes a continental breakfast on the large covered porch. The 40-acre site offers excellent walking opportunities, and horseback riding can be arranged. Rooms $125 for a single night, $95 per night for longer. Two-room suite $155.

BED & BREAKFAST INNS Stone Hedge Inn (800-859-1974 or 828-859-9114; fax 828-859-5928; www.stone-hedge-inn.com), 222 Stone Hedge Lane, P.O. Box 366, Tryon, NC 28782. This 1934 mansion, made of stacked fieldstone taken from the property, makes a charming site for this small inn and restaurant. Located 3 miles north of Tryon in the shadow of the Blue Ridge, the original house combines its vernacular local stonework with elements of art deco and Mediterranean architecture, all framed by spectacular views over the 28-acre estate. The inn consists of the main house, a guest house, and a tiny poolside cottage—all made of the same stacked fieldstone; a swimming pool sits between the three buildings. All six guest rooms are large enough to have a sitting area. The two rooms in the main house are the most formal, with antique furnishings complementing their sculpted plaster ceilings. The three guest house rooms and the single roomed poolside cottage tend to be more casual and contemporary. Its restaurateur owners run a fine small restaurant in the main house (see *Dining Out*), and the included breakfasts are predictably excellent. Rooms $100–115, suite with kitchen $130.

✐ **Tryon Old South Bed and Breakfast** (800-288-7966 or 828-859-6965; www.tryonoldsouth.com), 27 Markham Rd., Tryon, NC 28782. All year. Located in a residential neighborhood near downtown Tryon, this restored 1910 mansion is surrounded by wide lawns, old oaks, and azaleas. Its common areas and four rooms are filled with antiques, the rooms individually themed. Also on the property is a modest 1930s house, remodeled into a handsome guest cottage with full kitchen. The rate includes a full southern breakfast. Rooms $65–95, cottage $125.

✐ **The Foxtrot Inn** (888-676-8050 or 828-859-9706; www.foxtrotinn.com), P.O. Box 1561, 800 Lynn Rd., Tryon, NC 28782. This attractive 1915 home in a Tryon residential neighborhood has four guest rooms. It has a heated swimming pool, and mountains are visible through the old trees that frame the house. Both the common areas and the rooms are furnished in elegant antiques, with rooms attractively decorated to individual themes. Some have separate a private sitting room. A full breakfast is included. $75–115.

The Oaks Bed and Breakfast (800-893-6091 or 828-749-9613; www.theoaksbedandbreakfast.com), 339 Greenville St., Saluda, NC 28773. Built in 1895 for a local banker, this fine old Victorian house in a Saluda neighborhood has a witch's-hat turret, a wraparound porch with turned woodwork, and gables in all directions. Porches have plenty of wicker furniture, and common areas (including a living room, dining room, and library) are furnished in a combination of Victorian antiques and comfortable sofas and chairs. Four rooms in the main house are elegantly furnished with antiques, and the turret room has a separate sitting room (in the turret); three of these rooms are en suite, while the turret room has a private bath down the hall. Two suites (both en suite), located in a separate guest house, have separate sitting rooms and a deck or balcony, and are furnished with antiques or locally handcrafted furniture. The price includes a full breakfast. Rooms $115–125, suites $175.

✍ **Gaestehaus Salzburg** (877-694-4029 or 828-625-0093; fax 828-625-0091; www.gaestehaussalzburg.com), 1491 Memorial Hwy., Lake Lure, NC 28746. Austrian-born innkeeper Werner Maringer and his wife, Patricia, have built their Lake Lure B&B in the folk style of the Alpine borders. Located on a woodland plot on the east side of town just off US 74A, this AAA three-diamond inn has three guest rooms, all furnished in a traditional Alpine style with natural wood accents. There's a pool and hot tub by the gaestehaus, as well as the excellent German-Austrian restaurant Das Kaffeehaus (see *Eating Out*). The traditional German breakfast consists of fresh-baked breads and fresh fruits, the Kaffehaus's scrumptious Austrian pastries, soft-boiled egg (in a cup), and a selection of cold cuts, cheeses, and sausages. In addition to the B&B, they have a cottage on the property, and a set of eight modern condo-style efficiencies. Rooms $82–95, including breakfast. Cottage $145, efficiencies $125.

Ivivi Lake and Mountain Lodge (866-224-7740 or 828-625-0601; fax 828-625-8841; www.ivivilodge.com), 161 Waterside Dr., Lake Lure, NC 28746. This strikingly contemporary inn sits on a hill overlooking Lake Lure and the Blue Ridge. The imposing, modernist glass entrance is framed with undressed timbers. Inside, the house is decorated with contemporary European furniture and art objects from southern Africa. The dining room, where the full breakfast is served, is surrounded by plate glass and spills onto the adjacent flagstone patio, with wide views westward over the lake and toward Hickory Nut Gorge. The seven rooms are large and luxurious, with floor-to-ceiling windows and contemporary decor with an African theme. Included in the tariff is breakfast and an evening cruise on Lake Lure with wine and hors d'oeuvres. $255–350.

The Wicklow Inn (877-625-4038 or 828-625-4038; fax 828-625-0435; www.thewicklowinn.com), US 64/74A, P.O. Box 246, Chimney Rock, NC 28720. This attractive 1947 Colonial house sits in the middle of Chimney Rock Village on US 74A, by the Rocky Broad River. Innkeeper Jack Ryan named it for his native Wicklow Mountains in Ireland, and gives the inn an Irish flavor. The six comfortable rooms are beautifully furnished in a simple, country style. The three downstairs rooms all have a private entrance opening onto the garden or a deck overlooking the river. Upstairs, two charming rooms share a sitting room, while the third room has its own private sitting area and a dining alcove. Full breakfasts include seasonal fruits, muffins and scones, and specialty dishes.

CABIN RENTALS **Sandy Cut Cabins** (828-749-9555; www.sandycutcabins .com), P.O. Box 386, Saluda, NC 28773. Open all year. These two modern cabins are located on 15 acres near Saluda, set between the North Pacolet

River and the Saluda Grade, an active freight railroad. The cabins are clad in stained clapboard, one built in a simple mountain style with a full porch, the other more contemporary with a deck. Both have full kitchen with dishwasher, and either a hot tub or a whirlpool bath. First night $100–150, afterward $75–100 per night.

✳ Where to Eat

EATING OUT The Purple Onion Café and Coffee House (828-749-1179; www.purpleonionsaluda.com), 16 Main St., Saluda, NC. Lunch 11–3, dinner 5–8; closed Wed. and Sun. This small upscale eatery occupies a well-kept storefront in downtown Saluda. Its menu offers California-style cuisine, with lots of fresh and exotic ingredients. It has a good wine list and a selection of microbrews. Lunches feature salads, sandwiches, soups, and pizzas—a simple menu that conceals some exotic fare ("bulghur, mint, parsley, garlic, peppers, carrot, lemon, and olive oil served with tomatoes, cucumbers, feta, purple onion, pita and kalamata olives") seldom spotted in southern street-front cafés. Dinner menus add some more elegant entrées, such as London broil marinated in fresh ginger, soy, and lime, or roast pork tenderloin with fresh rosemary and portobello mushrooms.

Old Rock Café (828-625-2329; fax 828-625-9610), US 64/74A, Chimney Rock, NC. Located in Hickory Nut Gorge right outside Chimney Rock Park, the Old Rock Café offers salads, burgers, trout, and seasonal specials. In addition to indoor dining, they have tables on a large deck overlooking the Rocky Broad River.

Das Kaffeehaus Austrian Pastry Shoppe (828-625-0093; www.gaeste haussalzburg.com/shoppe.html), 1491 Memorial Hwy., Lake Lure, NC. Wed.–Sat. Lunch 11–2:30, dinner by reservation only 6–8. Part of the Gaestehaus Salzburg Bed and Breakfast on the east end of Lake Lure, Das Kaffeehaus offers freshly made Austrian pastries and authentic German entrées. You'll find it off US 74A down its own private drive, deep in the woods, built in the folk style found in the Alpine borders where restaurateur and innkeeper Werner Maringer was born. A selection of a dozen Austrian pastries will tickle your sweet tooth, while hot lunch entrées include sausages, goulash, potato pancakes, and crêpes. Dinners are more formal and require reservations; entrées include a variety of traditional German pork and sausage dishes. They have a full selection of German wines and beers. Pastries $2.50–3.50, lunch $5–8, dinner $12–16.

DINING OUT The Orchard Inn (800-581-3800 or 828-749-5471; fax 828-749-9805; www.orchardinn.com), US 176, Saluda, NC. Wed.–Sat., 7 PM by reservation only. Well known for its fine dining, the Orchard Inn is a 1910 National Register country hotel south of Saluda off US 176 in the scenic Pacolet River Valley. It's a fine old building, sitting on a grassy hilltop, with wide verandas wrapping around its front and sides, elegantly furnished with antiques. The dining area occupies a glassed-in porch overlooking the gardens and vineyard. The elegant and exciting four-course meal includes a choice of four entrées with fresh seasonal vegetables, soup, salad, and choice of dessert, plus hors d'oeuvres. Gentlemen should wear coats and ties. The Orchard has an excellent wine list, although the choices below $25 a bottle are extremely limited. $39 plus gratuity.

The Pine Crest Inn (800-633-3001 or 828-859-9135; fax 828-859-9135; www.pinecrestinn.com), 85 Pine Crest Lane, Tryon, NC. Breakfast and dinner. Reservations requested. The restaurant as well as the lodgings at the Pine Crest Inn have received the AAA four-diamond rating. Located in the hotel's historic main lodge, its two dining rooms are decorated as an English tavern. The menu, designed by executive chef Brian Binzer, features new American cuisine and favors original taste combinations with distinctive flavors. For an appetizer, seared scallops may be combined with celery root/sweet onion puree and an orange cream; an entrée may marry a pork tenderloin with pears, sweet onion marmalade, blue cheese, and a Marsala-scented reduction. An extensive wine list is available. Breakfast $6–8, dinner entrées $20–29.

Stone Hedge Inn and Restaurant (800-859-1974 or 828-859-9114; fax 828-859-5928; www.stone-hedge-inn.com), 222 Stone Hedge Lane, Tryon, NC. Dinner Wed.–Sat. 6–9, reservations encouraged. Sun. brunch, noon–2:30. Part of Tryon's Stone Hedge Inn, this casually elegant little restaurant occupies a delightfully eccentric building, a 1934 vacation mansion built entirely of local fieldstone in a style combining art deco and Mediterranean. Views from its brightly lighted dining room face out over 28 rolling acres of meadows and forests towards the Blue Ridge, only a few miles away. Much of the menu is simple, elegant fare—a Black Angus filet mignon wrapped in bacon, grilled

to order, and served with mushroom caps; a veal top round cutlet, lightly breaded and sautéed in clarified butter. A unique chicken dish is prepared every evening, along with other specials. Dinner $16–25.

✳ Entertainment

Tryon, NC
The Tryon Little Theatre (828-859-8322), Fine Arts Center, 34 Melrose Ave. This local amateur theater performs four plays a year at the Tryon Fine Arts Center. Plays $10, musicals $15.

The Pickin' Parlor (828-894-8091). First Friday of each month, 7–9 PM. This monthly jam brings local musicians together for folk and bluegrass music. It's held in one of two Tryon art galleries, usually the Fine Arts Center, but occasionally the Trade Street Café and Gallery. Donations at the door.

Saluda, NC
The Purple Onion Café (828-749-1179), 16 Main St. On Saturday night, downtown Saluda's Purple Onion Café features live acoustic performances in a coffeehouse atmosphere, tending toward folk and alternative music. Performances start at 8; dinner service ends at 9 (but you can order desserts and coffees until closing); performances typically end at 10.

✳ Selective Shopping

Lake Lure and Hickory Nut Gorge, NC
Edie's Good Things (828-625-8054; fax 828-625-8054; www.ediegood things.com), Chimney Rock, NC. Daily 9–6. This Chimney Rock gallery represents the work of fine craft artists from the western Carolina

mountains. The store features hand-woven basketry, hand-thrown pottery and clay pieces, hand-blown glass, hand-carved wood, handmade metal pieces, and much more.

A Touch in Time (828-625-1902), Bat Cave, NC. Daily 10–5:30. A wide-porched 1902 Victorian farmhouse, overlooking US 74 in Bat Cave (at the high end of Hickory Nut Gorge), carries a wide variety of crafts.

Hendersonville, NC

Silver Fox Gallery (828-698-0601), 508 N. Main St. This downtown Hendersonville gallery presents "art for living," as they put it—art for the home, practical and otherwise. Representing around 50 artists, Silver Fox has a large and varied selection of contemporary fine crafts and arts, including wall art, wearable art (including jewelry), glass art, clay, metal, papier-mâché, and wood. Their selection can have a whimsical touch, and they have a special selection of "horses and hounds."

Saluda, NC

Heartwood Contemporary Crafts Gallery (828-749-9365; www .heartwoodsaluda.com), 21 E. Main St. Mon.–Sat. 10–5 PM, Sun. noon–5. This downtown Saluda gallery features American fine crafts with a strong contemporary flair. Handsome, roomy, and brightly lighted, the historic storefront offers a wide range of items—handmade wearables, jewelry, paper, paintings, fine porcelain, stoneware, glass, metal, and wood.

Saluda Mountain Crafts Gallery (828-749-4341), 1487 Ozone Dr. Don't let the interstate-side location fool you; this is no chintzy gift shop. Located in a rusticized modern building by I-26's Exit 28, Saluda Mountain Craft

Gallery stocks original craft art with a traditional tone, featuring the works of local and regional artists. They carry pottery, woodworking, decoys, handmade furniture, woven art, jewelry, cornhusk dolls, children's toys, and books. They have a wide front porch with rocking chairs, and a quilter upstairs every Saturday. Best of all, the store right next door is a fine soda fountain that makes its own ice cream.

✳ Special Events

SPRING St. Patrick's Day Parade and Celebration. A parade through downtown Tryon, NC, is followed by live music, an antique car show, and plenty of food.

The Blockhouse Steeplechase (800-438-3681 or 828-859-6109; fax 828-859-5598), Tryon, NC. Late Apr. Ticket sales to the public begin on Feb. 15. Gates open at 10 AM. Races start at 2 PM. The Tryon Riding and Hunt Club has been holding this sanctioned steeplechase annually since 1947. Race day activities include a parade of hounds, antique carriages, the Parade of the Old Tryon Foot Beagles, and awards for Best Tailgate Picnic and Most Creative Hat. The 1-mile kidney-shaped track, located at the Foothills Equestrian Nature Center (FENCE), sits in a hollow surrounded by low hills. Spectators' tickets gain them a parking space within view of the track, and they watch the races from their car (or mingle about and admire each other's tailgate picnics and hats). The cheapest seats are in the infield, while the most expensive seats are hillside and RV parking. Walk-ins cost $60 per person at the gate, including off-site parking. Carload $80–125, RV $200; must be purchased in advance.

SUMMER Blue Ridge Barbeque Festival and Foothills Crafts Festival (828-859-7427). Mid-June. The official barbeque competition of North Carolina with a high-quality juried art fair in Tryon, NC's Harmon Fields (on the north end of town). Several of the 80-plus barbeque contestants, as well as other food vendors, sell food to the public. The craft fair offers a limited number of booths in each category, with booths going to the best artists; content is strictly limited to original-design fine crafts and arts.

Tryon Riding and Hunt Club Horse Show (800-438-3681 or 828-859-6109; fax 828-859-5598), Tryon, NC. Mid-June. This hunter-jumper show has been held in Tryon since 1928. It's a 4-day event at the FENCE equestrian center—one of a number of such events held throughout the spring and summer months.

Annual Coon Dog Days (828-749-2581). Early July. This annual coon dog show has been held in Saluda since 1964. Along with the coon dog judging is a coon dog race, a craft fair, a parade, live music, and a street dance. Free.

AUTUMN Any and All Dog Show (800-438-3681 or 828-859-6109; fax 828-859-5598), Tryon, NC. Early Oct. A Tryon tradition since 1933, this show has categories such as Most Interesting Tail, Looks Most Like Master, Best Costume, Most Doubtful Ancestry, Best Trick, Happiest, and (of course) Best Horse-Show Dog.

Foothills Highland Games (828-859-2050). First weekend in Nov. This 2-day event, held at Harmon Fields on the north side of the town of Tryon, NC, features Scottish athletic competition, the calling of the clans, bagpipe bands, Scottish dance, border collie demonstrations, live (nonbagpipe) music, and Scottish food.

WINTER Tryon Christmas Stroll. First weekend in Dec. Downtown Tryon, NC, celebrates Christmas with carriage rides, refreshments, an open house, carol singing, and a craft sale. Nearby, Saluda, NC, has its Home Town Christmas open house and celebration, while Columbus, NC, has a Christmas parade the next day.

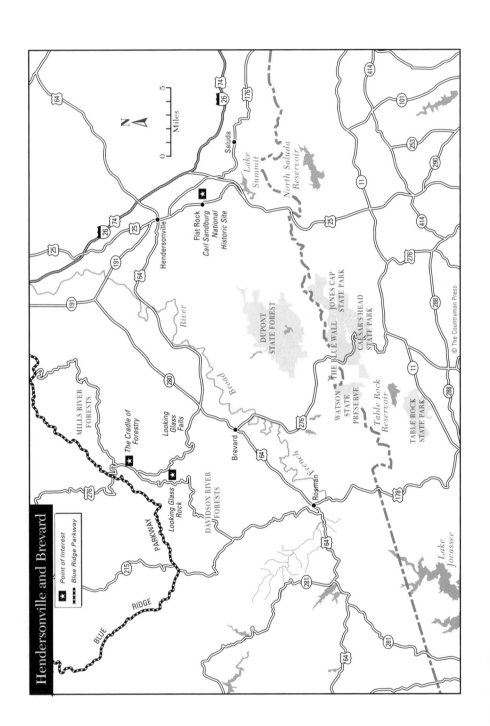

Hendersonville and Brevard

■ Point of Interest
★ Blue Ridge Parkway

BLUE
RIDGE
PARKWAY

215

276

MILLS RIVER
FORESTS

★ The Cradle of
Forestry

Looking
Glass
Falls

★
Looking Glass
Rock

DAVIDSON RIVER
FORESTS

281

281

64

64

Lake
Jocassee

Rosman

Brevard

64

280

64

191

191

64

25

Hendersonville

191

25

26 74

25

64

Saluda

74

26 74

176

Broad Branch

Broad River

River

178

288

11

276

25

11

414

276

253

290

101

414

Flat Rock
★ Carl Sandburg
National
Historic Site

Lake
Summit

North Saluda
Reservoir

DUPONT
STATE FOREST

THE BLUE WALL

JONES CAP
STATE PARK

CAESAR'S HEAD
STATE PARK

WATSON
STATE
PRESERVE

Table Rock
Reservoir

TABLE ROCK
STATE PARK

288

N

0   5
Miles

© The Countryman Press

THE BLUE RIDGE:
HENDERSONVILLE & BREVARD

At the far northern border of South Carolina, the hot, humid southlands end abruptly at the foot of a remarkable cliff. Two thousand feet high and 35 miles long, it's known as "the Blue Wall" by South Carolinians. Its western half is part of the Blue Ridge, here many miles south of the Blue Ridge Parkway; its eastern half is a side ridge called the Saluda Ridge. Its crest forms the boundary between South and North Carolina. In back of this crest, in North Carolina, sits a high perched valley, bowl shaped, with small mountains at its center. This valley is large enough to contain two North Carolina counties, high enough to be cool and pleasant in summer, and mountainous enough to be exceptionally beautiful. This chapter describes this valley, its two county seats—Hendersonville and Brevard—and the mountains that surround it.

Since the construction of the Buncombe Turnpike in the 1820s, rich South Carolinians have fled here in summer, escaping the sticky heat of Charleston and Columbia. Antebellum second homes are still scattered throughout this valley, as are vacation homes from every historic period thereafter. Today these historic homes play host to elegant inns and sophisticated restaurants. Art galleries dot brick-front main streets. Two symphony orchestras and the State Theater of North Carolina headquarter in these tiny rural towns, and a major classical music festival stages full-scale operas from its own lakeside campus. Tourism here is refined, cultured, and understated.

Hendersonville and Brevard offer excellent shopping and restaurants in their revived and restored downtowns, and both have a good choice in bed & breakfast inns. Hendersonville, the larger and more industrial of the two, plays urban host to the elegant 19th-century tourist settlement of Flat Rock, only a few miles south. Brevard, much deeper in the mountains, is quieter, with more of a small-town atmosphere; its summer music festival, held on its own lakeside campus, is one of the cultural highlights of the mountains. The valley itself is largely flat, so much so that the French Broad River wanders through it in a long series of tightly twisted meander loops. A series of small mountains runs up the middle of the valley, however; near Brevard, the westernmost of these low mountains make up the waterfall-rich DuPont State Forest.

Henderson County Travel and Tourism (800-828-4244 or 828-693-9708; fax 828-697-4996; www.historichendersonville.org), 201 S. Main St., Hendersonville, NC 28792. Mon.–Fri. 9–5; open weekends in-season. The visitors center occupies its own building on the south edge of downtown Hendersonville, just beyond the old county courthouse.

The Greater Hendersonville Chamber of Commerce (828-692-1413; fax 828-693-8802; www.hendersonvillechamber.org), 330 N. King St., Hendersonville, NC 28792. This private organization concentrates on promoting its member businesses, leaving tourism to the county's Travel and Tourism Authority.

Transylvania County Tourism Development Authority (800-648-4523 or 828-883-3700; fax 828-883-8550; www.brevardncchamber.org), 35 W. Main St., Brevard, NC 28712. The visitors center for the combined chamber of commerce and Tourism Development Authority is in a small storefront in the center of downtown Brevard.

The Pisgah National Forest, Pisgah Ranger District (828-877-3265), 1001 Pisgah Hwy., Pisgah Forest, NC 28768. Located on US 276, 4 miles north of Brevard, this National Forest Service visitors center has interpretive displays, a bookstore, and an information desk as well as the administrative offices of the Pisgah District.

GETTING THERE *By auto*: From I-26, 24 miles south of Asheville, NC, take **US 64** (Exit 18) west. You'll hit the north edge of downtown Hendersonville, NC, in 2 miles, and the north edge of downtown Brevard, NC, in another 20. Other routes, including those with U.S. highway numbers, are not recommended for any purpose other than sightseeing down steep and winding mountain roads.

By air: **Asheville Regional Airport** (828-684-2226; fax 828-684-3404), 708 Airport Rd., Fletcher, NC. Asheville's small regional airport is located 15 miles south of downtown off I-26, Exit 9 (NC 280). It's actually closer to Hendersonville than it is to downtown Asheville—9 miles compared with 13. It's 20 miles from Brevard. This lovely little airport is virtually unchanged since the 1950s—a low, rambling, white concrete structure with orange stripes, its boarding gates rambling outward from a central lobby. Despite its old-fashioned appearance, it has daily service from Atlanta, Cincinnati, Pittsburgh, Raleigh, and Charlotte, with 20 to 25 flights daily. Several car rental agencies are located within or near the airport.

By train: **Amtrak** (877-276-2767; www.amtrakcrescent.com). This is the only mountain location to have a reasonably convenient train connection. Hendersonville, NC, is 35 miles from the Amtrak depot in Greenville, SC, served twice daily by the Crescent from New York to Atlanta and New Orleans—a train with its own web site.

By bus: **Greyhound Bus Lines** (800-229-9424; www.greyhound.com). Hendersonville, NC, has twice daily bus service via Greyhound; Brevard, NC, has no bus service.

MEDICAL EMERGENCIES **Margaret R. Pardee Memorial Hospital** (828-696-1000; www.pardee-med.org), 715 Fleming St., Hendersonville, NC. This full-service major regional hospital offers 24/7 emergency room service from its campus on the northwest edge of downtown Hendersonville.

Pardee Urgent Care at Four Seasons (828-697-3232; www.pardee-med .org/urgentcr.htm), 205 Thompson St., Hendersonville, NC. Mon.–Sat. 9–9, Sun. noon–6 PM. This walk-in clinic, run by the area's regional hospital, is located near the I-26 intersection with US 64, just off US 64 (behind the Taco Bell), toward Hendersonville.

Transylvania Community Hospital (828-884-9111; www.tchospital.org), Hospital Dr., Brevard, NC. This small but full-service local hospital is located just east of Brevard off US 64.

✷ Wandering Around

EXPLORING BY CAR **Driving through the Pisgah National Forest**. This 40-mile drive winds its way through the heart of the Pisgah Forest, the forests that George Vanderbilt brought into his Biltmore Estate in 1889. In the early decades of the 20th century, when giant logging companies were devastating much of the Smoky Mountain forest, Vanderbilt's foresters tended these forests with thought and care. Today they are very beautiful.

Start at **Lake Powhatan Recreation Area**, turning onto the gravel FS 479. Your road follows **Bent Creek** gently uphill through increasingly handsome mixed forests, then climbs steeply to the Blue Ridge Parkway on the crest of the Pisgah Ridge. Cross the parkway and continue downhill on the gravel Forest Service road (FS 5000), winding downhill for nearly 6 miles to **North Mills River Recreation Area**. Turn right onto the gravel Yellow Gap Rd. (FS 1206). For the next 12 miles, Yellow Gap Rd. climbs two ridges, follows three streams, and enters four high-mountain coves. Watch how the mature forests change from the rich diversity of the coves to the dry oak and pine forests on the ridge-lines. The last of the coves is known as **The Pink Beds**, named for its rhododendron displays in June, and the center of Vanderbilt's early forestry operations.

Yellow Gap Rd. ends at US 276; turn left and follow the highway for 1.5 miles, passing The Pink Beds Picnic Area and the Biltmore's historic forestry school, **The Cradle of Forestry in America**. Then turn right onto FS 475B, another gravel forest road. This road takes you around the west side of the gigantic schist monolith **Looking Glass Rock**, best viewed from the Blue Ridge Parkway. In 3.5 miles the road passes through **Gumdrop Gap**, the trailhead for rock climbers attacking the north face of Looking Glass Rock, and drops down into the lush valley of Rockhouse Creek. Look for the attractive **Slick Rock Falls** on your left about 1.5 miles into the valley. In 2.75 miles you reach the Davidson River at **Johns Rock**; turn right onto FS 475, passing the **Pisgah Center for Wildlife Education**, a first-rate museum on wildlife management and conservation. This gravel road follows the Davidson River for nearly 5 miles upstream through a popular hiking area with many trailheads, topping out at **Gloucester Gap** to descend 3 miles to NC 215. Turn left on NC 215 to reach US 64 at

LOOKING GLASS FALLS.

US 276

The 46-mile scenic drive down US 276 is a perfect way to get acquainted with this part of the mountains. For its first 15 miles this route passes through the **Pisgah National Forest**, descending steeply off the Pisgah Ridge. In less than 4 miles the highway passes a Forest Service picnic area at **The Pink Beds**, named for its rhododendrons, and **The Cradle of Forestry in America**. In the

Rosman, NC, in 7.6 miles; Brevard and Hendersonville, NC, are east (left) on US 64.

EXPLORING ON FOOT **A Pisgah Forest hike**. Looming 1,000 feet over the **Pisgah Center for Wildlife Education**, the long expanse of gray cliff known as **Johns Rock** is hard to resist. This 6-mile loop climbs from the Pisgah Center to the top of Johns Rock, with good Pisgah Forest scenery along the way and a stunning panoramic view at the top. The path, named **Cat Gap Loop Trail**, starts at the far end of the Pisgah Center's parking lot. It follows a lovely little mountain stream, staying level for half a mile then turning south and starting its steady climb up a side valley known as Horse Cove. In 1.5 miles from the parking lot (and a climb of 500 feet), a side path peels off right across the stream and next 5 miles the highway drops into a gorgelike valley, passing **Slide Rock**, a popular swimming hole, and **Looking Glass Falls**, a classic river-over-a-cliff waterfall. A quarter mile later, a paved side road leads right to the **Pisgah Center for Wildlife Education**.

Leaving the national forest, US 276 immediately turns and follows four-lane US 64 to Brevard, NC, temporarily losing its charm but picking up a wide array of roadside services. After 3.4 miles of this the highway reaches the middle of **Brevard**, turns, and becomes Main Street through Brevard's handsome old downtown. It quickly leaves Brevard to follow the old, slow, meandering **French Broad River** for 2 miles, then enters a long series of straight stretches through pastoral scenery; look for craft artists' studios and galleries scattered about. Five miles south of Brevard, the twin waterfalls of **Conestee Falls** cascade beside the highway. At 11 miles south of Brevard, a left turn onto paved Cascade Lake Rd. leads to the **DuPont State Forest** with its first-rate waterfall walks.

Soon the highway crosses the Blue Ridge and suddenly tips over the edge of the world. No other road gets so up close and personal with South Carolina's **Blue Wall**. The highway follows the flat top of a side ridge for 3 miles out into the cliff lands, reaching **Ceasars Head State Park** with its stunning panoramic views and walks to gorges and waterfalls. Then the highway drops down off the ridgetop and switchbacks wildly down the steep slopes of the Blue Wall. In 7 miles of continuous twists the highway drops 2,200 feet to the floor of the South Carolina Piedmont. Five miles into this (it will feel longer) you will reach a graffiti-prone roadside rocky bald called **Bald Rock**, with wide views over this sudden end of the mountains to the endless flatness of the Deep South. Four miles later, at the base of the mountain, look for **Wildcat Falls** on your left, with a nature trail following the stream. In 4 more miles the highway reaches the flatlands, with views over fields toward the Blue Wall.

up to Johns Rock, reaching the summit in another mile (and another 500 feet up). The views north take in the gorgelike valleys of the Davidson and Looking Glass Rivers, the gray cliff-sided dome of Looking Glass Rock, and the mile-high crest of the Pisgah Ridge. From the summit, the trail heads south along the rock's narrow ridgeline, reaching a trail intersection in two-thirds of a mile. While all three choices will take you back to your car, this walk follows the right-most trail, **Cat Gap Bypass**. This path circles around the high forests above a little side valley, then merges with the Cat Gap Loop Trail (which has strayed uphill away from Johns Rock since we last met it). Follow the Cat Gap Loop Trail downhill along a dry ridgeline, then past the **Picklesimer Fields**, and down Cedar Rock Creek to the Pisgah Center.

A DuPont Forest waterfall walk. Four lovely waterfalls, each with its own unique personality, group tightly together at the center of the DuPont Forest. A single walk to all four waterfalls, following a roaring mountain river most of the way, takes a total of 5 miles with 750 feet of total climbing. To reach the trail-head parking, take US 276 south of Brevard 11 miles to Cascade Lake Rd.; then take Cascade Lake Rd. north 2.4 miles to its fork with Staton Rd.; then take Staton Rd. 2.3 miles (passing the Agfa plant) to a parking lot on the left just after a bridge.

Your first destination is **Hooker Falls**—through the gate at the end of the parking lot, then a third of a mile along the river on a level old road. Here the Little River, 130 feet wide, pours straight down over a 13-foot ledge. Retrace your steps to the parking lot, then cross the river on the paved road bridge to con-tinue upstream on the opposite bank. As the scenery becomes more mountainous the trail ascends to a view of **Triple Falls** on the Little River—three sep- arate cascades that together drop 120 feet. From here a path leads to the base of the falls, and a roadbed leads to a picnic shelter. Continue on the main trail, first uphill, then along the riverbank. As your trail goes uphill again, a side trail along the river leads to the base of **High Falls**, where the Little River slides straight down a 150-foot cliff. The main trail continues uphill to views from the top of High Falls, then more views from a picnic shelter.

At this point you have walked 1.75 miles and climbed 250 feet, and you are 1.4 miles from your car (downhill all the way). If you want to continue, there is one more waterfall nearby, a tall slide rock on Grassy Creek that will add 2 miles and 500 feet of climbing to your walk. Cross the Little River on the bridge upstream from High Falls, then continue left on Buck Forest Rd. (at one time the main road through these parts). After about a mile, you will cross Grassy Creek on a bridge, then turn left on Imaging Lake Trail (another old roadbed, leading a couple of miles to a pretty little lake built by the film factory in years past). The newly built path to the base of **Grassy Creek Falls** is just beyond, to your left.

Raven Cliff Falls on the Blue Wall. South Carolina's Blue Wall is a rugged and difficult area; with few exceptions, its rewards must be earned by hard effort. This walk is comparatively easy—by Blue Wall standards. By any reasonable standard, it's a tough day hike. However, with a 400-foot waterfall at the end, it's well worth it.

The 4- to 8-mile round-trip walk to Raven Cliff Falls, one of the tallest in the East, follows a well-built foot path in **Ceasars Head State Park**, 13 miles south of Brevard, NC, on US 276. Trailhead parking is a mile north of the park's head-quarters. For the first mile the path follows the gently rolling ridgeline along the top of the cliff wall, passing through handsome forests with occasional views over the Blue Ridge, with about 300 feet of climbing and dropping. At the intersection with **Gum Gap Trail**, continue left on **Raven Cliff Falls Trail**, dropping into the rugged terrain around the waterfall. The trail will drop 700 feet in the next 0.9 mile, and you will have to reclimb every step on your way back. At the bottom of the trail is an observation deck giving a wide view across this narrow, forested gorge to the waterfall, a strong cataract that hurls down the cliff in three large jumps. When it's time to go back, you have 1,000 feet of climbing to reach

your car, for a round trip of 4 miles. If you are feeling energetic, you an double
this length and add 300 feet of climb by taking the right-hand fork at Gum Gap
Trail, leading around to **Naturaland Trust Trail** and a suspension bridge over
the waterfall—another first-rate view from a completely different angle.

✳ Villages

Hendersonville, NC. This busy little city of 10,000 sits in a wide valley 20 miles
south of Asheville via I-26. A successful small center of commerce, it's surrounded
by a ring of modern, sprawling development, its highways busy and noisy. Its
quiet little downtown, however, is a wonderful place. Almost completely preserved from the early 20th century, it has five blocks of Italianate redbrick
storefronts, with wide, landscaped sidewalks and free street parking; downtown
shopping is varied and sophisticated, and the choice of restaurants is excellent.
The town's most historic (and ritzy) neighborhoods stretch westward from downtown along 5th Ave., then up a little mountain on the 1920s-era Laurel Park
Hwy.—ending at **Jumpoff Rock**, a lovely city park with a high-view rock.

Flat Rock, NC. This attractive village of 2,500 residents stretches along US 25,
3 miles south of Hendersonville. Like many southern settlements, it lacks a well-
defined center; shops and inns are spread out along the highway, widely separated by tree-lined fields. Flat Rock has been a tourist destination since the late
1820s, when the stagecoach road known as the Buncombe Turnpike (following
the route of modern US 25) made it accessible to wealthy South Carolinians. By
the 1850s Flat Rock was a fashionable
summer destination for heat-struck
southerners who could afford it, and
not even the Civil War could alter
this. Today it remains genteel and
beautiful, a village of elegant country
inns and fine restaurants hidden down
remote lanes. Flat Rock was the home
of Carl Sandburg and his wife for 22
years (1945–1967); the antebellum
Carl Sandburg Home and modern
goat farm are a National Historic Site,
a wonderful example of an early Flat
Rock plantation.

Brevard, NC. This small mountain
town of 6,800 people, the seat of Transylvania County, sits on a hillside by
the French Broad River, 20 miles west
of Hendersonville via US 64. The main
approach to town on US 64 doesn't do
it justice, passing through several miles
of sprawling industry and commercial
development before briefly diving in
and out of the town's center. Leave the

THE HENDERSON COUNTY COURTHOUSE IN
HENDERSONVILLE.

Jim Hargan

DOWNTOWN BREVARD.

Jim Hargan

main highway to explore the traditional center of town, however, and you will find a perfectly preserved redbrick downtown filled with interesting shops, galleries, and cafés, surrounded by well-kept old neighborhoods with lovely little parks and plenty of trees. Brevard gains a surprising level of cultural sophistication from **Brevard College**, its small Methodist liberal arts college, and its first-rate summer program for aspiring young professional musicians, the **Brevard Music Center**.

✳ Wild Places

THE GREAT FORESTS The Pisgah Forest. The Pisgah National Forest wanders through much of western NC, with important tracts stretching from the edge of the Smokies to Roan Mountain and on to the slopes of Grandfather Mountain. To most people in North Carolina, however, "the Pisgah Forest" is the great stretch of wildlands on the south slopes of the Pisgah Ridge, north of Brevard and Hendersonville.

Originally part of George Vanderbilt's Biltmore Estate (see "Asheville & the Blue Ridge Parkway"), this area's forests were carefully tended and restored by Vanderbilt over a 30-year period. Vanderbilt's foresters had set up America's first forestry college in log cabins on this 100,000-acre tract to train the assistants they needed; its buildings, still preserved, make up the core of the forestry museum, **The Cradle of Forestry in America**. More than a century later, Vanderbilt's Pisgah Forests are remarkably diverse and beautiful, with a network of gravel roads and hiking trails leading to its scenic wonders.

The Pisgah Forest splits naturally into two halves. To the east, the **Mills River** and its tributaries drain a series of watersheds. To the west, the **Davidson River** drains southward toward the headwaters of the French Broad River. In the center, roughly straddling these two areas, runs **US 276**, a winding and scenic drive that links many of the finest sites of the forest. Gravel forest roads run cross-grain through the area, giving ready access to most corners of the forest. The Blue Ridge Parkway, running along the mile-high crest of the Pisgah Ridge, lets you drive up to the high points of many of these trails and enjoy their best views without raising a sweat. These tracts are multiple-use national forest lands, not wilderness, yet they are largely given over to outdoor recreation, with little or no logging. Trails are extensive and well developed, with the majority open to bicycles and horses as well as hikers.

DuPont State Forest (828-251-6509; fax 828-251-6541; www.dupontforest .com), 14 Gaston Mountain Rd., Asheville, NC. This 10,300-acre NC state forest, purchased from the DuPont Corporation in 1997, lies in a high plateau 13 miles south of Brevard via US 276 and Cascade Rd. (SSR 1536). It's noted for its many waterfalls and slide rocks, and excellent views from a number of exceptionally large rocky balds. Its forests are young and varied, and its slopes are much gentler and shorter than other mountain tracts. It has four lakes, one of them quite large—remnants of old real estate schemes and summer camps. It has nearly 100 named trails, most of them old roadbeds—and nearly all of these gentle old paths are open to bicyclers and horses as well as walkers. In the middle of this large, popular recreation site sits a large film factory, formerly DuPont and now Agfa, like a hole in a doughnut. Access to the plant is strictly prohibited—and this means you. Access to everything else is free and open.

About a quarter of this forest, including nearly all of the prime recreation sites, was seized by the State of North Carolina in 2000 from a developer who had started to construct an exclusive gated community on the site; you can thank him for the beautiful new picnic shelters strategically placed by streams, waterfalls, and lakes.

For the traveler, the DuPont Forest is worthwhile for its seven major waterfalls and rock slides, the views from its large rocky balds, and its refreshingly easy walking. The largest and most remarkable waterfalls are on the Little River, easily reached from paved roads. The **DuPont Forest walk** (see *Exploring on Foot*) describes a stroll to three of these from a roadside parking area at the center of the forest. A second scenic area can be reached from a trailhead parking lot on Cascades Rd., about 2 miles north of US 276 (10 miles south of Brevard). From here, easy trails lead to **Bridal Veil Falls**, a wide, tall waterfall with a high water volume that you can walk behind, featured in the movie *The Last of the Mohicans*; to **Cedar Rock**, claimed as the longest rocky bald in the Blue Ridge, with panoramic views; and to **Corn Shoals**, a slide rock and popular swimming hole. A loop walk to all three points is 4.4 miles long with 950 feet of total climbing. (Hint: Do Cedar Rock first, and the Corn Shoals swimming hole last.)

The Mountain Bridge Wilderness of South Carolina. Rising 2,000 feet nearly straight up from the South Carolina Piedmont, this clifflike 35 miles of the Blue Ridge and Saluda Ridge is known as "the Blue Wall." The terrain is extraordinarily beautiful, with lush forests, deep gorges, huge waterfalls, and high cliffs. It's also extremely difficult—a rough and broken land with extreme elevation changes in short distances. Much of this wild territory is protected by the State of South Carolina in a series of state parks and state heritage preserves, while other large tracts are protected by private conservation foundations and city watersheds. Altogether these state, local, and private conservation tracts make up more than 40,000 acres of coterminous wildlands, termed "The Mountain Bridge Wilderness and Recreation Area" by the state government.

Three state parks make up the bulk of the recreational opportunities in this area. **Table Rock State Park**, on the western edge of this chapter's region off SC 11, centers on an outlying dome of hard, gray rock that looms 2,000 feet above the park's lakeside picnic area; history buffs will want to check out its extensive CCC architecture, listed on the National Register. **Ceasars Head State Park**, bisected by US 276 in the center of the region, protects a long series of cliffs and waterfalls—the only place on the Blue Wall with clifftop views you can drive to. **Jones Gap State Park** protects the upper reaches of the Middle Saluda River, with some spectacular cliff scenery.

RECREATION AREAS **Table Rock State Park** (864-878-9813; fax 864-878-9077), 158 E. Ellison Lane, Pickens, SC. Daily 7 AM–9 PM. Built in 1936, this 3,000-acre park preserves a 3,100-foot mountain dome, plus enough historic CCC architecture to place the entire park on the National Register of Historic Places. The central attraction is, of course, Table Rock, a cliff-sided outlier of the Blue Ridge that towers 2,000 feet above the picnic area—a horizontal distance of only 1.4 miles. Most visitors enjoy the view from the lovely little lake or the wildflower meadows at its base, but more than a few climb the very steep 3.5-mile trail to its peak, for wide views over the Blue Ridge and out over the level plains of the Deep South. The park has a CCC picnic area on a small lake, CCC-built log rental cabins, a lakeside restaurant with dining room views toward Table Rock, and a nature center.

Ceasars Head State Park (864-836-6115), 8155 Greer Hwy., Cleveland, SC. Apr.–Sep., 9–9; Oct.–Mar., 9–6. Bisected by US 276, Ceasar's Head State Park occupies a 3,200-foot cliff-faced side ridge projecting out into South Carolina's Blue Wall country. A roadside overlook offers stunning views over the rugged Blue Ridge, toward Table Rock and the plains of the Piedmont. Nearby a visitors center has an information desk, gift shop, and exhibits on area history. **Raven Cliff Falls**, at over 400 feet one of the tallest in the East, is in this park.

Jones Gap State Park (864-836-3647), 303 Jones Gap Rd., Marietta, SC. Apr.–Oct., 9–9; Nov.–Mar., 9–6. This 3,300-acre park protects the rare forests and unique rock formations at the foot of the **Cleveland Cliffs** along South Carolina's Blue Wall. Rugged (but well-maintained) paths climb the high cliffs, follow side ridges, or explore the **Middle Saluda State Scenic River**. At the park's headquarters up a quiet rural lane off SC 11, the park's Environmental Education Center has nature exhibits, and the CCC-era **Cleveland Fish Hatchery** has been restored and stocked as a demonstration.

PICNIC AREAS **Silvermont Park**. This funky Brevard, NC, city park offers good picnicking three blocks south of downtown on US 276. It takes up the house and grounds of a historic neoclassical brick mansion—but with no attempt at restoration. Quite the contrary; the house itself, used for meetings, is in bad shape, and much of its extensive formal gardens has been paved over with tennis and basketball courts. Still, it has a nicely kept, shady picnic area with a good playground, as well as a lovely little herb garden and a gravel exercise path through a forest garden.

North Mills River Recreation Area. At the end of the paved North Mills River Rd. and the start of two scenic gravel Forest Service roads, this Forest Service site offers picnicking in a great hemlock grove by a mountain river.

The Pink Beds Picnic Area. This National Forest Service picnic area sits just off the Blue Ridge Parkway on US 276. Apart from the famous rhododendrons for which it is named (and which display in June), it's notable for its attractive and level loop trail, which leads to beaver dams (and may be flooded by beaver ponds).

✻ To See

HISTORIC SITES ✍ ♿ **The Cradle of Forestry in America** (828-877-3130; fax 828-884-5823; www.cradleofforestry.com). Run by the National Forest Service, this historic site is on US 276, 14 miles north of Brevard and 3.5 miles south of the Blue Ridge Parkway. May–Oct., 9–5. When George W. Vanderbilt founded Asheville's Biltmore Estate as his private residence in the 1880s (see "Asheville & the Blue Ridge Parkway"), he surrounded it with vast tracts of forestlands, including much of the Pisgah Ranger District of the Pisgah National Forest. With no scientific forestry in existence in America at the time, Vanderbilt imported professional foresters from Germany to manage his forests—first the German-trained American Gifford Pinchot, then the German scientist Carl A. Schenck. With no trained assistants or staff available in the U.S., these scientists were forced to start a training school on Biltmore property. This training school is now preserved as The Cradle of Forestry in America, a beautiful and fascinating collection of historic log structures. The tour starts at the large modern museum, where historic and modern forestry practices are explained. Then a loop trail leads to the historic site, with a log schoolroom, store, and cabins (including some built in a properly German style by Dr. Schenck), where craft demonstrations are held. A second loop trail leads through a demonstration of historic forestry practices. $5 adults, $2.50 children.

✦ ㅎ **Carl Sandburg Home National Historic Site** (828-693-4178; fax 828-693-4179; www.nps.gov/carl), 81 Carl Sandburg Lane, Flat Rock, NC. Open all year, 9–5. In 1945 poet and scholar Carl Sandburg and his wife, Paula, moved from Michigan to Flat Rock, NC. Mrs. Sandburg was a dedicated goat farmer and serious goat breeder, and the mild climate of Flat Rock was a superior place to raise goats. They purchased Connemara, a large farm with a beautiful antebellum house and a large pond, at the center of Flat Rock. Carl Sandburg remained at Connemara until his death in 1967; a year later, it became Carl Sandburg National Historic Site, part of America's National Park System.

Connemara would have been worthy of preservation under any circumstances. One of the oldest farmsteads in this region, it was built in 1838 as a vacation home for a rich South Carolinian, Christopher Memminger, later treasury secretary for the Confederate States of America. His heirs sold it to a Captain Smyth (it was known locally as The Smyth House when the Sandburgs bought it), and Smyth's heirs sold it to the Sandburgs with 240 acres of farmland and forest. Despite this history, the National Park Service realizes that nothing more distinguished has happened to this fine old house than the Sandburgs. They keep the house, the grounds, and the goat farm the way Carl and Paula left them.

Connemara is an extraordinarily beautiful place, easily worth a full day's exploration. From the roadside parking lot, you walk along a lovely pond with views toward a meadow-covered hill and the columned old house. The path crosses a wooden bridge, then

A RESTORED LOG CABIN AT THE CRADLE OF FORESTRY IN AMERICA.

Jim Hargan

climbs along wood fences and through meadows for a third of a mile to the surprisingly modest house, with its columned porch and lush azaleas. The basement visitors center has a small bookstore and information desk. From there you can tour the house, carefully preserved the way the Sandburgs left it, a slice from a warm and comfortable life in the 1940s. From the house, you continue up into the farm area with 21 buildings preserved from the Sandburg era. It's still a functioning goat farm, and kids wander out from the giant red barn to greet visitors. Beyond the goat dairy, walking paths lead through woods to mountaintop viewpoints. Free admission to grounds and goat barn. House tours are $3 for adults, children under 17 free.

Historic Johnson Farm (828-891-6585; www.mountainwonders.com/johnson farm/), 3346 Haywood Rd., Hendersonville, NC. Tue.–Sat. 9–2:30, with guided tours at 10:30 and 1:30; May–Oct., closed Sun. and Mon.; Nov.–Apr., closed Sun.–Tue. Run by a not-for-profit on behalf of the Henderson County school system, this 15-acre museum complex preserves a late-19th-century tobacco farm. It centers on a restored brick 1870s farmhouse listed on the National Register and furnished as a late-19th-century farm residence. There are nine other historic structures, all original to the farm, including a boardinghouse and a barn museum. $3 adults, $2 students.

CULTURAL SITES Brevard Music Center (888-384-8682 or 828-862-2100; fax 828-884-2036; www.brevardmusic.org), 1000 Probart St., Brevard, NC. From its beautiful lakeside campus on the north edge of Brevard, the Brevard Music Center furnishes summer instruction in professional music practice and theory for talented, serious musicians from age 14 to postcollege. Its 50 faculty members teach 400 students each summer. Brevard's unique program emphasizes performance experience with professional musicians under real-world conditions—the sorts of rehearsals and audiences that students will encounter in their first professional jobs. For this reason the Music Center sponsors the annual Brevard Music Festival—two months of performances in which the Music Center's students perform with top-ranked professionals. Founded in 1936 as a band camp, the campus consists of 145 rolling, wooded acres with around 100 separate buildings and two lakes. Its main venue, the **Whittington-Pfohl Auditorium**, is open sided, with seating both under cover and on the open lawn by Milner Lake.

CONNEMARA, THE HOME OF POET CARL SANDBURG.

Jim Hargan

MUSEUMS ✍ ♿ **Pisgah Center for Wildlife Education** (828-877-4423; fax
828-877-4792), Pisgah Forest, NC. Daily 8–5. Located 10 miles north of Brevard, NC, this wildlife museum "sponsored by the sportsmen of North Carolina" (actually, the North Carolina Game and Fish Commission) is 1.5 miles off US 276 down a signposted, paved forest road. Deep in the Pisgah National Forest, the small museum occupies a beautiful site at a working fish hatchery, bordered by the rocky Davidson River and with views up toward the gray cliffs of Johns Rock. Inside the small, gray government-style museum building are a gift and bookshop; exhibits follow a stream from the mountains to the sea, including aquaria of mountain, Piedmont, and coastal species. Then the museum path leads outside for an easy streamside walk, with first-rate exhibits on Appalachian forest ecology, wildlife, and management. The museum tour ends with a walk through the working fish hatchery, its long concrete troughs filled with trout. Given the ownership of this museum, as well as its being funded by hunting and fishing licenses, expect a subtle pro-hunting (and an unsubtle pro-fishing) slant to the displays. There is a good picnic area at the far end of the parking lot, as well as trails to the top of John's Rock with stunning views. Free.

Western North Carolina Air Museum (828-698-2482; www.wncairmuseum .com), Hendersonville, NC. Afternoons on Wed., Sat., and Sun. This small air museum, run by local enthusiasts, has beautifully restored and fully operational small historic aircraft, including World War I fighters and small private aviation craft. It occupies a modern metal hangar on the grounds of Hendersonville's small airport, south of town off US 25 on Brooklyn Ave. Free.

The Jim Bob Tinsley Museum and Research Center (828-884-2347; www.jim bobtinsleymuseum.org), 20 West Jordan St., Brevard, NC. May–Nov., Tue.–Sat. 10–4; Dec.–Apr., Tue.–Sat. 1–4. This nonprofit museum in a historic downtown Brevard storefront houses the collections of cowboy singer and Brevard resident Jim Bob Tinsley. It features western memorabilia and cowboy music material, while other sections contain displays of Transylvania County history. There's a special section on local waterfalls, featuring art and photos from Jim Bob and others.

GARDENS AND PARKS **Skytop Orchard** (828-692-7930; www.skytoporchard .com), Flat Rock, NC. From US 25, turn west onto Pinnacle Mountain Rd. and follow the signs. Aug.–Oct., daily 9–6. Located on a side road off US 25 near the center of Flat Rock, this U-pick apple orchard has stunning views from 50 acres of handsome orchards straddling the Blue Ridge. Pickers have 20 varieties of apples to choose from; there are also hayrides, farm animals to pet, picnicking, and a farm stand during the picking season.

Conestee Falls. Although signs along US 276 south of Brevard, NC, advertise a residential subdivision named Conestee Falls, there is an actual waterfall and it is definitely worth a stop if you are in the area. You'll find it behind the development's real estate office alongside the main highway, 6 miles south of town. A well-built path leads perhaps 100 feet to a railed overlook with an excellent view over a double waterfall.

South Brevard Park. This local park, two blocks west of downtown Brevard, NC, on US 64, offers a small but worthwhile native plant garden. Covering perhaps half a block, it has a wide range of flowers blooming from April through October, displayed from a system of wide rectangular paths with plenty of benches.

Jumpoff Rock Park. This local park outside Hendersonville, NC, offers panoramic 270° views over the valley of the French Broad River, toward the mile-high crest of the Pisgah Ridge, from a large projecting rock. To find it, take 5th Ave. west from downtown Hendersonville; then continue on Laurel Park Hwy., never turning off onto any of the confusing maze of side roads, until you reach its end, 4.4 miles from downtown. Actually, Laurel Park Hwy. is a hoot—a genuine 1920s-era main road, complete with its original concrete surface, that curves uphill through an old, wealthy,

Jim Hargan

A 1929 CURTISS ROBIN AT THE
WESTERN NORTH CAROLINA AIR MUSEUM.

mountainside subdivision with 80-year-old mansions spread through the trees. Jumpoff Rock Park, at its end, is a landscaped picnic and walking area, where the clifflike sides of this small mountain become undeniable cliffs. Apart from the views, this is a pleasant, cool, and attractive spot.

✳ To Do

BICYCLING **Backcountry Outdoors** (828-884-4262; www.backcountryoutdoors .com/bike.html), 18 Pisgah Hwy., Pisgah Forest, NC. This outdoors supply store, located north of Brevard on US 276, specializes in outdoor activities in the Pisgah National Forest, and particularly in mountain biking. They will rent you a fine trail bike and help you find a good trail; they offer guided mountain bike tours of these forests as well. $28–38 per day for trail bike rentals.

FISHING **Davidson River Outfitters** (888-861-0111 or 828-877-4181; fax 828-883-2167; www.davidsonflyfishing.com), 4 Pisgah Hwy., Pisgah Forest, NC. This full-service fly-fishing shop, located north of Brevard at the intersection of US 64 and US 276, dispenses good advice as well as arranging guide service to the rich streams of the Pisgah National Forest. Their web page is worth checking for information on local streams. Guide services $125–200 half day, $215–325 full day.

GOLF **Etowah Valley Country Club and Golf Lodge** (800-451-8174 or 828-891-7022; www.etowahvalley.com), 450 Brickyard Rd., Etowah, NC. Open all year. Three nine-hole courses give a choice of play in this championship course, noted for its mountain views and beautifully landscaped floral edges. $31.

Crooked Creek Golf Club (828-692-2011), 764 Crooked Creek Rd., Hendersonville, NC. Located just south of Hendersonville, this mainly rustic course follows a stream along a valley bottom, with water in play on 12 of its 18 holes. The clubhouse occupies an old Warner Bros. retreat. $15.

Highland Lake Golf Course (828-692-0143), 111 Highland Lake Rd., Flat Rock, NC. Open all year. This nine-hole course near the center of Flat Rock (not part of the Highland Lake Inn resort) is fairly level, with four water hazards. $9 (nine holes).

HORSEBACK RIDING **Pisgah Forest Riding Stables** (828-883-8258), Avery Creek Rd., Pisgah Forest, NC. Located north of Brevard, NC, off scenic US 276 on a national forest road, this stable offers 1- to 3-hour trail rides inside the Pisgah National Forest, with destinations that include views and a waterfall. $20 per hour per person.

WHITEWATER ADVENTURES **Headwaters Outfitters** (828-877-3106; www .headwatersoutfitters.com), Rosman, NC. Apr.–Oct., daily 9–5. This is something you don't see often—a canoe outfitter in the deep mountains. Located at the start of 20 miles of serpentine flatwater, Headwaters Outfitters offers canoe and kayak sales, rentals, and shuttled trips on this unique and beautiful stretch of the French Broad River. Other services include tubing on nearby mountain streams, overnight canoe trips, and guided kayak tours of the gigantic wilderness reservoir, Lake Jocassee. $20–37 for canoe or kayak trip with shuttle service, $7–15 for tubing trips with shuttle service, $30 per day for renting canoes or kayaks.

✳ Lodging

COUNTRY INNS AND HOTELS **The Claddagh Inn** (800-225-4700 or 828-697-7778; www.claddaghinn.com), 755 N. Main St., Hendersonville, NC 28792. Open all year. This lovely old inn sits on downtown Hendersonville's Main St., a large late-Victorian mansion surrounded by lawn and shaded by giant oak trees. It's an oasis of calm charm within an easy stroll of downtown's first-rate restaurants and shopping. The three-story Classical Revival house, listed on the National Register, features an extra-wide wraparound front porch with interesting double columns and a roofline that curves around the edges of the cheerful yellow walls, and a cute second-story balcony. Inside, common areas include an elegant front parlor, a cozy wood-paneled library with piano, books, and fireplace, a dining room with table seating, and a convenient second-floor parlor; all are carefully furnished from the late Victorian period, a step back to when the house was new. The 14 en suite guest rooms, all comfortable to large in size with telephone, television, and air-conditioning, are individually furnished in Victorian antiques and reproductions. Some have special features, such as Room 215's private second-story sunporch with its parquet floor and wicker furniture. The third floor is split between two suites, each with two bedrooms and a sitting room. Guests are treated to a hearty country breakfast and an evening glass of sherry. Jan.–Apr., $89–125; May–Dec., $105–150.

The Woodfield Inn (800-533-6016 or 828-693-6016; www.woodfieldinn .com), US 25 S., P.O. Box 98, Flat Rock, NC 28731. Open all year. In operation since its founding in 1852, this National Register antebellum stagecoach inn sits on 28 acres at the center of Flat Rock. Surrounded by landscaped parkland, the 18-room Italianate structure has wide verandas on its first and second floors. The en suite rooms are individually themed with Victorian decor, including antiques; guests can choose rooms with private veranda, whirlpool tub, and views. The hearty breakfast is served in the inn's restaurant, which also offers lunch and dinner to the public. Apr.–Dec., rooms $119–149, suites $169–189; Jan.–Mar., $79–109.

The Angelique Inn (877-698-7819; 828-883-4105; www.angeliqueinn .com), 408 S. Caldwell St., Brevard, NC 28712. Open all year. This remarkable Victorian mansion sits near the center of Brevard, a block off US 64. The house, situated on a 2-acre knoll with lawns, gardens, and shade trees, is an elaborate three-story fantasy of columns, gables, dormers, verandas, projections, bay windows, a circular whatsis at the corner of the wraparound porch, and a witch's-hat turret. Inside are high-ceilinged, wood-trimmed common rooms filled with Victorian antiques. The rooms are also unique—three suites, each furnished in Victorian style including antiques, and each with an equipped kitchen (along with private bath, TV, phone, and air-conditioning). The largest (and most expensive) suite has a full kitchen, sunroom with sofa, and formal dining room; the other two suites have a large bedroom area, restricted kitchen

facilities, and a small eating area. This is not a bed & breakfast; breakfast is not served to guests. Suites $85–110. Off-season and weekly discounts apply.

RESORTS **The Highland Lake Inn** (800- 635-5101 or 828-693-6812; fax 838-696-8951; www.hlinn.com), Highland Lake Rd., P.O. Box 1026, Flat Rock, NC 28731. This 180-acre full-service resort in the center of Flat Rock has a modern inn and a historic lodge overlooking a lovely little lake. Resort amenities include fishing, lake swimming, pool swimming, canoeing, paddleboating, volleyball, horseshoes, and on-site walking trails. The site itself is beautiful, gently rolling and tree covered, with an extensive organic farm operation that supplies its first-rate restaurant. The contemporary inn has 16 large and airy rooms, some with whirlpool bath, wet bar, fireplace, or private patio, as well as several common sitting areas. The historic lodge, recently renovated, has 20 more rooms, with common areas that include a recreation room and a bar. Modest cabin duplexes, simple structures with board-and-batten walls and covered porches, make up the economy end of the lodgings, while quaint cottages with full kitchens make up the high end. Inn rooms $149–215, lodge rooms $144–180, cabins $109–130, cottages $209 and up.

BED & BREAKFAST INNS ✔ **The Flat Rock Inn** (800-266-3996 or 828-696-3273; www.bbhost.com/flatrock inn/), 2810 Greenville Hwy., P.O. Box 308, Flat Rock, NC 28731. Open all year. A classic four-room B&B, this 1888 National Register mansion sits comfortably off US 25 on its own tree-shaded property at the center of the village of Flat Rock. Originally built as a summer residence for a wealthy Charlestonian, its wraparound porches and second-story balconies peek out from between the trees. The large, quiet lawn and garden gives plenty of room to relax and enjoy the country air, swing from a hammock, or throw a few horseshoes. Homemade afternoon sweets are served from the wide porch or in the parlor. Inside, the common rooms are beautifully decorated in Victorian antiques. Comfortable sofas and chairs face a fireplace, with plenty of interesting books to read, while a traditional formal dining room furnishes the venue for the gourmet country breakfasts. A butler's pantry has tea and custom-blended coffee for guests, as well as a guest refrigerator well stocked with wine and ice cream as well as the usual soft drinks. Each of the large air-conditioned guest rooms is individually furnished in Victorian antiques and has a private bath; two have private porch. $85–145.

The Mary Mills Coxe Inn (800-230-6541 or 828-692-5900; fax 828-692-3343; www.marymillscoxeinn.com), 1210 Greenville Hwy., Hendersonville, NC 28792. Open all year. This seven-room inn occupies a National Register–listed mansion on the south edge of Hendersonville on US 25. Built in 1911 by a wealthy widow, the three-story pebbledash-sided Colonial Revival house is surrounded by its wraparound porch. During parts of the day and evening, the downstairs functions as the elegant Gables Restaurant; in the morning, it's the venue for elegant breakfasts served to the inn's guests. Upstairs, the seven en suite guest rooms have individual European decor. Differences in the

room give guests the choice of working fireplace, Jacuzzi bath, and wet bar. $140–160.

Mélange Bed and Breakfast (800-303-5253; fax 828-697-5751; www.melangebb.com), 1230 5th Ave. W., Hendersonville, NC 28739. This five-room B&B occupies a 1920 Colonial Revival mansion in an upscale residential section of Hendersonville. A tree screen protects the 3 acres from the street; behind the screen, the large house is surrounded by lawns and gardens in elaborate Mediterranean-style gardens, with four fountains. Surprisingly, the interior of this simple Colonial design is an elaborate French Empire concoction, first installed by a 1960s francophile owner and lovingly restored by the current owners. Common areas—which include an elaborate foyer, parlor, living room, formal and informal dining rooms, and a book-filled study—may have 11-foot ceilings, marble floors, mahogany trim, high mirrors, and (of course) elaborately elegant furnishings. All five en suite rooms are large, with decor both luxurious and comfortable; features (varying by room) may include wood-burning fireplace, whirlpool bath, sitting area, wet bar, and a private deck. Full gourmet breakfasts are served on a flagstone patio in the rose garden, weather permitting. Rooms $125–155, suite $165–185.

The Apple Inn (800-615-6611; www.appleinn.com), 1005 White Pine Dr., Hendersonville, NC 28739. This B&B occupies a 1930s-style house in a quiet suburb of Hendersonville. Built as a vacation home by a wealthy South Carolinian, the Apple Inn sits in the middle of 3 acres of lawns and gardens, making a pleasant environment for its porch and deck. The individually decorated en suite rooms can be country or Victorian in style, with antiques and reproductions. Homemade breakfasts are served on the porch or inside. $98 for rooms, $150 for two-bedroom suite.

Rose Tree Bed and Breakfast (800-672-1993 or 828-698-8912), 1 Boxwood Dr., Flat Rock, NC 28731. This two-suite B&B occupies a large 1910 home in the center of Flat Rock. The two-story house, renovated in 1998, sits on its own 6 acres of property with a wide wraparound porch and a bright, airy interior. Common spaces include a large parlor with a fireplace, grand piano, and plenty of books, and a traditional, formal dining room where the full breakfast is served. This classic B&B has only two rooms, both two-room suites with in-room refrigerator and flowers freshly cut from the inn's garden. $145.

The Red House (828-884-9349; www.brevardnc.com/business/redhouse/redhouse.htm), 412 W. Probart St., Brevard, NC 28712. Open all year. Located four blocks from downtown Brevard and eight blocks from the Brevard Music Center, the Red House is arguably the town's most historic structure. Established as a trading post before Brevard existed, it served as the town's first train station and as the founding location for Brevard College, a local four-year liberal arts school. The inn sits on a hill just north of downtown, surrounded by lawns. Painted brick red, it has first- and second-story wraparound porches and third-story dormers. Inside, it's furnished with Victorian antiques in rather a country style, including the four guest rooms.

The rate includes a full country breakfast. $65–99.

Chestnut Hill Bed and Breakfast (828-862-3540; fax 828-862-3803; www.bbonline.com/nc/chestnuthill/), 400 Barclay Rd., Brevard, NC 28712. Apr.–Oct. Built as a summer home in 1856, this National Register–listed antebellum mansion sits on a wooded hillock surrounded by hay meadows. Three miles south of Brevard, on a rural lane off US 276, Chestnut Hill offers lovely views over the French Broad River from its two-story gingerbread veranda, as well as gardens and woodland walks on its 80-acre tract. $125–185.

Key Falls Bed and Breakfast (828-884-7559; fax 828-884-8342; www.keyfallsinn.com), 151 Everett Rd., Pisgah Forest, NC 28768. This large two-story farmhouse from the 1860s sits on 35 acres by the French Broad River, 3 miles east of Brevard. Its well-kept gardens and meadows give views toward the river and the mountains beyond, while the large property contains a pond, tennis courts, and hiking trails (including one to the lovely Key Falls, on site). Comfortable common areas and five guest rooms are furnished with Victorian decor, including antiques. The room rate includes a full breakfast. $75–95.

CABIN RENTALS **Lakemont Cottages** (800-597-0692 or 828-693-5174; fax 828-693-5174; www.lakemontcottages.com), 101 Lakemont Dr., Flat Rock, NC 28731. Open all year. Lakemont features 14 modestly styled modern cottages spread around a rolling, wooded tract south of Hendersonville, not far off US 176. A small lake (or large pond) makes up the centerpiece of this little village. Cottages have separate bedroom and full kitchen, as well as enclosed porch. Credit cards are not accepted. Apr.–Oct., $60–100; Nov.–Mar., $60–90.

✳ Where to Eat

EATING OUT Cypress Cellar (828-698-1005), 321-C N. Main St., Hendersonville, NC. Located in a roomy, airy space below sidewalk level in downtown Hendersonville, the Cypress Cellar features authentic dishes from southern Louisiana for lunch and dinner. It's a bright and friendly space, with furniture made from Louisiana cypress. The lunch menu features hot Cajun dishes as well as sandwiches and burgers, including muffulettas and po-boys on bread from Gambino's of New Orleans, fried green tomatoes on jalapeño cheddar grits, gumbo, red beans and rice, jambalaya, and crawfish cakes. The dinner menu drops the sandwiches and adds a variety of steak, pasta, and seafood entrées. On weekend evenings it's a popular venue for live music. Lunch $5–7, dinner $6–15.

Rocky's Soda Shop and Grill (828-877-5375), 38 S. Broad St., Brevard, NC. Mon.–Sat. 11–5:30, Sun. noon–5; extended hours in summer. This nostalgic storefront in the center of downtown Brevard has burgers, hot dogs, and sandwiches, but the emphasis is on its old-fashioned soda fountain. Counter service with round stools and round tables with red-backed wire chairs, its decor steps back in time half a century—as do its ice creams, floats, sundaes, and banana splits.

DINING OUT ♿ The Gables Restaurant (800-230-6541 or 828-692-5900; www.marymillscoxeinn.com), 1210 Greenville Hwy., Hendersonville, NC. Dinner Mon.–Sat. Located in the elegant Victorian Mary Mills Coxe Inn on the southern edge of Hendersonville, on US 35, the Gables Restaurant serves American and international dishes in a setting of European antiques. The restaurant area—downstairs from the inn—wanders through two large parlors and fronts on the wraparound porch. Its tiny bar is paneled with book-filled shelves. The menu changes daily; an appetizer of venison sausage ravioli with smoked garlic cream sauce might precede an entrée of duck breast with orange Zinfandel sauce or fresh Thai snapper with tomato saffron broth. $35–40, including appetizer and dessert.

The Highland Lake Inn (800-635-5101 or 828-696-9094; fax 828-696-8951; www.hlinn.com/restaurant.htm), Highland Lake Rd., Flat Rock, NC. Breakfast 7:30–10, lunch 11:30–2, dinner 5–9; closed Sun.; closed Jan.–Apr. The dining room of the Highland Lake Inn describes its fare as "fine country garden cuisine." The description is literal; Highland Lake's vegetables, salads, and even herbs and seasonings come as much as possible from the inn's organic gardens. Sitting on 180 lakefront acres in Flat Rock, just off US 25, this attractive restaurant offers all three meals to nonguests. Lunches, which start at $9 and go into the "market price" range, offer salads made from their own garden vegetables, and sandwich favorites with a difference—half-pound burgers topped with caramelized shallots, apple-smoked bacon, and local farm cheese; chicken melts with roast breast meat topped with tomatoes and chives, topped with Muenster cheese and oven-baked on focaccia bread. The extensive dinner menu marries fish, fowl, or meat with exciting combinations of vegetables and cheeses, and includes some impressive vegetarian dishes. Lunch $9-plus, dinner entrées $15–23.

✴ Entertainment

Flat Rock Playhouse (828-693-0403; www.flatrockplayhouse.org), Flat Rock, NC. The **State Theater of North Carolina**, a professional Actors' Equity company, performs nine or so productions at its barnlike theater on US 25. $20–27.

Hendersonville Symphony Orchestra (828-697-5884), Hendersonville, NC. Hendersonville is probably the only small-town rural county seat with its own full-sized symphony orchestra. Made up of talented local musicians, it's led by music director and conductor Thomas Joiner, professor of violin and orchestra activities at Furman University and concertmaster of the Brevard Music Festival. Performing at various local venues (including the high school auditorium), its typical concert season includes a pops concert, a Christmas concert, and a couple of traditional classical concerts with guest soloists. $15.

✴ Selective Shopping

Downtown Hendersonville, NC
Hendersonville's five-block downtown remains utterly dominated by turn-of-the-20th-century two- and three-story buildings facing the landscaped Main Street. The main highway, US 25, splits down one-way streets that flank the back sides of these downtown blocks, leaving Main to shoppers and

people looking for parking places. Now one of the classier shopping districts in the mountains, downtown's old storefronts are dominated by art and fine-craft galleries, antiques shops, gift shops, specialty shops, and restaurants—90 retailers and eateries in all. The Main Street shopping district is bordered on the north by US 64 and on the south by the old and distinguished (but decrepit) Henderson County Courthouse. Parking is free along Main Street, and 25¢ for 2 hours on four metered lots along US 25.

✇ **Dad's Cats** (828-698-7525; www.dadscats.com), 221 N. Main St. Dad's Cats one-ups your normal model railroad shop with a large selection of model industrial cranes and construction equipment. Owned by a retired design engineer who specialized in earthmoving equipment, the shop specializes in limited, serial-numbered diecast scale models. They also have model cars, trucks, fire equipment, and—yes—train layout items, as well as educational toys and collectible model horses.

♿ **Brevard Music Festival** (888-384-8682; 828-884-2011; www.brevard music.org), Brevard, NC. June–Aug.; the box office opens in April. Students at the Brevard Music Center combine with top-notch professional musicians to put on a summerlong series of performances—typically 50 or so. Events include symphony orchestras, chamber music, popular music, musicals, and fully staged operas. Typically $7–25; some performances and seats may be higher.

Wickwire Fine Art/Folk Art (828-692-6222; fax 828-692-6870; www.wickwireartgallery.com), 330 N. Main St. This commercial fine art gallery features a wide variety of arts and fine crafts from local and regional artists. Its artists include three Smithsonian artisans and two artists who have been declared North Carolina Living Treasures.

JRD's Classics and Collectibles (877-640-7968 or 828-698-0075; fax 828-692-3816; www.jrdclassics.com), 226 N. Main St. JRD's specializes in memorabilia and collectibles from the 1950s—particularly those from soda shops. Their ever-changing inventory of reproductions and restorations includes soda machines, jukeboxes, pinball machines, slot machines, diner decor, gas pumps, telephones, diner furniture, and neon, as well as recently issued collectibles. They perform their own restorations, including vintage slot machines.

Henderson County Farmer's Curb Market (828-692-8012), 221 N. Church St. May–Dec., Tue., Thu., and Sat. 8–2; Jan.–Apr., Tue. and Sat. 9–1. Located just outside downtown behind the Old County Courthouse (facing southbound US 25), this non-profit organization has 137 vendors, all of whom are from Henderson County and all of whom offer only locally made or grown items. In continuous operation since 1924, it features some vendors now in their third or fourth generation.

Flat Rock, NC
Hand in Hand (828-697-7719), 2713 Greenville Hwy. Tue.–Sat. 10–5. This fine-craft gallery, specializing in professional local artists, occupies an unprepossessing roadside brick building toward the center of Flat Rock.

In it are a wide variety of fine crafts, both traditional and contemporary, as well as a quilting store.

Forge Mountain Foods (800-823-6743 or 838-692-9470; fax 828-692-6135; www.forgemountain.com), 1215 Greenville Hwy. This small specialty food company maintains its outlet store in an attractive modern building along US 25. Forge Mountain makes a wide variety of traditional southern-style gift foods—jellies, jams, fruit butters, honey, molasses, sorghum, syrups, relishes, ciders, candies, shortbreads, cakes, hams, and that sort of thing—and sells them all from this roadside company store.

Downtown Brevard, NC
This four-block classic small-town Main Street centers on its beautiful and well-kept Transylvania County Courthouse. For the past decade it's been evolving from rural downtown to an upscale shopping district; you can still get your hair cut and shoes repaired, but you can browse for art and antiques as well.

Number 7 Arts (828-883-2294), 7 E. Main St. This fine art and craft cooperative, sponsored by the Transylvania County Arts Council, is made up of local artists selected by an impartial jurying process. It displays a wide range of media and styles, and always has a local artist-member on hand.

Red Wolf Gallery (828-862-8620), 3 E. Main St. This fine art gallery represents well-known professional artists, mainly from the Appalachian region, with a decidedly contemporary slant.

The Forest Place (828-884-4734), 100 S. Broad St. This ecology-oriented gift and bookshop is owned and operated by The Cradle of Forestry

Interpretive Association, a nonprofit organization that supports The Cradle of Forestry in America and other educational efforts of the Pisgah National Forest. You'll find a wide range of books, gifts, art, toys, and educational materials, all dealing with forest ecology in the Blue Ridge and Smoky Mountains.

Cedar Mountain Community

This rural community, stretched along US 276 ten miles south of Brevard, is home to several highly respected craft artists who maintain galleries and open studios.

Mountain Forest Studio (828-885-2149), Greenville Hwy. Mon.–Sat. 10–5. This white stucco farmhouse on US 276, 3 miles south of Brevard, holds the studios of potter Mary Murray. It features the work of several other local artists as well.

LADY'S SLIPPERS DECORATE THE FOREST FLOOR.

Jim Hargan

✳ Special Events

SPRING Poetry Celebration at the Carl Sandburg Home (828-693-4178). Last weekend in Apr. This 2-day festival, sponsored by the National Park Service on the grounds of the Carl Sandburg Home National Historic Site, features poetry readings by schoolchildren, college students, and well-known guest poets, in addition to poetry workshops.

Johnson Farm Festival (828-891-6585). Last Sat. in Apr. This fundraiser for the nonprofit organization that runs the Johnson Farm museum features mountain crafters and musicians (including fiddles and dulcimers), old-time mountain food, craft exhibits, and farm demonstrations—as well as the full range of museum features. $5 adults, $2 students.

SUMMER The North Carolina Apple Festival (828-697-4557; www.ncapplefestival.org), Hendersonville, NC. Labor Day weekend. This 4-day festival in downtown Hendersonville celebrates the local apple industry. Six blocks of Main Street are filled with 150 vendors and two music stages, while apple-related activities and demonstrations go on throughout the county. The festival ends with a downtown Labor Day parade.

AUTUMN ✎ Brevard Halloween Festival (828-883-3700). Last Sat. in Oct. This annual festival features a costume parade, crafts, food vendors, and music.

The Great Smoky Mountains National Park

3

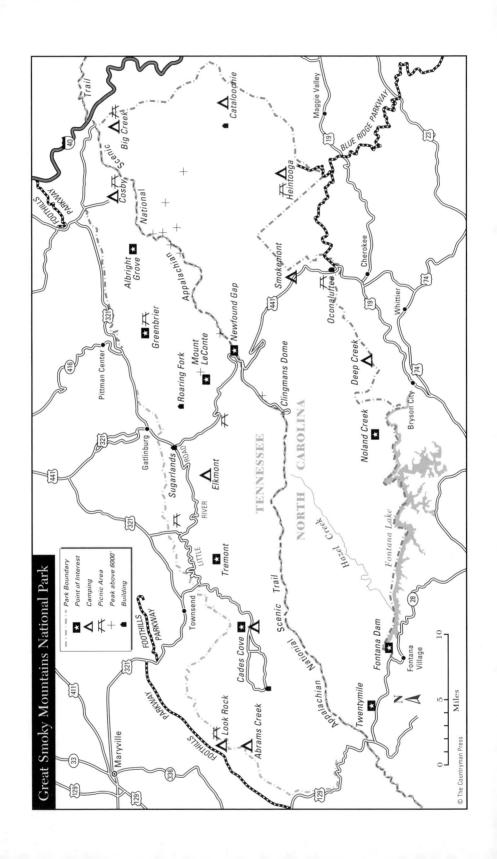

Great Smoky Mountains National Park

Legend:
- ⬛⭐ Park Boundary
- ⭐ Point of Interest
- △ Camping
- ⛺ Picnic Area
- + Peak above 6000'
- ■ Building

TENNESSEE

NORTH CAROLINA

Maryville

Pittman Center

Gatlinburg

Townsend

Cades Cove

Look Rock

Abrams Creek

Sugarlands

Elkmont

Tremont

Greenbrier

Albright Grove

Roaring Fork

Mount LeConte

Newfound Gap

Clingmans Dome

Cosby

Big Creek

Cataloochie

Heintooga

Smokemont

Oconaluftee

Deep Creek

Noland Creek

Hazel Creek

Fontana Lake

Fontana Dam

Fontana Village

Twentymile

Bryson City

Whittier

Cherokee

Maggie Valley

BLUE RIDGE PARKWAY

FOOTHILLS PARKWAY

Appalachian National Scenic Trail

LITTLE RIVER ROAD

Trail

Miles

0   5   10

N

© The Countryman Press

THE GREAT SMOKY MOUNTAINS NATIONAL PARK

The Great Smoky Mountains make up the craggy climax to the Southern Appalachians. While the nearby Black Mountains may be taller by a few dozens of feet, no other eastern range is steeper, more twisted and knotted, or more rugged. The Smokies run as an unbroken wall for 60 miles along the state line, blocking North Carolina from Tennessee with a cliff-walled razor's edge that has mile-high gaps and 6,000-foot peaks. Then, at Tricorner Knob, the Smokies suddenly twist south, change their name to the Balsam Mountains, and run as a mile-high wall for another 45 miles. Behind this great L-shaped range (to its south and west) lie a tangle of tall knotted mountains with deep gaps and slashing narrow valleys.

While the Smokies may have missed the honor of having the highest peak in the East, they are without doubt the most difficult, rugged, and impenetrable range in the Southern Appalachians. Where most eastern mountains struggle to push their peaks more than half a mile above sea level, the Smokies and the Balsams quickly reach an elevation of three-quarters of a mile—then stay there, or higher, for 100 miles. Indeed, the ridge stays a mile above sea level for 50 miles (in four stretches), with 107 mile-high peaks and gaps. Mile-high peaks and gaps are so common in these ranges that folks haven't bothered naming 35 of them, a nonchalance unheard of in other eastern ranges. Slopes plunge 4,000 to 5,000 feet nearly straight down from these high ridges to narrow valley floors, then jump straight up to the next ridge. This tangle of valleys and ridges forms a chaotic nonpattern in which all ridge names are arbitrary. Other mountains may be as tall, but the Smokies and the Balsams are the worst barrier.

Mountains this tall make their own climate. Valley floors as low as 800 feet above sea level have a warm southern climate with oak and pine forests. Looming above these valleys, the mile-high ridgelines extend into a subarctic climate zone typical of Canada, dominated by spruces and firs (known locally as a "balsam forest"). Between these two forest types you'll find every type of hardwood forest imaginable, changing by slope, elevation, local rainfall, exposure to the sun, history, and pure luck. The trees cover nearly every slope, no matter how steep, with the most rugged slopes covered in "laurel hells"—dense tangles of rhododendron and mountain laurel. High rainfall, on some ridges more than 100 inches a year, can bring about a lush temperate rain forest of wondrous variety and beauty, where springs ooze out of the rocks to become raging rivers within 3 miles. With all this variety, it comes as no surprise that the Great Smoky Mountains National Park is an International Biosphere Reserve, said to contain more tree species than Europe.

In these tangled ridges, stage roads and railroads followed the few river valleys with any width, while towns and farms followed the roads. Away from the railroads and turnpikes, settlement fanned out among the steep draws and coves as a thin cover of small subsistence farms. A high-mountain family would live in a one-crib log cabin and grow the food they planned to eat—mainly corn—in a small, steep plot cleared by girdling trees. They would probably have a log barn with a horse or mule and a few cattle, as well as a corncrib, a chicken coop, and (perhaps) a springhouse. Uphill, where it was too steep to farm, the ancient forest spread to the ridgeline; the menfolk hunted the forest, but did not log it. These small plots spread up streams wherever there was enough land to grow a little corn. The Great Smoky Mountains National Park preserves quite a number of these high-mountain farmsteads, some as major open-air museums, others as cabins sitting by a path.

The national park combines all these areas of interest—scenic grandeur, ecological diversity, and pioneer history. It forms a half-million-acre oval with the highest and most difficult ridges running lengthwise along its center, and roads penetrating in from its periphery. Only one road, the popular Newfound Gap Rd., penetrates deep into the park's interior to emerge on the other side. All other roads skitter along its edge, or run up valleys to dead-end at the mountain wall. Those roads lead to all sorts of places—wide views, deep forests, noisy rivers, beautiful waterfalls, and quaint log farmsteads. And footpaths. Over 800 miles of foot and bridle paths penetrate the national park's backcountry. If you stay in your car, you will miss most of the park.

The Great Smoky Mountains National Park is run as a wilderness experience. Apart from campgrounds and camp stores, there are no restaurants or lodgings inside the park. The largest concentration of rooms and restaurants is at Gatlinburg, TN, a congested tourist town at the park's main entrance. To the west of Gatlinburg, the settlement of Townsend, TN, offers a quieter alternative. On the North Carolina side, much of the land bordering the park is within the Qualla Boundary, the reservation of the 10,000-member Eastern Band of the Cherokee Nation; its tribal town of Cherokee straddles the park's main entrance in North Carolina. Not too far away are the unspoiled county seats of Bryson City and Sylva, each with an excellent choice of B&Bs and restaurants.

GETTING ALONG IN THE NATIONAL PARK **Fishing**. Inside the national park, fishing for rainbow and brown trout is allowed year-round; you must have a state license, use a single hook on an artificial lure, and not take brook trout (a native species the National Park Service is trying to restore). Despite the fact that the NPS stopped stocking streams over 30 years ago, the fishing is excellent, and most streams are at their trout population maximums. Fishing within the **Qualla Boundary** requires a tribal license but no state license; fishing on some streams is limited to tribal members.

Bicycling. For the most part, the National Park Service treats bicycles as vehicles on a par with autos, and requires them to follow the same rules. As a practical matter, this limits bicycling opportunities—the automobile roads are narrow, shoulderless, and crowded. There are some exceptions. The scenic drive from **Cades Cove** up **Parsons Branch Rd.** and back on the **Foothills Parkway** is well suited for bicycles, as is the loop around **Heintooga**. The NPS allows bicycles up the **Deep Creek** and **Indian Creek Trails** near Bryson City, NC, even though it's closed to vehicles. Last and best, the wonderful **Cades Cove Loop Rd.** is closed to automobiles on Wed. and Sat. mornings until 10, to allow bicyclists and walkers to enjoy it without noise and fumes.

Day Hiking (800-436-1200; www.nps.gov/grsm/gsmsite/roadinfo.html). Day hiking is unrestricted in the national park, and this guide includes many suggested paths. Paths are normally high in quality, wide and properly graded (although maintenance may vary in quality). Nearly all paths are forest walks, including those along ridgetops—forests cover even the steepest slopes in the Smokies.

Two dangers confront even the casual walker. The first is bears, discussed elsewhere. The second, and by far the more deadly, is hypothermia, followed by dehydration and exhaustion. Hypothermia—sudden body cooling leading to disorientation —can occur even in the hottest weather when altitudes exceed 5,000 feet and rainstorms blow up suddenly. Exhaustion and dehydration can occur whether or not a person is overcooled, particularly when pulling up a 25 percent gradient that stretches for miles without break. In either case, a disoriented person can wander off the trail—a very dangerous place to be in this twisted, craggy land. The park service posts a daily web report on trail conditions, weather, trail closures, and bear problem locations.

SNOW DUSTS THE HIGHEST ELEVATIONS OF MOUNT LECONTE.

Jim Hargan

Backpacking Couch potatoes may be surprised to learn that backpacking in the Great Smoky Mountains National Park is so popular that it has had to be rationed for the last 30 years. The rationing system takes the shape of backcountry camping permits required for overnight trail use. The most popular backcountry areas require reservations and assigned camping spots. Less visited areas have fewer restrictions. This system has succeeded in its goal of spreading backpackers throughout the park, instead of concentrating them in the hundreds along the **Appalachian Trail (AT)**. You can get a permit from any of the ranger stations, or by calling in advance of your trip.

Many people are interested in hiking the AT, as a special and famous place. Day hiking the trail is unrestricted, and this book includes suggestions. Still, this trail remains badly overcrowded by backpackers at all times of the year except the dead of winter, and is strictly regulated by the permit system. Here as elsewhere, the AT has three-sided shelters with shelf bunks every 5 miles or so, but these are completely full nearly all the time. Overuse can make these camping spots unpleasant. In addition, there are bear problems, because bears sometimes raid the AT camping areas for food. It's a good idea to backpack down other park trails, or on sections of the AT outside the park. Near the park, the **Cheoah Mountains** section of the AT is a good alternative, as are **Max Patch** and **Standing Indian Basin**.

Automobile Camping (800-365-2267; http://reservations.nps.gov/). Most campgrounds close seasonally; ask in advance. Auto-based camping is allowed at 10 campgrounds, all of them scenic but primitive, with unheated toilet rooms, no hookups, no electricity, and no showers. Despite these conditions the national park campgrounds are extremely popular and fill up fast. You can get reservations at the most popular campgrounds—**Cades Cove**, **Elkmont**, and **Smokemont**. Of the remaining first-come, first-served campgrounds, **Deep Creek** is an excellent alternative to the Big Three, with a convenient location right outside Bryson City, NC, a fair amount of room at 92 spaces, and some neat waterfalls. But on a really hot summer's day, try to get into **Balsam Mountain Campground** on the Heintooga Spur Rd.—at 5,300 feet, one of the coolest places in the park. If you want remoteness, the 12-site **Abrams Creek** is hard to beat; you may be 2 hours from Gatlinburg, TN, or Cherokee, NC, but the campground is lovely, the footpaths are some of the park's easiest and most beautiful, and the fishing is great. $12–17.

Pets. The Great Smoky Mountains National Park is definitely not a pet-friendly place; the National Park Service sees them as an environmental risk, period. Pets are prohibited on all trails, to the extent that through-hikers on the Appalachian Trail are required to kennel their dogs until they clear the park. Dogs are allowed only in the overlooks and picnic areas, and they must be on leashes at all times.

Bears. The park's first-ever black bear fatality happened in March 2000, on the Little River Trail about 4 miles from Elkmont. In this incident, two bears attacked two adult hikers without apparent provocation, killing one and guarding the body—as bears do a carcass they intend to eat—until rangers could arrive and kill the animals. Bears are extremely dangerous. They should never be approached or fed.

GUIDANCE Smoky Mountain Host of North Carolina (800-432-4678 or 828-293-0787; fax 828-524-2416; www.visitsmokies.org), 4437 Georgia Rd., Franklin, NC 28734. This innkeepers' organization will help you find a room throughout the North Carolina side of the Smoky Mountains. They run a large, friendly visitors center on US 441 south of Franklin, near the Georgia state line.

GATLINBURG & THE NORTHEAST QUADRANT

T he great majority of the 10 million people who visit the Great Smokies every year get their first sight of the national park from the tourist town of Gatlinburg, TN. With 3,800 full-time residents, this intensely busy collection of motels, restaurants, and shops straddles US 441 as it passes up a narrow valley and into the park. Brought into existence by the millions of visitors who have visited the park every year since the end of World War II, Gatlinburg tempts would-be nature lovers away from the park with a carnival-like atmosphere. It also plays host to an exceptionally large and rewarding craft community, with 80 or more craft artists perpetuating mountain traditions.

Whatever the attractions of Gatlinburg, the Great Smoky Mountains National Park remains the main event, with its main entrance abutting the southern edge of town. The park preserves a solid wall of mountains whose highest peaks loom a mile over Gatlinburg's main street, and whose crest extends 30 miles in both directions without a break. Despite its clifflike slopes, this mountain front is covered with the richest and most varied forest in North America, a forest where 130 tree species form nine distinct ecosystems (including successional fields and heath balds). In the areas of the park nearest Gatlinburg, visitors are faced with a wide range of exceptional sites. Views encompass the great crest of the Smokies, so high that the hills around Gatlinburg appear flat next to them. Old-growth forests form groves of giants, trees that tower 150 feet in the air on trunks 15 feet across. Waterfalls range from graceful, lacy curtains to raging torrents that plunge over 90-foot cliffs. Historic log homesteads, barns, and mills remain scattered about the hills above Gatlinburg. While some of these sites can be reached by auto, this is very much a walker's park, and most of the best sites are well removed from the noise and fumes of the park's busy main roads.

GUIDANCE **Gatlinburg Department of Tourism** (800-343-1475 or or 865-436-2392; www.ci.gatlinburg.tn.us/tourism/tourism.htm), 303 Reagan Dr., Gatlinburg, TN 37738. This City of Gatlinburg agency runs the convention center and works with the chamber to promote the area. It runs a small visitors center in the center of town, on the corner of US 441 and US 321, at the third traffic light.

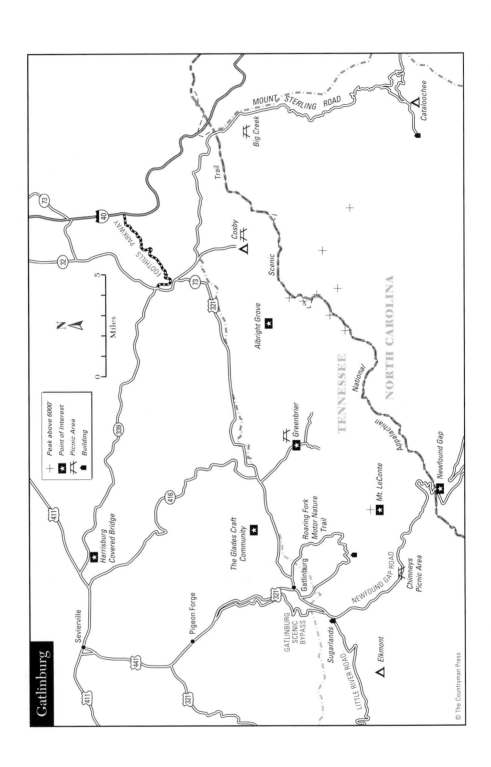

Gatlinburg

N

Miles
0   5

Peak above 6000'
Point of Interest
Picnic Area
Building

MOUNT STERLING ROAD

Big Creek

Cataloochee

Trail

FOOTHILLS PARKWAY

Cosby

Scenic

Albright Grove

Greenbrier

TENNESSEE

NORTH CAROLINA

National/

Appalachian

Mt. LeConte

Newfound Gap

Harrisburg
Covered Bridge

The Glades Craft
Community

Roaring Fork
Motor Nature
Trail

NEWFOUND GAP ROAD

Chimneys
Picnic Area

Sevierville

Pigeon Forge

Gatlinburg

GATLINBURG
SCENIC
BYPASS

Sugarlands

Elkmont

LITTLE RIVER ROAD

© The Countryman Press

Gatlinburg Visitors Center (Chamber of Commerce) (800-900-4148; fax 865-430-3876; www.gatlinburg.com), 811 E. Parkway, P.O. Box 527, Gatlinburg, TN 37738. The Gatlinburg Chamber of Commerce cooperates with the National Park Service to run this large welcome center on US 441 at the eastern entrance to the town. It offers help and information from both the NPS and the Gatlinburg Chamber, as well as a park-oriented bookstore run by the Smoky Mountains Natural History Association. It's also a major terminus (with free parking) on Gatlinburg's elaborate trolley network, making it a good place to park while visiting the rest of the town.

Sugarlands Ranger Station (865-436-1291; www.nps.gov/grsm/), 107 Park Headquarters Rd., Gatlinburg, TN 37738. The administrative headquarters for the national park is located just behind the Sugarlands Visitors Center, outside Gatlinburg. If you are looking for a place for walk-in information, try either **Sugarlands Visitors Center** on the Tennessee end of the Newfound Gap Rd., or **Oconaluftee Visitors Center** on its North Carolina end.

Mount LeConte Geology Web Page
(http://geology.er.usgs.gov/eespteam/Mtleconte/). This web page, sponsored by the U.S. Geological Survey at the request of the National Park Service, gives detailed information on the geology of the Smoky Mountain Front, accompanied by a large number of color photos to aid in rock identification. Rockhounds and geology enthusiasts will want to look up the detailed descriptions (with photos) of the geology along each of the trails up Mount LeConte. The USGS team responsible for this page has compiled a similar page for Cades Cove.

GETTING THERE *By car*: To reach Gatlinburg, TN, from any direction (including south), take Interstate 40 to TN 66 (Exit 407), then go south on TN 66 to pick up **US 441** in Sevierville, TN. Gatlinburg is 13 miles south of Sevierville on US 441. Don't worry about getting lost; Gatlinburg is well signposted the entire distance.

By air: If you are staying on the Gatlinburg side of the Smokies, you will want to fly into Knoxville's **McGhee Tyson Airport** (865-970-2773), 255 Alcoa Hwy., Alcoa, TN, a full-service regional airport with on-site car rentals. It's a 44-mile drive from Gatlinburg, more than half of it down two-lane roads; expect it to take at least 1¼ hours. If your primary destination is the Cades Cove area of the park, you should note that the Cades Cove entrance at Townsend, TN, with a full range of tourist facilities, is only a 20-mile drive from the airport via multilane highways.

By bus: There is no regularly scheduled bus service into Gatlinburg. Many tour operators offer bus tours to Gatlinburg; check with your travel agent.

MEDICAL EMERGENCIES Fort Sanders Sevier Medical Center (865-429-6100; www.fssevier.com), 709 Middle Creek Rd., Sevierville, TN. Despite its Sevierville address, Sevier (pronounced *Severe*) Medical Center is located in Pigeon Forge, 1.2 miles east of US 441 on Middle Creek Rd.; if you are coming from Gatlinburg, you will find this to be a right turn, 7 miles north of downtown. A branch of Knoxville's massive regional hospital company, Covenant Health,

Sevier is a small, full-service local hospital with surgery facilities and a 24/7 emergency room.

Gatlinburg First Med Walk-in Clinic (865-436-7267), 1015 E. Parkway, Gatlinburg, TN. Mon.–Fri. 9–3, Sat. 9–2. This walk-in clinic is located on the east end of Gatlinburg on US 321.

✳ Wandering Around

EXPLORING BY CAR **The Newfound Gap Road in Tennessee**. Built in 1932 as a scenic tourist highway, the Newfound Gap Rd. climbs the steep Tennessee face of the Great Smoky Mountains National Park to top out in the 5,048-foot-high Newfound Gap. From there the highway enters North Carolina to descend to Cherokee, a beautiful stretch with spectacular views. This two-lane highway is a fairly easy drive as mountain roads go, but heavy traffic and inconsiderate drivers can make it slow going. You'll enjoy it more if you approach it as a recreational drive, taking plenty of time to pull over and enjoy the scenery.

Most people start this drive at the national park entrance at the south edge of Gatlinburg. A better plan is to start at the north end, entering the **Gatlinburg Bypass** from the southbound lanes of US 441 a mile south of the Smoky Mountains/Gatlinburg Visitors Center. This 5-mile scenic parkway, part of the Great Smoky Mountains National Park, winds along the mountain slopes west of Gatlinburg with two stunning 180° views over the town and toward the high slopes of Mount LeConte. This little-used road will zip you around Gatlinburg and into the park just south of the Sugarlands Visitors Center to join the Newfound Gap Rd. proper. For the next 2 miles the highway curves gently uphill through a young hardwood forest growing on the site of the former Sugarlands community. A nature trail and two "quiet walkways" give you an opportunity to explore the forests for signs of its former inhabitants—old foundations, chimneys, tuliptrees growing on abandoned fields, even a motel and some paved roads and concrete bridges. After that the highway climbs above Sugarlands for sweeping views over the valley and toward the face of Mount LeConte. At 5 miles you will reach the streamside **Chimneys Picnic Area**, where a nature trail explores a virgin cove hardwood forest. Now the highway becomes more rugged as it climbs away from the valley, with good views to the **Chimney Tops**, two gigantic rock spires protruding from the ridgeline above. Beyond that, the highway goes through a 360° pigtail curve, circling over itself to gain a high, gentle-floored stream valley. When the road finally runs out of valley it switchbacks steeply up to become a ledge cut into cliffs, a low stone wall guarding its downhill edge. Finally it reaches **Morton Overlook**, with striking views into the deep valley below and receding ridges beyond. **Newfound Gap**, with its large parking lot, views, and Appalachian Trail access, is just beyond.

Roaring Fork Motor Nature Trail. This nature trail for the car-bound leads down old farm roads that once wandered through the settlements south of Gatlinburg, TN, before this area was included in the Great Smoky Mountains National Park and allowed to go back to forests. This scenic drive starts in downtown Gatlinburg, turning onto Historic Nature Trail (that's the name of the street) from US 441 at the eighth traffic light. Continue past the lovely little

Mynatt Park to enter the national park just beyond. The road goes through gentle curves to climb through hardwood forests to the **Bud Ogle Place**, a log cabin with running water piped in using hollow logs. Just beyond, the road breaks into a mile-long one-way loop through **Cherokee Orchards**, an apple orchard and commercial nursery until 1940. As the road loops uphill and around (to return to the Bud Ogle Place), turn onto the one-lane, one-way Roaring Fork Motor Nature Trail to the right. Passing the **Baskins Creek Trail** in a quarter mile, the road twists up to a ridge with a good view, then twists around to a second ridgeline with a great view—westward, toward Sugarlands, with receding ridges fading into the background. Passing the **Grotto Falls Trailhead**, the road twists through a hemlock forest, then follows a boistrous creek; look for the stone wall on its opposite side. After half a mile, a parking lot will mark the far end of the Baskins Creek Trail and the second historic site—a log cabin and outbuildings overlooking a small waterfall. Not after, the road reaches the **Ephraim Bales Place**, a modest dogtrot log cabin and barn, with an impressive stone wall marking the location of the old farm road. Half a mile farther, the road passes the last and most colorful of the four sites, the brightly painted **Alfred Reagan Place**, with a restored horizontal wheel "tub mill" by the stream. A double stream crossing marks the point when the stream drops suddenly down into a small gorge, the road following it on a ledge hewn into the rocky slopes above. Here are dramatic views down the stream, and two wonderful waterfalls dripping down the rocks above the road. The road finally leaves the park to reenter Gatlinburg; return to downtown by taking the turn to the left.

EXPLORING ON FOOT **Five popular hikes near Gatlinburg**. These five hikes, all within 10 miles of Gatlinburg, TN, are overwhelmingly popular. Each is extraordinary, even by Smoky Mountain standards, with a magnificent view, remarkable feature, or beautiful waterfall. Each is well maintained (one is paved) and capable of handling its visitors, although parking can be a problem. In fact, the only thing wrong with any of these hikes is their lack of solitude. On a sunny weekend, expect these hikes to be more like a carnival than a wilderness experience.

1. **Laurel Falls Trail**, 4 miles west of Sugarlands Visitors Center on Little River Rd. This 1.3-mile paved trail, partially blasted through solid rock by the CCC in 1935, leads past a view to a strong 75-foot waterfall.

2. **Chimney Tops Trail**, 6.7 miles south of Sugarlands Visitors Center on Newfound Gap Rd. This 2-mile uphill slog leads through old-growth forest to a popular, but dangerous, clifftop viewpoint. This is a really bad place to take children.

3. **Alum Cave Trail**, 8.6 miles south of Sugarlands Visitors Center on Newfound Gap Rd. The lowermost 2 miles of this Mount LeConte access trail feature huge boulders, an interesting geological formation known as Arch Rock, old-growth forests, and spectacular views from exposed bluffs.

4. **Grotto Falls** (on Trillium Gap Trail), 3.5 miles from Gatlinburg on the Roaring Fork Motor Nature Trail. This easy 1-mile walk leads through mature forests to a large waterfall.

5. **Ramsey Cascades Trail**, at the end of the left fork within the Greenbrier area. This difficult hike (an eight mile round trip distance with two thousand feet of climbing) runs through old growth forest with giant hemlocks and tuliptrees, to end at an exceptionally beautiful 90-foot waterfall.

Old settlement walks near Gatlinburg. One of the best ways to escape the crowds near Gatlinburg, TN, is to take a walk through the old mountain settlements of **Sugarlands** and **Baskins Creek**, abandoned in the 1930s to make way for the national park. These interconnecting paths are so close to Gatlinburg that you can start from the center of downtown, do them both in a day, and return to where you started—a total distance of 11 miles with an elevation gain of 1,600 feet. If you want to try this loop hike, follow the downtown sidewalk toward the park, then continue along the pretty riverside **Gatlinburg Trail** to the national park headquarters at Sugarlands, a level 2-mile stroll past old homesites and a lovely cascade.

Old Sugarlands Trail starts near the park headquarters (where you can park)—across the Newfound Gap Rd., over the bridge, and on your right. This little-used path follows old abandoned roads, some once paved, through the heart of the Sugarlands community. You will walk past foundations, stone walls, stretches of abandoned macadam, old automobile bridges, and a CCC camp beneath the trees. The walk is 4 miles to the Cherokee Orchards Rd.; the first 2 miles are particularly interesting, and nearly level.

To continue the loop walk, pick up **Trillium Gap Trail** at the end of Old Sugarlands Trail. This trail goes through an old commercial apple orchard absorbed into the park in 1942 and still shows signs of its former use. This trail connects with the next walk.

Baskins Falls Walk follows a little-used path 1.75 miles through an old settlement to a lovely waterfall. Its trailhead, marked BASKINS CREEK TRAIL, is just beyond the start of the Roaring Fork Motor Nature Trail. This trail climbs up a piney ridge, then descends into a small canyon with some impressive bluffs. As the main trail turns away, a side path continues downhill along the stream to Baskins Falls, a 30-foot plunge that settlers used as a shower in summer. This is the end of the official path, where most folk return to the main trail and go back to their cars.

You may want to continue ahead, however, along Baskins Creek to Gatlinburg, to complete the loop. This little-used informal path (a "manway" in park parlance) follows the banks of the creek through the heart of another old community. This rough, overgrown walk passes many signs of the old settlement, as well as wildflowers and beautiful stream views. The path leaves the national park and enters Gatlinburg at the end of the town's Baskins Creek Rd.; follow the paved roads downhill to return to downtown.

✴ Villages

Gatlinburg, TN. In the late 1920s Gatlinburg was just another poor mountain crossroads. It was where the road up from the flatlands reached the foot of the Smokies—a fork with a general store and a gas pump. From here, the highway

ALBRIGHT GROVE

Named for a National Park Service administrator who did much to ensure the park's integrity from developers, Albright Grove is a remarkable stand of virgin old-growth forest. It's a moderate hike, 6.7 miles round trip with 1,600 feet of uphill climbing, all through forests. The trailhead is hard to find. Go 15.5 miles east of downtown Gatlinburg, TN, on US 321, then turn right onto Baxter Rd. by Smoky Mountain Creekside Rentals; from there, turn right at the T intersection with Laurel Springs Rd., going a short distance until you reach the park service sign for the Maddron Bald Trail.

You will hike uphill on the **Maddron Bald Trail** for 3 miles to reach Albright Grove, walking along an old settlement road through forests that have grown over former farms. After half a mile you will pass one of the old farmhouses, a chestnut log cabin with a shake roof, built by Willis Baxter in 1889. The old settlement road ends after 2 miles, and the forest becomes deeper, dominated by large hemlocks; you are now entering a classic Appalachian cove hardwood forest, with a rich variety of old, large trees. At 2.8 miles the **Albright Grove Loop Trail** forks right to enter a segment of the forest that has never been logged. Giant tuliptrees (yellow poplars) exceed 25 feet in diameter; similar gargantuan hemlocks and beeches are scattered about, as are huge silverbells, the signature tree of the cove forest. In all, the loop trail leads through this cathedral-like forest for two-thirds of a mile before returning to the Maddron Bald Trail. To go straight back to your car, turn right; it's downhill all the way.

Strong hikers may be interested in taking a left here, going deeper into the wilderness and higher up the mountain. This path reaches a large, wild heath bald on remote Maddron Bald, with 360° views over the Smokies Crest and down into Tennessee—an addition of 6.5 miles and 1,800 feet of climb added to an already long walk.

(now the Newfound Gap Rd.) wandered into the Smokies to a dead-end at the poverty-stricken community of Sugarlands, also known as "Blockader's Heaven" according to a local moonshine expert. Then came the park. Gatlinburg found itself the main entrance to a park that attracted a million automobile-driving visitors in 1941. Within 20 years all those tourists had turned the mountain crossroads into a small city.

Gatlinburg is a city built for tourists. It's still centered on that old fork in the road, but now the fork is a busy multilane intersection in the middle of a crowded downtown. Here two-story buildings, jammed against the sidewalk and each other, are filled with every sort of tourist enticement imaginable—gift shops, restaurants, candy shops, old-timey photo places, sideshows (labeled "museums" and "attractions"), amusement rides . . . you name it. It has more than a passing

resemblance to a really large county fair, complete with bad parking, high prices, and a stiff dose of hucksterism. It's easy to complain about it, but it's a lot more fun to grab a corn dog and enjoy it.

Unlike Cherokee, NC, Gatlinburg is continuously tearing itself down and rebuilding itself. Its downtown is crammed into a narrow river gorge, a single block wide and a mile long, so that real estate is at a premium. The entire length is built continuously with commercial structures two to three stories high, attached to each other and the sidewalk. The latest commercial craze has been to take what had been normal-sized stores and turn them into "malls" with tiny shops opening onto a central corridor. This has allowed the number of downtown shops to multiply like rabbits, with small merchants scrambling to offer something new and different to browsing tourists. Behind this long, thin downtown strip, scores of motels with thousands of rooms climb down to the river and up the mountainsides.

Apart from this full-time street fair, Gatlinburg has a serious, mountain-oriented side. On the rural east side of town, the **Glades** area hosts a community of 80 craft artists—some newcomers, others from old mountain craft families. A series of crafter-owned shops strings out along this scenic mountain cove, with members of the community prominently displaying a logo certifying that they make what they sell. Indeed, most have their studios in their shops, and will welcome you in as they work.

Gatlinburg traffic is always slow, and it can grind to a stop during the high tourist season. If you wish simply to get beyond town to the other side, take the Gatlinburg Bypass, a scenic road maintained by the National Park Service. Outside the winter season, there is no street parking in downtown Gatlinburg. Instead, downtown parking is in a couple of city garages at a stiffish $1.50 per hour, plus an outdoor lot near the auditorium at a somewhat lower price. As an alternative, you can park for free at the visitors center at the north end of town or the city hall at the east end of town on US 321, and take a trolley ($0.25–2).

Pigeon Forge, TN. This sprawling suburb of Gatlinburg, 6 miles north of downtown, consists of a 2-mile string of chain restaurants and franchise motels stretching along a six-lane segment of US 441. Pigeon Forge's landscape is that of a recently built-up area on the edge of a large city, with no real mountain views or traditional mountain culture. If you long for the certainty of familiar surroundings and brand names you recognize, you will certainly find them at Pigeon Forge. If you want to immerse yourself in mountain scenery and culture, however, you might want to look elsewhere.

Sevierville (*SeVERE-vull*), TN, is the seat of Sevier County—the county that contains Gatlinburg. Travelers along US 441 will see little of it beyond a continuous suburban-style sprawl that merges seamlessly with Pigeon Forge. Two blocks off the highway, however, lies a quaint old downtown centering on an old brick courthouse with a statue of Dolly Parton in front. Many businesses in the foothills of the Smokies sport Sevierville addresses, even though they are not particularly near town.

Cosby, TN, is a dispersed rural settlement with no defined village center, stretching along US 321 about 16 miles east of Gatlinburg. It offers access to the little-visited northeastern fringe of the Great Smoky Mountains National Park, but services are slight and choices are limited.

❋ Wild Places

THE GREAT FORESTS **The Smoky Mountain Front**. A drop of rain, falling on the highest point of Mount LeConte, travels through 7 miles of wilderness before it reaches the river in downtown Gatlinburg, TN. It also drops 1 mile vertically—in all likelihood the longest slope in the eastern United States. This slope is wet as well as steep, with 7 feet of rainfall in a typical year. This combination of high rainfall and high, steep slopes does more than create big rivers and impressive waterfalls; it also creates one of the richest temperate forests in the world.

Start at the top, with that drop of water on the 6,593-foot peak of Mount LeConte. You'll be in a boreal forest, an extension of the great sub-arctic forest that covers much of Canada, whose Christmas tree species

A BRONZE SCULPTURE OF DOLLY PARTON BY JIM GRAY SITS OUTSIDE THE SEVIERVILLE COUNTY COURTHOUSE.

Jim Hargan

of spruce and fir form a forest canopy over thin, rocky soils. Below that will be a mosaic of forest types: New England–style hardwood forests, oak–hickory forests, beech–maple forests, pine–oak forests on warm, dry ridgelines, northern riverine forests along many streambanks. Unique to the Smokies and other nearby mountains is the cove hardwood forest, with the greatest species richness in temperate North America. A cove forest can mix and match as many as 25 tree species in an acre of old growth, covering a thick shrubby understory that bursts into colorful blooms every spring—rhododendron, mountain laurel, flame azalea, dogwood, redbud, silverbell. These thick forests cover even the steepest slopes with trees that grow 6 to 10 stories high.

And there's a lot of slope that has to be covered. The front of the Smoky Mountains at Gatlinburg forms an unbroken wall 65 miles long. The central 56 miles of that wall, immediately behind Gatlinburg, stays continuously above 4,000 feet, with half of that length more than a mile high. On the western (TN) side of the crest, the Smokies drop to a valley that appears flat bottomed from a crest-top viewpoint, and stretches off to the horizon as far as the eye can see. On the eastern (NC) side, other mountains, nearly as tall, fill the view in a confused jumble.

Access to this great forest is either from the **Newfound Gap Rd.**, or from a series of four trailheads along its perimeter: **Roaring Fork Motor Nature Trail**, **Greenbrier Picnic Area**, **Cosby Picnic Area**, and **Big Creek Picnic Area**. All five of these trailheads are gateways into rich and varied forests, with stunning wildflowers, roaring rivers, large waterfalls, and magnificent views. Almost without exception, the hiking and horse trails that lead from these trailheads are well built, well kept, and incredibly beautiful; it should go without saying that nearly all of them are very steep as well.

RECREATION AREAS **Greenbrier Picnic Area**. Six miles east of Gatlinburg, TN, on US 321, a right turn onto a narrow paved lane leads 4 miles up a broad valley named **Greenbrier Cove**. Inhabited by scattered farms in the 1920s, Greenbrier Cove is now grown over by a young riverside forest along the noisy, boulder-strewn **Middle Prong of the Little Pigeon River**. The modest, pleasant picnic area is 2.5 miles up the lane. In another half a mile, a side road crosses the Middle Prong at a particularly scenic spot, then winds through forests to the start of the **Ramsey Cascades Trail**, one of the park's most popular hikes. Straight ahead, the road follows **Porters Creek** to end at a gate in 1 mile. You can park here and continue up the road on foot. This was once the road to a farming community; you will pass old stone walls, steps leading up hills, boxwoods and roses growing rank where houses once stood. At the end of the road, in a mile, a short path leads right to an old cantilevered barn in the woods, and a log cabin nearby.

STATE CHAMPION HEMLOCK IS MEASURED BY VIRGINIA RUSSELL, NC FOREST SERVICE OFFICIAL, IN THE JOYCE KILMER MEMORIAL FOREST.

Jim Hargan

Cosby Picnic Area is at the far northeast corner of the Tennessee Smokies; go 18 miles east of downtown Gatlinburg on US 321 to TN 73 at Cosby community, then right 0.4 mile to TN 32, then right 1.3 miles to a park service lane on the right. This lane leads 2 miles into the national park, through a rich forest growing on a fan of river deposits at the foot of the Smokies. This forest is particularly beautiful in spring, when it gets its color early, and fall, when its color lingers a few extra days. The picnic area at the upper end of the road (there is also a campground here) is small and forest covered, along the lovely Cosby Creek. You will find a trailhead to the **Lower Mount Cammerer Trail**—a lengthy footway along the middle slopes of the Smokies, lower here than at Gatlinburg. The first 1.5 miles of this well-built path, climbing only 260 feet, is definitely worth your while. At first it leads along old roadbeds, with stone walls indicating a formerly settled area. Then, after half a mile, the old roads end and the trail (built by the CCC in 1935) rises gently for a mile to **Sutton Ridge**. A side trail uphill to the right leads to a wonderful view out over the foothills and the Great Valley. Beyond, the trail descends slightly to **Riding Fork**. You'll find a lovely little cascade upstream to your right, a place where the water trickles and dashes over the rocks in dozens of little steps—a good place to turn around.

Big Creek Picnic Area. This remote valley hides just over the state line in North Carolina, at the extreme northeast tip of the park. The drive there is part of its charm. Take US 321 east to Cosby, TN, then turn right onto TN 32. This narrow road must set a state record for twists as it slowly feels its way through a lovely young hardwood forest on the park's northeast flank. There's a really nice view or two at first; then the forest closes in, and the road becomes a serpentine tunnel through the trees for mile after mile after mile . . . You cross the state line and the Appalachian Trail at the same time, then descend quickly on the now gravel road to an intersection. The right turn takes you into the Big Creek area; straight ahead leads to Cataloochee; and the left turn takes you through the attractive settlement of Waterville to I-40, for a much faster return to Gatlinburg, TN.

Once at Big Creek you will be on a narrow gravel road that leads 1 mile into the park, to end at a creekside camping and picnic area. The picnic tables sit near the lovely Big Creek, noisy and full of rapids, sheltered by tall, young hardwoods. Beyond the picnic area, the road continues on up the stream as a foot- and horse path. Logged in the 1920s, this valley is now covered by a healthy young forest of tall tuliptrees and maples; the stream, visible frequently to the left of the road, is exceptionally beautiful. At 1.4 miles up this gentle roadway is **Midnight Hole**, a 6-foot cascade between two large boulders into a deep pool. At 2.1 miles is **Mouse Falls**, where the creek pours 20 feet over gray stone.

PICNIC AREAS **Chimneys Picnic Area**. This large picnic area offers forest-shaded tables strung along the Little Pigeon River, 7 miles from Gatlinburg, TN, on the Newfound Gap Rd. It's attractive, cool, and quiet, even on a busy summer day. A nature trail explores the Smokies' unique hardwood cove forest, leading three-quarters of a mile to a virgin old-growth stand. Picnickers should note that Chimneys is the last picnic area on the Newfound Gap Rd. for 22 miles—the next place to picnic is Collins Creek, way on the other side of the mountain.

Mynatt Park. This attractive city park inside Gatlinburg, TN, offers a number of forested, streamside picnic tables in a quiet residential neighborhood, as well as a full range of recreational facilities (including tennis, if you remembered your racquet). Parking is adequate. You'll find it a mile from downtown on Historic Nature Trail.

✳ To See

HISTORIC SITES **Harrisburg Covered Bridge**. Go east from Sevierville on US 411 for 4 miles; turn right onto TN 339, continuing onto TN 35, for a total of 1 mile; then turn right onto Harrisburg Rd. for 0.2 mile to the bridge. Built in

1875 by a local mill owner, this simple wood truss bridge spans a gap between two high bluffs above the East Fork, in this scenic rural location 5 miles east of Sevierville, TN. As with all true covered bridges, the cover protected the heavy wood trusses from rotting; the wood trusses, in turn, allowed the bridge to span the long distance between the bluffs. (Doubting Thomases in the TN DOT have stuck a big concrete pier in the middle, just in case.) The covered truss bridge still carries local traffic on this pastoral back road, thanks to a 1972 restoration funded by the local DAR chapter.

MUSEUMS **Sugarlands Visitors Center** (865-436-1291; www.nps.gov/grsm/), 107 Park Headquarters Rd., Gatlinburg, TN. Located outside Gatlinburg at the start of the Newfound Gap Rd., the Sugarlands Visitors Center has an information desk, gift shop, exhibits, a multimedia show, and a native plant garden. Its exhibit area explores the Smoky Mountains' unique environment in detail. Still, its most rewarding feature is its least visited: **Fighting Creek Nature Trail** leads you on a 1-mile ramble through forest growing on old farmland; it will take you along an old wagon track, along a stream, past stone walls and springs, to a restored log cabin deep in the woods.

Galleries and Gardens of the Arrowmont School (865-436-5860; fax 865-430-4101; www.arrowmont.org), 556 Parkway, Gatlinburg, TN. Weekdays, normal business hours. The prestigious Arrowmont School, founded by the Pi Beta Phi Fraternity for Women, has occupied its campus in the middle of downtown Gatlinburg since the 1920s—long before downtown Gatlinburg existed. You'll find it to be a string of handsome buildings ranging from old log cabins to contemporary structures, ranging up from busy downtown in beautiful parklike gardens. Five galleries in the main educational facility, a 1970 prairie-style homage that echoes the mountain peaks behind it, display works of faculty and students, as does a sculpture garden farther up the site. The campus starts behind the venerable Arrowcraft Shop on US 441, in the center of downtown just south of River Rd.

REALLY NEAT PLACES **Great Smoky Arts and Crafts Community** (800-565-7330; www.artsandcraftscommunity.com), P.O. Box 807, Gatlinburg, TN 37738. This scenic rural cove on the east side of Gatlinburg has been known as a center for mountain crafts for over half a century. An 8-mile loop road, well signposted off US 321 three miles east of town, runs through the center of this crafters' community, becoming increasingly beautiful as it draws away from Gatlinburg's center; along it, small craft shops sit in meadows with views over the low mountains of the foothills. Since 1978, the craft artists of the Glades have formed their own association, the Great Smoky Arts and Crafts Community, limited to Glades crafters who feature their own work in their own studios. There are now more than 70 such studio-galleries displaying the "Arts and Crafts Community" logo. According to member and porcelain artist Judy Baily, "People feel free to take their time in our shops. Many times they ask us a lot of questions about what we do, and we are glad to spend time with them." These fine crafters, rather than the downtown souvenir shops, are Gatlinburg's main attraction for serious shoppers.

Foothills Parkway East. This short length of the long-delayed Foothills Parkway links I-40 with US 321—sort of a shortcut for people heading from Asheville, NC, to Gatlinburg, TN. It's worth a visit, even if it's out of your way. This 6-mile section of parkway climbs to the 2,200-foot top of **Green Mountain**—the first foothill beyond the northeast end of the Smokies. Overlooks give panoramic views of the Great Smoky Mountains as they rise almost a mile above the foothills and valleys in front of you; other viewpoints look westward, over the foothills as they descend in waves into the Great Valley.

✳ To Do

CRAFT AND ENVIRONMENTAL SCHOOLS ♿ **Arrowmont School of Arts and Crafts** (865-436-5860; fax 865-430-4101; www.arrowmont.org), 556 Parkway, Gatlinburg, TN. In the early 20th century, the Pi Beta Phi Fraternity for Women founded the Settlement School just south of the mountain crossroads known as Gatlinburg, a charitable effort to bring schooling into the remote coves and hollows of the Smoky Mountains. Today known as the Arrowmont School, it has evolved over the years into one of the mountain's premier craft schools. Still occupying its original 70-acre campus at the center of Gatlinburg, it offers 1- and 2-week intensive residency courses in a wide variety of craft arts. $280 per week tuition; room and board available for $205–470 per week for a single adult; other fees may apply.

✐ **The Smoky Mountains Field School** (865-974-0150; fax 865-974-0154; www.ce.utk.edu/Smoky), 600 Henley St., Suite 105, UT Conference Center Bldg., Knoxville, TN. Courses run spring through late fall. This cooperative program between the National Park Service and the University of Tennessee offers outdoor walking-based courses, taught by experts. The range of courses is truly incredible, from the expected offerings on Smoky Mountain plants, animals, and history, to special programs in the arts and nature writing, to wonderfully specialized programs on such topics as land snails and slime molds. A typical course will meet in a picnic area inside the park, then travel (most likely, walk) to the course's various locations over a period of 4 to 8 hours. Many of the courses are specifically structured for parents to share with their children, with separate courses aimed at parents with teens and parents with youngsters. The Field School's headquarters is far outside the park, at the University of Tennessee's Knoxville Campus. Half-day programs range $12–18; full-day programs are typically $42; multiday programs (mostly camping) are mostly $84–148 for 2 or 3 days.

FISHING **Old Smoky Outfitters** (865-430-1936; www.oldsmoky.com), 511 Parkway, #201, Gatlinburg, TN. This downtown fishing shop offers guide service for both stream and lake fishing. $135 for half-day trips, $200 for full-day trips, $225 for full-day lessons.

GOLF **Bent Creek Golf Village** (800-251-9336 or 865-436-2875; www.bent creekgolfcourse.com), 3919 E. Parkway, Gatlinburg, TN. This par-72 golf course, designed in 1972 by Gary Player, is located at Pittman Center, 10 miles east of

Gatlinburg on US 321. Its first nine holes play along the valley bottom, while the more challenging second nine climb up and down the mountainside. Owned by Sunterra, there are a large number of time-share condos available for rent along the course, as well as some very nice cottages. $30–35 for nonmembers; $20 for nine holes.

Gatlinburg Golf Course (800-231-4128 or 865-453-3912; fax 865-429-1945; www.ci.gatlinburg.tn.us/golf/golf_course.htm), 520 Dollywood Lane, Pigeon Forge, TN. Open all year. Owned by the City of Gatlinburg, this 1955 Bob Cupp–designed course is noted for its dramatic 12th hole—teeing over a 200-foot drop down a clifflike slope to reach the green 194 feet away. This handsome 6,282-foot course offers beautiful views along its length, plus a lake on the 18th. $31–55 for 18 holes.

HIKING AND CAMPING A Walk in the Woods (865-436-8283; www.awalkinthe woods.com), 4413 Scenic Dr. E., Gatlinburg, TN. Erik and Vesna Plakanis offer half- and whole-day guided nature walks within the Great Smoky Mountains National Park, as well as custom trips and backpacking trips. All walks include a guide, car shuttles, and a picnic lunch. They also rent camping equipment. Appalachian Trail hikers should note that the Plakanises offer through-hiker support. $17–19 for half day, $38–50 for full day.

SKIING Ober Gatlinburg (865-436-5423; www.obergatlinburg.com), 1001 Parkway, Gatlinburg, TN. Open all year, except for the first 2 weeks in Mar. (dates vary). Ski season runs Dec.–Feb.; summer amusement park Apr.–Nov. You can drive to the ski slopes of Ober Gatlinburg, but it's a lot more fun to take the Swiss-made cable car from downtown Gatlinburg. The enclosed cars sweep over the Gatlinburg rooftops, up a hollow, and over a ridge to a panorama—Mount LeConte towering on the right, the much lower hills of East Tennessee on the left, and Gatlinburg deep in the valley directly below. The clean and orderly ski hall, which doubles as a fun center in summer, is a wide-spanning metal building with exposed girders and a sloping floor of exposed concrete. Inside, county-fair-style concessions surround a skating rink, with the floor spiraling down. The eight ski trails have a longest run of 5,000 feet and a maximum drop of 600 feet, with a maximum elevation of 3,300 feet.

MAILBOXES LINE A COUNTRY LANE OUTSIDE GATLINBURG.

Jim Hargan

Cable car from downtown Gatlinburg, $8 (discounted from lift ticket). Lift ticket $25–35 per day ($12 night only). Skating $7 for 3 hours. Amusement rides $2–6.

STABLES **McCarters Riding Stables** (865-436-5354). One of two national park concessionaires operating in the Gatlinburg area, McCarters offers trail rides in the Sugarlands area of the park, near the Sugarlands Visitors Center.

Smoky Mountain Llama Treks (865-428-4606; fax 865-428-4940; www.smoky mountainllamatreks.com), 1839 Creek Hollow Way, Sevierville, TN. Open all year. Sandy Sgrillo offers a variety of llama treks from her headquarters just outside Pigeon Forge. Short treks explore Bluff Mountain, while longer treks visit the mountaintop meadows of Max Patch. Half-day and full-day treks feature a gourmet lunch, while the overnighter has a four-course steak or salmon dinner served on china and crystal (brown-bagging welcome). $15 for a 1-hour hike with snack; $35 for a half-day hike with gourmet lunch; $50 for a full-day hike with gourmet lunch; $100 for an overnight camping trek with dinner and breakfast.

Smoky Mountains Stables (865-436-5634). The second of two national park concessionaires in the Gatlinburg area, Smoky Mountain Stables offers trail rides up the little-visited Dudley Creek area of the national park from a stable on US 321, 4 miles east of downtown.

WHITEWATER ADVENTURES ✍ **Rafting in the Smokies (Pigeon River Outdoors, Inc.)** (800-776-7238 or 865-436-5008; fax 865-436-6360; www.raftingin thesmokies.com), P.O. Box 592, Gatlinburg, TN. Mar.–Oct. From their downtown Gatlinburg location, this company runs whitewater rafting trips on the Class III–IV Pigeon River (shuttling half an hour to the river), and float trips on a smooth section of the same river. The intermediate-level rapids of the Pigeon —more thrilling than the better-known Nantahala River—are restricted to children over eight who weigh more than 60 pounds, but the float trip is open to anyone over the age of three. $42 for Pigeon River whitewater rafting, $20 for Pigeon River smoothwater floating.

✍ **Smoky Mountain Outdoors** (800-771-7238 or 865-430-3838; www.smoky mountainrafting.com), 453 Brookside Village Way, Gatlinburg, TN. This out-fitter offers Pigeon River whitewater rafting adventures and leisurely floats from their headquarters deep in the country, on the banks of the Pigeon River a mile down Hartford Rd. from Exit 447 off I-40, on the Tennessee side of the state line. They maintain a location in Gatlinburg as well, on the east side of town on US 321.

✍ **USA Raft** (800-872-7238 or 423-487-4303; www.usaraft.com/pigeoninfo.htm), 3630 Hartford Rd., Hartford, TN. This West Virginia rafting company maintains an outpost on the Pigeon River in the Hartford community, just off I-40's Exit 447, just beyond the TN–NC state line. They offer guided adventure rafting on the Class II–IV rapids of one section of the Pigeon, and family rafting (for children over five) on another section of the same river.

✳ Lodging

BACKPACKERS' CABINS **Mount LeConte Lodge** (865-429-5704). Mid-Mar.–mid-Nov. Deep within the national park's backcountry and accessible only by hikers, Mount LeConte Lodge sits just shy of the 6,593-foot peak of Mount LeConte. This collection of log buildings and primitive cabins is surrounded by old balsam forests, with only a short walk to wide sunset and sunrise views off clifftops. Hikers stay in bunk beds (linens and blankets supplied) in tiny board-and-batten cabins, heated by kerosene and lighted by oil lamps; there's no electricity or running water at LeConte Lodge. Meals, served in the rustic lodge and included in the price, are plain and hearty—not surprising, as the food has to be packed in by llama. On any given day it's the coolest place to stay in the South—typically 20° cooler than nearby Knoxville. It's also one of the rainiest and foggiest (and no, they won't give you a rain check on your reservation). If the weather cooperates, however, you will experience the finest sunrises and sunsets anywhere in the South, from clifftops 1.25 miles above sea level. Reservations are required, and very hard to get. Try calling the first week in October for the following year.

COUNTRY INNS **Eight Gables Inn** (800-279-5716 or 865-430-3344; www .eightgables.com), 219 N. Mountain Trail, Gatlinburg, TN 37738. Open all year. Rated four diamonds by AAA, the Eight Gables Inn sits in forests on the northern edge of Gatlinburg, 2 miles from downtown and a short distance off a section of US 441 maintained as a scenic corridor. Built in the 1990s, the handsome, stylized exterior is reminiscent of a prosperous Victorian farmhouse, with wide porches (complete with rocking chairs, swings, and checkers), high windows, powder-blue clapboarding, and two gables on each side. Inside, a large common area occupies half or more of the first floor. Comfortable sofas and easy chairs group around the large windows and the two wood-burning fireplaces, and a pot of coffee sits on a sideboard by the stairwell. In the middle, an impressive hardwood staircase sweeps upward, then splits into three spurs under an octagonal dome to reach the eight upstairs rooms, each under its own gable. There are 16 rooms in all—eight upstairs, four downstairs, and four in an adjacent "cottage," a homelike annex that blends quietly into the woods. All rooms are comfortable and full sized, theme furnished with reproduction antiques. Breakfast is served promptly at 9, and consists of a main dish, sweet pastry, and fresh fruit, with orange juice. Guests typically gather before breakfast for coffee and a chat by the fire, or to read a morning paper on the wide veranda. In the evening, a homemade sweet and coffee offers another chance to socialize. At lunch (except Mon.) the breakfast area becomes an elegant luncheon spot, the Magnolia Tea Room (see *Eating Out*). Low season $89–149, high season $109–189, including breakfast and evening sweet.

Hippensteal's Mountain View Inn (800-527-8110 or 865-436-5761; www.hippensteal.com), P.O. Box 707, Gatlinburg, TN 37738. Open all year. Prominent Gatlinburg watercolorist Vern Hippensteal and his wife, Lisa, own and operate this modern luxury inn on a hilltop deep in the countryside east of town. Set on 25 acres, the three-story inn has one of the finest views in the area, a sweeping 180° panorama over dense forest toward the high wall of the Great Smoky Mountains. Even better, every single one of the 12 rooms has its own share of this view from a wide covered porch furnished with rockers. Purpose-built during the 1990s, the three-story inn and its two-story annex have an old country look about them, with covered porches on every floor, French doors, and floor-to-ceiling sash windows. The inn's ground floor is taken up by a large common area, with many sofas and easy chairs grouped around small tables and a large stone fireplace. A separate glass porch holds the elegant little dining area, with marble floors polished to a glassy finish. Rooms are large, furnished with antique reproductions around a gas log fireplace, with two-person Jacuzzi and separate shower. Each room is themed around one of Vern's watercolor prints of the Great Smoky Mountains; you'll also find Vern's prints on all the walls of the halls and common rooms. A hearty full breakfast is served between 8 and 10. $149 for in-season and winter weekends, $95 for winter weekdays, including breakfast.

Blue Mountain Mist Country Inn (800-497-2335 or 865-428-2335; fax 865-453-1720; www.bluemountain mist.com), 1811 Pullen Rd., Sevierville, TN 37862. Open all year. Built as a country inn in 1987, this AAA three-diamond B&B looks like a turreted Victorian farmhouse, powder blue and surrounded by wide porches. Located in the hills above Pigeon Forge on the innkeepers' 60-acre family farm, its hilltop vantage point

offers wide views toward the Great Smoky Mountains 7 miles away. The 12 rooms are ample in size and elegantly furnished with antiques and heirloom quilts. Five simple clapboard cabins are luxuriously furnished, and include Jacuzzi and kitchenette. All rooms and cabins include a full breakfast and evening dessert. $115–145 for inn rooms, $135–159 for cottages.

Hilton's Bluff B&B Inn (800-441-4188 or 865-428-9765; fax 865-428-8997; www.hiltonsbluff.com), 2654 Valley Heights Dr., Pigeon Forge, TN 37863. Open all year. A modern cedar-sided building conveniently located just outside Pigeon Forge (on a dead-end residential road off US 321), Hilton's Bluff has 10 nicely decorated, country-themed rooms. Each has its own door to a balcony or deck, and half have two-person Jacuzzi. Common areas, all brightly lighted and carefully decorated, include a den with a fireplace and a recreation room with bumper pool and darts as well as table games. The cedar-clapboard building, in a plain modern style, is amply supplied with decks, porches, and balconies; it sits on a well-landscaped property surrounded by forests on all sides. $79–129, including full breakfast.

COUNTRY RESORTS The Buckhorn Inn (865-436-4668; fax 865-436-5009; www.buckhorninn.com), 2140 Tudor Mountain Rd., Gatlinburg, TN 37738. Open all year. Located in the beautiful, rural Glades area east of Gatlinburg, within the Arts and Crafts Community, this historic inn offers an elegant and gracious experience at an old-fashioned 1930s resort. Set in the midst of its own 25 private acres, the inn is surrounded by meadows and woodlands carefully set out by its original founder. From the approach road the inn appears as a simple, modest white-painted wood structure; it turns its more elegant side to the Smokies, with a lovely view over wildflower meadows and hemlock forests to the peak of Mount LeConte. With no TV or radio in the historic main structure, the Buckhorn Inn appeals to those who want quiet and meditation. The grounds encourage this with profuse wildflowers, a fishpond, and a labyrinth. Inside, a large common room and dining room occupy much of the ground floor, with sofas and easy chairs facing a fire. The six inn rooms are theme decorated with English country antiques and reproductions, and range in size from comfortable to large; the least expensive room is a charming two-level retrofit on the inn's old central tower (which held a water tank during the 1930s). Attached to the old inn is a new annex with three new luxury suites—each with its own sitting area, gas log fireplace, and Jacuzzi—and a large new common area. Down from the main inn are seven kitchenette cottages in a 1930s style, with porches, decks, and wide picture windows overlooking the meadows. Breakfasts are hearty and fresh, with a choice of four items from a menu that changes daily. Dinners are also served daily, but are not included in the price (see *Dining Out*) Inn rooms $115–130, cottages $130–150, guest houses $200–250 for up to four adults, including breakfast.

Christopher Place, An Intimate Resort (800-595-9441 or 423-623-6555; fax 423-613-4771; www .christopherplace.com), 1500 Pinnacles Way, Newport, TN 37821. With a four-diamond AAA rating, this luxury retreat sits on a remote site north of Cosby on English Mountain. A modern structure purpose-built as a deluxe country inn, Christopher Place looks for all the world like a colonial mansion, perched high above the valley and surrounded by meadows with wide views. It has more amenities than other country inns, with a pool table, heated outdoor pool, tennis, fitness room, sauna, on-site trails, and llama trekking. Most rooms are large, with private sitting areas; all are elegantly furnished, and all have some special feature. The restaurant serves a hearty breakfast and offers an elegant table d'hôte evening meal for $25 (available to the public with a 24-hour reservation). $150–300.

BED & BREAKFAST INNS **Berry Springs Lodge** (888-760-8297 or 865-908-7935; fax 865-428-2814; www.berrysprings.com), 2149 Seaton Springs Rd., Sevierville, TN 37862. Open all year. A farmhouse-style lodge built in 2000, this nine-room B&B is located deep in the hills above Pigeon Forge. Quiet and remote, its hilltop location offers spectacular views over the foothills toward the Great Smoky Mountains, 7 miles to the south. The rooms are handsomely theme furnished with reproduction antiques; each has a fireplace and a private door to either a deck, porch, or balcony with a view. A large common area is comfortably furnished with plush sofas and chairs—a great place to read a book by the fire. $89–169, including full breakfast.

7th Heaven Log Inn (800-248-2923 or 865-430-5000), 3944 Castle Rd.,

Gatlinburg, TN 37738. This modern log home with five guest rooms faces the seventh green of the Bent Creek Golf Resort, 10 miles east of Gatlinburg in Pitman Center. Four log-walled rooms on the first floor face the green and share a common recreation room with a pool table and kitchenette. The fifth room, larger than the others, has a Jacuzzi and its own private entrance and porch, with views over the golf course to the Smokies. A full breakfast and evening dessert is included in the tariff. $87–137.

Morley House Bed and Breakfast (800-299-8389 or 865-430-3399; www.innsnorthamerica.com/tn/Morley House.htm), 4559 Powdermill Estates Rd., Gatlinburg, TN 37738. Open all year. This large private house, recently built in a traditional country style, sits on 5 wooded acres just north of the Glades Crafts Community. Two guest rooms are each elegantly furnished with reproduction antiques; each has queen bed, private bath with Jacuzzi tub, and private entrance. The price includes a full homemade breakfast and evening dessert. $79–99.

Chilhowee Bluff Bed and Breakfast (888-559-0321 or 865-908-0321; fax 865-774-3308; www.chilhowee bluff.com/index.html), 1887 Bluff Mountain Rd., Sevierville, TN 37876. This modern four-room B&B sits in the Bluff Mountain area above Pigeon Forge, a steep, rock-bound mountain on the outward edge of the Smokies, 7 miles from the national park. All of the four rooms are beautifully decorated with country- style antique reproductions, and three of them are extra large—sitting area with plush furniture around a fireplace, two-person whirlpool tub, the works. Breakfasts are large and luxurious. Standard

room $85–99, suites with sitting areas and Jacuzzis $125–159.

Gremmy's Garden (888-592-9518 or 865-908-2709; fax 865-774-1994), 724 Sharp Rd., Sevierville, TN 37876. This French-country-style house isn't near much of anything but lots of beautiful countryside; it's well out into the low mountains of Harrisburg, east of Sevierville. Beautiful, wide views, and immaculate accommodations in four rooms in the main house, plus two full "mother- in-law" apartments. Elegant country-style furnishings are found throughout the commons and rooms. Amenities include walking trails, screened gazebo, hot tub, and recreation room with pool table. House rules prohibit smoking and alcohol. $99–129 for standard rooms, $139–149 for suites with kitchens, including breakfast and dessert.

MOTELS Gatlinburg, TN, has several thousand motel rooms, and nearby Pigeon Forge, TN, has several thousand more. Gatlinburg tends more toward independent motels, set tightly on small pieces of property, frequently with unusual architectural flourishes. Pigeon Forge units are more interstate style—chain motels, of standard construction, surrounded by large parking lots and fronting on a six-lane highway. Some of the more interesting-looking Gatlinburg motels sit along the river, a block below downtown. Contact the chamber of commerce (see *Guidance*) for more information.

✳ Where to Eat

EATING OUT **The Magnolia Tea Room** (800-279-5716 or 865-430-3344; www.magnoliatearoom.com), 219 N. Mountain Trail, Gatlinburg, TN. The large, brightly lit dining area of the Eight Gables Inn serves as the venue for this informal luncheon spot. Built in the style of a Victorian farmhouse, its large windows and French doors open onto a wide wraparound porch with rockers and swings. The menu concentrates on simple, well-prepared foods—soups, salads, sandwiches, a special, and dessert—all made to order from fresh ingredients. An easy walk from the trolley terminal at the Gatlinburg Visitors Center, the Magnolia Tea Room is a calm and quiet respite from downtown's noise and crowds.

Smoky Mountain Brewery and Restaurant (865-436-4200; www .smoky-mtn-brewery.com), 1004 Parkway, Gatlinburg, TN 37738. Lunch and dinner. This tavern and pizzeria has its own on-premise microbrewery, the only one in Gatlinburg. A two-story eatery toward the back of the Calhoun Village retail area, it is decorated in rough wood and 1950s-style furniture and flooring. The atmosphere is neat and the food is great, but the real story is the beer. If you have any taste for beer, you will want to try their fresh brews, with a selection of five regular beers that the brewmaster continues to refine and adjust: a Czech-style pilsner, a mellow German-style black porter, an American-style (only good) light lager, an Irish-style red ale, and a mild English-style brown ale. The food is made with the same attention to detail, with original twists on old favorites. The pizza is excellent, and the sandwiches are made with bread baked fresh on the premises. Next door, **Calhouns** is run by the same people and presumably has the same high-quality food; it is more of a sit-down restaurant, with

ribs and steaks dominating the menu. Sandwiches and salads $6–8, dinners $10–15.

The Fox and Parrot Tavern (865-436-0677), 1065 Glades Rd., Gatlinburg, TN. Gatlinburg's best place for a friendly meal won't be found among the tourist-crowded downtown shops; instead, it sits above photographer Brian Papsworth's first-rate gallery in the Glades Arts and Crafts Community. Brian's Fox and Parrot Tavern re-creates the atmosphere and spirit of a great village local in the heart of England. It's a place where locals and visitors meet and talk over a game of darts while enjoying a locally brewed ale and a freshly prepared bar meal. Every item on the menu is made from scratch on the premises. A dozen items are traditional British pub fare, with a savory twist for spice-loving American tastes—meat pies, bangers, ploughman's lunch, and corned beef top the list. A dozen or more American bar favorites are made as well, including a really good chili. Desserts are first-rate, including an amazing Eccles cake, a Scots pastry filled with rum-soaked raisins. Draft ales include imports and local brews from nearby towns, while the lengthy bottles list is filled with imports and microbrews; standard American beers are unavailable. Ale lovers should note that Brian tries to stock a cask-conditioned ale on a hand pump during the season. Meals $5–6.50, desserts $2.50–3.00; beer runs from $3 for a 12-ounce bottle to $5 for a 20-ounce draft.

DINING OUT The Buckhorn Inn (865-436-4668; fax 865-436-5009; www.buckhorninn.com), 2140 Tudor

Mountain Rd., Gatlinburg, TN. Open all year. Gatlinburg's historic resort inn offers an elegant yet friendly dining experience. The Buckhorn offers only one seating for the small number of tables in its 1938 main lodge, so that service is attentive and food is prepared specifically for each table. The lodge furnishes an intimate atmosphere, with sofas grouped around a large hearth, encouraging conversation. All diners are seated at one time and presented with five courses of a fixed menu; reservations are required, because preparation starts long before the seating time. The imaginative and exquisitely prepared food varies daily, but tends to combine familiar favorites in new and exciting ways. Located in a dry area of the county, the Buckhorn has no wine list, but welcomes you to bring your own and charges nothing for corkage. $25 per person; reservations required.

✳ Selective Shopping

Downtown Gatlinburg, TN

"We don't want to be noticed as T-shirt City, USA," the mayor of Gatlinburg once told a reporter, but "evidently it's easier to make a dollar selling T-shirts than anything else." Yes, downtown Gatlinburg has a lot of T-shirt shops. However, there are a lot of other shops as well: old-timey photographs, tattoo parlors, NASCAR memorabilia, wedding chapels, souvenir stores, fudge shops, funnel cakes, gaudy jewelry, four different Thomas Kincade stores (the California-based "painter of light"), museums of the curious and weird (filling the role of sideshows), amusement arcades, even carnival rides. It's easy enough to sneer at this "rundown, haphazard collection of buildings

ranging from the good to the bad to the ugly," as did the Sonoran Institute in a report funded by the Gatlinburg Chamber of Commerce; "Gatlinburg is widely viewed as one of the most unattractive and inappro-priate gateways to a national park in the United States," the institute sniffed. But it's also easy to relax and have fun at this giant unofficial permanent state fair. Message to the Sonoran Institute: Grab a funnel cake, guys, and chill.

This book finds four downtown sites particularly worth visiting. In this section you'll find Arrowcraft, a craft shop older than the downtown that surrounds it, and Beneath the Smoke, Ken Jenkins's wonderful combination of nature shop and photographic art gallery. Elsewhere are listings for the lovely Arrowmont School (see *To See*) and the fascinating cable lift to Ober Gatlinburg (see *To Do*), with its sweeping panoramic views.

Arrowcraft (865-436-4604; fax 865-430-4440; www.southernhighland guild.org/arrowcraft.html), 576 Parkway. Off-season, daily 10–6; summer and fall, Mon.–Sat. 10–8, Sun. 10–6. The Arrowcraft crafters gallery predates the downtown area that crowds around it on all sides; this wandering log building has been selling fine crafts by local artists since 1926. Originally part of the adjacent Arrowmont School of Arts and Crafts, it is now run by the not-for-profit Southern Highland Craft Guild and features only items handmade by SHCG artists.

Beneath the Smoke (888-818-2262 or 865-436-3460; www.kenjenkins .com), 446 E. Parkway, Suite 12. Beneath the Smoke is Gatlinburg nature photographer Ken Jenkins's homage to the Great Smoky Mountains, an 8,000-square-foot nature store, outfitter, bookshop, and gallery of Ken's stunning wildlife and scenic photography.

The Glades Arts and Crafts Community, TN

Out of the 70 or more craft artists who are members of the Arts and Crafts Community in Gatlinburg's scenic, rural Glades neighborhood, it's impossible to select only three or four "best" or "most worthy." The listings that follow are more in the line of appetite whetters than anything else. Poke around and choose your own favorites.

The Historic Cliff Dwellers (865-436-6921), 668 Glades Rd. Constructed in 1933 as an art gallery and studio, for decades this distinctive, multigabled wood structure served as a landmark in downtown Gatlinburg. When threatened with demolition in 1995, artists Chris and Jim Gray moved it to its present site at the heart of the Glades Community. Now the historic structure houses a fine-craft cooperative, showcasing the works of its eight member artists. These include spinning, weaving, pottery glass, decorative paper, watercolor, doll and basket making, and stuffed animals.

Next door is owner Jim Gray's studio and gallery, **Church Mouse Gallery** (865-430-3735; www.jimgraygallery .com). Daily 10–5. A watercolorist and sculptor, Gray creates a wide range of landscapes, portraits, and florals—by no means all of the Smokies, although Smoky Mountain scenes predominate. The detail and colors of his watercolors are remarkable, as are the liveliness and sympathy of his sculpture—which include the statue of Dolly Parton in front of the Sevier County Courthouse.

Gatlinburg Ceramics (865-436-4315). Judy Baily has been handcrafting fine porcelains in her Glades studio-gallery for 30 years, taking each piece painstakingly from raw kaolin to finished ceramic. The bulk of her work is in a traditional, even Victorian, in style, but her range is wide. She is frequently in her studio, visible from the showroom, and welcomes visitors.

Ogle's Broom Shop (800-443-4575 or 865-430-4402). One of the original craft studio-galleries in the Glades, David Ogle is a third-generation mountain crafter, native to Gatlinburg. He produces a variety of traditional mountain brooms, walking sticks with carved handles, wooden toys, doll furniture, and carved birds.

G. Webb Gallery (865-436-3639; www.gwebbgallery.com), 2160 Tudor Mountain Rd. Watercolorist G. Webb specializes in highly detailed studies of local landscapes; recent works include the Temple Feed Store in Sevierville and the Emerts Cove Bridge near his home. His Glades Community gallery occupies a restored 1910 board-and-batten farmhouse surrounded by wildflower gardens and giant hemlocks.

✳ Special Events

SPRING **Annual Spring Smoky Mountain Wildflower Pilgrimage** (865-436-7318; www.wildflower pilgrimage.org), 115 Park Headquarters Rd., Gatlinburg, TN. Last week in Apr. For over half a century, a group of East Tennessee organizations has sponsored this weeklong exploration of the national park's spring wildflowers. There are exhibits and vendors at the Gatlinburg Convention Center, but the real action takes place in a long series of field trips into the park—by foot, bicycle, and automobile. Wildflower walks predominate, but there are daily field trips for birders, and specialized trips for geology, plant identification, medicinal plants, moss, algae, fungi, insects, spiders, salamanders, bats, bears, old-growth forests, second-growth forests, logging, history, folk art, plant sketching, photography, and environmental issues. $10 adults, children under 12 free; other fees may apply.

The Cosby Ramp Festival. Since 1954, Cosby, TN, has celebrated that pungent herald of spring, the ramp. A ramp is a type of wild onion also known as a wild leek. It has a sweet, mild taste with a hint of garlic, but is notorious for the strong odor it leaves behind. One of the first plants to emerge in spring, the ramp has traditionally been a center of community celebration in the mountains—typically a ramp supper given by the volunteer fire department. The Cosby Festival is unusual in being a big shindig thrown for tourists as much as locals, with a full slate of mountain and bluegrass music.

Gatlinburg Scottish Festival and Games (800-568-4748), Gatlinburg, TN. Third weekend in May. This traditional Scottish festival includes bagpipes, drums, Highlands dancers, sheepdog demonstrations, entertainment, clan tents, and Scottish food (yum!), in addition to Scottish games. It's held in Mills Park, a largish city park near the Glades Crafts Community.

SUMMER **Fourth of July celebrations**. Gatlinburg, TN's July 4 celebrations start promptly at midnight, with a night parade through downtown that includes marching bands, lighted floats, and helium balloons. During the day there's a "River Raft Regatta" in which unmanned craft race down the river in the middle of town.

WINTER **Winterfest Kickoff**. Nov. 14. Gatlinburg, TN, starts its season of winter illumination—light displays that continue through Christmas to Valentine's—with a festival at the Ripley's Aquarium featuring a chili cook-off, live music, clowns, and magicians, as well as trolley tours of the lights. Christmas hayrides start 2 weeks later and continue through most of December.

New Year's Eve Space Needle Spectacular. A New Year's street party centers on downtown Gatlinburg, TN's Space Needle attraction, with a ball drop and a stunning display of fireworks launched from the 340-foot observation tower.

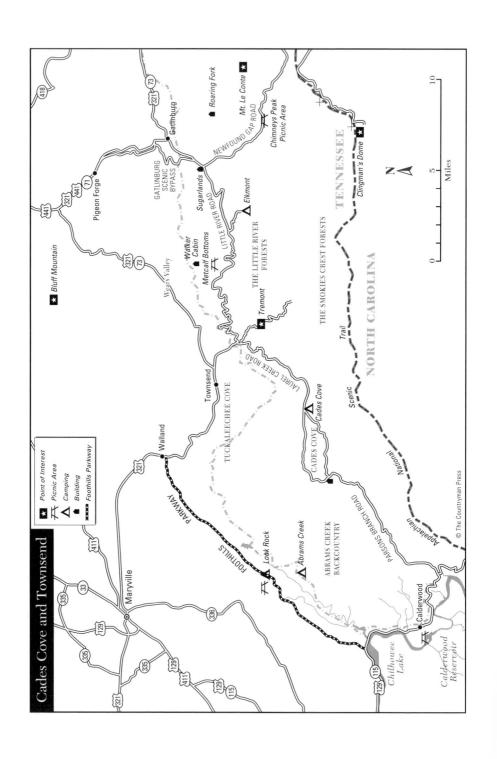

Cades Cove and Townsend

Point of Interest ★
Picnic Area ♿
Camping ⛺
Building ▪
Foothills Parkway ▪▪▪▪

★ Bluff Mountain

TENNESSEE

NORTH CAROLINA

418

321

73

Gatlinburg

321 441 71

Pigeon Forge

441

321

73

Wears Valley

GATLINBURG
SCENIC
BYPASS

Walker
Cabin ♿
Metcalf Bottoms

LITTLE RIVER ROAD

Sugarlands ▪

♿ Elkmont

★ Roaring Fork

NEWFOUND GAP ROAD

Mt. Le Conte ★

Chimneys Peak
Picnic Area

THE LITTLE RIVER
FORESTS

★ Tremont

LAUREL CREEK ROAD

Townsend ▪

TUCKALEECHEE COVE

THE SMOKIES CREST FORESTS

Clingman's Dome ★

Walland ♿

411

321

Maryville ◎

33

335

129

336

335

336 129

411 129

321 115

FOOTHILLS

PARKWAY

♿ Look Rock

⛺ Abrams Creek

ABRAMS CREEK
BACKCOUNTRY

⛺ CADES COVE
Cades Cove

PARSONS BRANCH ROAD

Scenic

Trail

Appalachian

Calderwood ▪

129 115

Chilhowee
Lake

♿

Calderwood Reservoir

© The Countryman Press

N

0 5 10
Miles

TOWNSEND, CADES COVE &
THE NORTHWEST QUADRANT

This quadrant of the Great Smoky Mountains National Park contains one of the most beautiful and rewarding sites in the eastern United States—the remarkable Cades Cove, a large flat-bottomed valley covered in pastureland, dotted with log cabins, and surrounded on all sides by great mountain walls. The National Park Service maintains this huge valley, 5 miles long and nearly 2 miles wide, as a 3,000-acre outdoor museum of pioneer life, with 12 major structures and many more outbuildings. An 11-mile-long, one-way loop road skirts the cove's edge, giving wide views and easy access to all its sites.

The drive to the cove tells another story. The twisting paved road follows the bed of a historic logging tramway along a roaring mountain stream—as do most of the roads in this part of the park, the former lands of the Little River Lumber Company. The handsome young hardwood forests you see in these parts have grown since the NPS gained control of the stripped-out land in 1940. Two old lumber camps, at Elkmont and Tremont, offer recreation opportunities, while the scattered remnants of the Little Greenbrier farming community survive in a little-visited corner of the woods.

Outside the park, another large cove straddles the main highway (US 321). Tuckaleechee Cove furnishes a scenic mountain setting for a variety of B&B inns, resorts, cabin rentals, cafés, and restaurants. It also contains the main settlement of Townsend, TN, a former logging town where restaurants, shops, and motels spread along the four-lane highway. It has a visitors center in a new log building in the center of town—a good place to get oriented. Townsend is a lot less trafficked and more mountainy than the Gatlinburg–Pigeon Forge area, for those who prefer a more personal, homelike experience and are willing to do without chain restaurants.

GUIDANCE & ↑ **Smoky Mountain Convention and Visitors Bureau** (800-525-6834 or 865-448-6134; www.smokymountains.org), 7906 E. Lamar Alexander Parkway, Townsend, TN 37882. Normal business hours, every day. This nonprofit organization, dedicated to promoting economic growth and tourism in the Blount County area of the Smokies, maintains a visitors center in a modern log building in Townsend, including a good gift shop and displays of local artists, as well as a staffed information desk. Free.

Great Smoky Mountains National Park ranger stations. The National Park Service maintains a ranger station at Cades Cove with a staffed information desk. You'll find it off to the left as you enter the cove, in the main recreation area across from the camp store. For general phone inquiries, it's best to call the Sugarlands Visitors Center (see "Gatlinburg").

Cades Cove Web Page (www.nps.gov/grsm/cchome.htm). Maintained by the National Park Service, this web page gives a good overview of the cove.

GETTING THERE *By car*: Townsend, TN, is on **US 321** between Maryville and Gatlinburg, TN. If you're approaching from the south or west, take the interstate to Knoxville, TN, then take I-140 and US 129 to Maryville; Townsend is another 20 miles via US 321. From the north or east, follow I-40/81 to TN 66 (Exit 406), northeast of Knoxville. Take TN 66 to Sevierville, then follow US 441 south until US 321 branches off right at Pigeon Forge; Townsend is 15 miles farther on.

By air: **McGhee Tyson Airport** (865-970-2773; fax 865-970-4113; www.tyson .org), 2055 Alcoa Hwy., Alcoa, TN, serving the Knoxville area, is about 20 miles from Townsend, TN. It's large enough to have all the major car rental agencies on site, which is just as well; there is no bus service into Townsend.

By bus, train, or public transportation: The Townsend, TN, area has no railroad, no bus service, and no public transportation.

MEDICAL EMERGENCIES **Blount Memorial Hospital** (865-983-7211), 907 E. Lamar Alexander Parkway, Maryville, TN. Located 20 miles west of Townsend on US 321, this 250-bed regional hospital serves all of Blount County from the county seat of Maryville. It has 24-hour emergency facilities.

Blount Health Clinic (865-983-0093), 1503 E. Lamar Alexander Parkway, Maryville, TN. Mon.–Fri. 5–10 PM, Sat. 10 AM–6 PM, Sun. noon–6 PM. This is an after-hours walk-in clinic near Blount Memorial Hospital, 20 miles west of Townsend on US 321.

Park Med (865-977-1455), 117 Gill St., Alcoa, TN. Mon.–Fri. 8–5, Sat. 8–1:30, Sun. 12:30–3. This is a walk-in clinic located just beyond downtown Maryville on TN 35, then three blocks left on Gill St. It keeps regular business hours on weekdays, and shortened hours on weekends.

✳ Wandering Around

EXPLORING BY CAR **Driving the Little River Railroad**. To the east of Cades Cove, 23 miles of park roads follow the railroad beds of the Little River Lumber Company. By the time this company finished logging in 1940, they had laid over 400 miles of railbed, mostly to dead ends in the valleys they were logging. These abandoned railbeds form many of the hiking trails and nearly all of the roads in this part of the park.

Starting at the **Cades Cove Picnic Area**, this drive follows Laurel Creek Rd. out of the cove toward Townsend, TN. Just beyond the Schoolhouse Gap

Trailhead the highway takes to the old logging railbed, acquiring its even gradients and sharp curves. Frequently the road becomes a narrow shelf cut into the mountain slope, with the stream racing along on one side and a vertical rock face on the other. You'll pass a tunnel and a waterfall, then the side road to Tremont, before you reach the fork to Townsend (1 mile left) at a great swimming hole with a sandy beach. From there, the old railbed goes right, following the Little River upstream. Now the road/railbed winds sharply while hugging this full-volume, cascading river. Views over the river are continuous for miles, with many opportunities to fish, wade, or admire the scenery. At **The Sinks** (parking right, over the stone bridge) there's a clifftop view of a stone bridge framed by two large waterfalls. A few miles farther down the road you will reach the **Metcalf Bottoms Picnic Grounds** and a side road leading to the historic **Little Greenbrier Community** and **Wear Cove**. When you reach the side road to **Elkmont**, take it; you will still be following the old railbed. Abandoned buildings and a security fence mark the start of the old lumber camp, then a long straight stretch of road follows Elkmont's railroad siding. The paved road ends at the parking area for the **Little River Trail**, which continues to follow the railbed upstream. A gravel road, right, leads to the **Elkmont National Historic District**, an early-20th-century vacation settlement.

The foothills of Cades Cove. The Foothills Parkway, part of the National Park Service's scenic highway system since the 1930s, has only two short completed segments. This scenic drive follows the longer of the two segments, Chilhowee (*kill-HOW-ee*) Mountain, for 17 miles, using historic old roads to make a loop trip.

To start this scenic drive, go through Cades Cove to the **Cable Mill site**, then take Forge Creek Rd. through young forests growing up on abandoned fields. In 2 miles Parsons Branch Rd. forks right. This is one of the earlier pioneer roads out of the cove, and the only motorable road that preserves the look and feel of a 19th-century turnpike—9 miles of twisting, steep, one-lane, one-way gravel road. It climbs in and out of small mountainside defiles as it rises; forests near the streams have giant hardwoods and hemlocks, while forests on the dry ridgelines have small pines and oaks. You'll reach the first of many fords at 2.7 miles; these fords consist of a concrete ramp into, then out of, a small stream. The road tops at **Sams Gap** (2,780 feet), then drops into a steep defile so narrow that it's forced into a dozen fords before it ends at a historic 20th-century road—US 129.

US 129 is a relict of the 1930s Works Projects Administration; built for a Depression era when cars were few and slow, it is so curvy that motorcyclists use it for rallies. Turn right. US 129 spends the next 5 miles twisting under giant power lines that lead from Alcoa hydropower lakes upstream (see "Robbinsville & Tellico Plains"). Views climax as the highway occupies an entire ridgetop, and the **Little Tennessee River** twists through a deep canyon below. Just beyond is the turnoff to the **Calderwood Power Station**. The highway finally descends to the banks of **Chilhowee Reservoir**, with 3 miles of wide and continuous views across the lakes. Turn right onto the Foothills Parkway.

Wide shouldered, straight, and easy, the parkway curves gently up Chilhowee Mountain to its dry, sandstone ridgeline. Once there, you'll get the first of many

LOOKING SOUTH OVER THE COVE TOWARD THE METHODIST CHURCH.　Jim Hargan

CADES COVE LOOP ROAD

The 11-mile, one-way Cades Cove Loop Rd. furnishes a scenic ramble through the national park's most historic and beautiful corner. Meandering through forests and fields, with sweeping views toward the Smoky Mountains, this lane passes 10 separate historic sites, each one preserving one or more pioneer-era structures from the cove's past.

To reach the start of the Cades Cove Loop Rd., enter the park at **Townsend**, TN, and follow the signs 7.3 miles to Cades Cove. The loop road

sweeping views east toward the high crest of the Great Smoky Mountains National Park. Along this stretch, the **Look Rock Recreation Area** offers picnicking and 360° views from an observation tower. From there the Foothills Parkway goes more than 3 miles without a view, then makes up for it with a westward view over the flat Tennessee Valley—a great sunset location. The parkway ends a few miles later, 7 miles from Townsend on US 321.

EXPLORING ON FOOT 🐾 ✐ **Tremont Logging Camp walk**. The Little River Lumber Company did its best to jam a full-gauge railroad into every stream valley between Elkmont and Cades Cove, TN. Eighty years later these old lumber begins with views over horse pastures to the crest of the Smokies, then wanders through forests and meadows for more than a mile to the **John Oliver Place**, a handsome log cabin set back a quarter mile from the road, visible over wide meadows.

Another 2 miles of winding through forests takes you to (or near) three of the cove's four 19th-century churches, including the lovely little **Methodist Church** set splendidly in wide meadows to the right of the road. From there the loop road passes through broad hay fields for more than 2 miles, giving some of the widest views from any paved road in the national park. Two miles into the hay-field stretch, a split-rail fence on the right frames views over wildflower meadows toward a large farmstead—the **Cable Mill area**, for many the high point of the loop with its visitors center, working water mill, restored farmhouse, cantilevered barn, collection of pioneer farm tools, and craft demonstrations. Another good reason to stop: Cable Mill has the only toilets on the loop road.

From Cable Mill, the loop road runs through forests, passing the **Cades Cove Nature Trail** on the right, to the **Dan Lawson Place**, a log cabin behind split-rail fences. Half a mile farther on sits the elaborate **Tipton Place**, with its impressive cantilevered barn. The final cabin on the loop, the modest **Carter Shields Cabin**, is 0.85 mile beyond, in an open glade rich in spring dogwoods. The loop road reaches its end 2 miles later, after passing through young, open forests with meadow views.

A final word of warning: Loop road traffic can be very bad. It's one lane wide with no passing, so you'll go no faster than the slowest car on the loop. On a weekend the loop road can become a parking lot, with traffic inching forward slower than a walking pace. There's a great alternative, though: On Wednesday and Saturday mornings (until 10 AM) the loop road is open to bicyclists and walkers only.

railroads can make for some great walking, combining wide, even paths and easy gradients with stunning streamside views. This quiet stroll follows one such path, starting from the old logging settlement of Tremont and going up the railroad grade used to log out Lynn Camp Prong.

You'll find the trailhead, with ample parking, at the end of the Tremont Rd., at the old town site. Constructed in 1925, **Tremont** operated for 8 years as the company stripped the upstream valleys bare of timber. Tremont had a hotel, general store, electrical generator, machine shop, doctor's office, and combination church/school/movie theater (known as the House of Salvation, Education, and Damnation)—now all gone. A brochure, available from a roadside kiosk at the end of the Tremont Rd.'s pavement, gives details of family life in the Tremont Camp as well as a map of the town.

A footbridge perches on old railroad piers in the center of the former town; a flat place beyond marks a siding and a fork in the railroad. Take the left grade up **Lynn Camp Prong**, a strong mountain torrent full of water in the driest weather, with many cascades in its narrow, steep valley. You'll immediately notice the coolness of this valley, and the fine smell of mountain water that hangs in its moist air. Straight young hardwoods and hemlocks shade the path and fill the valley on both sides. In a quarter mile the grade gives a clear view straight toward a 30-foot waterfall, where the stream slides down a great exposed dome of a rock. From here the grade gives lovely views of rapids, then another set of waterfalls, before reaching a set of still pools. For the next half mile the stream continues to furnish good views of small cascades, still pools, moss-covered boulders, and trees clinging to high bluffs. Then the valley becomes more U shaped, allowing the railroad to straighten and retreat from the more dramatic and difficult terrain to a flat valley floor. This is a good place to turn around.

Chestnut Top Trail. Cades Cove ranger Steven McCoy calls Chestnut Top Trail "the best wildflower walk in the Smokies, both for variety and sheer numbers." Located right outside Townsend, TN, this well-maintained footpath follows the ridgeline of Chestnut Top Lead just inside the national park boundary. You'll find the trailhead half a mile inside the park on the Townsend entrance road, at the large riverside parking lot. The trail starts by climbing the slope above the road, shaded by straight young hardwoods. Frequent limestone outcrops indicate the source of the lush wildflowers—rich limestone soil, similar to that of Cades Cove, supports a diverse ecosystem here.

As the path climbs away from the road, the trees become large and the forest more open. Hemlocks reach 2 feet in diameter and rhododendrons arch over the path as you reach a narrow but beautiful view over Townsend and the mountains beyond the park. Then the trail gains the ridgeline and leaves the tiny limestone cove, to enter a dry pine forest with a rocky outcrop floor and a rich pine smell. Continuing gently uphill, the path reaches a second gap, where trees cover a clifflike plummet on the left; listen for the river noise from this direction, as you have spent nearly a mile doubling back to a point 400 feet above the trail's beginning. As the trail continues up the ridgeline, the forest gradually yields to a dry ridgetop pine–oak forest, very sunny and dusty with a faint smell of dry rot on a hot day. When the trail levels and enters the fourth gap, you've gone 2 miles and climbed 800 feet; it's a good place to turn back. If you continue, the path will climb another 300 feet and lose it again before reaching the **Schoolhouse Gap Trail** in 2 more miles.

✳ Villages

Townsend, TN. Founded as a lumber mill town in 1901, Townsend sits on the first piece of flat land outside the national park boundaries, straddling the main road into this area of the park. This makes it the closest town to **Cades Cove**, and the closest collection of travel facilities (including food and gasoline) for the cove's 2 million annual visitors. Nevertheless, Townsend has always been dwarfed in popularity by Gatlinburg (23 miles east on US 321), and this has allowed it to retain much of the character of a quiet mountain cove. Today it consists of a scattered (but increasing) number of modest commercial buildings widely spread along a 2-mile stretch of four-lane US 321. It retains little of its past as a mill town apart from a worthwhile (and free) small museum at the mill site, and it lacks any real town center or historic structures. Views are good, though, and the town parallels the lovely Little River as it exits the Smokies. Townsend has only a scant few franchise motels and eateries, but

VALLEY MEADOWLANDS OUTSIDE TOWNSEND LOOK TOWARD THE SMOKY MOUNTAINS.

Jim Hargan

it does have a decent selection of craft shops, antiques shops, souvenir shops, and independent motels and restaurants. Traffic and parking pose few problems, even at the height of the season.

Wear's Valley (also known as Wear Cove), TN, is a wide rural valley just outside the park's boundary between Townsend and Gatlinburg. Although isolated by bad roads for many years, Wear's Valley started getting tourists when US 321 entered it in 1980. Since then it has become a popular spot for second-home subdivisions; its open views over rolling meadows are increasingly apt to include a large number of modern houses. A side road, Little Greenbrier Rd., leads 2 miles into the park, ending at Metcalf Bottoms.

✳ Wild Places

THE GREAT FORESTS **The forests of the Smoky Mountain Crest**. The Smokies Crest forms a giant half circle around the southern edge of Cades Cove. Lower here than at Gatlinburg, TN, the crest rises abruptly from the 1,940-foot **Deals Gap** at the park's southern edge to reach 4,700 feet at **Parsons Bald**— and then sticks at that elevation for most of its 12-mile arc around the cove. Although the Smokies formed a barrier here as well as elsewhere, it was a porous barrier, broken by a network of footpaths that allowed a low but steady commerce between the cove people and North Carolina. The cove folk would use these paths to bring their cattle up to graze in the great grassy balds that straddle the ridgeline. These balds, probably formed by the Cherokees and enlarged by the cove settlers, are some of the most varied and beautiful places in the park, with stunning views over the Smokies Crest and the infinitely receding ridges of North Carolina. Today's park trails retrace the old pioneer paths, ascending steadily through handsome young forests to the great mountaintop meadows above the cove at **Gregory Bald**, **Russell Bald**, and **Spence Bald**. Several of these paths make a challenging but doable all-day hike, with elevation gains between 2,000 and 3,000 feet and 6 to 12 miles of hiking one way.

The forests of the Little River. When the Tennessee National Park Commission started buying land for the Great Smoky Mountains National Park in 1925, the Little River Lumber Company owned the entire Little River drainage, some 77,000 acres. The company agreed to sell the land for a national park, but only if they could retain logging rights for 15 years. The commission agreed; after all, how many trees could they harvest in 15 years? The company attacked the slopes, stripping them of every tree they could sell before the deadline came and logging ended forever. They beat the deadline by a year, denuding the virgin forests of the Little River by 1939. Then they took up the last of the rails from the railbeds, disassembled the Townsend mill, and turned control of the wrecked Little River Basin over to the National Park Service. The logging company had purchased a huge tract of old-growth forest, removed every tree, left a destroyed land bereft of economic value—and sold it to the government for a 50 percent profit.

The forests you see today are a product of this clear-cut logging—a forest of young, straight hardwoods, mostly less than 70 years old. Hiking trails are more plentiful than you might expect, and many of these trails are remarkably easy and well built. Little wonder—they follow the gentle, even grades of logging railbeds, up the streams to end at the great mountainous wall of the Smokies Crest.

Lower Abrams Creek backcountry. The national park extends westward of Cades Cove to take in 60 square miles of rugged, little-visited backcounrty centered on the lower reaches of Abrams Creek. This is a jumbled region of low ridges, with elevations seldom reaching 3,000 feet—short, stubby, linear ridges, placed close together between parallel creeks. The entire backcountry is thickly forested, with dry pinelands on the ridges and rich mixed hardwoods and hemlocks along the creeks. Access is by foot and horse only, with three trails running across the lay of the land and many more occupying the linear streambeds. **Abrams Creek Trail**, the only well-used trail in the area, follows the gorge of Abrams Creek as it cuts through the middle of these ridges, while the beautiful old cove roads, **Cooper Rd.** and **Rabbit Creek Rd.**, allow easy and lonely walking through the backcountry's northern and southern marches. All three of these access trails start in Cades Cove and converge at the **Abrams Creek Ranger Station** at the western edge of the park in Happy Valley (best reached from Happy Valley Rd. at US 129 just east of the Foothills Parkway, then follow the signs). This ranger station has a fine little campground, a couple of picnic tables, and good fly-fishing access.

RECREATION AREAS Cades Cove Recreation Area. This large, tree-shaded recreation area sits at the beginning of the Cades Cove Loop Rd., a short distance down the paved road on your left. Its lovely streamside picnic area follows **Abrams Creek** as it flows into the cove from the mountains on its east. Just beyond is the large, wooded campground, the most popular in the park. Between the two is a recreation hall and camp store in a 1950s-style building, and a ranger station with an information desk; you can rent bicycles at the camp store. Across from the ranger station, a concessionaire-run stable offers trail rides.

Although the official picnic area is very nice indeed, serious picnickers will want to bring a blanket and enjoy the fine meadows on the cove floor. **Hyatt Lane** is a particularly good place to look for picnic spots, as is the stretch of loop road between the **Primitive Baptist Church** and the **Elijah Oliver Cabin**.

PICNIC AREAS **Metcalf Bottoms Picnic Area**. This large picnic area, 10 miles west of Townsend, TN, on the Little River Rd., occupies a long, flat-bottomed wide space on the otherwise twisty and cliff-sided **Little River Gorge**. Now covered in tall forest, this used to be a small, isolated farm and a whistle-stop on the Little River Railroad. Metcalf Bottoms nearly always has a large choice of tables along its long riverfront—a particularly calm and wadable stretch of the Little River. Little Greenbrier Rd. sneaks out behind this picnic area to the Little Greenbrier historic area, then out of the park to Wear's Valley.

Look Rock Picnic Area. This striking picnic area, about halfway along the Chilhowee (*kill-HOW-ee*) Mountain section of the Foothills Parkway, features a row of picnic tables along a rock precipice, the view only partially blocked by tree stubbornly growing in the rock cracks. This is a dramatic, breezy place for a warm summer's lunch. The nearby observation tower, built in the 1960s and given to casual vandalism, offers fine views west over the flat lands of Tennessee's Great Valley.

Calderwood Power Station Recreation Area. This remote, lovely recreation area off US 129 is owned by the Alcoa corporation and is open to the public daily 8–4. The Alcoa road goes south from the highway to a lakeside fork; the right fork follows the lake through grassy meadows, then swerves left onto a short causeway pier out into **Chilhowee Reservoir**. Here you'll find a few picnic tables and a portable toilet—and views, a full circle of views over the lake to the surrounding mountains, from this quiet and serene spot well out into the lake. Returning, be sure to take the left fork for three-quarters of a mile to admire Calderwood Power Station, a handsome industrial Gothic structure in red brick, built by Alcoa in 1928 and still used by them to help power their aluminum smelters in nearby Maryville, TN.

✷ To See

CADES COVE HISTORIC SITES **The John Oliver Place**. The first log cabin on the Cades Cove Loop Rd., the John Oliver Place may well be the most visually impressive. It sits a quarter mile off the paved road, clearly visible across a meadow, framed by a split-rail "worm" fence, set against a backdrop of hardwood forest and steep slopes. Like all cove log cabins, its logs are planked—hewn with flat fronts and backs—to prevent rot from entering along their rounded undersides. It works; the John Oliver Cabin has been standing for over 180 years. The cabin is built as a single log cube, one log in length, with logs that interlock with dovetail joints—the same type of joint still used in making good-quality cabinet drawers. The dovetail joints left large gaps between the logs, which the farmer chinked with mud mortar. Inside, the cabin is a single large room heated by a fireplace, with a second-story loft. The chimney is set outside the cabin against the gable end, and is made of local stone held with mud mortar. Southerners will see nothing unusual in this, but northerners might wonder about the heat loss from an outside chimney. The mountain people preferred it cool, particularly after a long day of cooking in the middle of summer. At night the sparse furniture would be moved out of the way; parents and girls would sleep downstairs, while the boys would sleep in the loft.

Primitive Baptist Church. Cades Cove's Primitive Baptist Church was organized in 1826; the surviving church building is an 1887 white frame structure a third of a mile down a gravel road. The Missionary Baptist Church (see below) is a short distance down the loop road.

Why two Baptist churches in such a small community? The Primitive Baptists were (and are) a deeply conservative and traditionalist group. They believed that every person should remain in the place given by God, and that missionary work was interfering with God's will for the heathen and a first step toward establishing a permanent, paid priesthood. In contrast, the upwardly mobile Missionary Baptists encouraged people to improve their position through business activity, had little fear of a permanent minister class, and funded missionaries. During the Civil War the Primitive Baptists were strongly pro-Union; God had created the Union, and to rebel against it was to rebel against God's will. Although the Primitive Baptist Church stopped meeting during the Civil War, its members resisted the Confederacy and formed a way station of the Underground Railroad that smuggled escaped Union prisoners to safety. For this they were targeted for assassination by Rebel marauders who would cross the border from North Carolina, receiving information from Rebel sympathizers in the cove. This viciously homicidal pattern repeated itself in isolated coves on both sides of the TN–NC border (see Shelton Laurel Backcountry Area in "Asheville's Rugged Hinterlands").

THE JOHN OLIVER PLACE.

Jim Hargan

Methodist Church. The current building is the prettiest of the cove's three churches, a beautifully proportioned 1902 white frame structure with a bell set in a small tin-roofed steeple. Built by a cove carpenter and blacksmith who later served as its minister, it replaced an old log church that the congregation had used since the 1820s. Like the other two surviving cove churches, it has a pioneer cemetery. Large meadows stretch uphill from it, a good place to ramble for views and wildflowers.

Missionary Baptist Church. The cove's Missionary Baptist Church was formed in 1839 by dissidents from the

Primitive Baptist Church. It, too, went inactive during the Civil War, its congregation split between Unionists and Rebels; it reorganized after the war without its Rebel families. The current white frame building dates to 1915, and served the congregation until it closed in 1944. Springtime visitors should look for the daffodils in the back of the church, planted by the cove's CCC troop in the 1930s to form the phrase "Co. 5427."

Elijah Oliver Place. The Elijah Oliver Place is a pleasant half-mile walk from the loop road. Elijah Oliver, a son of John Oliver, built this cabin after the Civil War. It's larger and more elaborate than his father's cabin, with an attached wing and a board-and-batten enclosure on the porch. It's interesting to note that Elijah used smaller logs than his paw had 40 years earlier; great trees had become harder to find in the cove. You'll find a number of interesting log outbuildings near the cabin, including a springhouse used to protect the cabin's water supply.

& **Cable Mill Historic Area and Visitors Center**. This complex of seven historic buildings occupies the site of the cove's mill, store, and most prosperous farm. When founded by John P. Cable in 1870 it had a gristmill and sawmill, both powered by a large overshot wheel that got its water down a long millrace from Mill Creek. The water mill is still in business, its overshot wheel turning its huge grist stones every weekend in season. The short walk along the millrace to the modest milldam is interesting and peaceful. The adjacent frame house, built from lumber sawed at the Cable Mill, was a store and boardinghouse run by "Aunt Becky" Cable from 1887 until her death in 1944, 10 years after becoming part of the national park. It's now furnished it like a late-19th-century cove boardinghouse. Nearby are all the outbuildings of a prosperous cove farm: a smokehouse, corncrib, barn, and sorghum mill. A large cantilevered barn houses a collection of farm wagons and implements. The cantilevered barn, a folk form unique to these mountains, uses two log cribs as a foundation for a large loft that's cantilevered out on all sides. Hay was stored in the large loft, stables created in the cribs, equipment kept dry under the overhang, and wagons pulled through the space between the cribs.

When you're scheduling your cove loop tour, be sure to check for craft demonstrations. These can include sorghum milling, blacksmithing, dyeing, and flint knapping, as well as milling corn. Every October the hay fields beside the Cable Farm are mowed with authentic 19th-century horse-drawn equipment.

Henry Whitehead Place. In the 1880s Matilda Gregory's husband deserted her and their son; in this emergency, her brothers quickly erected a crude log cabin for them. Then, a few years later, Matilda married Henry Whitehead, a widower with three daughters. Whitehead built them a fancy new cabin, attached to Matilda's tiny, crude one. The Whitehead Cabin is made of logs milled to 4 inches thick at the Cable sawmill, fitted snugly together, and covered with milled clapboards. It's the most sophisticated log cabin in the cove, and it's attached to the crudest. You'll find it three-quarters of a mile down Forge Creek Rd., a side road just beyond the Cable Mill entrance.

Dan Lawson Place. This well-built 1856 cabin is made of large hand-hewn logs fitted tightly together, with a frame extension added some years later. It has two log outbuildings, a granary and a smokehouse. Located at the intersection with Hyatt Lane, it is the most visible log cabin from the floor of the cove. Its split-rail fences provide space for wildflowers and a favored subject for photographs.

The Tipton Place. Col. "Hamp" Tipton, a Mexican War veteran who lived in nearby Tuckaleechee Cove, built this frame house in the early 1870s for his daughters, who taught school in Cades Cove. In the 1880s the Tiptons sold the house to a blacksmith, James McCaulley, who built a smithy that still stands behind the house. Quite a farmstead survives from McCaulley's era. In addition to the smithy, there's a smokehouse and woodshed in the front yard, and a corn-crib and cantilevered barn across the road.

The Carter Shields Cabin. Little is known of the history of this modest log cabin, set in a lovely glade 2 miles from the end of the loop road. It's named for George Washington "Carter" Shields, a wounded Civil War veteran, who lived in it with his wife 1911–1922.

OTHER HISTORIC SITES ✐ The **Little Greenbrier Community** is one of the least known and least visited historic sites in the national park. To find it, take Wear Gap Rd. from the middle of the Metcalf Bottoms Picnic Area (see *Picnic Areas*) half a mile to a gravel road on the right, then another half mile up this narrow gravel road to its end. You'll be parked by a one-room log schoolhouse. The schoolhouse started life as a church—hence the incongruous presence of a pioneer cemetery on the hill above it. The Greenbrier schoolhouse is still in use, being the site of special classes for the schoolchildren of Blount and Sevier Counties. With a bit of luck you'll find it open and class in session, with a full set of turn-of-the-20th-century texts and teaching aids. The teacher uses an old map

THE GREAT SMOKY MOUNTAINS SURROUND THE HISTORIC DAN LAWSON PLACE.

Jim Hargan

of Greenbrier Community that shows how these woods used to be filled with a network of cabins linked by paths and tracks.

One of those cabins still survives. Across the road from the cemetery a gated jeep track dives into the forest of young, handsome hardwoods. A lovely and nearly level walk, the track follows Little Brier Creek upstream for a mile, then goes right at a fork to cross the stream and continue a quarter mile to the **Walker Place**. This fine log cabin, set in a clearing with a springhouse and barn, was the home of the Walker sisters, who refused to move out of the park and continued to live in their family cabin until the 1960s. No other site in the park gives quite the feeling of remoteness, of quiet, and of simplicity as the Walker Place.

Elkmont National Historic District. In 1908 the first logging train climbed the Little River Gorge to the new lumber camp, Elkmont—then a typical company town, temporary but with a full range of services for the lumbermen and their families. However, the 18-mile rail journey up the Little River Gorge was so scenic, and Elkmont so cool and pleasant during the summer's heat, that tourists started coming up the rail line to stay at the modest little company hotel. By 1912 there were so many tourists coming to Elkmont that the company built a luxury hotel, the Wonderland, and subdivided a lovely nearby valley for vacation homes. These early-20th-century vacation developments, popular with Knoxville's powerful elite, easily survived the lumber camp's closure in 1926. In fact, they survived until 1992, an enclave of privilege inside the national park.

Why did the National Park Service allow the vacation homes of Knoxville's socialites to survive while they systematically demolished 6,600 farms, homes, and businesses? Many have jumped to the obvious conclusion—but the NPS maintains that no one received any special treatment. When the NPS condemned the privately held lands, they gave all the landowners the option of retaining a lifetime lease in exchange for giving up much of the purchase money. Mountain folk, who had to earn a living, took the money and left, while the Elkmont vacation home owners accepted the lease option. Then, in 1972, the Elkmont elite used their clout to gain a 20-year extension from Congress. Enraged, the NPS formally stated their intention of tearing down every structure in Elkmont as soon as they got control. By then, however, Elkmont was a National Historic District, with 69 of its structures on the National Register of Historic Places. This made the park's wholesale demolition plan illegal, and required independent review and approval for any substitute plan.

The NPS is still insisting on tearing down five dozen listed structures, and no outside agency will approve such wholesale historic destruction. The historic district has been in this bureaucratic limbo for more than a decade, while the National Park Service allows its buildings to deteriorate. Meanwhile, the cottage community is unfenced and open to anyone who wishes to see this bit of park history. To find it, continue down the Elkmont Rd. past the Little River Trailhead. Nearly all of the cottages have serious structural damage—so enjoy them from a safe distance, and respect the historic integrity of these listed structures.

MUSEUMS ✒ **The Little River Railroad and Lumber Company Museum** (865-448-2211), Townsend, TN (town center on Old Hwy. 73). Mon.–Sat. 10–2,

Sun. 2–6. Between 1902 and 1938 the Little River Lumber Company stripped over half a billion board feet of lumber from the Great Smoky Mountains and milled it in Townsend. This small local museum seeks to preserve the memory of the days when logging, not tourism, dominated the mountains of Tennessee. Headquartered in a historic railroad depot moved in from nearby Walland, this volunteer-run museum contains a first-rate collection of local logging artifacts. The artifacts are interesting in themselves, and are arranged intelligently to give a thorough and coherent picture of Smoky Mountain logging and the way of life it briefly created. If you're lucky, you'll be shown around by a volunteer such as Georgia Bradshaw, who can expand on the exhibits with tales from her own childhood in the lumber camps high in the mountains. Outside the museum sits one of the Little River Lumber Company's original Shay engines—an amazing sight with its huge geared wheels.

SPECIAL PLACES ✧ ⬆ **Tuckaleechee Caverns** (865-448-2274), 825 Cavern Rd., Townsend, TN. Follow the signs south from US 321, just east of Townsend. Apr.–Oct. 9–6; late Mar. and early Nov., 10–5; closed mid-Nov.–mid-Mar. The limestone-floored Dry Valley, just a mile east of Townsend, is home to one of the most dramatic show caves in the Southern Appalachians, Tuckaleechee Caverns. The 170-step descent (no disabled access) leads to a deep underground river, then follows it for half a mile. The 75-minute tour passes underground water-falls, rapids, and sandy beaches on a gently curving stretch of stream. Long stretches of the path appear to travel through a western-style canyon, with steep rock walls rising on all sides. Stalactites, stalagmites, and flowstone of all sorts decorate the cave walls. The path ends in one of the South's largest underground rooms open to the public, big enough to hold three football fields and containing a stalactite column five stories tall. Tuckaleechee Caverns is lighted with uncol-ored incandescent lamps—this cave doesn't need to be frilled up with colors. It's particularly dramatic in rainy weather, when its underground river rises and the waterfalls become lively. Because the path is not a loop, the total tour requires a mile's walk and 340 steps, so be prepared. $9 adults, $5 children 5–11, free for children under 5.

Bluff Mountain. Take US 321 three miles west of Pigeon Forge; go right on Walden Creek Rd. for 0.6 mile to Goose Gap Rd.; then go 0.6 mile up Goose Gap Rd. to turn left onto Bluff Mountain Rd. Any view aficionado will consider Bluff Mountain a real find. It's the last real mountain in the Smokies foothills—a steep, rocky, cliff-lined protrubance into the flatness of Tennessee's Great Valley. Bluff Mountain Rd., a narrow, steep, paved lane, leads to the very top of Bluff Mountain, with wide views from (you guessed it) high rocky bluffs. Nowhere else can you see how dramatically the Appalachians rise from the flatlands below, and how villages like Pigeon Forge are jammed into deep, narrow valleys. The views are at the very top of **Bluff Mountain Rd.** (4.3 miles from its start on Goose Gap Rd.), then left along the ridgetop on **Dupont Springs Rd.** You'll find two wonderful views along the 1.2 miles of this paved dead-end lane, then a third view a short walk through the gate at the end of the road—a panorama over the entire flatness of the Great Valley. On the way up, look for **Smoky**

Mountain Llama Treks, offering short treks up one of Bluff Mountain's high stream valleys.

✳ To Do

BICYCLING Faced with jammed auto traffic on Cades Cove Loop Rd., a large number of people prefer to bicycle around the 11-mile valley-bottom loop. In order to accommodate all these cyclists, the National Park Service closes the loop road to automobiles on Wednesday and Saturday until 10 AM during the summer season. Nor is the cove the only good place to cycle; the Smoky Mountain Visitors Bureau in Townsend, TN, has an excellent brochure giving detailed descriptions of eight back road jaunts throughout the area. You can rent bicycles from a concessionaire in the cove or from a shop in Townsend.

✔ **Cades Cove Bike Shop** (865-448-9034), Maryville, TN. Daily, Apr.–Oct. This national park concessionaire offers reasonable daylong rentals on sturdy, well-kept machines. They are located at the Cades Cove Camp Store at the start of the Cades Cove Loop Rd. $3.25 per hour, $16.25 per day.

✔ **Little River Village** (865-448-2241), 8533 TN 73, Townsend, TN. This bicycle rental operates from a large camp store in the middle of Townsend.

ENVIRONMENTAL PROGRAMS ✔ **The Great Smoky Mountains Institute at Tremont** (865-448-6709; fax 865-448-9250; www.nps.gov/grsm), 9275 Tremont Rd., Townsend, TN. Multiday programs run all year; reservations are required. For more than 30 years the Great Smoky Mountains Institute at Tremont has been giving youth and adult programs in environmental topics from their headquarters in the old YCC camp near Tremont. The Tremont Institute offers an immersive, intense experience with a great deal of group interaction, in the setting of a rustic camp surrounded by deep forest. While many of the activities are for school groups or professional educators, the institute also offers regular programs for the general public, typically 3- to 5-day residency programs with extensive outdoor time; meals are taken in a large mess hall. Youth and teen camps are scheduled throughout summer, while adult multiday programs include nature observation, wildflowers, geology, fall colors, photography, backpacking, and elderhostels. Most adult programs last 2 or 3 days and cost $120–375, including room and board.

FISHING Little River Outfitters (865-448-9459), 7807 E. Lamar Alexander Parkway, Townsend, TN. This large outdoor specialist offers

TWILIGHT SETTLES OVER THE COVE.
Jim Hargan

LOOKING ACROSS THE MEADOWS TOWARD THE GREAT SMOKIES.

fishing guides and a fly-fishing school in addition to a large line of gear and clothing. Owner Byron Begley is a fly-fishing expert.

GOLF ♂ ♿ **Laurel Valley Country Club** (800-865-4770 or 865-448-6690), 702 Country Club Dr., Townsend, TN. Open daily. The Laurel Valley Country Club is a modest but comfortable facility at the center of a large gated community a scant 3 miles east of Townsend. Fully open to the public, its 18-hole, par-70 golf course offers sweeping views toward nearby Rich Mountain (the northern border of the Great Smoky Mountains National Park), only half a mile away. Despite its stunning mountain scenery, the course is not unusually hilly or dramatically sloped. Its small clubhouse has a sports bar and restaurant (both very nice), as well as a swimming pool. Guaranteed tee times are available, but not required. Weekends $50 nonresidents, $40 residents; weekdays $40 residents, $30 nonresidents.

RAFTING AND KAYAKING ♂ **River Romp Tube Rentals** (888-862-2633 or 865-448-9097), 8203 TN 73, Townsend, TN. Located at the intersection of US 321 and TN 73 at the center of town, River Romp offers tube floats (with shuttle service) on the calm in-town section of the Little River.

STABLES ♂ **Davy Crockett Riding Stables** (865-448-6411), 505 Old Cades Cove Rd., Townsend, TN 37882. Located in scenic, rural Dry Valley east of Townsend, the Crockett Stables specializes in groups, but welcomes walk-ins for 1/2- to 2-hour guided rides; longer rides, including overnighters, are available by appointment. You can find the Crockett Stables by following the signs for Tuckaleechee Caverns, which is nearby.

♂ **Next To Heaven Stables** (800-407-2231 or 865-448-9150), US 321 (Wears Valley Rd.), Townsend, TN. Mon.–Sat. 10–5:30; closed Sun. This stable, located 3 miles east of Townsend on US 321, offers guided and unguided rides.

♂ **Cades Cove Riding Stables** (865-448-6286), 4025 E. Lamar Alexander Parkway, Walland, TN. Apr.–Oct., daily 9–5; closed Nov.–Mar. This national park concessionaire operates guided trail rides within Cades Cove, from a well-kept stable across from the picnic area. If you visit the cove early in the morning, you'll see their horses grazing the wide fields at the start of the loop road. They also offer carriage rides and hayrides inside Cades Cove.

✳ Lodging

COUNTRY INNS Maple Leaf Lodge and Cabins (800-369-0111 or 865-488-6000; www.mapleleaflodge.com), Apple Valley Way, Townsend, TN 37882. This new log inn, constructed in 2000, sits on a large tract of woods and meadows adjacent to the center of Townsend. Each of its 12 rooms is individually decorated, some with elegant antique reproductions, others with handmade log furniture with lots of character. The price includes a hearty country breakfast and afternoon tea. The log cabins, with either one or two bedrooms, all have whirlpool tub inside and hot tub on the porch outside, along with rockers and swing, wood-burning fireplace, cable TV, and private phone. The property has 3 miles of nature trails, with views over meadows toward the Smokies. Jan.–Mar., rooms $110–150, cabins $90–140; Apr.–Sep., rooms $120–170, cabins $100–140; Oct.–Dec., rooms $130–190, cabins $110–170.

COUNTRY RESORTS Blackberry Farm (800-862-7610 or 865-984-8166; fax 865-983-5708), 1471 W. Millers Cove Rd., Walland, TN 37886. Open all year. Formerly a 1920s-era summer estate on 1,100 acres adjacent to the national park, Blackberry Farm has evolved into a luxurious 44-room mountain resort. United by an architecture that combines the American shingle style of the original Main House with motifs from England's Cotswold District, the resort's facilities spread across 100 landscaped acres in groupings of large houses and small cottages. The landscaped grounds give the appearance of a thoroughbred horse farm through which guest can hike, bicycle, or jog on 7 miles of hiking paths and 3 miles of paved jogging trails; there are tennis, basketball, and shuffleboard courts, a swimming pool, and bicycles available to guests. All rooms are individual and unique, decorated in a simple, elegant English country style; the selection ranges from the original rooms in the historic Main House, to newer rooms in the Guest House, to suite-sized cottages, and on up to full-sized houses with all facilities. The elegant candlelight dinners are available to guests only, and are included in the room rates (excluding wine and beer) along with breakfast, a picnic lunch, a light tea, and ample daylong snacks. Executive chef John Fleer presents guests with his own "Foothills Cuisine," combining East Tennessee country flavors with haute cuisine preparation in a way that remains true to the original country sources. For those unable to choose which luxury to try next, a tasting menu gives the chef's own choices of three courses, to which sommelier Matthew Regen matches a different glass of wine for each course. Standard rooms run $495–695 per night. Cottage suites run $845–945 per night. All of these tariffs include three full meals and access to most on-site facilities (including bicycles) at no extra charge. A private three-bedroom house with meeting room and kitchen runs $1,895.

BED & BREAKFAST INNS ♿ **The Richmont Inn** (865-448-6751; fax 865-448-6480), 220 Winterberry Lane, Townsend, TN 37882. Open all year. The first thing you notice about the Richmont Inn is its remarkable architecture. Inspired by the unique local cantilevered barns, this modern purpose-built small hotel has a planked log ground floor and a much larger second and third floor cantilevered out a good 10 feet in all directions. Located on 11 wooded ridgeline acres, the Richmont offers a quiet and intimate experience, combining spectacular views toward Rich Mountain and the national park with lovely woodland walks. But the Richmont is really distinguished by its rooms and its food. The 12 rooms, ranging in size from cozy to full-sized luxury suites, are each individually decorated around a theme from Smoky Mountain history, and each has either a fireplace, a private balcony, or both. A trio of third-floor suites are decorated in Native American themes, each with wood-burning fireplace, private balcony, skylight over the king bed, and spa tub for two. Room rates include a full gourmet breakfast and a candlelight dessert worthy of the finest restaurant. Separate antique log buildings house the **Cove Café**, an intimate dinner place specializing in fondue, and a gift shop. Golfers receive a discount on the Laurel Valley golf course only a short walk away (see *Golf*). $115 for the smaller rooms and the disabled-access Asbury; $135–165 for the larger rooms. Two luxury suites (no kitchens) are available in a separate building for $220. All tariffs include full breakfast and evening dessert.

CABIN RENTALS Although the Townsend area has only a few bed & breakfast inns, it has an enormous number of high-quality cabin rentals at very reasonable prices. The listings below are just a sampling of the units available to you, chosen to give the flavor of this area. With nightly rental rates competitive with local B&Bs and Gatlinburg, TN, motels, these cabins—all with full kitchens and separate living, dining, and bedroom areas—are the bargains of the Smokies. And while the fellowship of a B&B is nice, there is something to be said for enjoying a mountain view from your own porch.

🐾 ✂ ♿ **Mountain Mist Cabins** (800-686-9288 or 865-448-6650; www.mtnmistcabins.com), P.O. Box 162, Townsend, TN 37882. Open all year. When Earl Lamb retired, he returned to the farm in Tuckaleechee Cove where his father had been born and raised. He found it grown up after half a century of abandonment, a pine-forested hollow along the abandoned pioneer road. On this old family farm, Earl has created a small community of country-style cabins, each set in its own woods separate from the others. Distinctive red tin roofs sit above full-sized wraparound porches; walls are sided with rough-cut 12-inch planks. Each porch has rockers and a hot tub. Inside, doors are handmade, and on-site wood is used for decorative accents with the log country furnishings. Fireplaces are finished in local stone, with gas log insets. $100–140 per night; ask for off-season rates.

🐾 ✂ **Blue Smoke Cabins** (865-448-3068; www.bluesmokecabins.com), 1233 Carrs Creek Rd., Townsend, TN 37882. Open all year. Retired fireman Ron Brady and his wife, Linda, run this collection of handsome log cabins high on top a pine ridge 3 miles north of town. These well-furnished, roomy cabins have fine views from the rocking chairs and hot tubs on their wide porches, yet each cabin is completely isolated from its neighbors. You'll find the site's gravel roads to be mountainy verging on breathtaking, but within the abilities of the family sedan. $85–95 in-season, $75–85 off-season.

Bradley Mountain Retreat (877-766-5915 or 865-448-6842; www .smokycabins.com/bradley_mtn_ retreat.htm), 339 Bradley Retreat Rd., Townsend, TN 37882. All year. This ridgetop site southwest of Townsend offers stunning views over the town toward Rich Mountain. The roomy log cabins, set far enough apart on this wooded site to offer good privacy, are furnished comfortably and with a lot of personality; all have porch and hot tub. Also on site is a two-story log building with three motel-style kitchenettes, at a greatly reduced price. Cabins $85–95, motel-style kitchenettes $40.

Carnes' Log Cabins (865-448-1021; fax 865-448-8076; www.carnes logcabins.com), 214 Tom Henry Rd., P.O. Box 153, Townsend, TN 37882. Open all year. Small pets are allowed, with restrictions; please call well in advance. Richard and Yvonne Carnes have built a lovely little community of four hand-hewn log cabins, conveniently located in a hollow above Townsend. The cabins form a rough circle around the end of the approach drive, scattered in a wooded, grass-floored glade that gives privacy without impeding the views. The roomy cabins, which range from one to three bedrooms, have rocking porch, fireplace, and whirlpool bats. Typically

$85–150 a night, with the higher rates in summer and Oct.

Gilbertson's Lazy Horse Retreat (865-448-6810; www.thesmokies .com/lazy_horse/), 938 Schoolhouse Gap Rd., Townsend, TN 37882. Open all year. Melody Gilbertson boards horses and their people from her spread in scenic Dry Valley, 4 miles southwest of Townsend. Horses board in 10 indoor box stalls in a handsome and well-kept modern barn, with half an acre of paddock surrounded by wooden fences. Their people get stabled in four cabins: two modern log cabins, a small house, and a farmhand's cabin right by the barn. This is a great location for trail riders, with 12 horse trails within 14 miles. $85 per night for the three large cabins, $65 per night for the smaller Cowboy Cabin. Horses $10 per night.

Hideaway Cottages and Log Cabins (865-984-1700; www.hide awayjo.com), 102 Oriole Lane, P.O. Box 653, Maryville, TN 37803. Open all year. These seven cottages occupy the center of convenient Black Mash Hollow, a scenic, wooded side valley linked to central Townsend, TN, by a short one-lane mountain road. These charming cabins range from modest and homey to elaborate and luxurious. All are handsomely furnished with antique and modern items, with fireplace and porch. All guests have access to a private, 5-acre streamside meadow with a pavilion and picnic area. $85–155 per night, with price reflecting size and luxuriousness; off-season rates available.

Old Smoky Mountain Cabins (800-739-4820 or 865-448-2388; fax 865-448-9917; www.oldsmokycabins .com), 238 Webb Rd., Townsend, TN 37882. All year. Possibly the oldest cabin rental in Townsend, Old Smoky has a wide range of properties scattered about, including a number of roomy, well-appointed log cabins. Their centerpiece property is a small modern hotel in a quiet rural location just north of town, with three suites overlooking a pool. All their cabin rentals have free access to the pool as well. $85–125; smaller, less expensive units available.

Whisperwind Cabin Rentals (800-993-9928 or 865-448-1979; fax 865-448-6555; www.whispercabins.com), 1177 Shuler Rd., Townsend, TN 37882. Open all year. Cheryl Hobbes offers seven cabins in Dry Valley, each on a separate property but none far from her house and office. These excellently kept rentals cover quite a range, from a modest little cabin to a large luxury house; all properties offer privacy, and some are very secluded. Various cabins offer log construction, mountain views, whirlpool bath, hot tub, wide porch, and great room with cathedral ceiling; Cheryl's excellent brochure, with first-rate professional photography, gives a full and accurate description of each unit. $75–135 per night.

CABIN RESERVATION SERVICES

Laurel Valley Cabin Rentals/ White Oak Realty (877-448-2040 or 865-448-8040), 125 Townsend Park Dr., P.O. Box 247, Townsend, TN 37882. A reservations service with many properties in the Laurel Valley development, on or near the golf course. Their Sequoyah Village collection of vacation cabins, deep within a ridgetop forest in Laurel Valley, offers roomy, modern cabins, each set deep in its own woods with whirlpool bath and wood-burning stone fireplace.

"Bear"ly Rustic Cabin Rentals (888-448-6036 or 865-448-6036; www.townsendcabin.com), 7807 E. Lamar Alexander Parkway, Townsend, TN 37882. All year. A reservation service for renting second homes, they offer a selection of more than two dozen homes through a color brochure and a web page.

Dogwood Cabins (888-448-9054; www.dogwoodcabins.com), 7016 E. Lamar Alexander Parkway, Townsend, TN 37886. A reservations service managing and renting second homes. Some accommodations, such as The River Loaf Farm, offer horse stalls and fenced grazing on site.

✳ Where to Eat

EATING OUT ✿ **Doolittles** (423-448-0199), 7837 E. Lamar Alexander Parkway, Townsend, TN. This small coffee shop in the center of town offers huge deli sandwiches on Italian flatbread, a selection of fresh-ground gourmet coffees, fresh-baked cakes and cookies, and hand-scooped ice cream (a choice of locally made Mayfield or fancy import Ben & Jerry's). It's a good place to relax and cool down a bit. Sandwiches $4.95–6.95, coffee $1.50 and up.

Trailhead Steak House (865-448-0166), 7839 E. Lamar Alexander Parkway (US 321), Townsend, TN. Open for dinner all year. Grill your own steaks on the Trailhead's large, open outdoor grill! Actually, owner Tim Byrd is a masterful griller with an obsession with quality. Most people prefer to let Tim do the work while they relax in this western-themed restaurant, enjoying the large, flavorful salad, homemade bread, and a cold beer. Apart from four types of steak, Tim will grill up Alaskan halibut or salmon, caught wild and flown in, local trout, chicken breasts, kebabs, or shrimp; all get a treatment of his lightly seasoned olive oil. Steaks $16.95–19.95, other entrées $10.95–15.95, sandwiches $6.95–8.95.

Smokin' Joes (865-448-3212), 8215 TN 73, Townsend, TN. Open all year for lunch and dinner; hours vary with season. Smokin' Joe is producing real barbeque the old-fashioned way; as you walk up to the modest restaurant, the aroma of oak and hickory smoke fills the air. Founder Joe Higgins is a farm-raised South Carolinian who learned the fine art of barbeque as a boy, during his family's seasonal hog butchering. He barbeques slowly—his ribs take 8 hours—creating a meat that's moist, smoky, flavorful, and falling apart. The ribs are spectacular, with the lightest of crust on the outside. Sides are made from scratch, and include barbequed pinto beans as well as everyone's BBQ favorites. Save room for dessert, as they make their own hot cobblers. Sandwiches $2.50–4, and add $2 for two sides; dinners $6.95–10.95, including two sides and bread.

✳ Entertainment

The Pickin' Porch at Nawgers Nob, Townsend, TN. Twice a week, on Tuesday and Saturday, local musicians and performers show up in front of Mike Clemmerer's dulcimer shop in the Nawgers Nob craft community. Mike will play a bit and introduce the other acts. Dave "Buffalo Bill" Nelson is a regular with his warm cowboy whimsy, and the local Creek Mountain Band is frequently on hand for some country and bluegrass. It's free, but don't forget your lawn chairs.

♪ ↑ **Appalachian Music at the Community Center**, Walland, TN. Every Friday night, year-round, local musicians come to the Walland Community Center to jam. What happens next depends on who shows up; bluegrass musicians might be playing in one room while old-time fiddlers hold court in another.

Mountain Music Program, Cades Cove, TN. The Great Smoky Mountains National Park sponsors a program of authentic Appalachian mountain music monthly at the Cades Cove Amphitheater, next to the camp store. In these programs, skilled musicians perform the historic music and ballads of the Smokies and talk about this heritage music. Traditional dance may also be performed. This event occurs on the third Saturday of every month, June–Oct.; for details, call the Gatlinburg Visitors Center (800-900-4148).

✳ Selective Shopping

Townsend, TN

↑ **Wood-N-Strings** (865-448-6647; www.clemmerdulcimer.com), 7645 E. Lamar Alexander Parkway. Mike Clemmer handcrafts fine Appalachian stringed instruments, from fiddles to the strange and beautiful stringed psaltery. But his favorites are dulcimers, lovingly crafted from walnut, cherry, or butternut. Mike is a soft-spoken man, as gentle and as sweet as the mountain instruments he loves, and he never seems to tire of showing off his sweet-toned dulcimers. His handmade dulcimers typically range $150–500, depending on material and decoration.

♿ ↑ **Earthtide Gallery** (865-448-1106), 7645 Lamar Alexander Parkway. With the Earthtide Gallery, Beryl

Lumpkin has assembled a truly astonishing variety of fine craft pieces—all from local artists. Occupying a newish log structure in the center of town, the gallery has baskets, furniture, glass, pottery, jewelry, wooden bowls, sculpture, and photography, ranging from traditional to the most vividly imaginative. One or more of their 70 represented artists is frequently on hand for craft demonstrations.

&. ⬆ **Larry Burton Art Gallery** (865-577-8350; www.larryburton gallery.com), 7142 E. Lamar Alexander Parkway. Prominent watercolor landscape artist Larry Burton keeps his gallery of original watercolors and art prints in a modern log building next to the popular gift shop **Apple Valley Farms**. Larry's watercolors are highly detailed and accurate renderings of Smoky Mountain scenes using soft, muted colors—in contrast to other artists, who feature bright colors and idealized subjects.

✴ Special Events

SPRING ✐ **Townsend in the Smokies Spring Festival and Old Timers Day** (800-525-6834 or 865-448-6134; www.smokymountains.org), 7906 E. Lamar Alexander Parkway, Townsend, TN. Last week of Apr., 9–6. This free weeklong festival, held in a large grassy field behind the Townsend Visitors Center, features daily live bluegrass music, craft demonstrations, and wildflower walks, with occasional special features such as storytelling, antique tractors, and a barbeque competition. Events include a barbeque cook-off, the Nawgers Nob Arts and Crafts Show at the Nawgers Nob Craft Village west of town, and Old Timers Day in Cades Cove. Most events are free.

AUTUMN ✐ **Townsend Fall Heritage Festival and Old Timers Day**, Townsend, TN. Last weekend in Sep. For those who can't make it to Townsend's Spring Heritage Festival, they repeat it in fall. That's okay—it's enough fun to be worth doing twice a year. Like its spring counterpart but shorter, the fall festival fills a weekend with bluegrass music, craft demonstrations, bake sales, and antique tractors, as well as parallel events at Nawgers Nob and Cades Cove.

Cades Cove Fall Harvest Hayride. Each evening, last full week in Oct. The National Park Service collaborates with the Cades Cove Stables concessionaire to offer this evening hayride around the Cades Cove Loop Rd. The cove is at its best in the evening, and never more beautiful than in fall—but this hayride has something special. As you progress around the cove, you meet people from the cove's history: a cove farmer, a Cherokee, perhaps an escaping Union soldier or a Confederate raider.

BRYSON CITY & THE SOUTHWEST QUADRANT

Bryson City, NC, sits at the southern edge of the Great Smoky Mountains National Park, within a deep, narrow bowl surrounded by mile-high peaks. To the north looms the third tallest peak in the eastern United States: Clingmans Dome, 6,643 feet above sea level, and 0.93 mile above Bryson City's small-town main street. To the south lie the knotted peaks of the Cowee Mountains, within the Nantahala National Forest. Between these two ranges the Tuckaseegee River drains a deep, narrow valley, where fertile bottomland supplies half a dozen produce stands. Bryson City, straddling the Tuckaseegee, is a fine old-fashioned southern country town whose lively little downtown spreads between the old railroad depot and the old main highway.

Although (or perhaps because) the national park's tallest and steepest region abuts Bryson City, only limited areas of the park's backcountry can be reached easily by automobiles starting from Bryson City. The Deep Creek area, reached down a paved local road, centers on a lovely stream noted for its waterfalls. The seldom-visited Lakeshore Dr. (aka The Road To Nowhere) offers a short, scenic drive down a dead-end park road, with access to Noland Creek, a former mountain settlement cut off by the rising waters of Fontana Lake. Farther west, the waters of Fontana Lake block the park's backwater all the way to Fontana Dam; even farther, the remote Twentymile Ranger District has worthwhile (and little-visited) walks.

Thirteen miles southwest of Bryson City lies the Nantahala Gorge, a deep tree-lined canyon. US 19 runs along the floor of the gorge, allowing easy access to numerous whitewater outfitters—a popular destination on a hot summer day. There's a scenic drive for this area as well, extending well upstream from the popular areas to explore some deep gorge scenery and waterfalls.

Other parts of the Bryson City area are dominated by scattered farms separated by private woodlots and the great tracts of the Nantahala National Forest. Most of the national forest lands around here are used for forestry and have little recreation development. The one exception is the Tsali Recreation Area on Fontana Lake, developed for off-road bicycling. In addition, a tract known as Big Laurel is worth a visit, with large meadows and a stunning waterfall.

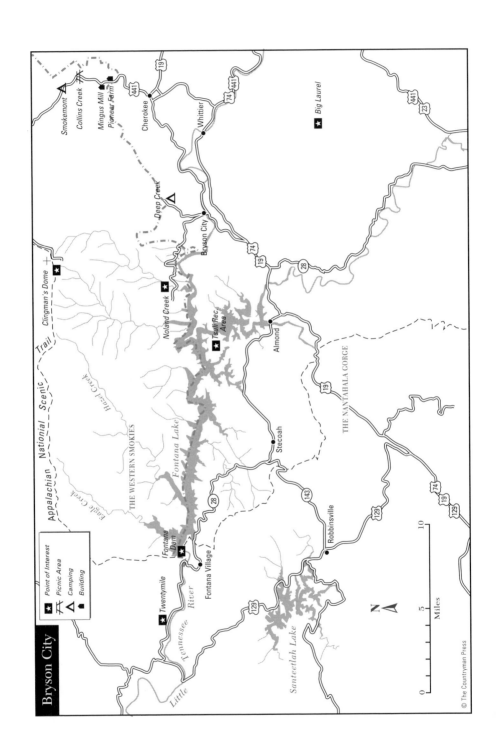

Bryson City

Point of Interest ★
Picnic Area ⚏
Camping △
Building ■

Smokemont
Collins Creek
Mingus Mill
Pioneer Farm
Cherokee
441
19
441
Whittier
74
441
23
Big Laurel ★

Deep Creek △
Bryson City
74
19
28

Clingman's Dome ★
Appalachian National Scenic Trail
Noland Creek ★
Tsali Rec. Area ★
Almond
19
THE NANTAHALA GORGE

Hazel Creek
THE WESTERN SMOKIES
Fontana Lake
Stecoah
143

Eagle Creek
28
Robbinsville
123
74
19
129

Fontana Dam ★
Fontana Village
129

Twentymile ★
Tennessee River
Little
Santeetlah Lake
129

N

0   5   10
Miles

© The Countryman Press

GUIDANCE Swain County Chamber of Commerce (800-867-9246 or 828-488-3681; www.greatsmokies.net), P.O. Box 509, Bryson City, NC 28713. The chamber is located at the center of downtown Bryson City, immediately adjacent to the old courthouse. You'll find it well staffed and extremely helpful. When the train is in town, they open a substation in an old red caboose within easy walking distance of the depot.

The Great Smoky Mountains National Park ranger stations. For backcountry permits and other related questions, visit the ranger station at Deep Creek, in the campground. The nearest visitors center, with a desk staffed 7 days a week, is at Oconaluftee, 2 miles north of Cherokee, NC, on US 441.

Wayah Ranger District, Nantahala National Forest (828-524-6441), 90 Sloan Rd., Franklin, NC 28734. The 15,000 acres of Nantahala National Forest in the Bryson City, NC, area are run from the Wayah Ranger Station in Franklin, 33 miles south via the four-lane US 74 and US 441.

GETTING THERE *By car*: Bryson City sits at the far western end of the four-lane **Smoky Mountain Expressway** that links North Carolina's rugged western counties with the rest of the state. For this reason, it's almost always easiest to approach it from the east, even if it means driving out of your way. You can pick up the expressway from Asheville, NC, by following I-40 west to US 64, or from Georgia by following US 441 north into North Carolina, reaching US 74 at Dillsboro.

NINETEENTH-CENTURY BRICK BUILDINGS LINE EVERETT ST. IN DOWNTOWN BRYSON CITY.
Jim Hargan

By air: **Asheville Regional Airport** (828-684-2226; fax 828-684-3404), 708 Airport Rd., Fletcher, NC. Located 15 miles south of downtown Asheville off I-26, Exit 9 (NC 280). Service from Atlanta, Cincinnati, Pittsburgh, Raleigh, and Charlotte, with 20 to 25 flights daily. Several car rental agencies are located within or near the airport—and because Bryson City has no bus service from Asheville (or anywhere else), you'll have to rent a car. The 70-mile driving distance is a stop-free expressway virtually the entire distance, and should take about 1¼ hours.

By bus or train: Bryson City, NC, has no bus or train links to the outside world. Like most of these poor mountain counties, Swain County has no rural bus system.

MEDICAL EMERGENCIES **Swain County Hospital** (828-488-2155; www
.westcare.org/patientsvisitors/swain/swainvisitorinformation.html), 45 Plateau St.,
Bryson City, NC. A rare survival from earlier days, this fully accredited small-
town hospital has 48 beds, general surgical facilities, and a fully staffed Level II
24/7 emergency room. You'll find it on an obscure residential side street, uphill
from the train depot; look for the blue hospital signs on the north side of the
depot.

✳ Wandering Around

EXPLORING BY CAR **Driving the Nantahala Gorge**. This scenic drive follows
the Nantahala Gorge, a 1,600-foot-deep, heavily forested gorge carved by the
Nantahala River. It starts 13 miles west of Bryson City, NC, on US 19, as that
highway drops into the gorge to follow its floor. The highway hugs the river
closely, with many places to pull over and admire the scenery. You will only have
to wait a few minutes to see kayakers paddling furiously through the rapids and
rafters carried happily with the current. After 8 miles US 19 continues straight
ahead, but the gorge swings left in an almost perfect right angle; follow the
gorge left onto Wayah Rd.

Now the gorge turns rugged, its river violent and boulder-strewn beneath black
rock walls—the scenery of a western gorge moved into the lush East and covered with trees. The highlight is **Camp Creek Falls**, a 200-foot jet of water
pouring over the sheer rock wall of the gorge, 2.6 miles up Wayah Rd. In another mile Wayah Rd. climbs out of the gorge without making any noticeable curve;
once again, the gorge has swerved 90°. Here you turn right onto Old River Rd.,
a good gravel road maintained by the Nantahala National Forest. You'll immediately cross **Whiteoak Creek**, with an impressive 20-foot waterfall visible on
your left from the concrete bridge. Beyond, the gorge is less rugged and the
river smaller. The Nantahala River passes over a beautiful small waterfall, then

INDIAN CREEK FALLS IN SPRING.

Jim Hargan

becomes starved for water by the TVA's Nantahala Dam, only a few miles upstream. In another mile the road catches up with some of that missing water—a giant penstock crosses the road, then follows it for half a mile. Old River Rd. ends at a T intersection with paved Junaluska Rd. (SSR 1401). A left turn will take you 2.5 miles back to Wayah Rd.; follow it left to US 19 in a bit less than 10 miles.

The remote western Smokies. The waters of giant Fontana Lake isolate much of the western Smokies from casual visitors. As a result, it has little by the way of development to intrude upon its stunning scenery. To explore this area by car, pick up NC 28 westbound, 9 miles west of Bryson City, NC, on US 74. Chances are you'll find this section partly four lane and partly under construction—a regional development project surviving from Lyndon Johnson's War on Poverty in Appalachia and scheduled for completion in 2008. (If you are visiting after 2008, you may find this section named "US 74.") In 10 miles you'll pass the sleepy village of **Stecoah**, NC, off on side roads to your left. Shortly beyond, NC 143 peels off to the left, a shortcut to Robbinsville, NC, and the corridor for the four-lane highway. From here, NC 28 becomes a lot more steep and curvy. Views will open up on your right, including a wonderful 180° sweep over Fontana Lake toward the crest of the Smokies from a wayside picnic area.

You'll reach the turnoff to **Fontana Dam** after 22 miles. It's worth a visit for the good views and generator tours at its visitors center—but the biggest thrill is driving over the narrow dam top, high above the gorge below. Turn left at the far end (inside the national park) for a great view of the dam. Continue on NC 28 to the **Little Tennessee River**; now NC 28 hugs the river, impounded as **Cheoah Lake**, with several beautiful views. In 8 miles you will reach the national park's remote Twentymile section, then reach US 129 in another 3 miles. Go left on US 129 for 2 miles to an old bridge over the Little Tennessee River. Here you will get a good view of **Cheoah Dam**, a 265-foot structure built in 1919 by Alcoa. This was the site of Harrison Ford's dramatic dam jump in the 1992 movie *The Fugitive*.

EXPLORING ON FOOT OR BICYCLE **Deep Creek Trail**. This easy path, following an old pre-park road up Deep Creek, is well known for its three beautiful waterfalls, as well as its lovely streamside scenery. The gravel road portions are open to bicycles and make a pleasant, beautiful morning's ride; bicycles are prohibited on the footpaths. You'll find the trailhead at the end of Deep Creek Rd., just inside the national park.

Walkers should start with the quarter-mile spur trail to **Junywhank Falls**, which leaves the northwest corner of the parking lot. Junywhank Falls is a thin trace of water that hurls itself over a 50-foot ledge, dashes under a wood log bridge, then bounces down another 30 feet of rock. Be sure to take the footpath to the log bridge for the best views, then return the way you came.

For Deep Creek Trail, walk or bike up the old roadbed a quarter mile to view **Tom Branch Falls**, a side stream that enters Deep Creek by pouring over a 30-foot rock wall. Farther along, the track follows Deep Creek as it bounces over rapids and rock shelves, then climbs above it to give views up the deep V-shaped cleft. At two-thirds of a mile the old road forks at a bridge where Indian Creek pours in from the side, through a chute into a still pool that throws rippling reflections onto the overhanging rocks. Both forks are open to bicyclists. Walkers will want to take the right fork—then listen for the roar of a waterfall. A short side trail leads to the base of the third and most impressive waterfall, **Indian Creek Falls**. Here a wide wall of water pours over a 50-foot ledge into a deep, still pool with a natural pebbly beach. A short distance beyond the side trail, the main path offers a good view over the top of the falls. Return the way you came.

EXPLORING ON FOOT Noland Creek Trail. Up until 1942 Noland Creek was the site of a streamside settlement, 50 or so families in scattered farmhouses that ranged from log cabins to modern bungalows. Then the Tennessee Valley Authority built Fontana Dam and flooded their road access. Rather than rebuild the road, the TVA condemned the Noland Creek community, evicted its residents, and donated their land to the Great Smoky Mountains National Park. To visit their old community, take Lakeshore Dr. to the trailhead at Noland Creek Overlook. You can go either up or down the valley—but the more interesting parts of the trail are up the valley, a 4-mile walk along an old road at a steady upward gradient of 6 percent. Although the National Park Service demolished nearly all of the structures in Noland Creek for safety reasons, signs of the settlement still remain. Boxwoods and roses grow rank around old homesites, where a set of steps or an old chimney might poke up through the trees. Because the valley was never logged, the forests are extraordinarily beautiful, a combination of old woods and young trees growing in former farmland.

At 3.7 miles, the track enters a flat-floored stretch known as **Solola Valley**, a heavily settled area named for the Cherokee word for "squirrel." The remains of this settlement include the ruins of a large mill, its wheelhouse foundations emerging from the streambed. At 4 miles a side trail, the **Springhouse Branch Trail**, leads uphill to the left, passing house and field ruins to reach a large old-growth forest in three-quarters of a mile. At 4.2 miles an unmarked side trail leads uphill a short distance to a cemetery, still used by the families evicted from Noland Creek. Another quarter mile leads to a nice waterfall—a good place to turn around.

A Twentymile walk. The western backcountry of the Great Smoky Mountains National Park has numerous choices for good walks, all the more enticing for being remote and little used. Most are cut off from roads by the waters of Fontana Dam, and require boat access. A collection of little-used trails radiates out from the Twentymile Ranger Station on NC 28 nine miles west of Fontana Dam (and 37 miles west of Bryson City, NC).

Like many of the trails in these parts, the **Twentymile Creek Trail** follows a pre-park road—in this case, an old narrow-gauge lumber railroad built in the 1920s and converted to a jeep track by the CCC. Closed to autos and bicycles, it makes for gentle and pleasant walking through attractive young forests, grown up since this area was logged 80 years ago. After a mile it reaches **Twentymile Cascades**, where the little Twentymile Creek jumps down a steep sloping rock about 40 feet high. At 3 miles the track reaches a trail intersection at **Proctor Field Gap**, where remnants of stone walls and old foundations poke up through the level forest floor.

At this point, you have climbed 1,000 feet above the Twentymile Ranger Station. Should you continue on the old track (to the right), you will gain another 1,500 feet in only 1.5 miles—a steep pull. When you finally reach the ridgeline you will be on the **Appalachian Trail**. A third of a mile to the right (and uphill, alas) is the **Shuckstack Fire Tower**, with one of the finest panoramic views anywhere in the Smokies. To your north the entire Smoky Mountain Crest marches along the horizon, while the deep gorge of the Little Tennessee River cuts across the ridges that recede forever into the south.

✳ Villages

Bryson City, NC. Visitors to Bryson City will find it a handsome town of about 1,500 inhabitants, with an old-fashioned downtown stretched into a T shape and possessing a full range of services. The **Old Swain County Courthouse** sits by the main downtown intersection and furnishes an unmissable landmark. It's guarded by a World War I doughboy instead of the traditional Confederate soldier, showing Swain County's post–Civil War origin. The town's Main Street follows US 19 east and west from the Old Courthouse, ending at the town's beautiful hilltop cemetery. Down from the courthouse, the downtown district crosses the Tuckaseegee River to reach the old railroad depot, now housing the **Great Smoky Mountain Railroad** with daily scenic excursions. Parking is ample and free. Apart from its quaint downtown with some interesting shops, Bryson City offers some of the better lodging and dining in the mountains, with several first-rate establishments in town or nearby.

The Nantahala Gorge. Located 13 miles southwest of Bryson City, NC, along US 19, this 8-mile-long gorge has recently acquired its own community of tourist-oriented businesses, drawn by the increasing popularity of rafting and kayaking on the Nantahala River. Most of it consists of roadside businesses of recent and undistinguished architecture, separated by long stretches of beautiful national forest land. Apart from the outfitters, you'll find several places to eat and at least one good lodge. Traffic can be slow on a warm summer weekend,

THE OLD SWAIN COUNTY COURTHOUSE IN BRYSON CITY.

Jim Hargan

with lots of pedestrians, cars entering from parking lots, and old repainted buses loaded high with inflated rafts.

Almond, NC. Formerly a riverside stopping place along US 19, 9 miles southwest of Bryson City, the settlement of Almond was flooded in 1942 by the rising waters of Fontana Reservoir. US 19 moved elsewhere, and the remnants of the village rose up the mountain slope until they were just above the high-water line. The NC 28 bridge over Fontana Reservoir, in the center of Almond (if Almond is big enough to have a center), gives good views over the giant lake. Some Nantahala Gorge businesses have Almond addresses.

Stecoah, NC. This tiny village off NC 28, 18 miles west of Bryson City, is the main population center in this remote corner of the Smokies. Its old stone school, now being renovated into a community center, marks the center of town. It has few services beyond gas, a café, and a couple of general stores.

Fontana, NC. Fontana Village was founded in 1942 as the construction camp for Fontana Dam. After the dam was completed in 1944, the construction camp became a resort. And so it remains—the main administrative building converted into a lodge, and the temporary workers' quarters becoming a small city of modest vacation cabins. A log cabin in the center has displays on pioneer life. The surrounding countryside is very remote, with few facilities. You'll find Fontana Village 31 miles west of Bryson City on NC 28.

✳ Wild Places

THE GREAT FORESTS **The southwest quadrant of the Great Smoky Mountains**. The high crest of the Smokies sweeps southwest from Bryson City, NC, starting some 10 miles north of town and 4,800 feet above it. For much of this area the crest comes to a sharp, rocky point and drops down almost clifflike—but still covered by trees more typical of New England or Canada than the South. In other places, the crest becomes wide and rolling, the scene of great open meadows. Side ridges branch off to the south, separating valleys that drop straight down to a sharp point, with scarcely enough bottomland to contain a fierce little river. Before the park was created in the 1930s, these valleys frequently contained roads that would peter out at high dead ends—some made by farmers, others by loggers. In 1944 many of these roads were cut off from the rest of the world by the waters of the newly impounded Fontana Lake, running along the southern edge of the park for 24 miles. Today they are hiking trails.

Within the wild southwestern quadrant of the park, two areas are easily reached from Bryson City: **Deep Creek** and **Noland Creek**. These valleys were once heavily settled, their upper reaches valued for hunting—effectively protecting them from the destructive large-scale logging that decimated many of the more remote valleys. Instead, these valleys had either been selectively logged, leaving a continuous cover of old hardwoods, or cleared for pasture, leaving rich, well-conserved soil that supported fast-growing, healthy forests when abandoned. Both valleys are rich in traces of their former inhabitants (although all the structures have been removed for safety reasons), and the upper slopes of Noland Creek preserve some large stands of old-growth forest.

Big Laurel. Take US 23/74 east of Bryson City, NC, to the Whittier exit, then follow the signs for the Smoky Mountain Golf Course through Whittier and beyond; when you reach the golf course, just keep going on Conley Creek Rd., which becomes a steep and narrow (but well-maintained) Forest Service road as it climbs up to Big Laurel. This recently acquired tract of national forest land centers on a high meadow-covered valley perched near the top of Cowee Mountain, a scenic 16-mile drive southwest of Bryson City. At this time the Forest Service is protecting the meadows and keeping up the roads—and little else, leaving this little-known cove in its natural state. At the far end of the cove a jeep track heads gently downhill to your right, leading in half a mile to the lovely **Alarka Creek Falls**, a 30-foot set of waterfalls, framed by rhododendrons, with a Japanese garden type of beauty. (To find the waterfall, look for an unsigned side trail on your left.) A word of caution: Visitors during the October leaf season will find the whole area taken over by bear hunters.

RECREATION AREAS **Tsali Recreation Area**. This large recreation area on the shores of Fontana Reservoir, devoted to off-road bicycling and horseback riding, occupies the site where the Cherokee Tsali hid with his family during the Trail of Tears—a turning point, as it happened, in the 1838 expulsion of the Cherokees from their homeland. Federal troops tracked Tsali and his people to these remote cliffs overlooking the Little Tennessee River, and took them peacefully, but younger men in the group hid weapons and killed most of their captors, allowing their clan to escape. The local Qualla Cherokees—legally inhabitants of North Carolina and not part of the Cherokee Nation being expelled—saw this as simple murder, and helped track down and execute the killers, taking and executing Tsali without help from federal troops. As a result of this chilling episode, the federal officer in charge of the district ruled that the Qualla could remain on their lands. Today the Qualla make up the Eastern Band of the Cherokee Nation, in Cherokee, NC.

This is the story told by the federal troop's official records. More details are available from the stories told by the Qualla and recorded by Smithsonian anthropologist James Mooney in the 1890s. Tsali's womenfolk had been attacked by federal troops, and the clan had fled to protect them. The young men were determined that no such outrage would be repeated, and took murderous action to protect their family from the brutal troops. Tsali voluntarily gave himself up to his tribal leaders, knowing he would be executed, to save the remainder of the Cherokees in North Carolina.

This large recreation area features 39 miles of marked bicycle and horse paths, ranging from old roads to

BIG LAUREL FALLS ON ALARKA CREEK.
Jim Hargan

🚲 🚂 **The Great Smoky Mountain Railroad in Bryson City** (800-872-4681 or 828-586-8811; fax 800-872-4681; www.gsmr.com), Dillsboro, NC. All year; schedule varies. As a major visitor attraction, the Great Smoky Mountain Railroad takes second place only to the national park itself. Organized to save a dead-end freight spur line from closing, its imaginative management has revamped it into a touring excursion line by day, with 53 miles of spectacular mountain sightseeing, steam and diesel engines, and a wide variety of special events. By night, this Cinderella railroad becomes a freight line again. The railroad runs excursions from two centers, its headquarters in Dillsboro (see "Sylva & Dillsboro"), and Bryson City, NC's historic old depot. Of the two, Bryson City has the more scenic tours, and its fine small-town depot, surrounded by old brick shops, is certainly charming.

The Bryson City depot hosts three basic excursions. The most popular excursion crosses **Fontana Lake** on a high old iron trestle, the follows the lakeshore up into the flooded lower reaches of the Nantahala Gorge. It stops for lunch at **Nantahala Outdoor Center**, then travels up the gorge to its end, returning the way it came. An alternative trip travels the same route but omits the lunch stop at NOC; instead, it uses the extra time to continue past the end of the gorge through spectacular mountain scenery to the small mountain town of **Andrews**, NC. A third variant follows the same route as the first Nantahala Gorge excursion—but its passengers disembark at the head of the gorge to raft their way back. As with the Dillsboro excursion, you will have a choice of an open excursion car, an air-conditioned Crown Coach, or an adults-only club car—a beautifully restored historic lounge car; unlike the Dillsboro excursion, the club car has wine and beer service. $28–33 for diesel, $33–38 for steam; $5 extra for Crown Coach and $7 for club car. Rail 'n Raft excursions are $64 per adult.

rough tracks. Paths lead to lake and mountain views, wildflower meadows, and old homesites, through a predominantly pine forest. But don't expect to see the rugged gorges that sheltered Tsali's family; they are all under the waters of **Fontana Reservoir**. There's also a boat ramp and a small picnic area.

PICNIC AREAS **Deep Creek Picnic Area**. Small by Smoky Mountains National Park standards, this ample picnic area offers stream-cooled air under a hardwood forest. It's less than 3 miles from Bryson City, NC, by well-marked paved roads, but quiet and away from traffic. The Deep Creek walk (see *Exploring on Foot or Bicycle*) starts nearby, leading to three impressive waterfalls.

Picnicking in the Nantahala Gorge. The Nantahala Gorge's major picnic area is the **Ferebee Memorial**, 1.3 miles south of the Nantahala Outdoor Center on

US 19. It centers on a memorial, carved in local marble, to Percy B. Ferebee, who donated the Nantahala Gorge to the American people. It's a very pleasant area, with a few tables scattered over a grassy, tree-shaded field; the Forest Service charges a dollar for its use, on the honor system. In addition to this major site, the North Carolina Department of Transportation operates four free roadside tables, each set a mile or so from the other, and each with a river view.

Riverfront Park in downtown Bryson City. This fine small riverside picnic area with a pavilion is located in the center of Bryson City, NC, at the new Swain County Courthouse. The picnic area is shaded by trees and rhododendrons, and has a short, lovely riverside walk that gives you views of the backs of the downtown buildings across the river. A flock of Muscovy ducks hangs along the river and will be sure to pay you a visit as soon as you start eating. The courthouse is an attractive modern structure on Mitchell St. two blocks west of downtown's Everett St., and its picnic area is on the river on its west side.

TVA Park on Old NC 288. Old NC 288 is the gravel road along the north shore of the Little Tennessee River that was flooded by the rising waters of Fontana Reservoir in 1944. It leaves Bryson City as Bryson Walk, runs along the river past a large lumber-drying kiln, changes its name to Old 288, then slowly drops toward the lake surface to disappear under the water. The TVA has converted the last half mile of the old road into a linear picnic ground with a large boat ramp at the end. It has six tables, each set a tenth of a mile from the next. All tables are on grassy swaths with shade trees, and all have wide views over the lake toward the mountains beyond. To find it, take Bryson Walk west out of town—it's the first left beyond the railroad depot, by the collection of old brick shops.

✳ To See

GARDENS AND PARKS The **Bryson City, NC, cemetery** occupies a tree-shaded hilltop at the west end of downtown. It's worth a visit for its lovely views over the town's Main Street, as well as a nice view of the Smoky Mountains. Its graves include a Thomas Wolfe angel—one of the angel statues imported from Italy by Wolfe's father and described by Wolfe in a famous passage in his novel *Look Homeward Angel*. Another, nearly identical angel statue sits in a cemetery in East Flat Rock, NC, but the Bryson City Wolfe angel has the distinction of gazing over the Great Smoky Mountains. Nearby is the grave of writer and historian Horace Kephart, a plaque set on a large boulder.

ONE OF THE MODELS FOR THOMAS WOLFE'S NOVEL *LOOK HOMEWARD, ANGEL*.

Jim Hargan

OTHER **Yellow Branch Cheese** (828-479-6710; www.yellowbranch.com), Yellow Branch Farm, 136 Yellow Branch Circle, Robbinsville, NC. Sat. 2–5, or by appointment; or just drop by. This family-owned organic dairy, near Fontana Dam off NC 28, produces farmstead cheese from their own cows. It's a pretty, little place, a ways up a valley and not far from Fontana Lake. The fat, sassy cows produce a high-quality, all-organic milk that yields a mild, buttery, full-bodied cheese. They make a jalapeño cheese from organic peppers they grow themselves. Next door is **Yellow Branch Pottery**, the studio and gallery of potter Karen Mickler, open Tue.–Sat. 2–5. It's worth a visit, too, and Karen sells the Yellow Branch cheese. The Mountain Hollow Bed and Breakfast is nearby. Free.

Fontana Dam (423-988-2431), 804 US 321 N., Suite 300, Lenoir City, TN. Sitting at the base of the Smoky Mountains 22 miles west of Bryson City, Fontana Dam is the tallest dam in the eastern United States, blocking the gorge of the Little Tennessee River with a concrete wall 480 feet high and over half a mile wide at the top. Built in a great hurry between 1942 and 1944, Fontana was an emergency wartime project, intended to ensure that the Knoxville, TN, area had enough electrical power for the strategically important Alcoa aluminum plant and the top-secret Oak Ridge Research Laboratory. Its impoundment created the 29-mile-long Fontana Lake, flooding the gorge of the Little Tennessee River and forcing the abandonment of half a dozen mountain communities.

Fontana Dam is an impressive sight, and well worth a visit. A modernist visitors center sits at its southern end, with a large observation deck giving fine views of the mammoth structure. From the center, those wanting to tour the dam take an inclined tram down the gorge wall to the generators at the base. A public road crosses the 2,600-foot dam top to national park trailheads on the opposite side—a fascinating drive.

✳ To Do

BICYCLING **Euchella Mountain Bike Outfitters** (800-446-1603 or 828-488-8835; www.main.nc.us/Euchella/details.html), Almond, NC. This mountain bike outfitter offers specialized mountain bikes for riding the trails of Tsali, as well as guided trips and twice-weekly (in summer) Youth Wilderness Sports Days for teenagers. Headquartered from a large forested tract near the mouth of the Nantahala Gorge, they offer a variety of lodge and cabin rentals at a variety of prices. $30 per day front-suspension mountain bike rental.

FONTANA DAM AS SEEN FROM THE FONTANA DAM OVERLOOK.
Jim Hargan

Nantahala Outdoor Center (888-662-1662; www.noc.com), 13077 US 19 W., Bryson City, NC. NOC offers a large range of mountain and road bicycling programs, from simple rentals to overnight trips. $25–42 for 1-day bicycle rentals, depending on type of bike. Also see *Whitewater Adventures*, below.

Jim Hargan

THE NANTAHALA RIVER IS ONE OF THE MOST POPULAR VACATION DESTINATIONS IN THE REGION.

GOLF Great Smoky Mountain Country Club (800-474-0070; www .smokymountaincc.com), 1112 Conleys Creek Rd., Whittier, NC. Located in Conley Creek Valley, this 18-hole par-71 course climbs the mountainsides 500 feet above the clubhouse. Views are stunning, and the play is challenging, even though only four holes play uphill.

STABLES Nantahala Village Riding Stables (828-488-9649), Bryson City, NC. Summer, daily 9–6:30; spring and fall, Fri.–Sun. 10–5; closed winter. Guided trail rides in the Nantahala Gorge area, 9 miles west of Bryson City. From $12 for 1 hour to $80 for an all-day ride; $150 for a 2-day trip.

WHITEWATER ADVENTURES Nantahala Outdoor Center (800-232-7238; www.noc.com), 13077 US 19 W., Bryson City, NC. This complex of half a dozen handsome buildings straddles both the Nantahala River and the Appalachian Trail, and qualifies as a tourist attraction all by itself. The employee-owned NOC offers kayaking and rafting, mountain biking, instruction at a variety of levels, three restaurants, cabin rentals, and an outdoor store. $18–35 per person for a variety of inflatables, in both guided and unguided trips; price varies by season and day of week.

Endless Rivers Adventures (800-224-7238 or 828-488-6199; fax 828-488-2259; www.endlessriveradventures.com), 14157 US 19 W., Bryson City, NC. This outfitter offers whitewater rafting on the Nantahala and other rivers, as well as workshops for kayaking and rock climbing, and fly-fishing guide service. $19–45 per person for a variety of inflatables, in both guided and unguided trips; price varies by season and day of week.

Rolling Thunder River Company (800-408-7238 or 828-488-2030; www .rollingthunderriverco.com), 10160 US 19 W. Bryson City, NC. Rolling Thunder offers a variety of inflatable rentals as well as guided raft trips on the Nantahala and other rivers. They have on-site camping and a bunkhouse. $17–32 per person, depending on type of rental, time of year, and day of week.

Wildwater, Ltd. Nantahala (800-451-9972 or 828-488-2384; www.wildwater rafting.com), Almond, NC. This outfitter offers a variety of guided and unguided rafting trips, as well as the popular Raft and Rail trip in association with the Great Smoky Mountain Railroad. $19–34 per person for a variety of inflatables, in both guided and unguided trips; price varies by season and day of week.

USA Raft (800-872-7238; www.usaraft.com), 1104 US 19 W., Bryson City, NC.

This Rowlesburg, WV, company has a presence in the Nantahala Gorge, offering raft trips and inflatable rentals.

❋ Lodging

COUNTRY INNS AND HOTELS ✐ **The Fryemont Inn** (800-845-4879 or 828-488-2159; www.fryemontinn .com), P.O. Box 459, Bryson City, NC 28713. The main lodge and restaurant are open mid-Apr.–Thanksgiving; suites are open all year. Built by timber baron Amos Frye in 1923, this National Register lodge sits on a hill above downtown Bryson City, with sweeping views from its wide front porch. The inn's large grounds are beautifully landscaped with native rhododendrons and hemlocks, isolated and very quiet. The bark-clad lodge has a large, comfortable lobby, filled with original Craftsman-style furniture, a large wood fire on cold days, and wide doors that open onto the porch when it's warm. The dining room, with many trout specialties, is a classic early-20th-century lodge room with a fine bar (see *Dining Out*). The 37 en suite rooms in the main lodge all have wormy chestnut paneling and simple, comfortable furnishings in a country style; queen bed rooms are small (and less expensive), while rooms with king or two double beds are quite large, with separate sitting areas. Room tariffs include a full breakfast and dinner, ordered from the menu, at the inn's dining room. A separate building, constructed in 1940 as a recreation hall, has been redone into large and comfortable "fireplace suites," each with a living room with fireplace, a separate king bedroom, and a wet bar. These suites, open all year, include breakfast and dinner during the season when the restaurant is open, with the tariff sharply discounted during winter when the restaurant is closed and meals are not included. Children are permitted in the main lodge, but not the fireplace suites. Main lodge $70–135, with two-bedroom units $150–186, including breakfast and dinner. Suites $137–196, including breakfast and dinner, when the restaurant is open; otherwise $75–150, with no meals.

Charleston Inn Bed and Breakfast (888-285-1555 or 828-488-4644; www .charlestoninn.com), 208 Arlington Ave., Bryson City, NC 28713. Open all year. Built by a local attorney in 1927, this large house sits on a wooded piece of property on a hillside within town. Beautifully renovated in 1996, the Charleston Inn has 20 rooms—6 in the main house, and 14 in an annex built in the 1940s and converted to excellent-quality rooms. In the main house, the common rooms are elegant and comfortable; a game room opens onto a glassed porch through French doors, while a bright TV room has sofas and easy chairs. The main feature, however, is the dining room, a glassed wing with French doors on three sides, shingle walls, exposed beams, and hardwood floors. The French doors open onto an elaborate multilayered deck with mountain views over the town and a seven-person hot tub in a corner. All rooms are carefully decorated with new furniture in an elegant English country style. The main house's 6 rooms are more like bedrooms in a wealthy home, while the annex's 14 rooms are larger, with separate sitting area and semiprivate porch. $75–165 per night.

✐ **Historic Calhoun Country Inn** (828-488-1234; fax 828-488-0488;

www.calhouncountryinn.com), 135 Everett St., Bryson City, NC 28713. Open all year. Innkeeper Sue Hyde was raised on her mother's stories of Bryson City's Calhoun Hotel, where she worked as a cook—the good country food and warm country welcome that the old owner, Granville Calhoun, had brought to it. Now Sue has restored this 1920s depot hotel to its glory days as a country hotel. Its public rooms are large, bright, and airy, with hardwood floors, Oriental rugs, and comfortable plush sofas; beyond, French doors open onto an extra-wide front porch whose rockers overlook downtown Bryson City's Everett St. The rooms are reminiscent of a fine old country hotel—small to medium in size, bright, with antiques mixed into the decor. The third-floor rooms face a large common area outfitted as a library; some have telescopes. Of the 23 rooms, 8 have shared baths; 4 on the second floor share two baths, and 4 on the third floor share one bath. The price includes a hearty country breakfast served in the sunny dining room. $65–135 per night, including breakfast.

RESORTS Hemlock Inn (828-488-2885; fax 828-488-8985; www .hemlockinn.com), Galbraith Creek Rd., P.O. Box 2350, Bryson City, NC 28713. Open May–Oct. Built as a country inn in 1952, the Hemlock Inn sits just 3 miles from the Great Smoky Mountains National Park's Deep Creek area, on its own 50 acres down a paved country lane. A low, modern structure of rustic gray wood, this AAA three-diamond-rated facility has a large common area and two motel-style wings. The common area has wide views over grassy fields from its

porch and deck, with comfortable country-style seating around a fireplace, and a large dining area. Breakfast and dinner—both included in the tariff—are hearty country fare, authentically mountain and made fresh from scratch on the premises. Meals are served family style, with the food placed in great bowls in lazy Susans in the middle of round tables. Rooms have pine paneling and attractive country furniture, but are small. $137–155.

BED & BREAKFAST INNS The Randolph House (800-480-3472 or 828-488-3472; www.randolphhouse.com), 233 Fryemont Rd., P.O. Box 816, Bryson City, NC 28713. Open May–Oct. Amos Frye built the Randolph House in 1895 as his personal home, nearly 30 years before he built

THE NANTAHALA RIVER AS IT PASSES THROUGH THE GORGE.
Jim Hargan

the grand Fryemont Inn across the street. For the last quarter century it's been the seat of a fine restaurant and B&B, owned and operated by Frye's great-niece Ruth Randolph Adams and her husband, Bill. Downstairs is the luxurious and intimate dining area where guests take dinner as well as breakfast. Upstairs are seven cozy, romantic bedrooms, decorated with antiques—some from the original house. $140–160 per night, including full breakfast and dinner.

Folkestone Inn Bed and Breakfast (888-812-3385 or 828-488-2730; fax 828-488-0722; www.folkestone.com), 101 Folkstone Rd., Bryson City, NC 28713. Open all year. This beautifully restored 1920s farmhouse sits slightly off the paved Deep Creek Rd. a quarter mile from the Great Smoky Mountains National Park. It's a bit of a cross between a Victorian farmhouse and a large bungalow, set in a grove of giant spruces by a tiny stream. A wide full-front porch faces Deep Creek with comfortable chairs, with another porch on top serving the second floor. The front parlor has Victorian farm furnishings and a potbellied stove, while the rustic breakfast room is faced with tall windows on three sides. The 10 comfortable rooms feature Victorian and country reproductions, including 3 ground-floor rooms with stone flag floors and low tin ceilings. This facility is also horse friendly, so you can stable your horse at a barn one block away, making it easy to enjoy Smoky Mountain trail riding in the area. Summer and fall $82–108, winter and spring $75–98.

Mountain Hollow Bed and Breakfast (828-479-3608; www.mountain hollowbb.com), 124 Possum Hollow Rd., Robbinsville, NC 28771. This Victorian-style house, modern-built on a 35-acre tract near Fontana, has turrets, gables, and a wraparound rocking porch lined with gingerbread. Inside, decor is country Victorian, elegant and simple; each of the four rooms is individually theme decorated with Victorian antiques and reproductions. One room is a suite, with a separate turret sitting room and a whirlpool bath. A full breakfast is included, taken in a turret breakfast room or on the porch. $55–125.

MOTEL **Cold Springs Country Inn** (877-500-4114 or 828-488-3537; www .coldspringscountryinn.com), 435 Cold Springs Rd., Bryson City, NC 28713. Open all year. This restored 1955 road-side motel takes you back to the early days of automobile touring. Originally known as the Sundowner Motel, the 10-room facility was built from local stone on what was then US 19 but is now a quiet back country lane, Cold Springs Rd. It's a quiet, comfortable spot, with plenty of grass and shade. The comfortably-sized rooms have their original paneling of locally milled tongue-and-groove wood—wormy chestnut, pine heartwood, poplar— with funky early-1950s white tile bathrooms in fine condition. The new owners have decorated each room individually to its own theme, using all-new furniture and mattresses (kings, queens, and doubles). Breakfast is an ample continental buffet, served in the paneled lobby. $55–75 per night.

CABIN RENTALS **Falling Waters Adventure Resort** (800-451-9972; fax 864-647-5361; www.fallingwaters resort.com), 10345 US 74 W., Bryson City, NC 28713. Although well known in the Pacific Northwest, luxury yurts are a new concept in the South.

These are tents, round in shape, pitched on a wood platform. However, these are not ordinary tents. They're 16 feet in diameter, with French doors opening up onto wood decks, skylights over the queen-sized four-poster beds, and area rugs on the polished knotty-pine floors. Not to mention ceiling fans, refrigerators, and coffeemakers. This is definitely the luxury end of tent camping. $72 per night for a luxury yurt.

Hidden Creek Cabin Rentals (888-333-5881; www.hiddencreekcabins .com), Bryson City, NC 28713. These four cabins overlook Hidden Creek on 23 private acres just outside the Lakeshore Dr. entrance to the Great Smoky Mountains National Park. Two of the cabins are traditional second homes; one is a modern log cabin; and one is a 1930s farmhouse. All four are on a stocked trout stream, and each has its own seven-person hot tub on an outdoor deck. The wooded property includes an 1850 log cabin. Although the cabins have a great atmosphere of quiet and remoteness, they are actually quite convenient to Bryson City and the four-lane US 23/74 for ready access throughout the region. $100 per night, $650 per week.

CABIN RESERVATION SERVICES **Yellow Rose Realty** (828-488-2797; fax 828-488-9855; www.yellowroserealty .com/vacation.php), 150 Bryson Walk, P.O. Box 326, Bryson City, NC 28713. This local Realtor manages 50 or so vacation properties throughout the Bryson City and Cherokee area.

✳ Where to Eat

EATING OUT **Everett Street Diner** (828-488-0123), 52 Everett St., Bryson City, NC. Tue.–Sun. 7–3. This busy café may occupy a brick storefront in downtown Bryson City, but it's no grits-and-grease small-town eatery; the Everett Street Diner offers an upscale menu filled with fresh foods and intelligent recipes. Inside you'll find indirect lighting, bamboo chairs, dark green carpets, and light gray walls hung with original art. A house salad is based on mixed greens (with nary a piece of iceberg lettuce in sight), its bitter peppery flavor balanced by the sweetness of the homemade raspberry vinaigrette. The chili, made fresh, is vegetarian, filled with black beans and chunks of tomatoes. Other menu items have the same twist—old favorites given a goose with fresh ingredients and imaginative combinations of flavors. Despite this decidedly big-city sophistication, you'll find the prices remain downtown Bryson City. Breakfast $3.65–4.95, lunch $5.25–6.95.

DINING OUT ✒ ♿ **The Fryemont Inn** (800-845-4879 or 828-488-2159; www.fryemontinn.com/dining.htm). Breakfast 8–10, dinner 6–8 (until 9 Fri. and Sat.); bar opens at 5 PM; closed winter. The historic Fryemont Inn, on a hill overlooking Bryson City and the Great Smoky Mountains from its wide porch, opens its dining room to the public for breakfast and dinner mid-Apr.–late Nov. This large room is well in keeping with a 1923 mountain lodge, with its wood rafters, polished hardwood floors, giant stone fireplace (with a wood fire cackling merrily away in chilly weather), and wormy chestnut paneling. Its full-service bar is comfortable and quiet, with lots of old wood and two pool tables. Chef and co-owner George Brown Jr. has developed a thoughtful menu of trout (served four different ways), ham (sugar or salt cured), lamb, and beef, always cooked fresh and served with family-style side dishes. Breakfasts emphasize simple country foods, well prepared: eggs, omelets, French toast, and pancakes. Breakfast $5–6.25, dinner $12–19.

Relia's Garden Restaurant (828-488-2176). Sun.–Thu. noon–9, Fri. and Sat. until 10; closed winter. Terraced herb gardens, curved and stepped like an amphitheater, flank the entrance walk to the fanciest of the Nantahala Outdoor Center's three restaurants. The handsome modern building, clad in unpainted board and batten, also steps up in multiple levels, with wide porches and high-pitched roofs. Entrées emphasize fresh ingredients and careful use of herbs, frequently from the garden outside. Sandwiches and salads $5.25–8.95, entrées $8.95–15.95.

Nantahala Village Mountain Resort and Meeting Center (800-438-1507 or 828-488-2628; www .nvnc.com), 9400 US 19 W., Bryson City, NC. This 200-acre resort and conference center, a local tradition since 1948, sports an excellent restaurant in its new lodge. The large dining room features a cathedral ceiling and plenty of wood trim; large windows offer a wide sunset view deep into the Nantahala Gorge, then over the mountains. Dinner entrées run from the simple (fried chicken, rib-eye steak) to the imaginative (spinach mushroom strudel). Expect the simplest entrées to be fresh and well prepared, such as a local trout, butterflied and sautéed in butter and herbs, served with capered butter. $8–17 for dinner entrées.

✳ Selective Shopping

Bryson City, NC

You don't really expect a small-town main street to be a center for high-fashion shopping, yet it can have its charms. Bryson City furnishes some interesting storefronts in an L-shaped district radiating from the old courthouse. Foremost among these is **Clampett's Hardware**, which maintains a separate store for farm-related products that may well have the single most compelling collection of country items in the Smokies. Next door, watercolor artist Elizabeth Ellison maintains her studio and gallery from a small storefront. A bit farther down, **The Charleston Station** offers antiques and gifts from an attractive early-20th-century house. And don't forget to stop for lunch at the Everett Street Diner (see *Eating Out*).

The depot area. Bryson City's classic small-town depot, on the north edge of downtown, is once again lively with passenger traffic—this time on the Great Smoky Mountain Railroad. And just like in the old days, the depot area is coming alive with small shops. A quilt shop and discount bookshop occupy the old car dealership on one side, while the old brick buildings across the street hold a variety of shops, including one specializing in mountain fiddles. Sideways across the street are more old brick storefronts with antiques and collectibles, with one shop specializing in what can only be called redneck humor (example: a skimpy bikini emblazoned with a Confederate battle flag).

✳ Special Events

SPRING **Dogwood Train Ride** (800-872-4681). Late Apr. The special Great

Smoky Mountain Railroad excursions are always extra fun, and this one has the added attraction of benefiting the local Rotarians' scholarship fund. The 4½-hour train ride into the Nantahala Gorge includes a barbeque lunch and plenty of spring color.

Heritage Day Festival (800-867-9246 or 828-488-3681), Bryson City, NC. Memorial Day. This annual celebration of mountain heritage features traditional food, music, and crafts, as well as a toy duck race on the Tuckaseegee River.

SUMMER Singing in the Smokies (828-497-2060), Inspiration Park, Bryson City, NC; follow the signs from the Ela exit off US 23/74 east of town. This gospel music festival, sponsored by the successful Bryson City male gospel group The Inspirations, features a large number of gospel groups over a week centered on the Fourth of July. Seating is on the grass, with a large, covered area when it rains. You're welcome to bring a lawn chair and a picnic meal, although both are available on site from concessionaires. A shorter version of the festival is held on Labor Day weekend and in the middle of Oct. $12 for evening sings, $15 for all-day sings.

Freedom Fest on the River (800-867-9246 or 828-488-3681). July 4. Bryson City, NC's town celebration takes place in its attractive Riverfront Park, with live entertainment, food, crafts, and fireworks.

Folkmoot USA (800-867-9246 or 828-488-3681). Late July. Bryson City, NC, hosts three groups of international folksingers and dancers in their native costumes as part of this major mountainwide folk celebration.

Fireman's Day Festival (828-488-9410), Bryson City, NC. Labor Day. Apart from the music, entertainment, crafts, and barbeque dinner, this fund-raiser for the local volunteer fire department features a Parade of Fire Trucks and a Miss Flame competition.

AUTUMN Nantahala Village Fall Dinner Concert Series (800-438-1507 or 828-488-2826). Nov.–Dec. After the tourist season winds down and night starts falling early in the evening, the excellent restaurant at Nantahala Village schedules a series of dinner concerts, where musicians from the Asheville Symphony perform their choice of acoustic music. Typical music might include a guitar duo, a jazz trio, or a quintet playing Celtic and mountain instruments. The full dinner, included in the charge, has a choice of three entrées (one of which will be a steak or prime rib, with the other two being more adventuresome chicken, fish, or vegetarian fare). $35 per person, including dinner.

WINTER Bryson City Merchants Christmas Parade and Festival (800-867-9246 or 828-488-3681). First Sat. in Dec. Sponsored by the merchants of Bryson City, NC, this Christmas celebration features a parade with floats, bands, horses, and clowns; a breakfast with Santa; an auction; special discounts for shoppers; and a local theater presentation. A week later the Rotarians sponsor "A Visit from Inn to Inn," visiting five historic old inns decorated for Christmas, with plenty of Christmas music and hors d'oeuvres (tickets $15 single, $25 couple).

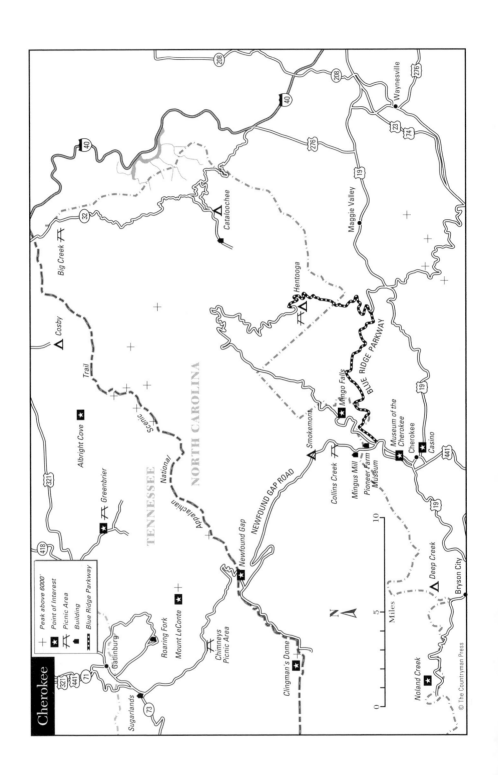

CHEROKEE & THE SOUTHEAST QUADRANT

T his chapter covers the southeastern quadrant of the Great Smoky Mountains National Park and the adjacent lands of the Qualla Cherokees. It includes the rugged and remote ridges that run down from the Smokies Crest into the North Carolina half of the national park; the large Cherokee Reservation, properly known as the "Qualla Boundary," on the park's southern edge; the populous tourist area now called Maggie Valley, NC; and the remote mountain coves of Cataloochee and Little Cataloochee, NC, once heavily settled and now preserving mountain heritage deep within the national park.

This corner of the Smokies was settled by traditionalist Cherokees in 1819, led by the respected Chief Yonaguska. Known as the Qualla, they wished to avoid both the white settlers and the Europeanized leaders of the Cherokee Nation; they built their riverside villages along the Oconaluftee deep in the Smoky Mountains, on land uncoveted by whites and outside the Cherokee Nation. In 1838 President Andrew Jackson supported the State of Georgia in its efforts to expel the Cherokee Nation, seize its land for white people, and send the Cherokees west to the "Indian Territory" (now Oklahoma). The result was the genocidal Trail of Tears, where federal soldiers forced Cherokee families from their houses at gunpoint into holding compounds, then on a long and brutal trudge in the dead of winter. The Qualla were not part of the Cherokee Nation, however, and legally not subjected to the expulsion; after much debate, federal authorities allowed the Qualla to stay. Today, the Qualla are the Eastern Band of the Cherokee Nation, their tribal headquarters of Cherokee located on the border of the national park.

The Great Smoky Mountains National Park wraps around the north side of the Qualla Boundary. Despite a mile-high landscape of knotted ridgelines separated by deep valleys, this quadrant offers some amazing opportunities to explore by car. The Newfound Gap Rd., built in 1932 to bring tourists into the newly formed national park, runs through the center of Cherokee then up the Oconaluftee River to reach a high ridge, for some of the best views in the park. From the top of the Newfound Gap Rd., a side road leads along the crest of the Smokies to Clingmans Dome, the highest point in the park. From the bottom, the Blue

Ridge Parkway wraps along the park's southern border, for wonderful views of the Smokies Crest and the receding ridges of the North Carolina Blue Ridge—then generates a scenic spur road that dives deep into the park's backcountry. East of the Qualla Boundary, the national park preserves the remote Cataloochee Cove, with its twisting gravel roads, wide meadows, and historic farmhouses.

GUIDANCE **Cherokee Visitors Center (Cherokee Tribal Travel and Promotion)** (800-438-1601 or 828-497-9195; fax 828-438-1601; www.cherokee-nc .com), P.O. Box 460, Cherokee, NC 28719. The visitors center offers information and brochures from a small stand-alone building in the center of Cherokee, by the Pizza Inn.

GETTING THERE *By car*: Cherokee, NC, is located at the main south gate of the Great Smoky Mountains National Park, at the intersection of **US 441** and **US 19**. Because US 19 is a narrow, winding two-lane road between Maggie Valley and Cherokee, it's nearly always faster to use the nearby freeway, **US 74**, to US 441 a few miles south of town. If your destination is Maggie Valley, NC, rather than Cherokee, approach it via **US 276**, either from I-40 or from US 74 in Waynesville, NC.

By air: **Asheville Regional Airport** (828-684-2226; fax 828-684-3404), 708 Airport Rd., Fletcher, NC. Located 15 miles south of downtown Asheville, NC, off I-26, Exit 9 (NC 280). Service from Atlanta, Cincinnati, Pittsburgh, Raleigh, and Charlotte, with 20 to 25 flights daily. Several car rental agencies are located within or near the airport—and you will need a rental car, because there is no bus service to Cherokee. The 66-mile trip is on four-lane highway all the way, and should take about $1\frac{1}{4}$ hours. From the airport, take I-26 north to I-40; then I-40 west to US 23/74; then US 23/74 west to US 441; then US 441 north to Cherokee.

By bus or public transportation: Cherokee, NC, has no bus service, and no public transportation. Greyhound has daily bus service into Waynesville, NC, 9 miles from Maggie Valley, NC; however, no public transportation links Maggie Valley with the bus terminal.

MEDICAL EMERGENCIES **Cherokee Urgent Care Clinic and Pharmacy** (828-497-9036), El Camino Plaza, US 19 N., Cherokee, NC. Weekdays 9:30–4:30. This walk-in clinic welcomes travelers with non-life-threatening illnesses or injuries. It's located by Harrah's Casino, and must be accessed either through the Harrah's parking lot or the parking lot of the El Camino Motel.

Serious emergencies. From Cherokee, the closest 24/7 emergency room is in the small **Swain County Hospital** (828-488-2155; www.westcare.org/patients visitors/swain/swainvisitorinformation.html), 45 Plateau St., Bryson City, NC (11 miles away); find it on an obscure residential side street, uphill from the train depot; look for the blue hospital signs on the north side of the depot.

The nearest full-service hospital is **Harris Regional Hospital** (828-586-7000; www.westcare.org), 68 Hospital Rd., Sylva, NC; it's a mile east of town on US Business 74, just off the easternmost of the three Sylva exits on US 23/74. Sylva is 18 miles from Cherokee.

Maggie Valley is about 10 miles from **Haywood Regional Medical Facility** (828-456-7311), 90 Hospital Dr., Clyde, NC. This major regional hospital has a walk-in clinic on its campus, as well as a full-service emergency room. Take US 19 to US 23; exit onto NC 209, then parallel the freeway to Jones Cove Rd.

✳ Wandering Around

EXPLORING BY CAR **The Blue Ridge Parkway and the Heintooga Spur Rd**. The Blue Ridge Parkway's final 13-mile section runs from Soco Gap on US 19 to the Newfound Gap Rd. just inside the Great Smoky Mountains National Park. From **Soco Gap**, the parkway climbs uphill through forests for the next 3 miles—a particularly fine stretch for spring wildflowers, reaching the Heintooga Spur Rd. (described later) at **Wolf Laurel Gap**. From here the parkway picks its way down a side ridge, dropping 3,200 feet to reach the Oconaluftee River. Although heavily forested, the terrain is rough enough to require five tunnels, and the parkway gets its share of views. The best views are found on a 2-mile stretch between **Big Witch Gap Overlook** and **Noland Divide Overlook**, where the wall-like Great Smoky Mountains are framed in June by a stunning rhododendron display. There are more good views near the end, where the **Oconaluftee River Overlook** gives an aerial of the Mountain Farm Museum. The parkway ends at an intersection with US 441 just outside Cherokee, NC, and just inside the Great Smoky Mountains National Park.

Back on the parkway, the unusual and fascinating **Heintooga Spur Rd.** (mentioned above) loops 27 miles through the park's Balsam Mountain backcountry, a leisurely forest drive that ends deep in the Qualla Boundary. The first of the spur's three major views arrives quickly, at **Mile High Overlook**—as its name implies, a 5,280-foot overlook with a 180° view toward the Smoky Mountain Crest. At 3.6 miles the road reaches **Black Camp Gap** and enters the national park; a pyramidal Masonic Monument sits a short distance off the road. From here the road is a pretty forest drive that climbs gently to **Balsam Mountain Picnic Area** on a high ridgetop. Shaded by a handsome old spruce forest, this high, windy spot is definitely the place to cool off on a summer day. It also has the second of the road's three views, known as **Heintooga Overlook**, at the far end of the picnic area—a broad view sideways over the high crest of the Smokies, renowned for its fine sunsets.

From the picnic area, the road becomes a one-lane, one-way gravel road, of dependably good quality. The road is so narrow as to be a car path through the great overhanging trees; fortunately, you don't have to worry about oncoming traffic. The third and last view comes 2 miles into this segment, a 90° degree vista southward over the deep canyonlike valleys of the Smokies toward the Qualla Boundary. Six miles later the road reaches **Pin Oak Gap**, an important backcountry trailhead, and finally drops away from the high ridgeline into the stream valleys below. At 22 miles the road bottoms out at **Round Bottom Horse Camp** and becomes two way again as it follows a lovely little stream to enter the Qualla Boundary. In 3.5 more miles it reaches Big Cove Rd., its first real intersection since it left the Blue Ridge Parkway. A left turn will bring you to Cherokee, NC, in 11 miles.

THE HEART OF THE SMOKIES

On the North Carolina side, the Newfound Gap Road climbs through the heart of the Smokies to reach a mile-high gap in the center of the range. In doing so, it wanders past a pioneer log farmstead and a wooden water mill, follows a torrential mountain river, then climbs to stunning views of the endlessly receding ridges between the Smokies and the Blue Ridge. Once at the top, an old spur road (unchanged in appearance from the 1930s) follows the crest of the Smokies to the park's highest peak, Clingmans Dome.

The Newfound Gap Road in North Carolina. It's good to get an early start, both to avoid the crowds and to catch a sunrise. For a sunrise go straight up to the top, then go down to the first overlook on the NC side, where the sun will rise over a deep mountain cleft. After the sun is up, you'll want to go on up to **Newfound Gap** to enjoy the way that the early-morning sun lights up the road as it dives into the deep valleys. From there the spur road to **Clingmans Dome** has more sunrise views.

While the Newfound Gap Rd. continues northward to descend into TN and Gatlinburg, this drive goes down the NC side, south toward Cherokee. The road drops down from Newfound Gap onto the crest of **Thomas Divide**. For the next 3 miles the road twists along the narrow ridgeline, giving panoramic views over the deep valleys of the Smokies, toward the twisted high ridges of the Cowee and Nantahala Mountains. On many mornings, the early light will be reflecting off great sheets of fog that blanket the valleys thousands of feet below, with the ridgelines poking through like archipelagoes. The road finally plunges down the side of Thomas Divide to give one final view over a sharp-sided valley and back up toward Newfound Gap. A quiet walkway on the left follows the original 1932 roadbed, abandoned in the 1960s; it looks like a footpath along a grassy terrace, with bits of asphalt occasionally showing through. After that, the road loops down into the valley for a long, easy streamside drive, reaching the Oconaluftee River at the **Kephart Prong Trail**.

From here the road hugs the river closely, sometimes looming over it from a high granite wall, sometimes swerving away from it through grassy meadows. Along this segment you'll pass **Collins Creek Picnic Area** at 10.6 miles and **Smokemont** at 12.5 miles. Beyond are two first-rate historical sites: **Mingus Mill**, a restored turbine water mill, and the **Oconaluftee Farm Museum**, a reconstructed mountain farm complete with crops, gardens, and farm animals. At the end of this drive, the Newfound Gap Rd. loops around broad meadows with wide views toward the log farm museum and the mountains beyond. On the far side of the meadow, the Blue Ridge Parkway makes its southern terminus. Just beyond is the park boundary and the town of Cherokee. **Clingmans Dome Scenic Drive**. This 7-mile spur road follows the crest of the Smokies westward from Newfound Gap to its dead end at Clingmans Dome. It's the easiest way to enjoy the unusual Canadian-style spruce–fir forest found only at the highest elevations, as this high-altitude road stays inside the forest most of its length. This forest (known locally as "balsams") is an isolated remnant of a great subarctic forest that blanketed the Southeast at the peak of the last ice age—preserved here by the subarctic conditions at the top of the Smokies.

More than any other park road, the Clingmans Dome Spur Rd. has the look and feel of a 1930s WPA scenic drive. It's narrow and twisting, shaded by the balsam forest crowding its edge, with trimmed rock walls on the downhill side. Its cuts are too modest to provide the wide views of a more modern highway, and its shoulders are frequently too narrow to pull off and park. The first view (0.4 mile from the beginning) is one of the best, a 5,200-foot-high bird's-eye straight down **Beech Flats Prong** to the Oconaluftee Valley, with the Newfound Gap Rd. curving away below. Your next landmarks are an **Appalachian Trail (AT)** access point (at 1.2 miles) and an interpretive nature trail about the spruce–fir forest (at 2.5 miles). You can combine both interests at the next trailhead (3.5 miles), however, where a short access trail leads to the AT, then half a mile left and uphill through a fir forest devastated by insects (the woolly adelgid, an illegal immigrant from Europe) to views and wild berries on the peak of **Mount Collins** (6,188 feet, the 25th tallest in the East). Then, at 5.3 miles, **Webb Overlook** gives another fine view eastward. But save some film for the final overlook at the road's end, with wonderful panoramic views east, south, and west over endless mountain ranges—another good place for a sunrise. At the end of the overlook is the paved path that leads to the summit of **Clingmans Dome** as well as a great AT walk. The walk to the wildflower-framed views from Andrews Bald starts here as well.

A high ridge walk on the Appalachian Trail. This 3-mile walk follows the Smoky Mountain Crest westward from Clingmans Dome, staying above 6,000 feet with stunning views into both Tennessee and North Carolina. Starting at the Clingmans Dome Overlook parking lot, go a short distance down the **Forney Ridge Trail** to the **Clingmans Dome Bypass Trail**. This little-used cutoff will save you some climbing, while leading past some good meadow views into North Carolina. After a third of a mile you gain the AT on the high, sharp ridge of the Smokies Crest. From here are first-rate views into Tennessee, toward Elkmont and over the side ridges that fall steeply downward to the foothills. Turn left onto the AT. You will be hiking along a razorbacked spine of a ridge, with grass growing between exposed rocks and long views over both North Carolina and Tennessee. The trail will remain more or less level to **Mount Buckley**, then start a moderate but inexorable drop, losing 1,000 feet in the next 2.5 miles. The trail remains scenic, passing through grassy areas and forests— but don't forget that going up this slope is going to be a lot more difficult than going down. When you decide to turn around, stay on the AT until it reaches the **Clingmans Dome Observation Tower**, to pick up a few good views you missed on the way out.

Andrews Bald walk. The high grassy balds of the Smokies remain one of the most important features of the park, playing a major part in its environmental diversity. They are also one of the most beautiful features—wide, ridgetop meadows, scattered with brushy azaleas, rhododendrons, and laurels, a riot of wildflowers all spring and early summer, with wide views the rest of the year. Ironically, these balds are disappearing as a result of the National Park Service's conservation efforts. It seems these balds were brought into their present form by settlers using them for summer cattle pastures—and they return to forest after grazing stops. Since the NPS eliminated grazing over 70 years ago, all the balds have shrunk, and some have disappeared altogether. Today the rangers maintain just two of the many balds, and those at a fraction of their former size: remote Gregory Bald, and Andrews Bald.

Although Andrews Bald is a short 3-mile hike, it's no level stroll. Starting from the high ridge at Clingmans Dome, it drops 600 feet in 0.9 mile, then rises 150 feet before the final 175-foot drop to the large ridgeline meadow. It offers wide views over North Carolina and Fontana Lake, framed by rhododendrons and azaleas in June. Not surprisingly, it's a popular walk, so expect a fair amount of company along the way.

Cataloochee Cove drive. Once the most heavily settled corner of the Smokies, Cataloochee is now the most remote part of the Great Smoky National Park accessible by car. To reach it you most drive over miles of narrow, winding gravel road, through deep forest. Once there you will find yourself in a wide valley, floored with broad meadows, dotted by historic buildings, and surrounded by mountains.

Start your drive to Cataloochee at the intersection of US 276 and I-40 (Exit 20), 6 miles north of US 19 near Maggie Valley, NC. Near the intersection you'll find a side road, Sutton Town Rd. (SSR 1331), heading west. Take it; then take the right fork in 1.5 miles onto Cove Creek Rd. (SR 1305). This switchbacks steeply uphill, then over a mountain and into the national park (turning into a gravel road along the way). When you reach the bottom you will find an intersection with a paved road, part of a long-abandoned project to turn Cataloochee into a major tourist attraction; turn left. The paved road winds through young forests, past a small campground, to an intersection with a gravel road in wide meadows. Here stands the 1905 **Will Messer Barn**, beside a small ranger station with an information desk. Continue along the paved road to the left, passing through meadows to the lovely little 1898 **Palmer Methodist Chapel**, still occasionally used. Nearby is the 1901 **Beech Grove School**, a one-room schoolhouse authentically furnished. After that the road turns gravel, continuing through meadows with wide, pastoral views. The road passes between a large barn and a 1906 Victorian-style farmhouse, the **Caldwell House**. Beyond, the auto road ends at a gate, but the old farm road continues to the **Woody House**, an 1866 log cabin with a 1910 addition. Return to the Will Messer Barn and ranger station, then turn left onto the gravel road. In a short distance (through more meadows) you will reach the attractive **Palmer House**; Uncle Fate Palmer built this dogtrot log cabin in 1860, and his descendants added the hand-planed interior paneling (in 1905), brightly painted weatherboarding (1910), and kitchen wing (1924). Just beyond, the gravel road enters the woods, then reaches a T intersection. The right fork goes back to Cove Creek Rd. and Maggie Valley. The left fork leads a few miles to an old road (now a trail) up to the Little Cataloochee Community. This 5-mile walk leads to three more historic sites: the 1864 log **Hannah Cabin** with its handmade brick chimney; the hilltop **Little Cataloochee Baptist Church**, topped by a handsome belfry and steeple; and the scant remains of the **Cook Place and Messer Farm** at the top of the road. Back at your car, continue on the gravel road, leaving the park in 3 miles to pass through 9 miles of meadows and farmlands. When you reach the road to the Big Creek area of the national park, turn right into Waterville, NC, reaching I-40 in 2 miles.

EXPLORING ON FOOT **Kephart Prong Trail**. Kephart Prong is a lively mountain stream named for Horace Kephart from nearby Bryson City, NC; the town's librarian, "Kep" was a prominent national park activist and an outdoors writer who authored *Our Southern Highlanders* in 1913. This easy walk on the North Carolina side of the Newfound Gap Rd. follows an old road for 2 miles along a lovely mountain stream to a small trail shelter. It is particularly interesting for the remains of a Civilian Conservation Corp camp hidden in the woods along the trail. The well-signposted trailhead parking lot is 3.75 miles north of Smokemont, on the right.

✳ Villages

Cherokee, NC. The main administrative center of the Qualla Boundary since the 19th century, Cherokee sits astride US 19 and US 441, hard against the southern boundary of the Great Smoky Mountains National Park. It's much smaller and more modest than Gatlinburg, and its parking and traffic isn't quite so bad. Much of its modest appearance is due to rules within the Qualla Boundary restricting land possession to tribal members; this has discouraged outside business investment and kept Cherokee in sort of a 1950s time warp.

Here's the layout. US 441 goes north–south, while US 19 goes east–west. Cherokee sits at their intersection, with modest businesses stringing outward along these highways. The most densely developed area, called DOWNTOWN CHEROKEE on road signs, straddles US 19 just east of US 441. Compared to the Tennessee tourist towns, "Downtown Cherokee" is startlingly retro, with a look and feel that have changed surprisingly little since the early days of park tourism. Old-fashioned open-front souvenir stands, bursting with an astonishing variety of trinkets, still dominate "Downtown." Shops trundle out stuffed bears on wheeled platforms. Giant sheet-metal tepees sit on flat 1950s roofs, and totem poles hold up porches. "Roadside chiefs" dress up like Great Plains Indians and sit in front of fake tepees.

The real center of Cherokee gathers around its government complex on US 441 about a mile north of "Downtown." The buildings here show standard government styles from the 1930s through the 1990s, with two new parks (**Oconaluftee Islands Tribal Park** and **Veterans Tribal Park**), the first-rate **Museum of the Cherokee Indian**, and **The Qualla Arts and Crafts Mutual**, the Eastern Band's craft cooperative, as well as the Cherokee Historical Association's outdoor drama and 18th-century Cherokee village.

Big Cove, NC. One of the five original towns of the Qualla Boundary, today's Big Cove is a large, scenic mountain valley following the gorgelike Raven Fork. To a visitor, it's most significant as the site of most of the commercial campgrounds, some good cabin rentals, and the spectacular **Mingo Falls**.

Maggie Valley, NC. This tourist strip town formed in the formerly beautiful Jonathan Creek Valley in the 1950s, when a new highway was built eastward from the Qualla Boundary and designated US 19. Sprawling suburban-style development slowly grew up along the new highway; now, 50 years later, the development is nearly continuous. Maggie Valley is not a convenient place to stay when visiting the Great Smoky Mountains National Park, as it has no park entrance, and the Cherokee entrance is 20 miles away by a narrow, winding, steep two-lane road. Still, the Blue Ridge Parkway is nearby, as are the Heintooga Spur Dr. and Cataloochee Cove.

✳ Wild Places

THE GREAT FORESTS The forests of the Oconaluftee Valley. The Newfound Gap Rd. from Cherokee, NC, to Gatlinburg, TN, gives access to the large drainage basin of the Oconaluftee River. While this was the home of the Qualla Cherokees since 1819, the Qualla preferred the better lands toward the bottom of the drainage, and left the upper slopes as hunting grounds. The tribe did not bother to purchase much of this land when they constructed the Qualla Boundary in the mid–19th century, allowing Champion Paper of Waynesville, NC, to acquire it in the 1890s.

As with their Waynesville tracts (see "Waynesville & the Blue Ridge Parkway"), Champion's doubtful stewardship led to large-scale ecological catastrophe. Fires and floods swept over their badly managed clear-cuts so viciously as to destroy large forests, creating meadows and even rocky cliffs that exist today. Paradoxically, the largest of these sites is now a renowned beauty spot, **Charlie's Bunion**, 4.5 miles west of Newfound Gap on the Appalachian Trail—an excellent, if long and tiring, day hike. Champion prized these high upper slopes for their giant spruce and fir trees, which yielded superior paper pulp. However, they logged the lower slopes with similarly enthusiastic abandon, removing every tree they could sell. They abandoned the Oconaluftee drainage in 1929 as a result of the Great Depression; the forests you see have been recovering since that date.

At the northeast edge of this forest Great Balsam Mountains split off from the Great Smoky Mountains to run south for another 45 miles. Nearly all of this length is above 4,000 feet—there is one deep gap, **Balsam Gap**—and a majority of it tops a mile in elevation. The Balsams have 14 peaks over 6,000 feet, while the Smokies get the credit for another five 6'ers at the Smokies–Balsams intersection. This remote and beautiful area is best reached from **Pin Oak Gap** (see *Exploring by Car*).

RECREATION AREAS **Balsam Mountain Picnic and Camping Area**. Part of the Great Smoky Mountains National Park, Balsam Mountain (also known as Heintooga) is certainly the place to be on a hot summer day. At 5,300 feet above sea level, it's the highest, coolest, and windiest picnic area and campground in the park. It may also be the loveliest, set in a fine old balsam grove. A very short walk takes you to **Heintooga Overlook**, with a sweeping 180° view over the entire Smoky Mountain Crest—probably the best place in the park to enjoy a sunset. To reach Balsam Mountain from Cherokee, go 12 miles up the Blue Ridge Parkway, then 7 miles up the Heintooga Spur Rd.

Smokemont was originally a timber camp, the headquarters of Champion Paper's logging operations in the Oconaluftee drainage during the first three decades of the 20th century. Champion valued the high ridges above the Oconaluftee for their spruce trees, which produced high-quality pulp for paper, and the company's aggressive logging practices led to the disastrous fires that created the meadows and cliffs around Charlie's Bunion similar to the huge fire-caused mountaintop meadows of the Shining Rock Wilderness. The Great Depression caused Champion to simply walk away from Smokemont in 1929; when the National Park Service took it over in the late 1940s, they removed nearly every trace of the polluted, deteriorating lumber camp and converted it to a recreation area. Today it holds a large campground, a livery concessionaire (see *Stables*), and a variety of trailheads.

Newfound Gap. This high gap marks the point where the Newfound Gap Rd. crosses the crest of the Smokies. Not surprisingly, it's heavily visited, with a huge parking lot. A monumental stone platform at its eastern edge served as the site of the 1940 dedication ceremony, personally attended by President Franklin Roosevelt (who gave a speech from it); nearby is a narrow, but impressive view of the highway wandering down the Tennessee side. The Appalachian Trail runs by the dedication platform and furnishes a steep but beautiful day hike (9 miles round trip) to **Charlie's Bunion**, a massive cliff with sweeping panoramic views. An overlook south of the platform has interpretive plaques and a handsome 180° sweep over the upper Oconaluftee drainage basin on the North Carolina side.

Clingmans Dome. At 6,643 feet, Clingmans Dome is the highest point in the national park and the second highest peak in the eastern United States. It offers some of the best views in the Smokies. Many of these views can be found at its large cresent-shaped parking lot, almost a quarter mile long, with a continuous south-facing panorama so broad that you have to walk its entire length to take it all in. The rest of the views are from the dome's large, modern observation deck, a concrete pillar surrounded by a huge spiral ramp, a steep quarter mile up a paved trail from the parking lot. Clingmans Dome is a major trailhead, where the **Appalachian Trail** reaches its highest point and the **Forney Ridge Trail** descends to beautiful Andrews Bald before it plunges deep into the NC backcountry. It has flush toilets and drinking water in season, but no picnic tables. Access is by the Clingmans Dome Spur Rd., which is closed in winter.

PICNIC AREAS Collins Creek Picnic Area. This large, lovely picnic area is scattered along three loops through a cool, streamside forest, 6.65 miles up the Newfound Gap Rd. from the park's boundary in Cherokee, NC. Despite the fact that it is the only picnic area on the North Carolina Newfound Gap Rd., it is little used, possibly because it has no recreation opportunities besides eating outdoors. Even its one CCC hiking trail has been closed for 30 years—a pity, because it climbed through a virgin forest to a good view.

Oconaluftee Islands Tribal Park and **Veterans Tribal Park**. Isolated from the center of Cherokee, NC, by the waters of the Oconaluftee, Islands Park is an oasis of cool, quiet loveliness. Its picnic tables are widely scattered through a forested glade and linked by an interpretive nature/history trail. Unfortunately, there is only limited parking on the gravel road shoulder by the bridge. The nearby Veterans Park in the center of the town's government district also has picnic facilities as well as ample parking. Both parks have full facilities.

SNOW DUSTS THE PEAK OF CLINGMANS DOME.

Jim Hargan

THE BLUE RIDGE PARKWAY Soco Gap. The parkway intersects with US 19 in this high (4,345-foot) gap. Soco Gap has had some sort of trail in it since the early 19th century, but its great elevation and clifflike sides have always prevented it from being a major entry point to the Smokies; it received its current highway, US 19, only in the 1950s. Apart from its height and steepness, it's had another barrier to travel: It may well be the snowiest U.S. highway in these mountains, frequently having deep snow when most other areas have had only a cold drizzle. This is not always a bad thing. Although this section of the Blue Ridge Parkway is invariably closed in winter, you can drive up to Soco Gap on the plowed and salted US 19, park on the intersection verge, and join in the other families sledding, cross-country skiing, throwing snowballs, and building snowmen along the closed parkway. For other times of the year, if you need facilities at this exit, drive 4 miles east on US 19 to Maggie Valley, NC.

HISTORIC SITES Mountain Farm Museum. Located in the Great Smoky Mountains National Park on the Newfound Gap Rd. 1.35 miles outside Cherokee, NC, the Mountain Farm Museum is one of the most complete, and one of the most handsome, exhibits on mountain farm life anywhere in the Southern Appalachians. Unlike sites in the more famous **Cades Cove** (see "Townsend, Cades Cove & the Northwest Quadrant"), the Mountain Farm Museum portrays a full-sized operating farm—flowers along the porch, furniture in the house, corn in the field, chickens in the coop, and a horse in the barn.

The farmstead consists of log structures, all built around 1900, moved in from remote areas of the park (where other such buildings were being destroyed as safety hazards). The log farmhouse is a solid two-story structure with a kitchen wing and two porches, built in 1902 by local farmer John Davis. Today the farmhouse is furnished in late-19th-century style, and docents in period costume explain the way of life. The Davis House is surrounded by hand-split pickets and planted with beds of native flowers. The barn anchors the other end of the site.

Original to this location, it's a large cantilevered log barn with an oversized clapboarded hayloft overhanging log cribs. Inside are examples of late-19th-century farm equipment, a horse, several stray chickens from the nearby coop, and a cat. The horse is a friendly old creature who loves to meet gentle and well-behaved children.

Between the two main structures lies a working late-19th-century farmstead. Corn grows behind high, strong split-rail fences; beans and squash grow among the corn, a standard mountain practice. A vegetable gar-

THE FARMYARD AND BARN AT THE MOUNTAIN FARM MUSEUM.

Jim Hargan

den, protected by pickets, grows a riot of tomatoes, squash, beans, and peas, as well as flowers for the kitchen table. Gourd birdhouses provide natural insect control. Log outbuildings include a corncrib, a chicken house, a springhouse, a smokehouse, an apple house with a stone foundation, a gear shed, a blacksmith shop, a pigpen, hollow-log beehives, and a sorghum press.

Adjacent to the Farm Museum is the modest **Oconaluftee Visitors Center**, with an information desk, bookshop, and interpretive exhibits housed in a classic Depression-era stone building.

Mingus Mill is a late-19th-century gristmill restored to operation, located on the Newfound Gap Rd. a short distance beyond the Mountain Farm Museum. In its time it was a modern facility, with two grist stones powered by an efficient store-bought turbine instead of the old-fashioned hand-carpentered overshot wheel. You can scramble under this large clapboarded building to see the turbine in operation, then go inside to watch the miller operate the great grist stones and buy a pound of stone-ground cornmeal. Its most impressive part, however, is its elevated millrace, standing 20 feet off the ground as it passes into the building to fall into the turbine. There's a short, pleasant walk that follows the millrace to the mill's small log dam on Mingus Creek.

WATER SPILLS OVER THE MILLRACE AT MINGUS MILL.

Jim Hargan

MUSEUMS The Museum of the Cherokee Indian (828-497-3481; www.cherokeemuseum.org), US 441 and Drama Rd., Cherokee, NC. This handsome 1970s wood building—constructed to evoke the surrounding mountain peaks—is located in town at the intersection of Drama Rd. and US 441, 1.25 miles north of US 19. One of the most intriguing, involving, and moving museum experiences in the western mountains, the Museum of the Cherokee Indian displays a mix of carefully chosen artifacts with artworks and state-of-the- art museum technology to tell the story of the Cherokees clearly, simply, and beautifully. Starting with the Cherokee creation myth, the museum leads visitors gently through the ages, from Archaic times, to the pre-Columbian Cherokee culture and way of life, through their contact with Europeans and the chaotic dislocations that ensued, and ending with an emotional account of the Trail of Tears, the violent relocation of most of the Cherokees to Oklahoma. The museum, which is a wholly independent not-for-profit, has a first-rate gift shop. $6 adults, $4 children.

Oconaluftee Indian Village (828-497-2315; fax 828-497-6987; www.ocona lufteevillage.com), Cherokee, NC. May 15–Oct. 25, daily 9–5:30. Built in 1952 by the Cherokee Historical Association, the Oconaluftee Indian Village authentically re-creates an 18th-century Cherokee settlement. Thatched log cabins group around a seven-sided council house, where Cherokee crafters in period costume demonstrate traditional tribal arts. $13 adults, $6 children.

The Qualla Arts and Crafts Mutual (828-497-3103; fax 828-497-4841), Cherokee, NC. Located in a low-slung 1960s-era building across the street from the Museum of the Cherokee, the Qualla Mutual is a craft cooperative and gallery for several hundred crafters who are enrolled members of the Eastern Band. A museum area has a series of glass-case wall displays that explain the varieties of contemporary Cherokee crafts, including their history, style, materials, and methods: stone carving, basket weaving (several kinds), pottery, masks, dolls, wood carving, jewelry. The main area of the building contains a large shop that wanders through several rooms, offering every kind of Cherokee craft at a wide range of prices. All crafts for sale are handmade by members, and carry an authentication mark.

GARDENS AND PARKS **Mingo Falls Tribal Park**. One of the most beautiful waterfalls of the Smokies, Mingo Falls is the highlight of a modest tribally run park and campground in Big Cove. A short, steep track leads a quarter mile uphill to the base of the falls—a lacy curtain of water hung over a 100-foot cliff. You'll find it 6 miles north of Cherokee on Big Cove Rd.; turn left at Saunooke Village, then just keep going.

SPECIAL PLACES ***Unto These Hills*** (866-554-4557 or 828-497-2111; www .oconalufteevillage.com), Cherokee, NC. June 14–Aug. 26, except Sun.; preshow entertainment starts around 7:45 PM. Founded in 1950 by the nonprofit Cherokee Historical Association, this large-scale outdoor pageant, performed by 100 actors and dancers over three stages, presents the history of the Cherokee people from their contact with Hernando de Soto to the Trail of Tears. $14–16 adults, $6–16 children.

Harrah's Cherokee Casino (800-427-7247 or 828-497-7777; fax 828-497-5076), 777 Casino Dr., Cherokee, NC. Open 24/7. The Eastern band owns, and Harrah's operates, this large, luxurious video gaming emporium, a short distance east of Cherokee on US 19. This new facility includes three restaurants and a 1,500-seat theater. Added recently is a 252-room, 15-story high-rise luxury hotel, conveniently connected to the casino, which houses an indoor swimming pool, fitness center, and gift shop and displays local Indian crafts and artwork throughout.

✳ To Do

FISHING **Fishing on the Qualla Boundary** (828-497-5201). North Carolina's record brown trout (at 15 pounds, 2 ounces) was caught on the Qualla Boundary in 1990. The boundary has 30 miles of trout streams open to visitors, plus several trout ponds. The tribe stocks these streams twice a week in season, and has a creel limit of 10 fish per day. Unlike the national park, you need no state fishing license; you must have a Tribal Fishing Permit, however, which costs $7 per day (children under 11 free with permitted adult). Permits are sold in most campground stores, outfitters, tackle stores, and general stores in the boundary.

GOLF **Maggie Valley Resort** (800-438-3861 or 828-926-6013; fax 828-926-2906; www.maggievalleyresort.com), 1819 Country Club Rd., Maggie Valley, NC. This 18-hole par-72 course, constructed in 1961, winds uphill from the center of Maggie Valley, with excellent views of the surrounding peaks. $51 for 18 holes.

STABLES **Smokemont Riding Stables** (828-497-2373), Cherokee, NC. May–Oct. This national park concessionaire offers guided horseback rides in the Smokemont area.

Cataloochee Ranch Stables (800-868-1401 or 828-926-1401; www.cataloochee -ranch.com), 119 Ranch Dr., Maggie Valley, NC. Apr.–Nov. Part of Cataloochee Ranch, this stable offers trail rides on the ranch's spectacular 1,000 acres of mile-high ridgetop meadows and forests and into the adjacent Great Smoky Mountains National Park. Half day (2–3 hours) $45, with $5 discount to ranch guests. Full day (7 hours), including lunch, $100, with $10 discount to ranch guests.

✳ Lodging

If you are looking for a B&B in Maggie Valley, NC, you'll find quite a choice. However, Cherokee, NC, has only motel rooms (2,500 of them) and cabins—no B&Bs, country lodges, or resorts. A sampling of good Cherokee cabin rentals is given below. You can also rent a private vacation home in the Cherokee area from either Apple Real Estate in Dillsboro (see "Sylva & Dillsboro") or Yellow Rose Realty in Bryson City (see "Bryson City & the Southwest Quadrant"). There are a number of first-rate B&Bs and small country hotels a short drive from Cherokee, also listed in the Sylva and Bryson City chapters.

COUNTRY RESORTS **The Swag** (800-789-7672; fax 828-926-2036; www .theswag.com), 2300 Swag Rd., Waynesville, NC 28785. Given four stars by Mobil Guides, this large log inn sits in a grassy swale 5,000 feet high, at the end of a 2.5-mile driveway that climbs over 1,000 feet in elevation. Remote and quiet, the views from its wide porches and balconies are spectacular. Rooms range in size from cozy to huge, each distinctively decorated with antiques and heritage quilts. Each room has its own special features—log walls, stone accents, fireplace, balcony, view, hot tub, steam shower, or loft. Three log cabins (one with its own billiard room) give additional choices. The tariff includes three gourmet meals each day: a full breakfast, a picnic lunch, and an elegant, relaxed dinner. The 250-acre site includes a pond, a waterfall, a 3-mile nature trail with fine views, and four sheltered hideaways for a little private relaxing in the woods. Rooms $265–515, cabins $395–580, including all meals.

Cataloochee Ranch (800-868-1401 or 828-926-1401; fax 828-926-9249;

www.cataloochee-ranch.com), 119 Ranch Dr., Maggie Valley, NC 28751. The Cataloochee Ranch has been operating from its current 1,000-acre ridgetop spread since 1938, under the ownership of the same family. It sits in sweeping mountaintop meadows above 5,000 feet high, directly above central Maggie Valley at the end of Fie Top Rd. Its main compound has a log lodge with six rooms, a modern conference building with four rooms and two suites, and nine log cabins. The tariff includes a buffet breakfast and a family-style dinner with traditional southern cooking; there are frequent barbeques as well. The ranch offers horseback rides at an extra fee, as well as hiking trips (both on its beautiful site and into the adjacent Great Smoky Mountains National Park), pond fishing, an outdoor swimming pool, and such activities as storytelling, clogging, square dancing, wagon rides, bonfires, and marshmallow roasts. Rooms $145–200, suites $210, cabins $195–275.

BED & BREAKFAST INNS **Timberwolf Creek Bed and Breakfast** (888-239-3203 or 828-926-2608; www.timberwolfcreek.com), 391 Johnson Branch Rd., Maggie Valley, NC 28751. This classic luxury three-room B&B is in a modern ranch-style house by a mountain stream, on a side road convenient to central Maggie Valley. The rooms are beautifully furnished with antiques, and have views (either mountain or stream) and two-person hot tub. The common area has plush country furniture around a stone fireplace, with beverages and fresh-baked goods on the counter. Full gourmet breakfasts are included. $195–245 per night.

CABIN RENTALS **Grandview Cabins** (828-497-1356; P.O. Box 1503, Cherokee, NC 28719. Open all year. "My grandfather owned all that land," observes Bob Ensley, owner of the Grandview Cabins, as he looks out from the porch of one of his modern, beautifully furnished log cabins. "He planted corn on that bottomland," he says, pointing to a level area of the town bustling with recent development. The Grandview Cabins are located in the center of Cherokee, with a wide and unobstructed view over the western parts of the town toward the mountains beyond. The four log cabins are roomy and well appointed, with covered porches that face the sunrise, rockers, fireplaces, and good kitchens. The two-bedroom units are small houses with spacious living rooms and separate bedrooms, perfect for a family or two couples. The one-bedroom units are studios, each with an ample great room/kitchen and a large offset bath, and each beautifully decorated. The Grandview Cabins have a very convenient location, a few hundred yards uphill from the intersection of US 19 and US 441 in the center of town. $100 per night.

Sycamore Log Cabins (828-497-9068), P.O. Box 563, Cherokee, NC 28719. Joyce Welch's three log cabins form a quiet little group along side Big Cove Rd. adjacent to the boundary of the Great Smoky Mountains National Park. These well-kept, recently built log homes have a great room with kitchen, plus two bedrooms. Each has a porch with rocking chairs, and is furnished in a rustic style. $65–95 a night, depending on season.

Great Smoky Mountain Log Cabins (828-497-6182; www.gsmcabins .com), 1056 Adams Creek Rd., Cherokee, NC 28719. Bud and Sheila Lambert keep two sets of cozy log cabins, one in the pastoral Olivet Church area south of Cherokee, and another up Owl Branch, a more heavily settled section of the Qualla Boundary. All but two of the cabins are modern milled log structures with a combined living area and kitchen, plus two bedrooms and either a hot tub or a whirlpool bath. All of the cabins have wide covered porches with rocking chairs, and gas fireplaces in the living areas, and all are furnished with comfortable, new furniture in a country style that fits the spaces well. Most beds are doubles, with a few queeens. $85–95 a night.

Boyd Mountain Log Cabins (828-926-1575; www.boydmountain.com), 445 Boyd Farm Rd., Waynesville, NC 28786. Set on a 150-acre private farm in Maggie Valley's scenic Hemphill Creek area, these six log cabins are all authentic, restored pioneer structures ranging from 150 to 200 years old. These cozy, comfortable historic cabins set in beautiful meadows, by or near a fishing pond; all have full porch and fireplace, with upstairs bedroom(s). $130 per night.

✳ Where to Eat

EATING OUT Frankly, this is not a good area to search for a memorable meal. The three restaurants inside Harrah's Casino all serve reliably good food, and there are several decent buffets for the all-you-can-eat crowd. Motel restaurants at Cherokee's Holiday Inn and Best Western are also reliable. There are some first-rate restaurants in nearby towns, however; see the chapters on Sylva and Bryson City, NC (both near Cherokee), as well as Waynesville, NC (near Maggie Valley).

✳ Selective Shopping

Cherokee, NC

Drama Rd. gift shops. Two locations on US 441 and Drama Rd., 1.25 miles north of US 19. Not surprisingly, the first-rate **Museum of the Cherokee** has a first-rate gift shop. Spacious, handsome, and full of stuff, this store has Cherokee art and crafts, books, children's toys and books related to the museum, as well as a fascinating selection of tasteful and relevant gewgaws and knickknacks. **The Qualla Mutual**, a Cherokee crafters' cooperative, is just across the street and simply bursting with even more good stuff—all of it handmade on the Qualla Boundary, and carrying a certificate of authenticity from the U.S. Bureau of Indian Affairs.

Great Smokies Fine Art Gallery (828-497-5444; www.greatsmokies art.com), Cherokee, NC. This storefront in the Saunooke Village area of Cherokee combines limited-edition prints by Native American artists with Native American crafts and North Carolina handcrafted furniture. With this mix, the shop has the comfortable feel of a luxuriously furnished home. Western Native American artists as well as Eastern Band artists are among those represented.

The Old Mill (282-497-6536), 3082 US 441 N., Whittier, NC. This large old clapboard mill, painted white and with a huge steel overshot wheel, ground corn through most of the 20th century. Nowadays it sell a wide variety of items, including locally made jams and honeys, stone-ground corn-meal (ground at a nearby mill—the Old Mill's workings were destroyed in a 1980s burglary), salt-cured country hams, Coca-Cola memorabilia, rocks, local and Cherokee crafts, and rural antiques and collectibles. It's a fun place to browse, with all sorts of neat stuff jammed into odd corners. The Old Mill is located on US 441 south of Cherokee, outside the Qualla Boundary.

✳ Special Events

SPRING **Honor the Elders Day**. Mid-Mar. Cherokee stickball, a ceremonial (and very exciting) sport, combines with traditional dances and food, at the Cherokee Ceremonial Grounds.

Ramp and Rainbow Festival. First weekend in Apr. Ramps—the mountain wild leek, with a taste redolent of both onion and garlic—traditionally

herald the coming of spring throughout the Blue Ridge and Smoky Mountains. This festival at the Cherokee Ceremonial Grounds celebrates the coming of spring with ramp and rainbow trout dinners, along with craft and fishing vendors.

SUMMER **Fourth of July Powwow**. The tribe celebrates the Fourth of July weekend with a powwow dance competition, arts and crafts displays, Native American foods, and a fireworks display, at the Cherokee Ceremonial Grounds.

Maggie Valley Arts and Crafts Festival. Second weekend in July. Sponsored by the Maggie Valley Civic Association, this festival at the Maggie Valley Civic Center features over 100 craft vendors, plus food and entertainment. It's repeated on the third weekend in October.

South of the Smokies 4

Jim Hargan

SOUTH OF THE SMOKIES

Mountains extend southward from the Great Smokies through North Carolina, to meet the Blue Ridge near the state line. These ridges are high and steep sided, with most peaks above 4,000 feet and many topping a mile high. They zig and zag around with no obvious reason, hemming in narrow-bottomed little valleys. The major rivers—the Tuckaseegee, the Nantahala, the Little Tennessee, the Valley, the Hiwassee, the Tellico—can run obediently between two low ridges, then turn suddenly to cut a deep gorge straight through a high barrier.

Early roads and railroads tried to pick their ways through the least difficult gaps and gorges, with settlements following. The state legislatures broke the mountains into increasingly small counties in a vain attempt to create courthouses within horseback distance of most of the settlers. Today, these courthouses sit at the center of compact old downtowns in small county seats—Sylva, Franklin, Robbinsville, Hayesville, and Murphy, all in North Carolina.

These are the lands in which the Cherokees made their last stand in the East. The Cherokee Nation gave up their most rugged areas to the European invaders, hoping to satisfy the land hunger and live unmolested in the lower mountains of northern Georgia and southeastern Tennessee. When the invasion failed to abate, the tribe fought its battles in the American courts—only to discover that the whites simply ignored their own courts when they did not like the results. In 1838 the Jackson administration, disobeying a U.S. Supreme Court order, forcibly removed the Cherokees from their lands, marching them to Oklahoma on the bitter Trail of Tears on which many hundreds died. The modern town of Murphy, seat of Cherokee County, occupies the site of one of the concentration camps used to gather the Cherokees for the forced march. Today the Robbinsville grave of Chief Junaluska, who had saved Jackson's life during the battle of Horseshoe Bend, is the sole monument to the Cherokee Nation in these lands. (The Qualla Boundary, modern home of the Eastern Cherokees, is outside the final boundaries of the old Cherokee Nation.) Some 600 descendants of Cherokees who escaped the expulsion form a community at Snowbird, also near Robbinsville.

More than most other eastern mountains, these southern ridges are dominated by public ownership, with settled areas sometimes little more than islands in a sea of forest. In North Carolina, the Nantahala National Forest owns the

SASSAFRAS FALLS IN THE NORTHERN UNICOIS.   Jim Hargan

majority of the mountain slopes; in Tennessee, it's the Cherokee National
Forest. Where the Blue Ridge overlaps into South Carolina, the Sumter National Forest takes over, and in Georgia the Chattahoochee National Forest rules
the roost. All four of these national forests maintain ranger stations in the major
towns throughout this area, and these stations always have staffed information
desks, books, and maps. As with all national forests, public recreation (including
hunting) is permitted nearly everywhere; these are not national parks or conservation areas, however, and active logging continues on many government-owned
tracts.

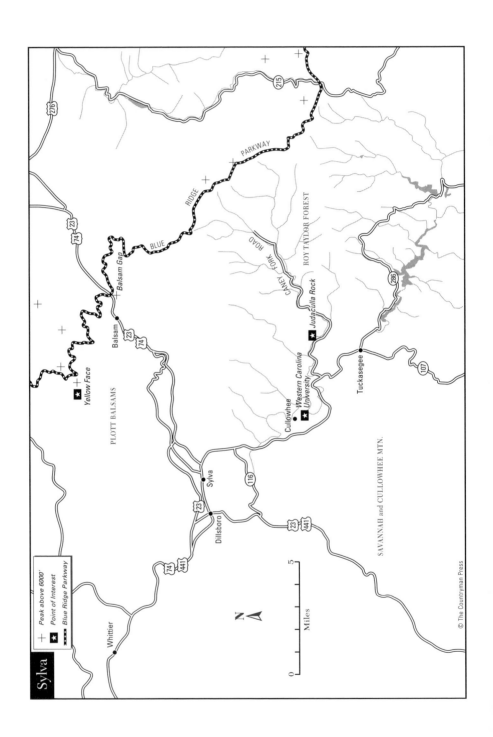

Sylva

Peak above 6000'
Point of Interest
Blue Ridge Parkway

© The Countryman Press

N

Miles

0   5

276

74
23

Balsam Gap

BLUE   RIDGE   PARKWAY

215

Yellow Face

PLOTT BALSAMS

Balsam

23
74

CANEY FORK ROAD

ROY TAYLOR FOREST

Judaculla Rock

286

Western Carolina
University

Cullowhee

Tuckasegee

107

Sylva

116

Dillsboro

23

23
441

74
441

SAVANNAH and CULLOWHEE MTN.

Whittier

NEAR THE PARK: SYLVA & DILLSBORO

The tall, jumbled ridges of the Smokies don't end at the national park boundaries. The high peaks and deep valleys continue south of the Great Smoky Mountains National Park to encircle the beautiful little county town of Sylva, NC, and its sister burg, Dillsboro, NC. Nestled deep in a valley formed by the Tuckaseegee River, Sylva and Dillsboro remain redbrick and white clapboard Victorian villages, surrounded by deep forests and mile-high summits. Other places have more chain restaurants and franchised motels; Sylva and Dillsboro are rich in authentic, old-fashioned comfort.

Sylva and Dillsboro command a deep mountain valley that has long served as the gateway to North Carolina's western mountains, including the Smokies. Ten miles to the east, the unusually deep and gentle Balsam Gap furnishes the only real break in the solid wall of the Smokies and their southward extension, the Great Balsam Mountains. In pioneer days the Rutherford Trace, a glorified footpath, ran through Balsam Gap to serve as the main route westward as late as 1850—an astonishing level of isolation, considering that railroads were entering much of the South by that time. In 1855 the Smokies' first wagon road, the Nantahala Turnpike, opened through Balsam Gap to Dillsboro and Bryson City, NC, then on through the Nantahala Gorge to Tennessee. It took the railroad almost 30 more years to reach this isolated backwater, paralleling the Nantahala Turnpike the entire way. US 74 roughly parallels the turnpike, while the Great Smoky Mountains Railroad carries passengers on the old railroad.

Dillsboro was the original pioneer settlement; nearby Sylva, founded as a railroad siding, slowly acquired most of the businesses and jobs. Today Sylva is the main town, a sleepy county seat little changed from the 1940s, with brick storefronts marching up to a grand old county courthouse crowning a green hill. Adjacent Dillsboro is a village of nicely kept white clapboard Victorian buildings, with one of the Smoky Mountains' finest concentration of craft and gift shops. To the south, the settlement of Cullowhee, NC, marks the center of a twisted knot of tall mountains and deep valleys. Throughout this area, your choices of restaurants and B&Bs are unusually good (just as the usual chains and franchises are largely missing), the towns are small and unspoiled, and the scenery is spectacular.

Access is good, with expressways leading to the Great Smoky Mountains in 15 miles and the Blue Ridge Parkway in 10 miles.

GUIDANCE **Jackson County Chamber of Commerce** (800-962-1911 or 828-586-2155; www.mountainlovers.com), 773 W. Main St., Sylva, NC 28779. This countywide chamber handles both Sylva and Dillsboro tourist information. Its new walk-in visitors center occupies part of the beautifully renovated Hooper House, right by the old courthouse on Main Street. If you have any questions about the towns and valleys west of the Balsams, their web site is the best place to start looking for answers.

The Jackson County Home Page (www.main.nc.us/jackson/). Sponsored by the mountains' not-for-profit Internet cooperative, MAIN (Mountain Area Information Network), the Jackson County Home Page is a thorough and well-designed repository of community information and links about the western slopes and valleys of the Great Balsam Mountains.

GETTING THERE *By car*: Sylva and Dillsboro, NC, sit near the intersection of **US 441** and **US 23/74**, both excellent four-lane highways—scenic and lightly traveled access for visitors from the south, east, and west. Visitors from points north will find the Great Smoky Mountains National Park firmly in the way; while sightseers will enjoy crossing the park on the scenic **Newfound Gap Rd.** (formerly US 441) from Gatlinburg, TN, anyone wishing to make time should take **Interstate 40** around the east side of the Smokies, picking up US 23/74 at Canton, NC, about 30 miles east of Sylva.

By air: The nearest airport is the **Asheville Regional Airport** (828-684-2226; fax 828-684-3404), 708 Airport Rd., Fletcher, NC; it's located 15 miles south of downtown Asheville off I-26, Exit 9 (NC 280). There's service from Atlanta, Cincinnati, Pittsburgh, Raleigh, and Charlotte, with 20 to 25 flights daily. Several car rental agencies are located within or near the airport—and you'll need to rent a car, because the Sylva area has no bus service. It's a 45-minute drive, four lane all the way, via I-26, I-40, and US 74.

By bus, train, or public transportation: There is no bus or rail service to this area, and there is no local bus service.

MEDICAL EMERGENCIES **Harris Regional Hospital** (828-586-7000; www.westcare.org), 68 Hospital Rd., Sylva, NC. Sylva's regional hospital is small but full service. It is a mile east of town on US Business 74, just off the easternmost of the three Sylva exits on US 23/74.

MAIN ST. IN DOWNTOWN SYLVA.

Jim Hargan

EXPLORING BY AUTO **The Nantahala Turnpike**. In 1855, when most of America was being linked together by iron rails, the Smokies finally got their first wagon road, the Nantahala Turnpike. This 14-mile scenic drive gives the look and feel of traveling down the old turnpike. On the way it offers good views of the 1882 railroad, including two fine old trestles and the second steepest railroad grade in the East.

Start 10 miles east of Sylva, NC, on the four-lane US 23/74 in **Balsam Gap** near the Blue Ridge Parkway; follow the signs to the old resort settlement of **Balsam**. This road (SSR 1701) quickly reaches the railroad and runs parallel to it, past the abandoned Knights General Store, then crosses the railroad to pass the grand old **Balsam Mountain Inn**, a 1905 railroad hotel still in operation and restored to elegance. Continue past the inn (on SSR 1700), then make a right onto Dark Ridge Rd. (SSR 1705). Here you'll follow an isolated mountain valley downhill through lovely remote scenery. Soon both the road and the stream cross under a fine old steel truss railroad bridge, a working piece of history from the late 19th century. After another mile of this remote mountain valley, this route turns left onto the former WPA-era main highway, Old US 19/23, at a T intersection. This particularly scenic section snakes through the gorge carved by **Scott Creek**, zigging and zagging past the railroad. At one point the road passes over the railroad just as the railroad passes over the creek—a double bridge. Half a mile later, the railroad flies over both the road and the creek. From here, the road (and the railroad) passes into wide valleys.

As you enter the town of **Sylva** some miles later, Old 19/23 bends left to return to the main highway. You can stay on the old turnpike by taking a right onto Chipper Curve Rd., then another right uphill onto the alleylike Allen St. At first it seems odd that the turnpike avoids entering Sylva—but of course Sylva didn't exist when the turnpike was built. The turnpike was actually trying to miss valley mud and floods, pretty typical behavior for an early-19th-century coach road. As Allen St. enters Sylva, follow residential streets down and left to the city hall, then right on Municipal St. to Grindstaff Cove Rd. and a quick right zag onto Old Dillsboro Rd. You have now recovered the turnpike route as it climbs and twists along hillsides to a panoramic view of the town of Sylva, which fills the valley bottom the turnpike was so careful to avoid. At the bottom of the hill, the Old Dillsboro Rd. returns you to US Business 23, the early-20th-century automobile road that replaced the turnpike.

EXPLORING ON FOOT **Plott Balsams Walk**. Close to the popular Waterrock Knob, this little-used 1.3-mile round trip follows the spectacular 5,800-foot ridgeline of Plott Balsams to the 6,032-foot peak of Yellow Face. Recently blazed, it's part of the Town of Sylva, NC's effort to open up Plott Balsams for outdoor recreation. You will find the trail along the side of the parkway opposite the intersection with the Waterrock Knob Spur; the closest parking is an eighth of a mile up the spur road at the **Cut-off Ridge Overlook**.

The trail immediately dives into a high-altitude "balsam" forest. Like all such forests in the Balsam Mountains, it's undergoing a drastic ecological transition as

Jim Hargan

THE OLD JACKSON COUNTY COURTHOUSE IN SYLVA.

Sylva, NC. The county seat of Sylva snuggles in a narrow side valley of the Tuckaseegee River, under the mile-high peaks of Plott Balsams. Its four-block downtown hugs the hillside above Scotts Creek, so that each old brick storefront has a basement on Main Street that comes out at street level on Mill Street. Main Street is not so much restored as unchanged, frozen in a time where people went downtown to shop in tiny old brick buildings; with establishments such as **Jackson's General Store** and **Schulman's Department Store**, it's like stepping back into the 1940s. Main Street ends at a flight of

the death of most of the firs (due to woolly adelgid infections) clears out the forest canopy and allows a host of other species to gain a foothold. Look for berries and wildflowers where forest giants once shaded a floor of needles, moss, and rocks. In a quarter mile the path reaches an open meadow with sweeping views east and south along the plunging slopes of the Balsams. Beyond, the trail climbs up a narrow, rocky ridgeline through tall spruces, gaining 300 feet in elevation; occasionally it clambers up a rocky outcrop, with mosses and dwarf trees to give the look of a Japanese garden. Near the top of the peak, the trail scrambles left around a large outcrop to follow a rocky ledge to another stunning view. From here you can see the little settlement of **Balsam** hugging the slopes of the mountain, with **Balsam Gap** slashing through the mountain so deeply that it steps climbing a tall green hill—past a fountain, then past a Confederate soldier statue, and on up to the column-and-dome **Old Courthouse**. With its exterior recently restored, the Old Courthouse makes a stunning landmark visible as far away as the Blue Ridge Parkway (from Grassy Mine Ridge Overlook, MP 437). The Old Courthouse is especially beautiful in spring when framed by dogwoods, but is worth a visit at any time for its views over Main St. toward the Blue Ridge Parkway and the 6,000-foot peaks of the Great Balsam Mountains. Downtown street parking is free and plentiful.

⟙ **Dillsboro**, NC. During the 19th century Dillsboro was the main town of the Tuckaseegee Valley, thriving decades before a nearby railroad siding was named "Sylva." Then a series of floods repeatedly inundated Dillsboro's low-lying downtown, driving its businesses uphill to find drier land along the Sylva siding. By 1970 upstream dams had solved the flood problem, but it seemed too late—Dillsboro was little more than a ghost town, with most of its old buildings abandoned. But things started to change. Craft artists discovered that its roomy old buildings could be rented cheaply and started moving in. The Hartbarger family acquired the town's railroad hotel, the **Jarrett House**, and returned it to its former glory as a fine old B&B and country-style restaurant. Then a set of investors bought out the recently abandoned freight railroad and turned it into a successful excursion line, the **Great Smoky Mountain Railroad**. Now Dillsboro is a beautiful old-fashioned village, reminiscent more of Old New England than the New South. Its two-block historic district, made up largely of original buildings tastefully restored, is crammed with more than 40 shops and craft studios. Opposite the historic district, the Great Smoky Mountains Railroad hauls freight at night and tourist excursions during the day, with scenic journeys departing from the nearby towns of Andrews and Murphy, NC, as well as Dillsboro.

appears only as a gash; on a roiling summer day, rain clouds will sail through the gap half a mile below you. The viewless 6,032-foot peak of **Yellow Face** (39th highest in the East), covered in blueberry and blackberry meadows, is a short distance beyond. This is a good place to turn back. If you decide to go on, the trail continues through high-mountain meadows, knife-edged outcrops, and balsam forests to reach **The Pinnacle**, with panoramic views, adding 6 miles and 2,100 feet of rugged climbing to your journey.

✳ Villages

Whittier, NC. At the turn of the 20th century Whittier was the roughest town in the district. The favored siding of the large logging companies, Whittier was well known for its brawls along its saloon-lined main street. A hundred years of time and a modern freeway have both taken their toll, and Whittier is now a sleepy collection of a few scattered buildings 7 miles south of Cherokee, NC. Two of the oldest surviving structures now house **Whittier, a Dream Remembered**, a delightful museum run as a labor of love by a townswoman. Three miles east of town on US 74 you'll find the Smoky Mountains' largest collection of **flea markets**, open weekends May–Oct. Whittier is off US 74 at a marked exit, 12 miles west of Sylva; you'll pass the flea markets on the way there, about 9 miles west of Sylva.

Balsam, NC. When the railroad finally crossed the 3,550-foot Balsam Gap in the 1880s, it became the highest point in the East to receive regular passenger service, and a resort village grew up around its small depot. By 1908 it had acquired a large wooden hotel, the **Balsam Mountain Inn**—now beautifully restored to a luxury full-service country inn, with gourmet food. The village is a quarter mile south of the four-lane US 23/74, signposted down local roads. It remains the highest and coolest place to stay in this area, as well as the closest to this section of the Blue Ridge Parkway.

Cullowhee, NC. Settled in the 1850s, this rural community is located at the place where the upper Tuckaseegee Valley narrows from a broad plain to a narrow gorge. Since 1889 it has been home to **Western Carolina University**—founded as a high school for training teachers, now a state university with 6,500 students and graduate programs in the liberal arts, sciences, business, and education. Cullowhee remains unincorporated, and has only a scattering of businesses on the northern edge of the university.

✷ Wild Places

THE GREAT FORESTS **Plott Balsams** is a high side ridge running at right angles to the main crest of the Great Balsam Mountains from Sylva to Waynesville, NC. Stretching for 23 miles, it has four peaks over 6,000 feet in a central section that maintains continuous mile-high elevations for 7.5 miles. The eastern two peaks, **Plott Balsam** (6,088 feet, 31st in the East) and **Mount Lyn Lowry** (6,240 feet, 19th in the East), are on private lands; Mount Lyn Lowry is topped by a giant electrified cross, the site of an annual Easter-morning prayer service. The western half of the range, with 6'ers **Waterrock Knob** (6,292 feet, 16th in the East) and **Yellow Face** (6,032 feet, 39th in the East), is largely public, split between the Blue Ridge Parkway, the Nantahala National Forest, and the Town of Sylva watershed—now being developed by the town into Pinnacle Park. Much logged in the early 20th century to support Sylva's paper mill, Plott Balsams is covered in a variety of mature second-growth hardwood. The high crest is mainly covered in the subarctic spruce–fir "balsam" forest, with isolated meadows and rocky outcrops offering impressive views. Waterrock Knob has a popular (and very steep) 1-mile trail to its summit, while Yellow Face can be easily reached in a pleasant 2.6-mile forest walk.

National forest lands near Sylva. In addition to Plott Balsams, this area has two substantial national forest tracts, both very beautiful and worthwhile, and neither with any meaningful recreation development. To the south of Sylva the large **Roy Taylor Forest**, named for a former congressman for this area, lies on the west slope of the Balsam Mountains below the Blue Ridge Parkway; it's mainly a logging area for the Nantahala National Forest. Across the Tuckaseegee River, the **Savannah Mountain/Cullowhee Mountain** tracts occupy the broken peaks to the south and west of Cullowhee, NC—a large and beautiful tract of mature second-growth hardwood forest that the Forest Service has not developed for public use in any way. In both cases, recreational use is possible (including camping, fishing, hiking, and hunting), but limited by a lack of trails, out-of-date maps, and possible logging operations.

PICNIC AREAS **East Laporte River Access Area**. Daily 8 AM–dusk. This shady riverside picnic area, run by Jackson County Parks and Recreation, sits on the Tuckaseegee River 4 miles south of Cullowhee, NC, on NC 107. It offers several simple recreational facilities, the best of which is a little pebble beach where kids can splash in this calm mountain river.

Mark Watson Park, Sylva, NC. Daylight and early-evening hours. This Jackson County park sits on the west side of town, on US Business 23, just behind the Old Courthouse. Although mainly a neighborhood recreation park, it has a number of tables under a pavilion, well away from highway noise. Its main points of interest are a number of WPA-style stone structures, including a long set of steps going up to Sylva's beautiful Old Courthouse with its sweeping views.

Dillsboro River Access Area. Daylight hours. This pretty little City of Dillsboro, NC, park sits on the Tuckaseegee River across the street from the Riverwood Crafters on River Rd., a short distance east of US 441; its entrance might be hard to spot. It has a handful of tables and barbeque pits on a very scenic riverside location.

✳ To See

HISTORIC SITES **Judaculla Rock**. Signposted off NC 107, 3 miles south of Cullowhee, NC. A state historic site in scenic Caney Fork Valley, Judaculla Rock is a large boulder completely covered by pictograms, sitting in on the edge of a lovely mountain meadow. The Cherokees credited the rock to their god of the hunt, Judaculla, a terrifying giant who lived in Judaculla Old Fields on the high Balsams crest. Examine the rock closely, and you can see the imprint of Judaculla's seven-fingered hand. Scholars cannot agree on the age or meaning of these carvings, or even if they were carved by the Cherokees. This mysterious site is located in a beautiful mountain valley with lovely views over its meadow. There is no office, visitors center, or even toilets on site—just a few parking spaces in a field, and the strange stone.

CULTURAL SITES ☂ **Mountain Heritage Center** (828-227-7129; www.wcu.edu /mhc/), Western Carolina University, 150 H. F. Robinson Bldg., Cullowhee, NC. Year-round, weekdays 8–5; Apr.–Oct., Sun. 2–5. Closed on university holidays. Run by Western Carolina University and located in its administrative building, this small museum tells the story of the pioneers who settled the deep coves and high hollows of the Smokies, and their descendants who followed the pioneer way of life. There are also changing displays on such diverse topics as black-smithing, mountain trout, and handcrafting. In addition to running the small museum and maintaining a 10,000-item collection of mountain artifacts, the center publishes scholarly and educational material, puts on educational programs, and co-sponsors the highly popular Mountain Heritage Day in Cullowhee on the last Saturday in September. Free.

Western Carolina University (828-227-7122; www.wcu.edu), Western Carolina University, Cullowhee, NC. The campus, Hunter Library, and A. K. Hinds University Center are open at all reasonable hours. The Belk Building Art Gallery is open weekdays 8–noon and 1–5. The most beautiful of the mountain colleges and universities, "Western" (as it is known) is a collection of redbrick buildings crowded into the narrow head of the Tuckaseegee Valley. Founded as a high school for teachers in the 1880s, its earliest buildings were constructed of materials carried in by pack mules. Although it now sits at the end of a modern four-lane highway, NC 107, it retains its sense of remoteness. One of the 16 campuses of the University of North Carolina, this 6,500-student university offers bachelor and graduate degrees in the liberal arts, sciences, business, and education.

Visitors can gain year-round enjoyment from Western's superb native mountain landscaping, particularly lovely in late spring when the rhododendrons and flame azaleas bloom. Western also sponsors the **Highlands Botanical Station**, the finest garden as well as the premier botanical collection in Smoky Mountains. Western's large **Hunter Library** houses a first-rate collection of mountain historical material, including the Kephart diaries. Casual visitors should enjoy the scenery and the views, visit the on-campus **Mountain Heritage Museum**, then check out the two permanent art galleries, one in the Belk Building and the other in the A. K. Hinds University Center. Free.

MADISON HALL AT WESTERN CAROLINA UNIVERSITY.

Jim Hargan

✎ ☂ **Whittier, a Dream Remembered** (828-497-7589), 29 Main St., Whittier, NC. Take US 74 for 12 miles west of Sylva to Exit 72, then take the first left onto Main St. Fri. and Sat. 10–5 and 7–8:30 PM; Sun. noon–3. Whittier resident Gloria Nolan runs a home repair service during the week, and opens her wonderful small museum in an old wooden storefront on the weekends. Centered on the history of Whittier, it features a

150-square-foot scale model of Whittier at the turn of the 20th century, as well as a collection of artifacts, family names, old photos, and newspaper articles. The front of her museum is her large and delightful display of Christmas miniatures and toy trolley engines, *A Little Bit of Christmas*. Admission is free; a first-rate gift shop adjoins the museum.

SPECIAL PLACES ✎ ⬆ **The Great Smoky Mountains Railroad in Dillsboro** (800-872-4681 or 828-586-8811; fax 828-586-8806; www.gsmr.com), Dillsboro, NC. All year; schedule varies. When Norfolk Southern Railroad announced that they would close the dead-end spur line that passed through Dillsboro to Murphy, NC, the western mountain counties faced the loss of their only railroad. To prevent this, private investors bought the 100-year-old freight line and formed it into the Great Smoky Mountains Railroad. As a small spur line, this dead-end run to the back of beyond would make money where the giants failed by using a simple formula: Carry freight at night, but tourists during the day. It's been wildly successful. The railroad runs year-round excursions on both steam and diesel engines (diesel tickets are cheaper) from Dillsboro and Bryson City, NC, on its 53 miles of track—and you'd better get a reservation if you want to make sure you have a seat.

Regular excursions from Dillsboro follow the Tuckaseegee River downstream, passing mountain settlements and forest-covered slopes. Highlights include a long tunnel dug by convicts, and the site of the train wreck staged for the movie *The Fugitive* (including the wrecked engine, still lying on its side by the tracks). The Dillsboro excursion ends at a historic depot in the center of the pretty little county seat of Bryson City, where passengers have time to try the local shops and restaurants before the return trip. Prices depend on the comfort level of the passenger car, with the cheapest being open cars and the most expensive being reconditioned club cars. The open cars give the best views and are great fun in good weather, but on a hot or rainy day most grown-ups will prefer the air-conditioned Crown Coach cars with their extra-large windows. In addition to these regular excursions the railroad runs many special trains: twilight dinner trains, murder mystery trains, trains that take in the entire 53 miles in one go, special Tommy the Tank Engine trains (with a real steam engine), a local microbrew train, an annual Santa Train, and a New Year's Gala Train. Diesel engine $26 adults, $13 children for open or standard cars. Steam engine $31 adults, $15 children for open or standard cars. More luxurious cars cost extra, as do special trains.

✳ To Do

FISHING **Smoky Mountain on the Fly** (828-586-4787; www.smokyonthefly .com), 100 Round Top Trail, Sylva, NC. All year. William R. Cope specializes in fly-fishing for trout in mountain streams. A local resident from an old pioneer family (try counting all the local places with *Cope* in their names), Willie knows just about everything about fly-fishing, the Smoky Mountain backcountry, and fly-fishing in the Smoky Mountain backcountry. Like all good guides, Willie will not only take you to the good places but also teach you what you need to know to catch the big one. A full-time guide, Willie is licensed by the State of North Carolina and permitted for guide service within the Great Smoky Mountains National Park and the Nantahala National Forest. He offers half-day, full-day, and backcountry trips, and will provide equipment if needed.

WHITEWATER ADVENTURE ✐ **Tuckaseegee Outfitters** (800-539-5683 or 828-586-5050; www.tuckfloat.com), Dillsboro, NC. Daylight hours, May–Oct. Dillsboro's Tuckaseegee River is much gentler than the raging Nantahala at nearby Bryson City; you might not want to train for the Olympics on the Tuckaseegee, but (unlike the Nantahala) you can take small children on it. Tuckaseegee Outfitters offers nonguided rentals of inflatables for downstream floats and paddles on the scenic, if unchallenging, Tuckaseegee. They drop you off at Dillsboro and give you a map; you make your own way downstream for a very pretty, and mildly exciting, 4.5 miles. Minimum body weight for rafting on the Tuckaseegee is 40 pounds (compared with 60 pounds on the Nantahala). You'll find Tuckaseegee Outfitters on the river, 5 miles west of Sylva, NC, on US 74/441. $15–28 per person, depending on the type of inflatable.

✐ **Blue Ridge Outing Company** (800-572-3510 or 828-586-3510; www .raftwithkids.com), 5472 US 74 W., Whittier, NC. Daylight hours, May–Oct. Located in the flea market complex 8 miles west of Sylva, Blue Ridge Outing offers guide assisted float trips on the Tuckaseegee River (a guide with every group), open to families with children as young as 4. Trips are 3½ hours, of which 2½ hours are on the river. Adults $32–42, teenagers $27–37, children $22–32.

✐ **Carolina Mountains Outdoor Center** (888-785-2662; www.cmoc-rafting .com), Whittier, NC. Daylight hours, May–Oct. Located on the Tuckaseegee River in Dillsboro, NC, Carolina Mountains Outdoor Center offers immediate starts with a shuttle at the end of the 4.5-mile downstream float. All trips are unguided on inflatables. Their handsome modern facility has changing rooms. $10–15 per person.

WILDERNESS EXCURSIONS Slickrock Expeditions (828-293-3999; www.slickrock expeditions.com), Cullowhee, NC. Burt Kornegay has been a professional guide since 1971, as well as being a freelance writer and past president of the North Carolina Bartram Trail Society. His Slickrock Expeditions offers several unusual and interesting wilderness excursions in the western mountains of the state.

✳ Lodging

COUNTRY INNS AND HOTELS ♿ **The Balsam Mountain Inn** (800-224-9498 or 828-456-9498; fax 828-456-9298; www.balsaminn.com), P.O. Box 40, Balsam, NC 28707. All year. This beautifully restored Victorian railroad hotel is located well off the main road in Balsam Gap, two-thirds of a mile from the Blue Ridge Parkway's inter-section with US 23/74. It was built in 1908 to take advantage of the cool summer temperatures at what was then the highest passenger depot in the East, with the dormered third story added at the last minute to ensure that passengers at the depot could spot the hotel over the trees. Built for coolness, the inn's 100-foot-long front is completely lined with a columned porch filled with rocking chairs and side tables, with a second porch topping it on the floor above. Both porches are lined with screen doors and full-length windows to bring plenty of cool mountain air into the hotel. The comfortable lobby runs the full length and width of the building, with polished hardwood floors, country antique furniture, a games area, and a 2,000-volume library. The 50 rooms all have original beadboard walls and ceilings. Each room has comfortable rustic-style furniture covered in bright fabrics, with original prints on the walls and either two double beds or a king; 16 of the rooms are expanded to include a large sitting area, and 8 are two-room suites. The breakfast (included in the tariff) is cooked to order and extremely good, while dinners (extra, by reservation) are of truly exceptional quality (see *Dining Out*). $100–110 for regular room, $110–130 for larger room, $135–160 for two-room suite (no kitchen), including breakfast.

The Jarrett House (800-972-5623 or 828-586-0265; fax 828-586-6257; www .jarretthouse.com), P.O. Box 219, Dillsboro, NC 28725. Open May–Dec. This three-story wood hotel in central Dillsboro has been in continuous operation since 1884, when it was built to serve the railroad depot. Like everything else in Dillsboro, it had fallen on hard times when Jim and Jean Hartbarger bought it in 1975 and converted it to a modern high-quality inn. The hotel's most dramatic feature is its triple-level porches, allowing plenty of cool rocking on every floor; its old wood siding is now clad in aluminum, and the porch rails are decorative wrought iron. Most of

the first floor is taken up by its well-known and popular restaurant, with seating for more than 200 (see *Eating Out*). Its rooms have been restored to the look and feel of an old country hotel, furnished in antiques, including many 19th-century pieces from the original hotel. All rooms are en suite, and nearly all rooms have from one to three double beds. $70–95 per night, including a full country breakfast served country style in the restaurant.

BED & BREAKFAST INNS **The Chalet Inn** (800-789-8024 or 828-586-0251; www.chaletinn.com), 285 Lone Oak Dr., Whittier, NC 28789. All year. Located in the Barkers Creek section of Jackson County down a tangle of paved country lanes, the Chalet Inn is only 2.4 miles from the four-lane US 23/74/441. Innkeepers George and Hanneke Ware have created an Alpine gasthaus deep in the Smoky Mountains, on 22 wooded acres in a gentle, isolated hollow. The inn's grounds are landscaped around a spring-fed mountain stream, and the surrounding hills are woven with footpaths. A grassy lawn provides full picnic and barbeque facilities for guests. The seven guest rooms are beautifully decorated, combining European flair with American amenities. All rooms have private balcony or porch, and all have views over either the landscaped grounds or the mountains. Breakfast at the Chalet Inn is served in the style of a German gasthaus buffet: authentic German breads, muesli from Switzerland, German cold cuts, fresh-baked pastries, fresh fruit, and egg casserole—all served up by George and Hanneke in authentic Alpine dress. Rooms $80–102, suites $130–180, including full breakfast. Cabin rentals $450 a week.

The Freeze House (828-586-8161; fax 828-631-0714; www.freezehouse bnb.com), 71 Sylvan Heights, Sylva, NC 28779. This large, hilltop redbrick bungalow sits in a quiet Sylva neighborhood, on a shaded property large enough to be registered as a Backyard Nature Preserve by the National Wildlife Federation. Its L-shaped porch, wrapping around two sides of the house, furnishes a cool, shaded location for full-sized country breakfasts as well as a good place to rock and enjoy the view over the old Nantahala Turnpike to Sylva's Mark Watson Park. The Freeze House has been in the same family since it was built, and has been open to visitors just as long. Restored and modernized in 1995, the Freeze House offers three large and comfortable upstairs rooms, flooded with light from banks of gable-end windows, with comfortable, homey furnishings and a variety of bed arrangements, from double to king. There are also two guest houses adjacent to the property, available for weekly and monthly rental. $75 per night for B&B rooms, including full breakfast; cottages are $400–600 per week.

☼ ♂ **The Dillsboro Inn** (866-586-3898 or 828-586-3898; www.dillsboro inn.com), 146 North River Rd., P.O. Box 270, Dillsboro, NC 28725. Open all year. This small B&B lodge overlooks a dam waterfall on the Tuckaseegee River, a short distance outside Dillsboro. It has 300 feet of landscaped riverfront, including a small fishing pier and a sitting area. Guests can enjoy wide views over the river and the falls from a large deck, or from a wood-burning hot tub. The Dillsboro Inn has two rooms and three suites (without kitchen facili-

ties). All of the rooms are large and comfortable, with contemporary decor that contrasts pleasantly with the rustic exterior, exposed beams, and board-and-batten walls. $80–140 for the rooms, $140–180 for the suites. All tariffs include a full breakfast.

The Olde Towne Inn (888-528-8840 or 828-586-3461; www.dillsboro-olde towne.com), 300 Haywood Rd., P.O. Box 485, Dillsboro, NC 28725. Open Feb.–Dec. This large 1878 wood farmhouse in the center of Dillsboro has a wide, full-length front porch where you can sit in a rocking chair and watch the town's historic center immediately below. The old farm parlor now furnishes a homelike lounge, while halls remain lined with original beadboard (horizontal on the main wall and vertical on the wainscot). Its four rooms and a suite are spacious and comfortable, with country-style furnishing and quilts. A fifth room, less expensive than the others, is much smaller and shares a bath with the owner. While this inn has many steps, both down from the covered parking and up from the street, it gives ready access to the heart of Dillsboro. Rooms $75–90, suite $105–135. All tariffs include full breakfast.

♿ **The Applegate Inn** (800-353-0377 or 828-586-2397; fax 828-631-9010; www.applegatebed-breakfast .com), 163 Hemlock St., P.O. Box 1051, Dillsboro, NC 28725. Located on Scotts Creek in the center of Dillsboro, the Applegate Inn sits secluded by trees and its roomy garden, separated from the Great Smoky Mountain Railroad and the Front Street shops by only a footbridge. A large, screened gazebo sits cantilevered over

Scotts Creek, directly opposite the track where the steam engine is prepared for its tasks. With only a single level and no steps, the Applegate looks like a modern ranch house. Its five rooms and three mini suites (two with kitchens), however, are first-rate, recently redecorated to the highest standards of style and comfort. Breakfast is served on the covered porch overlooking the garden and the creek—even in rough weather, when plastic shades and outdoor heaters protect the guests (inside dining is also available). Ask innkeeper John Faulk about a hayride pulled by his restored John Deere tractor. $70–100, including full breakfast.

The Squire Watkins Inn (800-586-2429 or 828-586-5244), 657 Haywood Rd., P.O. Box 430, Dillsboro, NC 28725. All year. This large 1880 Queen Anne mansion sits on a grassy hill just outside Dillsboro's center. Its gardens are spectacular. Designed by the prominent mountain landscape architect Doan Ogden in the early 1950s, they step down the slope in a series of rock wall terraces, each terrace hung with a rich display of seasonal color. A pond sits at the top, serving as a sunrise lure (easily viewed from the porch) to squirrels, rabbits, and raccoons. As an added bonus, the Great Smoky Mountain Railway's steam locomotive chugs through the garden. Inside, light floods in from high windows, allowing breezes cooled by the wide front porch overlooking the inn's lawn and gardens. A second porch upstairs gives easy views from the bedroom floor, while square corner towers add visual interest to the front and fascinating odd angles to the corner rooms. Furnished completely in Victorian antiques, the four

upstairs rooms are spacious and comfortable; all rooms are en suite and air-conditioned. The property also has three housekeeping units behind the main house, 1930s-style board-and-batten kitchenettes, very well kept and charmingly furnished in a country style. Rooms $75–85, including full breakfast. Housekeeping units $68–95 a night, $375–400 a week.

The River Lodge (877-384-4400 or 828-293-5431; www.riverlodge-bb .com), 619 Roy Tritt Rd., Cullowhee, NC 28723. All year. River Lodge would be notable for its friendly hosts, Cathy and Anthony Sgambato, for its 6 carefully landscaped acres with sweeping views, for its peaceful

THE SQUIRE WATKINS INN, A FORMER 19TH-CENTURY MANOR HOME.

Jim Hargan

600-foot waterfront on the trophy-fish-producing Tuckaseegee River, for its comfortable and well-decorated rooms, or for its gourmet breakfasts. But what you really notice is the Great Room, a gigantic space serving as the guest lounge. Its walls are of century-old hand-hewn logs, each a foot in diameter, salvaged from derelict local cabins and barns by the building's architects in 1970. Inside, old barn timbers support the massive roof span, while stairs made of half logs flow up to the second story. The decor, both in the Great Room and in the guest rooms, combines Victorian oak, country vernacular, Mission-style designs, and Native American motifs. Guest beds, either queen or two twins, are unique creations, handmade in the Smokies of whole logs. All rooms are en suite; most have either a claw-footed tub with a separate shower or a double-sized shower. A suite has a sitting area with its own stone fireplace and whirlpool bath, with a wood spiral staircase to the loft sleeping area. Rooms $109–139 peak season, $99–129 off-peak; suite $200 peak, $190 off-peak. All tariffs include full breakfast.

CABIN RENTALS 🐾 ✍ ♿ **Mountain Creek Cottages** (877-525-4933 or 828-586-3588; www.mountaincreek cottages.com), 2672 Dicks Creek Rd., Whittier, NC 28789. All year. Located 2.5 miles up a paved mountain from the four-lane US 23/74/441, these four cabins share a beautiful streamside grove of giant hemlocks, laced with paths and centered on a log gazebo. These older cabins have been recently renovated by owners Marybeth Druzbick and Patrick Hinkle; all are bright, clean, roomy, and comfortably furnished with full kitchens and

queen or king beds. The Druzbicks also own the three small houses that make up the **Eagle's Nest Cottages**, and manage four private homes for weekly rentals. Cabins and cottages $70–90 per day, $420–540 per week; houses $105–150 per night, $630–900 per week.

🐾 ✍ **Fox Den Cottages** (800-721-9847 or 828-293-0828; www.foxden cottages.com), P.O. Box 129, Cullowhee, NC 28723. All year. As you drive to Talmadge Fox's log cabin rentals, 3.4 miles south of Cullowhee, you might get the feeling of delving deep into the recesses of the Southern Appalachians—wildflowers grow along fences and by barns that only look abandoned; hound dogs sleep on porches. Fear not—Fox Den Cottages are completely modern, roomy, well furnished, and immaculately kept. They are set together on their own high slope tract, with enough land to give privacy and a feeling of remoteness. Some cabins have mountain views, and all have large porches and rockers, wood-burning fireplaces, and oak floors. It's 30 miles from the Great Smoky Mountains National Park, but less than 4 miles from Western Carolina University. $375–600 per week; daily rates available during the off-season.

CABIN RESERVATION SERVICES 🐾 ✍ **Apple Realty** (800-766-2775 or 828-586-3450; fax 828-586-2485; www.applerealty-mgt.com), 998 US 441 S., Sylva, NC 28779. This Realty company leases and maintains over 50 private units. They take credit cards, but charge an extra 3 percent fee. You'll find their office on US 441 south of town. Typically $512–877 per week.

✷ Where to Eat

EATING OUT *⌂* **The Jarrett House** (800-972-5623 or 828-586-0265; fax 828-586-6257; www.jarretthouse .com), P.O. Box 219, Dillsboro, NC 28725. Open May–Dec. Lunch daily 11:30–2, dinner Fri. and Sat. 4–8. This historic inn in central Dillsboro, in continuous use for 120 years, continues its tradition of good, plain food and plenty of it. Choices never vary: It's salt-cured ham (fried or baked), fried chicken, or deep-fried fish— catfish for lunch, local trout for dinner. Meals are served with sides of coleslaw, candied apples, buttered potatoes, green beans, pickled beets, and hot biscuits. Lunch is served as a plate, while dinner is served family style, out of big bowls. Desserts consist of vinegar pie, cobblers, and French silk pie. No beer or wine service. Lunch $9, dinner $11–12.50, beverages $1, desserts $1.25–2.25; substantial discounts for children.

Golden China Restaurant (828-586-9079), 744F E. Main St., Sylva, NC. Sun.–Thu. 11–9:30, Fri. 11–11, Sat. 5–10. This modest restaurant in an old motel is a pleasant surprise— friendly, sparkling clean, with food that's fresh, imaginative, and authentic. De Tong Chen and his family offers wonderful specialties, perfectly spiced and beautifully presented, along with a long list of traditional favorites prepared with equal care. The Golden China has wine and beer service, so you can enjoy an ice-cold Tsing Tao with your meal. Specialties $8.95–15.95, dinner menu $5.95–8.95, seafood $8.95–12.95.

Dillsboro Smokehouse (828-586-9556), 403 Haywood Rd., P.O. Box 269, Dillsboro, NC 28725. Mon.–Sat. 11–8, Sun. 11–3. This friendly spot in central Dillsboro is definitely where the locals go. It features hearty, fresh food, including old-fashioned mountain barbeque. Typically $5–11 per person.

The Well House (828-586-8588), US 441, Dillsboro, NC. Sat.–Wed. 11–5, Thu.–Fri. 11–8. This Dillsboro café, in the basement of the Riverwood Crafters across the river from the main town, specializes in deli sandwiches, fresh salads, homemade soups, and made-from-scratch desserts. Owner and manager Mike Dillard has been in charge for 16 years, and continues to pursue quality over convenience. Inside it's roomy, if a bit dark, with many booths and an actual 19th-century well in one corner (still used for irrigation water). Long a popular lunch stop, they've recently added dinner entrées on Thu. and Fri., including prime rib, Cuban pork chops, and chicken with saffroned rice. They'll pack you a picnic box if you ask them. Salads and sandwiches $2.95–4.95.

DINING OUT **The Balsam Mountain Inn** (800-224-9498 or 828-456-9498; www.balsaminn.com), Balsam, NC. 6–10 PM, by reservation. This 1908 railroad hotel, half a mile off US 74/23 near its intersection with the Blue Ridge Parkway, offers fine dining in a remote, rural setting. The hotel itself is worth a visit just to admire its authentically restored late-Victorian architecture and 100-foot-long porches on two floors. The hotel's old dining hall has now become an exquisite restaurant without losing any of its early, earthy flavor, a place where classical columns contrast with beadboard paneling. A small side room displays early tourist maps of the Smokies, and an enclosed porch offers more seating with large, bright windows. The menu typically combines several traditional items, such as fresh-baked mountain trout or filet mignon, with two or three surprises, like shrimp and crabmeat au gratin in a sherry cream sauce, or apple-smoked pork with caramelized leek sauce. A sophisticated wine list completes the experience. Typically $15–25 per person, excluding alcohol.

Lulu's Café (828-586-8989; www .luluscafe.com), 612 Main St., Sylva, NC. Mon.–Sat.11:30–9. This handsome restaurant, occupying three red-brick storefronts in downtown Sylva, has gained a wide reputation for its sophistication and intelligence. With nearly the same staff now as at its start in 1989, Lulu's offers a high degree of continuity—in quality and service—combined with an ever-evolving menu. That menu specializes in blending complementary flavors in new and original ways—like a catfish sandwich in which the catfish is crusted in pecans and baked, or portbello mushrooms grilled in a basil-orange glaze. The lunch menu offers stunning and original salads and sandwiches, with specials such as black bean and sweet potato enchiladas and seafood gumbo offering more entrée-like fare. At dinner the sandwiches disappear, replaced by a selection of entrées and specials, typically non-traditional and frequently adventurous. Spicing is subtle, with small differences in flavor clearly distinguishable. Lulu's wine list is as sophisticated as the rest of the menu; the beer list includes a choice of several microbrews and imported ales. Typically $7–12 per person, excluding alcohol.

Spring Street Café (828-586-1800), Sylva, NC. Lunch and dinner Tue.–Sat., brunch Sun.; closed Mon. The Spring Street Café has acquired quite a reputation in its brief existence. Set in a bookstore basement down a side street from Sylva's downtown, it's a full-service lunch and dinner restaurant. Its menu is adventuresome, with exotically spiced free-range chicken, trout, shrimp, and vegetarian dishes. Despite this distinctly un-mountain cuisine, it has become instantly popular with the locals, and comes highly recommended. Lunch salads and sandwiches $3–7.95, lunch entrées $5.25–7.85, dinner $5.95–13.95, Sun. brunch $3.75–7.95.

✳ Selective Shopping

Sylva, NC
Jackson's General Store (828-586-9600), 582 W. Main St. Mon.–Thu. 9–7, Fri.–Sat. 9–9; closed Sun. For many years occupied by Sylva Dry Goods, this two-sided downtown store has old wood fixtures, a mezzanine balcony, and a worn hardwood floor that dates straight back to the Depression. One side has casual clothes with an outdoors bent, while the other side is filled with country-style crafts, cards, and doodads.

Livingston's Photo (828-586-2814), 526 W. Main St. It's always good to know where you can find a good camera shop when you're on the road. This full-service shop in downtown Sylva, with a wide selection of equipment and supplies spread over two storefronts, is as good as anyplace in the mountains.

Dillsboro, NC
Without any doubt, Dillsboro offers the best shopping in this area. Nearly

all of its 40-odd stores are interesting. This sampling is slanted toward those shops that feature local artists and crafters—truly unique offerings.

L. Kotila, Watercolors (828-631-1996), 85 Webster St. Mon.–Sat. 10–5. Linda's subtle and highly detailed watercolors treat contemporary rural life with affection and respect. Stop by her shop and chances are you'll find her working on a new watercolor or a commissioned portrait. She offers several outstanding series of framed art prints. One such series portrays the unique village atmosphere of Dillsboro through winter festivities and merrymaking; another features meticulous portraits of Father Christmas, warm and humorous.

Dogwood Crafters (828-586-2248), 90 Webster St. Daily 9:30–5:30. This modest log building at the western edge of Front Street hides half a dozen rooms jammed floor to ceiling with every kind of country craft and fine art imaginable. As the outlet store for Jackson County's Dogwood Crafters Cooperative, this volunteer-staffed shop offers the work—handmade and deeply original—of the cooperative's 100 local members. You'll find quilts, wall hangings, stained glass, watercolors, fancy bird feeders, Christmas decorations, pottery, baskets, calligraphy, lace, knick-knacks, bric-a-brac, and souvenirs of all sorts.

Mountain Pottery (828-586-9183), 152 Front St. Normal retail hours during the season; restricted hours off-season. May close for lunch. This brightly lit shop, with full windows running down to its wood floors, offers a large and varied selection of fine art pottery by owner Rick Urban

and other mountain potters. You'll find pottery that's bright, earthy, traditional, sexy, humorous—anything but ordinary. More often than not, Rick will be working on new pieces in a large open studio area on one side of the gallery.

The Dillsboro Chocolate Factory (877-687-9731 or 828-631-0156; fax 828-631-0156; www.dillsboro chocolate.com), 27 Church St. Mon.–Sat. 10–5. The aroma of melting chocolate mixes heavily with that of hot espresso as you walk in the door of this tiny candy and coffee factory. Owners Randy and Susan Lyons make their own fine chocolate candies and scratch fudges, while stocking several varieties of gourmet chocolates. There's only one table inside, but outside are café tables under some fine old birches—and coffee and chocolate can be a perfect pick-me-up in the middle of an afternoon.

⇡ **The Riverwood Crafters** (828-586-2547), US 441 S. Year-round, normal retail hours daily; individual shops may vary. Located across the river from the main part of town, this fine old Victorian structure now

BRANT BARNES OF RIVERWOOD CRAFTERS THROWING A POT.

Jim Hargan

houses a fine-craft gallery, a pewter maker, a potter, a stained-glass maker, a café, a used-book store, and a couple of first-rate gift shops. All three of the crafters welcome visitors into their studios, adjacent to each of their shops. Potter Brandt Barnes combines the traditional with a vivid and subtle color sense—and perhaps a touch of whimsy as well. Stained-glass artist Ivor Pace operates in a more romantic style, reminiscent of Tiffany, lush with nature motifs; a partially enclosed porch has been converted into a perfect display area. The Riverwood Pewterers are the oldest crafters in the area, authentic mountain crafters with a continuous history in Dillsboro dating back to the Depression; their simple, elegant hand-hammered ware speaks to an earlier time.

Whittier, NC

⬆ **Stuff and Such** (828-497-7589), 29 Main St. Fri. and Sat. 10–5 and 7–8:30 PM; Sun. noon–3; closed Mon.–Thu. (but check, as Gloria opens when she is working in her museum). This gift shop features a large selection of homey, locally made crafts in one of the few old wooden storefronts surviving in Whittier. It's run by Gloria Nolan as part of her local museum Whittier, a Dream Remembered, which is attached.

✳ Special Events

SPRING Greening Up the Mountains Festival. Late Apr., Sylva, NC. A combination of three smaller festivals, this downtown street party combines Appalachian heritage with environmental themes.

SUMMER Dillsboro Heritage Festival. Mid-June. Dillsboro, NC, kicks off the tourist season with this large and popular street fair, featuring crafters who demonstrate their talents at their booths, along with performances by regional musicians.

THE TUCKASEEGEE RIVER, WITH THE GREAT SMOKY MOUNTAINS IN THE BACKGROUND.

Jim Hargan

Sylva Independence Day Celebration. July 4. Sylva, NC, celebrates Independence Day with bluegrass street dances and fireworks over the beautiful hilltop courthouse.

AUTUMN Mountain Heritage Day. Last Sat. in Sep., Cullowhee, NC. The largest and most distinguished heritage festival in the NC Smokies, Western Carolina University's Mountain Heritage Day features live performances, craft demonstrations, and a midway with over 200 mountain crafters and artists. Now in its third decade, this annual event draws tens of thousands of people to Western's beautiful rural campus.

WINTER Dillsboro Lights and Luminaire. First two weekends in Dec. Dillsboro, NC, merchants end the season with a nighttime program

DILLSBORO EASTER HAT PARADE
Easter Sunday, Dillsboro, NC. Months before tourist season begins, Dillsboro residents celebrate the coming of the first flowers of spring by dressing up in creative hats and parading through the center of town, escorted by antique cars. Totally uncommercialized and completely local, this is great fun.

of Christmas lights, candle-lined streets, regional music, homemade treats and hot beverages served in the shops. A special train, sponsored by the Smoky Mountains Railroad, brings families in from Sylva, NC.

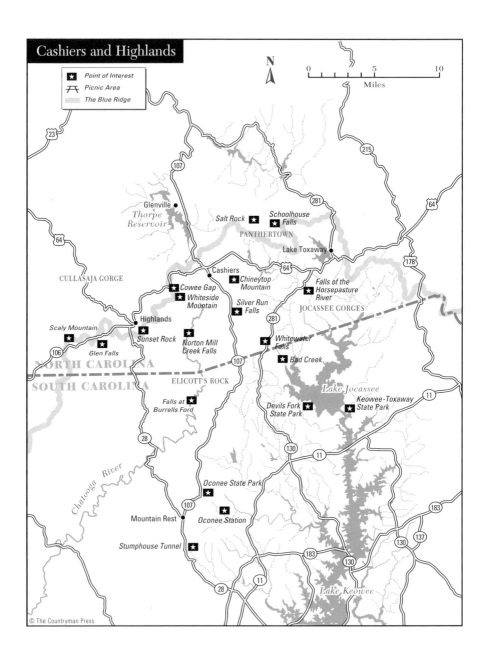

Cashiers and Highlands

★ Point of Interest
🎪 Picnic Area
    The Blue Ridge

N

0   5   10
Miles

23

107

281

215

64

178

64

Glenville
Thorpe Reservoir

Salt Rock ★

Schoolhouse ★ Falls

PANTHERTOWN

Lake Toxaway

CULLASAJA GORGE

Cashiers
★ Chineytop Mountain

64

★ Cowee Gap
★ Whiteside Mountain

Silver Run ★ Falls

Falls of the ★ Horsepasture River

JOCASSEE GORGES

Scaly Mountain

★ Highlands

★ Sunset Rock

281

106

★ Glen Falls

★ Norton Mill Creek Falls

★ Whitewater Falls

107

★ Bad Creek

NORTH CAROLINA

SOUTH CAROLINA

ELICOTT'S ROCK

Lake Jocassee

★ Falls at Burrells Ford

Devils Fork ★ State Park

Keowee-Toxaway ★ State Park

11

28

130

11

Chatooga River

★ Oconee State Park

Mountain Rest

★ Oconee Station

107

183

130

137

Stumphouse Tunnel ★

183

130

28

11

Lake Keowee

THE BLUE RIDGE: CASHIERS & HIGHLANDS

I n this area the Blue Ridge has one of its more creative moments. Just to the east, it has just come off its long run as the Blue Wall, a solid granitic mass rising straight up from the plains of South Carolina. Now it retreats suddenly to the north, its crest lined up with the North Carolina towns of Lake Toxaway, Cashiers, and Highlands. Extending south of this crestline, well into South Carolina, it twists into a mass of hard rock ridges, many separated by deep gorges in which rivers rage over high waterfalls. Here the scenery mixes charming valleys with great gray cliffs; lovely little streams drain these valleys, only to fall off their edges in a fierce plunge over a waterfall. Much of this scenery is highly accessible from US 64, which runs east–west near the crest of the Blue Ridge, or from NC/SC 107, which runs north–south.

GUIDANCE **Cashiers Travel and Tourism Authority** (828-743-5941; fax 828-743-9446; www.cashiers-nc.com), P.O. Box 238, Cashiers, NC 28717.

Highlands Area Chamber of Commerce (282-526-2112; fax 828-526-0628; www.highlandschamber.org), P.O. Box 404, Highlands, NC 28741. This chamber maintains a visitors center in the middle of downtown, just off Main St. on US 64.

Nantahala National Forest, Highlands Ranger District (828-526-3765), 2010 Flat Mountain Rd., Highlands, NC 28741. The ranger station for this part of the Nantahala National Forest is located down rural Flat Mountain Rd. east of Highlands; follow the signs from US 64. They have an information desk and small bookshop.

Sumter National Forest, Andrew Pickens Ranger District (864-638-9568; fax 864-638-2659), 112 Andrew Pickens Circle, Mountain Rest, SC 29664. In South Carolina most of the public forests are within Sumter National Forest. Their ranger station is located at the southern end of this chapter's area, on SC 28 just north of its intersection with SC 107.

GETTING THERE *By car:* This isolated area straddles the Blue Ridge Crest between the towns of Franklin and Brevard, NC. No modern, high-quality road enters this area. Even its one U.S. highway, **US 64**, was engineered in 1923 and never upgraded. The best of the bunch is **SC/NC 107**, heading north from Walhalla, SC, to Cashiers, NC; its two lanes are full sized, its curves are engineered, and it has a real shoulder most of the way. All the other roads are substandard.

By air: The closest and most convenient airport is **Greenville-Spartanburg International Airport**, although **Asheville Regional Airport** isn't much farther. In both cases you will have to drive a rental car some distance on mountain roads. Atlanta's airport is about 3½ hours away.

By anything else: Highlands and Cashiers, NC, like the rest of the western mountains, have no bus or train service. Highlands does have a shuttle service, however: The **Highlands Transportation Company** (828-526-4113) will pick you up from any of the regional airports (Asheville, Atlanta, Greenville), as well as take you to a restaurant once you're in Highlands.

✳ Wandering Around

EXPLORING ON FOOT **Walking the Blue Ridge**. The Blue Ridge in this area is best explored on foot. **Panthertown Valley** is certainly one of the best walking and biking areas, although you will need to buy a map from the Forest Service (see *Guidance*) if you intend to stray off the gravel roads. High Hampton's **Chimneytop** and **Rocky Mountains** are probably the most exciting hikes in the area. Of course, the view off the highest cliff in the East, at **Whiteside Mountain**, is pretty hard to beat. The rivers that drain the Blue Ridge are pretty impressive, too. The **Horsepasture River** has a whole series of waterfalls in a deep gorge—remarkable, but just a taste of the 60,000-acre **Jocassee Gorges** now under development. And for a quiet riverside walk, the **upper Chattooga River** from Bull Pen Bridge is exceptional.

✳ Villages

Highlands, NC. The town of Highlands sits in a large bowl at the crest of the Blue Ridge, at an elevation above 4,000 feet. It was founded as a resort town in the 1870s, and numerous buildings date from the 19th century. It remains a high-end resort town, with a large summer population of Atlanta and Florida socialites. Strict zoning have left it looking more like a New England village than a southern town, nearly devoid of sprawl and chain stores. It is a desert for those reliant on McDonald's stands and their ilk, and heaven for travelers who appreciate local, independent shops and cafés. A four-block downtown lines Main St. with a wide variety of shops in an eclectic mix of buildings from every era. Parking is free and plentiful. Still true to its 19th-century origins, Highlands has quite a variety of small independent hotels, and almost no motels.

Cashiers, NC. Pronounced *CASH-ers*, this town was until recently little more than a crossroads post office and general store at the intersection of US 64 and NC 107. Since 1845, when South Carolina's Hampton family established their **High Hampton** hunting lodge there, Cashiers has drawn wealthy South Carolina socialites. In recent decades its popularity with the wealthy has increased. The low hills around High Hampton have become crossed with narrow roads and

EXPLORING BY CAR THE CULLASAJA GORGE

West of Highlands, NC, US 64 follows the bottom of a rough little gorge carved into the backside of the Blue Ridge by the Cullasaja River—the 8-mile-long Cullasaja (*Cul-la-SAY-jah*) Gorge. The current roadway is utterly unchanged since being built in the 1920s; its modernization ceased in the 1930s, when the CCC developed its scenic features for tourism. That is how it stands today—a highway built for farm wagons and Model Ts, running through a rugged mountain gorge, and lined with national forest sites with lovely CCC architecture. Leaving Highlands, it passes by **Lake Sequoyah**, one of the long lakes that meander through the town's neighborhoods; look for the dam on your left. Half a mile farther, lacy **Bridal Veil Falls** drops 30 feet from an overhanging cliff. Modern US 64 passes in front of the falls (a concession to safety made in 1954), while the original highway's roadbed still goes underneath the falls, maintained and drivable—very possibly the only such highway in existence. In three-quarters of a mile on the left, the Cullasaja River plunges 50 feet over a large overhang to form **Dry Falls**, so named because the footpath passes underneath the overhang, allowing walkers to pass dry (mostly) behind it. A mile farther, **Cliffside Lake Recreation Area**, with lakeside and clifftop walks, and a CCC picnic area, turns off right. Shortly after that the gorge road becomes rough and woolly, with plenty of twists and turns. Four miles from Cliffside the road becomes a narrow ledge carved into a perpendicular granite cliff, with barely enough room for two cars to pass each other. Views over the gorge are spectacular. There is just one place to park, however: on the left, with room for only about four cars. Don't miss it—it's your only chance to view 200-foot **Cullasaja Falls**, a stunning double cataract. The gorge drive ends suddenly, dropping out onto flat farmlands in a suddenly widened valley.

DRY FALLS IN CULLASAJA GORGE.

Jim Hargan

crusted with hidden mansions, and a downtown area has slowly grown up around the old crossroads. You will now find Cashiers a full-service town, although you might have to ask where to find something. There's an Ingles Supermarket a mile east of town on US 64, the only chain supermarket in this chapter's area.

Lake Toxaway, NC. Founded in 1903 as a resort for the ultra-wealthy, the town's fortunes collapsed when its dam broke in 1916. With the dam rebuilt in 1961 the settlement has come back to life, but remains mostly a crossroads community at the intersection of US 64 and NC 281, east of Cashiers.

✳ Wild Places

THE GREAT FORESTS Panthertown Valley (locals say *Painter-town*) is a wide, flat-bottomed bowl perched high up on the crest of the Blue Ridge, between Cashiers and Lake Toxaway, NC. The valley has two access points, one on each side. The western gate is reached from Cashiers, an interesting and beautiful drive that crosses the Blue Ridge Crest twice: Take US 64 west 1.8 miles to a left on Cedar Creek Rd. (SSR 1120), then climb 2.1 miles to a right on Breedlove Rd. (SSR 1121), which you follow to its end in 3.5 miles. The eastern gate is reached from Lake Toxaway: Take NC 281 north from US 64 for 0.8 mile to Cold Mountain Rd. (SSR 1301), which you follow to its end in 5.5 miles.

Part of the Nantahala National Forest since 1989, this area is noted for its high cliffs, waterfalls, sandy-beached swimming holes, and incredible biological diversity. Previous private owners installed a network of gravel roads and rough tracks, making the valley easy to get around by foot or mountain bike—motor vehicles are strictly prohibited.

Jocassee Gorges. In this area the Blue Ridge shifts north, leaving a maze of hard rock side ridges and outliers extending south into South Carolina. While this terrain stretches between Lake Toxaway and Highlands, NC, the eastern half (between Lake Toxaway and Cashiers, NC) is the rougher—a land of narrow, cliff-sided gorges and tall waterfalls. Duke Power acquired most of this area for its hydroelectric potential during the 1960s, building **Lake Jocassee** in the 1970s and the **Bad Creek Project** in the 1980s. In the 1990s Duke negotiated with a group of governments and conservation organizations to convert most of the remaining land into public conservation lands, with the remaining Duke properties having conservation easements and public access via wildlife management programs. By 2001 the conversion was complete, and the 60,000-acre Jocassee Gorges Tract had been created.

The tract possesses immense value for its biological diversity, rugged scenery, and many waterfalls. However, it is now split between six different entities (NC State Parks, SC State Parks, NC Wildlife Resources, Nantahala National Forest, Sumter National Forest, and Duke Power), and recreational plans are not yet complete. Meanwhile, existing recreational facilities at **Horsepasture River** and **Whitewater Falls** give some taste of the wonders to come.

Chattooga Wild and Scenic River and Ellicott Rock Wilderness. The Chattooga River rises at the base of Whiteside Mountain, then flows southward through deep, boulder-strewn gorges. Lower sections may be known for their kayaking, but this area is much too rough and dangerous. Instead, it's the haunt of hikers and bank fishermen, with most of its length within national forests and followed by footpaths. Public access starts at **Whiteside Cove Rd.** (SSR 1107, off NC 107, 1.7 miles south of Cashiers), where this country lane crosses a clear mountain stream—the Chattooga near its headwaters. A short walk upstream on a fisherman's trail leads to a pretty little waterfall and a sand beach. Downstream are more waterfalls and a rough gorge, reached by walking trails from **Bull Pen Bridge**. From here the river runs through Ellicott Rock Wilderness, declared by Congress in 1975. Easiest foot access is from **Burrells Ford** in South Carolina, where the **Chattooga River Trail** follows the left bank both up- and downstream.

RECREATION AREAS **Cliffside Lake Recreation Area**. This Nantahala National Forest recreation area, inside the Cullasaja Gorge, has a lovely little lake underneath cliffs. Paths lead around the lakeshore and up the cliffs for some really excellent views. The park features classic CCC architecture from the 1930s, including a gazebo at the top of the cliff and a number of picnic shelters. The picnic area sits by the lake, under a canopy of tall old trees.

Bad Creek Power Station. You don't normally think of a power station as a recreation area. Bad Creek, however, is a different type of hydropower station. This Duke Power pumped storage facility floods a bowl-shaped valley perched high in the mountains near the SC–NC border, just south of **Whitewater Falls**. Its purpose is to create extra hydropower during peak demand periods; Duke actually pumps water up to this reservoir during slack times, then runs it through the Lake Jocassee turbines when it's needed. Duke occasionally opens it for tours. More to the point, they always allow recreationists to enter the site during daylight hours (you can leave, but not enter, after dusk), to use the network of hiking trails. The most prominent feature is **Lower Whitewater Falls**, over 300 feet high and every bit as beautiful as the more famous waterfall upstream. Because the lands are closed to hunting, this is a good place for October backcountry walking. You will find it just inside South Carolina on NC 281/SC 130; you will need to sign in at the visitors gate.

PICNIC AREAS **Ravenel Park**, Highlands, NC. Adjacent to the Highlands Botanical Gardens, this town park follows a narrow, winding lakeshore through a residential area. Such lakes are a typical and charming feature of Highlands neighborhoods, and Ravenel makes for a good picnic spot.

Oconee State Park (864-638-5353), 624 State Park Rd., Mountain Rest, SC 29664. Located at the far southern end of the Blue Ridge's craggy outliers, just off SC 107, this South Carolina state park offers lakeside recreation as well as picnicking. The CCC built most of this lovely little park's buildings in the 1930s.

In addition to Oconee State Park, there are several Sumter National Forest picnic areas along SC 107, starting just below the state line.

✳ To See

ALONG THE BLUE RIDGE The Blue Wall (see "Chimney Rock & Saluda") section of the Blue Ridge ends suddenly. The crestline of the Blue Ridge sweeps backward, well into North Carolina, and the space between the retreating crest and the line of the Blue Wall is filled with a jumble of hard rock ridges. Those jumbled ridges are separated by spectacular gorges, with an incredible concentration of waterfalls. Back at the crest—now running from Lake Toxaway through Cashiers and into Highlands, NC—the Blue Ridge is up to its old tricks, with great gray cliffs plunging down its south face, and gentle slopes leading to high valley bowls on its north face. This makes for a unique treat: wide views from the highest cliffs in the East, over a massive jumble of deep gorges and craggy mountains—and all of it easy to reach from those gentle north slopes. Here are a few of the best spots, from east to west.

Schoolhouse Falls. Here the headwaters of the Tuckaseegee River plunge over an overhanging 20-foot ledge into a large pool, not half a mile from the crest of the Blue Ridge. Schoolhouse Falls is the most accessible of Panthertown Valley's waterfalls; like many such waterfalls, it has formed a grotto, which protects a variety of rare ferns and other plants. The large pool is a popular swimming hole. Schoolhouse Falls are located on the western edge of Panthertown Valley in the Nantahala National Forest, only two-thirds of a mile from the gate at the end of Cold Mountain Rd. (SSR 1301).

Salt Rock. Naturalist and biographer George Ellison has called this "one of the most delightful views in the southern highlands." Salt Rock sits above the western end of Panthertown Valley in the Nantahala National Forest. It is a large rocky bald, decorated with moss and wind-dwarfed trees, that gives a wide panorama of the cliff face of the Blue Ridge rising straight up from Panthertown Valley. You will find it a very easy quarter-mile walk down the gravel road from the gated end of Breedlove Rd. (SSR 1121), with the bald on the left through a tree belt.

Chimneytop Mountain and **Rocky Mountain**. Cashiers, NC, sits at the feet of these two craggy outliers of the Blue Ridge. Rocky Mountain, on the north, provides a long, smooth, gray cliff that serves as backdrop to Cashiers and the High Hampton golf course. To its immediate south, Chimneytop pokes a tall, narrow, black crag up through the trees. The High Hampton Inn includes both peaks in their 1,400-acre resort, and maintains exciting (and none too easy) hiking trails to the tops of both. These trails lead to breathtaking views over Cashiers, along the cliff-sided Blue Ridge, and toward Whiteside Mountain.

Cowee Gap. Here's one you can drive to. When US 64 crosses the Blue Ridge Crest between Cashiers and Highlands, NC, it opens up a broad panorama over the headwaters of the Chattooga River. Rocky and Chimneytop Mountains are ahead of you; the part of Whiteside Mountain known as the Devils Courthouse is to your right. This overlook comes up quickly on a very sharp bend, so be alert.

Whiteside Mountain. Reputed to be the highest continuous cliff in the East, Whiteside projects a mile out into the valley of the Chattooga River from the Blue Ridge Crest. Its gentle north slope, typical of the Blue Ridge, makes for a moderate walk to the clifftop. The view must be seen to be believed—and the loop path follows this clifftop for a mile, opening up new vistas at every turn.

Like most Blue Ridge cliffs, these start off as gentle rock slopes that get gradually steeper; a foolhardy hiker can get quite a ways down before noticing the extraordinary danger. A failed tourist attraction in the 1950s, the attraction's old tram bed makes for an easy but viewless walk to the top, where a loop trail follows the cliff line back to the parking lot. Whiteside is part of the Nantahala National Forest, which may charge a parking fee.

Sunset Rock. Part of the town of Highlands, NC's Ravenel Park, Sunset Rock is a large bald overlooking Highlands. It sits on one side of the Blue Ridge Crest, here an unimpressive little ridgeline, with Sunrise Rock on the other side. From Sunset Rock this little mountaintop town looks particularly quaint and attractive, its downtown surrounded by forests and framed by mountain ridges. On the other side of the ridge, Sunrise Rock gives more limited views over the face of the Blue Ridge. You can walk up to Sunrise Rock from the Highlands Nature Center, or drive up a rough gravel road that goes right from Horse Cove Rd. (SSR 1603) to follow the Blue Ridge.

Glen Falls. Just west of Highlands, NC, a violent little stream called the East Fork throws itself straight down the Blue Ridge escarpment, dropping 800 feet in half a mile. On the way down it forms three impressive waterfalls, each one bigger than the last. The Nantahala National Forest path goes straight down as well, using interminable steps to drop through old-growth forest to views of the waterfalls.

Scaly Mountain. Scaly Mountain anchors the western end of this segment of the Blue Ridge. It has a large, south-facing rocky bald that gives broad views over the low ridges that drop into Georgia. Access is by the Bartram Trail, a long-distance path that retraces the steps of 18th-century naturalist William Bartram. From NC 106 south of Highlands, NC, turn right onto Turtle Pond Rd. (SSR 1620), then left onto gravel Lickskillit Rd. (SSR 1621); as you top a gap, look for a place to park. The Bartram Trail goes left 1 mile to Scaly Mountain, a 500-foot climb.

WATERFALL COUNTRY Between Highlands and Lake Toxaway, NC, the Blue Ridge Crest pulls back northward into North Carolina. Downhill to the south, great jumbled knots of ridges extend into South Carolina, separated by deep valleys cut through the hard rock. Underneath one of these narrow gorges, a particularly hard and stubborn layer of rock will suddenly give way, letting floodwaters crash down into softer stone, breaking it, carrying it downhill into the flatlands. This is waterfall country.

Falls of the Horsepasture Wild and Scenic River. In 1986 the U.S. Congress acted to stop a California

WHITESIDE MOUNTAIN, VIEWED FROM WHITESIDE COVE.

Jim Hargan

carpetbagger from destroying the little Horsepasture River in a hydroelectric scheme, by declaring it a Wild and Scenic River—the result of an extraordinary campaign by local residents. Waterfalls were the reason for this unusual congressional action—five of them. Three are easily accessible from NC 281 south of Sapphire, NC, via a Nantahala National Forest path. Nearest the highway is **Drift Falls**, a 30-foot slide rock with a large swimming hole at the bottom. Ten minutes farther down the excellent path is **Turtle Back Falls**, which looks like water rolling over a turtle's back, with a 15-foot drop into the pool beneath. Some of the foolhardy (and you may doubt the "hardy" part) use this as a slide rock as well. Nobody uses the next waterfall as a slide rock. **Rainbow Falls** drops 150 feet straight down in a roar of water that puts up a perpetual mist in which rainbows form. Farther downstream the path becomes much steeper and quite difficult, leading to **Stairstep Falls** and **Windy Falls**.

Whitewater Falls. One of several waterfalls claimed as the "tallest in the East," Whitewater Falls is an impressive sight. Located in the Nantahala National Forest, off NC 281 near the state line, it carries a huge flow of water 450 feet straight down in three great jumps. It has carved a great bowl for itself, and a projecting ledge (a short, flat walk from the parking lot) gives an unobstructed view of its entire length. The old pioneer-era road ran right by this waterfall, and its roadbed can be walked to its top. Downstream, **Lower Whitewater Falls** can be reached from Duke Power's Bad Creek facility just south of the state line; drive right up and ask the guard at the gate.

WHITEWATER FALLS.

Jim Hargan

Falls of the Jocassee Gorges (828-966-9099 for North Carolina's Gorges State Park). The first two waterfall entries are classic Jocassee Gorge waterfalls, fortunate enough to have public protection for many years. As this book went to press, North and South Carolina had not yet finalized plans on how they intend to develop the remaining 53,000 acres of the Jocassee Gorges, purchased in 1999 from Duke Power. Neither state has designed a trail network, much less started construction. A pity—the 7,500-acre Gorges State Park in North Carolina has inventoried 13 major waterfalls on only 14 percent on the land, and this may be an undercount. Stay tuned.

Silver Run Falls. The only difficulty in exploring this isolated piece of the Nantahala National Forest is finding the parking area. It's on NC 107, 3.92 miles south of US 64, near Cashiers, NC. It's a wide gravel area on the left, and if it's summer there are cars parked there. This is a justifiably popular swimming hole. The falls are lovely, one of those active little rivers that throws itself over a 15-foot ledge.

Norton Mill Creek Falls. From US 64 in Cashiers, NC, go south on NC 107 for 6.9 miles to Bull Pen Rd., SSR 1603, then west 5.1 miles to the spectacular steel truss bridge with wonderful views of the Chattooga River far below; park where you can. One of the finest swimming holes in the mountains, this little gem is little known and little visited—possibly because it's a bit of a walk. From the steel bridge, the **Chattooga River Trail** leads upstream 3 miles through a lovely riverine forest in a deep gorge, to this small, beautifully formed waterfall with a large, deep pool and sand beach. There's a steel footbridge over it, which the Forest Service helicoptered in.

Falls of the Chattooga at Burrells Ford. The rough side mountains of the Blue Ridge extend deep into South Carolina. Three attractive waterfalls can be found grouped around the Burrells Ford Bridge over the Chattooga River. (You'll find Burrells Ford Rd. 13 miles south of Cashiers on NC/SC 107, on the right.) Burrells Ford forms a sort of mini recreation area along a smooth stretch of the Chattooga River, in South Carolina's Sumter National Forest; it has many good places to fish, a primitive camping area that can double as a picnic area, and a network of trails that leads to (among other things) three waterfalls. You will find trailhead parking a bit uphill from the bridge. For **Spoonauger Falls**, go to your right up the Chattooga River Trail for a short half mile; this small stream stair-steps 40 feet down a cliff on your left. Straight ahead, the path continues to the Ellicott Rock Wilderness, following the Chattooga. For more waterfalls, however, return to Burrells Ford and continue across the road on the Chattooga River Trail. Very shortly (inside the camping area) a side trail will lead a third of a mile uphill to **Kings Creek Falls**, another 40-foot drop but much more violent than Spoonauger. Return to the Chattooga River Trail and continue downstream for another 3 miles to reach **Big Bend Falls**, down a fisherman's path on your right (listen for the noise of the waterfall). This is a 25-foot waterfall stretching the width of the Chattooga, with a 12-foot plummet over an overhang onto an equally large cascade. The trail doesn't end here—it continues another 4 miles, following the Chattooga through a deep gorge, reaching SC 28 in 10.5 miles from Burrells Ford.

BIG DAMMED LAKES **Lake Glenville**. This large lake, 3,500 feet in elevation, sends out long, thin arms into many former valleys in the Glenville, NC, area, north of Cashiers on NC 107. The highway skirts the lake for some distance before swerving away as it reaches what passes for central Glenville (still a dispersed mountain community). Lakeside scenery is very mixed, with much forest, a number of farms and meadows, and a slowly but steadily increasing number of subdivisions. A winding narrow lane (SSR 1157) turns left off NC 107 on the north end of Glenville, first reaching a nice county park with picnicking and a boat ramp, then crossing the impressive World War II–era dam (with a free boat launch on the other side). The lake is owned by Duke Power; its water flows through a giant pipeline to a hydropower station at Tuckaseegee. By the way, it's officially known as "Thorpe Reservoir," but if you call it that no one will know what you're talking about.

Lake Toxaway (800-443-0694; www.laketoxaway.com), Lake Toxaway, NC. This is the lake that would not die. The Toxaway Company, established in 1896, aggressively developed Sapphire and Toxaway, NC, as resorts for the rich. In 1903 they built Lake Toxaway and placed a giant luxury hotel on its shore. It seemed to be a roaring success, filling with millionaires who would park their private railroad cars on a special siding built for that purpose. The company flared out in 1911, however, going into bankruptcy. In 1916 the Lake Toxaway Dam failed, sending a wall of 5.4 billion gallons of water straight down the mountainside; you can still see the scoured-out trail it left just below the US 64 bridge. The grand inn was abandoned, then dismantled for scrap in 1947. In 1961 a group of investors purchased the dried-up lakebed and rebuilt the dam, selling lots once again around the lakeside. Only a few of the original mansions remain along the rebuilt Lake Toxaway, the most remarkable being the Moltz Mansion, now the **Greystone Inn**. The lake itself is private, closed to the public.

Lake Jocassee floods 7,600 acres of Blue Ridge valleys in South Carolina, just below the state line. It's part of a massive hydropower operation by Duke Power, in combination with Lake Keowee to the south and the **Bad Creek project** to its north. Most of the lands to the north of Jocassee have been owned by Duke Power since the 1960s, protecting them from development; now they are in public ownership as the 53,000-acre Jocassee Gorges area. Lake Jocassee sends long, thin arms deep into this wilderness, allowing easy access to some remarkably remote areas. There are boat ramps at Devil's Fork State Park, on SC 11 east of SC 107.

HISTORICAL SITES **Stumphouse Tunnel**. This local park, at the far southern edge of the Blue Ridge's outliers, preserves the mortal remains of an extraordinarily overambitious antebellum railroad project. In 1850—a time when no accurate maps existed of the Blue Ridge and Smoky Mountains—the Blue Ridge Railway made a serious attempt to run a road straight across the Southern Appalachians. At Stumphouse Tunnel, the railroad tried to breach the first rock face of the Blue Ridge and failed. The tunnel was to be well over a mile long, and was mainly completed when the venture collapsed in 1859. Today a local park keeps the south end of the tunnel open for 500 feet, with a nice picnic area nearby. (Up to 1994 you could go 1,600 feet into the tunnel, viewing a giant air shaft at midway, but a roof collapse has closed that part of the tunnel.)

Oconee Station State Historic Site (864-638-0079), 500 Oconee Station Rd., Walhalla, SC. Two miles off SC 11 north of Walhalla—by coincidence, just downhill from Oconee State Park. Open for tours on weekends. A South Carolina state park, this stone-built colonial Cherokee trading post sits in grassy fields at the bottom of the Blue Ridge's last outlier. The adjacent **Richard's House** dates from the same era.

The Church of the Good Shepherd. This lovely little Episcopalian church, located off NC 107 in Cashiers, NC, was built in 1896 to serve the town's summer colony. Listed on the National Register, it's a particularly handsome example of the rustic Gothic style then favored by the Episcopal and Catholic churches. It is still in use, the center of a year-round parish since 1982.

✳ To Do

GOLF **High Hampton** (828-743-2450; www.highhamptoninn.com/golf), NC 107 S., Cashiers, NC. Designed by George Cobb in 1956, this 18-hole course is noted for its outstanding beauty, including wide views of the cliffs of the Blue Ridge reflecting in the glassy surface of Hampton Lake. $35.

Trillium Links (828-464-3800), 48 Links Dr., Cashiers, NC. Designed by Morris Hatalsky in 1998, this 4,000-foot-high course is part of a land development project in the Glenville Lake area north of Cashiers. $95–125.

Sapphire Mountain Golf Club (828-743-1174), 50 Slicers Ave., Sapphire, NC. This 1982 Ron Garl course, part of a large modern resort and subdivision development east of Cashiers on US 64, features mountain scenery from its narrow and undulating fairways (including a hole that plays over a waterfall). $65.

JUST FOR KIDS ✐ **Highlands Youth Adventures** (828-526-2174; www.high landsadventures.com), Highlands, NC. This organization sponsors summer weekday trips for kids ages 9–15, with a different program each day. They furnish lunch and snacks, equipment, and transportation, for daily programs of horseback riding, mountain biking, whitewater rafting, tubing, rock climbing and rappelling, and high ropes and zip lines. $59–89.

GARDENS AND PARKS
Highlands Botanical Garden (828-526-2602), Highlands, NC. At the center of Highlands sits a very special botanical garden. Run by Western Carolina University, the 30-acre Highlands Botanical Garden is a biological reservoir of native species and a serious research station for mountain botany, ecology, and biology. The garden is highly informal in its design and layout, a skillful modification of the found environments that safeguards and showcases the specimens. Paths loop around a lakeshore thick with lily pads, climb along sheltered streambanks, and break into old cove forests. The gardens were established in 1962, but the research station has been there since the 1930s and has the look and feel of an old-time ranger station. On site, facing Horse Cove Rd., is the **Highlands Nature Center**, a nature museum open seasonally. **Ravenel Park** is adjacent, and **Sunset Rock** is an easy walk up a footpath.

STABLES Arrowmont Stables and Cabins (800-682-1092 or 828-743-2762; www.arrowmont.com), 276 Arrowmont Trail, Cullowhee, NC. All year, Mon.–Sat. 8–5. Arrowmont provides horses for guided trail rides on 6 miles of trail on their remote 200-acre property in the high mountains north of Cashiers, near Glenville. They also have two cabins, older but clean and well kept, as well as group camping in bunk cabins left over from when the property was a boys' camp. $25–50.

Sapphire Valley Stables (828-743-9574), US 64 W., Cashiers, NC. Part of a large resort development at Sapphire, east of Cashiers on US 64, this stable offers 1-hour trail rides. $25.

Giddy Up N Go Riding Stables (828-526-4531), Buck Knob Rd., Highlands, NC. Located in the Highlands area, this stable offers ½- to 2-hour trail rides.

WHITEWATER ADVENTURES Rafting the Chattooga River. The Chattooga River does not become floatable until has put the high cliffs of the Blue Ridge well behind. The National Forest Service, which owns nearly all of the river, sets the upper limit of the floatable river at the SC 28 highway bridge—the southern end of this chapter. Two large regional float companies are licensed by the Forest Service to run trips on the Chattooga below SC 28: the **Nantahala Outdoor Center** and **Wildwater Rafting**. See the Bryson City chapter for full information on both.

✳ Lodging

COUNTRY INNS AND HOTELS The Old Edwards Inn (888-526-9319 or 828-526-9319; www.oldedwardsinn .com), P.O. Box 1778, 4th and Main, Highlands, NC 28741. Open all year. The oldest building in downtown Highlands, the 1878 Old Edwards Inn is a country hotel in the grand old manner. It's a distinctive three-story brick building with a beautiful stone entrance; a long wooden annex with a second-story veranda, almost as old as the main building, houses the excellent Central House Restaurant (see *Dining Out*) and additional rooms. A lovely little garden sits in the space between the two buildings, separated from the Main Street sidewalk by a hedge. Furnishings are elegant late-19th-century country in style, with beautiful wall stenciling a major feature found in all 20 rooms; most have balcony, and some have sitting area. A full breakfast, included in the tariff, is ordered off the menu in the restaurant. Apr.–Dec., $115–150; Jan.–Mar., $85–105.

The Highlands Inn (828-526-5899; www.highlandsinn-nc.com), P.O. Box 1030, 420 Main St., Highlands, NC 28741. This classic wood coaching inn, listed on the National Register, has dominated downtown Highlands since 1880. A long, low three-story building, its second-story veranda covers the sidewalk for most of a block. Completely renovated in 1989, it has been carefully decorated with authentic antiques and reproductions typical of a late-19th-century inn. The 31 rooms range from cozy to large in size, and some have separate sitting area. The tariff includes an extended continental breakfast. $94–174.

The Main Street Inn (800-213-9142 or 828-526-2590; www.mainstreet -inn.com), 270 Main St., Highlands,

NC 28741. Built in 1885 and restored in 1998, this farmhouse sits in the middle of Highland's Main Street shopping district, surrounded by its own oak-shaded lawns. The 20 guest rooms are individually theme furnished in antiques and reproductions; some have individual sitting area or balcony. In some rooms, cathedral ceilings reveal the original hardwood beams from 1885. A large country breakfast is served, and afternoon tea greets guests as they come in from shopping or touring. $95–185, including breakfast and tea.

🐾 ✍ **Kelsey and Hutchinson Lodge** (888-245-9058 or 828-526-4746; fax 828-526-4921; www.k-h lodge.com), 450 Spring St., Highlands, NC 28741. Located on a side lane two blocks from downtown Highlands, the Kelsey and Hutchinson (named for Highlands's founders) is a 1997 reconstruction of the 1883 Lee's Inn, a favorite Highlands destination for many decades until it burned down in the 1980s. The 3.5 acres of land includes several surviving outbuildings of the Lee's Inn, two of which have been beautifully restored for additional rooms. More business friendly than many historic inns, the K&H has meeting rooms, concierge services, a gift shop, dataports in every room, and 24-hour voice-mail service. Rooms are beautifully decorated with knotty-pine paneling and gas fireplace; most have whirlpool bath, and some are available with balcony or porch, and sitting area. The **Chestnut House**, also on the property, has two bedrooms, living room, dining room, and full kitchen. Tariff includes a continental breakfast. The K&H is pet friendly, with a special VIP program for pets. Rooms

$82–222, Chestnut House $162–262. $15 pet fee.

The Chandler Inn (888-378-6300 or 828-526-5992; www.thechandlerinn .com), P.O. Box 2156, US 64 and Martha's Lane, Highlands, NC 28741. Open all year. This three-diamond AAA inn is one of the more unusual facilities in Highlands. Located on the east side of town on US 64, it consists of several wooden buildings grouped tightly around a central garden area, linked by decks and walkways. A modern complex, it has a rustic look and feel, with well-tended gardens; although convenient to the main highway, it's very quiet. All 15 oversized rooms have a private entrance onto the interconnecting decks. A hospitality room has morning coffee and home-baked goods; guests eat their breakfast by the fireplace, or take it out onto the decks or back into their rooms. $65–160, including continental breakfast.

RESORTS **High Hampton Inn and Country Club** (800-334-2551 or 828-743-2411; www.highhamptoninn .com), P.O. Box 338, Cashiers, NC 28717. Located in Cashiers, this 1,400-acre resort has been run by the McKee family since 1922. It's older than that, however—Wade Hampton, a South Carolina planter (and later a Confederate general, then governor and senator), established the High Hampton estate as the family summer home in 1845. The entire resort is a National Historic District, with 17 of its buildings listed on the National Register. Most of these buildings date from the 1920s and '30s, built as part of the resort. The main inn is a classic rustic lodge built in 1933, noted for its walls clad in chestnut bark, and for the wide views from its wraparound veranda. The large Hampton Lake, beside the main building, opens up vistas to the wide front of the Blue Ridge, which flanks the lake with great gray escarpments and granite crags. Two wonderful hiking trails lead to the tops of these crags—all on High Hampton property. The 117 rooms are rustic, with board-and-batten paneling from wood logged on the estate and simple country furniture. The tariff includes three meals a day, plus afternoon tea on the veranda; meals are hearty country fare, prepared fresh from scratch, and served buffet style. At dinner, gentlemen are expected to wear coats. Wine and beer are available with dinner, and an adjacent bar has mixed drinks. The resort has an impossibly scenic golf course, tennis, and boat rentals, all at a reduced tariff for guests. $178–228 for two people in one room, including all meals.

The Greystone Inn (800-824-5766 or 828-966-4700; fax 828-862-5689; www.greystoneinn.com), Greystone Lane, Lake Toxaway, NC 28747. This resort complex, given four diamonds by AAA, centers on a six-level Alpine-style 1915 mansion, built by local heroine Lucy Moltz (who lived there until her death in 1970). The mansion occupies a grassy hilltop peninsula in Lake Toxaway, and stair-steps down the slope in stone terraces to the waterside. Since becoming a resort in 1985, the 13 guest rooms and suites in the Moltz Mansion have been supplemented by 14 suites in two new buildings; all rooms are individually decorated with antiques and reproductions. The resort strives to present gourmet meals to its guests, all included in the tariff—a full break-

fast, an afternoon tea on the sunporch, wine and hors d'oeuvres before dinner, and a formal dinner with menu choices and dessert by the inn's pastry chef. An evening champagne cruise is offered free to guests, as are canoeing, kayaking, powerboating, waterskiing, tennis, and lawn games. Golf privileges are available at nearby Lake Toxaway Country Club. Rooms $315–415, suites $415–595, including breakfast, dinner, afternoon tea, and a range of activities.

BED & BREAKFAST INNS **4½ Street Inn** (888-799-4464 or 828-526-4464; www.4andahalfstinn.com), 55 4½ St., Highlands, NC 28741. Located in a residential neighborhood a few blocks from downtown Highlands, the 4½ Street Inn occupies a sprawling old farmhouse with a wraparound porch and a large back deck. Comfortable and homey, its 10 rooms have handmade quilts on the beds and terrycloth bathrobes in the closets. The tariff includes a full gourmet breakfast (including homemade granola and cheese grits), fresh homemade cookies, and an afternoon wine hour with hors d'oeuvres.

Colonial Pines Inn (828-526-2060; www.colonialpinesinn.com), 541 Hickory St., Highlands, NC 28741. Located in a residential neighborhood not far from downtown Highlands, the Colonial Pines occupies a large mid-20th-century plantation-style house on 2 acres. It's surrounded by landscaped, shaded lawns, with gardens that supply the breakfast table with fresh produce and herbs. Common rooms have a cozy, 1940s look with country furniture, redbrick fireplace, and knotty-pine paneling. The knotty pine carries throughout the six rooms and one kitchenette apartment, which range in size from cozy to large. $85–150, including a full breakfast.

Toad Hall Bed and Breakfast (828-526-3889; www.toadhallb-b.com), 61 Sequoyah Point Way, Highlands, NC 28741. Open all year. This five-room B&B occupies a former family complex, built in the 1950s on a peninsula in Lake Sequoyah, an easy mile's drive from downtown Highlands. This small human-made lake, wandering through the hills on the west side of town, offers lovely views, frequently with a glassy-surfaced reflection; the inn has a nice dock and canoes for guests. Toad Hall (named for Kenneth Grahame's *Wind in the Willows*), the main building of the complex, is principally the owners' residence and the elegant, log-sided dining room, with a large picture window overlooking the lake. Four of the rooms are in the next building, Badger Hall; all are large, individually decorated, with whirlpool tub and either a balcony or terrace. The fifth room is a cottage with a separate living room, a stone, wood-burning fireplace, and a kitchenette. All five rooms enjoy the full breakfast in the main hall. Rooms $120–200, cottage $130–225.

Innisfree Victorian Inn (828-743-2946; www.innisfreeinn.com), NC 107 N., P.O. Box 469, Glenville, NC 28736. This small country hotel, rated four diamonds by AAA, is an elaborate Victorian fantasy on the shore of Glenville Lake, 6 miles north of Cashiers off NC 107. The three-story modern structure, purpose-built in a Victorian style to serve as an inn, has full wraparound verandas and decks on the first two floors, with wide views over the lake. Victorian antiques fill the bright common rooms, and an octagonal table in a turret room serves as the formal dining area for breakfast. The 10 rooms, ranging from standard size to very large, are individually decorated, each with its own Victorian theme. Whirlpool baths, private verandas, and fireplaces are available. $119–300.

Millstone Inn (888-645-5786 or 828-743-2737; fax 828-743-0208; www.millstoneinn.com), US 64 W. 119 Lodge Lane, Cashiers, NC 28717. Open Mar.–Dec. This 1933 vacation lodge, a mile west of Cashiers and well off US 64, faces its two bark-shingled bay wings over the headwaters of the Chattooga River toward a tree-framed view of crag-topped Whiteside Mountain. Converted from a private home in 1952, Millstone features wide lawns with spectacular views, a large sitting room with a millstone embedded in the fireplace, and 11 comfortable rooms. The rooms are decorated in a country rustic style, with local hardwood paneling. The main lodge has seven of the rooms, with four more in an annex built in 1952; some have balcony, while others have separate sitting room. $131–198.

A MISTY MORNING ON LAKE SEQUOYAH.

Jim Hargan

CABINS **The Cabins at Seven Foxes** (828-877-6333; fax 828-862-4132; www.sevenfoxes.com), P.O. Box 123; on Slick Fisher Rd., Lake Toxaway, NC 28747. Located 4 miles north of Lake Toxaway on the Blue Ridge, this group of five new cabins sits on 6 wooded acres. These one- and two-bedroom cabins, modestly styled on the outside, are comfortably furnished with antiques and reproductions, each with its own theme. All cabins have porch, gas fireplace, fully equipped kitchen, and quilts. $100–255 per day, $630–1,395 per week.

The Cottage Inn (877-595-3600 or 828-743-3033; fax 828-743-0199; www.cottageinncashiers.com), 71 Brocade Dr., US 64 E., Cashiers, NC 28717. This collection of 14 cottages sits on 10 acres just east of Cashiers, off US 64. The cottages range widely in size and style, but tend to be modest and simple, yet handsome and well kept. All have an efficiency kitchen (some lack an oven), a living area, and a porch or deck, and all but one have a fireplace. On the property, and open to all cottage renters, are an indoor swimming pool and a hard-surfaced tennis court, as well as hammocks and a picnic area. A lodge, with four en suite rooms and a conference room, provides a venue for business meetings or family reunions. $90–155 per night.

✪ ♿ **Devil's Fork State Park** (864-944-2639; www.discoversouthcarolina.com/stateparks/parkdetail.asp?pid=1355), 161 Holcombe Circle, Salem, SC 29676. This South Carolina state park, located on the western shore of Lake Jocassee, has 20 large modern cabins in a contemporary/rustic style, with a large screened porch. Each has a living room with a fireplace, a kitchen, and either two or three bedrooms, and 11 have lake views. $99–132.

✳ Where to Eat

EATING OUT **Pescado's Highland Burrito** (828-526-9313), N. 4th St., Highlands, NC. Lunch and dinner. This downtown Highlands Mexican eatery prepares its food from scratch using fresh ingredients. Specialties are large California-style burritos,

THE BLUE RIDGE MOUNTAINS REFLECTED IN A SMALL LAKE NEAR CASHIERS.

Jim Hargan

tacos, quesadillas, and salads, with plenty of fresh-made salsa.

Carolina Smokehouse (828-743-3200), US 64 W., Cashiers, NC. If you find yourself at a loss for a good, simple roadside eatery, this is your place. It occupies a plain little building with a covered deck, west of Cashiers on US 64. Inside it's just as plain, but clean and with a decor centering on old automobile tags. The barbeque is fresh and tasty, with a sweet tomato-based sauce, served up with the classic sides, and reasonably priced.

DINING OUT **On the Verandah** (828-526-2338; www.ontheverandah.com), 1536 Franklin Rd., Highlands, NC. Dinner daily; Sun. brunch. Located west of Highlands on US 64, this family-owned restaurant occupies an old 1920s speakeasy overlooking Lake Sequoyah, with lovely views over the lake from its deck or enclosed veranda dining areas. Inside, the bright and attractive dining room is dominated by founding owner Alan Figel's collection of more than 1,300 bottles of chili sauce (any one of which diners are welcome to try). The menu features a fusion of Caribbean, South American, and Asian approaches, always with fresh, local ingredients emphasized. As you might expect from someone with 1,300 bottles of hot sauce, at least a couple of items will feature fresh, unusual chili peppers, and the mild dishes tend to be richly flavored. This restaurant has a 200-bottle wine list, and a wine bar with an extensive choice of wines by the glass.

Ristorante Paoletti (828-526-4906), 440 Main St., Highlands, NC. Dinner Mon.–Sat., June–Oct. This downtown Highlands storefront restaurant offers fine Italian dining with a rich choice

of foods that go well beyond red sauce on pasta. The Paoletti has a long menu of gourmet pastas with a wide variety of treatments, any of which may be ordered as a main dish or as a side to one of their entrées—veal, lamb, fish, chicken, and filet mignon. Their wine list includes over 800 bottles. Appetizers $6–9; pastas $14–19 à la carte, $9–14 as an accompaniment; entrées $19–33.

The Central House Restaurant (888-526-9319 or 828-526-9319), 4th and Main, Highlands, NC. Located in the center of downtown Highlands, in the Old Edwards Inn, the Central House offers a casual lunch for shoppers and a gourmet dinner after the day is done. Crab soup, onion soup, an array of fresh green and fruit salads, imaginative sandwiches, and fresh fish entrées highlight lunch, which may be served inside or in the inn's lovely garden. Dinner menus have a large selection of fresh seafood, cooked to your order the way you prefer, with steak, chicken, pork, and lamb entrées also available. Recipes are simple, merging fresh flavors in straightforward ways.

✳ **Entertainment**

Highlands Playhouse (828-526-2695), Oak St., Highlands, NC. This respected summer theater performs plays and musicals in its shingle-clad playhouse behind downtown Highlands.

Highlands Chamber Music Festival (828-526-9060), Highlands, NC. This summer series of chamber music performances is held at the Episcopal Church of the Incarnation, in July and August.

✳ Selective Shopping

Highlands, NC

Highlands's large concentration of million-dollar vacation cottages ensures that it has an equally large concentration of antiques shops and art galleries. In fact, Highlands has had a first-class collection of antiques shops for a number of decades, about half in its quaint downtown and the other half scattered about town. The chamber of commerce lists 16 antiques shops and art galleries, with five more craft galleries and shops, 14 gift shops, and two bookstores.

Scudders Gallery (828-526-4111), 352 Main St. Open all year. Established in 1925 (in Silver Springs, FL), Scudder's has antiques auctions every night at 7:30. During the off-season, it can be the town's primary form of evening entertainment. Definitely a high-end antiques dealer, their stocks include Oriental carpets, estate jewelry, furniture, silver, paintings, and other art. Catalog sales are held the second and fourth Sat., June–Nov., at 11 AM. You will find it in downtown Highlands.

Country Inn Antiques (828-526-5036), 4th and Main. Specializing in antiques from the American South, this downtown Highlands shop is filled with furniture and knickknacks. The shop features American country furniture and accessories, vintage glass, and decorative smalls, as well as early textiles and architectural adornments.

The Old Red House (828-526-9201), 5th and Main. This shop specializes in fine handmade quilts, with a choice of around 250 antique quilts and 75 modern quilts handmade by six local quilters; the provenance of each quilt is known in detail. The shop also offers vintage linens, antique fishing equipment, and local crafts. It has two locations; the original Old Red House is south of downtown Highlands on NC 106, while the new shop is downtown.

The Christmas Tree (800-523-6558). In downtown Highlands for over a quarter of a century, the Christmas Tree offers just about everything you could put on, under, or near a tree. It has a particularly large selection of miniatures, and is a Department 56 Gold Key Dealer.

Cashiers, NC

Basketworks (828-743-5052), NC 107 S. Located south of Cashiers's center, this shop features locally made smoke vine baskets, as well as Shenandoah Valley antiques, 18th-century antique botanicals, dried and handmade silk flowers, and a range of gift items.

Lyn K. Holloway Antiques (828-743-2524), US 64 and NC 107. Located behind the bank at the center of town, this cottage-based shop is set off by its attractive gardens. It features French, English, and American antiques, and specializes in American lazy Susan tables.

✳ Special Events

SUMMER Symphony Under the Stars (828-743-9941). July 4. The Charleston Symphony Orchestra performs on the banks of Lake Sapphire, east of Cashiers, NC.

AUTUMN Cashiers Annual Chili Cook-off. Mid-Sep. This annual chili cook-off, sponsored by the Cashiers Chamber of Commerce, has live music.

FRANKLIN & THE NANTAHALA MOUNTAINS

The headwaters of the Little Tennessee River carve out two of the Southern Appalachians' most impressive ridgelines: the Cowee Mountains and the Nantahala Mountains. Between the two lies the deep, flat valley of the Little Tennessee, along with the little gem-mining town of Franklin.

The Nantahala Mountains (pronounced *Nanna-HAY-luh*) dominate this area, with their stunning waterfalls, spectacular cliff views, wilderness rivers, and quaint CCC picnic areas. The Nantahala ridgeline forms a straight, steep edge running north between the Little Tennessee River and its western tributary, the Nantahala River. From its southern end, where it intersects with the Blue Ridge at Big Butt (near Pickens Nose), to its northern terminus at Wesser, the Nantahala ridgeline carries the Appalachian Trail through 30 miles of thick, deep forest little disturbed since logging stopped.

East of this mountain system lies the Little Tennessee Valley and the bustling county seat of Franklin. For centuries before the coming of the Europeans, this valley was the center of Cherokee civilization. It supported a chain of settlements known as the Middle Villages, each village ranging from half a dozen homesteads to groups of 30 or more dwellings. In 1817 the Cherokee Nation ceded the upper Little Tennessee Valley to the government of North Carolina and retreated to the lands west and south of the Nantahalas. Settlers trickled in; after 10 years the valley had enough population to warrant its own county government, with its seat at the Cherokee village of Nikwasi, now named Franklin for a former governor. Another 30 years after that the valley received its first decent road, a turnpike that linked Franklin with Asheville and Murphy, NC, crossing the Nantahalas at Wayah Gap.

Gem mining started in the upper Little Tennessee Valley in the 1870s. To be more accurate, corundum mining started in the 1870s, and the corundum mines kept kicking up gem-quality rocks. Corundum was (and is) a valuable industrial abrasive, being the second hardest substance found in nature and considerably more plentiful than the hardest, diamonds. Usually corundum is found as an opaque, milky-white rock, but when crystallized in an exceptionally pure form it becomes either rubies or sapphires (depending on the trace elements that add

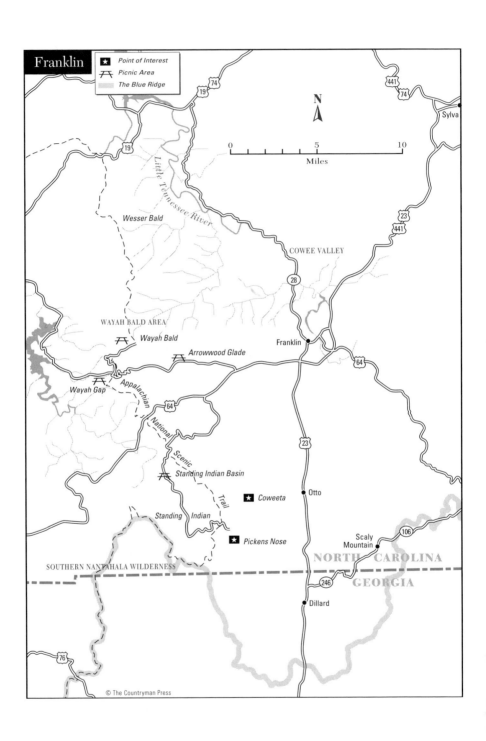

Franklin

★ Point of Interest
🏕 Picnic Area
▓ The Blue Ridge

N

0   5   10
Miles

74
19
441
74

Sylva

Little Tennessee River

19

Wesser Bald

23
441

COWEE VALLEY

28

WAYAH BALD AREA

🏕 Wayah Bald

Arrowwood Glade

Franklin

64

🏕 Wayah Gap

Appalachian

64

National

Scenic

🏕 Standing Indian Basin

23

★ Coweeta

Otto

Trail

Standing   Indian

★ Pickens Nose

Scaly
Mountain

106

SOUTHERN NANTAHALA WILDERNESS

NORTH CAROLINA

GEORGIA

246

Dillard

76

© The Countryman Press

color). While the quality of the occasional gemstone impressed Tiffany's and attracted investors in the 1890s, a reliable source for the gemstones was never found. Commercial corundum mining ended with World War II, and today gemstone mining is a popular recreational pursuit.

GUIDANCE **Franklin Area Chamber of Commerce** (866-372-5546 or 828-524-3161; fax 828-369-7516; www.franklin-chamber.com), 425 Porter St., Franklin, NC 28734. The Franklin Chamber handles tourism promotion and visitor relations for all of Macon County. Their visitors center is located south of downtown Franklin on US Business 441.

Nantahala National Forest, Wayah Ranger District (828-524-6441), 90 Sloan Rd., Franklin, NC 28734. The ranger station for the Nantahala Mountains is located 1.6 miles west of downtown Franklin, just off Old US 64 (now known as Old Murphy Rd., SSR 1442). They have a staffed information desk during business hours, and can help with maps of the Nantahala backcountry.

GETTING THERE *By car*: Franklin, NC, has excellent highway connections with the outside world. Its main north–south highway, **US 441**, is a modern four lane. From the west, **US 64** is a well-engineered two lane with gentle curves and wide shoulders. From the east, however, US 64 is a mess, unmodernized since it was built in 1923; take **US 74** to US 441 at Dillsboro, NC, instead.

By air: Franklin is over an hour from Asheville, NC, and about 3 hours from Atlanta on good roads. Atlanta is usually cheaper.

By bus or train: Franklin has no bus or passenger train service. **Road Runner Driving Services** (828-524-3265) offers shuttle services from all regional airports, as well as driving services within the area.

MEDICAL EMERGENCIES **Angel Medical Center** (828-524-8411), 120 Riverview St., Franklin, NC. This local hospital is located a few blocks north of downtown on Riverview St.

✳ Wandering Around

EXPLORING BY CAR **The Nantahala Mountains**. *Leg 1*: US 64 west from Franklin, NC, 3.8 miles; right on Old Murphy Rd. (SSR 1442), then 0.2 mile; left on Wayah Rd. (SSR 1310), 8.7 miles; right on Wayah Bald Rd. (a Forest Service road) 4.2 miles. Return to US 64. Many curves; a steep, gravel forest road. *Leg 2*: On US 64 westbound, 2.2 miles; left on Old US 64 (SSR 1448), then 6.4 miles to Wallace Gap; left on paved FS 71, then 1.7 miles to the end of the pavement at national forest campground; continue left uphill on gravel FS 71 to Pickens Nose.

These two legs use the predecessors to modern US 64 to explore the Nantahala Mountains, topping the crest both times. The first leg follows the 19th-century coach road, while the second follows the early-20th-century's first attempt at a paved auto road.

The first leg follows a handsome creek valley up past the CCC **Arrowwood Glade Picnic Area**, then heads into deep woods. It switchbacks steeply up to

Wayah Bald; only ignorance of the mountain's true layout could be responsible for putting the 1850 coach road through this high, cold gap. Look for **Bertie's Falls** on the left as you switch upward. Once in Wayah Gap, this leg follows a very steep gravel forest road for over 4 miles, mostly along the Nantahala Crest. Be sure to stop for the **Wilson Lick Ranger Station** on your left, an attractive historic site preserving a very early station. At the top you will get good views from the picnic area parking lot, but be sure to walk up the quarter mile to the stone **Wayah Bald Tower** for some remarkable panoramas. Go back the way you came.

The second leg leaves modern US 64 to the left, to follow the original US 64 auto road designed and constructed in the 1920s, replaced only in the late 1970s. It's a dramatic climb; try to picture a fully loaded semi, circa 1975, coming down-hill toward you with smoking brakes. When you top out, leave the old highway to take the paved Forest Service road into the **Standing Indian Basin**. This is a beautiful forest drive along a lovely wild river, then uphill on a good gravel road to waterfalls and a stunning clifftop view.

EXPLORING ON FOOT **Standing Indian Basin** is an outstanding hiking area, with varied and interesting scenery easily reached by a variety of loop trails. For an easy leg stretcher that samples the best of Standing Indian, take in the two waterfalls, then follow up with a walk out to Pickens Nose. See *To See*.

✳ Villages

Franklin, NC. An early pioneer town, Franklin has been a major market center for the surrounding mountains since stagecoach roads converged here in the

THE CIRCA-1911 WILSON LICK RANGER STATION.

Jim Hargan

1850s. Today it has a handsome and shoppable downtown of three square blocks, with lots of businesses sprawling outward along its U.S. highways, US 441 Bypass, US Business 441, and US 64. It sits in the middle of a broad flat valley, straddling the Little Tennessee River with low hills that wouldn't look out of place in the Piedmont. When the mountains get started, however, they kick in with a vengeance, with all local ridgelines surpassing 4,000 feet and the Nanta-halas reaching well above 5,000.

Cowee Valley. This remote and pastoral valley is dotted with so many old farm-houses and barns that it has been declared a National Historic District. Its rolling farmlands are framed by the tall forested peaks of the Cowee Mountains, and easily visited from a network of country lanes. But that's not why it's famous. No, it's the rubies. Cowee Valley has been a source of rubies since the 1870s. Not crummy, cloudy little industrial corundum specks, either, but big star rubies and sapphires, gem quality and weighing hundreds of carats. Gem-quality rubies are found in other mountain valleys as well, but the large majority of the local "gem mines" salt their dirt with low grade foreign semiprecious stones. This guide lists only those mines that provide unsalted pay dirt from their own property.

Otto, NC. South of Franklin, NC, the Little Tennessee River drains a wide, flat-bottomed valley that stretches to the state line and beyond. US 441 follows this valley south into Georgia, then on to Atlanta and Florida. Somewhere along this valley, between Franklin and the state line, Franklin ends and Otto begins. Otto is a broad rural community with no town center. For practical purposes, places in Otto are places that are way south of Franklin but still in North Carolina.

✳ Wild Places

THE GREAT FORESTS **The Southern Nantahala Wilderness**. Congress cre-ated this 24,500-acre wilderness to protect the great knot of mountains at the juncture of the Blue Ridge and the Nantahalas. Although only the northern slopes of the Blue Ridge are easily reached from Franklin, NC, the wilderness extends a great distance over the southern slopes as well, including large tracts in Georgia's Chattahoochee National Forest. The **Appalachian Trail (AT)** follows the crest of the Blue Ridge from Georgia to the Nantahala Mountains, then fol-lows the Nantahalas north.

These lands are extremely rugged, with knotted ridgelines and steep slopes. Nearly all the forests are second-growth hardwoods, as the entire area was logged between 1910 and 1940. The logging camp was located at the modern Standing Indian Campground, and logging railroads were built up the stream valleys. Some of these old railroad grades now make for attractive walking through nicely recovered riverine and cove hardwood forests.

The Forest Service owns perhaps twice again as much land in the immediate area that is not included in the wilderness but remains open to public recreation. This includes the entire **Standing Indian Basin**, adjacent to the wilderness on its north. Many good-quality trails start in the Standing Indian area, with good trail-heads on its gravel access road, and extend into the wilderness; by connecting

Jim Hargan

BIG LAUREL FALLS IN STANDING INDIAN BASIN.

RECREATION AREAS **STANDING INDIAN BASIN**

Established as a Nantahala National Forest campground in the 1950s, on the site of a logging camp from the 1940s, the Standing Indian Basin has evolved into a major outdoor destination. It encompasses the headwaters of the

these trails, hikers and backpackers can make a wide variety of loops. One ambitious loop day hike (or good overnighter) starts at the Standing Indian Campground trailhead, hikes up the railroad grade along Kimsey Creek to the AT, then climbs **Standing Indian** on the AT for wonderful views; hikers can return to their cars by half a dozen different alternative paths.

The Wayah Bald area. The highest peak in the northern Nantahalas is not Wayah Bald. It is Wine Springs Bald, a mile to the south and a good 100 feet higher. No one cares. Everything in this area is named for Wayah Bald, including the Nantahala National Forest's ranger district. It has its own gravel road, 4.5 miles long, climbing 1,100 feet just to reach it. It has one of the oldest ranger stations in the East on its slopes, preserved as an historic site. It has a stone lookout tower that's been there since 1912 and is simply beautiful. And it has views that just won't quit.

Wayah Bald marks a rough halfway point in the northward march of the Nanta-

Nantahala River, surrounded by the 5,000-foot peaks of the Blue Ridge and the Nantahala Mountains. The highest peaks on its south are protected in the Southern Nantahala Wilderness. Lower down, the lands are open to logging and other such operations.

No doubt much of the interest in this area comes from the fact that the **Appalachian Trail (AT)** makes a three-quarters circle around the Standing Indian Campground, allowing weekenders to do a 2-night backpack on the AT and return to their car. There are now a large number of trails that loop down and up, allowing any number of different routes from a single camping space at the center. For the auto-bound hiker, this is a unique place.

The scenery is worth the attention it gets. The Nantahala River runs merrily through a narrow flat-bottomed valley, lined with meadows. The trout fishing is said to be excellent, and there are lots of places to pitch a tent. While all the upstream slopes were logged in the early 20th century, they were selectively cut and recovered quickly to form impressive forests. The side streams are violent and lovely, and higher streams have mighty waterfalls, including **Big Laurel** and **Moony Falls**. The high ridgeline of the Blue Ridge and the Nantahalas has wide views from grassy balds at Standing Indian, and from sheer crags at **Pickens Nose**.

A gravel road, FS 71, cuts southward to the heart of this district. From it most of the paths radiate. It is a worthy drive, passable by all but the wimpiest automobiles to Pickens Nose; SUVs can continue down it into **Coweeta Hydrologic Laboratory** without difficulty.

hala Mountains. It's surrounded by huge expanses of the Nantahala National Forest, a lot of it purchased as soon as the Weeks Act established the national forest system in 1911. (That's why it has such an old ranger station.) Nearly all of the recreational development has centered on the **Nantahala Crest**, traversed by the Appalachian Trail from one end to the other. Downslope, the public lands roll on and on, cut by logging roads and open to those who don't mind entering trail-less areas armed only with 50-year-old USGS maps.

PICNIC AREAS **Arrowwood Glade Picnic Area**. Located on the road to Wayah Gap (Wayah Rd., SSR 1310), this is a classic CCC picnic area, little changed since the 1930s and simply beautiful. If you miss it, there is another nice national forest picnic area in Wayah Gap (on the left as you crest out), named **Wayah Crest**.

Standing Indian Picnic Area. Yes, you can picnic at Standing Indian. The picnic area, by the Nantahala River, is very beautiful and makes a great starting (or ending) place for further exploration.

✳ To See

IN THE MOUNTAINS The Nantahala Mountains dominate the Franklin area. Running almost due north from the Blue Ridge, the Nantahalas have always been a great green barrier, with more than a dozen peaks over 5,000 feet and only three gaps, which barely dip below 4,000 feet. The Blue Ridge, running east–west, merges with the southern end of the Nantahalas to form the backbone of the Southern Nantahala Wilderness and wall off the Standing Indian Recreation Area. There are many things worth exploring in these mountains, all of them in the Nantahala National Forest; a few of them are listed below, from south to north.

Standing Indian—The Mountain. Well over a mile high, Standing Indian dominates the Southern Nantahala Wilderness. It's also one of the tallest peaks on the Blue Ridge, just a foot shy of 5,500 feet. Known as "the grandstand of the Southern Appalachians," it has wide rocky balds with 180° views over the headwaters of the Nantahala River, framed by the 5,000-foot wall of the Nantahala Mountains. Reaching it is a bit of an adventure; paths up from Standing Indian Recreation Area are good, but climb a whopping 2,100 feet before reaching the top. There's an easier way up, however—a passable Forest Service road, FS 71, leads 6 miles to the Appalachian Trail at Deep Gap, reducing the hike to a short, steep 1,100-foot climb. You will find FS 71 on the left, 14.4 miles west of Franklin on US 64.

Waterfalls of Standing Indian. Two worthwhile waterfalls can be easily reached from the gravel road through the Standing Indian area. At **Big Laurel Falls**, 4.9 miles up from the campground, a large stream makes a 20-foot plunge over a ledge; the trail to it is half a mile long. At 5.6 miles past the campground, **Moony Falls** is just off the road to the right.

Pickens Nose. This easily reached high bald has wide and wonderful views over the much lower Georgia mountains to the south, and over the rich valley of the Little Tennessee River. A side ridge of the Nantahalas, it forms the eastern edge of the Southern Nantahala Wilderness. The path to it leaves the Standing Indian gravel road on the right, 8.7 miles from the campground, then follows a ridgeline for three-quarters of a mile, climbing 200 feet.

Coweeta Hydrologic Laboratory. The National Forest Service established this forest in 1933 to perform a series of in-depth, long-term experiments that would map out the precise relationship between forest cover and stream flow—at the time a hotly controversial subject on which there was almost no data. This involved altering the forest cover in a number of small stream basins, setting up a dense network of rain gauges and groundwater wells to measure water flowing into a basin, then measuring the water flowing over a weir at the bottom. These experiments have been crucial in improving conservation practices on public and private lands throughout the South.

Today's Coweeta continues these long-term experiments, using a multidisciplinary approach that includes detailed ecological studies, yielding data capable of addressing such questions as the effects of controlled burning or climate change. This is a serious research program, very active throughout its almost 6,000 acres.

While there are no recreational opportunities, Coweeta is happy to answer questions and give tours. The main Forest Service road through the center of Co-weeta, FS 83, is usually passable by passenger car (though steep, rough, twisty, and ill marked); it connects with the road through Standing Indian, FS 71, at Pickens Nose.

Wayah Bald. The 5,350-foot peak of Wayah Bald is crowned by a two-story stone tower that gives a full-circle panorama in all directions. There are more views from the nearby picnic area. The gravel Forest Service road to Wayah Bald climbs 1,100 feet in 4.5 miles; on the way it passes one of the first National Forest Service ranger stations ever built, now preserved as a historic site.

Wesser Bald. The last and the lowest of the Nantahala's major peaks, Wesser Bald (4,630 feet) may well have the best views. A viewing platform built on top of its old fire tower gives a complete circular panorama whose views down into the valleys below are unobstructed. It requires a 2-mile round-trip hike on the Appalachian Trail with an 800-foot climb; the trailhead, at **Tellico Gap**, is a 30-mile drive from Franklin. To reach it, take US 64 west from Franklin, NC, for 3.8 miles; turn right onto Old Murphy Rd. (SSR 1442), then drive 0.2 mile. Turn left onto paved Wayah Rd. (SSR 1310) and continue straight ahead for 13.4 miles, then go right on gravel Otter Creek Rd. (SSR 1365) for 3.9 miles to the Forest Service parking lot in Tellico Gap.

CULTURAL SITES **Macon County Historical Museum** (828-524-9758; www .genealogybookstore.com/publishing/macon/historical/historicalsociety.htm), 36 W. Main St., Franklin, NC. Mon.–Fri. 10–4. Downtown Franklin's 1904 Pendergrass Store still has the appearance of a turn-of-the-20th-century small rural department store, with its wood paneling and central stairs to a mezzanine balcony. These days, however, it's filled with historical artifacts and displays about the Franklin area, as part of a local history museum and research center run by the Macon County Historical Society. Free.

The Franklin Gem and Mineral Museum (828-369-7831; www.fgmm.org), 25 Phillips St., Franklin, NC. May–Oct., Mon.–Fri. 10–4. The old Macon County Jail in downtown Franklin housed prisoners from 1850 until 1970. In 1976 it became the site of the Franklin Gem and Mineral Museum, run by the local rockhound club, the very active Franklin Gem and Mineral Society. The building remains very much an old jail, with gem and mineral exhibits in the cells. One such exhibit contains gems and minerals from North Carolina, including a most rare and valuable piece—an 18th-century Wedgewood porcelain made from clay taken from Franklin (then a Cherokee village). Another exhibit has minerals from every state in the Union. There are displays of wire-wrapped jewelry, of fluorescent minerals, of Native American artifacts, and of fossils. Free.

Scottish Tartans Museum (828-524-7472; fax 828-524-1092; www.scottish tartans.org), 86 E. Main St., Franklin, NC 28734. Mon.–Fri. 10–5, Sun. 1–5. The official North American museum of the Scottish Tartan Society—the governing society for all tartans worldwide, located in Pitlochry, Scotland—occupies a storefront in downtown Franklin. Its museum displays Scottish tartans and relates them to Scottish history and culture. It has facilities for looking up family tartans, and a really great gift shop. The Scottish Tartans Museum sponsors the annual Taste of Scotland Festival. $1 donation per adult requested.

PARKS AND GARDENS Perry's Water Gardens (828-524-3264; fax 828-369-2050; www.tcfb.com/perwatg/Perryhom.html), 136 Leatherman Gap Rd., Franklin, NC. Mon.–Sat. 9–5, Sun. 1–5. Located in Cowee Valley, these extensive water gardens are on the site of one of America's largest commercial aquatic nurseries. Here you will see every conceivable type of water plant, but most especially water lilies, lotuses, and irises. Every pond has its own population of giant goldfish, which keep the area mosquito-free. Free.

✳ To Do

FISHING Great Smokey Mountain Fish Camp and Safaris (828-369-5295; www.fishcamp.biz), 81 Bennett Rd., Franklin, NC. This Little Tennessee River outfitter, just north of Franklin on NC 28 (near Cowee Valley), offers guided fishing trips, canoeing and kayaking, biking (including rentals), and a gourmet food store, in addition to the campground.

GEM MINING

Mason's Ruby and Sapphire Mine (828-369-9742), 6961 Upper Burningtown Rd., Franklin, NC. Apr.–Oct., daily 8–5. This ruby mine in the Nantahala Mountains west of Franklin allows miners to dig their own dirt, and does not practice salting. This mine is different from, and unconnected with, Mason Mountain Mine (which is near Cowee Valley and salts its dirt with foreign stones).

Sheffield Mine (828-369-8383; www.sheffieldmine.com), 385 Sheffield Farms Rd., Franklin, NC. Apr.–Oct., daily 9–5 (admissions close earlier). This long-established Cowee Valley mine—open to the public since the 1940s but in existence before then—features unsalted dirt from the property. This is one of the few places in the world where star rubies (purple-red rubies that form a star when cabachoned) can be mined. They also sell salted dirt, clearly labeled as such; they do not salt rubies or sapphires. Their web site has good information on ruby mining.

KILTS ON EXHIBIT AT THE SCOTTISH TARTANS MUSEUM.

Jim Hargan

GOLF Mill Creek Country Club (800-533-3916 or 828-524-6458; www.mcgolfresort.com), Mill Creek Rd., Franklin, NC. This 18-hole course, located on the west side of Franklin adjacent to Nantahala National Forest lands, offers very scenic play with wide mountain views. $40.

Franklin Golf Course (828-524-2288), 255 First Fairway Dr., Franklin, NC. This nine-hole course was built in 1929 as part of a subdivision just south of downtown Franklin. It offers convenient in-town play. $10.

Holly Springs Golf Course (828-369-8711), 115 Holly Springs Golf Village, Franklin, NC. A nine-hole golf course near Franklin that was built in 1976 as part of a housing subdivision. $20.

WHITEWATER ADVENTURES **The Little Tennessee River** is wide, smooth, and beautiful, passing through handsome farmland with wide views toward the Nantahala and Cowee Mountains. Popular with local canoeists and kayakers, it is undiscovered by the raft trip operators. However, the Smoky Mountain Fish Camp (see *Fishing*), on its banks near Cowee Valley, offers canoeing, kayaking, and tubing.

✴ Lodging

COUNTRY INNS AND HOTELS **The Summit Inn** (828-524-2006; fax 828-349-1246), 210 E. Rogers St., Franklin, NC 28734. This 1898 mansion, built as a private house, sits on a hilltop overlooking downtown Franklin, one block to its south. A white clapboard structure, its large veranda extends outward to flank the front entrance with two room-sized extensions—one of which has been converted into a sunroom, the site of the Summit Inn Restaurant (see *Dining Out*). Downstairs, the **Down Under Bar** fills the cellar's river stone walls with nightly music and dancing; its stone fireplace, pool table, and large-screen TV are always open to guests. The hotel has 14 rooms, individually decorated; only six have private bath. $59–99.

The Franklin Terrace (800-633-2431 or 828-524-7907; www.franklin terrace.com), 159 Harrison Ave., Franklin, NC 28734. This distinguished white wooden building, listed on the National Register, originally housed a school when it was constructed in 1887; it's been the Franklin Terrace Hotel since 1915. Extra-wide verandas cover both stories

of the building's long front, and columned porticos shelter the side entrances. Nowadays the B&B shares this building with an antiques shop— the shop taking up the downstairs and the B&B upstairs. The B&B has been returned to its 1915 original with period antiques in its nine carefully decorated rooms. $52–69, including a full breakfast.

BED & BREAKFAST INNS **The Snow Hill Inn** (800-598-8136 or 828-369-2100; www.bbonline.com/nc/snow hill/), 531 Snow Hill Rd., Franklin, NC 28734. This large 1914 house, once used as a schoolhouse, occupies 14 acres with views over the Little Tennessee Valley. A classic white clapboard farmhouse, its wide front porch looks out over gardens with a gazebo and benches, framing a view that takes in six mountain peaks. The eight rooms, all with private bath, are decorated with antiques and reproductions in a simple country style. The tariff includes a full breakfast in the bright and airy sunroom. $67–97 per night.

Heritage Inn (888-524-4150 or 828-524-4150), 43 Heritage Hollow Dr., Franklin, NC 28734. This attractive, old-fashioned house sits a short block away from downtown Franklin in a quiet residential neighborhood. Its wide, wraparound veranda overhangs an old stone terrace, right above the side street. It has five en suite rooms, one with a kitchenette. Included in the tariff are a full breakfast and evening wine and hors d'oeuvres. $75–95; discounts available for longer stays.

Blaine House Bed and Breakfast (888-349-4230 or 828-349-4230; www .blainehouse.com), 661 Harrison Ave., Franklin, NC 28734. This 1910 cottage sits on lightly traveled NC 28 on the north end of Franklin. With elaborate gables and dormers, its entrances framed with neoclassical columns and pediments, it has a lot of personality. Inside, it's carefully decorated with family antiques and heirlooms. Two cozy rooms are decorated in a simple, country style with quilts on the beds; the two large suites, with separate sitting areas, are more formally decorated. Gourmet breakfasts are served in a bright and airy sun-

room. Rooms $79, suites $99–109; discounts for longer stays.

✳ Where to Eat

EATING OUT **Mama's** (828-369-8185; fax -9597; www.mamasrestaurant .com), 21 Heritage Hollow Dr., Franklin, NC. Tue.–Sat. 6:30 AM–9 PM. Located in a wandering gray-sided building set among trees a scant block south of downtown Franklin, Mama's features standard American fare at reasonable prices, three meals a day. They make their own yeast rolls, vegetable soup, and pies fresh from scratch, and have a full line of sandwiches as well as hot entrées. Breakfast $2–4, lunch $4–6, dinner $6–11.

The Frog and Owl Kitchen (828-349-4112), 46 E. Main St., Franklin, NC. Mon.–Sat. 11–3. This downtown Franklin storefront café serves American fusion cuisine for the casual lunch crowd. It's a rare small-town treat when you're looking for a lunch that's light and sophisticated. Wine is available. $6–12.

YOU'LL FIND DOZENS OF MINES ALONG RUBY MINE ROAD.

Jim Hargan

The Chef and His Wife (828-369-0575; fax 828-369-1725), 15 Courthouse Plaza, Franklin, NC. Lunch and dinner. This popular eatery sits on the Courthouse Square in the center of downtown Franklin. Its food sits somewhere in the middle, too—fancier than standard southern fare, but not as out there as nouveau American fusion. Lunch features hot dogs (good ones), fresh half-pound burgers, and a variety of sandwiches (from roast beef on a kaiser to goat cheese and roasted red pepper on French bread). Dinners range from meat loaf and ribs, through a variety of steaks, to a good selection of fresh seafood. Lunch $4–6, dinner $9–15.

Fat Buddies Ribs and BBQ (828-349-4743; www.fatbuddiesribsand bbq.com), 311 Westgate Plaza, Franklin, NC. Mon.–Sat. 11–2:30 and 5–9. You will find this authentic pit barbeque in a suburban shopping plaza off the freeway portion of US 64 W. Meats are slow-cooked over a blend of hardwoods, and basted with Fat Buddies' own sauce. They smoke pork, beef, chicken, and baby back ribs, serving the results as a sandwich with fries or a platter with two sides. They also have a good choice of well-thought-out salads for the barbeque impaired, as well as Brunswick stew and black-eyed pea stew. They make four different barbeque sauces and five salad dressings, all from their own recipes. Most meals are in the $5–9 range; ribs cost more.

DINING OUT **The Summit Inn Restaurant** (828-524-2006; fax 828-349-1246), 210 E. Rogers St., Franklin, NC. Franklin's Summit Inn serves lunch and dinner in the sunroom, with views over downtown to the Nantahala Mountains. Weather permitting, there is additional dining on an outside patio. The straightforward menu features hand-cut steaks, seafood, and vegetarian entrées. A wine list is available. In the inn's cellar, a large bar has walls of native rock from the Little Tennessee River, a stone fireplace, pool, and live music and dancing.

❋ **Entertainment**
Pickin' on the Square (828-349-1212), Franklin, NC. There's free music and dancing every Saturday night at the gazebo on the square in downtown Franklin, in front of the County Courthouse. It starts with an open mike at 7 PM, with the main band—either bluegrass or gospel—coming on at 8 PM.

❋ **Selective Shopping**
Franklin, NC
Franklin is an important market center for its surrounding region, and so takes on more of the look of a contemporary southern town than many of its peers in the mountains. Its three-block downtown is definitely worth a stroll, with gift, antiques, and gem shops as well as two museums and a nice town square. Beyond that, a large number of shops string out for 2 or 3 miles along all of the main highway: at the exits along US 441 Bypass, US 441 south of town (the biggest concentration), US Business 441 north and south of downtown, and US 64 east and west of downtown.

Michael M. Rogers Gallery (877-918-5888 or 828-524-6709; www .sharethebeauty.com), 18 W. Palmer St. This well-known watercolor artist lives in Franklin and maintains a gallery downtown. He paints highly detailed and accurate scenes of nature in the Blue Ridge, the Nantahalas, and the Smokies, showing how weather highlights seasonal changes. His web site is worth a visit.

MACO Crafts, Inc. (828-524-7878), 2846 Georgia Rd. (US 441 S.); find it 2.5 miles south of town on US 441. This crafters' cooperative maintains an inventory of 10,000 items—all handmade by local crafters. The selection is juried for quality, but not for style; every possible kind of craft is here, from simple grandma-style crafts to sophisticated contemporary art. MACO is particularly noted for its handmade quilts, and carries a good selection of quilting supplies and fabrics.

Otto, NC
Spring Ridge Creamery (828-369-2958), 11856 Georgia Hwy. (US 441 S.). The small dairy selling its fresh products by the highway has become a rare sight in the North, and has long since disappeared from the South. So it's a surprise to see exactly that, sitting by US 441 north of the state line (about 10 miles south of Franklin). The Spring Ridge Dairy's Jersey cows graze in the meadows beside their shop. They stock the products of their dairy: milk, butter, and ice cream. Ice cream! Real ice cream made from cream. You may have noticed that all the ice cream shops and restaurants throughout the mountains stock the same brand of ice cream, one manufactured by a giant regional dairy using the latest technology from Modern Food Science. Stop by Spring Ridge and get the real stuff.

RICKMAN'S GENERAL STORE IN COWEE VALLEY.

Jim Hargan

Cowee Valley, NC
Rickman's General Store (828-524-2223), 259 Cowee Creek Rd. This traditional general store has stood at the entrance to Cowee Valley, north of Franklin off NC 28, since time out of mind. It beckons to visitors with its doorside collection of flags, stuffed bears, and whatnot; inside you will find gift items as well as the stock of a functioning general store.

Cowee Creek Pottery (828-524-3324), 20 West Mills Rd. Located a few blocks from Rickman's General Store, the former West Mills General Store is now a gallery of handmade pottery, made in a studio in the back of the old store.

✳ Special Events
SUMMER Taste of Scotland Festival (828-524-7472), Franklin, NC. Mid-June. Scottish food and Scottish music—what could be better? In this downtown Franklin festival people eat

their haggis with a bagpipe accompaniment, and call it good. You'll find dancing, sheepdog demonstrations, and lots of Scottish stuff to buy at this annual event, sponsored by the Scottish Tartan Museum.

Fourth of July Celebration, Franklin, NC. The chamber of commerce sponsors Franklin's annual Independence Day parade at the Macon County Recreation Park. Athletic competitions include a rubber ducky derby, a horseshoe tourney, a watermelon roll, a plunger toss, cow pattie bingo, and—for the under-five set—a tricycle race. There's plenty of food, and fireworks begin at dark.

Macon County Gemboree, Franklin, NC. Last week in July. This annual rock show brings in gem and mineral dealers from all over, as well as custom jewelers. Sponsored by the Gem and Mineral Society of Franklin, it's been running every year since 1965. $2 adults, free for children.

Folkmoot (828-452-2997). Last week in July. This major gathering of national folk dancing troupes, headquartered out of Waynesville, NC, uses Franklin as one of its venues.

Gem Capital Auto Club Antique Auto Show (828-369-0557). Labor Day weekend. This annual auto show, held at the Macon County fairgrounds, features a wide assortment of antique automobiles and trucks.

Macon County Fair, Franklin, NC. Mid-Sep. This classic county fair features livestock shows and sales, agriculture displays, food, crafts, and entertainment. Free.

AUTUMN **Pumpkin Fest**. Last Sat. in Oct. This downtown Franklin, NC, street fair has food, entertainment, crafts, games, a costume parade and contest, a pumpkin cook-off, a pumpkin rolling contest, and trick-or-treating for kids.

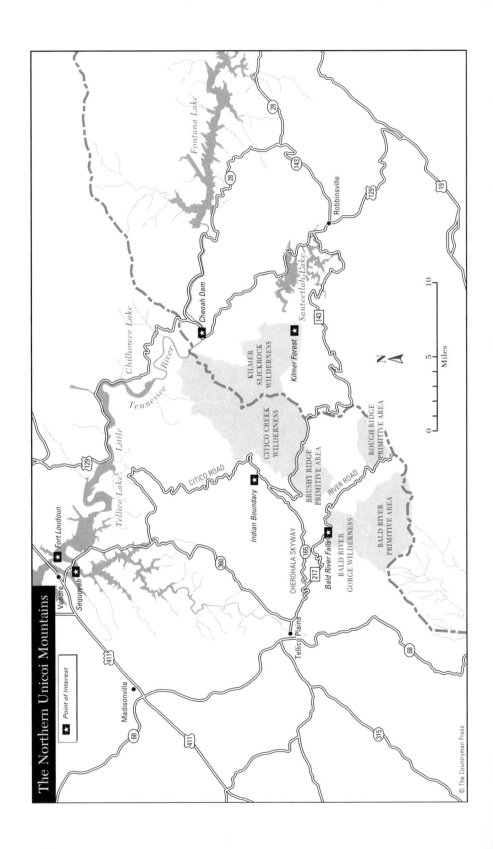

The Northern Unicoi Mountains

★ Point of Interest

Fontana Lake

28

143

Robbinsville

129

19

Chilhowee Lake

Cheoah Dam ★

Santeetlah Lake

143

KILMER
SLICKROCK
WILDERNESS

Kilmer Forest ★

Tennessee River

CITICO CREEK
WILDERNESS

N

Little

Tellico Lake

CITICO ROAD

BRUSHY RIDGE
PRIMITIVE AREA

ROUGH RIDGE
PRIMITIVE AREA

Fort Loudoun ★

Indian Boundary ★

RIVER ROAD

0   5   10
Miles

Vonore ●

Sequoyah ★

360

CHEROHALA SKYWAY

165

217

Bald River Falls ★

BALD RIVER
GORGE WILDERNESS

BALD RIVER
PRIMITIVE AREA

68

411

Madisonville ●

Tellico Plains ●

68

411

315

© The Countryman Press

THE NORTHERN UNICOIS:
ROBBINSVILLE & TELLICO PLAINS

South of the Great Smoky Mountains National Park, the Little Tennessee River cuts a deep gorge through the mountains, marking the end of the Smokies. The mountain range picks up again on the other side of the gorge, however, under a new name—the Unicoi Mountains. As with the Smokies to the north, the Unicois mark the line between North Carolina and Tennessee, and between the Nantahala and the Cherokee National Forests. The eastern side of the mountains, in North Carolina, looks to the tiny county seat of Robbinsville for shopping and services. The western side, in Tennessee, looks to the remote village of Tellico Plains.

Between these two small towns lies 40 miles of nearly unpopulated forestland. These huge, empty stretches of public land include 35,000 acres of congressionally declared wilderness (and another 20,000 acres of roadless and primitive areas)—a wonderful, and little-visited, recreational opportunity. Here you will find huge waterfalls, wide mountaintop meadows, thousands of acres of virgin and old-growth forest, and incredible views from high crags. You will also find long lakes that probe thin arms of stillwater deep into this wilderness, impounded behind four hydropower dams.

Until recently these two sides of the mountain could have been on different continents for all the interaction between them. There wasn't even a road between them until 1931—and that highway, US 129, has never been modernized. In 1997, however, the stunning recreational parkway known as the Cherohala Skyway finally opened after 20 years of construction. The Cherohala flies high above the valleys in broad sweeps along the crest of the Unicois, with constantly changing panoramas along its 25-mile length. It now links Robbinsville directly with Tellico Plains, bringing these two areas very close together and opening their huge wilderness to the outside.

GUIDANCE **Graham County Chamber of Commerce** (800-470-3790 or 828-479-3790; fax 828-479-9130), P.O. Box 1206, Robbinsville, NC 28771.

Monroe County Tourism Council (800-245-5428 or 423-442-9147; fax 423-442-9016; www.monroecounty.com), 4765 TN 68, Madisonville, TN 37354.

These are the people to contact for help in visiting Tellico Plains and the northern Unicoi Mountains of Tennessee. They have a visitors center at the county seat of Madisonville, about 10 miles north of Tellico Plains on TN 68.

Nantahala National Forest, Cheoah Ranger District (828-479-6431; fax 828-479-6784), Rt. 1, Box 16-A, Robbinsville, NC 28771. The ranger station for the eastern side of the Unicoi Mountains, including all national forest land around Robbinsville, is located on NC 143 northwest of Robbinsville, near Lake Santeetlah. This station is on the site of a historic CCC camp, and has some interesting exhibits and a nature trail on the subject.

Cherokee National Forest, Tellico Plains Ranger Station (423-253-2520), 250 Ranger Station Rd., Tellico Plains, TN 37385. This ranger station, set in a lovely little cove off the Tellico River, has an information desk and a bookstore, with a staff that is eager to answer your questions. It's also a fascinating and beautiful historic site in its own right, and has its own listing.

Tennessee Overhill Heritage Association (423-263-7232; fax 423-263-1670; www.tennesseeoverhill.com), P.O. Box 143, L&N Depot, Etowah, TN 37331. This private not-for-profit promotes tourism development in the southern Tennessee mountains.

GETTING THERE *By car*: The area around Tellico Plains, TN, is easily reached from **I-75**; take the TN 68 exit, and follow **TN 68** east to Tellico Plains. At any time other than winter, this is the best approach to Robbinsville from the west as well, following the **Cherohala Skyway** eastward from Tellico Plains. From any other direction (and from the west in winter), approach Robbinsville from US 19 to **US 129**.

By air: Knoxville and Chattanooga are the two closest airports.

By bus or train: There is no bus or train service to this area.

MEDICAL EMERGENCIES

In Tennessee
Sweetwater Hospital (865-213-8200), 304 Wright St., Sweetwater, TN. This is the nearest hospital to Tellico Plains, 23 miles north on TN 68.

In North Carolina
There is no hospital in Robbinsville or Graham County, NC. A call to 911 will bring the Robbinsville Rescue Squad (and you will be glad you supported them with a ramp dinner—see *Special Events*). The nearest hospital is the **Murphy Medical Center**, 36 miles away in Murphy, NC, via US 129 and US 19 S. Murphy also has an urgent care clinic, open every day.

✳ Wandering Around

EXPLORING ON FOOT **A Slickrock Wilderness walk**. Slickrock's isolation adds to its charm. Cut off from the rest of the world when Calderwood Lake flooded its entrance in 1928, Slickrock Creek has always been a difficult area to penetrate. Although the Kilmer-Slickrock Wilderness has been a national forest wilderness area since 1975, the Forest Service has long had the policy of doing nothing to improve its network of rough hunter's paths. Even a level hike is tiring and difficult because of the rough trail.

This walk takes the only reasonably level path into Slickrock, starting at US 129 at the **Cheoah Dam**. From the south side of the highway bridge, a Forest Service trail heads west along the steep slopes above **Calderwood Lake**, following the top of the Little Tennessee River's drowned gorge. After half a mile the trail climbs to an intersection; continue straight. When the trail starts to fall it is turning the bend to enter the **Slickrock Creek** basin; a sign marks the wilderness boundary. From here the trail follows the old lumber railroad along the creek, very rough from long abandonment, and a mere ledge in some places. Nevertheless, the forests are handsome, and the stream is very beautiful. At 2.6 miles from the trailhead the path reaches **Lower Falls**, an attractive 20-foot waterfall with a high volume. This is a good destination for a 5-mile return trip, although the creekside trail continues another 6 miles past a gorge and two more waterfalls. The many side trails lead high into the Unicoi Mountains, over into Joyce Kilmer Forest or the Citico Wilderness.

✳ Villages

Robbinsville, NC. The county seat of Graham County, NC, Robbinsville is a tiny (in 2000 its population was 747), down-at-the-heels town where life centers on the hardwood lumber mill and the small string of new franchise restaurants along the US 129 Bypass. Its Main Street, one block off US 129, has a one-block downtown next to the handsome 1942 courthouse, clad in local stone. Downtown Robbinsville was the location for the small-town shots for the 1994 movie *Nell* (staring Jodie Foster and Liam Neeson), playing itself; interiors depicting local stores (including 80-year-old **Sniders Department Store**, the local pool hall, and the local café) were shot in the actual businesses, sometimes with the employees as extras.

Tellico Plains, TN. This small town sits at the feet of the Unicoi Mountains in TN, tucked among low ridges and drained by the Tellico River. Farther west the mountains yield to the Great Valley, but here they remain in control. For many years Tellico Plains was a small industrial town, appealing to businesses that needed to reach mountain resources with a railroad. In the last few decades, tourism has grown as industry has retreated and as visitors have learned about the immense Cherokee National Forest wilderness and recreation lands that extend for dozens of miles from the town center. Today's Tellico Plains has

THE GRAHAM COUNTY COURTHOUSE IN ROBBINSVILLE.

Jim Hargan

A TRAIL AND FOOTBRIDGE LEAD TO AN OVERLOOK ON THE CHEROHALA SCENIC PARKWAY.

Jim Hargan

EXPLORING BY CAR: THE CHEROHALA SKYWAY
Leg 1: Start on NC 143 at Stecoah Gap (off NC 28 between Fontana and Bryson City, NC). Take NC 143 west to the start of the Cherohala Parkway, 17.9 miles. *Leg 2:* Continue on NC 143 uphill, now known as the Cherohala

a small, handsome downtown with antiques and art galleries, as well as some good places to eat and stay. The beautiful **Cherohala Parkway** starts (or ends) here on its long run along the Unicoi Crest, and the county is anchoring this scenic highway with a visitors center and museum on the town square. A colony of fine artists and crafters has been growing in the surrounding valleys, with the downtown **Tellico Arts Center** putting the spotlight on their work.

✳ Wild Places

THE GREAT FORESTS **Joyce Kilmer Memorial Forest**. In the 1930s the National Forest Service decided to dedicate a large, virgin forest to the poet Joyce Kilmer, author of "Trees," who was killed in World War I. They chose the forests of Little Santeetlah Creek, northwest of Robbinsville, NC, calling them "some of the finest original growth in the Appalachians." Today this watershed

Parkway. As the highway crosses into Tennessee, its designation changes to TN 165. End at the village of Tellico Plains, TN—39.7 miles. *Note*: There are no services between Robbinsville and Tellico Plains.

This drive enters the area as would a traveler from the Great Smoky Mountains, crossing the Cheoah Mountains at **Stecoah Gap**. Here the **Appalachian Trail** crosses the highway as it follows the crest of the Cheoahs. The parking lot gives views back toward the Smokies, while the road ahead gives a broad view over Robbinsville, NC, toward the Unicoi Mountains—your destination, 35 miles away. The highway drops into **Robbinsville**, using a nondescript bypass to go around it; the one-block drive downtown is worthwhile. At **Lake Santeetlah**, NC 143 turns off the main highway to follow the south side of the lake, passing the Forest Service headquarters and some attractive views over pastoral scenery. On this stretch the state highway is a twisting, intimate lane through remote countryside.

The start of the Skyway is obvious, not only because of its sign, but also because of NC 143's sudden return to full modern width and shoulders. With a design patterned after the Blue Ridge Parkway, the next 26 miles feature sweeping and ever-changing views. The Cherohala slabs and switches up a major side ridge of the Unicois, reaches the top, then slabs from gap to gap along the crest. Along the way it will reach elevations well over a mile high and pass near wide mountaintop meadows. For the first 15 miles the views are all eastward over the endlessly receding ridges of North Carolina. Then, as the Skyway crosses the state line at **Beech Gap**, the scenery changes to an abrupt and rugged drop into the Great Valley. At the bottom of the mountain the road turns left for a long, easy 12-mile ramble into the attractive village of **Tellico Plains**.

contains thousands of acres of never-cut old-growth forest, with trees reaching 20 feet in diameter. A 2-mile loop trail leads through some of the most dramatic forest, climaxing in a grove of huge yellow poplars. A separate trail, **Naked Ground Trail** (Trail 55), follows the valley uphill to its end, reaching the Unicoi ridgeline in 5 miles after a 2,700-foot climb; at the crest, the path to the right leads another 2 miles to stunning views from **Hangover Lead**. The original "Memorial Forest" has now become part of the much larger Kilmer-Slickrock Wilderness, which extends into Tennessee and combines with the Citico Creek Wilderness to protect 33,000 acres. With all this wilderness surrounding it, the original Joyce Kilmer Memorial Forest remains one of the best places to see the forests of the Appalachians as they appeared to Cherokee hunters and European settlers.

Kilmer-Slickrock Wilderness. This 17,400-acre wilderness, created in 1975, combined the Joyce Kilmer Memorial Forest with the adjacent stream basin drained by Slickrock Creek. The Slickrock Creek basin has been partially logged in the mid-1920s, but the 1928 impoundment of **Calderwood Lake** had drowned the loggers' railroad; after that, logging was abandoned, the land visited only by hunters and fishers. Today the Slickrock trails remain largely unimproved and unsigned, and the Slickrock experience remains one of deep and difficult backcountry. Trails interconnect among Slickrock, Kilmer, and the adjacent **Citico Creek Wilderness**, creating a large number of possible ridge and valley trips that combine old-growth forests with waterfalls and mountaintop meadows.

The Snowbird Creek forests. Follow NC 143 west of Robbinsville, NC, toward the Cherohala Skyway for 5.4 miles; turn left onto Snowbird River Rd. (SSR 1115) and go 3.1 miles; turn left onto SSR 1120 to its end at a Forest Service parking lot. Snowbird Creek drains the uppermost heights of the Cherohala Skyway, west of Robbinsville, NC, in the Unicoi Mountains. The Nantahala National Forest owns all of the Snowbird drainage, and protects it as a backcountry primitive area. A network of good-quality Forest Service trails follow the main creek (actually a tumultuous little river), its major side creek, and several nearby ridgelines. A 3-mile walk into the area brings you to a whole series of lovely waterfalls, including the beautiful **Sassafras Falls** on Trail 65 along Sassafras Creek.

FERNS FLOURISH IN THE RICH SHADE OF
JOYCE KILMER MEMORIAL FOREST.

Jim Hargan

The Cheoah Mountains form an east–west barrier between Robbinsville, NC, and the Great Smoky Mountains, with peaks as high as 5,000 feet and gaps above 3,000 feet. The **Appalachian Trail (AT)** runs along its crest, after first climbing 3,300 feet in elevation from the bottom of the Nantahala Gorge. The slopes of the Cheoahs have been subjected to logging by the Nantahala National Forest over the years, so that the AT remains the prime recreational resource of these mountains. It is most easily reached from NC 143 as it crosses the Cheoahs at Stecoah Gap, between Robbinsville and Fontana, NC. A 5.5-mile hike eastward (with 1,800 feet of climbing) leads to **Cheoah Bald** with a famous panoramic view.

Citico Creek Wilderness. Created in 1984, this 16,300-acre wilderness protects the western slopes of the Unicoi Mountains as they extend into Tennessee. The eastern slopes had already been protected by the 1936

Joyce Kilmer Memorial Forest and the 1975 Kilmer-Slickrock Wilderness; together, these areas protect 33,200 contiguous acres of mountain wilderness. Citico is noted for its deep stream valleys and violent little rivers, most with extraordinarily clean water. Its lower slopes were extensively and destructively logged in the 1920s, but a huge forest fire in 1926 destroyed the logging operation so thoroughly that it was abandoned, leaving the upper slopes untouched. Today's hiking trails follow the old lumber trams up the streams, past rapids and waterfalls, to enter the old-growth forest and eventually reach the crest of the Unicois. The **Cherohala Skyway** follows a side ridge along the southern edge of the wilderness, creating additional trailheads into the Citico's 57-mile trail system. If you have time for only a brief taste of this large area, take the short **Fall Creek Falls Trail** from the Skyway's Rattlesnake Rock Parking Lot; it leads 1.3 miles (with a 400-foot climb on the return) to a lacy waterfall on an 80-foot cliff.

The Tellico River and the Bald River Gorge Wilderness. The upper reaches of the Tellico River are almost entirely owned and controlled by the National Forest Service, mostly within Tennessee's Cherokee National Forest and easily reached from Tellico Springs. A paved scenic road, FS 217, runs along the river's bank, frequently flanked by gray cliffs as the Tellico digs its way deep into a gorge. At one point, FS 217 passes immediately by a huge waterfall, 100 feet tall and carrying a huge volume of water. This is **Bald Creek Falls**, and behind it is the 3,700-acre **Bald River Gorge Wilderness**, with a fine hiking path following the gorge bottom. Another 10,000 acres upstream from the Bald Creek Gorge Wilderness have received administrative protection as a series of Primitive Areas and provide some more remote opportunities for hiking, camping, and fishing. Not all of the stunningly beautiful wildlands of the Tellico River have received such careful handling by the National Forest Service. At the end of FS 217 at the state line, North Carolina's Nantahala National Forest sponsors the heavily used 8,000-acre Upper Tellico Off Road Vehicle Area in the high mountain basin that gives rise to the Tellico River.

RECREATION AREAS **Indian Boundary Recreation Area**. This small human-made lake nestles at the base of the Unicoi Mountains in Tennessee, 2 miles from the place where the Cherohala Skyway finishes its descent. A recreation area of the Cherokee National Forest, it has a picnic area by a sandy swimming beach, with impressive views over the lake toward the Unicoi Mountains. Take the easy loop path around this lake for more views and some pleasant woods walking. There's also a fairly large campground in this area.

PICNIC AREAS **Joyce Kilmer and vicinity**. Joyce Kilmer Forest has a very nice picnic area at its trailhead parking lot, but it does tend to fill up during the busy season. Heading back toward the Cherohala Skyway and Robbinsville, NC, you will find a table with a fabulous view toward the Unicois 2 miles from the Kilmer entrance road. Another 5.3 miles down NC 143 toward Robbinsville, a small national forest picnic area with a nature trail sits beside **Lake Santeetlah**.

Cheoah Point. This Nantahala National Forest recreation area sits on the shore of **Lake Santeetlah**, 7 miles north of Robbinsville off US 129. It has a nice picnic area and a sandy swimming beach on the lake, with views over the lake to the mountains beyond.

Along the Tellico River. Northeast of Tellico Plains, the Tellico River forms a recreation corridor within the Cherokee National Forest. Because of the steady tourist use along its scenic road, FS 217, the Forest Service has developed several picnic areas along it, as well as creating parking for fishermen and trail users, and designating several small primitive camping areas.

✳ To See

BIG DAMMED LAKES People frequently assume that the lakes that stretch through this area are part of the TVA—the Tennessee Valley Authority, a Great Depression hydropower project (still going strong). Not so. Only the huge Tellico Lake, completed in 1979, was a TVA project (along with Fontana Lake, upstream, completed in 1943). The four other lakes in this area are part of a project that long predated TVA, a completely private initiative of the Alcoa Corporation, still known as "Tapoco." Tapoco (which stands for "Tallassee Power Company") is a wholly owned subsidiary of Alcoa that owns and runs four major dams and the lakes behind them: Chilhowee, Calderwood, Cheoah, and Santeetlah. Built between 1917 and 1957, these four dams supply about half the power sucked down by the giant Alcoa smelter at nearby Maryville, TN, outside Knoxville. Although privately owned, all four lakes are open to recreational boating.

Tellico Lake. With nearly 25 square miles of surface area, this huge TVA lake backs up from the foothills of Tennessee to the feet of the Unicoi Mountains. In the late 1970s it became a symbol to environmentalists of development out of control, and a symbol to developers of environmentalism out of control, as the U.S. Supreme Court stopped the entire dam project to save an endangered species known as the snail darter. Congress sided with developers and amended the law to allow the dam to be completed, snail darters or not; the giant Tellico Lake started backing up in 1979. The entire lake is public land, as is much of its shore.

Chilhowee Lake. The newest of the four Tapoco projects, the 1957 Chilhowee Dam is just up the Little Tennessee River from the TVA's new Tellico Lake. It floods a deep gorge, providing a long, serpentine lake that extends 8.5 miles upstream but covers less than 3 square miles. The lower parts of the lake are hugged by US 129, with picnic tables and a boat launch. The upper half of the lake is remote from roads, accessible only from Alcoa's **Calderwood Power Station Recreation Area**.

Calderwood Lake. Alcoa built Calderwood Dam in 1928, the third of its four Tapoco dams. It's located a mile upstream from the end of their Chilhowee Lake—a mile that's typically dry, because Alcoa reroutes the river water through a large pipe to the downstream power plant. The narrow lake backs up into a deep gorge for 7 miles, lined by wilderness its entire length. No roads follow it, but US 129, meandering along a ridgeline high above it, gives a spectacular bird's-eye view. The long lake finally ends at the base of the next dam, Cheoah, where US 129 gives access to it.

Lake Santeetlah. Alcoa added Santeetlah to its Tapoco project in 1926. Its big dam blocks the Cheoah River, turning it dry for 9 miles as it sends its waters through a pipeline to a power station on Cheoah Lake, far below and far away. Lake Santeetlah has the best-developed recreational opportunities of all the lakes in this area, with two private marinas and a Nantahala National Forest boat ramp at Cheoah Point. Santeetlah has a long and highly convoluted shoreline, most of it owned by the Nantahala National Forest; there are many shoreline camping spots within the national forest, and views are spectacular.

HISTORIC SITES **Fort Loudoun State Historic Area** (423-884-6217), 338 Fort Loudoun Rd., Vonore, TN. Follow the brown signs south off US 411 at Vonore, just south of the bridge over the Tellico Lake. Don't be confused by signs north of the bridge pointing to Fort Loudoun Reservoir; that's a different place altogether, and in the wrong direction to boot. This very scenic state park occupies part of a forested island within the large Tellico Lake. Its centerpiece is a careful reconstruction of Fort Loudoun, a large British fortification that figured prominently in the conflicts among the Cherokees, the British, and the colonials. This palisaded fort, with formidable walls overhanging any attacking force, encloses a variety of military log structures furnished according to their original uses. Views from the fort are impressive, sweeping over the length of the large Tellico impoundment to the great wall of the Smokies and the Unicois. This is a favorite place for reenactment encampments, and the white tents and colorful uniforms add great charm to the scenery. A small museum sits near the fort, with exhibits interpreting life in the fort using archaeological finds, as well as a 15-minute video. Elsewhere on the grounds are walking paths and a very nice picnic area.

THE RECONSTRUCTED COLONIAL-ERA FORT ON THE SHORES OF TELLICO LAKE AT FORT LOUDOUN STATE HISTORIC AREA.
Jim Hargan

The Stewart Cabin. This minor site is a fun side trip from the Joyce Kilmer Forest or Cherohala Skyway. From the start of the Skyway, 2 miles south of Kilmer, FS 81 drops down to the right to cross Santeetlah Creek in a mile, with good views over this handsome creek (and good access for fishermen) from the bridge. Another 2 miles along, the Stewart Cabin sits in

THE STEWART CABIN. Jim Hargan

riverside meadows by the gravel road. It's a modest, handsome log cabin, framed by wildflowers and a split-rail fence. The Nantahala National Forest restored it, and preserves it as a historic site. Return the way you came.

Junaluska's Grave. Chief Junaluska was a respected Cherokee warrior who fought with Gen. Andrew Jackson against the Creeks at the battle of Horseshoe Bend (Alabama). Junaluska and his warriors saved Jackson's European troops from near-certain defeat, and turned the battle. The victory opened Alabama to European settlement. Years later, President Andrew Jackson signed the order that expelled Junaluska from his home near Robbinsville, NC, sending him with his tribesmen on the Trail of Tears to Oklahoma. In old age, Junaluska was given permission to return to Robbinsville; his grave, immediately outside town, is a sacred site of the Cherokee Nation.

Cheoah Dam. This is the most easily viewed of the Tapoco dams, built by Alcoa to supply electricity to their aluminum smelter in Maryville, TN. Built in 1919, Cheoah was (at 225 feet) the tallest dam in the world at the time, and had the largest turbines. It is now best known as the site of Harrison Ford's famous dam jump in the move *The Fugitive*—accomplished by tossing a dummy off the dam, combined with a matte to splice in the background. US 129 crosses the river just in front of the dam, with wonderful views of it, and more views from the side of the road. Take a gander at the industrial Gothic turbine station in the gorge under the dam, a beautiful piece of architecture instantly recognizable in the movie. The dam remains impressive nearly a century later, and gives you a good idea of the scale of Alcoa's early electrical project, very successful and still going full tilt. Incidentally, this section of highway is historic in itself—essentially unchanged since it was built in 1931, the first paved road into this remote corner of the mountains. The trailhead for the **Slickrock Wilderness walk** is downstream on the left.

Tellico Plains Ranger Station (423-253-2520), 250 Ranger Station Rd., Tellico Plains, TN. Off the Tellico River Rd. (FS 217—about 5 miles north of Tellico Plains via the Cherohala Skyway), down a scenic little drive that winds along a mountain stream through a lovely old forest. Mon.–Sat. 7–5. The earliest CCC camp in Tennessee, still in pristine condition, houses the offices of the Tellico Ranger District of the Cherokee National Forest. It's a nice place to drop by— scenic, historic, and friendly. The station is a collection of white clapboard buildings, built in 1937, centered on a small white-columned headquarters building. It's the administrative headquarters for about a sixth of the 633,000-acre Cherokee National Forest, and forest crews frequently come and go from its large, neat maintenance yard. The pine-paneled headquarters building welcomes visitors with an information desk with books and maps, as well as exhibits on the

CCC at Tellico, including a 1931 map of the Cherokee National Forest and 19th-century geological maps of the area. Free.

CULTURAL SITES **Sequoyah Birthplace Museum** (423-884-6246), Citico Rd., Vonore, TN. Follow the brown signs south off US 411 at Vonore, just south of the bridge over Tellico Lake. The museum is a short distance beyond Fort Loudoun State Park, on the right. Mon.–Sat. 9–5, Sun. noon–5. In 1821 Sequoyah, a nonliterate Cherokee silversmith living in northern Alabama, introduced a Cherokee syllabary—an alphabet in which each symbol represents a syllable rather than a sound. This astonishing feat made him the first, last, and only historic figure to invent an alphabet from scratch, having no previous knowledge of the concept of reading or writing. The Sequoyah Birthplace Museum, operated by the Eastern Band of the Cherokee Nation, presents exhibits on Sequoyah's life and accomplishments, as well as a full presentation of the succession of Native peoples in the Tennessee Valley along with the archaeological artifacts through which we know them. It also features a small exhibit area of Native American art and a very nice gift shop with a good selection of Cherokee and other Native American arts and crafts. $3 adults, $2 seniors, $1 children.

Cherohala Visitors Center at Tellico Plains. A joint project of Monroe County, TN, and the Monroe Chamber of Commerce, this visitors center on Tellico Plain's town square combines an information desk and exhibits on the new Cherohala Parkway with a historical museum about the Tellico Plains area.

✳ To Do

FISHING **Cherohala Outfitters** (828-479-4464; fax 828-479-9414; www .cherohalaoutfitters.com), 260 Snowbird Rd., Robbinsville, NC. Open all year. This guide and outfitting service, headquartered north of Robbinsville near Lake Santeetlah, the Snowbird area, and the Kilmer-Slickrock Wilderness, offers guided trips for both fly-fishing and lake fishing, as well as hunting trips for the Russian blue boar found in this area. They will guide for backpacking trips as well, and will arrange for prepared camping, where they furnish all equipment (except the sleeping bag) and set up the site in advance for you.

Cherokee Guide Service (877-223-3588 or 423-261-2747), 130 Payne Mountain Rd., Tellico Plains, TN. This guide service offers fishing and hunting trips throughout the Tellico River area, on lands of the Cherokee National Forest.

STILLWATER ADVENTURES **Santeetlah Marina** (828-479-8180; www .santeetlahmarina.com), 1 Marina Dr., Robbinsville, NC. Daily Apr.–Oct. This full-service marina is located on Lake Santeetlah, 5.2 miles north of Robbinsville just off US 129. They rent canoes, ski boats, and pontoon boats, as well as slips by the night and overnight vehicle and RV storage. If you are interested in boat camping, they have information on more than 50 informal camping spots on the long lakeshore within the national forest.

Dayton Camp Boat Rentals (828-479-7422). Daily, spring–fall. Located on the south shore of Lake Santeetlah, on NC 143 near Robbinsville, Dayton Camp rents canoes, johnboats, ski boats, and pontoon boats.

✳ Lodging

COUNTRY INNS AND HOTELS **Snow-bird Mountain Lodge** (800-941-9290 or 828-479-3433; fax 828-479-3473; www.snowbirdlodge .com), 4633 Santeetlah Rd., Robbinsville, NC 28771. Apr.–Nov. This 1941 rustic-style lodge sits high in the mountains above Lake Santeetlah, very near the Cherohala Parkway and Joyce Kilmer Forest. Built by a Chicago tour operator as a place to pamper tour guests after a visit to the Kilmer Forest, it features wide, spectacular views from its native stone terrace. The library and lobby are paneled in wormy chestnut taken from the site, and feature a stone fireplace and picture window facing the view; the furniture includes pieces made by local craftsmen for the original inn's opening. The lodge's rooms all have en suite private bath and are paneled in a variety of local hardwoods. An adjacent cabin has been recently renovated to hold two more rooms, both larger than the lodge rooms and sharing the cabin's porch. A new building, constructed to blend with the original structures, holds the six largest and most luxurious rooms. The room tariff includes a full breakfast buffet, a picnic lunch, and a gourmet dinner; the dinner varies daily, featuring fresh local ingredients in imaginative, international recipes. $175–320.

⚓ **The Blue Boar Inn** (866-479-8126 or 828-479-8126; fax 828-479-2415; www.blueboarinn.com/home .html), 1283 Blue Boar Rd., Robbinsville, NC 28771. Located on Lake Santeetlah, just off NC 143 near the Cherohala Skyway and Joyce Kilmer Forest. Built in 1950 as a hunting lodge by Cincinnati's Bruckmann

Brewery, the Blue Boar has been completely renovated into a elegant little bed & breakfast inn rated three diamonds by AAA. The unusual design combines features of both lodge- and cottage-style architecture with some inspiration from early tourist camps. The guest rooms, reduced in number to eight, all have outside private entrance with private porch. Inside, a sitting area is separated from the roomy sleeping area by an open arched wall. The decor is simple and elegant, both in the rooms and in the common areas. A full breakfast, included in the tariff, is served in dining room, as is lunch (open to the public), and dinner by reservation (see *Dining Out*). $95–135, plus 15 percent service fee.

RESORTS **Tapoco Lodge Resort** (800-822-5083 or 828-498-2435; www.tapocolodge.com), 14981 Tapoco Rd., Robbinsville, NC 28771. Alcoa constructed Tapoco Lodge in 1930, using it as a corporate retreat center until 1997. Alcoa built it north of Robbinsville off US 129, near the hydropower dams they owned (and still own) on the Little Tennessee River. (Alcoa needed—and still needs—an immense amount of electricity for their large aluminum smelter in nearby Maryville, TN.) Today's resort occupies the Tapoco Lodge in much the same spirit as the 1930s corporate retreat. The main lodge is an ivy-covered Georgian structure, simple and elegant in red brick. The second story contains rooms, as do a series of classic 1930s white clapboard cottages wandering up the hill. Between the lodge and the cottages are the swimming pool, fully restored and renovated in 1999, and the tennis courts; the lodge contains a large game room with pool and Ping-Pong tables. Furnishings are simple, 1930s style, with many pieces specifically built for the original lodge. The tariff includes a full breakfast, a light lunch, and a hearty southern-style dinner. The resort has 150 acres of property and adjoins the Nantahala National Forest; hiking trails extend from the lodge deep into the Kilmer-Slickrock Wilderness.

BED & BREAKFAST INNS The Magnolia House (800-323-4750 or 423-253-3446; fax 423-253-7400; www3.tellico.net/~hannans/mag.htm), 305 TN 165, P.O. Box 269, Tellico Plains, TN 37385. Mike Hannon is a print artist. His subtly colored traditionalist landscapes look like watercolors, but they are really the result of Mike's high-tech digital computer studio, in a back room of the Magnolia House. His wife, Elizabeth, runs Tellico Plains Realty from an adjacent room, and together they both run Magnolia House B&B in the remainder of this roomy and historic old farmhouse. Located conveniently near the town square on a large and grassy tract of land, this old farmhouse, with its friendly large porches, was built in several phases in the 19th century. Each of its three guest rooms has a king bed (one of which can be converted to two twins) and a comfortable sitting area with a sofa or futon, a small refrigerator, and a coffeemaker. The rooms are English style, with a washbasin and water closet in each room, and a common shower for all three rooms. Downstairs, a roomy and comfortable sitting area has coffee, a microwave, and a refrigerator stocked with juice and plenty of ice. Continental breakfasts include fresh

muffins and other breads, cereal, milk, and juice. Rates start at $49.95 single, $54.95 double.

CABIN RENTALS Tellico Vacation Rentals (866-253-2254 or 423-253-2253; www.tellicovacations.com), 113 Scott St., P.O. Box 906, Tellico Plains, TN 37385. These seven private cabins, scattered around Tellico Plains countryside, offer the comfort of an immaculately kept and handsomely furnished private house. Owned by Sandra and Weldon Pyron of the Tellico Arts Center, this rental service offers a careful selection of fine private homes, ranging from small and simple rustic structures to luxurious chalets. All are beautifully set in the East TN countryside; some have mountain views, others views over fields, rivers, or woods. $70–150.

The Historic Donley Cabin (423-253-2520; fax 423-253-2804), Tellico Ranger Station, Tellico Plains, TN 37385. Of all the lodgings listed in this guide, the Donley Cabin comes closest to an authentic pioneer experience. Owned and operated by the Cherokee National Forest, the cabin is located in the Tellico River area, 20 miles from Tellico Plains by gravel road—and a quarter-mile walk into the forest. It's a two-crib cabin dating to the 1860s and '70s; the earlier and cruder crib is said to have been built by a Civil War draft dodger who was hiding out, while the later, much more sophisticated crib was added by Jack Donley, a prominent local settler. Donley's descendants owned and used the cabin until selling it to the Forest Service in 1994. The Forest Service has since restored the cabin to its 1880 condition, as a typical example of a log farmstead that has grown organically through multiple ownerships and generations. It's a beautiful little cabin, sitting in a little wildflower meadow with a nice front porch. Guest accommodations are in period as well: two slab beds without mattresses, a table with chairs, and a fireplace. That's it. No bedding; no shower; no water; no toilet. There's a stream and an outhouse nearby. Despite the less-than-luxurious conditions it stays booked up, and reservations are required. $35 per night.

✳ Where to Eat

EATING OUT **Tellahala Café** (423-253-2880), 228 Bank St., Tellico Plains, TN. Sun.–Thu. 11–8:30, Fri.–Sat. 11–9:30. Don't be deceived by the modest appearance of the Tellahala Café, in a converted fast-food building near some edge-of-town strip shopping plazas. Inside is a warm, inviting place, with soft, rich colors and solid oak furnishings. The menu is imaginative and ambitious—and lives up to its promise, with a wonderful variety of fresh seafood, chicken, steak, and pasta, imaginatively seasoned and presented. Our meals included fillet of chicken breast grilled with fresh rosemary, and a large salmon fillet crusted with pecans and broiled to bring out the natural sweetness of the nuts. All food is made from scratch on the premises by a staff of experienced, trained chefs. The owners, Rich and Donna Leudemann, try to create a special, pleasurable experience out of each meal— and succeed. You can always find one or the other in the kitchen, or meeting guests in the restaurant. No liquor service is available, but guests are welcome to bring a bottle of wine; glasses will be provided without

charge. Entrées $8–14, with steaks higher; sandwiches, burgers, and salads $4–6.

Town Square Café and Bakery (423-253-2200), 704 TN 165, Tellico Plains, TN. Mon.–Thu. 6 AM–8 PM, Fri.–Sat. 6 AM–9 PM, Sun. 7–7. Years ago, nearly every town in the South had a friendly little storefront café on its square. Tellico Plains is lucky; it has Randy and Carol Martin keeping up this tradition in the Town Square Café and Bakery. This spotlessly clean eatery is paneled with warm pine planks and matching pine tables, for a real homey feel. The fresh food, prepared to your order, concentrates on traditional southern favorites, and Randy's chatty menu will tell you all about it with a series of articles on such subjects as Tellico Plains's history and his grandma's biscuits. Breakfasts (served anytime) concentrate on biscuits (with sausage gravy or spread), pancakes (light, tender, and tasting of buttermilk), and eggs, bacon, and sausage. Dinners feature country favorites such as fried chicken, country-fried steak, pork chops, country ham, and catfish; all dinners come with two sides, soup, and corn bread. They also serve a full range of salads, sandwiches, and burgers. Breakfast $2–7, dinner $6–9, sandwiches and burgers $2.50–5.

DINING OUT **The Blue Boar Inn at Lake Santeetlah** (828-479-8126; www.blueboarinn.com), 1283 Blue Boar Rd., Robbinsville, NC. Near Joyce Kilmer and the Cherohala Parkway, off NC 143. The first-rate restaurant of this elegant little B&B opens to the public for lunch, and for dinner by reservation only. The lunch menu focuses on sandwiches and salads, made with a flair. A steak or chicken sandwich has thinly sliced meat grilled, then served on fresh-baked baguette with provolone cheese, sautéed onions, and green peppers. Or try a sausage on a bun—in this case a third of a pound of wild boar or venison sausage on a fresh-baked French roll with sautéed onions, green peppers, mustard, and mayo.

✳ Entertainment

The Tellico Arts Center (423-253-2253), 113 Scott St., Tellico Plains, TN. The Tellico Arts Center sponsors eight or so events a year, centering on mountain music and storytelling (see *Selective Shopping*, below).

✳ Selective Shopping

Snowbird Indian Trading Post and Gallery (828-479-8653; www.snowbirdindian.com), Cornsilk Branch Rd., Robbinsville, NC. Follow NC 143 west of Robbinsville toward the Cherohala Skyway for 5.4 miles; turn left onto Snowbird River Rd. (SSR 1115) and go 1.8 miles; then turn left onto Cornsilk Branch Rd. (SSR 1119) and go 0.7 mile. Open normal business hours in-season; call for an appointment in winter. This modest building at the heart of the Snowbird Cherokee community has been a trading post since the early 20th century. Now it houses a craft cooperative for the Snowbird community, featuring the work of local Native American artisans.

Tellico Arts Center (423-253-2253; www.overhillarts.com/tac.html), 113 Scott St., Tellico Plains, TN. Tellico Plains's craft colony continues to grow, and this excellent not-for-profit gallery is at its center. Located a block off the Town Square on Scott St., the Tellico Arts Center hosts the work of 74 artists, all from the immediate area. The center occupies a large, handsome old redbrick building, filling the large loftlike space with a wide variety of fine art and craft art, from the traditional to the contemporary. Fabric art includes handwoven and felted llama items, hand-knit sweaters, quilts, and painting on fabric. Three metal artists display works. Pottery, beading, wheat weaving, leather work, stained glass, photography, soaps, candles, paintings, and mixed media are included. The center was founded and managed by Sandra and Weldon Pyron, one of whom is nearly always on hand to talk about East Tennessee art and artists, and to direct people toward other area galleries and open studios.

Coker Creek Gallery (423-261-2157), 206 Hot Water Rd., Coker Creek, Tellico Plains, TN. Nine miles south of Tellico Plains via TN 68, to Hot Water Rd., then a short distance west; the turn-off is well signposted. Apr.–Dec. 21, Tue.–Sat. 10–5; all other times and dates by appointment. Owners Kathleen and Ken Dalton, craft artists well known for their white oak basket weaving, have assembled a fine collection of craft art from close to 50 local and regional artists. Their large selection of pieces, jammed into a building the size of a small house, includes baskets (of course!), pottery, fine hand textiles, toys, metal sculpture, dolls, wood carvings, paintings, and some pieces that are just plain eccentric. While styles range from traditionalist to abstract, all their pieces are united by a high degree of technical competence and originality. Unlike most galleries, the Daltons buy their pieces outright from their artists—so they feature nothing that they wouldn't buy themselves. Prices are nearly always under $1,000, with a wide selection of pieces under $60.

Coker Creek Village (423-261-2310), Coker Creek, TN. Eleven miles south of Tellico Plains on TN 68. For many years Sanford Gray ran one of the more eccentric and entertaining sites of the southern mountains—a large "general store," where some items were for sale but most were his huge collection of antiques, memorabilia, and bygones. Unfortunately, the entire facility and its contents burned to the ground in the fall of 1999—a total loss. Now Sanford has rebuilt, creating a structure designed by himself ("the secret is to stay 10 days ahead of the builders," he says), a large structure combining planked log walls with a post-and-beam central area, the posts being whole logs from his property, complete with bark—a wonderful piece of folk art in itself. Although much of the new Coker Creek Village caters to groups and retreats, Sanford has re-created his general store in one part of his building, and given another corner to the Cherokee National Forest as a staffed information center. It's definitely worth a stop.

Sequoyah Birthplace Museum Gift Shop (423-884-6246), Citico Rd., Vonore, TN. Mon.–Sat. 9–5, Sun. noon–5. Concentrating on Native American art, with a special emphasis on Eastern Cherokee artists, this museum gift shop offers a wide variety of jewelry, pottery, sculpture, and other items. The gourd pots are particularly remarkable and attractive. Book lovers will enjoy browsing the small but extremely well-selected collection of Cherokee titles.

✳ Special Events

SPRING Fort Loudoun Bagpipes and Revelries (423-884-6217), 338 Fort Loudoun Rd., Vonore, TN. Apr. The Fort Loudoun Association sponsors this annual musical event in the center of the reconstructed fort. It features bagpiping, Highland dancing, Celtic music, and living history reenactments.

The Telliquah Native American Gathering, Tellico Plains, TN. Mid-Apr. This annual gathering of tribes features Native American ceremonies and crafts.

Graham County Ramp Festival (www.main.nc.us/grahamcoems/ramps), Robbinsville, NC. Last Sun. in Apr. Small communities throughout the North Carolina mountains traditionally support their volunteer fire departments and rescue squads with a ramp dinner. A ramp is a broad-leafed wild leek with a strong onion-garlic flavor, one of the first plants to poke through the snow in the mountain forests each spring. In the bad old days, people who were at the end of their winter food supplies would go into the forests and gather ramps as a healthy and hearty food until the crops came in. Ramps meant hope, and better things to come. And they taste good, too—both the greens and the bulbs are edible, and delicious. The Graham County Ramp Festival is just such a traditional community get-together at the Rescue Squad building on Moose Branch Rd. in Robbinsville. They want everyone to come in and enjoy ramps cooked with mountain trout, chicken, baked beans, hushpuppies, corn bread, potato salad, and dessert.

SUMMER Graham County Heritage Festival. July 4. This daylong Independence Day festival has events throughout the county, but centers on Robbinsville, NC. There's a parade, a duck race, tributes to war veterans, a townwide craft fair, and (of course) fireworks.

Cherokee Arts and Crafts Festival and the 18th Century Trade Faire, Vonore, TN. Second weekend in Sep. The Sequoyah Birthplace Museum sponsors an annual celebration that mixes Native American handmade crafts with Cherokee dancing, stickball, games, artists, reenactments, and storytellers. Meanwhile, the European settlers are whooping it up at the 18th Century Trade Faire, a few blocks down the road at Fort Loudoun State Historic Site. Hundreds of reenactors attract thousands of visitors to an authentic 18th-century trade fair at the gates of the fort, with period wares, food, and entertainment from music to fire eaters.

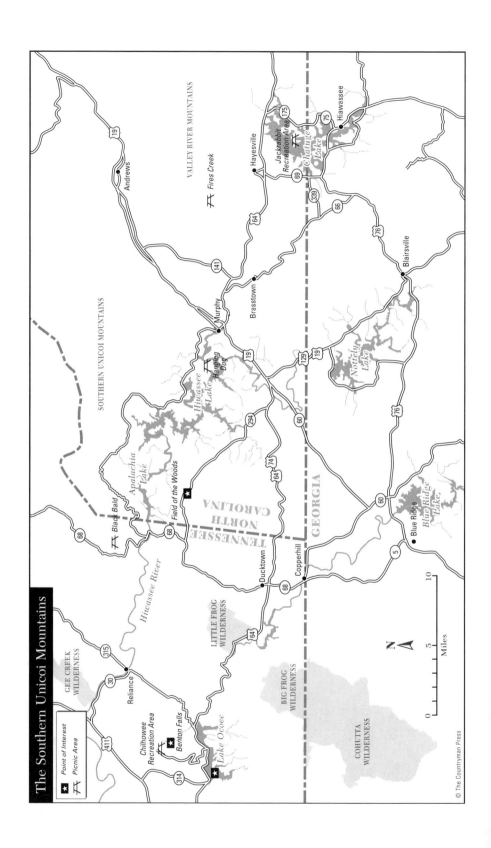

The Southern Unicoi Mountains

Point of Interest ★
Picnic Area 🏕

GEE CREEK WILDERNESS

315

30

Reliance

411

Chilhowee Recreation Area 🏕 Benton Falls

314

Lake Ocoee

Hiwassee River

68

🏕 Black Bald

Apalachia Lake

★ Field of the Woods

68

SOUTHERN UNICOI MOUNTAINS

🏕 Hanging Dog

Hiwassee Lake

Murphy

294

LITTLE FROG WILDERNESS

64

Ducktown

68

Copperhill

60

74

64

129

19

19

Brasstown

141

19

Andrews

VALLEY RIVER MOUNTAINS

🏕 Fires Creek

64

Hayesville

339

66

Jackrabbit Recreation Area 🏕

Chatuge Lake

175

75 Hiawassee

76

Blairsville

Nottely Lake

76

TENNESSEE
NORTH CAROLINA

GEORGIA

BIG FROG WILDERNESS

COHUTTA WILDERNESS

5

60

Blue Ridge

Blue Ridge Lake

N

0   5   10
Miles

© The Countryman Press

THE SOUTHERN UNICOIS:
MURPHY & THE COPPER BASIN

T he great massed knots of mile-high mountains that characterize the Smokies and the Blue Ridge start to slowly drop away as their ridgelines head south to the Georgia border. The area remains ruggedly mountainous; still, 4,000 feet becomes a high peak instead of a low one, and valley widths start being measured in miles instead of feet.

In this area Murphy, NC, serves as the main town for a broad valley that stretches for 60 miles east and west, and can reach 10 miles wide in spots. Drained by the Hiwassee and Ocoee Rivers, this valley can be softly pastoral in some places, ruggedly handsome in others. Apart from Murphy, the Hiwassee Valley contains the towns of Andrews and Hayesville in North Carolina, and Ducktown, Copperhill, and Reliance in Tennessee.

Here tourism turns from the mountain summits to the rivers beneath them. The Ocoee River, site of the 1996 Olympic whitewater competitions, furnishes nearly continuous Class III–V rapids. The Hiwassee River in Tennessee, noted for its exceptional beauty, is popular with fishers, canoeists (rapids are Class I–II), and hikers. A series of five large TVA lakes gives a wide choice of stillwater boating; this definitely includes wilderness exploration, as several of these lakes extend long, narrow arms for dozens of miles into remote national forest lands.

GUIDANCE **Cherokee County Chamber of Commerce** (828-837-2242; fax 828-837-6012; www.cherokeecountychamber.com/), 805 W. US 64, Murphy, NC 28906. The Cherokee County, NC, Chamber covers Robbinsville and the surrounding countryside.

Andrews Chamber of Commerce (877-558-0005 or 828-321-3584; fax 828-321-1356; www.andrewschambercommerce.com), P.O. Box 800, Andrews, NC 28901. The small town of Andrews, 16 miles north of Murphy on US 19, has its own chamber, with a visitors center in the center of town.

Clay County Chamber of Commerce (828-389-3704), P.O. Box 88, Hayesville, NC 28904. The Clay County, NC, Chamber covers the mountainous area east of Robbinsville, including the county seat of Hayesville.

Polk County–Copper Basin Chamber of Commerce (877-790-2157 or 423-496-9000; www.ocoeetn.org). The Polk County, TN, Chamber covers all of the Tennessee mountains in this chapter, including Ducktown and the Copper Basin. They maintain a visitors center in Ducktown.

Cherokee National Forest, Ocoee Ranger District (423-338-5201), Rt. 1, Box 348D, Benton, TN 37307. The national forest ranger station for this part of the Tennessee mountains is located on US 64 by Lake Ocoee. They have an information desk and bookstore.

Nantahala National Forest, Tusquitee Ranger District (828-837-5152), 201 Woodland Dr., Murphy, NC 28906. This ranger station covers all of the Nantahala National Forest around Murphy and Hayesville. Located off US 64 east of Murphy, it has a staffed information desk and sells maps of the forest.

GETTING THERE *By car*: This region's modern four-lane highway still follows (at least roughly) the tracks of the 1850s wagon road that crossed through this area from Asheville to the rich farmlands of Tennessee. Whether you approach from Asheville and I-40, or from Chattanooga and I-75, you need to take **US 74**.

By air: **Chattanooga Metropolitan Airport** (423-855-2200; www.chattairport .com) 1001 Airport Rd., Suite 14, Chattanooga, TN. This airport is the closest—only 80 miles from Murphy, NC, via US 74. Knoxville's airport is an extra 20-mile journey, at 100 miles away via I-75 and US 74. Asheville's is 35 miles farther, and Atlanta (which may be cheapest) is 50 miles farther than Chattanooga. You will have to rent a car in any case; none of the towns in this chapter has bus or train service.

By train or bus: This region has no scheduled train or bus service.

MEDICAL EMERGENCIES **Murphy Medical Center** (828-837-8161), 2002 US 64 E., Murphy, NC. This 50-bed local hospital is the closest 24/7 emergency facility for the Murphy area. It's a short distance east of town on US 64.

District Memorial Hospital, Andrews (828-321-1200), 415 Whitaker Lane, Andrews, NC. This 40-bed hospital in Andrews has a 24/7 emergency room and an evac helicopter. It may be closer than Murphy for many locations in the Hayesville, NC, area.

Copper Basin Medical Center (423-496-5511), TN 68, Copperhill, TN. A 44-bed local hospital with 24/7 emergency room service.

✳ Wandering Around

EXPLORING BY CAR **Driving the southern Unicois**. *Leg 1*: From Andrews, NC, follow Old US 19 (Main St. in town, Andrews Hwy./SSR 1428 out of town) and US 19 south to Murphy, NC. *Leg 2*: At Murphy, turn right (into town) at the traffic light where US 64 enters from the left. Go downhill through downtown to Lake Hiwassee; turn left onto Joe Brown Hwy. (SSR 1326). Follow Joe Brown Hwy. westward for 19.9 miles; head right onto SSR 1322 for 4.7 miles to a T intersection; then right on River Rd. 2.1 miles to TN 68. *Leg 3*: Take TN 68 south to Ducktown, TN, then take US 64/74 west to Lake Ocoee.

The first leg starts in downtown **Andrews**, an area of brick storefronts with a pretty, old depot. From downtown, stay on the old highway (crossing four-lane US 19) for the next 7 miles for a taste of old-style country driving with light traffic and wide mountain views. This passes through the former town of Marble, once a major marble quarry but now mainly abandoned; the courthouse in Murphy is clad in stone from this mine. The scenery continues pleasant as you regain the four lane.

Entering the lovely mountain town of **Murphy**, you will see a pretty wood church on the left, a good example of rural Gothic design favored by 19th-century Episcopalians. The **courthouse** is the main feature, looming over the entire downtown, and worth stopping to admire. Downtown continues to the bottom of the hill, lined continuously with shops and worth exploring. Past town, the road sweeps past **Hiwassee Lake**, then winds into farming valleys, over low ridges, and back to the lake several times. As this slow and pretty drive continues, the scenery becomes wilder, more wooded, with fewer homes. At the end of the drive the road follows a tumultuous creek down to the Hiwassee River, then follows the riverbank over the state line to a paved Tennessee highway.

The third leg follows TN 68 south through the wide valley that sweeps through the center of this region, then into the **Copper Basin** and **Ducktown** for a view of the old copper mines and the devastation they caused. (This view is being preserved as both a historic site and a reminder—the rest of the devastation is being cleaned up.) Heading west on US 64/74, the route follows the **Ocoee River Gorge**, with frequent view of this violent river and the three lakes that tame it. Near its end the road follows Ocoee Lake for 7 miles, with many views; **Chilhowee Mountain**, a fine recreation spot, is on the right up FS 77.

EXPLORING ON FOOT Hiking the Hiwassee River. The two great rivers of Tennessee's Unicoi Foothills, the Hiwassee and the Ocoee, are both completely controlled by upstream dams. Despite that, the two are a study in contrasts: The Hiwassee River is as mild and beautiful as the Ocoee River is rugged and violent. The Ocoee is best explored by raft or kayak, but the Hiwassee can be fully enjoyed on foot. The 19-mile **John Muir National Recreation Trail** follows the north bank of the river.

The most popular section of the John Muir is its western end, reached from FS 108, off TN 315 just north of Reliance, TN. This level section follows the river, with wide views of its rapids and rock formations; tall gray river bluffs tower on the left.

At the trail's halfway point, a remote and difficult trailhead gives access to its more remote and difficult areas. To reach this trailhead from Coker Creek, go south on TN 68, then follow the signs for COKER CREEK FALLS onto Duckett Ridge Rd., FS 22, and south onto FS 228 to its end. Coker Creek Falls' access road is impassable by passenger cars; FS 228 may be in very bad shape as well.

From this trailhead, follow the John Muir Trail right (west) to switchback up to the top of one of those river bluffs, with broad views over the river south. At the base of this climb, a short, hard side trail leads right to the bluff's foot for an intimate view of a riverine cliffside. Also from this remote trailhead, **Coker Creek Trail** goes uphill through a deep defile along a raucous stream to reach **Coker Creek Falls**; this entire walk has been declared a National Scenic Area.

Exploring the Unicoi Foothills wilderness. Despite their low size, the Unicoi Foothills are true mountains with rugged terrain, clifflike slopes, turbulent streams, and rich environments. Within these foothills, two small tracts of Tennessee's Cherokee National Forest have been declared wildernesses by the U.S. Congress. The Gee Creek Wilderness, with only 2,500 acres, occupies a small but rugged gorge on what is geologically the same mountain as the Chilhowee Recreation Area, just north of the Hiwassee River off US 411. The Little Frog Wilderness contains 4,600 acres of twisted mountain wilderness just west of Ducktown, TN.

The **Gee Creek Wilderness** centers on a small but extremely broken and rugged gorge carved into the hard rock side of the mountain. Two worthwhile trails extend from the trailhead. The first is a rough fisherman's path that follows the creek upstream, splashing through the creek and climbing over boulders. It leads through deep hemlock forests to three lovely waterfalls and a beautiful glade underneath a 150-foot cliff. The second trail climbs the ridgeline left to reach the mountain crest in 3 miles and a 1,400-foot climb—a difficult day trip rewarded by wide views from the cross-path that follows the level ridgeline. The trailhead is reached from a paved road off US 411, 1.8 miles north of the Hiwassee Bridge; there should be signs.

The **Little Frog Wilderness** protects a range of 2,000- and 3,000-foot peaks just east of Ducktown. Despite being adjacent to the Copper Basin areas devastated by acid rains in the 1860s and '70s, this rugged range has shown little obvious damage; before the restoration of the Copper Basin's vegetation, the contrast was very dramatic. Although logged in the early 20th century, the Little Frog's hardwood and pine forests are lush and beautiful, with a large number of wildflowers. Two trails penetrate the wilderness from US 64/74 west of Ducktown. The first climbs a mountain ridge uphill from the #3 Powerhouse on US 64, for varied ridgeline forests and occasional views; if you stay on it to its end, you'll travel 11 miles round trip and climb 900 feet. A few miles closer to Ducktown, a second trail starts on US 64/74 to climb through the center of the wilderness. This is a more difficult hike, crossing several creek valleys as it climbs into a gap, then descends to lovely little **Pressley Cove**.

✳ Villages

Murphy, NC. The largest town of this area, Murphy is a good-sized, somewhat sprawling place at the center of a very large valley. It has a lovely, well-developed old downtown that climbs a hill, making for interesting strolling. Within North Carolina it is famous for its early-20th-century **courthouse**, reputed to be the most beautiful in the state—a large and stately neoclassical structure completely clad in locally quarried marble. **Hiwassee Lake**, which starts 10 miles east of town, backs up into the village's residential areas.

Hayesville, NC. The tiny seat of Clay County (population just 350), Hayesville sits 2 miles off the main highway, US 64, east of Murphy. Isolated by the rugged Valley River Mountains, Hayesville remains nearly unchanged, a 50-year step back in time. It has a wonderfully beautiful **Town Square**—a 19th-century red-brick courthouse, framed by azaleas and rhododendrons, shaded by oaks, and with a little gazebo in front. The square is surrounded by tiny shops forming Hayesville's downtown. East of town, US 64 gives wonderful views as it climbs out of Clay County.

Andrews, NC. The small town of Andrews sits at the dead end of a wide, flat-bottomed river valley stretching northeast from Murphy to the Nantahala Gorge. The first large piece of flatland on the far side of the Nantahala Gorge, it was a natural location for a major siding on the railroad passing through the gorge. Like many railroad towns, Andrews declined for decades along with its line—now the **Great Smoky Mountains Railroad**. In the last few years its fortunes have been reviving, and its small but well-formed downtown of old brick store-fronts is beginning to attract new businesses. Andrews is the closest town to the isolated and beautiful **Nantahala Lake**; the road from Andrews to the lake, Junaluska Rd., follows the 1855 stagecoach turnpike.

Ducktown and Copperhill, TN. Ducktown is a small, compact hilltop village just off US 64/74. Reliant on copper mining from 1850 to 1987, it's a neat, whitewashed town dominated by modest workers' housing and a few small stores. Five miles south, Cop-perhill is considerably larger, with a well-formed downtown of brick store-fronts facing the Ocoee River. The area between Ducktown and Copper-hill, known as the Copper Basin, was utterly stripped of vegetation by acid rain during the 1860s and '70s, a by-product of the crude copper smelting methods then in use. The worst of the pollution ended in the 1880s, when local mines started recovering and selling the acidifying sulfur instead of spewing it into the air. Still, the vegetation didn't start to grow back until a revegetation effort in the late 20th century, and rural landscapes remain immature. Ironically, the sul-fur extraction outlasted the copper mining by almost two decades, the last sulfur plant closing in 2001.

THE COUNTY COURTHOUSE AND POLICE DEPARTMENT MUSEUM IN MURPHY.

Jim Hargan

Reliance, TN. This small town sits in the gorge of the Hiwassee River, tightly hugging TN 30. Noted for its concentration of old-fashioned small-town buildings, it's now a National Historic District. Look for the **L&N Watchman's House**, the **Vaughn-Webb Homeplace**, the **Hiwassee Union Church/ Masonic Lodge**, **Higdon Hotel**, and **Webb Brother's General Store**—all listed on the National Register. Just over the river north of the village, the **John Muir National Recreation Trail** gives an easy walk along the beautiful Hiwassee River.

✳ Wild Places

THE GREAT FORESTS **The Southern Unicoi Mountains**. The Unicoi Mountains end north of Murphy, NC, and Ducktown, TN, in a series of 4,000-foot ridgelines. Heavily forested in past years, the area is covered in second-growth hardwoods. Most of these mountains are in public ownership within the Nantahala and Cherokee National Forests. Nevertheless, recreational opportunities are few, and these peaks remain remote and little visited. Lacking formal trails, hunters and hikers use Forest Service logging roads and other old tracks, poorly documented on topographic maps.

The Unicoi Foothills. The Unicois do not end suddenly and dramatically. Instead, they decline into smaller ridges and wider valleys. These foothills remain mountainous in character, but with only 1,000 feet or less of local relief they lack the drama found only a few miles farther north. This is a land of wide valleys filled with attractive farms, with meadow views toward low mountains. It has a surprising amount of Cherokee and Nantahala National Forest land, including two wilderness areas, **Little Frog** and **Gee Creek**. Particularly on the Tennessee side, creeks tend to be full of water, dashing over cascades into lush, steep-sided gorges.

The Valley River Mountains. This 4,000-foot ridgeline isolates Hayesville, NC, from nearby Murphy and Andrews. Here two gapless ridges run southwest, surrounding Fires Creek. The entire mountain complex is owned by the Nantahala National Forest and made open to public recreation by a series of hiking paths, reached from the road to and past the **Fires Creek Picnic Area**. The terrain is quite rugged and covered with second-growth hardwoods, with few if any views; all the best scenery is along the creek. The area is very popular with local fishers and hunters.

The Cohutta and Big Frog Wilderness. Located at the southwest corner, straddling the TN–GA state line, is one the East's largest congressionally declared wilderness, at 45,000 combined acres. It encompasses a wild and rugged zone of 4,000-foot ridges, separated by violent rivers in steep defiles. It can be a real surprise; the approaches are through the much lower relief of the Unicoi Foothills or the nearly level Great Valley. Though heavily logged in the early 20th century, this area has rested for decades and now is covered by lush and attractive forests. The extensive trail network leads through every sort of mountain scenery imaginable, and the large size allows multiday backpacking loops. Like all national forest wilderness areas, it's open to hunters who wish to confront the wilds without their pickup trucks and ORVs; game is plentiful, and wildlife observation is excellent.

RECREATION AREAS **Ocoee Whitewater Center** (877-692-6050 or 423-496-5197; fax 423-496-1515), 3970 US 64, Copperhill, TN. Built by the Cherokee National Forest for the 1996 Olympic whitewater slalom races, this whitewater racing channel looks like an accidental product of nature. Not true—the course is completely human-made, carefully designed to test the skills of the world's top athletes. This stretch of the Ocoee appealed to Olympic officials precisely because it was (and is) dewatered by its upstream dam sending its water through a pipeline to a downstream power station. This allows large-scale manipulation of the Ocoee's dry riverbed and carefully planned water releases through the course. The center also includes a native plant garden, paved walkways, a hiking and biking trail on the **Historic Old Copper Rd.**, pools of water for wading or feeding fish, and a regional visitors center.

Jackrabbit Recreation Area is a large and handsome Nantahala National Forest site on the shores of **Lake Chatuge**, south of Hayesville, NC. It occupies a pine-covered peninsula extending far out into the lake. Its pine-shaded picnic area has excellent views over the lake toward the Valley River Mountains.

Hanging Dog Recreation Area. Three miles east of Murphy, NC, this attractive Nantahala National Forest recreation site gives access to **Hiwassee Lake**. It has a lovely picnic area, nice walking paths, a little pioneer cemetery, and lake views. You will find it off the Joe Brown Hwy., heading west from the Murphy town center.

Chilhowee Mountain Recreation Area. Chilhowee Mountain forms a 1,000-foot-high barrier on the far western edge of this district. Oval shaped, its sides are even and clifflike, but its top is a broad, gently sloping basin. The Cherokee National Forest's Chilhowee Mountain Recreation Area occupies that mountaintop basin. Its access road, FS 77, makes a dramatic climb straight up from Lake Ocoee. At the top are wide panoramas toward the Unicoi Mountains, over the Ocoee Gorge, and over the Great Valley of TN. Recreation facilities center on a lovely little lake, and include a fine picnic area. Walking paths lace through the mountaintop basin, including one to a 65-foot waterfall. To reach it, take US 64/74 west from Ducktown, TN, to Lake Ocoee, where FS 77 is on your right.

PICNIC AREAS **Fires Creek Picnic Area**. To reach the picnic area from the Hayesville Town Square, go north on Anderson St. (SSR 1307) for 0.4 mile; then left on Mission Dam Rd. (SSR 1300) for 4.5 miles; then right on Fires Creek Rd. for about 2 miles. Located in the Valley River Mountains north of Hayesville, NC, this small national forest picnic area has streamside tables shaded by a deep forest. The base of **Leatherwood Falls** is visible from the picnic area, and a short path leads to the top. The good forest road that leads to the picnic area, Fires Creek Rd., continues on to explore Forest Service lands in the Valley River Mountains, with many trailheads.

Buck Bald is located in the Cherokee National Forest north of Ducktown, TN; go north on TN 68 for 18.2 miles, then go right on gravel FS 311, following the signs on this rough but passable road for about 2 miles. The site of an old fire tower, this conical 2,350-foot mountain is crowned with open grassy lawns and a handful of picnic tables. Remarkable views in all directions make this a popular spot, despite its remoteness.

Hiwassee Dam. From Murphy, take US 64/74 west 7.6 miles to a right on NC 294; then north for 8.6 miles to a right on SSR 1314; then north for 5.2 miles to the dam. This TVA picnic area sits on a grassy hill, shaded by large old trees, with sweeping views over Hiwassee Lake and Dam; its paved back road goes right over the top of the dam.

Sugarloaf Mountain State Park (423-338-4133). This Tennessee state park sits at the base of Ocoee #1 Dam, giving access to the calm Lower Section of the Ocoee River as it flows out of the mountains and into the Great Valley. The park includes a scale model of the 1996 Olympic whitewater slalom race channel that is located upstream at the Ocoee Whitewater Center (see *Recreation Areas*).

✳ To See

BIG DAMMED LAKES The Tennessee Valley Authority—universally known as TVA—owns and operates six hydropower dams in this area. On the Hiwassee River in North Carolina, Chatuge near Hayesville controls the upstream flow, Hiwassee backs water up as far as Murphy, and Appalachia produces additional power near the state line. On the Ocoee River in Tennessee, the unimaginatively named Ocoee #1, #2, and #3 Dams break this fierce river to harness its power. The TVA, "a corporation clothed with the power of government" as Franklin Roosevelt described it, uses these and 43 other hydropower dams to produce much of Tennessee's electrical power. (The rest is produced by coal and nuclear plants, also owned by TVA.)

Lake Ocoee. Sometimes known as "Ocoee #1 Lake," this large lake was built in 1910 by a local power company and purchased by the TVA, which now runs it. It's another long, thin lake that floods the Ocoee Gorge, with a main pool over 7 miles long but with only 3 square miles of water surface. US 64/74 follows Ocoee Lake for its entire 7-mile length, giving continuous views and many recreational opportunities, ending with a good view of the old dam. Needless to say, this lake is a popular spot.

Upstream is **Ocoee #2 Dam**, built in 1913 and later purchased by the TVA. It serves merely to divert the river into a wooden flume that carries it to a downstream power plant, so that its impoundment is really very tiny. If you are interested in this old complex, you can see it from US 64/74. As you drive west from the Ocoee Whitewater Center, look for the #2 Dam on your left at 2.3 miles; watch for its flume on the other side of the Ocoee River for the next 4 miles; then look for the #2 Powerhouse.

Ocoee #3 Lake. Built by the TVA during World War II, this small, narrow lake covers a bit more than 4 miles of the Ocoee River downstream from Copperhill, TN. Recreational access is from US 64/74, 3.1 miles west of the TN 68 intersection. The #3 Dam controls the flow of the Ocoee River's Upper Section, the site of the 1996 Olympics.

Apalachia Lake. TVA's Apalachia Lake (yes, it's spelled with only one *p*) covers 9 miles of narrow Hiwassee River gorge between the state line and Hiwassee

Dam. It's little used by fishermen or other boaters, probably because it has no marinas, and its only boat ramp is in an isolated location. You will find the single boat ramp a short distance from the Hiwassee Dam.

Hiwassee Lake. Water from the TVA's Hiwassee Dam backs up into the town of Murphy, NC, 10 miles away. This long, skinny lake with many arms floods a long gorge of the Hiwassee River, with steep-sided hills rising out of the water, and the tall Unicoi Mountains visible to the north. Its main channel takes 20 miles to travel the 10 miles from the dam to Murphy, and its largest side channels extend another 10 miles—and nearly all of this 163 miles of shoreline are national forest lands. Recreational access is provided by the national forest at Hanging Dog, and by TVA at the dam—a worthwhile site in itself.

Chatuge Lake. This large lake, built by the TVA in 1942 for wartime power production, sprawls over 11 square miles of surface, extending from Hayesville, NC, south into Georgia and the town of Hiwassee. It has a broad open central area from which many arms extend deep into mountain valleys. This is a prime recreation lake, with private marinas and a very nice national forest recreation area. It is particularly noted for its beautiful views toward the Valley River Mountains to its north. There is a large amount of privately owned land along its 128 miles of shoreline, and many second homes.

Nantahala Lake. One of the most remote and beautiful hydropower lakes in the region, Nantahala was built in the 1940s by this region's local power company, Nantahala Power and Light (now Duke Power). It floods a rugged mountain valley 14 miles east of Andrews; to reach it, take Junaluska Rd. 13 miles to a right on Aquone Rd. (SSR 1310). Nantahala Lake has a T shape, with each of its arms 2 or 3 miles long and a quarter to half a mile wide. It's surrounded by 4,000- and 5,000-foot peaks on all sides that rise straight up out of the water; the west side and nearly all of the surrounding mountains are primitive national forest lands. This makes the lakeside scenery very wild and remote, particularly when viewed from Aquone Rd., which follows it for some length. There's a public boat ramp on Aquone Rd.

Release water from Nantahala Lake provides the dependable, high-quality whitewater sports in the downstream Nantahala Gorge. Like several other hydropower sites in these mountains, Nantahala's power station is located some miles from the dam; the river water is carried to it through pipes, leaving the channel "dewatered."

HISTORIC SITES Ducktown Basin Museum and Burra Burra Mine Site (423-496-5778; www.state.tn.us/environment/hist/stateown/ducktown.htm), 701 Burra Burra St., Ducktown, TN. Mon.–Sat. 10–4. When copper mining came to Ducktown in the 1850s, it was a remote and inaccessible mountain community. The ore was mined in the crudest way possible, using techniques already long abandoned in most of the industrialized world. These mining methods, practiced by dozens of independent miners scattered throughout the valley, pumped so much sulfur into the air that the mountain rains turned into a sulfuric acid bath, killing all the vegetation for miles around. This high a degree of acid rain ended in the 1880s, when more modern facilities recovered and sold the sulfur, but by then

Field of the Woods (828-494-7855), NC 294, Murphy, NC. Field of the Woods is 18 miles west of Murphy; take US 64/74 west for 10 miles, then go right on NC 294 for 8 miles. This "biblical theme" park, run by the Church of God of Prophecy, commemorates its founding with monumental art deco sculptures in poured concrete, including the world's largest Ten Commandments. It occupies the spot where A. J. Tomlinson professed to have received the revalation (in 1903) that led to the founding of the Church of God. (Tomlinson led a split from the Church of God in 1923, his group becoming the Church of God of Prophecy. Both groups are now major Pentecostal denominations.) It's a remarkable place. Its white arched entrance leads into a landscaped valley filled with Christian monuments. The most striking date to the park's founding in the 1940s and show a brilliant vernacular use of art deco elements in their curved, white-washed concrete. The enormous Ten Commandments are the most famous, covering a grassy hillside with 7-foot-tall concrete letters. The most impressive monument, however, is the Place of Prayer, a 320-step landscaped path lined with gigantic concrete tablets engraved with biblical verses, leading to a prayer garden with wide views. Other monuments include a reconstruction of Golgotha and the tomb in which Jesus was buried, and a hilltop garden displaying the flags of all nations where the Church of God has congregations. There is also a large gift shop. Free.

THE RECONSTRUCTION OF GOLGOTHA AT FIELD OF THE WOODS BIBLE PARK.

Jim Hargan

it was too late. A hundred years later the Copper Basin was still stripped bare of vegetation, restored only in the late 20th century at great effort and expense.

The Ducktown Basin Museum tells the story of the copper mines from the site of the 1899 Burra Burra Mine. Here the desolate ocher landscape survives, preserved as a National Historic District. Owned and operated by the Tennessee State Parks system, the museum sits above the mine, with exhibits (redesigned in 1996) that tell the story of the Cherokee expulsion from this valley, the subsequent European settlement, and the devastating copper mining. An overlook gives impressive views over the mine's flooded pit, and guided tours visit the mine's buildings.

CULTURAL SITES ♿ **John C. Campbell Folk School** (800-365-5724 or 828-837-2775; www.folkschool.org), 1 Folk School Rd., Brasstown, NC. From Murphy, NC, go east on US 64 for 4.6 miles to a right turn onto Settawig Rd., and look for the signs. Founded in 1925 by New England social worker Olive Campbell and named for her late husband, the Campbell School occupies 380 acres in the rural community of Brasstown, 7 miles east of Murphy, NC. The beautiful and well-kept campus looks like a large and prosperous farmstead, complete with barn and farmhouse—but these buildings hold studios and classrooms. The school sponsors an incredible list of 6-day courses, with a large number going on at once and the courses changing every week. While every aspect of folk and fine art crafts is covered, the school is particularly strong in wood, textiles, and baskets. They run a first-rate craft store, as well as sponsoring weekly concerts and bimonthly dances.

✳ To Do

BICYCLING **Ocoee Adventure Center** (888-723-8622 or 423-496-4430; www.ocoeeadventurecenter.com). This rafting company on the Ocoee River (see *Whitewater Adventure*) also has mountain bike tours and rentals. Rentals $30 a day, guided rides $39–75.

GLIDING **Chilhowee Gliderport** (423-338-2000), Reliance, TN. Weekends; weekdays by appointment. This full-service glider aircraft operation is located at the foot of Chilhowee Mountain, just outside Benton, TN, on US 411. They offer 20- and 30-minute rides, for a high, quiet perspective on the mountains. $69–99.

GOLF **Mountain Harbour Golf and Yacht Club** (828-389-4111), 100 Mountain Harbour Dr., Hayesville, NC. This 18-hole Hayesville course was built on rolling terrain in the early 1990s as part of a housing subdivision. $32–38.

Chatuge Shores Golf Course (828-389-8940), 260 Golf Course Rd., Hayesville, NC. This 18-hole course was built in 1972 as part of a lakeside subdivision on Lake Chatuge near Hayesville. It features scenic views over the lake toward the mountains. $18.

Cherokee Hills Golf and Country Club (828-837-5853), Harshaw Rd, Murphy, NC. Located east of Murphy, this 18-hole 1969 course has a reputation for difficulty, with hilly terrain and water hazards. $25.

ROCK CLIMBING **Outdoor Adventure Rafting** (800-627-7636; www.raft.com/ rock.htm), Ocoee, TN. This local rafting company (see *Whitewater Adventure*) sponsors rock climbing and rappelling instructions on a 75-foot limestone bluff on their own 20-acre compound, with all equipment provided. $11–29.

High Country Outfitters (800-233-8594; www.highcountryoutfitters.com). This Ocoee River whitewater outfitter runs rock climbing and rappelling instructions, and offers a guide/instructional service on the slope of your choosing. $125–245.

STILLWATER ADVENTURES **Lake Ocoee Inn Marina** (423-338-5591), Rt. 1, Box 347, Benton, TN. This marina on Lake Ocoee rents pontoon boats, fishing boats, and canoes.

WHITEWATER ADVENTURE The **Ocoee River** gained fame with whitewater enthusiasts as the site of the 1996 Olympic Games' whitewater competition. The river drains northward out of Georgia (where it is named the Taccoa River), through the center of downtown Copperhill, and then down through the mountains into Tennessee's Great Valley. In that final downhill stretch the Ocoee is controlled by three dams: Ocoee #3 Dam on the uphill end, then the much smaller Ocoee #2 Dam in the middle, and finally the large Ocoee #1 Dam at the downstream end. Below the #3 Dam is a long dewatered stretch of river, as the river is piped from the dam to a downstream power station. This forms the Upper River Section, the site of the Olympics, bone dry unless Ocoee #3 releases water. Downstream, between Ocoee #2 Dam and Ocoee Lake, is the Middle River Section, which receives regular water releases from Ocoee #2 specifically for whitewater sports—a practice that started in 1976. Both of these sections offer nearly continuous Class III–IV rapids, with predictably optimal water flows because of the dam controls. Trips that combine the two sections typically run the Upper Section, paddle into #2 Lake, have lunch on the lakeshore, and then portage around #2 Dam to start the Middle Section. Downstream from Ocoee #1 the river enters the Great Valley, becoming much calmer; this is where tubing trips are held.

Ocoee Outdoors (800-533-7767; www.ocoee-outdoors.com), Ocoee, TN. This local company was one of the earliest to lead rafting trips on the Ocoee, and has been operating here since 1977. They offer trips on the beautiful and mildmannered Hiwassee River, also in this area, as well as the exciting Ocoee.

Outdoor Adventure Rafting (800-627-7636; www.raft.com), Ocoee, TN. This company has a 20-acre site on the Ocoee, from which they run rafting and tubing trips, and hold rock climbing instruction.

Ocoee Adventure Center (888-723-8622 or 423-496-4430; www.ocoee adventurecenter.com), Rt. 1, Box 1500, Copperhill, TN. This outfitter runs both the upper and the middle river by raft and by kayak, has kayak instructions, and offers mountain bike tours and rentals.

High Country Outfitters (800-233-8594; www.highcountryoutfitters.com). This company maintains a 30-acre compound on the Ocoee River, with rental cabins and a campground. They run the Hiwassee as well as the Ocoee. They also do rock climbing instruction, lead backpacking trips (and do backpacking instruction), and run retail stores in Atlanta and Birmingham.

Nantahala Outdoor Center (800-232-7238 or 423-338-5901), Rt. 1, Box 222, Ocoee, TN. This large outfitter in nearby Bryson City, NC, maintains this location for its Ocoee River runs.

Wildwater, Ltd. (800-451-9972 or 423-496-4904). This South Carolina company maintains an outpost for Ocoee River rafting.

✳ Lodging

BED & BREAKFAST INNS **The White House** (800-775-4166 or 423-496-4166; www.bbonline.com/tn/whitehouse/), 104 Main St., Ducktown, TN 37326. This National Register–listed B&B sits within the Ducktown Historic District, in a residential area a block from the town center. It's a large white clapboard house with a wide wraparound porch, shaded by large trees. A classic B&B, it has three guest rooms, all with private bath and furnished with antiques. A full breakfast is included. $75–79.

The Company House B&B (800-343-2909 or 423-496-5634; www.bbonline.com/tn/companyhouse/), 125 Main St., Ducktown, TN 37326. This 1850 white clapboard house has wraparound porches that overlook the center of Ducktown's Historic District. Listed in the National Register, it was built by the local doctor, remembered for his service to the copper miners in those rough early years. The lovely water garden in the back has the biggest goldfish we have ever seen. The six guest rooms, comfortable and furnished in antiques, are named for local mines. A full breakfast is provided. $69–79.

The Lodge at Copperhill (423-496-9020; www.lodgeatcopperhill.com), 12 Grande Ave., P.O. Box 247, Copperhill, TN 37317. This European-style B&B is owned by gold-medal Olympic canoeist Joe Jacobi and his wife, Lisa. A large bungalow-style house built by the town doctor just off downtown Copperhill, this B&B has a large, attractively furnished common area. Like French *pensions*, the six guest rooms share four baths. The full breakfast, included in the tariff, can include fresh eggs, local cheeses, or mountain trout. $50 for two; set price of $25 per person, regardless of occupancy.

✐ **The Hawkesdene House** (800-447-9549 or 828-321-6027; fax 828-321-5007; www.hawkesdene.com), Phillips Creek Rd., Andrews, NC 28901. Located in a mountain cove above Andrews, this is a modern-built house, looking like a large old farmhouse with dormers, sitting in broad meadows with the mountains towering above. Llamas graze the meadows, ready to participate in treks to uphill waterfalls. The interior is elegantly furnished in antiques, with a great room dominated by a large stone fireplace and a bank of windows. The five private-bath guest rooms (one has its private bath across the hall) are all large enough for sitting areas, and one has its own kitchen (and yes, it gets breakfast, too). A set of two-bedroom cabins are also on the property, with the modest look of a late-1940s cottage but elegantly furnished inside; a very roomy three-bedroom cabin is off the site. Young children are welcome in the cabins only. $85–110.

Huntingdon Hall Bed and Breakfast (800-824-6189 or 828-837-9567; fax 828-837-2527; www.bed-breakfast -inn.com), 272 Valley River Ave., Murphy, NC 28906. This homey, 19th-century lawyer's house, not two blocks from downtown Murphy, has five guest rooms furnished in comfortable antiques. Common rooms have the same Victorian feel, and the sense of comfort continues with a bed turn-down and a locally made chocolate in the evening. Business travelers have long appreciated such touches as well as the availability of fax machines, phones, and a dataport (though not in the rooms). The excellent full breakfast is available on weekdays as early as 6 AM and as late as 9 AM. $75–98.

Park Place Bed and Breakfast (828-837-8842; www.bbonline.com/nc/ parkplace), 54 Hill St., Murphy, NC 28906. This circa-1900 farmhouse-style B&B is located in a quiet resi-dential section of Murphy, across from a city park. This comfortable private house is furnished with antiques and hand-knotted Oriental rugs; the two guest rooms are fur-nished with Victorian decor. Rates include a full gourmet breakfast. $80.

CABIN RENTALS **Stone Creek Cabins** (800-780-3459 or 423-338-2674; www.sccabins.com), 662 Mountain View Rd., Benton, TN 37307. All year. Five rustic cabins sit at the base of Chilhowee Mountain on 20 acres adja-cent to Cherokee National Forest. Cabins are sided with stained logs or clapboards; furnishings are country style, simple and comfortable, with wood paneling and floors. There's a volleyball court and fishing pond (catch and release) on site. $76–105 per night; discounts for longer stays.

Mountain Shadow Cabins (877-338-0652 or 423-338-0652; www .mountainshadowcabins.com), 285 Locke Lane, Benton, TN 37307.

FARMLAND IN THE UNICOI FOOTHILLS NEAR MURPHY.

Jim Hargan

These two modern log cabins sit in broad meadows by the Hiwassee River, north of Benton off scenic TN 30. Cabins have wide front porches, exposed log walls, fireplaces, and wood floors; furnishings are new and comfortable. Both cabins have full kitchens. Porches face the river, while the rear of the cabins have a view toward nearby Chilhowee Mountain over wide meadows. $100–110.

Welcome Valley Village (800-542-8567 or 423-338-9499; www.welcome valleyvillage.com), P.O. Box 577, Benton, TN 37307. This 17-acre property fronts the Ocoee River, just under Chilhowee Mountain and a short distance from US 64. Four modern log cabins are spaced apart for privacy, each with unique design and decor. All have full kitchen and porch, wood floors, and exposed log walls. Guests have a choice of river views, whirlpool tub, and/or wood-burning fireplace. A riverside dock and a meadow are lovely for outdoor activities. $60–155.

🏠 ♿ **Cobb Creek Cabins** (828-837-0270; fax 828-837-9424), 106 Cobb Circle, Murphy, NC 28906. The collection of seven cabins occupies a quiet, rural site just off US 19, southwest of Murphy. Each cabin is an individual (one is an apartment in the owner's 140-year-old farmhouse), but all share a high level of comfort. The site has a fishing pond, volleyball, and a horseshoe pitch. $65–88; discounts for longer stays; extra for hot tub use.

✳ Where to Eat

EATING OUT **El Rio Authentic Mexican Restaurant and Cantina** (423-496-1826; www.theblueridgehigh lander.com/elrios_mexican_restaurant), 23 Ocoee St., Copperhill, TN. This downtown Copperhill Mexican res-

taurant occupies a large and attractive two-story storefront, nicely decorated, with mezzanine seating and a tin ceiling. The menu includes the old favorites, then adds some old family recipes, topping it off with vegetarian specialties. All food is made fresh from fresh ingredients.

Iron Horse Grill (423-496-9991; www.theblueridgehighlander.com/iron _horse_grill), 50 Ocoee St., second floor, Copperhill, TN. Tue.–Sun. 11–9. Located in downtown Copperhill, this walk-up pub has a railroad theme, British beer, and some interesting and ambitious entrées among the sandwiches and burgers. Friday and Saturday nights feature live acoustic guitar and fiddle playing.

ShoeBooties Café (828-837-4589; fax 835-8508; www.shoebootiescafe .com), 25 Peachtree St., Murphy, NC. This downtown Murphy storefront eatery has deli sandwiches and salads for lunch, and steak, seafood, chicken, pasta, and chef specialties for dinner. Wine is available.

✳ Entertainment

The Licklog Players (877-691-9906 or 828-389-8632; fax 828-389-1642; www.licklogplayers.org), 301 Church St., Hayesville, NC. Organized in 1977, the Licklog Players are named for the notched log used to hold salt for grazing livestock (and a common place-name in the mountains). They are a community theater, presenting amateur productions from Hayesville's Peacock Playhouse.

Friday Night Concerts at the Campbell Folk School (828-837-2775), Murphy, NC. Most Friday nights the Campbell Folk School sponsors a showing of student work at 6:40 PM, followed by a music concert at 7:30 PM, featuring old-time mountain instruments and music. When weather permits, concerts are held in the Festival Barn, so bring a lawn chair or be prepared to sit on a hay bale. Free.

Saturday Night Dances at the Campbell Folk School (828-837-2775), Murphy, NC. Twice a month on Saturday, 8–11 PM. These community square and contra dances, with live music, welcome couples, singles, and beginners. $5 adults, $2 children.

✳ Selective Shopping

John C. Campbell Folk School Craft Store. Located on the beautiful campus of the Campbell Folk School east of Murphy, NC (see *Cultural Sites*), this craft shop has a juried selection of folk and fine arts by Campbell School students, faculty, and alumni.

Webb Brothers' General Store, Reliance, TN. This general store has been serving Reliance since 1936, from its store on the banks of the Hiwassee River on TN 30.

✳ Special Events

SPRING Polk County Ramp Tramp Festival (423-338-4053). Fourth week in Apr. This annual event at the Mc-Croy 4-H Camp near Copperhill, TN, begins with a trip to Big Frog Mountain to gather ramps, the pungent and delicious wild leek that heralds the coming of spring. When a bountiful ramp harvest has been assured, the bluegrass music and eating begin. A mountain tradition, the Ramp Tramp has been held every year since 1958.

Murphy Spring Festival (828-837-6821). First weekend in May. This downtown Murphy, NC, street festival features crafts, fun, food, and music.

THE CANTRELL BLACKSMITH SHOP AT THE JOHN C. CAMPBELL FOLK SCHOOL IN BRASSTOWN.

Jim Hargan

☙ **Ocoee Whitewater Games**
(423-496-2275), Copperhill, TN. Last
week in May. This multiday series of
professional whitewater competitions,
held at the 1996 Olympics venue (see
Recreation Areas), is always lively. In a
typical year there will be multiple
whitewater sports events here; check
with www.ocoeewhitewater.com to find
out what's happening during your visit.
$6 adults, $4 students, free for children under 10. Pets on a leash cost $5.

AUTUMN **Fall Festival at the Campbell Folk School** (800-365-5724 or
828-837-2775). First weekend in Oct.
Held annually since 1973, this festival
at the famous folk school boasts crafts,
food, live music, dance, children's
activities, and live demonstrations.

WINTER **Christmas Celebrations in
Murphy and Andrews**. Murphy,
NC, has a downtown Christmas street
festival on the first weekend in
December, with a Christmas parade,
arts, crafts, food, and entertainment.
A week later, nearby Andrews, NC,
has its nighttime Christmas parade.
**Annual Possum Drop at Clay's
Corner** (828-837-3797; www.clays
corner.com), 11005 Old Hwy. 64 W.,
Brasstown, NC. Every New Year's Eve
the good people of Brasstown, 7 miles
east of Murphy down a back road, gather at Clay's Corner (that's the general
store) and bring in the new year with a
ceremonial Lowering of the Possum.
There's a Miss Possum contest, a possum song contest, bluegrass music, and
the Little Brasstown Church Choir.
You can even buy a can of USDA-
approved possum from Clay's Corner.

INDEX

N

Y

Z